THE KENSINGTON RUNE STONE
Compelling New Evidence

Dr. Richard Nielsen • Scott F. Wolter P.G.

Layout and Design by: Jennifer Wreisner
Printed by: Sexton Printing

LAKE SUPERIOR AGATE PUBLISHING

ISBN 1-58175-562-7

Published by Lake Superior Agate Publishing
www.kensingtonrunestone.com
www.lakesuperioragate.com
swolter@amengtest.com
651-659-1345

Table of Contents

Dedication

To Janet, Grant, and Amanda Wolter, for putting up with *both* authors during the three years it took to research and then write, and rewrite this book, through its many arduous twists and turns.

Acknowledgements

The authors have received tremendous help and support from many people who we feel compelled to acknowledge. The following individuals provided assistance in locating important documents and photographs at the following institutions: **Farley Wirth** at the Kootenai Brown Pioneer Village at Pincher Creek, Alberta, Canada; **Heather Bigeck** at the South Dakota Historical Society; **Rachel Vaghts** and **Kathy Buzza** at the Luther College Library in Decorah, Iowa; **Mathew Thompson** at the Runestone Museum in Alexandria, Minnesota; **Craig Wright and the entire staff** at the Minnesota Historical Society library in St. Paul, Minnesota; **Lars Nylander** and **Gunilla Stenberg** at the Hälsinglands Museum in Hudiksvall, Sweden; **Kristian Berg** at the Historiska Museum in Stockholm, Sweden; **Patrik Ahlmark**, the pastor at Lye Church on the island of Gotland in Sweden; and **LuAnn Patton** at the Runestone Museum. We especially want to thank **Mel and Mary Conrad** for their continuous help locating information at the Douglas County Historical Society, and in Kensington, Minnesota. We want to thank the following people for sharing personal information about family members we researched: **Roxanne Miller, Irene Kralichek**, and **Mark Jensen**. Important documents were translated from Norwegian into English by **Edna Rude**, and from Swedish into English by **Lars Westman, Britta Blank**, and **Susanna Larsson**. The following individuals provided critical input to our research: **Janey Westin, Judi Rudebush, Dr. Charles Matsch, Dr. John Green, Dr. Paul Wieblen, Dr. Guy Gibbon, Professor James Knirk, Buff Parry, ProfessorBob and Betty Johnson,** the late **Dr. Robert Hall,** the late **Dr. Bryant Mather,** and the late **Tom Reiersgord.** Our thanks go out to the following individuals who provided thoughtful review of this manuscript: **Russell Fridley, John Bengtson, Dick Stehly, Runo Löfvendahl, Dr. Dick Ojakangas, Professor Michael Barnes, Professor Henrik Williams** and **Dr. Alice Beck Kehoe.** Many thanks to **Ann Warren** for her editorial advice. Both authors wish to express our sincere gratitude to **Lars Westman** and **Susanna Larsson** for being exceptionally gracious hosts and guides during our visits to Sweden. When we approached the **Ohman Family in Minnesota,** we were overwhelmed by their openness and willingness to help with our investigation. The **Ohman Relatives in Sweden** were equally supportive and forthcoming with any and all information, including the Ohman letters that they thankfully had saved. We also owe a great debt of gratitude to the following friends who provided encouragement and support during the three-plus years it took to complete this book, including **Richard Olson,** who also performed excellent work creating the numerous runic fonts that appear in the book, **Ruby Sabolik** and her late husband **Arlen,** the late **Jon Polansky, Barry Hanson, Jim Mavor, Gonzalo Leon, Einar Bakke, Gil and Marjorie Moe, Pryce Score, Ken Anderson, John Conner, Tony Maschadri, Edwin Larson, Paul Janke, Mike Ruddy, Gerard Moulzolf, Terry Swor, Jon Earl,** and **Gloria Farley.**

Cover Art

The watercolor painting on the cover of this book was painted by artist Dan Wiemer who also made the chapter icons as well as some of the maps. The painting includes hidden items that are related to subject matter in the book. We invite the reader to find nine of the mysterious characters found within the inscription (ᛔ, ᛩ, ᛩ, ᛘ, ᚷ, ᛅ, ᚱ, ᛖ, ᚭ), and Olof Ohman's signature. Go to www.kensingtonrunestone.com for a key to the hidden items. Wiemer also painted two watercolors for author Wolters' 2001 book, *The Lake Superior Agate: One Man's Journey*, one of which appeared as the cover of that book. To see more of Dan's work go to www.danwiemer.com.

Foreword

Alice Beck Kehoe

Richard Nielsen and Scott Wolter are hard scientists. They understand the methodology of science, and Inference, from data, to the Best Explanation-IBE, philosophers of science call it. Both scientists are experienced at serving as expert witnesses in court cases. Nielsen, with his doctorate in material science, realized that the question of the Kensington Rune Stone's authenticity likely could be answered with petrographic data. He engaged Wolter to examine the Rune Stone using current high-tech microscopy. The result was clear: the rune incisions are too weathered to have been carved as recently as the nineteenth century. QED, inference from the Petrographic data leads to the carved date for A.D. 1362 as the best explanation for its origin.

Wolter presented his petrographic data to an audience of archaeologists and anthropologists at a session of the Plains/Midwest Archaeological Conference happening to meet in St. Paul soon after the Petrographic tests were completed. To his surprise, the audience was cool. "We know it's a hoax." People insisted. Nielsen presented his research on Old Swedish vernaculars and rune variations at the same session, linguistic data that are much less familiar to Midwestern archaeologists than geology weathering, but that explained why the century-old rejection by professors of languages is no longer tenable. The Rune Stone itself stood at the front of the meeting room, letting everyone who came to it see, and feel, that its greywacke is a very hard stone, not a slab a hoaxer would be inclined to select for a remarkably long inscription.

I met Nielsen in the 1980s at a conference on pre-Columbian transoceanic contacts, receiving from time to time his ongoing discoveries of variant runes in medieval Scandinavian manuscripts. Barry Hanson, a chemical engineer, independently figured out, about 1990, that the Rune Stone ought to be examined by a contemporary petrographer. He found Nielsen on the Internet and the two agreed to work together to obtain the obvious tests. Nielsen asked me to advise as an archaeologist, which led to my putting him, Hanson, and Wolter on the Plains/Midwest Conference program. I contacted two of my colleagues, Senior Professor Guy Gibbon of the University of Minnesota, and recently retired professor Dale Henning, who is considered the foremost authority on the western Minnesota-adjacent region's pre-history. Gibbon and Henning heard the presentations and agreed that inference to the explanation supported authenticity of the 1362 date of carving.

It happens that both Gibbon and I have studied history and philosophy of science in order to better understand our field of American archaeology. We encountered a number of cases where an eminent authority figure's opinion closed off research, or a fashionable approach eclipsed empirical data. Initial lack of appreciation of the significance of Wolter's work did not surprise us, given textbooks' frequent mention of the Kensington Rune Stone as a classic hoax. Wolter and Nielsen proposed a day-long workshop presentation of the petrographic and linguistic data, along with discussion of historical circumstances of 1362 and 1989, the time the Rune Stone was discovered. Professor Gibbon was pleased to chair the workshop, at Fort Snelling in St. Paul, April, 2003, and to explain to the audience how the weigh of probability now lies on the side of authenticity (and had since the late 1960s when L' Anse aux Meadows excavations proved that the Norse had built a colony on Canadian soil). Still the representatives from the Smithsonian and Minnesota Historical Society could not give up their dogmatic insistence that 1898 linguists' opinion has to trump the hard data of geology and more than a century of advances in knowledge of Scandinavian languages, manuscripts, and North Atlantic settlements and trade.

Richard Nielsen had engaged Scott Wolter for the laboratory analysis of the Rune Stone carvings because Wolter enjoys a national reputation for expertise in petrographic analysis. The geologist, although a life-long Minnesotan, knew nothing about the Kensington discovery. When he encountered unaccustomed skepticism over his report, he went to the Minnesota Historical Society archives to look at his predecessor geologist's report, that of Newton Winchell. Wolter of course knew of Winchell, his name graces the University of Minnesota's Geology building. Reading Winchell's field notes and report, carried out ten years after the initial discovery, Wolter was deeply impressed by the pioneer researcher's thorough, well-considered fieldwork and conclusion that inference to the Best Explanation supported authenticity for the inscription-basically, the same weathering data Wolter confirmed at stronger magnification. Disrespect for Wolter's presentation puzzled the forensic petrographer, but disrespect for the scientist who had fathered Minnesota geology appalled him! Now Wolter systematically searched the Archives for clues to the rejection; what he has found is, as he says, "a scandal of scholarship," dismissal of leading geologists' evaluations, failure to publish or follow up letters validating the early settlers' accounts of the find, refusal to consider later judgments by the leading Danish archaeologist, Brønsted, and the distinguished American linguist Robert Hall.

What has been popularly held up as a classic hoax is now a classic example of dogmatic insistence on a hasty, inadequately-informed verdict. From a larger perspective, facile rejection of the Kensington Rune Stone inscription indicates the power of the Columbus myth, that the Americas had been hidden from the active world until the Admiral of the Ocean Sea rent the veil. Five centuries denigrating civilizations of America's First nations have been also five centuries pooh-poohing Norse history. Newton Winchell was not the only solid scientist whose conclusions have been ignored; the great early-nineteenth-century naturalist Alexander von Humbolt published comparisons of American and Old

World cultures to argue the probability of transoceanic contacts before Columbus, and in the twentieth century, so did the remarkable Cambridge biochemist and historian of Chinese science, Joseph Needham. Columbus and his Spanish backer were entrepreneurs who broke not a veil hiding America, but international law recognizing entitlement from first discovery-first discoveries indubitably made thousands of years ago by ancestors of the hundreds of millions owning American in 1492. European invasions intent on conquest and dispossessions have been "legitimized" by convoluted rhetoric claiming virgin wilderness, brute savages, and God's will. Not even a small expedition of Norsemen seeking sources for furs west of the familiar Canadian Atlantic regions could be admitted to the virgin land.

Richard Nielsen and Scott Wolter here give us a full account of the finding of that Norse expedition's memorial to their fallen comrades, clear presentation of the geological and linguistic data validating a precolonial dating, and, at last, publication of the ignored materials in the Minnesota archives. They offer, too, a few intriguing aspects of the inscription hinting of the text's writer's education by clerics and perhaps association with medieval military organizations. You readers may accept these more extensive possibilities. You must respect the Petrographic and linguistic data and Wolter's and Nielsen's inferences to the best explanation. Accept, too, that sorely beleaguered farmer Olof Ohman was an honest man. The notion that the Kensington Rune Stone is a late-nineteenth-century hoax is not supported by contemporary data.

Milwaukee, Wisconsin

September, 2005

Introduction

This book will present compelling evidence that the Kensington Rune Stone is a genuine medieval document. It is very important to understand that the position of both authors is the Kensington Rune Stone was *not* carved in the 19th century and therefore Olof Ohman was *not* involved in a hoax. Our goal is to earn the reader's trust that we have been honest and objective as we pursued our investigation. Time and again we found researchers in the past who, in our opinion, were not. These biased attitudes inevitably led to flawed investigations that only further clouded the questions and perpetuated myths about the Stone. There is a voluminous amount of information that we have sifted through attempting to make sense of it all. We want to encourage the reader to learn the different runes and symbols that appear in this book. It will make the experience more enjoyable and help in getting through the relatively complicated material about the runes and language of the inscription. It is important to discuss this information to reach a clear understanding of the origin of the artifact. We think we have been successful in clearing away most of the cobwebs that have clouded the truth.

As we formulated our factual conclusions about the authenticity of the Stone we were careful to steer clear of the word "believe" because it conjures a negative stereotype. We have heard people on both sides of the argument use this word and invariably get labled "true believers" or "naysayers." They were generally not considered objective and consequently their impassioned arguments usually fell on deaf ears. The other problem with the word believe, is that it implies an almost spiritualistic "leap of faith" in the Stone. Faith is fine in some arenas, but it only gets in the way of seeking answers to the many vexing questions about the Rune Stone.

The story of the Kensington Rune Stone is told through a systematic presentation of new evidence that covers history, geology, mathematics, linguistics, runology, and religion. We have tried hard to build our multi-disciplined case by considering only the factual evidence, void of surmise and conjecture, and to organize it in a logical way. Each chapter represents an important part of the investigation where newly discovered evidence is presented.

Much of this new evidence is truly startling and fits together in a consistent and cohesive way that was never before thought possible.

To fully understand the controversy it is important to understand how the investigations of the past got off track. In the chapter, "Scandals in Scholarship," we explain how the Kensington Rune Stone came to be so misunderstood by scholars who thought they had fully and completely solved the mystery of the inscription and then bragged about it. Throughout our investigation we uncovered many examples of researchers who lost their way. In some cases we found evidence where some investigators provided false information and even lied about the results of their research or exhibited irresponsible conduct.

Our investigation even turned up an important letter written by an over-looked first-hand witness to the discovery. Willie Sarsland's written testimony provides important new facts that are presented here for the first time. The implications of these facts cut the heart out of the credibility of a well-known Kensington Rune Stone detractor and his hoax theories.

This book was also written to try and set the record straight about the man who has been the central figure in the story since he discovered the stone over 107 years ago: Olof Ohman. The Larsson rune rows alone exonerate Ohman from the claim by most Scandinavian runologists that he invented six special runes of the Kensington Rune Stone. The Ohman family has endured over 100 years of accusations, ridicule and scorn. Mr. Ohman denied any involvement in the creation of the inscription for the 37 years he lived after he found the Rune Stone. In spite of this he was still made the scapegoat by scholars and disbelievers who labeled him a practical joker and a "prankster." What they failed to understand was they were really calling him a liar. The evidence presented here proves that Ohman was an honorable man who was telling the truth.

The gravestone of Olof Ohman resides in the Lutheran Church Cemetery, one mile north of Kensington, Minnesota. (SFW)

We have also made several exciting discoveries of important new evidence that bear directly on the Stone. One of the most important recent discoveries was made by the Ohman family in Minnesota in June of 2004. They located long forgotten boxes of books, letters and hundreds of photographs that came from the Ohman Farm in

Kensington. Going through those boxes with the family was like sorting through the jewels of a long lost treasure.

What has been the most rewarding part of this effort for us was to receive the complete support of the Ohman relatives in Sweden and the Ohman family here in America. They have embraced our efforts and provided important information that researchers in the past never had available to them. There have been many other people who have contributed helpful information in the pursuit of evidence and answers. We felt like the captains on a big team where everyone was working together with the "let the chips fall where they may" attitude. Without the help of these many people much of the amazing progress made would not have been possible.

In October of 2003, the Kensington Rune Stone traveled to Stockholm, Sweden, for the first time to be evaluated by modern Scandinavian scholars. Perhaps the most important result of the associated publicity the Stone received during this trip was the discovery of the Larsson rune rows (alphabet) documents purported to be from 1883 and 1885. The rune rows eliminated the chestnut that *the Kensington Rune Stone must be a modern artifact since six special runes had never been seen in Scandinavia and were invented by the carver.* Not surprisingly, naysayers immediately asserted that the Larsson rune rows would prove to be the death-knell of the Kensington Rune Stone. However, the authors realized immediately the Larsson rune rows would help immensely in demonstrating that the Kensington Rune Stone was medieval. The exhibition and lectures at the Stockholm Historical Museum also led to the discovery of a trove of letters written by Olof and Karin Ohman that most likely would not have happened if the Stone hd not caused such a stir of publicity in Sweden.

As we compiled our data an entirely new and unexpected line of compelling evidence emerged that has added an exciting new dimension to the history of the Kensington Rune Stone. Over the Christmas holidays of 2004 the authors spent days pouring through the photo record of the Kensington Rune Stone inscription taken and reported by author Wolter (2002). Armed with this new knowledge, the mysterious punch marks we documented three years earlier in the inscription, started to make sense. In June of 2005, the authors were able to review the notes made by three prominent Scandinavian runologists, Helmer Gustavson, James Knirk and Henrik Williams together with author Richard Nielsen during a visual examination of the Kensington Rune Stone at Sweden's Historical Museum in October of 2003. They identified three dotted R's (ᚱ, ᚱ, ᚱ), the double rune (ᚱ) possibly for "fp," a dotted L-rune (ᚠ) and the previously unknown, shallowly dotted (ᛘ) found in ᛘ man (10 men). Their observations are important and compliment our findings.

We also found numerous signs on the Kensington Rune Stone that we thought were the unmistakable mark of the medieval order of the Teutonic Knights, an order active in the Baltic and Gotland, Sweden, from its sanction by the pope in 1199 and 1525 when the Order became secular. The Knights Templar (known also as the Brethren of the Sword) amalgamated with the Teutonic Knights in the Baltic in 1237 after horrendous losses in battle.

The past five years, beginning with the new geological investigation of the Kensington Rune Stone, have arguably been the most interesting period in the history of the Stone. We thought it would help put many of the events that have occurred into proper perspective by a personal touch in a section called "My Experience with the Kensington Rune Stone" by author Wolter.

The story of the discovery of the Stone has been told countless times. Each version has a little different spin depending on the agenda of the storyteller. We decided to use a different approach by presenting the story in a couple of ways. The first is through a chronology of historical facts. We have put together a historical time-line that is divided into nine important blocks of time. Each block represents a period of time when a particular set of important events occurred. We thought the best place to begin the time-line was with the birth of the central character in the story, the Swedish American farmer Olof Ohman. Throughout the time-line we have reproduced all or portions of the original documents that illustrate an important event, statement or fact.

The Kensington Rune Stone is an extremely complicated story that has taken many twists and turns over the years. It should come as no surprise that there is such a diversity of opinions because for decades the arguments have been clouded and incomplete. It has taken a monumental effort to sort it all out. After sifting through the vast quantity of information and drawing upon our own personal experiences we are pleased to have the opportunity to present our view as to what it all means. As is so often the case, human fallibility has tripped up many who have attempted to solve the mystery. We have tried very hard not to suffer the same fate. We believe this is the first book about the Kensington Rune Stone that comprehensively addresses all aspects of the controversy.

As confident as we are in our conclusions, we are also aware that there is certainly more work that can be done. New discoveries related to the inscription are sure to be made in the future that will no doubt prove valuable. It was a shame that linguists had the artifact removed as an object of study for so many years. However, the Stone is now up off the canvass and is fighting hard for its rightful place in history to be recognized. Future research should also be conducted on several other runic inscriptions in North America such as the Spirit Pond Rune Stones, the Heavener Stone, the Noman's Land Island Rune Stone and others. These stones have all been dismissed for reasons similar to the

Kensington Rune Stone. Our position is ***not*** that these artifacts are genuine; it is that they need to be properly studied.

During the writing of this book, some of our reviewers expressed concern over the curious timing of our discovery of the involvement of a medieval monastic order in the story of the Kensington Rune Stone and the immensely popular <u>*fictional*</u> novel *The Da Vinci Code.* Although it may be perceived as planned, in reality it was pure coincidence. Exploring the history of the Templars and the Teutonic Knights arose from the need to explain the presence of the "X," the dotted "O" and the mysterious punch marks in the inscription. One stunning fact are the two words formed by the first six runes that appear to have been singled out by the carver: ᛨ ᚱ ᚷ ᚠ ᚢ ᚱ = Grail is (the a-rune in Gotland also stands for "ai"). These words certainly would have had important religious meaning to a member of a medieval monastic or military order. The intriguing text that immediately follows is "by two skLar." The word skLar remains a mystery. The evidence clearly points in the direction of the Templars/Teutonic Knights, suggesting an explanation that is arguably more interesting than fiction.

We also want the reader to understand that there are two distinct aspects to this book. The first is a comprehensive presentation of factual evidence that supports the authenticity of the artifact; the second is our attempt to explain the origin and meaning of some of the mysterious aspects of the inscription. It is a fact that the word "grail is" appears when the first six unique runes in the inscription are read in sequence; it is sheer speculation that it was what the carver intended. We implore the reader to avoid confusion between fact and speculation. It has been a wild and exciting ride chasing after the facts about this most interesting artifact. We hope you will enjoy reading about our discoveries and adventures with this amazing stone.

Kensington is shown at the apex of three watersheds made up of the Mississippi system discharging southwards to the Gulf of Mexico, the Red River system empting northwards to Hudson Bay, and then the Great Lakes system draining eastwards to the Atlantic. Easy ingress to Hudson Bay was demonstrated by the Dane Jens Munk in 1619. The likely finding place of the La Vérendrye stone is shown on the Milk River in Canada. Little-known Rockall, west of Scotland, likely explains historians' concern with an unknown island south of Iceland. Kensington is along the border between the northeastern plains and woodlands, the southwestern limit for wild rice and an eastern zone for buffalo herds. Helen Tanner stated, *"…that Kensington is on an upland from which flow the headwaters of rivers leading to three major water routes: the Minnesota, Red, and Mississippi Rivers."* Tanner suggests the Kensington party had considered building a trading post on the Kensington-area upland to facilitate collecting furs from Native American traders (Kehoe, 2005: 68). (Map by Dan Wiemer)

The Discovery

The story of the Kensington Rune Stone is complex, and sorting it out has taken a concerted effort. There are still questions about Norse explorers, the German Hanse and the Teutonic Knights, and other non-native peoples in North America prior to Columbus. However, the question of whether the Kensington Rune Stone is a 19th century hoax has been answered. The best way to review the discovery is to let people who were there tell the story in their own words.

In the fall of 1898 (see table, "When was the Kensington Rune Stone Discovered" on page 5), Olof Ohman was, *"engaged in grubbing upon a timbered elevation, surrounded by marshes, in the southwest corner of my land, about 500 feet west of my neighbor, Nils Flaaten's house and in full sight thereof."* (Ohman affidavit, July 20, 1909) *"The hill where the stone was found was without trees when the settlers first arrived some 20-30 years ago; but since that time a number of aspen trees have grown up there; it was an aspen that had grown over the stone, presumably 20 to 30 years ago. The man who found the stone has not lived on the land very long, but his honesty is not to be doubted."* (E. E. Aaberg of Kensington, Minnesota, to the editor of the *Skandinaven*, February 23, 1899)

"I can state that the stone in question was found under a poplar root. The stone was imbedded between these roots with the runes turned downward and the runes on the side turned toward the taproot. I cut off the outer root and also the taproot in the same place. Then the tree fell and the stone was revealed. I saw that the stone was thin. I simply put the grubbing hoe under it and turned the under side up so that the runes were exposed. My boy Edward was born in 1888. He was about 10 years old. He was the first to see that there was something inscribed on the stone. The boys believed they had found an Indian almanac. I myself also saw that there was something written. But to read it was a mystery to me." (Ohman to Upham, December 9, 1909)

"The finders of the stone were Ole Ohman and his sons, Ole E. and Edward Ohman." (*The Daily Inter-Ocean*, Chicago, February 21, 1899) One of the important, previously unknown facts to come from these accounts is that the oldest son, Olof Jr., was there when the Stone was discovered, along with his father Olof and his younger brother Edward. Olof Jr.'s presence is confirmed by a letter he wrote in 1957 that was found in the Ohman

documents in the summer of 2004 (see pages 206-208). *"I was ten years old and going to school at the time. As a rule we come home from school and brought lunch out to dad. We also helped him until he quit for the evening. This happened when we pulled this stump, an aspen or we called it a poplar tree. It was approximately eight to ten inches in diameter growing on top of the stone. Our neighbor, Flaaten, came over as he was grubbing across the section line – the line between my Dad's place and his. He was also quitting. Dad was disgusted about this stump, hard work and also stones. Just before we went home, Dad drove his grub hoe to see how deep it went into the ground. And as it happened it was flat under and we sluffed it up. Here I sat down on it and started to dig in the dirt with my hands as kids usually do and I suggested to dad that we take it home and use it for a doorstep. The story goes that it was used for a doorstep, but it never was. When I was sitting on the stone I told Dad we ought to take that home and put it in front of a door. Just then I discovered the carving on it. I told Dad that something was written on it."* (Edward Ohman interview with the Minnesota Historical Society, December 29, 1949)

"Upon washing off the surface dirt, the inscription presented a weathered appearance, which to me appeared just as old as the untouched parts of the stone. I immediately called my neighbor, Nils Flaaten's attention to the discovery, and he came over the same afternoon and inspected the stone and the stump under which it was found." (Ohman affidavit, July 20, 1909)

"My neighbor, Olof Ohman, who was engaged in grubbing timber about 500 feet [sic 1500] west of my house, and in full view of same, came to me and told me he had discovered a stone inscribed with ancient characters. I accompanied him to the alleged place of discovery and saw a stone about 30 inches long, 16 inches wide and 6 inches thick, which was covered with strange characters on two sides and for more than half their length. The inscription presented a very ancient and weathered appearance. Mr. Ohman showed me an asp tree about 8 inches to 10 inches in diameter at its base, beneath which he alleged the stone was found. The two largest roots of the asp were flattened on the inner surface and bent by nature in such a way as to exactly conform to the outlines of the stone. I inspected this hole and can testify to the fact that the stone had been there prior to the growth of the tree, as the spot was in close proximity to my house. I had visited the same spot earlier in the day before Mr. Ohman had cut down the tree and also many times previously – but I had never seen anything suspicious there. Besides the asp, the roots of which embraced the stone, the spot was also covered by a very heavy growth of underbrush." (Nils Flaaten affidavit, July 20, 1909)

"I am Swedish, born in Hälsingland, but I have never seen any rune stone before. The stone lay 44 feet above the present water level. The poplar tree was about 8 inches in diameter." (Ohman to Upham, December 9, 1909)

The tree stump and the roots that had been wrapped tightly around the Stone were observed by at least a dozen witnesses who gave written statements about what they saw. Their statements are consistent and indicate important facts. The trunk of the tree was about nine inches in diameter and at least twenty-five years old. The roots wrapped around the Stone were at least three inches wide and flattened from prolonged contact. Based on these statements, Olof Ohman, who had immigrated to America nineteen years earlier in 1879 and had lived on the property for only eight years, could not have been involved in a hoax.

Age of the Tree

Witness	Estimated Age	Diameter	Flat Roots, Size	Reference
Siverts to Breda	30-40 years			*Minneapolis Journal*, Feb. 22, 1899 Blegen, (1968, pages 129-131)
Olaus Olson May 16, 1899	25-30 years	10 inches	Observed the flatness of the roots	Blegen (1968: 137)
H. Holand October 1908	30 years by annual tree ring count	Did not observe tree	Did not observe roots	*Harper's Weekly* Oct. 1909
Olof Ohman July 20, 1909		10 inches	Observed the roots The small top root was 3 inches wide and flattened	Blegen (1968: 137) Affidavit
Nils Flaten July 20, 1909		8-10 inches	Observed the roots which were 3 inches wide and flattened	Blegen (1968: 139) Affidavit
Edward Ohman July 20, 1909		10 inches	Observed the roots which were 3 inches wide and flattened	Blegen (1968: 139) Affidavit
Roald Bentson July 20, 1909		8-10 inches	Observed the roots which were 3 inches wide and flattened	Blegen (1968: 140) Affidavit
Sam Olson July 20, 1909		8-10 inches	Observed the roots which were 3 inches wide and flattened	Blegen (1968: 140) Affidavit
Olof Ohman Dec. 9, 1909		About 8 inches	One root down the side and one across the back	Blegen (1968: 158) **Sketch** (see page 31)
Sam Olson Mar. 5, 1910		Tapered to 6 inches at 18 inches above base	Observed the flatness of the roots	Blegen (1968: 151) **Sketch** (see page 31) MHS Report

Witness	Estimated Age	Diameter	Flat Roots, Size	Reference
Joseph Hotvedt Mar. 5, 1910		Did not observe tree	Observed the stump and flatness of the roots	Blegen (1968: 152) Winchell's Field Note Book
John P. Hedberg Mar. 12, 1910	A great deal older than the time of the arrival of the first settlers (20 years before)	Did not observe tree	Observed the stump and flatness of the roots	Blegen (1968: 152)
Cleve van Dyke Apr. 12, 1910	12 years based on stump only*	Did not observe tree	Observed the stump and flatness of the roots	Blegen (1968: 152)
Edward Ohman Dec, 29 1949			One root down the side and one across the back	Interview in MHS files
Olof Ohman Jr. 1957		9-10 inches	One root down the side and one across the back	Ltr: Arthur and John Ohman. **Sketch** (see page 32)
Arthur Ohman Sept. 26, 1961		10 inches	Observed the flatness of the roots. One root down the side and one across the back.	Landsverk (1961: 52-6). **Sketch** (see page 459)
Olaus Flaten Oct. 2, 1961		8 inches		Landsverk (1961: 69-71)
John Flaten Oct. 2, 1961		8 inches		Landsverk (1961: 69-71)
Conclusions from above	Tree was at least 25 yrs old	Tree had a 9″ diameter	Roots were flat with 3″ wide roots over the top of the stone	

*Van Dyke's estimate is quite curious since he viewed the roots and stump at the same time as Sam Olson (Minnesota Historical Society Report), Olaus Olson (May 2, 1899), and John Hedberg (March 12, 1910), and the latter two both estimated the age of the tree to be twenty-five to thirty years. "As I remember it, we judged the tree to be about twelve years old." (Cleve W. Van Dyke letter to Newton Winchell, April 19, 1910)

When was the Kensington Rune Stone Discovered?

Witness	Recollection of Discovery Date	Reference
Olof Ohman	August 1898	Affidavit, July 20, 1909
Nils Flaaten	August 1898	Affidavit, July 20, 1909
Edward Ohman	August 1898	Affidavit, July 20, 1909
Roald Bentson	August 1898	Affidavit, July 20, 1909
Sam Olson	August 1898	Affidavit, July 20, 1909
Willie Sarsland	September 1898	Letter to Dr. Harold Cater, November 14, 1949

Based on the statements of the witnesses, the Stone was found in late summer (August or September). Newspaper accounts and Winchell's entries constitute second-hand information, and are superseded by the first-hand accounts. The Stone was discovered in August, according to a report by Knut Hoegh that appeared in *Symra* (1910, pp.178-189).

The Stone Goes to Kensington

"He [Ohman] found it under a tree when grubbing – he wanted I should go out and look at it and I told him to haul it in when he came (not thinking much of it) he did so." (J. P. Hedberg letter to Swan J. Turnblad, January 1, 1899)   *"In the first place the stone was brought in to my office in Kensington by the finder Olof Ohman. I took quite much interest in the same."* (J. P. Hedberg letter to N. H. Winchell, March 12, 1910)   *"The engraved stone was at first brought to the house and then to Kensington and was exhibited in a window by Hedberg or [sic and] Johnson."* (N. H. Winchell notebook entry on November 30, 1909)

"I kept the stone in my possession for a few days; and then left it in the Bank of Kensington, where it remained for inspection for several months. During this interval, it was sent to Chicago for inspection and soon returned in the same state in which it was sent." (Ohman affidavit, July 20, 1909)

Samuel Siverts' son, Ingvald T. Siverts, wrote two letters to Theodore Blegen in the 1960s. In the letter dated June 25, 1964, Ingvald wrote that his father and three companions hired a rig and brought the Stone, still covered in dirt, to the bank in Kensington, where it was placed in a back room. In another letter, dated June 29, 1964, Mr. Siverts wrote that the men who went to get the stone "drove out in a sleigh."

The Ohman and Siverts Copies of the Inscription

One major point of confusion over the history of the Kensington Rune Stone is the origin of the inscription copies made and sent from Kensington.

Ohman/Hedberg Copy

"Mr. Ohman made a transcription of the characters or runes carved on the stone and sent this through J. P. Hedberg in Kensington to Svenska Amerikanska Posten (SAP). We in turn sent it to Minnesota University where Professor O. J. Breda studied it and came to the conclusion that it was a mixed runic inscription, but believed that the whole thing was a practical joke created by someone who was familiar with runes and wanted to make fun of the learned professors. Nevertheless, a similar transcription was sent to Professor Curme at the University in Evanston, Illinois, and he asked for the stone to be sent to him, which was done." (*Svenska Amerikanska Posten*, February 28, 1899)

"The letter (with the Ohman Copy) which induced Professor George Curme of the German department of the University to undertake an investigation is similar to others which are known to have been sent (by Swan Turnblad at SAP) to the authorities of the Universities of Minnesota and Wisconsin and other leading institutions of the Northwest." (*The Chicago Tribune*, February 20, 1899)

"Convinced that they had found a relic of some kind, but not realizing the importance of it, the farmer took it to his minister, who advised him to acquaint the authorities of the Northwestern University. The letter was received several weeks ago at the University, and turned over to Professor Hatfield. Professor Hatfield being unable to make anything of it sent it to Professor George Curme, who carried the letter about in his pockets several weeks before he was able to make anything of it. The runic characters upon the tracing the farmer had made of them were somewhat inaccurate and difficult to decipher. After a few days of study, light began to break upon Professor Curme's mind of the value of the information that had accidentally come to him, and he realized that the tablet ought to come in to the possession of the University." (*Chicago Inter-Ocean*, February 21, 1899) It was in this article that Professor Curme's first translation appeared:

> A company of Norsemen are out on expedition of discovery from the Vinland of the West. We had camp along **with** two boats one day's journey from this stone. We go out daily and fish. One day after we came home we found a man red with blood and dead. Ave (good-bye). Rescue from fire. Has one ever had a comrade such as we have had. We are on our way to look after our ship, fourteen days' journey from this island.

This version is different from the copy at the Minnesota Historical Society currently labeled, *"Enclosed in J. P. Hedberg to Swan Turnblad."* That copy is actually the version that was sent to Breda, at his request, by Samuel Siverts of Kensington. The Ohman copy contains the word "with" in the 4th line, whereas the Siverts copy does not.

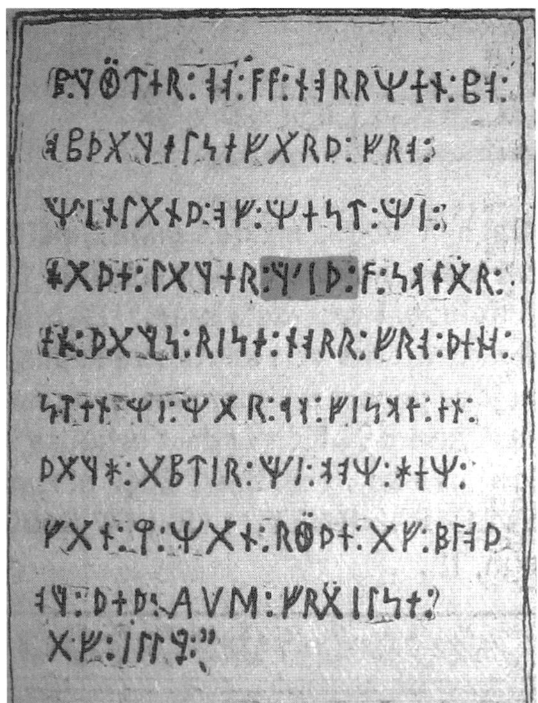

This copy of the inscription was made by Olof Ohman and sent to Swan Turnblad, editor of the *Svenska Americanska Posten*, by J. P. Hedberg on January 1, 1899. Ohman's version contains the word "with" (shaded) on the fourth line, which was omitted in the Siverts copy. The document was incorrectly thought by some investigators to be a pre-inscription draft. (Courtesy of the American Swedish Institute in Minneapolis, Minnesota)

Siverts Copy

The inscription copy by Siverts confused early investigators, and in the 1940s J.A. Holvik and others incorrectly asserted that it was a pre-inscription draft.

"About New Year 1899, I was first informed of the existence of the alleged runic inscription at Kensington." (Olaus J. Breda letter to Warren Upham, March 7, 1910)

"Mr. Ohman found a stone…and brought it to town where Mr. Hedberg, a businessman, copied the inscription and sent it for translation to SAP. The editors…sent it to the University where it was handed to Prof. Breda." (*Ariel* on January 14, 1899)

*At my request Mr. Siverts of K[ensington] sent me a rough draft of the inscription which I deci-
phered and read substantially in the same way that it was afterwards read by runic experts in
Norway.* (Olaus J. Breda letter to Warren Upham, March 7, 1910)

Professor Olaus Breda translated the Siverts copy that appeared in *Ariel*, a weekly publication of the University of Minnesota, on January 14, 1899. Breda was not working with
the Ohman copy because "with" is not translated. It appears that Breda requested the
copy from Siverts, a fellow Norwegian immigrant and someone he trusted, to check the
copy made by Hedberg.

> Swedes and Norwegians on a journey of discovery from Vinland west – we
> camped?? One day's journey north from this stone – we fished one day - after we
> came home we found men red with blood and dead – save from evil. Have men
> at the ocean to look after our ships. ? day's journey from this island. ? Year ?
> (Blegen 1968, page 20)

Breda sent a copy of the transcription to Professor Oluf Rygh in Olso. Rygh had an article published in the *Mogenbladet* (The Morning News) in Olso on March 12, 1899 that
included his translation, made from the Siverts copy (it did *not* contain the word "with"),
just as the translations were that appeared in both the *Chicago Tribune* of February 21,
1899, and the *Skandinaven* of February 24, 1899. (Wahlgren, 1958: Figs. 13, 15, 16) A
telegram was then sent to the *Minneapolis Tribune* on April 16, 1899, from Rygh, Sophus
Bugge, and Gustav Storm.

> *The manufacturer reveals himself to be a Swedish-American who has already become
> Americanized. Various English words have slipped in here or there. He has used sev-
> eral unusual runic symbols; where he has got these from is uncertain, but in any case
> they are evidence not for not against the genuineness of the inscription. Perhaps he has
> made up some of these symbols himself. In some cases he has not used the same symbol
> for two sounds (such as "a" and "ä" or "o" and "å"); a few times, he has used the wrong
> symbol carelessly.*

> **Goths and 22 Norwegians on discovery journey from Vinland of west.
> We had camp 2 sleds one day's march North from this stone. We were
> to fish one day. After we came home found 5 men red from blood and
> dead. AVM Save from ???illge(?)
> Have 5 men by the sea to look after our ships 14 days journey from this
> island. Years 1462.**

Since it is clear from their translation that Professor Breda and Rygh were not knowledgeable
about the pentadic numbers on the Stone, how would a carver in Minnesota in 1898 know?

Norwegian runic expert Oluf Rygh did recognize the pentadic numbers 8, 22, and 14, but misread 1362 as 1462. Rygh also did not know that Ꝑ stood for 10. Nielsen (1986) first identified this symbol as the Arabic number 10, which was known and used in Scandinavia by 1250. The recent discovery of the Larsson rune row from 1883 with the pentadic series from 1-10 confirms this pentadic number. The question remains as to how anyone in Minnesota in the 19th century could know it; a question that those who claim the Kensington Rune Stone is a modern artifact have not been able to answer.

The Larsson rune row copied in 1883 from earlier sources has the same two-blocked pentadic numbers (the bars start at the top of the vertical staff) as used on the Kensington Rune Stone. The Larsson rune row shows Ꝑ to be equal to zero, but on the Kensington Rune Stone it is equal to 10, which is the correct value, since the pentadic number series starts at 1.

This copy of the inscription, incorrectly labeled as being sent by J. P. Hedberg, was sent to Professor Olaus Breda at the University of Minnesota by Kensington resident Samuel Siverts. The shaded area indicates where the word "with" was omitted by Siverts and was missing from all of Professor Breda's translations. This shows Breda didn't use the Ohman/Hedberg copy in his work. (Minnesota Historical Society)

The Stone Travels to Chicago

"…It took considerable writing and argument to induce the farmer to part with his treasures, but he finally consented and the tablet was to have arrived yesterday. S[am] Olson of Kensington, in a letter to the Professor, vouches for the sincerity of Mr. Ohman. Mr. Olson states that a further witness to the find was Flaatens, and says if it is a hoax Mr. Ohman is innocent." (*The Daily Inter-Ocean*, Chicago, February 21, 1899)   Sam Olson (Flom's report, 1910)   crated up the Stone and sent it by rail in early February to Evanston, Illinois, for a scheduled arrival on February 25, 1899 at the home of Northwestern University Professor George O. Curme, but it arrived three days late on February 28, 1899. (*Chicago Tribune*, March 1, 1899)

Professor Curme spent the afternoon translating the inscription on the Stone and uncovered one or two places where the copy was wrong. He found a message in the inscription that was slightly different from the copy. His new translation was:

> Eight Goths from Sweden and twenty-two Norwegians, on an expedition of discovery from the Vinland of the West. We had camp **with** two boats a day's journey [north] from this stone. We went out fishing one day. After we came home we found a man red with blood and dead. Goodbye, rescue from evil. We have men at the ocean to look after our ship, fourteen day's journey from this island. Year 1362.

Once Curme saw the stone he could easily read the pentadic numbers, except for the 10 symbol. Unfortunately, some of his misunderstandings created the impression that there are some English words on the Kensington Rune Stone. The following table shows the words Curme mis-translated and their current knowledge:

Kensington Rune Stone	Current knowledge	Curme's Mistranslation
Vinland of West	Vinland to the West	The Vinland of the West
Skᚠar	Shelters? Hiding places? Ships?	boats
Blod og ded	blood and death	blood and dead
Havet	Either "the inland sea" or "ocean"	"the ocean" only
Opdagelse	taking up expedition	discovery expedition
Har ᛈ mans	There are 10 men	We have 10 men

The time the Stone spent with Professor Curme was very important from a geological standpoint. He examined the Stone along with amateur geologist John F. Steward and made some comments that were reported to the newspaper *Skandinaven*, and published on March 3, 1899. John Steward took the first known photographs of the Stone and likely offered valuable input to Professor Curme that were reflected in his comments about the weathering of the inscription. Even though the inscription had been scratched out shortly after its discovery, weathering was observed along the walls of the carved characters by both men.

"The letters of the inscription were evidently carved with a sharp instrument for they are clear and distinct in outline. But the fact that the upper edge of the incised line is rough and rounded as a result of the disintegration of the stone, while the bottom of the incisions is sharp and clear, shows plainly that many years must have elapsed since the inscription was cut." (Professor George O. Curme in the *Skandinaven*, March 3, 1899)

"The inscriptions are on the two cleavage surfaces of the stone, which have received no dressing. They are cut as with a 'diamond-pointed' tool. The grooves show no more newness than the natural surfaces of the rock; on the contrary all show age." (John F. Steward letter to Professor Ludwig F. A. Wimmer, October 15, 1899) Fortunately, Steward sent the photographs to the expert runologists Professor Ludwig Wimmer in Copenhagen, and Professor Adolf Noreen at Uppsala University in Sweden. The only photographs to survive are the four photos set sent to Wimmer.

> **8 göter ok 22 norrmen po opdagelsefärd fro Vinland of west.**
> **Vi hade läger ved 2 skjar en dags rise** (The Danish travel "rejse" with English spelling) **norr fro deno sten. Vi var of fiske en dagh äptir. Vi kom hem, fan 10 man röde af blod og ded** (The English dead "död") **AVM fraelse af illy** (The English ill "ondo").
>
> *Här 10 mans ve havet at se äptir vore skip, 14 dagh rise from deno öh, ahr 1362!*
>
> Noreen is the first one to read all the dots in ä correctly, with the exception **fraelse** [sic fräelse]), but he added two, in **färd** [sic **fard**] and skjar [sic skjar].

The scratching out of the runes (retooling) has not been fully appreciated by investigators. The 1949 letter written by Kensington resident Willie Sarsland provided eye-witness testimony that there was mud in the runes, which is consistent with the conclusion reached by N.H. Winchell's investigation in 1910. *"This difference was said to be due to the fact that the runes on the edge had been filled with mud and had been cleaned out by scraping them with a nail."* (Winchell report, April 21, 1910, page 19) *"It was during the noon hour, Olof, myself and my threshing crew started to remove some of the shale and deposits and the more we worked we noticed that someone had carved on this stone."* (Willie Sarsland letter to Dr. Harold Cater, November 14, 1949)

The facts that emerge from firsthand accounts of the discovery tell a straightforward, plausible story with no indication of a hoax. One way to investigate the facts surrounding the discovery is to search for clues using the most reliable witness still around today: the Stone itself. Geologist Newton Winchell performed an extensive examination of the Rune Stone in 1909. The next detailed investigation into the physical aspects of the Stone was performed ninety years later by Scott Wolter. Both Winchell and Wolter documented important evidence that bore directly on the age of the inscription and the discovery. Wolter's results are consistent with Winchell's findings, and they revealed several new facts published in this book for the first time.

The Geology of the Kensington Rune Stone

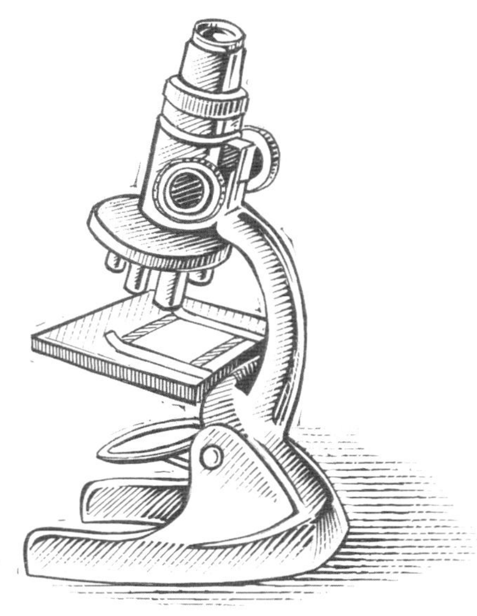

This chapter is essentially the report of an investigation into the geologic aspects of the Kensington Rune Stone and the relative age of the inscription that was performed by Wolter (2001, 2002, 2003) on July 14, 2000. An important part of the fieldwork consisted of a visit to the Runestone Museum in Alexandria, Minnesota, and to the discovery site on the Ohman farm near Kensington, Minnesota. In March 2003, chip samples were collected from tombstones (with permission) in the Hallowell Cemetery in Hallowell, Maine. American Petrographic Services Inc. in St. Paul, Minnesota, and the Materials Analysis and Research Laboratory at Iowa State University in Ames, Iowa performed laboratory analysis of the samples. In addition, the history of the Kensington Rune Stone was researched at the Minnesota Historical Society. Where appropriate, portions of relevant documents are reproduced here. Some of the information referred to in this report is contained in a previous report by American Petrographic Services (Job #10-01120, dated January 4, 2001). The Epigraphic Society funded this research and the report to them is published in ESOP #24 (Wolter, 2005). All photographs in this chapter were taken by Scott Wolter unless otherwise noted.

General Description and Physical Features

The laboratory work was essentially carried out with the same approach a pathologist would use when performing an autopsy. The only difference is that the "body" in this case is a 202-pound (91.6 kg) slab of very hard, durable rock. The following names were assigned to identify the six sides of the Stone:

1. **Glacial Face Side** – The relatively flat side that contains the first nines lines of the inscription (see figure 1).

2. **Glacial Top End** – Roughly perpendicular to the glacial face side, if the stone were set upright this side would be at the top (see color section, plate 4).

3. **Glacial Side** – This side rounds quickly to near vertical and runs the entire length of the stone (see figure 2). If you stood facing the upright stone, the glacial side would correlate to the right side.

4. **Glacial Back Side** – Somewhat rough and irregular, it is on the opposite side of the stone from the inscription (see figures 11 & 12).

5. **Glacial Bottom End** – This end tapers sharply, and was apparently intended to be set in the ground (see figure 13).

6. **Split Side** – Relatively flat with an irregular surface, the split side contains the last three of the twelve total lines of the inscription (see figure 18).

During the course of the examination, the large-scale features were documented first, followed by progressively smaller-scale features. The stone was reviewed visually, and by using reflected and transmitted light microscopy, as well as by scanning electron microscopy (SEM) and elemental mapping. The basic parameters of the stone were documented first.

<u>Approximate Dimensions</u>   <u>Weight</u>

31″ (79 cm) x 16″ (41 cm) x 5″ (14 cm) thick   202 lbs. (91.6 kg)

Figure 1: Overall view of the glacial face side of the Kensington Rune Stone, showing the first nine lines of the inscription.

Figure 2: The glacial side of the stone. The three dark gray vertical lines on the side are weathered joint fractures.

The stone is tabular in shape and about the size of a common tombstone. The overall angular shape was produced by roughly parallel fractures that developed while the stone was still part of the original bedrock. When intense pressure and stress that has built from deep within the earth over millions of years is released, it produces these orderly fractures called **joints**. A few of these joint fractures run parallel to each other across the face of the Kensington Rune Stone.

Figure 3: A prominent joint fracture running across the face side of the stone at a shallow angle to the inscription.

The face side is mostly a bluish-gray color with intermittent grayish-tan areas, and does not exhibit glacial striations (scratches). The first nine lines of the inscription are carved into this surface. A second set of smaller scale fracture planes called **cleavage**, that exhibit a repeatable, roughly parallel orientation are also observable on the stone's face. The cleavage was produced by heat and intense pressure from within the earth that stretched and aligned newly formed micas and other elongate minerals (minerals that are longer than they are wide). Five distinct cleavage planes, nearly parallel to each other, are visible on the face side.

Figure 4: Sunlight at a low angle highlights five distinct cleavage planes that step upward along the face of the stone. The long vertical step between two cleavage planes cuts deeply across six lines of the inscription.

Cleavage played an important role during the original carving of the inscription in that it caused the carver to change plans for the text's location as the carving progressed. The first line of the inscription begins at the far upper left side of the stone. The second line is indented about 3″ and begins on the uppermost cleavage surface. Close inspection of this area reveals where a character, an "O" rune (ᛂ), was carved that appears to have caused a piece of the rock to spall (flake) off when it was struck. Presumably, the carver started the second line at the far left edge, but lost most of the first word when the rock broke off flush with the cleavage plane below. We refer to this as the "Oh Shoot" area. The third line was also started on the upper surface at the edge of the area that had flaked off. The carver apparently regained confidence in the stability of the rock, because the fourth line was started at the far left edge. Whoever carved the inscription definitely had to be mindful of the unpredictable nature of fractures and spalling caused by the inherent aspect of cleavage in the stone. In other words, carving the stone was tricky because of the way it formed, millions of years ago, in layers that tend to split off when they're struck.

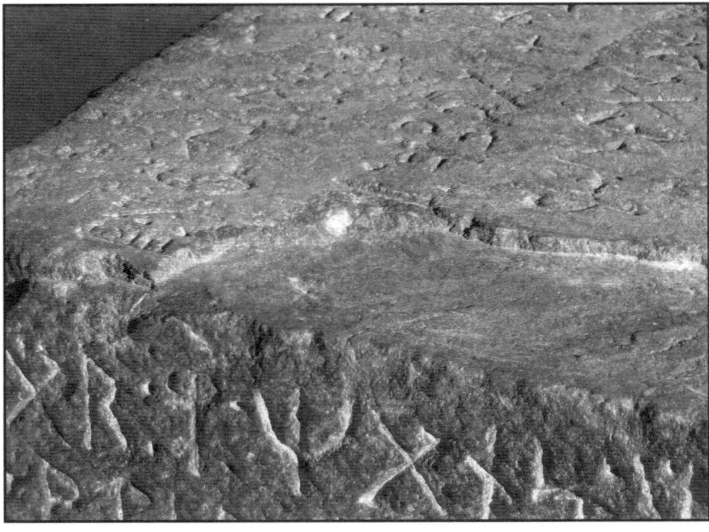

Figure 5: A relatively large piece of rock spalled off along the lower cleavage plane as the second line of the inscription was being carved (See figure 6). A dark gray, curved impact fracture is clearly visible on the edge of the stone directly above the ᛉ on the split side.

Figure 6: A pit was created when two runes were carved in the area between two cleavage planes on the face side (L-6, C-126, 127, 128, 129). (3.75X)

Another prominent feature on the face side is the white triangular area on the lower left side of the stone. This very thin layer (1-2 mm thick) is composed of a coarse-grained crystalline calcite ($CaCO_3$) that moved along the joint fracture system in solution, parallel to the face side of the stone, and was deposited in the crack millions of years ago. Within the calcite are elongate chlorite [$(Mg, Fe, Al)_6 (Al, Si)_4 O_{10} (OH)_8$] crystals, which exhibit a preferred orientation that is parallel to the long axis of the stone.

Figure 7: The relatively thin (3 to 5 mm), tan-white triangle-shaped area is composed of medium to coarse-grained calcite. The presence of aligned chlorite crystals indicates that the calcite was likely deposited by solutions that moved along the joint fracture system when the stone was still in the bedrock.

The hydrothermal calcite is important because several characters were carved into this area. Calcite is a relatively soft mineral (3 on the Mohs hardness scale which ranges from 1 to 10), so the way it weathers is much different than the rest of the rock, which is considerably harder. Microscopic examination using reflected light revealed that the characters carved into the calcite were less distinct and appeared to be more weathered than the characters carved into the graywacke. Additionally, there was no discernable weathering boundary or ground line observed that might indicate the stone was upright in the ground for a prolonged period. Further study of the weathering of the characters within the calcite area might yield additional information about the relative age of the inscription, but currently the only tests available are invasive and would deface the inscription.

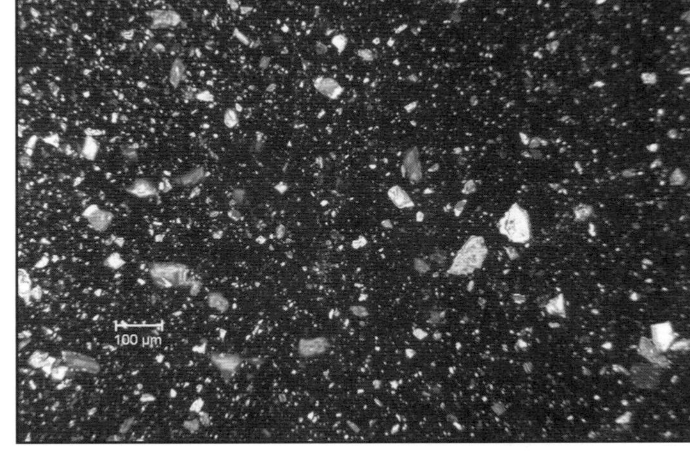

Figure 8: A sample of the relatively coarse-grained, angular calcite was scraped from the white triangular area on the face side of the stone. These grains exhibit 3rd order (brightly colored) birefringence when reviewed under cross-polarized light. (400X)

The glacial back side of the stone exhibits some very interesting features. A fiber-optic light source was directed at a very low angle across the back of the stone. What immediately became apparent were relatively deep (1 to 5 mm) glacial striations that run roughly parallel to the long axis of the stone. No other sides of the Kensington Rune Stone that exhibit glacial striations, which indicates that they were made when the stone was still a part of the bedrock. The glacier likely dragged rocks that were frozen at the base of the ice over the bedrock, creating the striations. The tabular-shaped stone was later dislodged from the bedrock and incorporated within the body of glacial ice. The stone was transported by a glacier, presumably into the Kensington area, and deposited when the glacial ice melted, roughly twelve to fifteen thousand years ago.

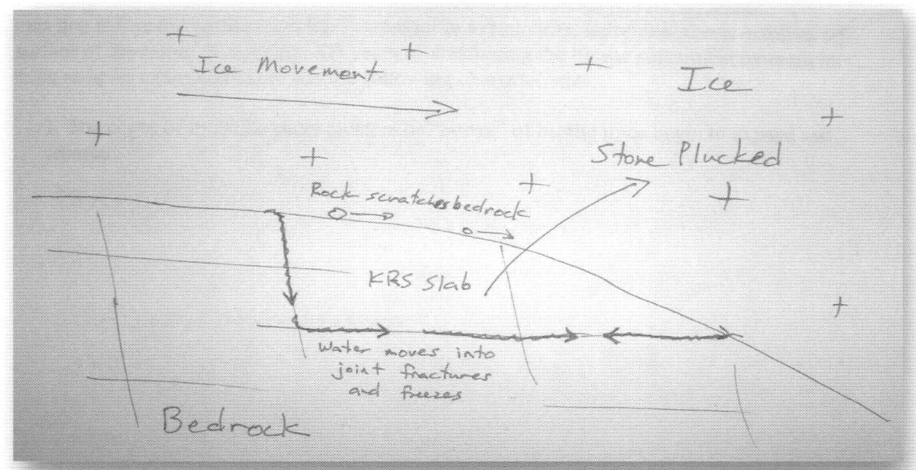

Figure 9: The likely origin of the Kensington Rune Stone involved the glacial back side being striated or gouged when the stone was still part of the bedrock. The stone was broken loose and carried within the body of the ice with little or no abrasion. The ice eventually melted and the stone was deposited as a surface glacial erratic (a loose rock left when the glacier receeded). (Sketch by Scott Wolter)

Figure 10: The relatively deep glacial striations on the back of the Kensington Rune Stone are highlighted by low angle fiber-optic light.

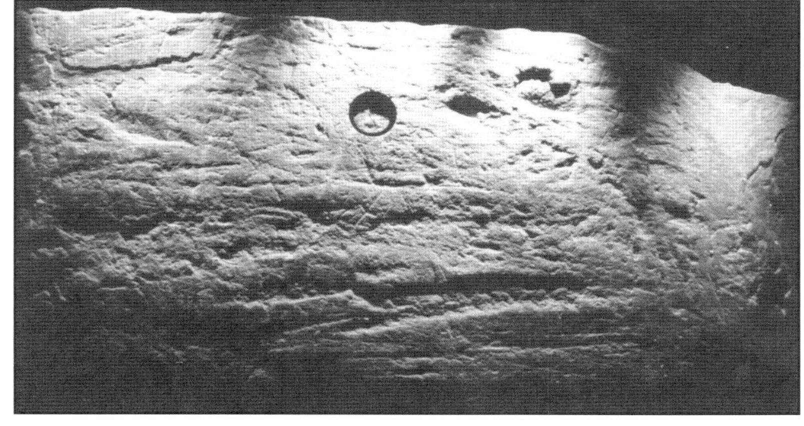

Two peculiar white lines extend across the glacial surface. Roughly parallel, undulating, and branching off at three locations, they appear to have been formed by the roots of the tree under which the Kensington Rune Stone was found. The white lineation closest to the middle of the stone turns downward over the relatively steep and rounded opposite (glacial) side.

Figure 11: Two white, roughly parallel, undulating and branching lineations trend across the glacially striated surface and down the glacial side of the stone.

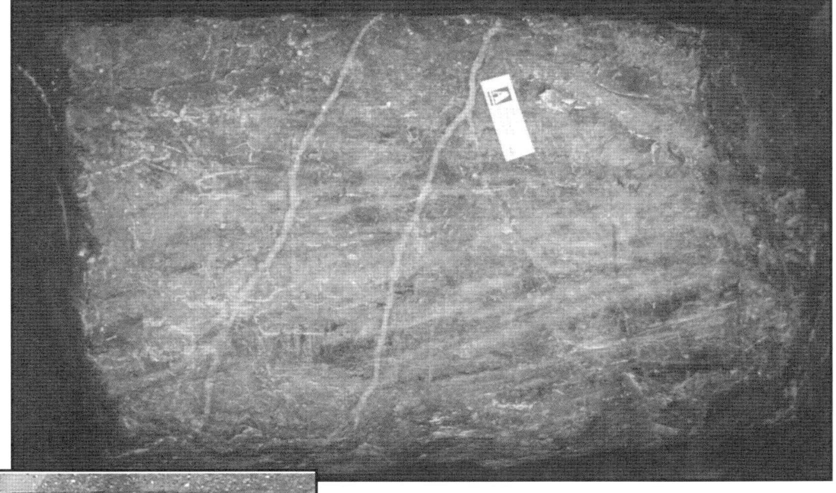

Figure 12: One lineation appears to continue over and down the glacial side and beyond the bottom edge of the stone (in this orientation).

There are intermittent areas of yellowish-white secondary calcite coatings on the sharp, tapered glacial bottom end. Numerous sand grains are bound within the coatings, commonly found on glacial erratics. During field work at the site where the Rune Stone was found, several glacial erratic boulders were observed with similar calcite coatings.

Figure 13: Yellowish-white, fine-grained secondary calcite coatings speckle the tapered glacial bottom end of the stone.

Figure 14: A heavy calcite coating on a granite glacial boulder was found at Rune Stone Park in Kensington, Minnesota. Many glacial erratics with calcite coatings were seen near the site, and are consistent with the coatings observed on the Kensington Rune Stone.

Another type of white surface coating was observed primarily along the top edge of the stone's split side. These deposits are scattered within several rune grooves and word separators. Scrapings of the material reviewed under polarized light indicate that the coatings are composed entirely of gypsum ($CaSO_4 + 2H_2O$). The Minnesota Historical Society reportedly made several plaster casts of the Stone in the 1940s. Since plaster is made of gypsum, these coatings are probably remnants from the casts.

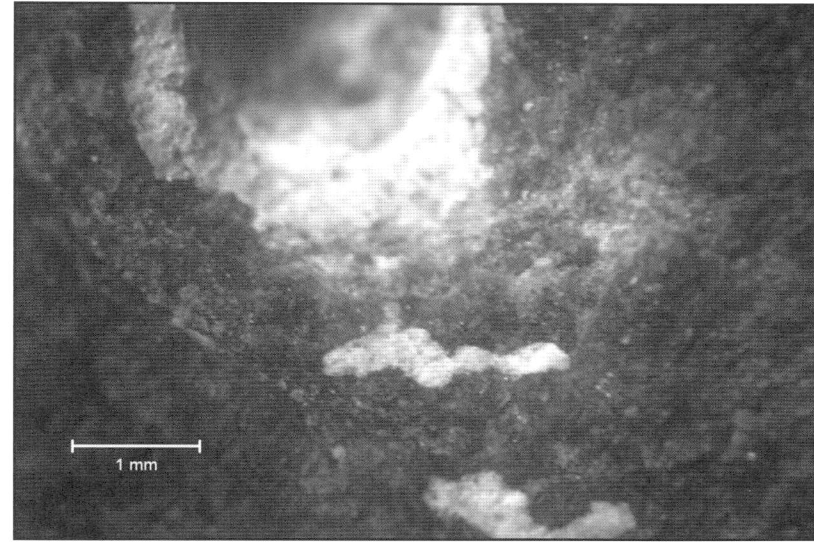

Figure: 15: Intermittent white coatings of gypsum occur within a word separator on the split side of the Kensington Rune Stone [L-10, C-236]. (30X)

Close examination of the sharpest edge, where the glacial side and the side containing the last three lines of the inscription meet, revealed at least six indentations. These rounded, conchoidal, fracture-like areas appear to be related to purposeful impact.

Figure 16: At least six indentations (at arrows) along the sharpest edge indicate areas of impact. The far left arrow indicates the location of the impact fracture in figure 17.

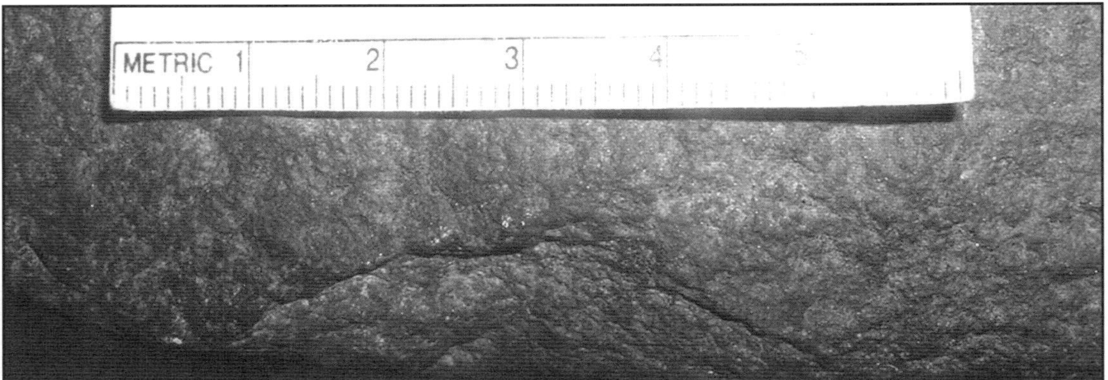

Figure 17: One of at least six rounded, conchoidal-like fractures along the top edge of the stone's split side.

The split side contains the last three lines of the inscription. This surface has a rougher overall texture, and a color that is a slightly darker bluish-gray than the other glacial sides. The stone appears to have been purposely shaped, or "dressed," prior to the inscription being carved. Seven of the nine lines on the face side begin immediately adjacent to the left edge, which confirms the carver planned his inscription on an edge that had been worked, not an irregular, naturally-occurring edge. Close inspection of the outside edges along this side of the stone reveals additional curved impact fractures. In December 2000, professional letter carver Janey Westin was asked to examine the stone. She agreed that the conchoidal fractures along the edge were produced by purposeful impact and that the entire split side had been broken off prior to carving the last three lines of the inscription.

Another important aspect of the stone is the weathering profiles of the different surfaces. All of the surfaces that have been weathering since being transported and deposited by glaciers have a similar appearance: a light bluish-gray color with noticeable small-scale pitting. The pitting is caused by complete dissolution of the softer and less stable minerals, micas, pyrite, and calcite (see thin section mineral identification on page 34). These surfaces have been exposed to weathering for at least twelve thousand years, the approximate age of the last glacial activity. The split side surface, however, has a darker overall gray color and does not exhibit the prominent pitting observed on the glacial surfaces. This surface appears to have been exposed to weathering for a significantly shorter period of time.

**Figure 18: The split side of the stone that contains the last three lines of the inscription and the Holand "H,"
which was carved by Hjalmar Holand after he took possession of the stone in 1907. The dark gray color and
rougher texture of this surface are different from all the other glacial-aged weathered surfaces.**

The Inscription

There are twelve lines in the original inscription, composed of two hundred eighty-seven individually carved characters. The first thing that jumps out when examining the inscription is that the carved characters are relatively fresh-looking. The bottoms of the grooves were scratched out by a sharp instrument, reportedly a nail, shortly after the stone was found, and with sufficient force to remove all weathering products that were previously present. This **retooling** crushed the constituent minerals in the stone, giving them a white appearance. Close examination of the characters reveals the color and texture on the walls of the grooves are different from other surfaces, which have the same darker gray color as the split side of the stone. These other surfaces represent areas where flakes of rock spalled off next to the main grooves at the time the stone was originally carved. **Flaking** is observed to some degree on nearly every character on the face side.

All of the characters on the face side, and approximately 75% of the characters on the split side, have been lightly scratched or completely retooled. The retooling on the face side appears to have been done with greater force than the split side, perhaps due to the face side's easier access. The retooling reportedly occurred shortly after the Stone's discovery in November of 1898; there are at least eleven documented references by witnesses or previous investigators to the inscription being scratched out.

Retooling (Scratching Out) of the Runes

Witness	Date	Retooling Statement	Reference
Professor George O. Curme	March 3, 1899	"It can be plainly seen that most of the letters have been scratched over with a sharp instrument after the stone was unearthed."	*Skandinaven,* Chicago Edition
John F. Steward Amatuer Geologist	October 15, 1899	"...cut *as with* a 'diamond-studded tool...'"	Steward letter to Ludwig Wimmer
Hjalmar Holand	1908	"…when the stone was found ten years ago some of the runes on the stone's edge were scraped by a sharp tool."	*De Norske Settlementers Historie,* Page 19
W. O Hotchkiss State Geologist of Wisconsin	April 4, 1910	"Most of the characters were unfortunately scratched – evidently recently, and, according to Mr. Holand, in cleaning the dirt out at the time the Stone was discovered."	Hotchkiss letter to Upham, MHS

N. H. Winchell, former State Geologist of Minnesota	April 10, 1910	"This difference was said to be due to the fact that the runes on the edge had been filled with mud and had been cleaned out with a nail."	MHS Report, Page 19
Knut Hough	1910	"Unfortunately, somebody scraped it a little, so a couple of the characters became more indistinct than they been."	*Symra*, 1910, pp. 178-189
Willie Sarsland	November 14, 1949	"Olof, myself and my threshing crew started to remove some of the shale and deposits and the more we worked we noticed that someone had carved on this stone."	Sarsland letter to Dr. Harold Cater, MHS
Professor Johannes Brøndsted	1950	"…approximately a hundred of the runes had been scraped, pricked, or chopped with iron."	Aarboger, page 67
R. H. Landon	February 23, 1956	"…the cuts had been deepened in recent times."	Landon letter to Johan Holvik
Emil Mattson	1965	"…they said Mr. Holand had the runes cleaned out with a chisel…"	*Park Region Echo*
Scott F. Wolter	January 4, 2001	"All of the original rune-form grooves on the face side and approximately 75% of the rune-forms on the split side have been lightly scratched or completely retooled."	KRS Report

MHS – Minnesota Historical Society

Close inspection of photographs taken by John F. Steward in March 1899 appears to show that the runes had already been retooled.

Figure 19: The split side's inscription retooling is apparent by the lighter color of the characters in this photograph taken by John F. Steward in March 1899. However, caution must be exercised when examining the four Steward photographs because there is evidence that some of the runes on the photos may have been retouched. (Courtesy of the Runestone Museum, Alexandria, Minnesota).

Figure 20: The first characters of the second and third lines in the shadow area of the split side appear as though the photograph may have been retouched. (Courtesy of the Runestone Museum, Alexandria, Minnesota).

sedimentary rock not easily weathered. Most of the characters were unfortunately scratched - evidently recently, and, according to Mr. Holand, in cleaning the dirt out at the time the stone was discovered. Some of the characters

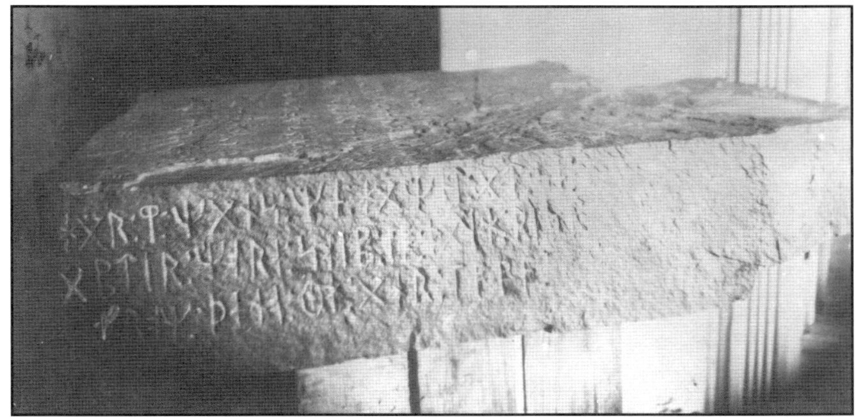

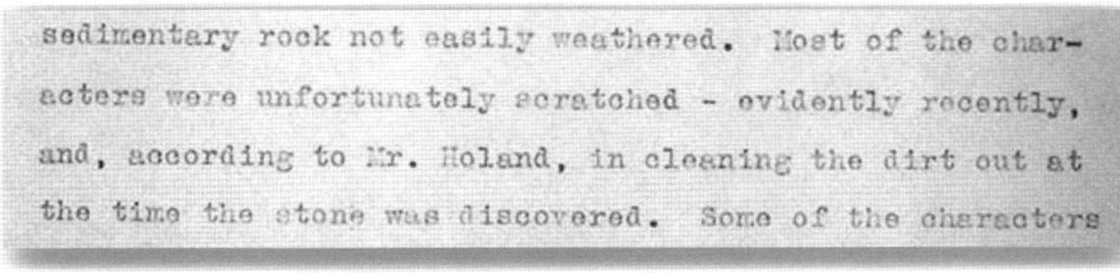

Figure 21: W. O. Hotchkiss letter to Warren Upham dated April 4, 1910. (Minnesota Historical Society)

There is one character on the stone that we know was carved relatively recently. Hjalmar Holand reportedly carved an "H" into the split side toward the bottom end of the stone when he took possession of it in 1907. This character does not exhibit any observable weathering (see figure 18).

Fortunately, on the split side inscription, many of the runes were weakly scratched and roughly a dozen were not scratched at all. These unscratched original characters have the same color, texture, and weathering features as the entire side into which they are carved. That means the split side's preparation, and the original carving of the characters were done at the same time. These characters are also important because they exhibit weathering features, such as iron oxide deposits. The iron oxide deposits developed from the decomposition of the minerals biotite and pyrite (FeS_2). These deposits were observed both within the original carved runes that were not retooled, and speckled intermittently throughout the entire surface of the split side. (see color section plate 7) Within some of the original grooves were small (~0.5 mm), iron oxide-coated open pits that indicate where pyrite crystals have completely weathered away. (see color section plate 8) No one knew how long these weathered pyrite pits took to develop until a fortuitous control sample, the "AVM Stone," was discovered. Analysis of pyrite observed in this stone yielded important information relevant to pyrite weathering in the Kensington Rune Stone inscription.

Figure 22: This brassy-colored pyrite crystal (0.2 mm in size) exhibiting cubic habit resided within a clear quartz sand grain just below the polished surface of the core sample taken from the Kensington Rune Stone. Parallel striations on crystal faces of pyrite were also observed. (220X)

The AVM Stone

In May of 2001, a large, approximately 2,500-pound (1,135 kg) granite gneiss boulder (also a glacial erratic) with an inscription on the top was discovered in a pile of boulders cleared from the fields. The stone was found within a few hundred yards northwest of the place the Kensington Rune Stone was discovered, and initially was thought by some to be related to it. The message contains thirteen carved characters including the letters "AVM."

The AVM Stone was extracted from its location on July 9, 2001, and delivered to the APS laboratory for examination in August of 2001. Close inspection of the carved characters in the lighter-colored, granitic areas revealed conspicuous rust-colored halos around actively oxidizing, exposed pyrite crystals. None of these decomposing pyrite crystals were observed on the glacial-aged surfaces of the stone because they had long ago weathered away.

Figure 23: A pyrite crystal exhibiting cubic habit and a gold-colored metallic luster under plane polarized and reflected light, in a thin section made from the core sample obtained from the AVM Stone. (100X)

Pyrite crystals observed at various stages of oxidation within the original carved surfaces of the AVM Stone were starkly different from the pyrite pits observed on the Kensington Rune Stone. The implication of this discrepancy became clear when a group of five individuals came forward in September 2001, and claimed they'd carved the inscription in the spring of 1985. Their rune stone hoax suddenly became an important control sample, because it gave us the opportunity to compare exhibited weathering of an inscription in a rock comprised of many minerals that make up the Kensington Rune Stone (biotite, quartz, orthoclase, plagioclase, chlorite, magnetite, and pyrite). Additionally, though at different oxidation stages, the pyrite crystals were of comparable size and distribution in both stones. Further, both inscriptions were exposed to the same weathering conditions with one important difference: the Kensington Rune Stone inscription was buried in the ground, whereas the AVM Stone inscription was exposed to an exterior weathering environment. The rate of weathering on an exposed stone should be greater and more severe than a stone that's buried in a neutral pH soil type as was the Kensington Rune Stone. Several additional factors would impact the rate of weathering at the surface, which would not be present in the ground, such as wetting and drying events; cycles of freezing and thawing; ultraviolet light exposure; ventification (wind polishing); and acid attack from decomposing plant material, animal feces, and lichen.

It should be noted that the Kensington Rune Stone was found in what's called the soil horizon (the Stone was reportedly found buried at an angle from within an inch of the surface to roughly four inches at the deepest point) of a limey glacial till that had a pH of 7.5, which is on the alkaline side of neutral. This relatively stable environment would tend to slow the rate of pyrite oxidation compared to the above-grade (above ground) environment. These factors all contribute to a reasonable and conservative comparison of the relative rate of pyrite decomposition between the two inscribed stones.

In 2002, the AVM Stone was returned to the farmers on whose property it was discovered, with the request that it be left outside to continue weathering. The stone's weathering is periodically observed. Active oxidation of the pyrite grains within the inscription was still occurring in June 2005. Because the pyrite crystals are still actively corroding within the AVM Stone inscription after twenty years of weathering (since June of 1985), the pyrite crystals on the original man-made surfaces of the Kensington Rune Stone must have taken longer than twenty years to completely decompose.

Photo-library of the Inscription

A digital photo-library of all 287 characters that comprise the inscription on the Kensington Rune Stone was generated during the period December 11 to December 13, 2002 (Wolter, 2002). At least two photos were taken of each character, using reflected light at both high and low angles with magnifications ranging from 3.75 to 64 times. These images were generated to gain a better understanding of the physical characteristics of the inscription, as well as provide a detailed database that can be used for research, educational, and security purposes.

During the generation of these images numerous features were documented that deserve mention. Previously undocumented round punch marks were observed both within and immediately adjacent to the carved lines of several characters. The punch marks *within* the carved lines are deeper than the grooves they were carved into. However, most of the punch marks *adjacent* to carved lines are actually shallower than the nearby grooves. Due to relatively large flaked areas in some of the runes, we suspect the carver cut shallower punches to avoid damage to the character. Several relatively short carved lines were also observed, some of which were previously interpreted to be rounded punch marks. The physical aspects of the inscription are directly related to the grain size of the minerals in the stone. The coarse sized minerals in the AVM stone created less precision by the carver which led to the reported "slip of the chisel" and misinterpretation of one of the runes (see pages 267-9). The Kensington Rune Stone is a much finer grained rock type allowing for a higher level of detail by the carver who appears to have been highly skilled. This fact made the chances of a slip of the chisel highly unlikely indicating the documented punch marks were intentional and require evaluation by qualified experts to decipher their meaning.

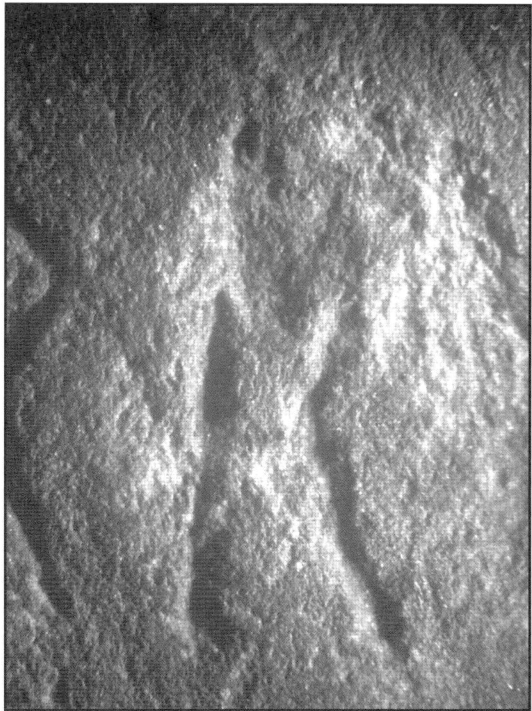 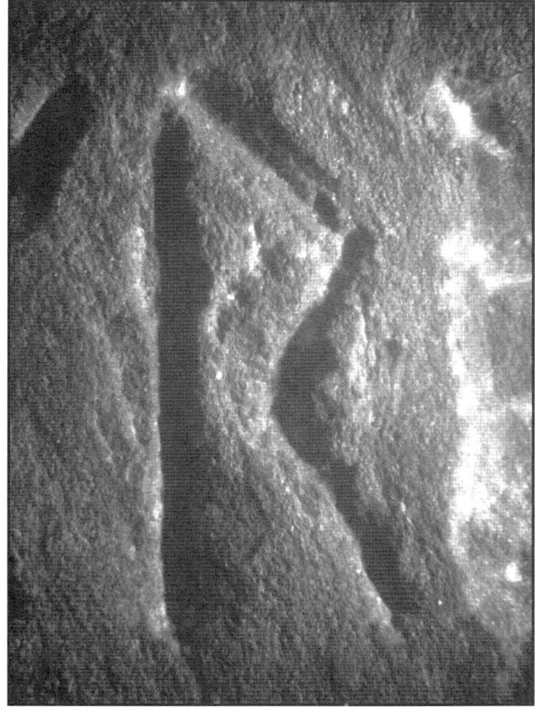

Figure 24: The upper portion of the R rune on the left was damaged during carving. The punch mark in the upper portion of the R rune on the right was carved to a shallower depth than the other lines, apparently to avoid damage due to flaking. Both photographs were taken with low-angle reflected light to highlight the carved lines (left: L-1, C-18; right: L-6, C-125).

Figure 25: A photograph taken with low-angle reflected light revealed an unusual rune-form (L-7, C-171).

Core Sampling

An important phase of the analysis involved obtaining a core sample from the Kensington Rune Stone. Several test specimens produced from the core enabled precise mineral identification and a more detailed study of the various weathered surfaces. An area on the glacial back side was selected that included a branching portion of the white lineation, and an apparent joint fracture. A water-cooled, diamond-studded coring bit cut the 1 ¹/₂″ (32 mm) diameter by 2″ (50 mm) long core sample.

Figure 26: A 1 ¹/₄″ (32 mm) diameter diamond-studded coring bit is positioned over the back side of the Kensington Rune Stone.

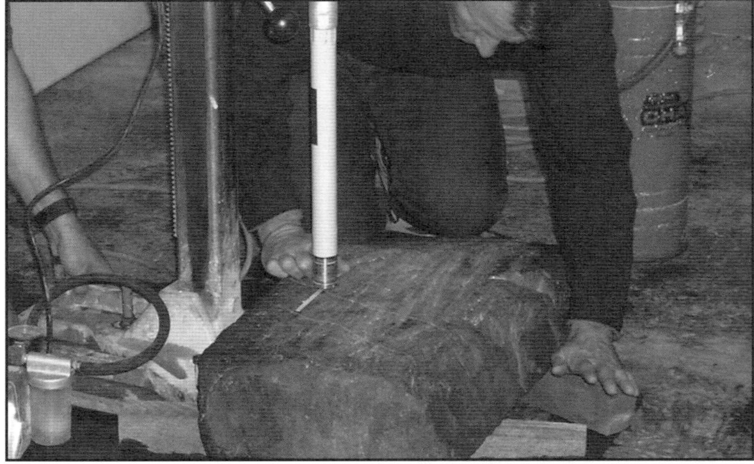

Once the sample was obtained, the top ¹/₂″ (13 mm) of the core was cut off. This top portion, shaped like a small hockey puck, was then cut, perpendicular to the top surface and across the white lineation, to create a cross-sectional profile of this feature. Examination of the polished profile revealed that the white lineation penetrated the rock to a depth of 1.5 mm; the whitened color was produced by chemical leaching of iron and magnesium elements from biotite minerals in the stone.

Figure 27: A cut and polished cross-sectional profile of a white lineation on the glacial back side of the stone. A yellowish fracture running sub-vertically from the top surface is unrelated to the white lineation. (5X)

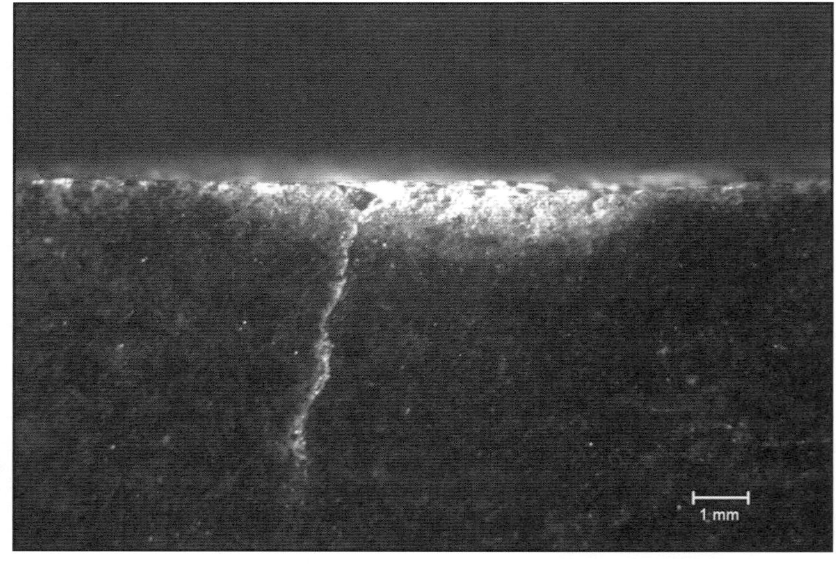

The pattern of the white lineation is similar to the description of the roots that wrapped over the stone at its discovery in recorded testimony, signed affidavits, and sketches by the witnesses. Olof Ohman, his sons Olof Jr. and Edward, neighbor Nils Flatten, and Kensington residents Roald Bentson and Samuel Olson all described the root as being about 3″ (76 mm) wide and flattened to conform to the stone.

Figure 28: Olof Ohman's December 9, 1909 letter included a sketch of the tree roots gripping the stone. Ohman labeled the sketch with the inscription side of the stone facing down. (Minnesota Historical Society)

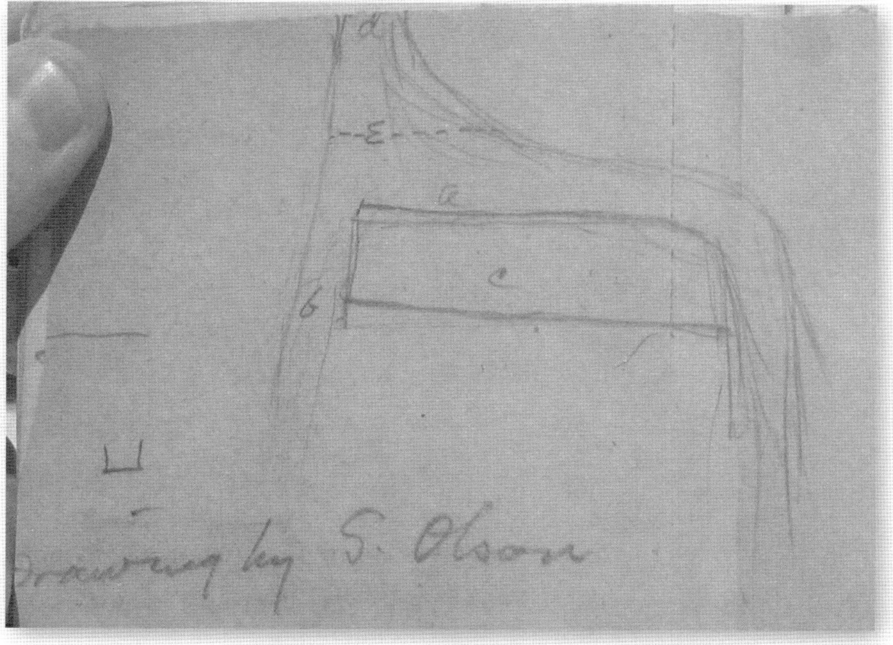

Figure 29: Sam Olson's drawing (March, 1910) of the roots over the back side of the Stone, which appears in Newton Winchell's field notebook. (Minnesota Historical Society)

Figure 30: Olof Ohman, Jr. wrote a letter to his brothers Art and John on April 2, 1957, that included a sketch of the roots going around the stone that is remarkably similar to the sketches made by his father and Sam Olson in 1910. (Courtesy of the Ohman Family)

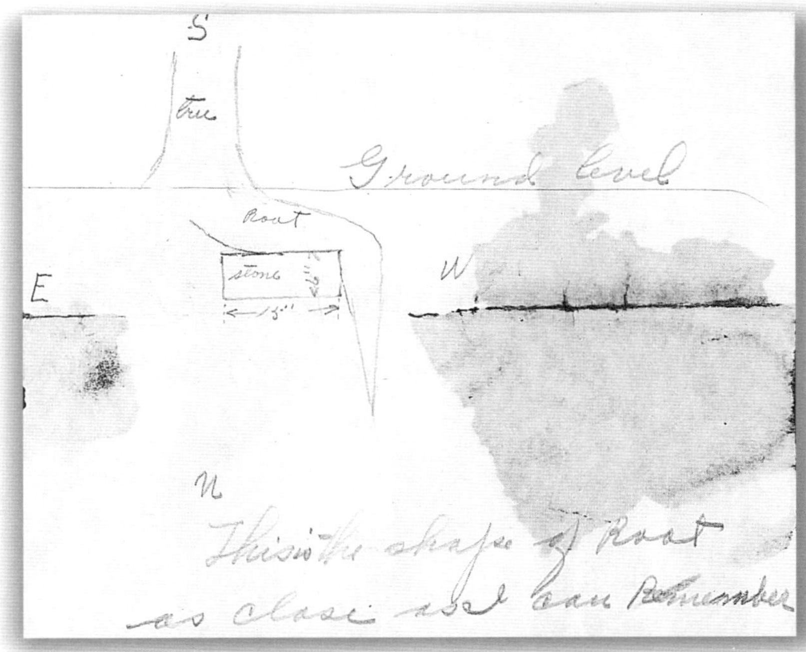

Interpretations
– Part I (Physical Aspects of the Stone)

1. The glacial striations running roughly parallel to the long axis of the stone, and only on the glacial back side, indicate they developed when the stone was still in situ (in the position it was found). After the scratches had developed when the stone was at the base of the glacier, it was plucked from the bedrock and carried within the body of the advancing ice. This relatively abrasion-free transport is responsible for the lack of striations on the other glacial-aged weathered surfaces.

2. The triangular, tan-white, relatively thin (3 to 5 mm), coarse-grained calcite on the glacial face side of the stone contained light green chlorite crystals that were aligned roughly parallel to the long axis of the stone. The aligned chlorite crystals indicate that they were deposited by hydrothermal solutions while the stone was in situ millions of years ago.

3. The yellowish-white, fine-grained calcite coatings with intermittent sand grains that were observed on the glacial bottom end of the stone, were deposited by percolating groundwater after the glacier deposited the stone. Similar coatings were found on many other glacial erratic boulders in the same area as the Kensington Rune Stone. These coatings suggest that all these boulders, including the Kensington Rune Stone, were likely deposited by glacial activity in the same general area roughly twelve thousand years ago.

4. The white lineations on the back side of the Kensington Rune Stone appear to have been formed by prolonged contact with the tree roots. The whitened color of the lineations was produced by chemical leaching of iron and magnesium elements from minerals in the stone (see figures 11 and 12), and the pattern of the lineations closely matches the descriptions and sketches of witnesses (see figures 28, 29 and 30).

5. There is an obvious discrepancy between the much larger size of the flattened root described by the witnesses and the $^1/_2''$ (13 mm) maximum width of the white lineations. Leaching must have occurred when the roots were relatively young, and smaller in size, because the highly active immature ends of the root ends seek out nutrients through chemical reactions. Recent research suggests that ectomycorrhizal fungi form a symbiotic relationship with a root, and excrete organic acids that enable the plant to take up essential nutrients directly from minerals found in the earth (van Breeman et al., 2001). As the leading ends of the roots grew downward, the nutrient-seeking phase of the root ends and the leaching stopped. Bark gradually formed around the root, and its diameter increased with age.

6. Numerous indentations and curved fractures along the split side edges of the stone indicate purposeful impacts (see figures 16 and 17), which suggest that the stone was first marked where an intentional break was planned. The stone was then broken off with a single, powerful blow along this impact plane, prior to the inscription being carved.

7. The white gypsum coatings observed on the split side of the stone are likely the remnants of plaster from the casts reportedly made in the 1930s.

Thin Section Analysis

Thin sections were cut from the core sample to properly identify the constituents of the stone. A glass slide was epoxied to the polished surface of the core at the $^1/_2''$ (13 mm) depth, the core was cut off, and the slice of rock attached to the slide was ground down to a thickness of approximately 25 microns. The section was then placed under a polarized light microscope and examined.

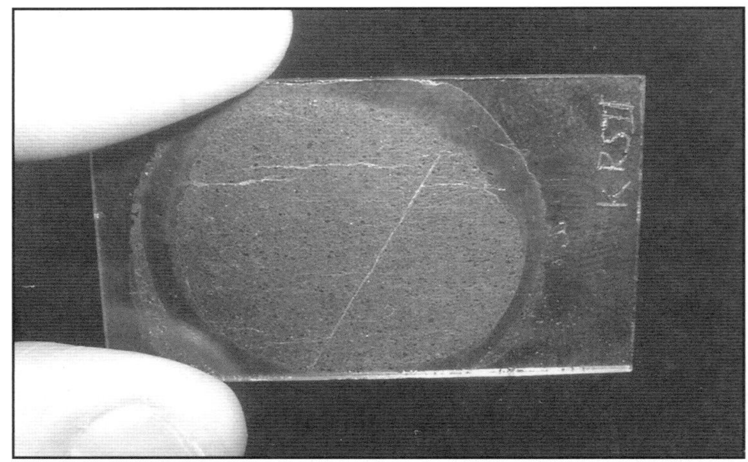

Figure 31: One of the thin sections made by cutting slices from the core sample. The core sample was examined for the purpose of identifying the constituent minerals.

The mineralogy of the Kensington Rune Stone is comprised dominantly of mostly angular, fine-grained quartz, orthoclase feldspar, and rock fragments. The elongate grains exhibit a preferred orientation that is sub-parallel (nearly parallel) with the foliation composed of various mica minerals (muscovite, chlorite, and biotite) that comprise the matrix. The presence of cleavage, a mild foliation, and the mineral chlorite indicate low-grade metamorphism. Several point counts were performed on two thin sections (300 points on each) cut from the core sample. The results of the point counts are averaged in the table below (personal communication, R. W. Ojakangas, 2003):

<u>Mineral</u>	<u>Estimated Modal Percent</u>
1. Muscovite-sericite	22.3
2. Quartz	20.5
3. Felsic volcanic rock fragments	18.0
4. Quartz-feldspar-mica (fine-grained)	14.7
5. Orthoclase feldspar	7.3
6. Chlorite	7.0
7. Biotite	5.5
8. Plagioclase	2.5
9. Leucoxene	1.3
10. Pyrite	0.7
11. Calcite	0.3
12. Hematite-magnetite	0.2
Total	100.0

Figure 32: Rock fragments, like this porphyritic felsic volcanic fragment under plane-polarized light, comprise roughly 18% of the Kensington Rune Stone. (100X)

The Kensington Rune Stone is a fine-grained meta-sedimentary rock called a meta-greywacke. The stone exhibits a strong preferred orientation of very fine-grained mica minerals (biotite, muscovite, and chlorite); in other words, these fine-grained mica are aligned and not oriented chaotically. A second, less obvious preferred orientation of micas suggests the stone was subjected to two different metamorphic events. This two-directional foliation of the mica minerals is a unique and diagnostic feature.

In the spring of 2003, Dr. Richard Ojakangas, professor emeritus of geology at the University of Minnesota Duluth, examined the thin sections of the Kensington Rune Stone and compared them with samples of other meta-graywacke in an attempt to identify the likely bedrock source. Dr. Ojakangas generated a triangle diagram that plotted the percentages of quartz, feldspar, and rock fragments of the Kensington Rune Stone, and compared it with other kinds of meta-graywacke. His conclusion was that the source of the meta-graywacke upon which the runes were carved probably is the Paleoproterozoic Animikie basin in east-central Minnesota (1.85 to 2.1 billion years ago).

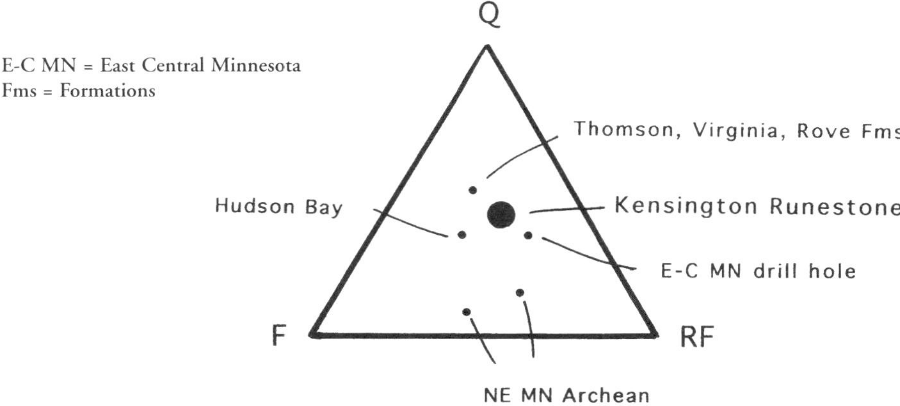

Figure 33: A triangle diagram plotting the relative quantities of feldspar (F), quartz (Q), and rock fragments (RF). The Kensington Rune Stone plots close to meta-graywacke from the Paleoproterozoic Animikie basin in east-central Minnesota (Ojakangas, 2003).

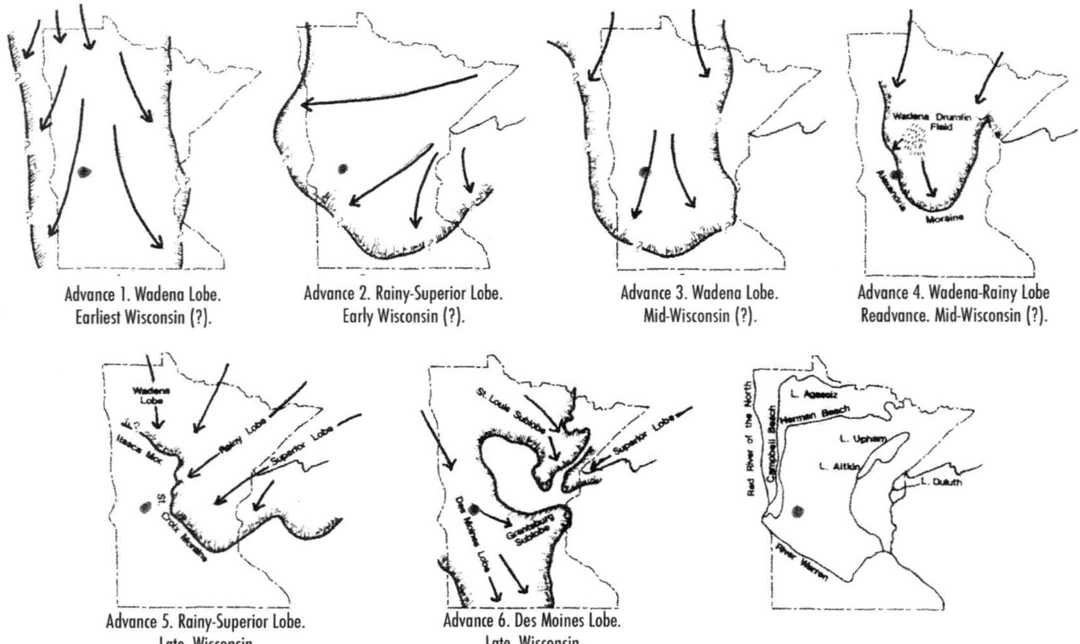

Figure 34: During the Wisconsin age glacial period, the general trend of the flow of ice was toward the south and southwest. It is quite reasonable for the Kensington Rune Stone to have originated from the Animikie basin, which is located generally "up ice" from Kensington (gray dot). (Map courtesy of Ojakangas and Matsch, 1982, p. 107)

Split Side Chip Sample

To better understand the weathering features of the original inscription, an additional sample was taken for analysis. Since the entire split side of the stone has the same appearance and physical characteristics as the original inscription, this surface must have experienced the same amount of weathering. Therefore, a sample taken from anywhere along this surface should yield similar weathering information. A ½" (13 mm) x ¼" (6.5 mm) x ⅛" (3.25 mm) sample was chipped from the split side of the Kensington Rune Stone using a hammer and chisel. This sample was then examined using scanning electron microscopy, energy dispersive analysis, and elemental mapping.

Figure 35: Location of the chip sample obtained from the split side.

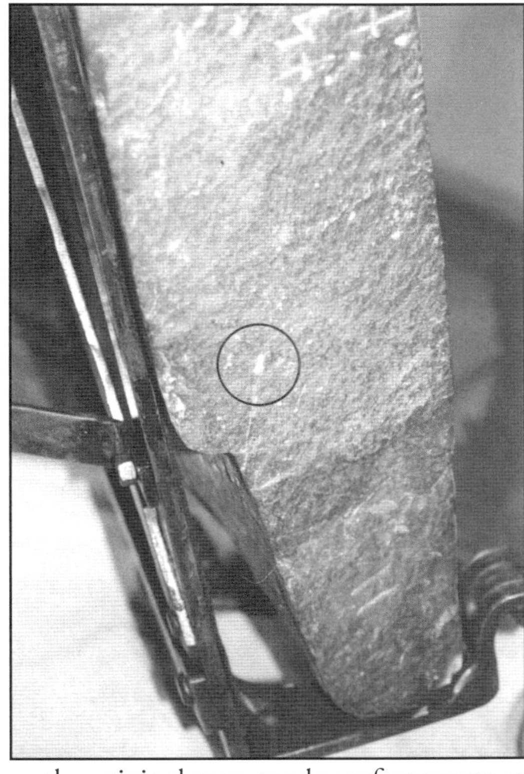

Scanning Electron Microscopy

The next phase of the testing program involved reviewing the core and chip samples using scanning electron microscopy (SEM) and energy-dispersive x-ray microanalysis (EDX). The Materials Laboratory at Iowa State University in Ames, Iowa analyzed the samples. Their microscope has low vacuum capabilities and does not require the use of a gold, carbon, or nickel coating of the samples. The Kensington Rune Stone samples were put directly into the chamber and analyzed. The bottom of the core and the back side of the chip where it had been broken off the stone were the first surfaces analyzed. These freshly fractured surfaces exhibited clean, un-weathered minerals that are the same as the original man-made surfaces were at the time they were carved.

The top of the core sample was examined in the areas adjacent to the white lineations, and was found to represent a glacial-aged surface that has experienced at least twelve thousand years of weathering. These surfaces exhibit fine-grained, uneven pitting with angular projections of exposed quartz and feldspar grains. Noticeably absent were any of the bladed mica grains that had long since weathered away. This advanced stage of weathering was in sharp contrast to the freshly fractured surfaces, which were rich with mica.

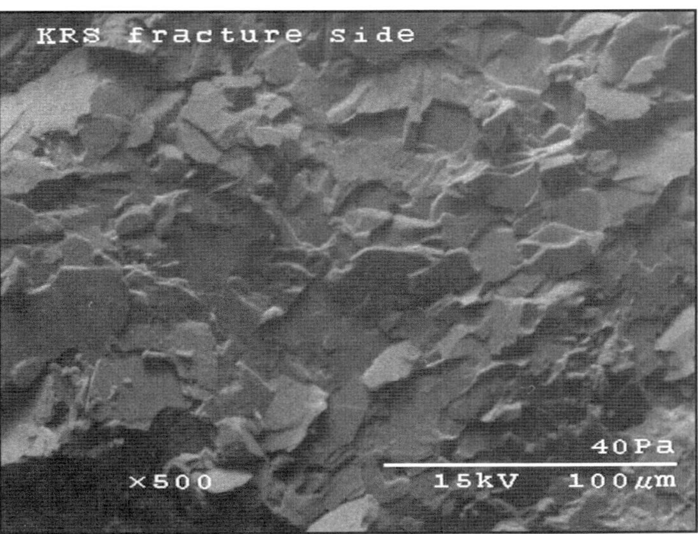

Figure 36: This SEM image shows numerous bladed-shaped biotite and muscovite mica minerals identified by EDX on the freshly fractured surface of the back side of the chip sample. (500X)

Figure 37: Scanning Electron Microscopic image of the glacial top surface of the core, which has experienced at least twelve thousand years of weathering. Compare to Figure 36, and note the absence of bladed mica minerals. (500X)

Lastly, the chip sample was examined, with particular attention to the state of the mica minerals that were exposed when the split side of the stone was made. The mica minerals were not observed on the "outside" surface of the chip, indicating that they had also weathered away completely.

Figure 38: An SEM photograph of the split side of the Kensington Rune Stone where the mica minerals are not evident. (500X)

How long did it take for the mica minerals on the split side and the original inscription to weather away? To try to answer the question other rock samples containing micas that have been weathering for a known period of time were analyzed. Chip samples from tombstones of various ages that contained the important mica minerals were obtained, in the hope that the study of these samples would yield a timeline of the minerals' decomposition.

The Tombstone Study

In March of 2003, twenty-three chip samples from slate tombstones were collected, with permission, in the Hallowell Cemetery in Hallowell, Maine. The tombstone death dates ranged from 1796 to 1865, which means that the slate tombstones were exposed to roughly the same weathering conditions as the Kensington Rune Stone for 138 to 203 years. The following list of criteria for the testing program that gave the most meaningful data:

1. In general, if all other conditions are the same, the smaller sized mineral grains will weather faster. To be most comparable, the mica minerals in the slate tombstones must have the same average grain size as the Kensington Rune Stone micas. Three of the twenty-three samples had a comparable mica grain size, and were identified as follows:

Sample Number	Decedent	Death Date	Years of Weathering (2003)
1	Richard Dummer	1806	197 Years
3	Gorham Dummer	1805	198 Years
22	Abner Lowell	1815	188 Years

The average age of weathering of the three samples was 194 years, plus or minus 5 years.

2. To ensure the tests were accurate comparisons, the weathering environment where the test samples were obtained must be comparable to the environment where the Kensington Rune Stone was found. The climate in Hallowell, Maine, is quite similar to the climate in Kensington, Minnesota with the one exception that Hallowell receives about 17 inches more rainfall annually, which would tend to accelerate the weathering rate.

Weather Records for Augusta, Maine, and Kensington, Minnesota.*

Annual Average	Augusta	Kensington
Temperature, °F	45	41.3
High, °F	55	51.3
Low, °F	36	31.7
Precipitation, inches	41.1	24.1

* Kensington data represents the average of Alexandria, Morris, and Fergus Falls, Minnesota. Weather data collected from www.weatherbase.com.

3. The samples for comparison should be obtained from both above- and below-grade. Only above-grade samples were collected because the ground was frozen and covered with a foot of snow. Subsequent below-grade studies have not been performed due to the difference in pH of the soil in Hallowell, Maine and the Kensington Rune Stone discovery site.

Figure 39: SEM images of the Kensington Rune Stone micas (biotite, muscovite, and chlorite) and the Lowell tombstone mica (biotite) below. The mineral grains, identified by energy dispersive analysis, are about the same size. (500X)

Figure 40: 1815 Lowell Fresh Surface at 500X.

An elemental map highlights selected elements of the surface of a freshly fractured tombstone chip sample. The backscatter image being mapped is in the upper left-hand corner. The relative brightness of areas in each panel is a function of the relative quantity of a given element as well as its atomic weight. The elements selected for this particular map were carbon (C), oxygen (O), sodium (Na), magnesium (Mg), aluminum (Al), silicon (Si), phosphorus (P), sulfur (S), chlorine (Cl), potassium (K), calcium (Ca), titanium (Ti), and iron (Fe). These maps help determine both the geochemistry and spatial relationships of the mineralogy (where minerals are in relation to each other) of the tombstone samples.

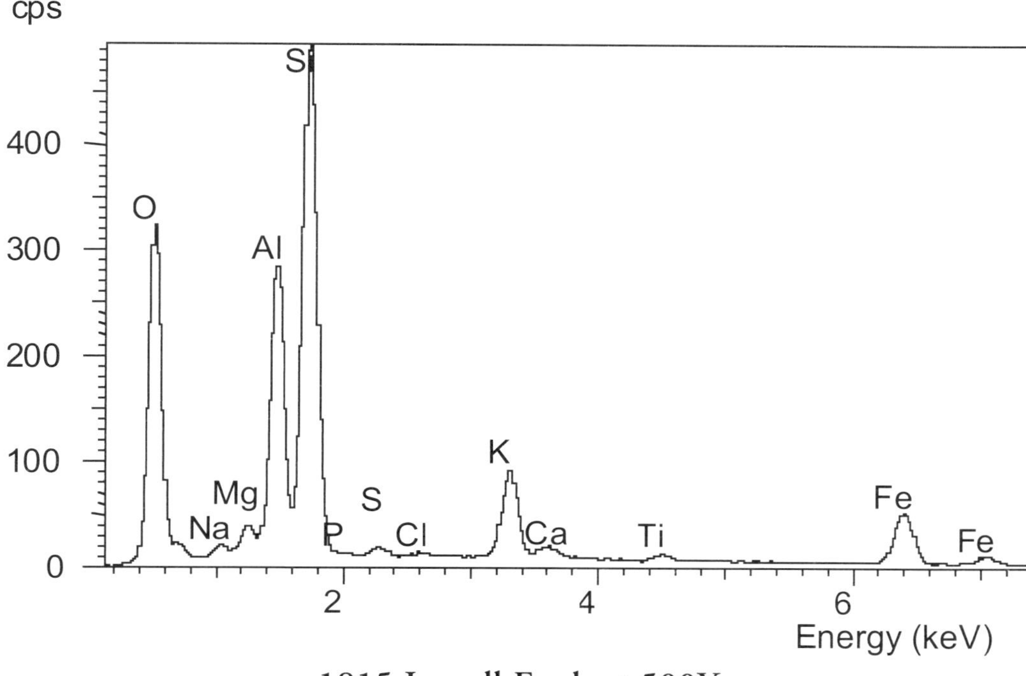

1815 Lowell Fresh at 500X

Figure 41: An energy dispersive analysis spectrum for the mineral biotite which was obtained from one of the tombstone chip samples. (Spectrum made by Jerry Armenson)

Figure 42: The Theresa Stratton tombstone (1802) and the equipment used for sampling. The climate in Hallowell, Maine is comparable to Kensington, Minnesota, save that Maine's climate receives more rainfall.   Because of the snow and frozen ground, only above-grade samples were obtained.

Figure 43: Tombstone chip samples being loaded into the SEM sample chamber.

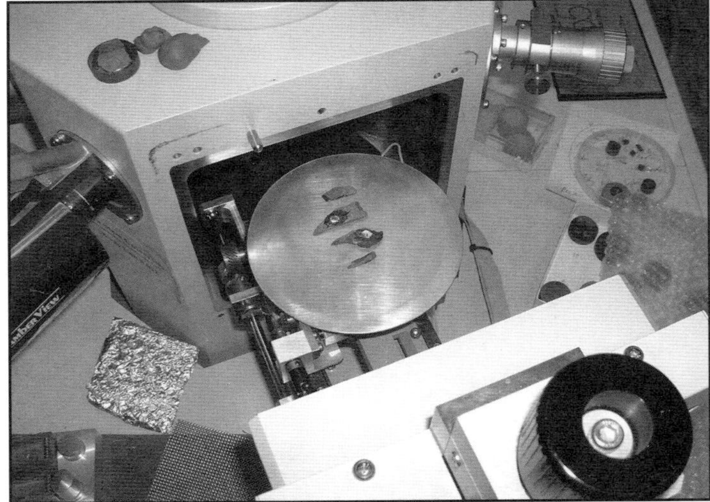

In general, the tombstone inscriptions looked very sharp and exhibited very little observable overall weathering. However, of the approximately one hundred slate tombstones reviewed that ranged from about 150 to 200 years in age (based on the death dates), the weathering features of the slabs generally consisted of the following:

1. Delamination along cleavage planes aligned sub-parallel to the faces of the tombstones.

2. Roughly parallel, linear fractures at various orientations across the tombstone faces.

3. Exudation (oozing out) of secondary minerals from within the fractures.

4. Intermittent iron oxide staining on exposed surfaces.

Figure 44: White-colored secondary deposits were observed exuding from sub-horizontal fractures traversing the face of a slate tombstone.

Microscopic review of the slate chip samples under reflected light revealed a considerable difference in color between the freshly fractured areas when compared to the weathered surfaces. The weathered surfaces are darker gray (see figure 46) and had a somewhat smoother texture.

Figure 45: Sub-parallel fractures and rust-colored iron-oxide deposits on the face side of the Richard Dummer (1806) tombstone.

Figure 46: The Abner Lowell (1815) chip sample showing the dark gray weathered area at left, and the light gray freshly fractured area to the right. (22X)

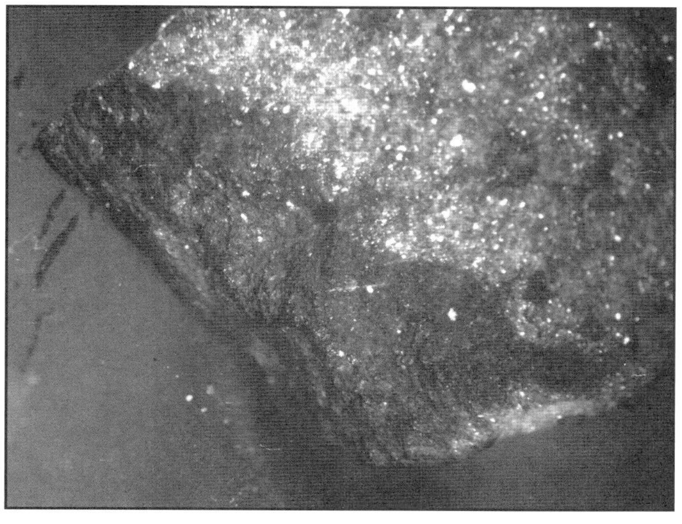

When examined in the SEM, the weathered surfaces of the three chip samples exhibited several features that were consistent with decomposition of the biotite mica. In general, the biotite grains exhibited both chemical and physical degradation. It appears that before the biotite completely weathers to vermiculite, individual sheets exfoliate (flake) off the surface of the stone. The process is similar to leaves falling off deciduous trees in the autumn. After roughly two hundred years of weathering, the biotite minerals exhibited the following characteristics:

1. The edges of multiple sheet clusters or "books" of biotite mica begin to expand and separate.
2. Individual mineral edges become rounded and frayed.
3. Pitting develops on the basal (flat) surfaces.
4. Individual sheets of biotite begin to exfoliate off the weathered surface.
5. Acid produced by lichen on the surface of the tombstone accelerates dissolution of biotite grains at an unknown rate. The amount of lichen development on slate tombstones is an important parameter in understanding the rate of weathering. Most of the tombstones sampled exhibited little to no observable lichen.

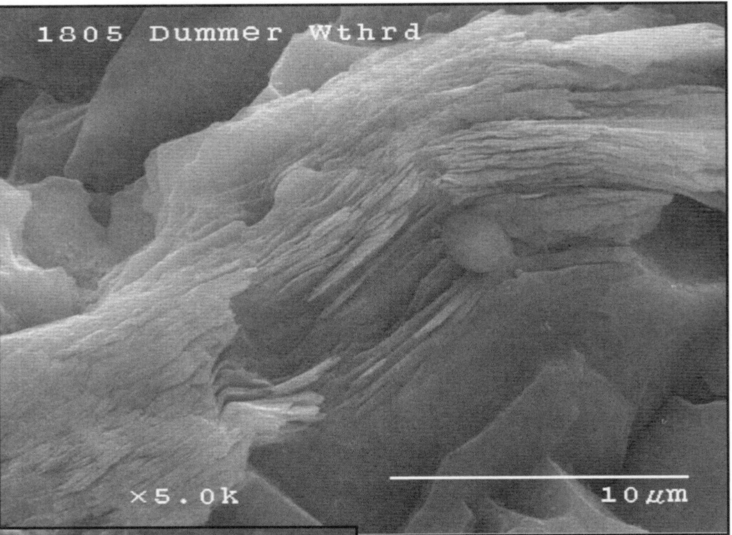

Figure 47: The edges of individual sheets of clustered biotite begin to expand and separate on the weathered surface of a slate tombstone after two hundred years. (5000X)

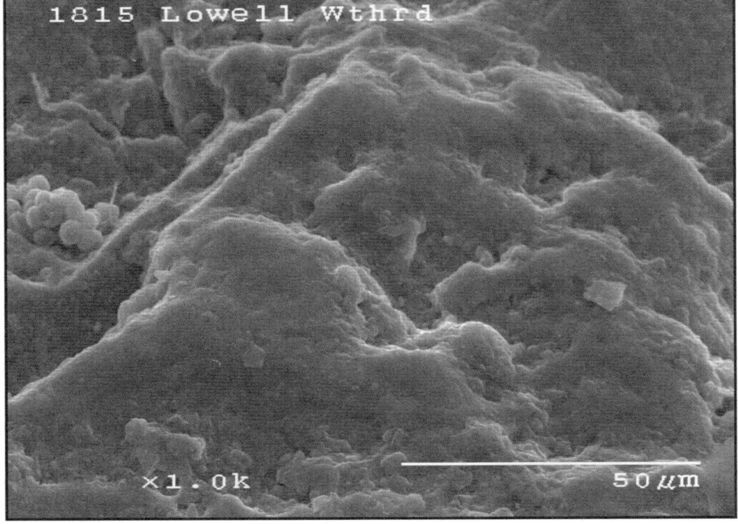

Figure 48: Rounded and frayed edges of biotite mica grains on the weathered surface. (1000X)

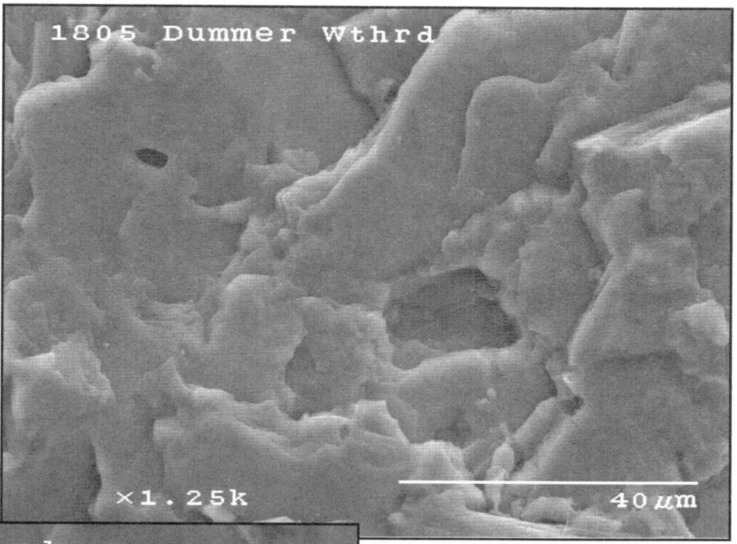

Figure 49: Large- and small-scale pitting was observed on the basal surfaces of weathered biotite grains. (1250X)

Figure 50: Individual sheets of biotite exfoliate off the weathered surface of the slate tombstone. (2000X)

Another factor of weathering that we need to be mindful of is that the Hallowell Cemetery is located within a few dozen yards of a railroad. Localized acid rain conditions were produced by the exhaust from the sulfur-laden coal of steam engines over a period of roughly two hundred years, which would certainly accelerate the weathering of all tombstones in the cemetery. Ironically, the slate tombstones are closest to the railroad. Even though we observed exfoliation of some biotite grains after two hundred years of weathering, the vast majority of the minerals at the surface were still intact.

Interpretation – Part II (Tombstone Study)

When we compare the tombstone data with the weathering of the original man-made surfaces on the Kensington Rune Stone, a statement about the inscription's relative age is possible. Since the biotite mica grains are generally in an advanced stage of deterioration on the tombstones after about two hundred years, and all of the mica minerals on the original man-made surfaces of the Kensington Rune Stone have weathered away (this includes the runes, flaked areas, the "Oh Shoot" area and the entire split side), the Kensington Rune Stone inscription must be older than two hundred years.

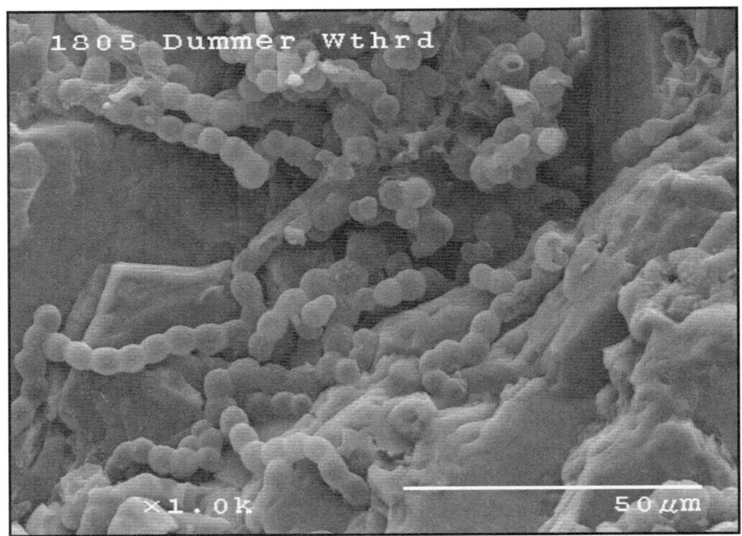

Figure 51: Tiny worm-like beads of lichen partially cover the surface of a slate tombstone. Acid produced by the lichen accelerates the weathering rate of biotite mica. (1000X)

It should be noted that although the dissolution of sheet silicates, including biotite, has been studied for decades, there are a number of new research opportunities. Hopefully, this ongoing tombstone research will add to the understanding of the weathering characteristics not only of micas, but other minerals as well.

Conclusions

Based on our observations, test results, research, and past experience, the following conclusions are appropriate:

1. The Kensington Rune Stone is a tabular-shaped, dark gray, meta-graywacke glacial erratic boulder. Based upon the mineralogy and geologic textures, the stone probably originated from the Paleoproterozoic (roughly 1.8 to 2.1 billion years before present) Animikie basin of east-central Minnesota.

2. Several curved fractures along the split side edge of the stone indicate purposeful man-made impact. The previously larger-sized stone was intentional broken down, or split, to its present shape prior to carving the inscription.

3. The dark gray color, rougher overall texture, and similar weathering profile of the entire split side match the flaking and non-retooled (unscratched) areas of the inscription, indicating that all these surfaces were made at the same time.

4. Approximately 95% of the runic inscription was cleaned out with a nail shortly after its discovery. This "retooling" removed weathering features from the bottom of the carved grooves and crushed the constituent minerals, which turned these surfaces

white. This "fresh" appearance of the inscription has led to confusion, bias, and misinterpretation of the inscription's relative age. Several runic characters in the last three lines of the inscription on the side of the stone were not retooled and exhibit original weathering features.

5. The white gypsum coatings on the split side of the stone appear to be remnants of plaster casts reportedly made by the Minnesota Historical Society in the 1940s.

6. The glacial back side of the Kensington Rune Stone exhibits two, approximately $1/2''$ (13 mm) wide, white, undulating and branching lineations. The white lineations were produced when iron and magnesium were leached from minerals in the stone by young tree roots. Because the pattern of the root leaching matches the description and sketches of three witnesses (Olof Ohman, Olof Ohman Jr., and Sam Olson), they were most likely made by the same tree under which the Stone was reportedly found.

7. Based on comparison with the still actively oxidizing pyrite crystals within the AVM Stone inscription carved in 1985, the completely oxidized pyrite pits observed in the original Kensington Rune Stone inscription took longer than twenty years of weathering to develop, as of June, 2005. This fact means Olof Ohman could not have perpetrated a hoax since he immigrated to the United States from Sweden in the summer of 1879, only nineteen years before the discovery.

8. Based on comparison of the weathering characteristics of biotite in the chip samples from the slate tombstones, the mica minerals in the original inscription of the Kensington Rune Stone took longer than two hundred years to completely weather away, which eliminates the possibility that anyone living in the late 19th century could have been involved in a hoax.

Plate 1: This aerial view of the Ohman Farm was taken in about 1995 and indicates the approximate discovery sites of both the AVM Stone (1985) and the Kensington Rune Stone (1898). (Photograph courtesy of the Douglas County (Minnesota) Parks Division)

Plate 2: The glacial surfaces, under reflected light, of the stone exhibit a lighter overall blue-gray color with noticeable pitting. This surface represents at least 12,000 years of weathering (50X). (SFW)

Plate 3: Under reflected light, the split side surface is a darker gray color and does not exhibit the prominent pitting of the glacial surfaces. This surface represents a weathered appearance that would have developed over a much shorter period of time than the glacial age surfaces of the stone (50X). (SFW)

Plate 4: On the glacial top end of the stone the far right side (outlined in red) has a darker gray area that has the same color and texture as the entire split side indicating it spalled off when the stone was reshaped. (SFW)

Plate 5: The dark gray areas adjacent to the white scratches (retooling) were produced by pieces of rock that flaked off when the original inscription was carved. These flaked surfaces have the same properties as the entire split side, which indicates that they were created at the same time (line 3, character 51) (7.5X). (SFW)

Plate 6: A sharp instrument crushed the minerals at the bottom of this rune groove turning the area white. A nail, reportedly used to clean the inscription shortly after its discovery, cut through the well-developed iron oxide deposits (line 10, character 217) (20X). (SFW)

Plate 7: Rust-colored iron oxide deposits within an original character on the split side (line 11, character 239) (10X). Notice also that the flaked areas have the same color, texture and weathering profile as the entire surface of the split side, which indicates the surfaces were made at the same time. (SFW)

Plate 8: Weathered pyrite pits (red arrows) with halos of iron oxide within a rune groove on the split side (L-10, C-213) (56X). (SFW)

Plate 9: The AVM Stone was found roughly in the middle of a pile of field-cleared glacial boulders. The yellowish-orange-colored lichen reportedly developed in the previous five years, when the adjacent wetland water level was raised roughly five feet because the outlet was dammed. (SFW)

Plate 10: The AVM Stone inscription was carved on a granite gneiss glacial boulder. Characters carved in the dark gray, roughly 2 inch (6.5 cm) wide band of biotite-rich schist were white in color. (SFW)

Plate 11: Rust-colored staining emanated from actively oxidizing pyrite crystals within the carved "V" character of the AVM Stone inscription.   This photo was taken in September of 2003, at which time the inscription was over eighteen years old. (SFW)

Plate 12: A rust-colored iron oxide stain was formed by a decomposing pyrite grain within a carved character (the red lines indicate the first carved letter, an "A," on the stone) in the lighter-colored granitic area of the glacial erratic "AVM" boulder (20X). (SFW)

Plate 13: An actively corroding pyrite crystal (red arrow) created a pronounced halo of iron oxide within a carved character on the AVM Stone (60X). (SFW)

Plate 14: The core sample location (yellow circle) on the glacial back side of the Kensington Rune Stone. (SFW)

Plate 15: The freshly fractured surface on the bottom of the core sample shows several white clusters of crushed minerals (mostly micas) under reflected light (50X). (SFW)

Plate 16: Elongated muscovite mica (yellow) grains are visible under cross-polarized light and aligned in two directions, at roughly 90 degrees to each other, which suggests two metamorphic events occurred that are unique to the Kensington Rune Stone meta-greywacke (200X).

Plate 17: The primary mineral constituents of the Kensington Rune Stone are mostly angular quartz, orthoclase, and plagioclase sand grains visible here under cross-polarized light (40X).

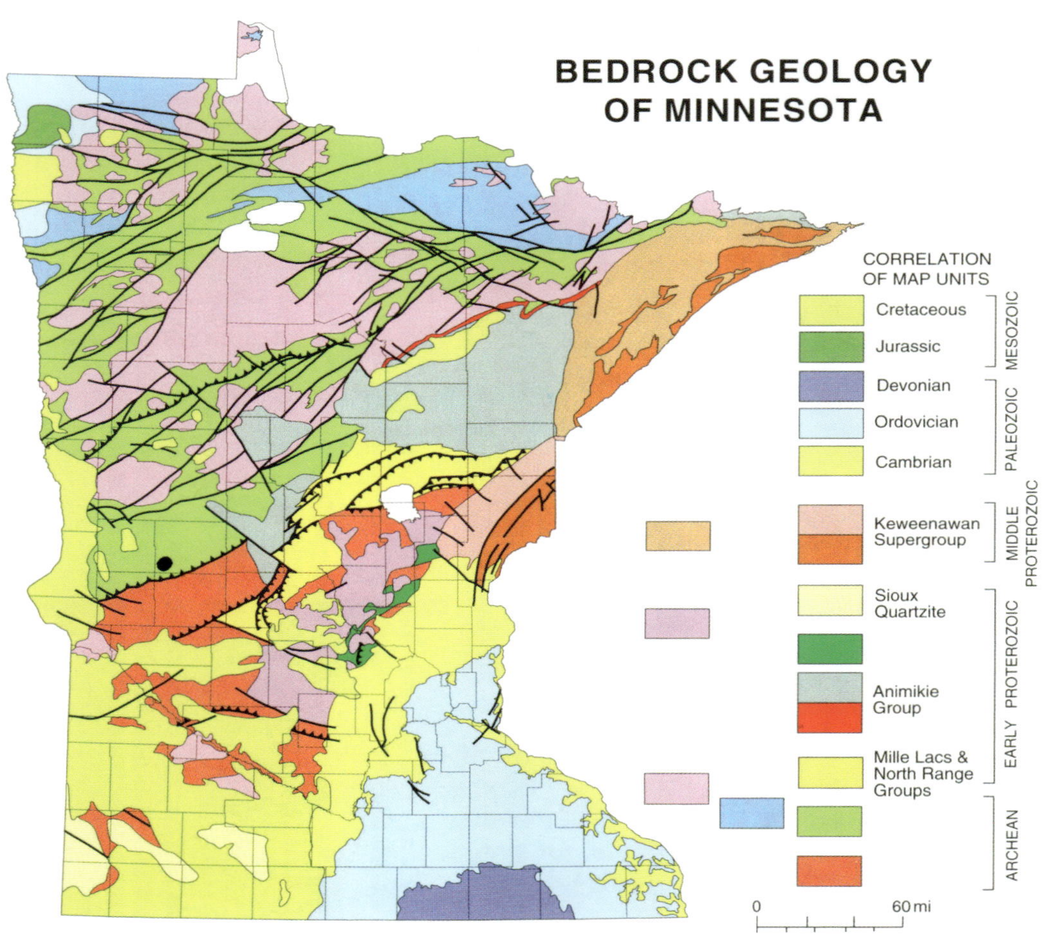

Plate 18: A geologic map of Minnesota shows the Animikie Group rocks, the likely source of the Kensington Rune Stone, located east and northeast of Kensington (black dot). Geologic map by the Minnesota Geological Survey, 1997, modified from Morey, G. B., compiler, 1996.

Plate 19: The characters used in the Dating Code in the Kensington Rune Stone inscription are highlighted in blue. If the two crossed runes (ᛨ and ᛏ) are used for the Sunday letter (B) and the Golden year number (14), along with the only pentadic number with a punch (ᛒ), the date calculated using the medieval Easter table is 1362. This appears to be a confirmation of the pentadic date at the end of the inscription so that it could not be altered. The characters used in the Mystery Code in the Kensington Rune Stone inscription are highlighted in red. The first six characters (ᛃ,ᚱ,ᚷ,ᚠ,ᚷ̆,ᚱ) have conspicuous punches within the lines or short chisel strokes. These apparent singled out runes in sequence spell in Swedish "Gral är" which in English is "Grail is." The punched M and ᛃ runes could stand for wisdom.

Plate 20: The green dots identify intentional punches that represent the use of a palatal R at the end of the words norR, in line 5, and waR in line 6. The use of dotted Rs in the Kensington Rune Stone inscription represents compelling proof of its medieval origin.   Photographs were taken by John Steward in March 1899.

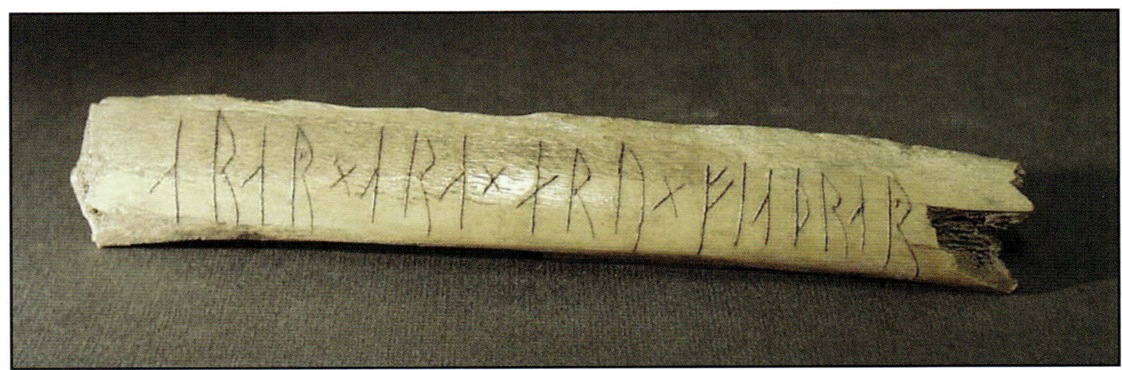

Plate 21: This carved bone was found during the excavation of a medieval site in Lund, Sweden in the 1930's and the inscription dates to about 1200 A.D. There are two dotted Rs carved in the inscription (DaRn 302, supplement 5) which translated into English reads, "The eagle's oars are [its] feathers."

Plate 22: In the 13th and 14th centuries the Baltic was a center of crusades against the pagans who lived on its southern coast from Lübeck in Germany to Estonia in the east. (Map by Dan Wiemer)

Plate 23: The island of Gotland in the Baltic Sea of Scandinavia was a bustling center of trade for centuries. In its heyday, the island supported over ninety churches. Many of these buildings preserved runic inscriptions from well before 1000 to as late as 1621. (Map by Dan Wiemer)

Plates 24 & 25: Inside Lye Church (top) on the island of Gotland the G 99 runic inscription is found on a medieval grave slab (bottom) mortared into the floor next to the altar. The inscription is dated twice (1449), once written out in runes (blue), the other using the Easter Table dating method (red). The carver identified the Sunday letter (R), the Golden year number (K) and the column is XII (12), incorrectly carved as XI (11). (SFW)

Plates 26 & 27: The beautiful Tofta Church contains the important G 195 grave slab inscription (bottom) which was broken up and buried under the floor in the distant past. Ironically, this probably prevented the inscription, carved into local limestone, from weathering away. Many medieval inscriptions are highly weathered or have completely weathered away.   (SFW)

Plates 28, 29, & 30: Many of the medieval grave slabs in Gotland are found outside the churches like the beautiful Hejnum G 242 inscription (above). Runic inscriptions that display symbols include a Templar-like cross on Rute G 319 (bottom left) and the six-pointed star on Vamlingbo G 8 (bottom right). (SFW)

Plates 31, 32 & 33: To defend themselves from periodic raids by pirates, the people of Gotland built defense towers next to at least six churches located along the coasts. Most of the defense towers, like the one at Gothem Church (above) along the east coast, and Sundre and Öja Churches (bottom left/right) on the west and southern coasts, are now in ruins. (SFW)

Plate 34: This reproduction of a Viking age picture stone near Ardre Church, circa 900, is typical of the era on the island of Gotland. The eight-legged horse on the upper part of the stone is the mythical figure called Sleipner. (SFW)

Plate 35: Templar-like crosses adorn the walls on both sides of the altar piece at Lojsta Church. (SFW)

Plates 36, 37, & 38: Many of the churches on Gotland with medieval wall murals have Templar-like crosses prominently displayed.   Left: Öja Church, Middle: Lye Church, Right: Fide Church. (SFW)

Plate 39: This medieval grave slab was one of three with runic inscriptions that have large Templar-like crosses carved on them at Othem Church on Gotland (G 283). (SFW)

Plates 40 & 41: The modern Ukna Church in Småland, Sweden in 2005. The Sm 145 runic inscription and the dotted-R first came to the attention of runologists in 1935 when the grave slab in the ruined Ukna Church was examined. The old Ukna Church was abandoned in the 1820's. (SFW)

Plate 42: The religious symbols M and W appear on this relic case (ca.1200) from Spånga Church in Uppland, Sweden.   Note the repeated X pattern in the trim.   This case is now in the Historiska Museum in Stockholm, Sweden. (SFW)

Plate 43: This foot-tall, gold gilded AVM was found in the secret room at St. Sulpice in Paris, France and was reportedly set aside for Count Maurepas. The letters "AVM" can clearly be seen. It is the only known artifact, other than the Kensington Rune Stone, to exhibit these characters in an apparently religious context.

Plate 44: Author Wolter stands next to the Sternarna (U 160, Risbyle, Täby) rune stone near Uppland on October 23, 2003. The stone was raised in the beginning of the 11th century and is the oldest rune stone in this area. Translated into English by author Nielsen the inscription reads, *"Ulvkätill and Gye and Une raised this stone in memory of Ulv, their good father. He lived in Slålhambri. God and God's mother help his spirit and soul, bestow upon him light and paradise."* (Photo by Lars Westman)

Plate 45: Swedish journalist Lars Westman stands next to a Viking age rune stone (U 164) outside Stockholm, Sweden, on October 24, 2003. (SFW)

Plate 46: Professor Michael Barnes stands next to a thousand-year-old rune stone (Sö 178) outside Gripsholm Castle in Sweden on October 25, 2003. The stone was found in 1730 and moved to the castle grounds in 1926. Translated into English by author Nielsen the inscription reads, *"Hälgulv and Olov. They raised both stones in memory of their brother Kätilmund and made this bridge in memory of Soma their mother. However, Brune her brother carved the runes."* (SFW)

Plates 47 & 48: The majestic twin spires outside the Gothic style Uppsala Cathedral (left) soar over 150 feet into the sky. At Vaksala Church outside Uppsala, Sweden, white engrailed Ms and Ws are painted in the triangle peak (right). (SFW)

Plate 49: Professor Henrik Williams kneels next to the rune stone fragment Frötuna Rasbo U 1003B which he examined in a wooded area outside Uppsala, Sweden in May of 2005. A double-dotted R is found on this fragment. (SFW)

Language and Runes of the Kensington Rune Stone

The Origin of the Runes and Language on the Kensington Rune Stone

For over a century certain details on the Kensington Rune Stone inscription were asserted to be powerful proof of a modern forgery. Most of these details are now fully explained by the close examination of the runes of Gotland that follows, and by the identification of Kensington Rune Stone traits that have a lot in common with the dialects of Gotland and East Götaland. This chapter begins with a section on the most compelling proof that the Kensington Rune Stone is medieval, the dotted ř (Patrik Larsson, 2002). Next is a section that demonstrates how many of the runic details on the Kensington Rune Stone are found in the medieval runic records of Gotland, followed by a section that deals with the mutual dialect traits to be found either in Gotland or East Götaland, with those on the Kensington Rune Stone. A section on the Easter Table derived date on the Kensington Rune Stone comes just before the last section, which deals with the recently discovered rune-rows on the Larsson documents discovered in Sweden in 2004, and the Yoke inscription which was discovered in Sweden in 2003.

The well-known phrase, "the devil is in the details" could not be more appropriate when it comes to the inscription on the Kensington Rune Stone. It is these details that give compelling proof that the runes and language of the Kensington Rune Stone are indeed medieval and could have been applied in the 14th century.

The Dotted R

The most compelling indication that the runes of the Kensington Rune Stone are medieval is the use of the dotted R found on the inscription. R represents a palatal r sound, but is a sound no longer found in Scandinavian. When the Kensington Rune Stone was discovered in 1898, runologists thought that the palatal R, designated by the pitch-folk or triton-shaped rune (⋔) was out of the language at the end of the Viking age (latest 1100). However, Otto van Friesen (1933: Fig. 64, 231-2) included (⋔) in his rune-row as applicable in Gotland until around 1300. In her recent doctoral thesis Snædal (2002) has shown that (⋔) was used in Gotland as late as the mid-1300s at Fide Church in inscription G 28 and that during the 1300s (⋔) was often applied incorrectly, as at Tofta Church Inscription G 195 of circa 1347. Therefore, the use of the palatal R on the Kensington Rune Stone would be in keeping with the times.

But there is something else that is very important. A special sign was introduced in medieval times for the palatal R, namely the dotted R (ᚱ̇). This rune form was documented in Ukna Church in Småland, Sweden on the southern coast opposite Gotland, and in Lund, Skåne, Sweden at the southern end of the Baltic. Both of these inscriptions were found in the 1930s, forty years after the Kensington Rune Stone was discovered.

The two dotted Rs (ᚱ̇ᚱ̇) present on the Kensington Rune Stone are definitive and compelling proof of its medieval origin. What follows is a comprehensive look at the dotted Rs on known medieval inscriptions and on the Kensington Rune Stone.

Ukna Church Inscription

In 1935 the dotted ᚱ̇ first came to the attention of runologists on an inscription (Sm 145) in the Ukna church in Småland, Sweden. The words iðräᚱ̇: boniᚱ̇, (your prayers) appear in the inscription with both Rs dotted. The dot was used to indicate the R sound, perhaps when pronounced with the tip of the tongue on the roof of the mouth. Jacobsen and Moltke (1942: 968) report this discovery in their manual of runes.

iðräR BöniR (your prayers)

This inscription (SM 145), from about 1300 was found in 1935 at Ukna Church near Kalmar, Småland, Sweden. The dotted Rs, the first painted and the second not painted in this picture, in this inscription are cited in Jacobsen and Moltke (1942: 968). (SFW)

Lund Bone 4 in Skåne, Sweden

The Lund Bone 4 in Jacobsen and Moltke (1942: 968) was discovered in 1938.

araR ara äru fiaþraR

Another inscription with two dotted **R**s was found in the 1938 excavation of a medieval site in Lund, Sweden from the Elder Middle Danish period, circa 1200 (see color section, plate 21). The Lund Bone 4 (Danish Rune Annex 5) has two dotted Rs in the words **fiaþraR** (feathers) and **araR** (oars) in the poetic expression "The eagle's oars are its feathers (wings)."

Dotted Rs on the Kensington Rune Stone

The first dotted R to be noticed on the Kensington Rune Stone was sighted by Erik Wahlgren in 1958 in the word **norr** (north), and can be seen on the inside cover of his book. Based on photographs, Wahlgren detected the sequence **RR** on line 5 of the inscription, but made no attempt to interpret it. Barry Hanson made a visual inspection in 2001, which indicated there was no intentional punch in the first R, and only the lower punch was present in the second R yielding **norR** (north). Wolter (2000) photo documented the dotted Rs in the words **GøteR** (Götalanders) and **lægeR** (camp). These dots are easily observed in the previously published photographs of the Kensington Rune Stone. However, Wolter's (2002) subsequent microscopic photographs under different lighting has allowed for better examination of the punches.

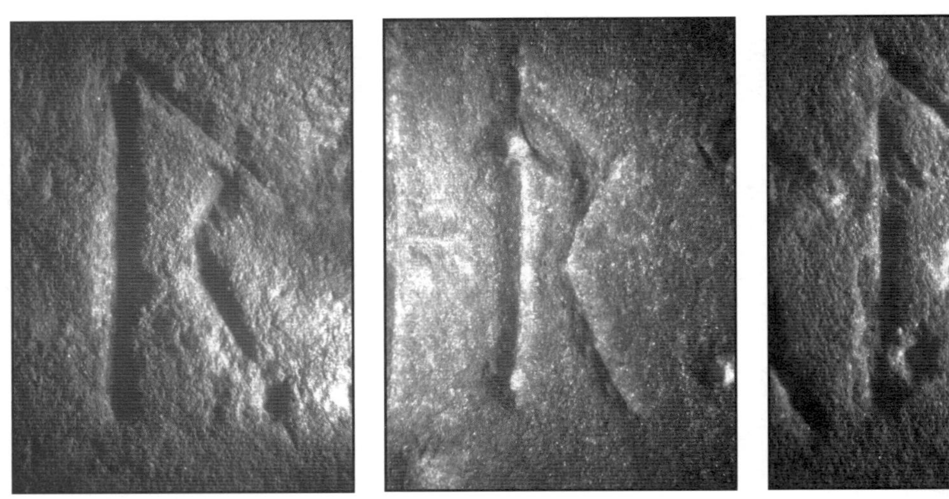

These three "R" runes on the Kensington Rune Stone have obvious punch marks (L to R: L-1; C-7, L-4; C-74, L-5; C-104, L-6; C-125). (SFW: 2002)

A fourth dotted R was documented by the authors in December 2004 in the word va (were). We sought out this particular dotted R when we realized that it would be ety-mologically correct.

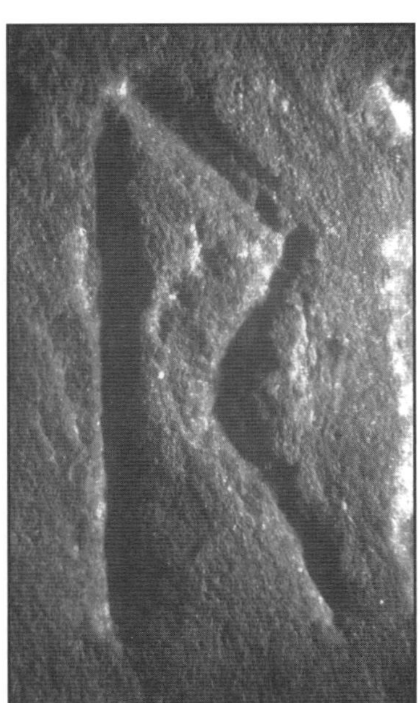

A punch in the upper part of the R in var (were) was documented in December 2004 (L-6; C-125) (from Wolter 2002). (SFW: 2002)

The dotted R in the word var (were), as seen here on a full sized cast of the Stone, has the original etymology. (SFW)

Compare **vahR** with the word *vaR* (were) in the G 370 inscription at Hablingbo Church on Gotland from circa 1150 (Snædal, 2002: Fig 4, 68-70). This word also has an h-insert sequence **–ahR,** a three letter sequence that is reminiscent of **ahr** (year) with its h-insert on the Kensington Rune Stone.

Prior to 1949, there were at least five known photographs taken of the Kensington Rune Stone, and the dotted R's are clear in all of them. Inexplicably, while Moltke (1949) stated that the photographs from Steward (1899) were so clear it was as if he had the Kensington Rune Stone on his desk, he did not observe the very dotted Rs he had reported with Jacobsen in 1942. In 1985, Moltke gave this advice on observing rune forms: *"But if there is any doubt, no photograph can ever take the place for the rune stone itself. Go and look at it."* If the runologist had taken his own advice he probably would have discovered this compelling evidence in favor of the Stone's validity as a medieval artifact.

 The palatal R usually occurs at the end of a word or syllable.

The word vahR (were), with a palatal R (ᛦ), appears in the G 370 inscription from Hablingbo Church on Gotland, circa 1150.

Examples of the correct usage of the palatal R (ᛦ) persist into the late 1300s in Gotland (G 28, G 282, G 289, and G 290). In the Norrlanda Church inscription G 151, both the r-rune and R-rune are used, indicating the carver's uncertainty about which r-letter to use. The fact that he used both would seem to indicate that the two sounds were beginning to coalesce.

The Norrlanda Church inscription (G 151), circa 1300, has the word eptirR (after). The last ᚱ rune has only the left arm, a Gotlandic unilateral ↿, as opposed to a bilateral R (ᚱ).

Examples of the correct usage of R (ᚱ) are present as late as the latter part of the 1300s in Gotland (G 28 Fide Church circa middle 1300s).

Dotted Rs Recorded by Swedish Investigators on Gotland

Five dotted Rs are described in runic inscriptions on Gotland, including G 57 Hemse, G 100 Lye, G 158 Gothem, G 70 Urgude, G 128 Guldrupe, and G 282 Othem Church, but their significance has been overlooked by examining runologists.

Hemse Church

The Hemse Church inscription (G 57) on Gotland, circa 1150, has an apparent dotted R documented by runologists as Gairaif. The dotted R was treated in the texts as a normal "r" without a dot. Author Wolter personally examined and photographed (right) this fragment at the Historical Museum storage facility in Stockholm, Sweden, on May 11, 2005, and believes this is an unintentionally chipped area. Author Nielsen however, pointed out that the chipped area occurs in the correct place in a word spelled with a palatal R as late as 1280 in Gotland. (SFW)

The Hemse Church inscription (G 57) on Gotland, circa 1150, contains a dotted R (ᚱ) that was curiously ignored in the text write-up for the name **Gairalf**. Acknowledging the dot yields **GaiRalf** and is etymologically correct for this name. The runologist Wessén went on to say that G 57 indicated an early transition of the palatal R to the modern r before 1150. Instead, it may indicate the first record of the dotted ᚱ on the island of Gotland. However, the chipped area must be examined further to determine if a punch was inserted in the loop of the R.

Lye Chruch

The G 100 Lye Church inscription has a dotted R at the end of the word byrℝ *byrþ* (birth), dated to 1449. (SFW)

Byrþ (birth) is the normal spelling, but for some reason the carver apparently heard a palatal R when he spoke the word and recorded it for þ. However, it is not etymologically correct.

Gothem Church G 158

A dotted ℝ was identified in the word þors (Sunday number Thor) by Pehr A. Säve in 1864. (SFW)

A dotted R was recorded by Säve on a grave slab in Gotland on the east edge of the inscription (G 158) at Gothem Church dated to 1305. þors (Thor) is the name of the þ-rune.

This ℝ is seen as the 5th rune from the end of the 7th line in the inscription. þors (Thors). When plotted on the Easter Table the Golden Year date on the G 158 inscription gives the year as 1305 (Snædal 2002: 142). In another surprising twist artist Pehr A. Säve had already noted the dotted R in this inscription (G 158) on Gotland in 1864, but its significance has remained unrecognized by runologists to this day. For one thing, the R is not etymologically correct, however by 1305 ⋏ was incorrectly applied for R in Gotland.

Urgude Inscription G 70 from Sproge Parish

This dotted R which is dated to 1514 on the G 70 Urguda inscription was likely a decoration from an earlier inscription since the palatal R was no longer used in speech. The inscription says Petar (Peter)

The G 70 inscription, called Urgude, is a dated inscription by the Easter table from 1514 and has a dotted R that could have been copied as a decoration from some earlier inscription(s) carved a century or two before. It's likely there were many other inscriptions that were still in good condition in 1514, but almost five hundred years later most are now either destroyed or weathered to the point where they are illegible.

Guldrupe Church

The G 128 inscription in plaster at Guldrupe Church, circa 1500, has an initial dotted R. The dot could be a decoration, or it could be a dotted R used as an e-vowel in eygþ (eyed).

The year 1500 is too late for the palatal R on Gotland, but in Guldrupe it is used initially, meaning that it could still represent a vowel sound. If not used as a decoration, this word might mean **eygþ** (eyed). This inscription would be the only one in which the dotted R is used as a vowel. In the Sm 145 Ukna Church inscription the dotted Rs are used for the palatal R sound, but in the same inscription (ᚤ) was used for y, since it is between two consonants, in the name þyrhilsär (Tyrgil's).

The Ukna Church inscription Sm 145, circa 1300, has an R (ᚤ) used for the vowel "y" between two consonants in the word þyrhilsär (Tyrgil's). (SFW)

Dotted Rs Recorded by the Authors on Gotland

The authors' investigation of the word aLliR (all) in the G 192 inscription at Västergarn Church revealed what might be the first dotted R on Gotland with the dot in the lower loop of the R. ALliR is etymologically correct with the terminal palatal R. This means there are now six dotted Rs found in Scandinavia. It would not be surprising if a number of other examples in Gotland remain to be discovered upon re-examination of previously studied inscriptions.

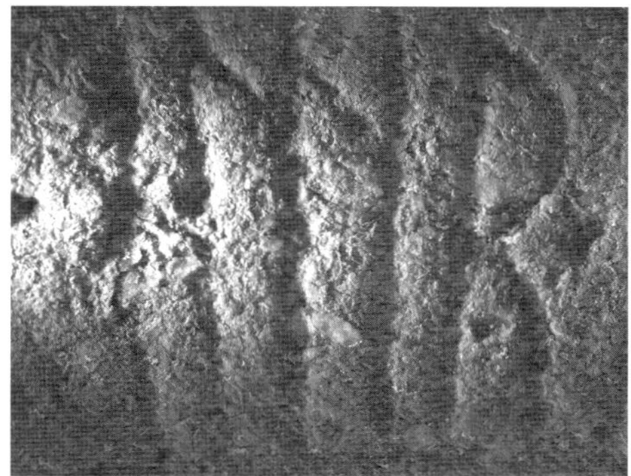

Another apparent example of the dotted R in the word aLliR (all) appears in G 192 inscription, circa 1400, at Västergarn Church. The dot in this R is in the lower area rather than the top section of the R. (SFW)

The G 282 inscription, from circa 1300s, at Othem Church has the etymologically correct I : R (you). (SFW)

Another apparent dotted R was discovered among the owner's tags recovered from the Bergen Wharf excavations of the 1960s. The inscription reads **BotlaifR a** (**BotlaifR** owns). It has a dotted R as would be expected for this date in Gotland as is also found in **ButraifR** with the palatal R = ᚼ in the G 207 Stenkumla Church inscription of circa 1150.

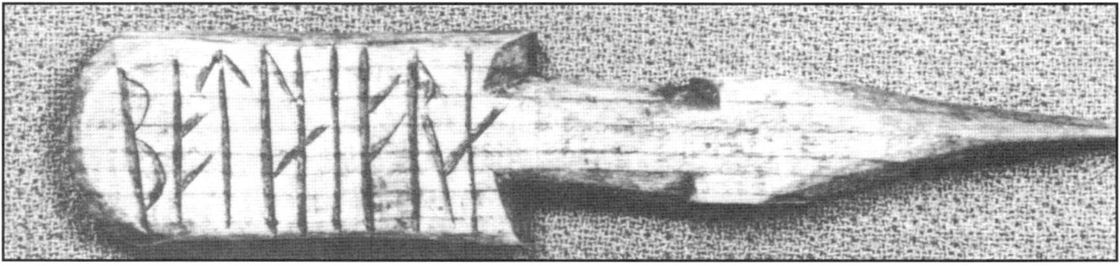

Norwegian Rune 670 was retrieved from between the 1198 and 1246 burn layers of the Bergen Wharf excavation in the 1960s. This is an owner's tag from Gotland and was used to identify wares.

Overstrikes of the R

A double dotted R with both dots on the main stave was found in this inscription (G 115), which dates from circa 1300, in the word botuiþr from the Gammelgarn Church on Gotland. (SFW)

Since the dots on the R in the word **botuiþr** are not at the same elevation as the word separator they may not indicate an overstrike. This usage is identical to the dotted R in the Kensington Rune Stone word **läge** (camp). A palatal R is not etymologically correct in **botuiþr** and it seems to be a placement of the shaft over a prematurely carved word divider.

The word lägeR (camp) on the Kensington Rune Stone that likely has an overstrike on the R.

The discovery of the dotted Rs on the Kensington Rune Stone seem to be undeniable proof of the inscription's medieval origin and the connection of the Stone's author in some way to the island of Gotland.

On the Förtuna fragment U 1003B, circa 1100, both R and r are used at this time (and) in the word -btiRr (after). The r-rune is regarded as an overstrike of the word divider. This rune stone fragment was discovered in 1923.

Thompson (1975: 136) referred to this inscription as the "strange dotted r-rune of 1003B." Runic commentators have considered this to be a correction for the placement of a prematurely placed double dotted word divider.

The Easter Table Dating Code

The year carved on the Kensington Rune Stone is given in pentadic numbers as 1362 (ΓꝼΡΓ). This method of dating is simple and uses minimal characters and space, so it's a benefit to the carver of the inscription. However, this type of date is potentially vulnerable to alteration. A simple stroke with a hammer on a chisel could make a fourth horizontal bar on the pentadic three (Ϝ to a Ϝ), which would easily change the date by a hundred years. We unexpectedly discovered a confirmation code on the Kensington Rune Stone that employs the Easter Table that the carver used to confirm the pentadic date. The Easter Table was commonly used by medieval priests to calculate important religious dates.

To our surprise, this method of dating seems to be used in runic inscriptions found on Gotland. There are more than a dozen inscriptions on Gotland that use the Easter dating system. We have chosen two examples from Sanda Church (G 182 and G 184) to illustrate the procedure used to extrapolate a date from the three dating items given. The three items required to calculate a date using the Easter Table include the Sunday Letter, the Golden Year number and the column number.

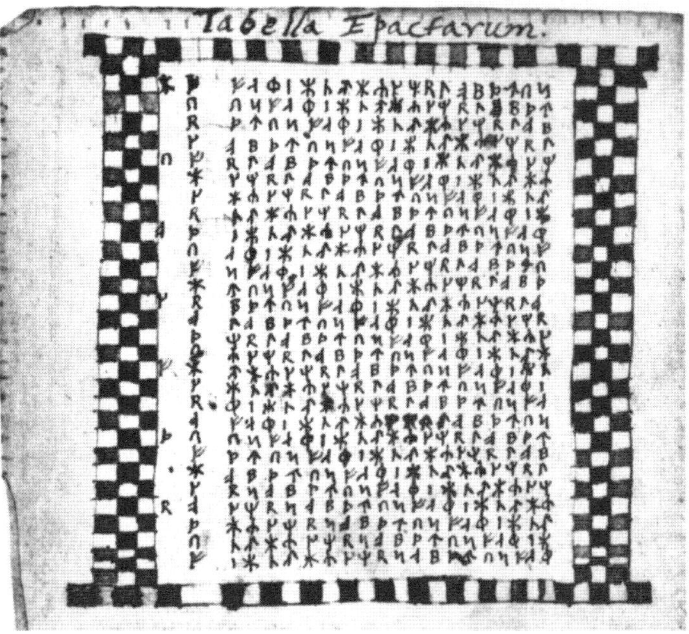

Table 1: This runic Easter Table was hand copied by Ole Worm from the Gotlandic calendar of 1328. This copy is from the manuscript he saw in 1622 from an old library in Jutland in Denmark. The table displays the 532-year period in runes for the perpetual calendar with 19 columns to the right of 28 rows. The two left most columns are the Sunday Letters columns that record the day that the first Sunday of the year occurs. The runes are converted to Latin letters and Arabic numbers in table 2. (Lithberg, 1939)

The Sunday Letters can be converted from runes to Latin letters or Arabic numbers.

Date of First Sunday	1	2	3	4	5	6	7
Runic Sunday Letter	ᚢ	ᚤ	þ	ᛂ	ᚱ	ᚠ	✳
Latin Sunday Letter	A	B	C	D	E	F	G

Sunday Letters

The Golden Year numbers can also be converted from runes to Arabic numbers by the conversion.

1	2	3	4	5	6	7	8	9	10	11	12	13	14	15	16	17	18	19
ᚢ	ᚤ	Þ	ᛂ	ᚱ	ᚠ	✳	ᛏ	I	ᛏ	ᚴ	ᛏ	B	ᚼ	Ψ	ᚻ	ᛏ	ᚫ	Φ

Golden Year Numbers

On Gotland, the Sanda Church bell has a runic inscription (G 184) that identifies the Sunday rune, the Golden year rune and the column number. When plotted on the Easter Table they yield the date the bell was made: 1493.

This bell hangs in the Sanda Church on the Island of Gotland. The inscription G 184 was cast into the bell and reads in English, "k is the Sunday letter and t is the Golden Year in the 13th column of the Easter Table." When cross plotted on the Easter Table these characters yield the year 1493. (SFW)

k suntahr tir brim o͡k i treta͡ntu rato

»**k** söndag(sruna) och **t** prim(runa) i trettonde raden (på påsktavlan).»

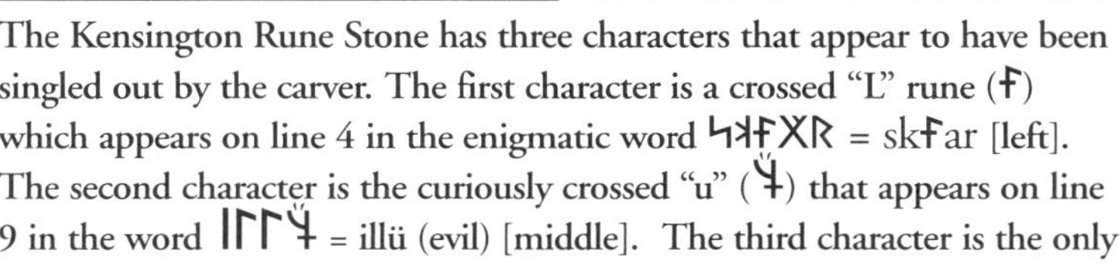

One of the many self-dated grave slab inscriptions from Gotland is from the Sanda Church (G 182) which was reported by Sjöborg (1822). It identifies the Sunday letter as ✱ and the Golden Year as Lahr—the name for the l-rune—in the 7th column of the Easter Table. When plotted on the Easter Table these characters yield the year 1324.

On the Kensington Rune Stone the Easter dating procedure involves using the two uniquely crossed runes, (⅄ = Ⴖ = "u") and (Ϝ = Γ = "l"). Since "l" is not a Sunday letter it is assigned as the Golden Year number, "u" is then the Sunday letter. The conversion tables yield a Sunday letter of B and the Golden Year number as 14. The third item needed was a column number. There are twelve individual pentadic numbers in the inscription. During the microscopic examination performed in 2002 a mysterious punch was observed within the carved lines of one of the numbers. Since it was the only number that had a punch we gave it a try. The first character in the inscription is a pentadic 8 that has a punch at the end of the second horizontal bar (Ᵽ). When the punched pentadic number eight on the Kensington Rune Stone is cross-plotted in Table 2 it marks the eighth column, which designates the years 1336 to 1363. The Golden Year number 14 appears twice in column 8, indicating the years 1343 and 1362. By using the Sunday Letter B, the year is confirmed as **1362**!

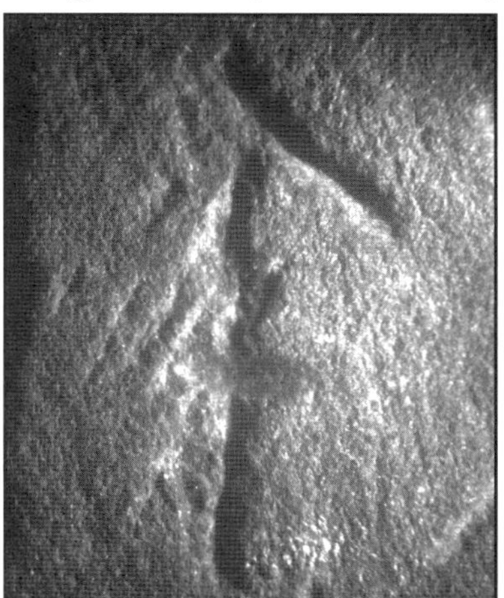
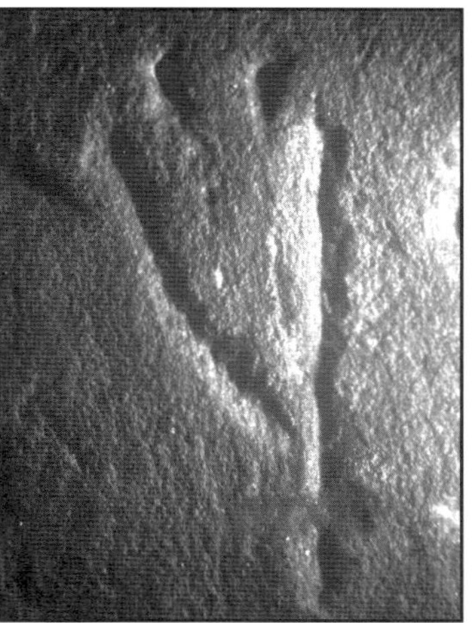
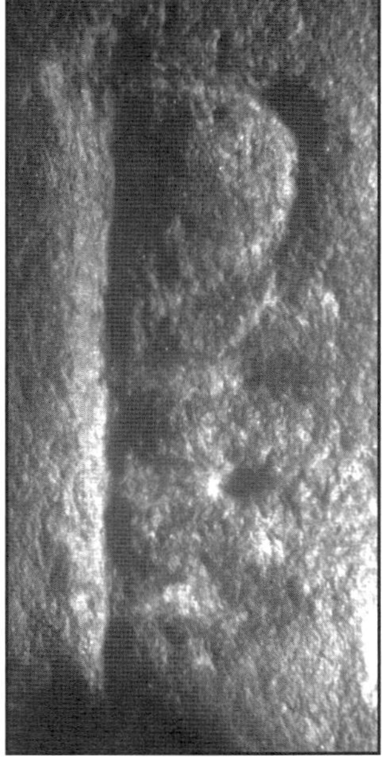

The Kensington Rune Stone has three characters that appear to have been singled out by the carver. The first character is a crossed "L" rune (Ϝ) which appears on line 4 in the enigmatic word ЧⴑϜXR = skfar [left]. The second character is the curiously crossed "u" (⅄) that appears on line 9 in the word ⏐ΓΓ⅄ = illü (evil) [middle]. The third character is the only one of the twelve individual pentadic numbers that has a mysterious punch carved at the end of the second horizontal bar of the eight [right]. This is the first character on the first line of the inscription. When plotted on the medieval Easter Table they yield the year 1362. This appears to be a code confirming the date carved in the inscription. (L 4, C 84; L 9, C 209; L 1, C 1) (SFW: 2002)

		I 1140—1167	II 1168—1195	III 1196—1223	IV 1224—1251	V 1252—1279	VI 1280—1307	VII 1308—1335	VIII 1336—1363	IX 1364—1391	X 1392—1419	XI 1420—1447	XII 1448—1475	XIII 1476—1503	XIV 1504—1531	XV 1532—1559	XVI 1560—1587	XVII 1588—1615	XVIII 1616—1643	XIX 1644—1671
G	F	1	10	19	9	18	8	17	7	16	6	15	5	14	4	13	3	12	2	11
	E	2	11	1	10	19	9	18	8	17	7	16	6	15	5	14	4	13	3	12
	D	3	12	2	11	1	10	19	9	18	8	17	7	16	6	15	5	14	4	13
	C	4	13	3	12	2	11	1	10	19	9	18	8	17	7	16	6	15	5	14
B	A	5	14	4	13	3	12	2	11	1	10	19	9	18	8	17	7	16	6	15
	G	6	15	5	14	4	13	3	12	2	11	1	10	19	9	18	8	17	7	16
	F	7	16	6	15	5	14	4	13	3	12	2	11	1	10	19	9	18	8	17
	E	8	17	7	16	6	15	5	14	4	13	3	12	2	11	1	10	19	9	18
D	C	9	18	8	17	7	16	6	15	5	14	4	13	3	12	2	11	1	10	19
	B	10	19	9	18	8	17	7	16	6	15	5	14	4	13	3	12	2	11	1
	A	11	1	10	19	9	18	8	17	7	16	6	15	5	14	4	13	3	12	2
	G	12	2	11	1	10	19	9	18	8	17	7	16	6	15	5	14	4	13	3
F	E	13	3	12	2	11	1	10	19	9	18	8	17	7	16	6	15	5	14	4
	D	14	4	13	3	12	2	11	1	10	19	9	18	8	17	7	16	6	15	5
	C	15	5	14	4	13	3	12	2	11	1	10	19	9	18	8	17	7	16	6
	B	16	6	15	5	14	4	13	3	12	2	11	1	10	19	9	18	8	17	7
A	G	17	7	16	6	15	5	14	4	13	3	12	2	11	1	10	19	9	18	8
	F	18	8	17	7	16	6	15	5	14	4	13	3	12	2	11	1	10	19	9
	E	19	9	18	8	17	7	16	6	15	5	14	4	13	3	12	2	11	1	10
	D	1	10	19	9	18	8	17	7	16	6	15	5	14	4	13	3	12	2	11
C	B	2	11	1	10	19	9	18	8	17	7	16	6	15	5	14	4	13	3	12
	A	3	12	2	11	1	10	19	9	18	8	17	7	16	6	15	5	14	4	13
	G	4	13	3	12	2	11	1	10	19	9	18	8	17	7	16	6	15	5	14
	F	5	14	4	13	3	12	2	11	1	10	19	9	18	8	17	7	16	6	15
E	D	6	15	5	14	4	13	3	12	2	11	1	10	19	9	18	8	17	7	16
	C	7	16	6	15	5	14	4	13	3	12	2	11	1	10	19	9	18	8	17
	B	8	17	7	16	6	15	5	14	4	13	3	12	2	11	1	10	19	9	18
	A	9	18	8	17	7	16	6	15	5	14	4	13	3	12	2	11	1	10	19

Table 2: This numerical Easter Table is a modern depiction using Latin letters and Arabic numbers (Lithberg, 1953: Table 65).   The 19 columns span a 532-year period from 1140 to 1671.

Inscription	Sunday Rune	Golden Year Rune	Column	Sunday Letter	Golden Year Number	Column	Year
G 182	⁎	⌐	*Sjunde* (seventh)	G	14	7th	1324
KRS	↯	⌐	ᛒ (eighth)	B	14	8th	1362
G 185	⌐	↑	*Trettonde* (thirteenth)	F	12	13th	1493

This dating computation table shows the values required to obtain a date using the Easter Table.

It should be noted that all the pentadic numbers on the Kensington Rune Stone, outside of the date itself, are related to the column 8 and the indicators for the Sunday number 2, since "22 (ᚠᚠ) Northmen" and "2 (ᚠ) sk⸺ar " appear, and then a "14 (ᚠᛅ) day journey" confirming the Golden Year number. These are the only pentadic numbers carved in the text. The other four numbers are two Arabic tens (ᚤ) and **en** (one), written out twice.

In 1993, author Nielsen did not have the benefit of two discoveries described in this book: the rune ↯ identified as a u-rune in the Larsson rune-row; and the punched 8 (ᛒ). Nevertheless, Nielsen (1993) proposed the following at that time: "The Kensington Rune Stone has no apparent Golden rune dating, but does have some unusual usage. No u-rune was used on the inscription, which is most unusual for this popular letter, and numbers 2 and 22 were used once, thereby confirming the Sunday rune (u is the second letter in the runic alphabet). The crossed ⱡ was used once, as was the number 14, thereby confirming the Golden rune [Year]. There were 8 Goths, which confirms column 8."

In Gotland, the dates were at one time spelled out in runes confirming the Easter Table date. If a rune were damaged or incorrect, then the alternate date served to preserve the dating information. An example of this is the G 99 Lye Church inscription, where the Sunday Rune is designated as "r" and the Golden Rune as "k", but the column number XII was carved incorrectly as XI (see color section, plate 25). However, the date of 1449 was also carved out in runes as, **af guz byrþ fiurtan huntraþ ar ok ainu are minna en V tihi ar** (from God's birth 1400 years and one less than five tens). If the reader consults the Easter Table it can be readily seen that the column should have been XII. This example illustrates the value of confirming a date using a complimentary method.

The Word Count Table below shows that the e was used 27 times on the Kensington Rune Stone. It is curious to note that 1362 appears on the 27th row of the 8th column of the Easter Table. This count includes the e in skⱢar (sklear)

U	ᛦ	illu	1
b	ᛒ	bloþ	1
ø	⊕	gøter, røþe, øh	3
R	ᚱ	gøteℝ, lägeℝ, norℝ, vaℝ,	4
p	ᛔ	po, optagelse, äptir, äptir, skip	5
ä	ᛉ̈	läger, äptir, fräelse, här, äptir	5
k	ᚴ	ok, skⱢar, ok : fiske, kom, skip	6
m	ᛘ	norrmen, kom, hem, man, mans, from, AVM	6
t	ᛐ	gøter, vest, sten, äptir, havet, at, äptir	7
g	ᚣ	gøter, optagelse, läger, þags, þagh, og, þagh.	7
l	ᚱ	opþagelse, vinland, läger, skⱢar, bloþ, fräelse, illy	7
h	ᚼ	haþe, þagh, hem, havet, þagh + Här, øh, ahr	8
f	ᚠ	farþ, fro, of, fro, fiske, fan, af, fräelse, af, from + hafþe	11
v, w	ᛁ	vinland, vest, vi, veþ, vi, var, vi, ve, havet, vore, AVM	11
s	ᛋ	optagelse, vest, skⱢar, þags, rise, sten, fiske, fräelse, mans, se, skip, rise.	12
i	ᛁ	vinland, vi, rise, vi, fiske, äptir, vi, illu, äptir, skip, rise	11
th	ᚦ	(þen)o, opþagelse, farþ, vinlanþ, haþe, veþ, þags, þeno, þagh, bloþ, þeþ, þagh, þeno	14
n	ᛏ	norr-men, (þen)o, vinland, en, norr, þeno : sten, en, fan, man, mans, þeno	14
o	ᛂ	ok, norrman, po, (þen)o, op-, fro, of, norr, fro, þeno, ok, kom, bloþ, vore, from, þeno	16
r	ᚱ	norrman, farþ, fro, skⱢar, rise, fro, äptir, røþe, fräelse, äptir, vore, rise, from, ahr.	6
a	ᚷ	opþagelse, farþ, vinlanþ, haþe, skⱢar, þags, var, þagh, fan, man, af, af, mans, havet, at, þagh, ahr, AVM	18
e	ᛏ	gøter, norrmen, (þen)o, opþagelse, haþe, vest, læger, veþ, skⱢar, en, rise, þeno, sten, fiske, en, hem, røþe, þeþ, fräelse, ve, hawet, se, vore, rise, þeno	27

This word count table of the Kensington Rune Stone is provided by the authors to serve as a database for future research. The table includes the spalled section as (þen)o, the "e" in skⱢar (sklear), and assumes there are four dotted Rs.

Comparing the Runes of Kensington and Gotland

The runes used on the Kensington Stone can be divided into two basic groups. The first group consists of the standard late Viking age runes that were still in use on Gotland at the beginning of the 1300s: ᛒ ᚽ ᚠ ᚵ ᚼ ᛁ ᛚ ᛘ ᚿ ᛔ ᚱ ᛋ ᛏ for **b, e, f, g, h, i, l, m, n, p, r, s,** and **t** respectively. The second group is comprised of three runes on the Kensington Rune Stone that have features similar to the medieval Gotlandic including the o-rune (ᚮ= ᚯ), the mirror image Latin K–rune (ᛍ), and a dotted l-rune (ᛛ). The remaining Kensington Rune Stone runes, not found in Gotland, are: ᚷ ᚷ̈ ᚯ ᚢ̈ ᛘ for **a, ä, ö, u** and **v** respectively. The special crossed l-rune (ᛜ) and the dotted R-runes (ᚱ, ᚱ, and ᚱ) on the Kensington Rune Stone are addressed separately.

The Crossed "L"

Perhaps the best example of a rune found on the Kensington Rune Stone that was completely bungled by past scholars is the infamous "j" or crossed "l" rune. The Danish runologist Erik Moltke said this rune was invented by the carver, that this form never existed in Scandinavia, and its absence was clear proof of forgery on the Kensington Rune Stone. Scholarly unfamiliarity with this rune is puzzling since it is clearly found in both the *Codex Runicus* circa 1319 (Thorsen, 1877), and the *Mariaklagen* circa 1325 (Brøndrum-Nielsen, 1929) documents.

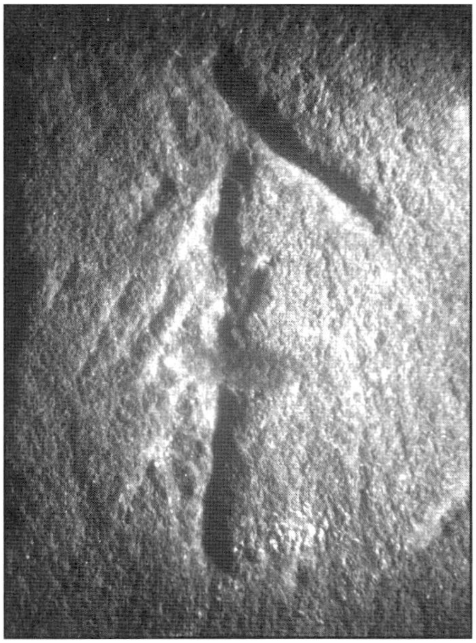

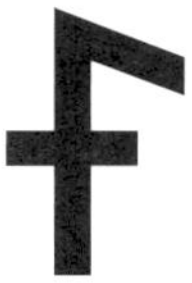

The equivalent of the dotted "L" rune on the Kensington Rune Stone is the crossed "L" rune ᛜ (L-4, C-84), which appears in the enigmatic word ᛋᛍᛜᚷᚱ = skᛜar. **(SFW: 2002)**

Prior to author Nielsen (1987), all investigators commenting on the Kensington Rune Stone inexplicability ignored the well-known evidence in the *Codex Runicus* and *Marlaklagen,* proclaimed the crossed l-rune (ᛜ) an invention of the carver, and therefore sure proof of a modern artifact.

Codex Runicus is a runic manuscript of the Scandian Law written in Danish circa 1319. Two crossed Ls can be seen in the first and last words (ᛋᛁᚠᚢᛁ and ᚴᛏᚠ) for silᚠi and päᚠ (silk and fine bedding) on the last line of the last page of the manuscript, which in this case is a ballad. This rune is found on other pages of the law document as well.

The Dotted L-Rune

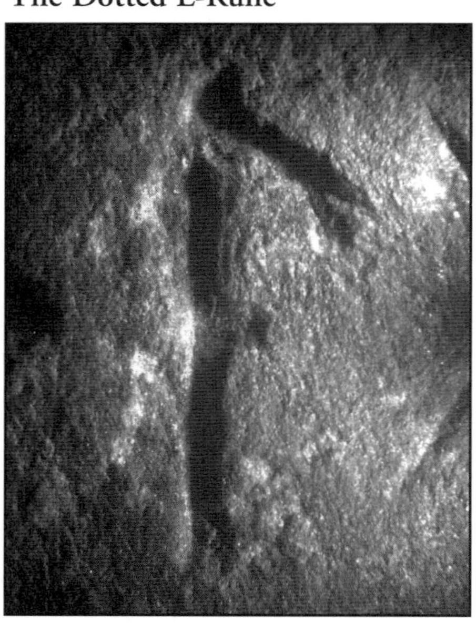

The Kensington Rune Stone has a dotted L-rune in ᛩᛁᚿᚠᚷᛅᚿ (Vinland). (L 3, C 49) (SFW: 2002)

The Kensington Rune Stone has a dotted L-rune in the word ᛩᛁᚿᚠᚷᛅᚿ (Vinland), but there is no reason to expect a long "l" here. The short horizontal stroke may be a mistake by the carver or it could have been copied from another inscription without the proper understanding of its meaning. There are several instances of this L in the medieval runic corpus of Gotland, some of which are listed and discussed here.

This grave slab (G 63) at the Silte Church, dated to late 1300s, contains a dotted L-rune in the word aLum (all). The first to discuss this dotted rune was Snædal (2002: 212), who identified the marking as indicative of a long L sound.

Among the dotted Ls found in the runic inscriptions on Gotland is G 163, circa 1300, from Mulde for ᚴᛁᛅᛚᛂᚱᛅ (kiaLera = cellar). (SFW)

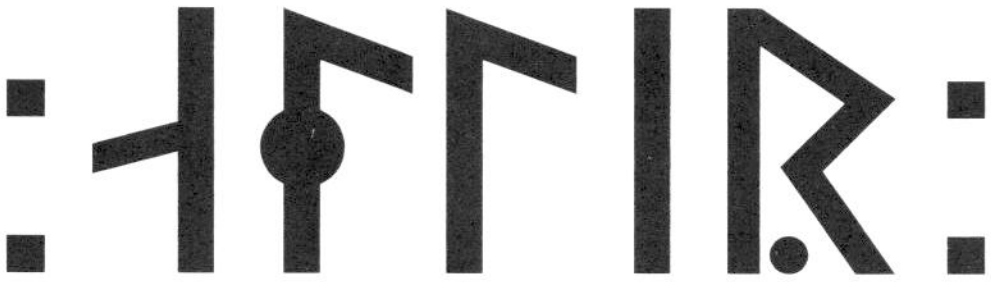

Another example of the dotted L appears in aLlir (all) in G 192, circa 1400, from the Västergarn Church. (SFW)

The ᚱ-rune

This unusual bind-rune was found on the Kensington Rune Stone by Wolter (2002) and appears to represent the combined u-rune and þ-rune. The u-rune could represent "f" in hafþe (had) which is appropriate for 1362. (L-4, C-67) (SFW: 2002)

The ᚱ-rune is the result of an afterstrike of ᚴ on the þ rune which yields *ᚼᛅᚱᛏ = **hauþe** > **hafþe** (had). We have not yet located another late medieval example of ᚴ used for "u" in Gotland, but the G 185 whetstone inscription, while undated, is considered a later medieval inscription. Bind-runes with the þ-rune are not uncommon on Gotland. Some examples are for **aþ**, for **uþ**, and **ouþ**  .

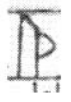

The G 185 inscription is as yet uninterpreted, but clearly has the Norwegian style u-rune in the sequence "nuihr." There were always good trade connections between Gotland and Norway and the existence of a Norwegian trade item or artifact with this feature would be no surprise. (SFW)

The use of "u" for "f" is found in a number of Norwegian inscriptions. The wooden ownership tag (N 648) was retrieved from just above the 1332 Bergen Wharf burn layer and begins with ᚼᛅᚢ : ᚠᚱᛁᛘᛁ = **haugrimi** for the name **hafgrimi.** N 655 and N 656, also from the Bergen Wharf, have **haluan ask** for **halfan ask** (half a box). Seip (1934: 98-99) shows "u" used for "f" inðhau e (had) in the same usage as the Kensington Rune Stone.

Examples of the Norwegian u-Rune (ᚴ) in Gotland

ᚠᚱᛁᚦᛘᚾᛏᚱ

The late Viking age Stenhuse G 186 inscription near Sanda Church from circa 1100 has the name Friþmuntr (Fridmund). This inscription has the shortened Norwegian stutt-style u-rune which the Kensington Rune Stone's bind-rune (ᚱ) could also contain. (ᛁ) is the Norwegian-style m-rune from the late Viking period.

This late Viking age inscription Stenhuse (G 187), circa 1100, contains two of what we call the "mule-shoe" u-rune (ᚴ), in (b)ruþur (brother?). Both this inscription and G 187 were on the door post of a stone house near Sanda Church. It is said that Norwegian King Olaf converted Gotland to full Christanity in 1030 and these inscriptions may come from that time period.

The K-Rune

The Viklau Church inscription's (G 133) inverted rune-row, circa 1400, has a Latin k-rune in the word Viko, seen in the circle at the center.

The Viklau Church inscription (G 133) has the only evidence that the Latin K-rune was used on Gotland. It was also used sporadically in Denmark and Norway, and on mainland Sweden in medieval times. Von Friesen suggested that the inscription read **Botuiþr i Viku Peders arfi** (Botvid i Vikers [?], Peter's heir). The Kensington Rune Stone k-rune (ᚴ) would then be the reverse image of this Latin K-rune. Had Wahlgren (1958: 116) seen this inscription, he would likely not have written of the Kensington Rune Stone, "The symbol for k is suspicious."

The Ψ-Rune

Sometimes runes were carved upside down, as seen in the discussion on G 133 at Viklau Church and in the G 33 Näs Church on Gotland.

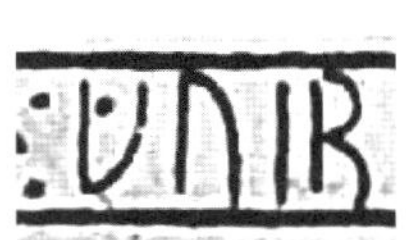 

The U-rune was used in a variety of ways in inscriptions on Gotland during medieval times. Variations included the upside down U in the word **yvir** (over), in the G 33 inscription at Näs Church, circa 1300.

In the Scandinavian runic inscriptions either the u-rune or the f-rune are used to express v/w and in at least two cases a u-rune carved within a u-rune was used (Moltke 1985:.429) and Johnsen (1990: 274)). The v/w-rune on the Kensington Rune Stone could be a combination of two inverted u-runes with a dot to have a distinction from "m" (Ψ).

The Scandinavian medieval manuscript letter combination "vu" was sometimes used for the w-sound (Seip, 1965), a combination of the inverted v-rune and u-runes.   Combining the v-rune (Ⴖ = Ʉ) and a u-rune (Ⴖ), resulting in Ψ + Ⴄ = Ψ could also be an explanation. Ψ also is not far removed from a dotted f-rune (Ⴄ) for a v/w-rune, which may be its origin. Some runologists we have spoken to do not have a problem with this, while others do. Conflicting opinions often enter into subjective reasoning situations.

The Double-Dotted Runes

The Gotlandic runic tradition used two, and sometimes three, vertical dots to denote the letter "y" in **yftir** (after) and other words.

The word Husfruy (housewife) with three dots occurs in the G 34 inscription at Näs Church, circa 1300. Two dots occur in the word yvir (over) in the G 103 inscription at Lye Church, circa late 1300s. (SFW)

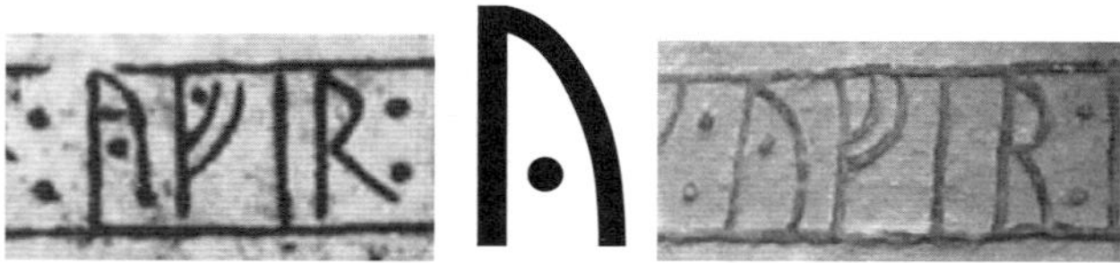

The author's inspection in 2005 showed that the G 42 inscription at Havdhem Church (left), circa 1500, has only one dot. Inscription G 65 at Sproge Church, circa early 1300s, also has one dot for y and both are found in the word yftir (after). (SFW)

The Bilateral N and T Runes

The Mästerby Church inscription (G 191) depicts the bi-lateral n (ᛁ) and t (ᛏ) runes, and dates from circa 1300. Both of these runes appear on the Kensington Rune Stone. Translated into English it reads, *"The maiden girl recites the prayer in the proper way."*

Had Wahlgren (1958: 115) known of the G 191 inscription he likely would not have written, *"The Kensington form of the rune n (ᚾ) had passed out of existence by the year 1100."* As it turns out Wahlgren was only 200 years short of evidence that shows the bilateral n was being used in the 14th century.

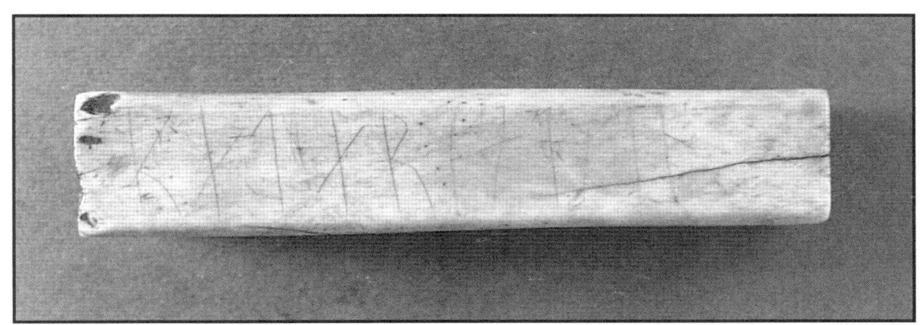

The Lund knife handle [DR 306] (Moltke 1985: 467) shows how the ä-rune approaches but does not complete with an X shape.   The inscription reads Pætær : gæd min (Peter guard me), and is apparently from the early medieval period.

The Split of the First Word on the Kensington Rune Stone

The first word on the Kensington Rune Stone is g:öter (Götalanders) which has a runic word divider after G.

The first word on the Kensington Rune Stone is **g:öter** (Götalanders) has a carved runic word divider after "g", which is the characteristic mark of two runic inscriptions in Gotland at Othem Church, G 282 and G 283. Here the first word in both inscriptions is **i : ᚱ** (you) divided in the same way.   This same feature is found in other localities, such as Ög 10, Sö 173, Sö 129, Sö 302, Sö 335 (3 times), Sm 5, and Sm 145 (Unka) and others.

The Othem Church inscriptions G 282 (pictured here) and G 283, circa 1400, both start with i : R (you). The inscription reads, **I : R BIÞIH : FÆF : FⱭRI :** (You must pray well for …). (SFW)

The majestic Othem Church on Gotland contains three very important medieval grave slabs (G 282, G 283 and G 284) with runic inscriptions and Teutonic Knight crosses.

Dialect Traits from Gotland on the Kensington Rune Stone

The runic inscriptions of Gotland and the Kensington Rune Stone have numerous language and orthographic traits in common. Erik Moltke (1949, 1951, and 1953) maintained that the Kensington Rune Stone word **og** (and) was impossible for the Swedish language in the 14th century. He asserted **og** proved the Kensington Rune Stone was a modern artifact, but two examples from Gotland prove that he was wrong. Henrik Williams was kind enough to supply two other examples from mainland Scandinavia in Norway with **og** in N 291 and in Sweden the word **yg** is found twice in U 1158.

An early example of the voicing of *k* to *g* occurs in the word ok (and) appears on the runic inscription G 182, dated 1324, from Sanda Church on Gotland. (SFW)

Another early example of the voicing of *k* to *g* appears in the word aug (and) on the Viking age runic inscription G 181, circa 1050 at end of the Viking age, also from the Sanda Church. (SFW)

E Dialect

Gotland is a recognized e-dialect region, as are the western reaches of West Götaland along the Göta River and in East Götaland (Brøndum-Nielsen 1927). Word endings on the Kensington Rune Stone, such as **fiske** (fish) rather than **fiska** (fish), indicate that it is an e-dialect.

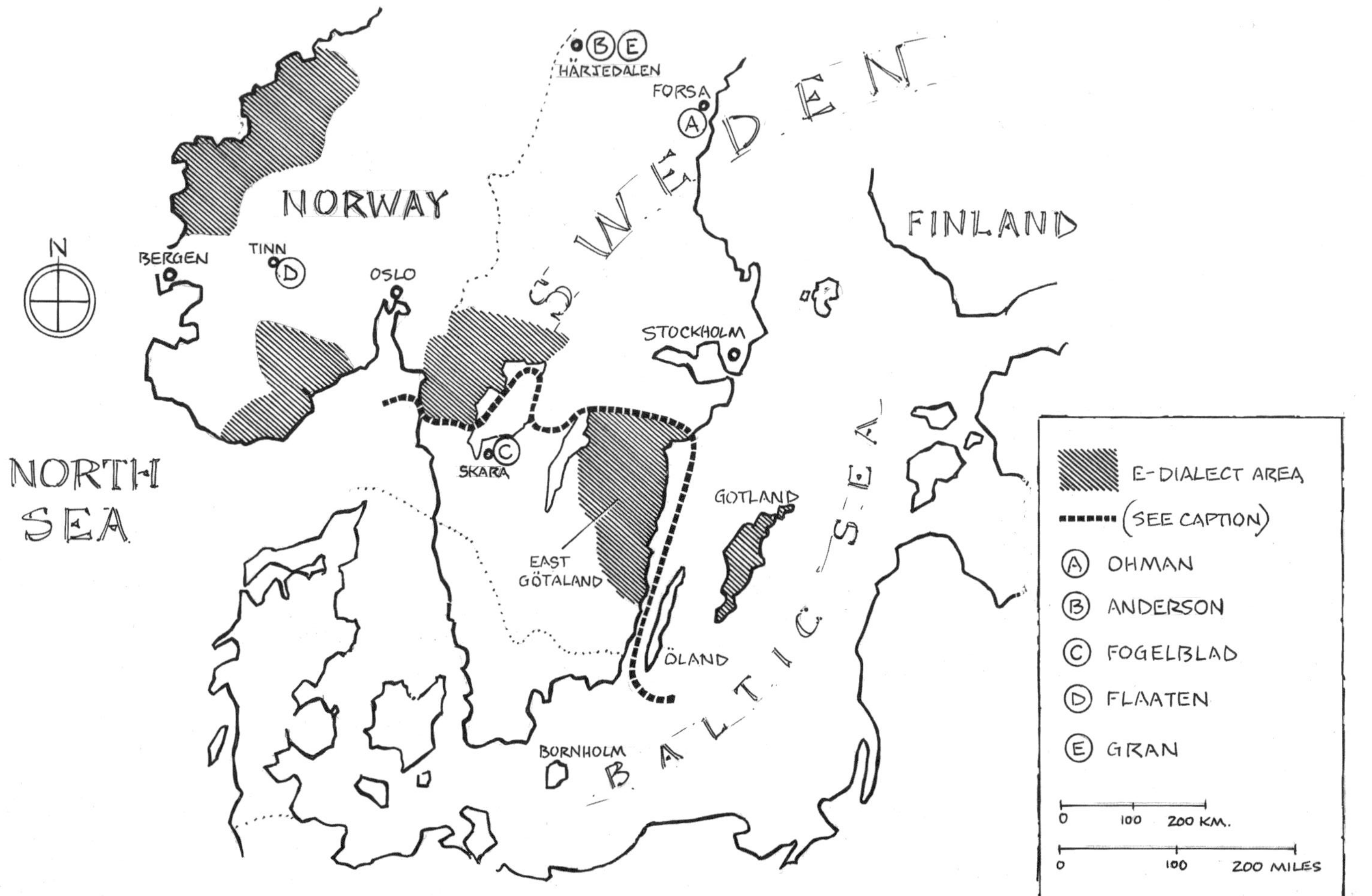

The shaded areas indicate where an "e"-dialect was spoken in Sweden and Norway during medieval times through the 19th Century. All the usual suspects, Andrew Anderson, Nils Flaaten, Sven Fogelblad, Olof Ohman and even John Gran, immigrated to the United States from regions that spoke an "a"-dialect. South of this heavily dashed line is the region in medieval times where the definite article "-et" (the) prevailed, as drawn by Brøndum-Nielsen (1927: Map 6). North of this line the "t" is dropped at the end of the definite article, thus leaving only "–e." The Kensington Rune Stone has the word hawet (the inland sea, the sea) indicating the writer most likely was from south of this stapled line. Since the Kensington Rune Stone text also displays an e-dialect, the conclusion is drawn that the writer was probably from East Götaland. The –et ending is standard Swedish to this day.

From, fråm (from)

Gotland is located southwest of the Estonian Islands where the Swedish dialect studies by Vendell (1882) indicate that both *from/fraam* (from) was used by descendents of earlier Swedish immigrants perhaps as early as 1220 when Denmark, and later Sweden controlled the Estonian Islands. Karl Martin Nielsen (1950) considered **from** to be a form with long a (fruam) reported by Axel Kock (1890) on the Estonian Island of Runö.

Ave Maria

On the eighth and ninth lines of the Kensington Rune Stone there is a unique Christian prayer that is a combination of the Lord's Prayer and Ave Maria. The early experts scoffed at the notion that Ave Maria would be used to ask anything such as "Save from evil." This usage had never been seen before and in the minds of experts it was inconsistent with common medieval religious practice. In Sven B. Jansson's 1949 paper, he said, *"A Catholic would never think of addressing such a prayer to the Virgin Mary...."* However, in 2000 the Massey twins found this type of address in prayer books from 1380 in the St. Birgitta monastery in Syon, England.(Collins, 1969:15) In 2003, Richard Nielsen and Henrik Williams found a possible variant of this hybrid prayer in Latin documented in the St. Birgitta cloister at Vadstena, Sweden. There was always a close association between Vadstena and the Cistercian abbeys in Sweden.

Abbreviations

A Cistercian would have been adept at Latin, of course, and could have easily used abbreviations in the Kensington Rune Stone inscription. In 1347, a Latin inscription was carved around a runic inner ring at Tofta church (G 195). This Latin inscription of 140 characters is abbreviated, but without abbrevation marks that were common in manuscripts (See color section, plate 27). The runic inscription at Tofta reads, "The year of our Lord 1347, on May 13th, [Sic 16th] the Sunday next after Jesus' Ascension date Siglaiv and his son Nikulas were killed. May their souls rest in peace, Amen." The Latin text for the outer ring is, ANNO: DO*mini*[:] M: CCC: XLVII: I*n* DIE[:] DO*minic*A: R*ro*XI*m*A: POST: ASCE*n*SIONE*m*: DO*mini*: OCCISI: S*un*T: SIGLEW[*us*: C]V*m*: FILIO + SVO: NICHOLAO: QVO*rum*: A*n*I*m*E: REQ*vi*ESCA*n*T: IN [:P]ACE: : AMEN III ID*us* MA*ii*. The character in the center (the reverse $\overline{Z}$) may be the trademark of the farm of the deceased.

When taking abbreviations into consideration, the text of the Kensington Rune Stone begins to look very logical for 1362. Considering the writing instruments of the day were a hammer and chisel, it would have been highly desirable to abbreviate whenever possible. The difficulty of carving rock, and the amount of time required to create an inscription, are the most likely reasons for the carver's decision to use the shorthand pentadic date, and may explain the contractions of *varum* to **var** (were), *komum* to **kom** (come), and *fanom* to **fan** (found). No abbreviation marks are visible on the Kensington Rune Stone, but neither were they used as expected on the Tofta Latin inscription, although it's common on Latin grave slab inscriptions.

Orthographic Traits

H-insert (Medial)

The last two words on the Kensington Rune Stone, **øh** and **ahr** (year), could have two medial h-inserts.

lhit *lit* (let) in the G 118 inscription from Anga Church, circa 1300, has an h-insert. (SFW)

Double Letters

Double consonants are common in runic inscriptions, and the Kensington Rune Stone has them in **illu** (evil), **norrman** (Norwegian) and **norr** (north). This same trait is found in several Gotlandic inscriptions with "rr" and "nn." The Kensington Rune Stone form þeno for þenno, which is used twice, has only a single "n." However, this doubling trait is not limited to Gotland, since "bb" is found in Sm 22 and Dr 38, dd in N 256 and NB 625, and "ff" in DR 172, DR 173. Such doubling can be found in modern Swedish as well.

Double L

The double l "ll" appears on the Kensington Rune Stone in the word **illu** (evil). It also appears in the word **allir** (all), on the G 195 inscription at Västergarn Church on Gotland.

An example of the double l appears in allir (all), in the G 192 inscription from the Västergarn Church, circa 1400s.

Double R

The Double r-runes are found in the Kensington Rune Stone words **norR** (north) and **norrmen** (Northmen). Double r-runes are also found in at least three inscriptions on Gotland.

Double r-runes are found in fyrre *fyre* (for) in the G 170 inscription from Hejde Church, dated to 1506, and frru *fru* (wife) in the G 178 inscription from Väte Church, circa 1300, and gerra *gera* (do) in the G 128 inscription from Guldrupe Church, circa 1500. (SFW)

In Gotland the G 242 inscription at Hejnum Church has the word **norþrby** (North City). The Kensington Rune Stone form **norr** < **norþr** results from the loss of "þ" due to the three consonant rule (no more than two consonants may be together in a word).

The same may be true of the Kensington Rune Stone with **norþr > norR**. The three consonant rule would also explain the Kensington Rune Stone form **norþrmen > norrmen** (Norwegian), whereby the middle consonant is dropped.

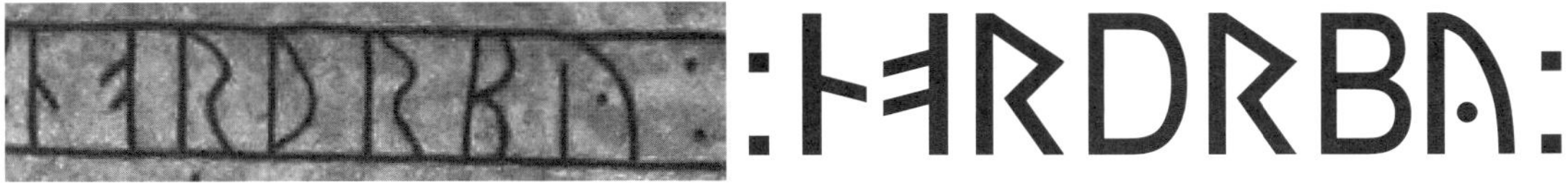

G 242 inscription at Hejnum Church, circa 1250, has norþrby (Norrby).

GH-Digraph as on the Kensington Rune Stone

The G 283 inscription from Othem Church has the word **akhnebo** > *agnebo* (Agne's farm) and Lärbro Church inscription G 294 has **aghnabo**. These inscriptions have the gh-digraph, just as the Kensington Rune Stone word **þagh** (day). Other inscriptions with this feature are Vg 217 [**akgi**], DR 111 [**lakhe = lage**], DR 469 [**khriþi = greþi**], and some Norwegian examples in N 269, NB 143, NB 249, etc.

Starting in the black mark above the Knights Templar cross in the G 283 inscription at Othem Church, circa 1400, are the words [a]khnabo *agnabo* (Agnes farm). This gh-digraph is also found on the Kensington Rune Stone. (SFW)

The þ Rune used for T.

The þ-rune was used for *t* in the words **optagelse** (reclaiming) and **teno** (this) on the Kensington Rune Stone. The þ-rune was sometimes used for *t* in Gotland as seen in the G 2 Sundre inscription in **sþan** *sten* (stone) and **liþ** *lit* (let). This is also seen in Sm 38, Sm 62, Vg 210 and many others in Sweden, and in Norway in N 72, N 155, N 351, NA 258, NB 181, and others.

The words sþan *sten* (stone) and liþ *lit* (let) appear in the G 2 inscription, circa 1400, at Sundre Church. Liþ was recorded by Linné in 1641, but the word has since weathered away.

If the initial þ-rune is used for *t* on the Kensington Rune Stone, **þagh** could also stand for **tagh > dagh** (day) and **þeþ > teth > deth** (death). In the dialect on the Gotlandic runic inscriptions, both **tag/dag** (day) and **to/do** (died) are found, and the use of the t-rune for "d" is common in almost all Swedish dialects.

Use of the Unilateral and Bilateral t-Rune in the Same Inscription

In the G 65 inscription at Sproge Church on Gotland, circa 1200, the word listana (grave slabs) is a medieval German word. This word used the bilateral t-rune ($\uparrow$). (SFW)

In the same G 65 inscription is Auþualtr (name) with a unilateral t ($\uparrow$). (SFW)

The Profile of the Carver

The runes of Gotland also answer other nagging questions on the Kensington Rune Stone. No longer is the Kensington Rune Stone the earliest record of **og** (and).   In addition, h-inserts abound in both initial and medial position on Gotland.

Robert Hall (1982: Appendix) first pointed to an old Indo-European type of sentence structure on the Kensington Rune Stone in which the beginning is constructed with a subject and modifier, but without a verb. This was then followed up by a pronoun and verb, as in the Kensington Rune Stone:

Subject: **8 Goths and 22 Norwegians**
Modifer: **on this journey of reclaiming far west from Vinland**
Pronoun: **We had camp by two…One day's march north from this stone**

This structure is found in many Gotlandic inscriptions such as the Näs Church G 33 inscription:

Subject: Rudvi
Modifier: daughter to Hägvid in Hagnastäde
Pronoun and verb: She placed this stone over her husband Botolv …

Another example is Hablingbo G 60:

Who: Katrin and Botvid and Nikulas
Modifier: <none this inscription>
Pronoun: They placed this stone over their good father.

Other Gotlandic inscriptions with this construction are Grötlingbo G 35, Urgunde G 70, Kullans G 78, Lye G 99, Väte G 178, Atlingbo G 201, Vall G 206, Stenkumla, G 207, and G 208. A profile of the author of the Kensington Rune Stone might look something like this:

Traits that could have been acquired in Gotland

The carver of the Kensington Rune Stone:

1. Was likely a Cistercian monk from the Gutnalia Cloister on Gotland, a carver of grave slabs and an avid reader of the hundreds of stones extant in 1360 on Gotland.

2. Created the rune-row from the runes he read daily as a priest in Gotland. He used common medieval runes: ᛒ ᛏ ᚠᚼᛁᛚᛘ ᚱᛍᚦ for **b, e, f, h, i, l, m, r, s,** and **þ** with some medieval runes that were being used in Gotland and Småland in the 1300s: ᛆ ᛒ ᛌ ᛐ ᛒ ᚱ ᚱ ᛐ for **a, L, k, n, p, dotted R,** and **t.**

3. Pronounced **norr** (north) and **norrmen** (Northmen) with a double rr.

4. Voiced *k* to *g* like cok > cog in English in low stress positions as found in **og < ok** (and).

5. Learned and used the Gotlandic calendar system of 1328. This system was introduced in the 1140s at a conference at Linköping Cathedral in East Götaland.

6. Learned use of the German loan words: **10 man** (10 men).

7. Was traveled, and had perhaps served in the Swedish-held Estonian islands at the head of the Bay of Riga where *from/fraam* (from) was a part of the dialect used by people there as late as the 19ᵗʰ Century.

8. Used new runes probably created with German orthography, which would have been well known by the learned Cistercians in Gotland, and used for the umlauts ü, ä, and ö. Gotlandic writing had no runes for monophthongs since Gotlandic language, called Gutnish, only used diphthongs, such as "ai" for ä and "au" and "ey" for ö.

9. Used pentadic numbers from his church calendar. Cistercians were adept with Arabic placement and numbers because they used the system to count boards and to compile church records. The Templars, an organization associated with the Cistercians, had introduced letters of credit, and knew Arabic placement very well.

10. Was aware of the use of palatal Rs, ᛦ, ᛈ and ᛥ, from reading numerous grave slabs, and used the dotted R in ᚤᚯᛏᛁᛦ (Götalanders), ᚺᛆᛱᛦ (north), and ᚤᚷᛦ (were). In keeping with what is known about Gotlandic practice the 1300s, some words would not be entymologically correct, like ᚺᛆᛱᛦ (north).

11. Continued to use þ and ð in his dialect on the Kensington Rune Stone for both the initial position like þeno (this), in the medial position (ð) like the **röþe** (red), and it final position (ð) like the Kensington Rune Stone **bloþ** (blood). The Kensington Rune Stone uses the þ seven times in initial position, two in the medial position and four in the final position. The Lye G 99 from 1449, 87 years after 1362, still used þ in all positions, 5 in the initial, 6 in medial, and 3 in the final position. The letter "d" is not used in either the Kensington Rune Stone or the Lye Church G 99 inscriptions.

12. Used the t-rune for "d," as in **tagr** (day) and **to** (died), and the þ-rune for "t". This leaves the possibility that **þagh** on the Kensington Rune Stone stands for **tagh** *dagh* (day) and þeþ stands for **teth** *deth* (death).

Kensington Rune Stone traits that could have been acquired in East Götaland

The Goths mentioned on the Kensington Rune Stone would have originated in Östergötaland, where three key dialect traits are found as on the Kensington Rune Stone:

1. An e-dialect (characterized by weak stress on the end of the word) as the endings in **optagelse** (taking up), **fiske** (fish), **röþe** (red), and **rise** (journey). Gotland also has an e-dialect.

2. Use of monophthongs, as found in **göter** (Götalanders), **röþe** (red), and **öh** (island). Gotland used diphthongs in 1362.

3. Use of the definite article -et in neuter as in the Kensington Rune Stone word **havet** (the inland sea), and not (the inland sea) **have,** as would be commonly found in the Swedish provinces to the north and west of Östergötaland, as per Brøndum-Nielsen's dialect map number 6 of 1927.

Östergötaland and Gotland were close not only geographically, but culturally as well, since Gotland was part of the diocese of the archbishop housed in Linköping, Östergötaland. He would have supplied the priests for the 92 churches in Gotland. By the 1300s this mainland influence was quite noticeable in the runic inscription.

The Carver

1. Had likely stopped at Ukna Church while traveling from Linköping to Gotland and had very likely seen the dotted Rs, such as ᚱ.

2. Knew the dative phrase **af blod og þeþ** (of blood and death) on the Kensington Rune Stone from the *Notes of the Priest of Vidum circa 1325* known as VGIV (West Göta Law IV) Collen 1827, which has the same dual noun construction as in *af forfalum ok dødæ* (of decline and death). (See Noreen: 1934)

3. Used the definite article –et in the neuter form **hav** (sea, inland sea) to form the Kensington Rune Stone **havet** (the sea, the inland sea). This characteristic places the carver from East Götaland, the only place that had both this form and an e-dialect.

4. Knew the Latin Matins of the St. Brigitta Vadstena Cloister located in East Götaland, where the phrase "Ave Maria Save from Evil" was used.

5. Could have been familiar with the Elder West Götalandic Law's writing of "þ" for "d."

6. Used an e-dialect, which was common to Gotland and East Götaland.

Appendix
A word-by-word discussion of the Kensington Rune Stone inscription is provided in the appendix.

The Kensington Rune Stone and the Larsson Rune Rows

The presentation of this new evidence reveals that numerous experts in linguistics and runology have missed significant evidence that supports a medieval origin of the Kensington Rune Stone inscription. Discovery of the Larsson papers has completely changed the perspective on the origin this inscription. For decades the burning question has been, "What is the origin of the Kensington Rune Stone alphabet?" Elements of the inscription had not been seen before, so it was assumed by some that the runes had been invented by a prankster. Swedish runologist Helmer Gustavsson wrote in the Fall 2004 issue of *Viking Heritage Magazine,* that the Larsson rune rows were likely a "secret" alphabet used by special tradesmen or Freemasons. This interesting idea opens up many possibilities. In 1554, Olaus Magnus reported that runic codes were used in besieged cites and army field camps to exchange secret messages (von Friesen 1933: 241). Von Friesen further stated that the Swedish War Archives contained evidence that a Swedish commander, de la Garde, used runes during the Thirty Years' War (1618-1648) for the same purpose, apparently taken from Bure (1599 and 1612), the father of Swedish runology. Is it possible that the Larsson rune row is a runic code of the same nature? A comparison with the Bure runes might shed light on this possibility.

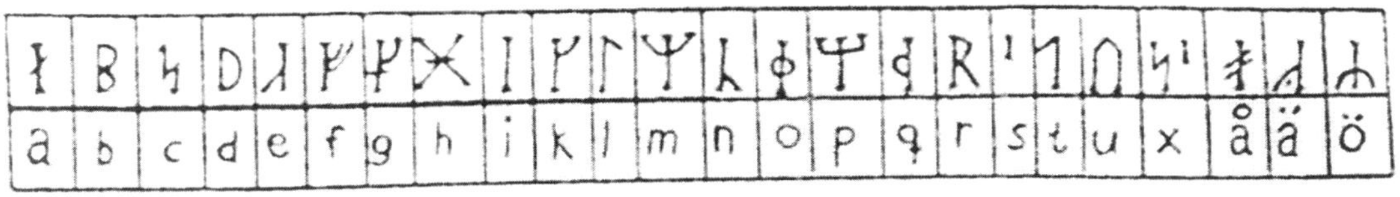

The 1599 Bure runes as cited by Gustafson in 1985.

The 1599 Bure rune row exhibits a major departure from the classic medieval rune row character of the Kensington Rune Stone as shown below:

Letter	KRS	Post-Reformation	Usual Post-Reformation Rune
c	ᛋ	Never used for s	ᛋ, C
d	ᚦ	Never used for th	D
e	ᛐ	Never used for e	ᚿ
g	ᛩ, ᚴ	Never used for g	ᚵ
o	ᚯ	Never used for o	ᛰ
p	ᛒ	Never used for p	ᛘ
t	ᛏ	Never used for t	1

Even when liberally compared to the Bure runes, the Larsson rune row of 1885 that was discovered in 2004 has only twelve similar runes.

As has been demonstrated, the Kensington Rune Stone inscription contains runes and other features that are unique, yet have parallels on the island of Gotland during the 14th century. The possibility of a Gotlandic author has never been considered before in spite of the fact that strong evidence in favor of such a connection has always existed. This book will show that there are yet other lines of evidence that indicate the Kensington Rune Stone is a medieval artifact carved with a medieval inscription, based on the runes of Gotland.

These symbols represent the Larsson rune row alphabet.

This alphabet is of the runes of the Kensington Rune Stone.

An analysis of the various runes yields several interesting observations.

In all, 13 Larsson runes are not used on the Kensington Rune Stone. These runes are for: c, e, g, n, o, p, q, r, x, y, z, å, and ö.

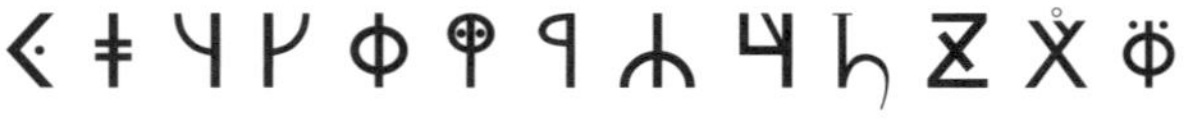

Nine Kensington Rune Stone forms are not seen on the Larsson rune row. These runes are for: e, g, l, Ł, n, r, R, s, and t.

The Larsson rune forms Ч, Ч, and Ψ are similar in form to the Kensington Rune Stone rune forms Ч, Ч, and Ψ. These three Kensington Rune Stone forms could possibly be explained as the following medieval forms:

1. The Kensington Rune Stone Ⴗ and the Larsson Ⴗ are mirror images of the normal medieval **g**-rune ⌐, with or without a dot.

2. The Kensington Rune Stone ⴎ and the Larsson ⴗ could be based on the German double-dotted "ü" used in 14th century Danish manuscripts in 1387 (Uldaler 1968: 142-5). This double dot analogy applies to the Kensington Rune Stone ✕ and the Larsson ✕.

3. The Kensington Rune Stone Ψ and the Larsson Ψ could be a combination of the inverted **v**-rune and **u**-rune for a **w**-rune. This is a medieval development because the manuscript letters "vu" or "uu" were combined to create the "w" sound (Seip, 1954).

The Larsson p-rune ⌀ has two dots, as does the classic medieval p-rune **B**. The p-rune **B** was not used after 1554.

If the Kensington Rune Stone rune row is in fact a runic code it must be of a medieval origin. The code is not meant to be so much a secret, but an indicator to a reader who understood the special signs that the message was genuine and written by a member of his own group. In 2001, author Tom Reiersgord suggested that a Christian monastic order, such as the Cistercians, may be related to the Kensington Rune Stone rune row. The Cistercian Abbey at Gutnalia on Gotland may hold the answer.

✕ rune for a

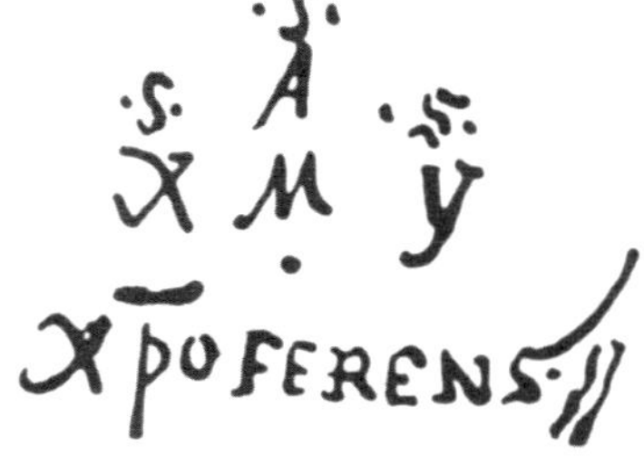

Christopher Columbus

Columbus' signature is the only other known link to the hooked X on the Kensington Rune Stone that we are aware of. This leaves the mutual Kensington Rune Stone ✕ and ✕ explained as medieval. Columbus has used the Greek CH = X with a hook. The last line of the signature reads ✗*risto*ferens. The Kensington Rune Stone has special dots in the sequence ✕MΨ (ämw) and since V and Y often used the same symbol. The 4th line of the signature is the same sequence **XMY**. Columbus' father-in-law was a Knight of Christ, an order directly linked to the Knights Templar in Portugal since 1312. The Portugese were on joint sea missions to Greenland with the Danish king in the latter part of the 1400s.

Larsson Rune Row Characters Similar to Forms in Gotland

Of the ten remaining Larsson rune forms, ᚲ ǂ ᚠ Φ ᑫ ᛦ Ч h Ƶ and X̊, six forms have readily identifiable medieval origins in Gotland and on mainland Sweden: ǂ ᚠ Φ ᑫ ᛦ and Ƶ.

ǂ-Rune for e

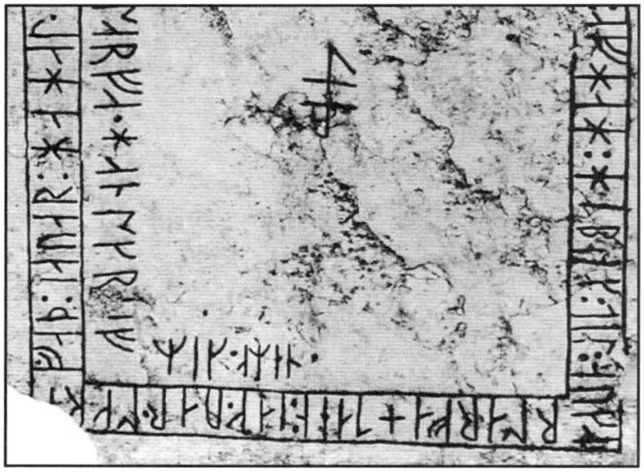

A grave slab in the Hemse Church (G 55), from the 1400s, depicts what could be the Cross of Lorraine ǂ on an L-rune Γ. This cross was originated during the first half of the 14th century in the province of Lorraine, which was German at the time. The Cistercians had strong ties to Lorraine and Burgundy in the 13th and 14th centuries. Similar crosses were used in early missionary times.

Φ-Rune for e in Norway

ᚼᛆᚿᛋᛘᛆᚱᛆᚠᛋΦᚿ

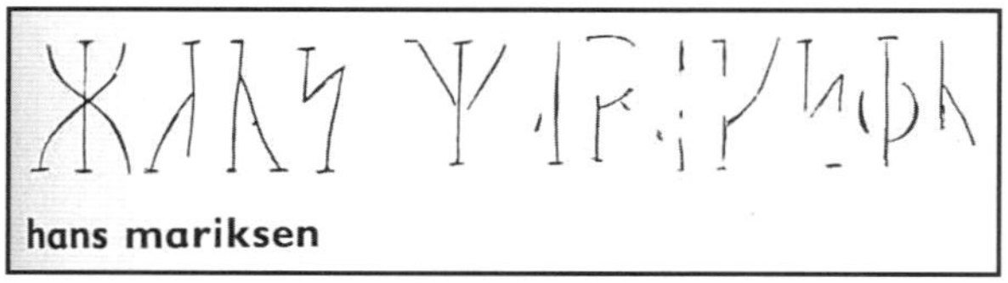

The painted Φ-rune for "e" in the G 105 inscription at Lye Church, circa 1500, occurs in the words ᚼᛆᚿᛋ ᛘᛆᚱᛁᚠᛋΦᚿ (Hans Mariksen).

Φ̈-rune for Ö

On the Larsson runes the post-Reformational o-rune (Φ) has been given double dots to yield Φ̈

ᚠ-rune for n and the ᑫ-rune for q

The Larsson n-rune and q-rune are seen in the 1544 rune row from Johannes Magnus. It is clear that the latter four runes were arbitrarily assigned to the last four Golden Year numbers 16-19, i.e. ᛦ ᛏ Ж and Φ.

Johannes Magnus' rune row (von Friesen 1933: Fig. 74, 241).

The Larsson r-Rune

Only on Gotland in the 1300s was the palatal rune R used for r, so its appearance in this capacity identifies Gotland as the likely origin of the Larsson rune row.

This segment of the G 195 inscription at Tofta Church on Gotland incorrectly uses the rune ᚴ for r in the word *husproyiu* (housewife), dated to 1347. (SFW)

ᶫ-Rune for Z

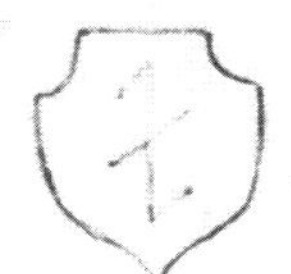

This 1863 drawing by runologist P. A. Säve shows a mark on a shield similar to one on a grave slab in the Tofte Church (G 197), from the 1300s, and to one in the center of inscription G 195, which is reversed.

The characters ❮ and ⦶ are similar to some figures in the Dalecarlian rune rows of the 1700s, but the hooked X has not been seen elsewhere. However, Columbus used a hooked Greek X for ch.

Summary

Our conclusion is that most of the Larsson runes are based on runic models later than the Kensington Rune Stone runes.

The Yoke is Modern

The Yoke inscription transcribed from runes to Swedish, and then to English:

Detta bärträ gorde iag den 10 September 1907
"This yoke made I the 10th of September 1907." (SFW)

The March 2004 article about the Kensington Rune Stone that was published in *Viking Heritage* Magazine is an appropriate place to start a discussion of the Månsta yoke inscription. Swedish runologist Helmer Gustavsson asserted that the Kensington Rune Stone runes were known in parts of Sweden during the 19th century and pointed to the Månsta yoke inscription as well as the painted inscription on the pulpit in Tåby church as proof. In his haste to dismiss the Kensington Rune Stone as modern, Gustavsson made critical errors. The yoke was carved in wood nine years after discovery of the Kensington Rune Stone, using runes that were consistent with newspaper copies of the inscription. The most glaring error gleaned from early newspaper reports is the omission of the "hook" on the Kensington Rune Stone double-dotted "ä" runes (X).

The Kensington Rune Stone has five double-dotted X-like "ä" runes with the hook (L 10, C 212). (SFW: 2002)

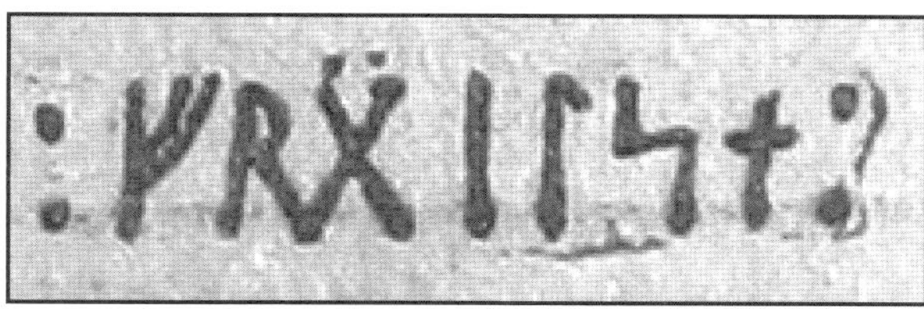

Several newspaper articles published in 1899 incorrectly had the same Kensington Rune Stone a-runes *without* the hook or the dots. The dots only appeared in Ohman's copy, which was published in *Svenska-Amerikanska Posten* on February 28, 1899.

The Månsta yoke inscription contains two double-dotted a-runes without hooks on the upper right arm. (SFW)

The p-rune (B), which occurs on both the Kensington Rune Stone and the yoke, is clear proof that the yoke is not from the post-Reformation period. The B-rune has never been documented in any inscription after 1550. In addition, Gustavsson did not discuss the fact that the s-rune in the yoke (ᛋ) also does not appear in post-Reformation inscriptions.

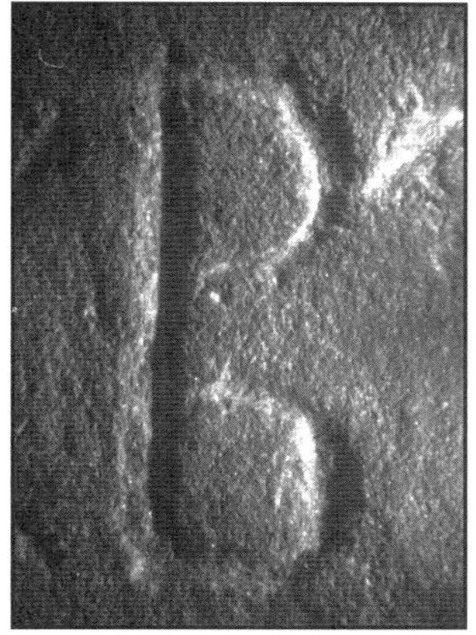

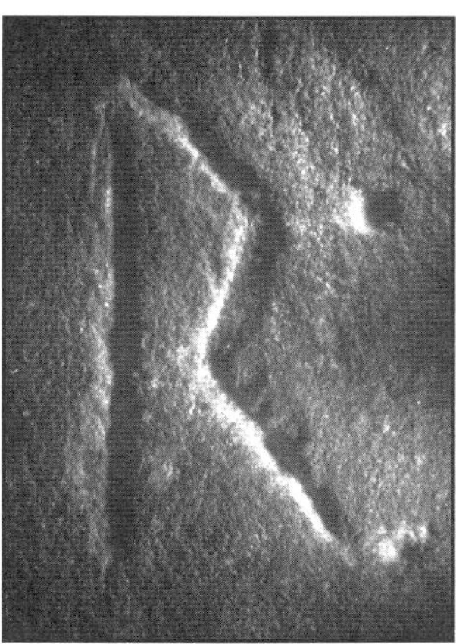

The p-rune (B) rune in the yoke inscription (left) and the Kensington Rune Stone (middle; L 6, C 145) has never been reported in a post-Reformation inscription (after 1550). The yoke's r-rune also differs from the Kensington Rune Stone (right; L 6, C 148) in that it is closed on the yoke. Additionally, the s-rune (ᛋ) on the yoke has never been seen in a post-Reformation inscription for "s." (SFW: 2002)

How did these specific runes get on the yoke in such detail and with such similarity to the runes on the Kensington Rune Stone? The answer is that they were most likely copied from one of several newspaper illustrations of the Kensington Rune Stone inscription published prior to 1907. The only source of such illustrations at the time was the Ohman copy, which was published in Minneapolis' *Svenska-Amerikansa Posten* in February 1899, since only Ohman's copy had the double dots indicated on the ä-rune (Ẍ).

Another curious feature of the yoke is the use of the closed r-rune (ᚱ). The Kensington Rune Stone does ***not*** have the closed "r," but some of the newspaper copies of the inscription prior to 1907 did. The bi-lateral t-rune (ᛏ) on the yoke is suspicious as well, since it is not seen in post-Reformation inscriptions in Dalecarlia.

Gustavsson cites the date on the yoke (1907, not 1908 as he reported) as additional proof that the Kensington Rune Stone alphabet was known in the 19th century because pentadic numbers were used with Arabic placement. The simple explanation is that the usage was copied from the newspaper illustrations. However, the carver of the yoke tipped his hand and revealed his lack of understanding of pentadic numbers by using the Arabic 10 (φ) for zero. This same mistake was made in the Larsson rune rows, which indicates that those pentadic numbers were also copied from an earlier document. Pentadic numbers were used for calendars, so there was no need for zero. During the Middle Ages, the Arabic 10 was only used on counting boards to conduct business and financial transactions, but for legal reasons the results were corrected to Roman numbers.

The four Arabic 10 renditions found in medieval manuscripts, φ Φ P Þ, are nothing more than a sign of 1 in the tens position and null in the digit box, where the square represents the empty digit box to the right, and the circle represents the empty pit for the pebbles of a counting board drawn on the ground.

Tens	Digits		Various signs for Arabic Number 10
I	Empty pit	=	φ
I	Empty pit	=	Φ
I	Empty box	=	P
I	Empty box	=	Þ

The 1907 date on the yoke inscription (left), and the pentadic numbers in the Larsson papers (1883 middle, 1885 right), all incorrectly use φ for zero, which indicates a lack of understanding of how these numbers were used in medieval times. (SFW)

The errors in the yoke inscription have a tell-tale consistency with the early published newspaper copies of the Kensington Rune Stone inscription and represent the most likely explanation for the yoke inscription. This is also a much simpler explanation than some unsubstantiated secret runic alphabet as alleged by Gustavsson. The insistence that the Kensington Rune Stone runes were derived from post-Reformation Dalecarlian runes is not supported by research (Gustavsson, 1985). In fact, the following runes of the Kensington Rune Stone differ considerably from the Dalecarlian runes published by Gustavsson himself.

Letter	KRS Runes	Dalecarlian Runes (after 1550)	Larsson II
A	ᚷᚷ	ᚷ	ᚷ
B	ᛒ	B	ᛒ
C	Not used	C	ᚲ
D		D, Þ	Þ
E	†	ᛐ	‡
G	ᛃ	ᚷ	ᛃ
K	ᚴ	ᛕ	ᚴ
N	ᚾ	ᚠ	ᛔ
O	ᛟ	φ	φ
P	ᛓ	ᛜ	ᛩ
R	ᚱ	R	ᛘ
S	ᛋ	'	ᛋ
T	↑	↑	↑
Þ	Þ		
U	ᚢ	∩	ᚢ
V	ᛦ	V	ᛦ

A comparison of the Kensington Rune Stone and Dalecarlian runes reveals significant differences, and indicates that the Kensington Rune Stone alphabet did *not* originate in Dalecarlia.

Hammarby Calendar Staff

The recently discovered Hammarby calendar staff and the Kensington Rune Stone are the only known artifacts (the Larsson rune rows are written documents) with pentadic numbers in Arabic placement used in a date (╟╚ ╠╟ = 1791). This alone provides additional proof that this concept was known prior to the 19th century.

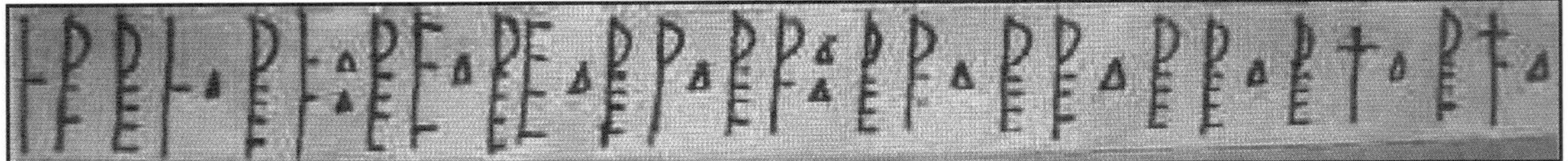

This calendar staff from 1791 has a series of pentadic dates from 1791-1801 with Arabic placement (Bloombum, 2004). These are for 1791, 92, 93, 94, 95, 96, 97, 98, 99, 00 and 01. The carver did not know to handle zero, since the last two numbers are incorrect. It would appear that the carver copied an earlier calendar staff where zero was not treated. This image is from the article "Runstaven på Linnés Hammarby" (The Runic Staff from Linné's Hammarby) written by Barbro Håkursen in 2004.

The Hammarby calendar stave, named after the home of the famous Swedish botanist Carl Linné, shows that utilization of pentadic numbers in Arabic placement was as feasible in concept in 1362 as 1791. The "old chestnut" that pentadic numbers could not be used in Arabic placement due to a lack of evidence has now been put to rest. The Hammarby calendar stave also demonstrates that a modern carver would not understand how to treat zero. This would mean he would have avoided zero in the text, but the Kensington Rune Stone has both **10 man** (10 men) and **10 mans** (10 of men) with zero handled correctly with the Arabic 10 (╠). Since Linné died in 1778 it is likely that his descendents produced this pentadic series, possibly from his notes.

The History of
Gotland and the
Teutonic Knights

History

Chronology of Events Important to the Island of Gotland

1029	St. Olof, King of Norway, converts Gotland to Christianity.
1030	The first three of what would be more than ninety churches (Stenkyrka, Atlingbo, and Fardhem) are built on Gotland.
1050	King of the Svear (Eastern Sweden) agrees to protect Gotland for an annual fee.
1100	Around this time the Bishop of Linköping in Östergötaland is appointed to oversee the Gotlandic churches. Gotland and Östergötaland begin a close connection, since they are in the same diocese.
1104	Archbishop is established in Lund and placed over all Scandinavia.
1139	The Dane Eskil becomes Archbishop of Lund.
1140	A Swedish flotilla sails up the Neva River and raids the east side of Lake Ladoga, but is destroyed, according to Russian records.
1161	German merchants are allowed to live in the city of Visby.
1162	About this time the Lübeck establish a trading center in Visby.
1164	The 180th Cistercian abbey since Clairvaux is founded by St. Bernard on Gotland at Gutanalia. The Cistercians will send many German, English, and French monks to Gutnalia.
1169	Denmark conquers the Wends of Rügen in their capital of Arkona, and the raids by pirates from Rugen cease.
	Pagan Estonian pirates from Ösel raid the Swedish islands of Gotland and Öland.
1170	Pope Alexander III declares a crusade against pagan Estonia.
1174	Estonians sack and burn Sigtuna, on the Måleren, in Sweden.
1185	Danes under Bishop Absalon of Lund conquer the Wends of Pomerania.
1191	The pope establishes the German Order of Teutonic Knights. The king of Denmark sponsors a crusade to the Holy Land.
1200	The Cistercian, Theoderic van Treiden, founds the Brethren of the Sword (Templars) in Riga.
1204	Around this time the Holy Spirit Church in Visby, Gotland is founded by Bishop Albert of Riga for the benefit of the Crusaders on their way to the Eastern Baltic.
1211	Papal bull for a crusade in the Eastern Baltic is issued.
1216	Pope Innocent III issues a papal bull to the Swedish king for crusade against Estonia.
1219	Estonia is conquered by Denmark and Brethren of the Sword (the junior arm of the Templars). Raids on Gotland from Estonia ceased.
1220	Swedish army in Estonia is defeated with huge losses.

1236   Gotland completes a trade pact with England. Gotland's prosperity increases due to trade and its support of the many papal crusades launched in the Eastern Baltic.

1250   Visby begins construction of the city wall.

1276   Gotland given rights to trade with Sweden on same basis as Riga, Hamburg, and Lübeck. Visby is a bustling city, the New York of its day, populated by many European traders. German and English words appear in runic inscriptions.

1285   The Swedish King exempts the Gotlanders from military duty, except for crusades, in return for the cessation of gunrunning to pagans in the eastern Baltic.

1288   The wall is completed around Visby. Gotlanders and German citizens of Visby are in civil war over trade. The German merchants of Visby are fined for building a city wall without the permission of King Ladulås. Visby's trade continues to flourish at the expense of the native Gotlanders, and Visby became an independent city.

1300   The dotted palatal R is used in the Ukna Church inscription located in East Götaland just opposite Gotland on the Swedish mainland.

1313   Gotland revolts over taxes to King Birger of Sweden. Birger's troops are defeated near Lärbro Church and Birger was held captive.

1318   Swedish King Birger outfits a Gotlandic fleet to relieve the fortress of Steneborg, held by Crown Prince Magnus Birgersson, but all the ships are captured. A new fleet is sent, but suffers the same fate. Birger then flees to exile in Copenhagen. Sweden, in pursuit of Birger, occupies Gotland.

1323   Sweden obtains part of Karelia north of Nöteborg, Russia.

1328   Runic Calendar of 1328 in use in Gotland.

1342   Unrest and executions in Visby result in many influential German families leaving the island.

1346   Danish Estonia sold to the Teutonic Knights for 10,000 marks.

1347   King Valdemar of Denmark rides south through Europe and embarks on a ship to Palestine and becomes a Knight of the Holy Suplechre.

1348   Swedish King Magnus embarks on a papal crusade in Russia at Nöteborg on Lake Ladoga. King Magnus returns to Sweden and Norway due to the rise of the Black Death.

1350   Black Death hit, Gotland particularly hard.

1359   The plague returns to Sweden. King Erik of Sweden and his family are stricken and die.

1360   Denmark conquers Öland and Skåne.

1361   Denmark conquers Gotland.

1390   Mecklenburg pirates construct forts in Gotland after Albreckt of Mecklenburg is dethroned as King of Sweden.

1397   The German Mecklenburg pirates conquer all of Gotland.

1398   Mecklenburg pirates on Gotland are defeated by the Order of Teutonic Knights.

1403   The Kalmar Union under Queen Margaret lands troops on Gotland at Silte.

1404   The Teutonic Knights force the surrender of the Kalmar Union troops.

1405   Denmark pays the Teutonic Knights to leave Gotland.

1420   About this time Erik of Pommeren, king of Sweden, starts to build Visborg Castle near Visby.

1436   King Erik of Sweden lives in exile at Visborg Castle.

1449   Sweden's King Erik is expelled from Visborg and Gotland by the king of Denmark. Visborg Castle is then torn down.

1525   Troops from Lübeck in Germany burn much of northern Visby. Gotland is then in a steep economic decline. Only one of six Visby churches can be supported there after.

1572   Runic calendar of 1572 in use in Gotland

1645   Gotland reverts back to Sweden by treaty with Denmark.

1806   Sweden offers Gotland to the Knights of Malta, who decline to accept.

1850   About this time Sweden restores the Gotland Churches (over ninety in number).

1864   P. G. Säve records a dotted R in Gothem Church in inscription G 158.

1935   The dotted R is discovered in Lund and Ukna Church in East Götaland, Sweden, which is a mere day's sail from Gotland.

1962   Sven Jansson and Elias Wessén publish runic inscriptions from Southern Gotland.

1972   The inscriptions from Middle Gotland are published by Elizabeth Svärdström.

2002   Dr. Thurgunn Snædal publishes her thesis on the runes of Gotland.

2004   Most of the runic inscriptions from Northern Gotland are now available on the web.

The first abbey in Gotland was founded by the Cistercians at Gutnalia in 1164. With the Reformation the abbey was abandoned, and now only the arches remain. (SFW)

The Cistercians built Roma Church on Gotland in a Romanesque style with Gothic vaulting. (SFW)

The eight-sided spire of Roma Church exhibits the Cistercian concept that heaven is represented by the eight-fold. The spire was thought to help obtain the inspiration of the Holy Spirit. The definition of "inspire" is "to affect as with a supernatural influence" and "inspiration" is "communication of ideas

from a supernatural source." Almost all the churches on Gotland have this eight-sided spire. The Cistercians and their brother group, the Knights Templar, introduced the ogive arch and Gothic style to Europe. Soon almost all the churches of Gotland rebuilt their naves in the Cistercian Gothic style used in the Roma Church.

In 1164 Cistercian Gutnalia was founded on Gotland on the ancient Gutna-ting site in the parish of Ruma (now called Roma). Gutnalia's establishment coincided with the Danish king's decision to attack pagan Estonia. In 1171, a papal crusade was declared against Estonia, and the Knights Templar and Teutonic Knights joined this call to war. Cistercian monasteries advanced together with the Templars, eastward along the southern Baltic shores at Dargun in 1172, Kolbarz in 1173, Olivia in 1186, and Edena in 1188. The Templars and Cistercians were firmly established in Riga by 1202.

In Gotland the co-operative and skilled monks of the Cistercian Abby at Roma introduced ashlar masonry during the construction of Follingbo Church in about 1200. These finely-cut stone blocks, called ashlars, were also used at Eskelhem Church during the same period. The principles of Freemasonry had taken root on the island of Gotland. Later, in the 1280's skilled Gotlandic masons joined French masons and architects imported for the construction of the Uppsala Cathedral in Gothic style. These masons returned to Gotland in the first quarter of the 1300s and erected the great Southern Chapel of the Cathedral of St. Mary's in Visby.

This runic inscription (G 216) was found in a telephone installation trench near the Cistercian Abbey of Gutnalia at Roma. The inscription reads: ormiga : ulfuair : krikiaR : iaursaliR : islat : serkiat. "Ormiga and Ulvair (were in) Greece, Jerusalem, Africa, and Iceland." These men were likely crusaders who traveled to the Holy Land during the king of Denmark's crusade circa 1200. (SFW)

The inscription found on a stone unearthed in a telephone installation near Gutnalia is a testament to the extensive travels of two men, Ormiga and Ulvair, who may have been crusaders with the Danish crusade of 1191 that started in Copenhagen and then proceeded to Bergen. The ships came from as far afield as Greenland, Iceland, and Gotland joined the ships assembled in Bergen for the journey to the Mediterranean.

Earlier, in 1110, King Sigurd left Norway with fifty ships and spent seven years on a crusade. They spent one winter in England, camped one winter in France, and another in Galicia, Spain. While in Portugal, they helped the king expel the Moors from the Cintra Castle near Lisbon. Sigurd fought the Moors in Majorca and Africa, and landed at Acre in Palestine. After visiting Jerusalem and helping to conquer Sidon in Lebanon, they proceeded to Constantinople where they exchanged the ships for horses. The men then rode back to Norway via Bulgaria, Hungary, Bavaria, Germany, and Denmark. Following World War II a map showing Vinland was found by chance in a library in Hungary. This map may have been left in Hungary by King Sigurd. The papal crusade in the Baltic to expel the pagans in Estonia lasted from 1171 to 1219 under the king of Denmark. Many papal crusades were established against the Finns and Russians by the Swedes as late as 1348. The latter failed under King Magnus of Sweden.

The present state of the Helge And (Holy Ghost) octagonal church in Visby is ruins. In the sketch of the church as it appears centuries ago, the M-form of the windows in the tower and the W form of the lower tower roof are visible. The spire is eight-sided, as if aspiring to the 8-fold nature of Heaven. (SFW)

Holy Ghost Church features an octagonal construction and is the only church in Sweden with this form except for Lärbro Church in Gotland, which was modeled after Holy Ghost.

Lärbro Church was inspired by Visby's Helge And Church, and was built in the early 14th century. Note the M form of the windows and the W form of the lower tower roof. Like most churches in Gotland the tower is eight sided. Note the weapons storage house to the left. (SFW)

From the latter part of the 1100s to 1349, several popes authorized

crusades in the Baltic, with the promise that Gotlanders who participated would have absolution of their sins for one year. If they were killed in battle all their sins would be absolved for their entire life. This lure attracted many young men from Gotland. The number of grave slabs adorned with Knights Templar crosses attests to the appeal of such papal promises. The Teutonic Knights also assisted in these campaigns and established a Cistercian monk as Bishop of Riga in 1200. This bishop established the octagonal Church of the Holy Spirit (Helge And) with an associated hospital in Visby immediately thereafter for the benefit of pilgrims and crusaders. The king of Sweden had his crusade against Finnish and Russian pagans in 1280, and in 1285 he exempted Gotlanders from crusader duty in return for the cessation of gunrunning to pagans in the eastern Baltic. Much of the history of this time has been lost. Swedish historians know of the defeat of an entire Swedish naval fleet and Swedish army in Lake Ladoga, Russia in 1140, but only from Russian accounts.

Haagensen and Lincoln's (2002) premise is that Bornholm was used as a base for the Knights Templar in the crusade against Estonia. Their proof of Templar influence is in the fantastic mathematics used in laying out the churches, particularly the round ones, on Bornholm. After Estonia was finally conquered in 1219, Gotland became a prime out-post of the German Hanseatic League that was based in the city of Visby on Gotland's west coast. Estonia was sold to the Teutonic Knights, the German branch of the Templars, in 1346 by King Valdemar of Denmark. The king was then spared from the Black Death that claimed one out of two Danes in the plague of 1349-50. The Black Death hit Gotland in 1350, as evidenced by the Lärbro Church inscription G 293. Both Visby and rural Gotland suffered a high death rate.

In Denmark, the bodies lay unburied for months. They were found on depopulated farms, along the roadside, stacked by the thousands in the churchyards. It was said the overpowering stench was everywhere, and the many bodies of those buried under the church floors made it impossible to hold more services. However, the church grew rich from the many gifts received from the departed and those made to appease the wrath of God. Valdemar, by agreement with the pope, received a third of the church income and most likely this helped save the king from his financial crisis.

After partially recovering from the Black Death, Denmark reclaimed their old eastern provinces of Halland, Skaane, and Bleking, that had been mortgaged to King Magnus of Sweden in the 1330s. In 1360, they took the island of Öland.

Gotland was considered a prize possession. It had also been greatly weakened by the breakout of the Black Death, nevertheless ships continued to call at Visby from all parts of Europe: Greenland, England, Iceland, Norway, German, Denmark, and Sweden ships. Next to the port in Bergen, it was the most active of the Hansa trading centers. Visby was home to seven churches for the traders from these lands, such as St. Clements for the

Danes, St. Mary's for the Germans, the Holy Ghost Church for the crusaders, the Russian Church with St. Clements, St. Catherins, St. Nicholas and St. Hans open to the Danes, Norwegians, Swedes, and Gotlanders. Gotland stationed agents in Bergen and the ship traffic was heavy between them.

Denmark invaded Gotland in 1361. In July of that same year the Danish army landed near Öja Church in southern Gotland, tarried in the south for two weeks, and reduced the defense towers there and at Flöjel Church on the way to its final battle outside the walls of Visby. A Latin inscription from the time says it all of the Danish Army: *"they burn our farms, put our men to the sword, all is woe."* Visby had been the center of the lucrative spice and fur trade from Novgorod (Nyrod = New City) in Russia. This city had been founded by Gotlanders many centuries before, but now the connection was lost. However, it appears that a new connection was made by the Gotlanders.

The spice trade had been closed forever by the Mongol invasions of the 1200s, but now the furs from the New World opened up new vistas. It was common knowledge that in 1289 that Erik, the king of Norway, had sent Rolf to seek men in Iceland to go to a new land, and that a Greenlandic ship from Markland had arrived with eighteen men in Iceland in 1347 (Rasmus Anderson, 1906). The tales of Leif Eriksson and Thorfinn Karlsefne had been circulated by the Hauk manuscript in the period 1299-1334, and the wealth that Karlsefne acquired by selling his cargo of timber and furs was part of the account. His widow Gudrud had even visited the kings of Denmark and Norway, and traveled to Rome in the 1020s. The church records of Adam of Bremen (and Lund was a daughter-cathedral of Bremen) stated that King Sven Estridson of Denmark had declared that *"Vinland was a well-known place from the many people that have traveled there and come back."* The special clams from New England found in the sand strata of Klagen off the northern tip of Jutland prove that ships from New England had anchored there in the 1200s and 1300s. In the other direction, the European periwinkle was found in the medieval sand strata of Halifax harbor. Both the clams and the periwinkle can only travel attached to bottoms of ships.

Additional evidence of travel to North America may be found in newly-discovered bills of lading from circa 1380-1420. These furs landed in London apparently aboard Basque ships with beaver that were bailed in the Canadian fashion, as opposed to being packed in barrels as those from Russia were. The Kensington party could have been just one of many to leave for the New World during the turmoil caused by the Danes, taking of Visby. By this time the sturdy cogs of the Hanse were fit for transatlantic sailing.

The defense tower next to Fröjel Church near the west coast of Gotland is now in ruins, most likely due to the assault of the Danes in 1361. (SFW)

The German Burgers built this wall around Visby between 1250 and 1288 without permission of the Swedish king, since Gotland was only loosely connected to Sweden at that time. This wall became useful in the civil war that ensued with the Gotlanders of the countryside in 1288. (SFW)

Visby was a walled town when the Danish army hacked to pieces the two-thousand-man Gotlandic army of farmers, including very young boys and very old men, in 1361. The Visby inhabitants looked down on this carnage from their walls but made no move to help. The citizens of Visby opened the city gate to the Danes, but not wanting to be guests of the city they hacked a portal in the wall sufficient for thirteen men to walk abreast. The army marched in through the gate and out through the breech in the wall shoulder to shoulder, but did not sack the town.

The 2,000 bloody, mangled, and hacked bodies were immediately buried in a hastily-dug pit on a hot summer day, the July 27, 1361. In the haste to cover the bodies, much armor and even moneybags were left. During the last century these bodies were exhumed and examined. Most had their left foot (the leading foot exposed under the shield) axed off and had received repeated vicious axe blows to the head. The experienced and professional Danish army showed no mercy against these brave lads and old men who had no idea what was in store for them with the arrival of modern warfare. The demonstration cowed the citizens of Visby, who had no stomach for such a fight. The next day, Visby was forced to give up all its treasure to avoid being razed by the Danes, and never really recovered. The plunder of its treasury was coupled with the city's loss of trade due to the introduction of larger, more powerful sailing ships introduced in the 14th century that could pass by the port at Visby.

The new types of high-endurance sailing ships that came into use in the 1300s doomed Gotland to a decline in trade, as she was no longer needed as a transit point. Such ships could sail from Russia all the way to England. Compared to earlier ships, in 1362 ships like this could sail relatively quickly from Gotland and reach territories of the King of Sweden in north Norway, Iceland, and Greenland. (SFW)

In the 1390s, the German Mecklenburgish pirates conquered Gotland, but the Teutonic Knights expelled them around 1398. The magnificent nave portal of Bunge Church opens up into a lofty Gothic interior that presents well-lighted murals depicting the battle between the pirates and the Order of Teutonic Knights. After landing in late 1403, the Kalmar Union troops were forced to surrender in May 1404. In 1408 the Danes had a ten-year stay to guard the interests of Visby for the Hansa, and paid the Teutonic Knights to leave Gotland. Shortly after, King Erik of Sweden began to build a well-fortified castle in Visborg just outside the north wall of Visby. After King Erik's exile in 1436 he tried to use this castle as a base to reestablish himself on the Swedish throne. The Danes forced ex-king of Sweden, now Erik of Pommeren, to leave in 1449, and Gotland remained Danish until 1645 when it reverted to Sweden by treaty. This episode led to the carving of two of Gotland's outstanding grave slabs at Lye Church, G 99 and G 100, that speak of a Jacob of Mannegårde killed by a canon ball from the Visborg castle.

It is the thesis of this book that among the eight Goths and twenty-two Norwegians of the Kensington Rune Stone party there likely was a Cistercian cum Teutonic Knight with knowledge of Latin, Old Swedish, the Gutnish dialect, and Middle Low German spoken by the Germans in Visby, which is only seventeen kilometers northeast of Roma. This scenario could explain the traces of Gutnish dialect words **og** (and); the Middle Low German-based forms **rise** (journey), **west** (west), and **10 man** (10 men); and the dotted umlauts (ᛘ̈, Ẍ, ⦶̈) on the Kensington Rune Stone.

Teutonic Knights and Knights Templar Symbols

Unraveling the Kensington Rune Stone mystery must start with St. Bernard of Clairvaux (1090-1153), who was the driving force in the expansion of both the Cistercians and the Knights Templar. The organizations worked hand-in-glove, beginning in 1128, and would exert a heavy influence on Gotland from the 12th century through the end of the Middle Ages. Bernard joined the first Cistercian monastery in Burgundy, France when he was in his early twenties. During his lifetime more than one hundred fifty monasteries were built, and over three hundred European abbeys were in planning when he died in 1152. He had unprecedented political and religious influence throughout Europe, and answered to no king or nation, only to the pope in Rome. He became the Protector of

the Knights Templar in 1128. Bernard selected the beehive for his sign and is the patron saint of beekeepers.

In this portrait of St. Bernard an apparent M can be seen in the folds of his right sleeve. The M is an ancient symbol for Wisdom. (Rev. Ailbe J. Luddy, *The Order of Citeaux*, 1932, p. 41)

These new cathedrals, such as Notre Dame in Paris (begun in 1163) and Chartres, south of Paris (begun in 1194) were inspired by the Templars and the Cistercians and were unlike anything seen before in Europe. Even modern methods cannot duplicate the finely made stained glass windows in these structures. The amazing architecture used in these structures involved mathematics that are still being re-discovered. The Templars learned mathematical secrets, such as how to calculate a ninth of a degree and a seven-pointed star, during crusades to the Holy Land. The seven-pointed star was used in the construction of Chartres, as seen in the diagram below, and in laying out the exact positions of churches in Bornholm (Haagensen and Lincoln 2002: 15-22, 57, 69-83).

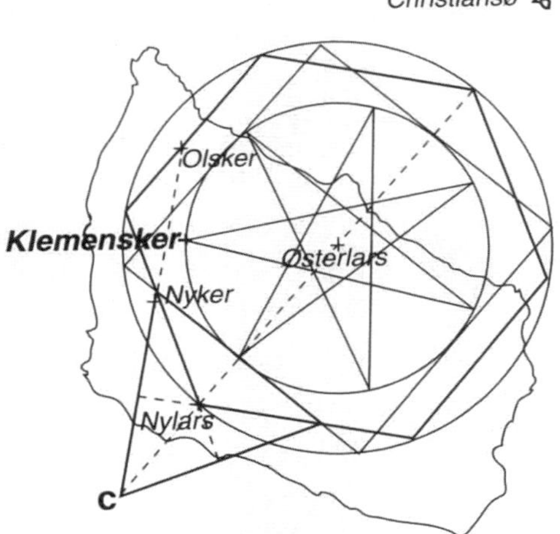

The seven-pointed star pattern on which the cathedral at Chartres is based, and the layout of the church-es of Bornholm (Haagensen and Lincoln 2002: 15-22, 57, 69-83), is the sure mark of the Knights Templar's mathematical ability because the seven-pointed star can not be developed by graphical means as the five-and six-pointed stars can.

At Hellvi church on Gotland a tell-tale seven-pointed star was carved over this portal (von Friesen 1933: Fig 68, 235). (SFW)

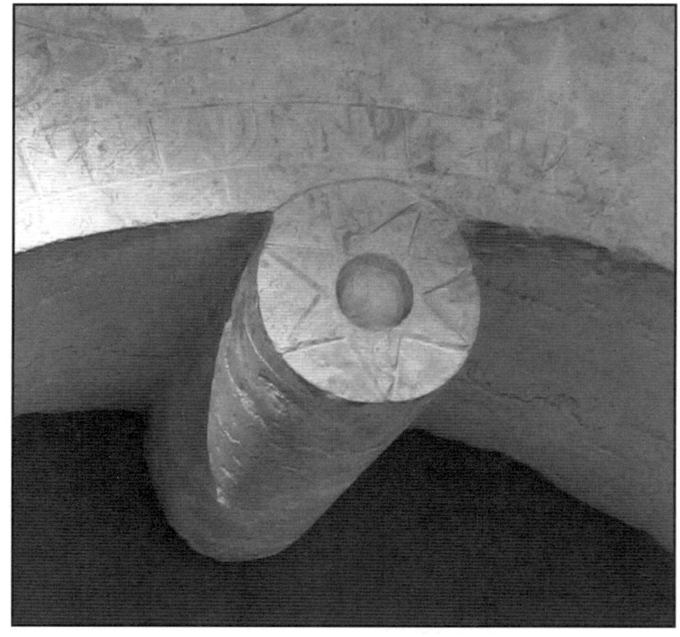

These Gothic cathedrals were soon followed by more, such as at Reims in 1211 and Amiens in 1221. The cathedrals at Bayeaux, Rouen, Evreux, Laon, were built in a pattern that traced the constellation Virgo across the landscape. Virgo has the star sign (♍) similar to M, which stands for "virgin." By the next century over eighty Gothic structures were complet-ed in the Cistercian-Templar model. The style of the magnificent cathedrals was aptly called Gothic, from a Greek word derivative meaning magical (Gardner 1996: 262-64).

Notre Dame soared to new heights with the innovative construction methods inspired by the Cistercians and Templars. The flying buttresses installed on Gothic Cathedrals, seen on the right side of the image, pass the weight load of the wall to an external curtain wall, which allows large stained glass windows to be installed (Cantor 1999: 42).

In 1996, Gardner (1996: 118) said, *"The Cistercians, Dominicans, Franciscans, and various other monastic orders of the era all followed a lifestyle separate from the episcopacy of The Roman Church. However, they shared a common interest in Mary Magdalene. In drafting the constitution for the order of Knights Templar in 1128, St. Bernard specifically mentioned a requirement for the 'obedience of Bethany, the castle of Mary and Martha'. It is evident that the Notre Dame cathedrals of Europe, which were wholly Cistercian-Templar instigated, were dedicated not to Jesus' mother Mary, but to 'our Lady' Mary Magdalene."* The Kensington Rune Stone seems to reveal startling and stunning symbolism about the Knights Templar's reverence for Mary Magdalene and esoteric Eastern religious beliefs that have become the unexpected, surprising thesis of this book.

Timeline for St. Bernard, the Cistercians, the Knights Templar, and the Teutonic Knights

This timeline includes events that were important to the Baltic Crusades and their aftermath.

1090 The child who would become St. Bernard of Clairvaux in Burgundy, France is born.
1098 Cistercians found first abbey in Citeaux, Burgundy.
1104 Archbishop establishes in Lund.
1113 St. Bernard joins the Cistercians.

1115	St. Bernard establishes Clairvaux, the second Cistercian abbey.
1119	Templars establish in Jerusalem by nine nobel-born Bugundian knights.
1128	The nine knights return and St. Bernard becomes protector of the Templars.
1140	A Swedish flotilla sails up the Neva River and raids the east side of Lake Ladoga, but are destroyed, according to Russian records.
1143	Cistercian Abbeys of Alvasta and Nydal are founded in East Götaland and Småland, Sweden. Cistercian Abbey of Herrevad founded in Denmark.
1145	Bernard's disciple, the Cistercian Egenius (1145-1154), is elected pope.
1153	St. Bernard dies after 125 Cistercian Abbeys are founded and 175 more planned in his lifetime.
1154	Cistercian Abbey of Esom founded in Denmark. Pope Eugenius dies.
1158	Cistercian Abbey of Vitskøl founded in Denmark.
1161	Cistercian Abbey of Sorø founded in Denmark. German merchants are allowed to live in Visby.
1160s	The Hanseatic League establishes its trading center in Visby.
1164	The Cistercian Fulco is appointed Bishop of Estonia. Papal crusade against Estonia is sanctioned. The 181st Cistercian Abbey founded on Gotland at Gutnalia. The Cistercian Alvastian monk from France is Sweden's first Archbishop with a seat in Old Uppsala.
1169	The Pagan Wends of Rügen are conquered by Denmark.
1170	Pagan Estonians raid Öland in Sweden. Papal Crusade against pagan Estonia is declared.
1172	Cistercian Abbey of Dargun established east of Rügen on Baltic Coast.
1173	Cistercian Abbey of Kolbatz established east of Dargun.
1181	Archbishop Eskil dies at Clairvaux after four years there as a simple Cistercian monk.
1185	The Wends of Pomerania are conquered by the Danes while under Bishop Absalon of Lund.
1186	Cistercian Abbey of Oliva founded in Pomerania (Poles by the sea).
1187	Cistercian Abbey of Eldena founded near present day Gdansk.
1191	The German Order of Teutonic Knights Abbey at Thorn, in what would become part of Prussia, is founded.
1192	King of Denmark sponsors crusade to the Holy Land.
1199	The Pope sanctions the German Order of Teutonic Knights to allie with the Knights Templar.
1200	Bishop Albert founds the Monastery in Riga and Holy Ghost Church in Visby.
1201	Around this time the Holy Spirit Church in Visby, Gotland, is founded by Bishop Albert of Riga for the benefit of the Crusaders on their way to Latvia. This church is associated with a hospital as well.
1202	The Cistercian, Theoderic van Treiden, founds the Order of the Sword Brethren (an offshoot of the Knights Templar) in Riga.
1211	The Cistercian, van Treiden, now becomes Bishop of Estonia. New Papal Bull for crusade in the eastern Baltic is issued.
1215	From 1210-1215 the Mongols conquer all of China north of the Yellow River. West Turkomens are forced westward and many East Turkomens fled the wrath of Genghis Khan.
1219	Estonia conquered by Denmark and Bretheren of the Sword, Bishop Theoderic is killed.
1220	Swedish crusade to Estonia crushed, and Bishop Karl of Linköping, Östergötaland, who was also the Bishop appointed over Gotland, is killed.
1226	Gotlandic trade pact with England allows extensive trade with English merchants including the Knights Templar and the Teutonic Knights.
1230	Pope Gegorius IX urges King Erik of Sweden to expel heathens from Tavastland, Finland.
1236	Pope Gegorius again authorizes a Finlandic crusade against the pagans, now under Swedish King Birger. He grants full rights to participants in the same manner as if they were on crusade to the Holy Land.
1237	After heavy battle losses from the Lithuanians, the Order of the Sword Brethren are amalgamated

to the Order of Teutonic Knights. Thus the order gains possession of Latvia, Estonia, and Lithuania, which were collectively known as Livonia.

1240   Swedish crusade to Russia is decimated on the banks of the Niva River.

After Kiev is sacked by the Mongols, the Teutonic Knights and the Poles lose the bloody battle of Lieglitz in Silecia to the Mongol army. Poland and Germany are saved from invasion when the Mongols pounce on Hungary instead. The king of Poland flees the battle and obtains haven in a Cistercian Abbey in Moravia.

1241   The Mongol army returns to Mongolia, never again to threaten Europe. However, the East-West trade route is now open.

1242   Teutonic Knights severely defeated on Lake Peipus by the Russians.

1258   Iraq and Persia fall to the Mongols.

1271   Marco Polo starts his journey to China.

1280   The king of Sweden, Magnus Ladulås, crusades against the Finnish and Russian pagans.

1285   The Swedish king exempts the Gotlanders from crusader duty in return for ending gun-running to pagans in the eastern Baltic.

1288   Gotlanders and German citizens of Visby engage in civil war.

1291   Crusaders lose Acre, their last stronghold in Palestine. The Knights of St. John (Hospitallers) transfer to the Greek island of Rhodes off the Turkish coast and conduct naval operations against the Muslims. The Knights Templar retreat to the Mediterranean island of Cyprus.

1295   Marco Polo returns to Venice.

1307   The Grand Master of the Knights Templar, Jacques de Molay is lured to France by the Pope to discuss the future of the Knights Templar. The French Templars, including de Molay are arrested by King Phillip the Fair on Friday the 13th of October.

1309   Teutonic Knights move base from Venice to Marienburg in Prussia and select a Baltic destiny. By the 1330s thousands of towns had been colonized in Prussia.

1310   German Templars exonerated in German courts of any wrongdoing. Many join the Teutonic Knights. French Knights Templar in German Lorraine do the same thing.
        Many English Templars flee to Scotland, a safe haven not under papal control.

1312   Knights Templar dissolved by Pope Clement V. Portuguese Templars are exonerated in court and change their name to the Knights of Christ.
        The Templar estates are awarded to the Knights of St. John.

1314   Jacques de Molay burned at the stake at Notre Dame in Paris by order of King Philip.

1323   Sweden obtains part of Karelia north of Nöteborg, Russia.

1346   Danish Estonia sold to the Order of Teutonic Knights.

1347   Swedish King Magnus mounts another papal Crusade against Russia.
        A Greenlandic ship with eighteen men arrives in Iceland from Markland, then sails on to Bergen.

1351   Azores placed on an Italian map.

1360   Denmark takes Öland, Bleking, and Skåne.

1361   Denmark then conquered Gotland. Visby pays dearly in silver to avoid destruction.

1368   The Mongols fall to the Ming Dynasty of China. East-West trade routes are closed.

1398   Mecklenburg Pirates defeated by the Order of the Teutonic Knights on Gotland.

1408   Teutonic Knights paid by Danish Queen to leave Gotland.

1410   The Order of Teutonic Knights is crushingly defeated at the battle of Tannenburg.

1447   At about this time Columbus is born in Majorca.

1467   The Order of Teutonic Knights is forced to be vassal to Poland and hold only Eastern Prussia, with the city of Koningberg as its base.

1468   About this time, Columbus marries Dona Felipa Perestello of Portugal in Lisbon. Her father, a Knight of Christ, is Governor of the island of Porto Santo, the smaller of the two Madeiras.

1477   Columbus visits Iceland, Ireland, and the Azores.

1492	Columbus discovers the West Indies. He hopes to recover the Holy Land by a pincer movement from the east, with Spain from the west, all funded with New World gold.
1498	Vasco de Gama rounds the Cape of Good Hope in Africa and discovers a route to India.
1502	The Livonia Brethren, as an arm of the Order, check the advance of Ivan III of Moscow.
1506	Columbus provides funds in his will for the recovery of the Holy Sepulcher in Jerusalem.
1523	The Knights of St. John lose Rhodes to the Ottomen Turks.
1525	The Order of Teutonic Knights reject the pope and become secular. Its Grand Master, Albrecht of Brandenburg, becomes the duke of Prussia.
1530	The Knights of St. John transfer to Malta as vassals to the king of Sicily. Annual tribute for the newly named Knights of Malta is a gold Maltese falcon, the origin of the famous statuette.
1558	Ivan the Terrible seizes Livonia from the Order. The Order concentrates on Prussia and tries to restore its power.
1736	Freemasonry in Sweden is suppressed by Swedish police.
1750	Around this time the new Swedish freemasonry is founded by the Swedish king.
1792	The Order's processions in France are nationalized following the French Revolution. French revenues are also nationalized by the French Assembly.
1798	The Knights of Malta surrender to Napoleon.
1806	Sweden, in war with Napoleon, offers to donate Gotland to the Knights of Malta (successors to the Knights of St. John), but the offer is declined.
1839	The Order reconstitutes in Austria and returns to its original purpose, which was charity.

Between 1143 and 1207, several Cistercians abbeys were established in Scandinavia: eleven in Denmark, six in Sweden, and three in Norway. Swedish abbeys at Alvastra in east Götaland and Nydal in Småland were founded in 1444. In 1150, mainland Sweden also added an abbey at Varnheim in Västergötaland. Julita in Sveland was first established at Viby on the Måleren near Stockholm, but was moved to Saba, which was also known as Julita, in about 1174. The early Cistercian nunneries in Sweden—Vreta, Askeby, Riseberga, Gudhem, Sko, Vårfruberga, and Solberga—also became well known around this time.

Many Swedes took the Crusader's Cross and fought in the Holy Land or joined the Baltic Crusades against the heathen Slavs in Latvia and Estonia. Swedish king Magnus Ladulås, born in 1200, had participated in both crusades as a youth, just as many other Swedes had done before and would continue to do after him. The Knights of St. John had a cloister in Eskilstuna. Beginning in the 13th century, the Order of Teutonic Knights owned farms in Sweden, and the city of Årsta was the seat for the Commandant of the Order in Sweden. Ordinary knights were first dubbed during the reign of King Ladulås in the latter part of the 1200s (Montelius, 1877: 478, 484).

There is no doubt that the French connection to Sweden was strong due to the Cistercian presence. This relationship allowed the Knights Templar, who had been disbanded by Pope Clement V in 1312, to simply join other existing orders in Sweden. The same opportunities existed with similar situations afforded to the Templars in both Spain and

Portugal. It is hard to imagine that the Templars even missed a beat in Sweden, and Gotland would have been a perfect base to continue their activities. Their efforts in the Baltic theater during this time were fully amalgamated with the Order of Teutonic Knights. Gotland was a safe haven with its population of German, English, Norwegian, Danish, Russian, Latvian, Estonian, and French in Visby. King Birger of Sweden was busy with other matters and had no time for papal matters. In about 1308, the Templars in Portugal were cleared of all charges against them and simply changed their Order's name to the Knights of Christ. Ships of the Order sailed with the same Red Pâté cross of the Templars before them. One of their churches at Tomar near Torres del Rio, Portugal, is still the best preserved model of a round Templar church. In Spain, the military orders reported directly to the king and were not under the power of the pope. German Templars were exonerated in German courts of any wrongdoing and could join the Teutonic Knights. English Templars fled to Scotland, which was not under papal power. According to Pike (1905: 820), "… Jacques de Molay and his fellows perished in the flames, but before his execution (in 1314) the chief of the doomed order organized and instituted what afterward came to be called the Occult, Hermetic, or Scottish Masonry. In the gloom of his prison, the Grand Master created four Metropolitan Lodges, at Naples for the East, at Edinburgh for the West, at Stockholm for the North, and at Paris for the South."

The Cathedral of Uppsala was still under construction, having been begun in 1270 under supervision of architects of the Cistercian-Templar school from northern France (see color section, plate 46). Furthermore, the masons were brought from Gotland for this work, and they returned to Gotland in about 1320. The Danes had used Gotlandic masons to construct their capital city, Tallin, in Estonia, which is why the stone buildings in Visby and Tallin are similar in form and construction techniques. Henry the Navigator (1394-1360), was a Grand Master, and Columbus's father-in-law was a Knight of Christ, as was Vasco de Gama. Columbus's mother-in-law gave Columbus her husband's sea-going charts, diaries (1394-1360), and records that covered his maritime service under King Henry the Navigator, as a Knight of Christ. Columbus became steeped in Templar lore, and may have even learned of the Kensington party on his visit to Iceland in 1477. The striking fact that Columbus has a hooked X in his name like the hooked X on the Kensington Rune Stone (1362) and those of the Spirit Pond rune stones (circa 1400) in Maine, gives one pause to speculate what else we don't know about Columbus. To our knowledge the Kensington and Spirit Pond rune stones and Columbus's signature are the only occurrences of the hooked X until the Larsson rune rows of 1883-5.

Columbus had a deeply religious side. Quoting Heer (1961: 155-6) on a letter to King Isabel and Ferdinand and Queen Isabela, " *I hold that the Holy Ghost can manifest Himself in Christians, Jews, Moors, and all sorts of men, and indeed not only in the wise but also in the simple.' Columbus's aim, as he expressly declared was to discover India and realize the old crusading dream of finally overcoming Islam by a huge pincer movement launched simultane-ously from the East and from the West."* Columbus harked back to his model, Joachim of Flora, an abbot of a house of Cistercians in Calabria, who died in 1202. Joachim had prophesized the coming reign of the Holy Ghost and the third millennium (Heer, 1961: 156).

In Haiti during his first voyage, Columbus wrote in his journal *"that Ferdinand and Isabella would now have funds sufficient to conquer the Holy Land"* (Durant 1957: 163). In his later years he collected prophecies to help prove that the time was right that Jerusalem should be returned to Christendom by Spain. In his will he left money *"for the recovery of the Holy Sepulchre in Jerusalem"* (Pohl 1986: 229).

Templar Crosses

A tombstone inside the Kilmory chapel at Loch Sween in Argyll, Scotland, bears the eight-sided stone cross in the typical Templar style. This style of cross is seen on numerous grave slabs and painted on the walls of most churches on Gotland (Baigent & Leigh, 1989: Figure 6).

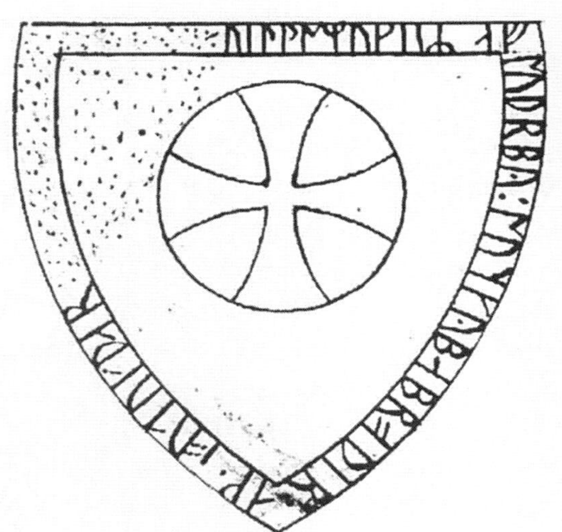

This inscription (G 245, Hejnum Church) on the island of Gotland contains a similar type of cross in the middle of the shield.

This Templar cross, circa 1200, was painted on the wall of Nylar Church on the island of Bornholm (Haagensen and Lincoln, 2002).

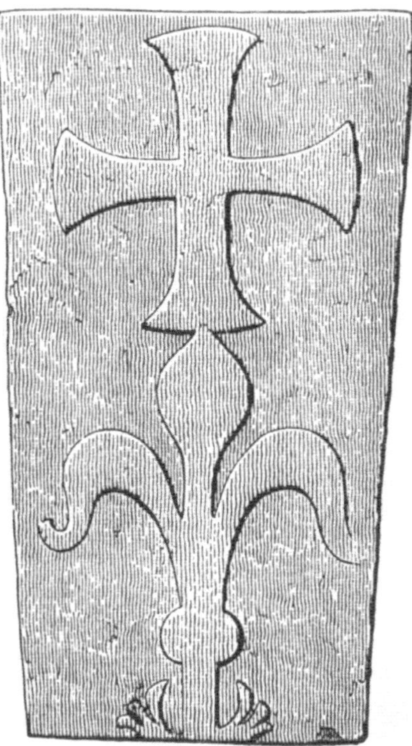

On the left is G 292, a Lärbro Church inscription on Gotland. This church also has an octagonal tower modeled after Holy Ghost Church in Visby. (SFW) On the right is a grave slab from Uppland, circa 1200s (Sölve Gardell II 1937: 126).

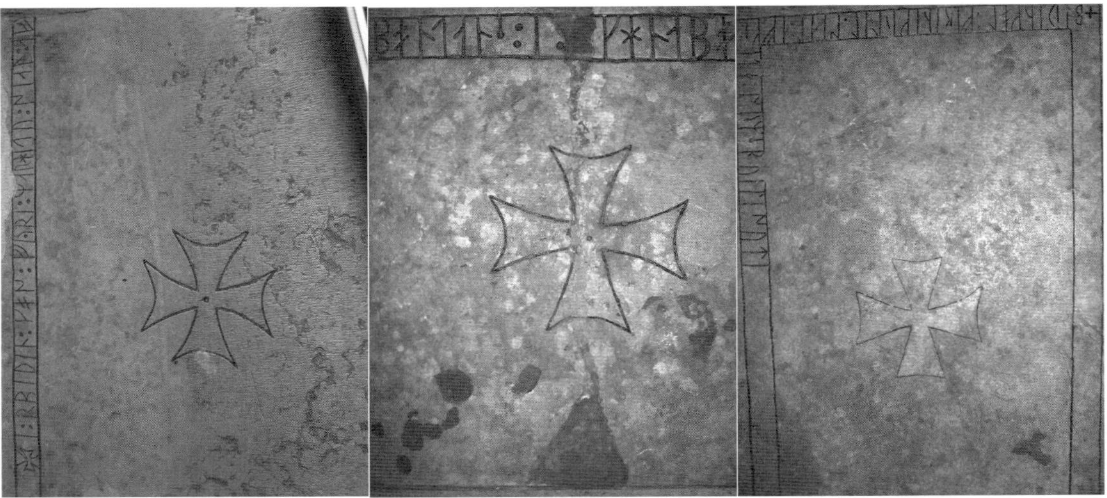

Templar crosses appear on three medieval grave slabs G 282, G 283, and G 284 at Othem Church on Gotland (circa 1400s). (SFW)

The 8-Fold of Heaven

The 8-fold pattern of the floral design is repeated in church spires on Gotland, which are 8-sided conical sections.

The defense tower stands next to the Gammalgarn Church, located near the central eastern coast of Gotland. The eight-sided spire is typical of most Gotlandic churches.(SFW)

Skull and Crossbones

A 17th century grave at Temple, Scotland (near Edinburgh). Note the mason's mallet to the right. (Baigent and Leigh 1989: Fig 28).

Three skulls and crossbones were carved on this grave slab at St. Maria Church in Visby. (SFW)

It has been said that the Jolly Roger of pirate fame has the flag of Knights Templar fleets as its origin. The presence of mason's tools on grave slabs is a typical Templar indicator from Scotland and Palestine. Mason tools are depicted in at least one wall mural and one sculpture on Gotland. One inscription, G 8 on Gotland, seems like the illustration of the chalice and the sword seen at Roslyn Chapel in Scotland.

To the left is a Templar tomb stone with a mason's square from Kilmory in Scotland. In the middle is a 13th century tombstone of a Templar Mason from the former Templar castle at Athlit, Palestine (Baigent and Leigh, 1989: Figures 7 and 25). This stone sculpture (right) at Öja Church on Gotland has a mason square and an architect's compass carved into the slab. (SFW)

Based on such illustrations, a mason must have carved the horizontal barred "o" rune ⌐|
on the Kensington Rune Stone instead of the usual downward angled **o**-rune, ⌐|. Likewise
the pentadic numbers on Kensington Rune Stone, with its horizontal bars at the top,
must have appealed to a mason (⌐ instead of the usual center bared ⊢).

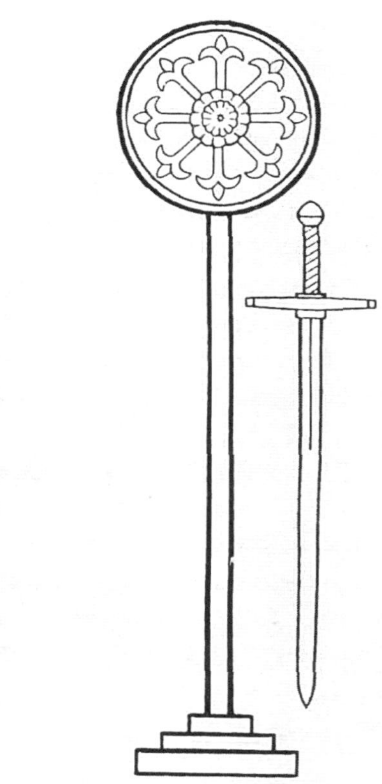

The Sword and Chalice of the Holy Grail

On the bottom end of the G 8 inscription on Gotland, (see
color section, plate 30) is an obvious X that resembles the
Greek letter "chi" which stood for Christ. The six-pointed
symbol below the cross at the top of the inscription could
be a sign of significance (as was the eight) rather than just a
decoration. Compare with the representation to the right
in Gardner 1996: 298.

A six-sided flower similar to the G 8 inscription appears in
the nearby Vamlingbo Church. (SFW)

Freemasonry

The row above from the Larsson papers shows the same code characters as seen in the French freemasonry code in lowercase below. However, the letters following s above do not correspond with the code letters below.

ABCDEFGHILMNOPQRSTUXYZ

These symbols are the French Masonic Code on Trestle Board (Beresniak 2003: 32) circa 19th Century.

The fifth sign from the left on this French Masonic gold arc is the Gotlandic s-rune. Four of the other symbols are found in the two Masonic alphabets shown above. (Beresniak 2003: 88)

The crest in the middle of this grave slab (G 344) on Gotland at the St. Pers Church in Visby is a variation of the unique Gotlandic S rune ( ) with a horizontal bar added to create a cross of Templar design beneath. Could this crest be symbolic of the Templar sword and the chalice? Surprisingly, this s-rune was present in French Freemasonry of the 19th century, as seen in the illustration of the golden arch, above. It is not, however, present on the Kensington Rune Stone.

In March 2004 the Larsson rune row was discovered in Sweden, prompted us to wonder if a secret society may have been operating in Sweden. To our surprise, we found it was certainly true, since Swedish authorities suppressed the freemasons, successors to the Templars, in 1736, but King Karl XIII of Sweden established the Swedish Masonic System with his brother King Gustav III around 1760, and the society is extant in Scandinavia today. All subsequent Swedish monarchs, including the late King Gustav VI, have held the position of Grand

Master of Swedish Masonry. The king maintained that he had acquired the secret files of the Knights Templar, and his portrait shows the regalia of the Knights Templar, with their banner in the background. (Haagensen and Lincoln 2002: 92-5)

This painting of King Karl XIII of Sweden shows him in full regalia as Grand Master of Swedish Masonry. Behind him is the red cross of the Knights Templar (Haagensen and Lincoln 2002). The Grand Master was referred to as the Master of Wisdom. (Photo courtesy of Sverre Dag Mogstad)

This door marks the entrance to the Freemason Order (Frimurarnas Logehus) on the island of Gotland that continue many of the centuries-old traditions to this day. (SFW)

Are there Teutonic Knight Signs on the Kensington Rune Stone?

The Cistercian-Templars are known to have been a force in the Baltic in 1362, and there is proof that the Templars issued letters of credit with secret validation codes. With these facts in mind, we began to wonder if the special punch marks (apparently not meant to alter the values of the runes) recently found on the Kensington Rune Stone might have something to do with Templar codes. The runes with these punch marks appear in the following order: G (ᛉ), Ä (ᛪ), M (ᛗ), and V (ᛘ).

It could be interpreted that ᛉᛪᛗᛘ is a coded word meant to be read by another member of the Order who knew what to look for and how to read it. Simply put, the message revealed who the carver was only to those who could understand it. GÄMV could have referred to God, Xrist (Christ), Maria, Holy Spirit, or perhaps it meant **gämo** (concealed), as V/W was often used for "o" in medieval manuscripts. The special dotted series of GÆV as *gämo* (hidden, protected) could also be understood to be *gömo* (hidden, protected) in the same way as *göre* and *gäre* (do) are the same word. On Gotland, *geara* (do) is a common runic spelling, and *gerre* was used for Old Swedish *görre* (did). Today it is *gemme* in Danish, but *gömma* in Swedish.

The concept of the Father, the Son, and the Holy Spirit was present in Europe for centuries. The Templars added a fourth concept, the female wisdom based on their experiences in the Holy Land, where god has been represented by four letters since ancient times. The four letters of the deity were JHWH in the tetragrammaton of the Hebrews, ADAD in Assyrian, AMUN in Egyptian, the Persian SYRE, the Greek ThEOS, and the Latin DEUS (Mackey 2004: 327). These letters represented the four gods: the Father, the Son, the Mother, and the Daughter.

In addition, the 10 (ᛘ) on the face and the 10 (ᛘ) on the side have a punch mark in the left side and right side of the circle, respectively.

The g-rune ᛉ could stand for God or **Gesus** (Jesus). One interpretation is the use of ᛉ as an initial for **God.** On the other hand, **Jesus** was often spelled with a G in runic inscriptions, and the Greek letter *chi* represented Christ (X, as in X-mass or Xmas). It is noteworthy that all seven of the g-runes on the Kensington Rune Stone are carved in mirror image, and only the first one is double-punched.

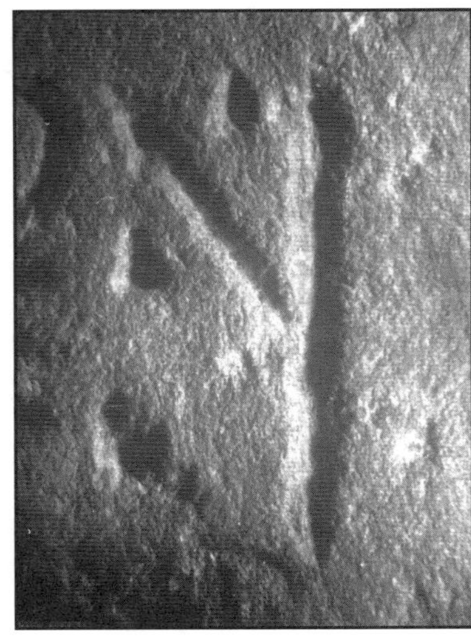

There are mysterious punches within the lines of four runes on the Kensington Rune Stone. L-1, C-3, has a punch in the upper left arm of the letter G. (SFW: 2002)

This grave slab from Gammelgarn Church (G 115) has two interesting features. It begins with a Templar-like cross that's followed by "Gesus Krist" (Jesus Christ). (SFW)

The first time Ӝ is used on the Kensington Rune Stone it has two punches in the leg (Ӝ). Since (Ӝ) appears in the Kensington Rune Stone **läger** (camp, resting place, grave?), could this be a reminder of Christ's resting two nights in the grave chamber?

L-4, C-71, has a punch in both feet of the letter ä. Is this an X for Christ (as in Xmas), and is the hook a representation of the chalice? The double-dotted X with two punch marks appears in the Kensington Rune Stone word läger (camp, resting place, grave). (SFW: 2002)

The punched M in AVM is likely for Maria.

:AVM:

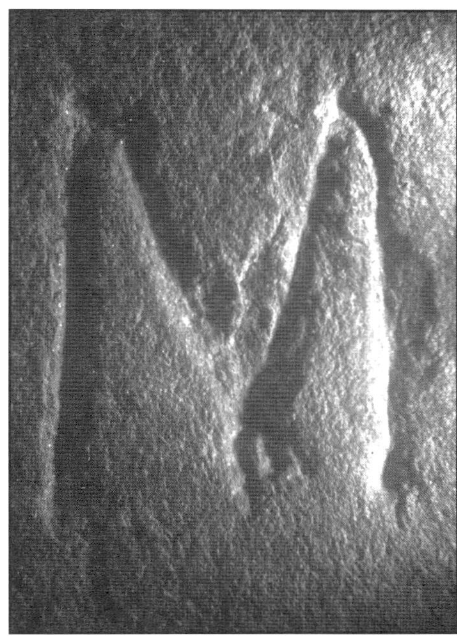

M.

The Latin M (M) in AVM (L-9, C-193) is punched at the base of the right leg and likely stands for Maria.(SFW: 2002)

The punched V in **havet** (the inland sea) might stand for the Wisdom of the Holy Spirit, particularly given that the punched series of GäMV could stand for *gömo* (hidden, protected) in Old Swedish. The fourth line of Columbus's signature has XMY, but no explanation as been made. The Kensington Rune Stone has ᛉMᛉ all with punches. Did Columbus see this sequence? Are these initials, X M Y, meant to stand for ᛉ M ᛉ? Is this another code?

The W-rune on line 10 of the Kensington Rune Stone inscription (L-10, C-227), has a punch at the bottom of the main stave. (SFW: 2002)

In Jan Provost's painting called "Christian Allegory,"

the upturned hands above the lower eye form a W (inverted M). Mary Magdalene is shown freeing the dove of the Holy Spirit that carries forth wisdom through the upturned hands. This inverted M can be seen as an architectural feature by the minister's upraised arms found in churches around the world even today, calling forth the wisdom of the Holy Spirit upon the congregation during a benediction.

A 15th century painting by Jan Provost, entitled "Christian Allegory," depicts Jesus and Mary Magdalene (Gardner 2002: Fig 4). The Kensington Rune Stone v/w-rune is much like the all-seeing eye and the upturned hands at the base of the picture.

The M may also represent the astrological symbol for Virgo. The roof line of the octagonal towers seen at both the Holy Ghost Church in Visby and at Lärbro Church outside of Visby forms a W, and an M when viewed from above. The Kensington Rune Stone v/w-rune (Ψ) and the **m**-rune (Ψ) are almost alike. The reader may have other explanations for these circumstances.

Is the Kensington Rune Stone v-rune with a punch at its base meant to be a representation of upturned hands forming a W on top of the Seeing Eye? The orb and all-seeing eye has its foundation in ancient Samaria around 2000 years BC. One is tempted to point out that the peculiar ⊕-rune on the Kensington Rune Stone might be seen to represent the male orb ♂ as ⊕ with the addition of the all-seeing eyes on the orb as the Kensington Rune stone rune ⊕. It is noteworthy that the word "orb" is a poetic word for eye. The eyeball is the globe of the eye. The eye socket is called an orbit due to the elliptical orbits common to planets and the shape of the eye. The eye is the sun and the orbit or eye socket is the elliptical orbit of Venus.

Is this the Orb of Christ seen in "Christian Allegory" with the all-seeing eyes and the cross interchanged?

Even the special punch marks on the Kensington Rune Stone might represent the all-seeing eye that the Knights Templar knew from the lore transmitted to them by the eastern mystics. Remember that the U.S. Treasury in the 1930s issued the new dollar bill with an all-seeing eye at the apex of a pyramid, without Secretary of the Treasurer Henry Morgerthau realizing its ancient origin and special meaning to certain occult societies. In other words, much has been forgotten about symbols of the past. (Mayer and Brysac: 1999)

The information that Nicholaus Roerich was responsible for the all-seeing eye on the dollar bill is attributed to Mayer and Brysa (1999). The truncated pyramid is also of particular significance (this pyramid is shown in the color section).

Nicholaus Roerich met Henry Wallace in 1929, who was the secretary of the treasury under Roosevelt from 1933 to 1941, and vice president from 1941-45. Roerich became of some influence with Wallace as well as with President Roosevelt. Quoting Meyer and Brysa (1999), "Roerich's influence was also suspected in another Wallace initiative, the

adornment of the one-dollar bill with the verso of the Great Seal, showing a pyramid crowned by an all-seeing eye. Wallace pointed out to an incredulous Treasury Secretary Henry M. Morgenthau, Jr. that underneath the (truncated) pyramid were the words *Novus Ordo Seclorum* (*Novus Ordo* can be read as Latin for "New Deal"), a politically relevant inscription, and the change was approved in 1935. "It was not 'till later,' Morgenthau wrote in his diary, 'that I learned that the pyramid…had some cabalistic significance for members of a small religious sect'." (Mayer and Brysac: 1999)

This portrait of Nicholas Roerich was painted by his son Svetoslav. In Roerich's hands is the sacred Rothenburg casket referred to in his wife's poem, "Legend of the Stone." (Courtesy of the Roerich Museum)

This painting by Nicholas Roerich is entitled, "Sophia—the Wisdom of the Almighty." Sophia is the Greek word for wisdom, as in Hagia Sophia Church (Holy Wisdom Church). (Courtesy of the Roerich Museum)

Some believe that for the Knights Templar, Mary Magdalene stood as the personification of wisdom on Earth. The truth is we do not know exactly what such a secret organization believed. Provost's painting may reflect the best information we have about Templar symbolism, since they were active in the 15th century as the Order of Teutonic Knights. Freemasonry gives an imperfect look back at the symbols used, and cannot tell us what their exact meaning was to the medieval mind. On the other hand, discoveries in the 20th century show that much of Jewish and Christian thought has parallels in ancient Samaria and Egypt. When the Second Crusade conquered Egypt, these religious ideas inspired the crusaders with radical new thoughts.

Are there signs on the Kensington Rune Stone that have meaning, both occult and mysterious? It appears so. From around 2000 BC, the Samarian king of the gods was symbolized by a dragon, and his consort the queen as an owl (Gardner 2001). The queen was charged with implanting wisdom, conveyed by a spirit or wind, just as the Holy Spirit is charged in Christian faith to this day. Similar thought and symbolism have been passed down through time from one nation to another, including Egypt.

A carving of the Sumerian goddess Lilith from 2000 BCE shows her with owl talons and wings (Gardner 2001: color section). The name derives from the Assyrian *Lulutu* (wind spirit) (Gardner 2001: 146). The M in Egyptian derives from the glyph for owl, a word beginning with M. Since the owl was considered the messenger for the Goddess of Wisdom, the concept of M could represent the wisdom of the Holy Spirit.

 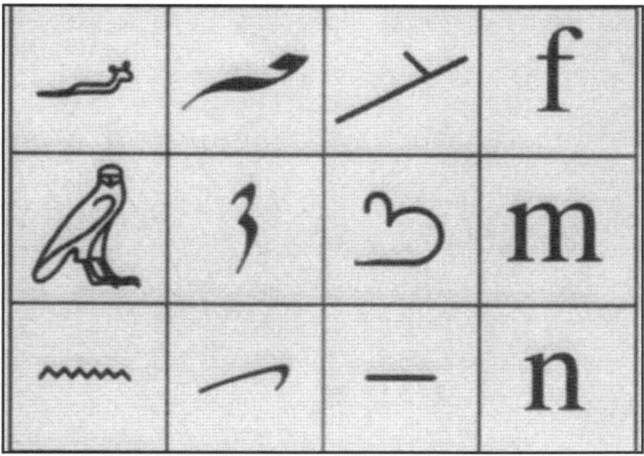

One suggestion is that M for wisdom comes from the Egyptian glyph for M, which is an owl that evolved from the hieroglyph carved in stone. M was the 13th letter in almost all alphabets, and since the owl was the bearer of news (mostly bad) it is possible that thirteen came to be regarded as an unlucky number because of its alphabetical position. (Courtesy of Time-Life Books, Dersin, 1996: 62, 82)

The brow of Lilith's owl is M-shaped. The M was a symbol for wisdom, and in eastern religious tradition the owls bore the Holy Spirit and its wisdom. Venus was called Mylitta in Assyrian (Durant, p. 245) and this may be the source of the letter designation for the Zodiac of Virgo (♍) and the concept of M for knowledge. Eastern mysticism captivated the Knights Templar, particularly what they apparently learned from the Druids in Lebanon. While their persecution, the Templars were accused of worshiping Baphomet, whose name comes from the Moorish *bufihimat* after the Arabic *abu-fihamet* (source or father of wisdom and knowledge) (Brigent et al, 1982: 62-3). Being accused of worshiping a god of wisdom and knowledge is good evidence of the Templars' high regard for the two characteristics. The cross of the Templars in effect has four stylized Ms, which stand for the four paths of wisdom, giving it eight points (again, the eight-fold represented heaven to the Templars). Apparently this cross was in use well before the time of Jesus and has no direct tie to the later crucifixion cross.

The Blood Cross of the Knights Templar (Gardner 1996:261). The four stylized Ms of this design represented the four paths of knowledge and wisdom to Templars. Excavations at the temple site in Jerusalem show that this type of sign seems to have existed many centuries before the Christian era.

St. Sulpice is in Paris is next to the Jesuit seminary of the same name. Because the Jesuits viewed the La Vérendrye Stone in Quebec and it was then sent to Count Maurepas in Paris, who was a church warden of St. Sulpice with a secret home constructed for him, St. Sulpice has been thought to be the place where the La Vérendrye stone was to be found (Parry, 2005). Recently, Parry was shown what he calls a Golden MA, actually an AVM, in Count Maurepas' secret room (see color section page 43), the only record of the sequence AVM other than the Kensington Rune Stone. This golden alter piece certainly symbolizes the three Templar themes of the chalice, the sword, and M for Wisdom. In medieval times AV stood for ave (hail) and M for Mary, hence "Hail Mary."

In June of 2005, Daniel Entin, who is the director of the Roerich Museum, forwarded a photograph reportedly taken in 1923, of the contents of the casket that Roerich received in Paris in 1923. The object appears to the authors to be a stone that has the tell-tale concave edges and appearance of an iron-nickel meteorite. Mr. Entin concurred with this assessment. One thing for certain is that the stone reportedly in the casket is *not* the inscribed La Vérendrye stone described by in Pehr Kalm's memoirs.

The stone on the cloth is actually a meteorite placed on a embroidered rendition of the all Seeing Eye. Perhaps M comes from the m in the word meteorite, an ancient Greek word, for certainly a shooting star had some significance to the ancient world. (Courtesy of the Roerich Museum)

St. Bernard's Cistercians worked hand-in-hand with the Knights Templar. The Cistercians built the first Gothic church on Gotland, Roma Church, after they arrived in 1164. A grave slab we now refer to as G 215 was partly hidden in its wall. This grave slab features five Ms, two in the top corners, one at the base of the cross, and one at each side. The same M and W symbols are found on a relic case from Spånga Church in Uppland, Sweden, circa 1200 (see color section, plate 42).

This grave slab from Roma Church (G 215) was found partially hidden in a wall, and features five stylized Ms carved on its face. The grave slab appears to have the proportion of two squares side by side, which conforms to Cistercians and Templar methods. (SFW) Note the series of Ws and Ms on the chancel roof of Lund Cathedral, circa 1200 (Montelius, 1877).

The Lund Cathedral (top) and Old Uppsala Church (bottom) both exhibit apparent templar symbols including M and W patterns, circa 1200 (Montelius, 1877).

Unexplained Punch and Stroke Marks on the Kensington Rune Stone

There is a double-hooked X on the Kensington Rune Stone, unexplained punches in the 10s, and strokes in the v/w-runes and g-runes rather than a punch, for which we have no clear explanation. These inconsistencies may be a code to authenticate the Stone to a reader who could understand the code. We know that Templars and Teutonic Knights were experts at coding their letters of credit, and such actions were second nature to them.

The Dual Hooked X

The first word with an a-rune X on the Kensington Rune Stone is in **optagelsefarþ** (taking-up journey, ascension). This a-rune in **farþ** (journey) is unique because it has two hooks rather than one. Perhaps the letter x, which also stood for Christ in the old Scandinavian expression X-mass, draws attention to Christ's journey or ascension to heaven.

The a-rune in the word optagelse (taking up) in the Kensington Rune Stone has two hooks L-2, C-38. (SFW: 2002)

The second X on the inscription has two hooks, and appears in optagelsefarþ (taking-up journey, ascension).

These special Kensington Rune Stone runes could be modeled after the Templar sacred geometrical schematic of the Varnhem Church, because its two diagonals, four corners of the square, and circle appear in these three runes.

Note how the ogive arches of the Cistercian Varheim Abbey Church make an X in each open square in this plan view of the church. This was sacred geometry to the Cistercians and the Knights Templar (Montelius, 1877).

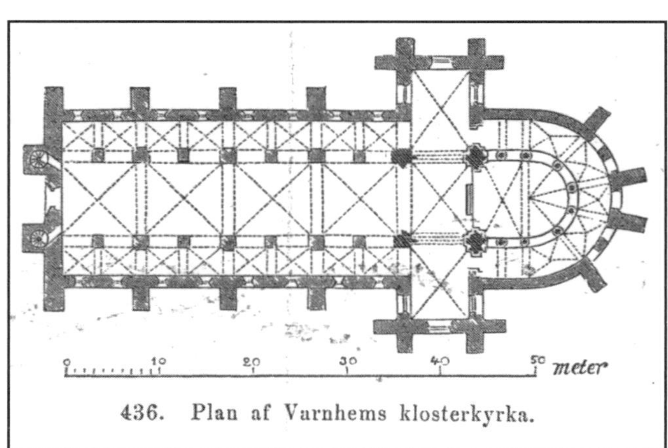

436. Plan af Varnhems klosterkyrka.

The equal sides of the sacred square are depicted by the common Kensington Rune Stone i-rune (|), while the special o-rune (ᴴ) and the special pentadic one (Γ) depict its square mason-like corners, and the e-rune (ᛐ) represents the four corners of the mason square. The carver also carved dots in the v- and g-runes with a chisel stroke rather than a punch, but no significance has yet been attached to these markings as of yet.

Another curious feature of the Kensington Rune Stone is the slightly angled vertical elongate strike, as opposed to a punch, in the upper left area of seven of the ten v-runes. Do these marks hold some special significance? (L to R: L-6, C-120; L-6, C-123; L-7, C-150) (SFW: 2002)

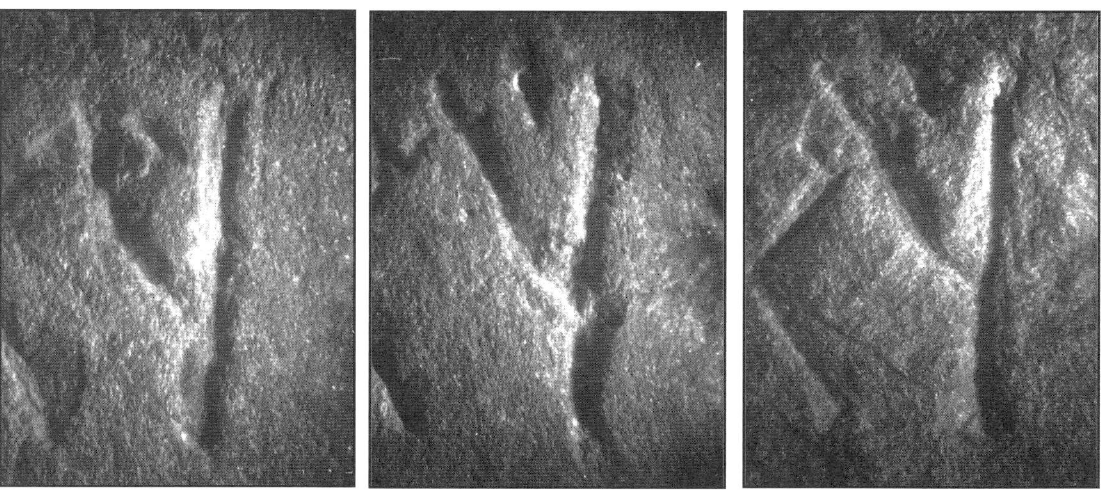

Seven of the ten g-runes also feature a slightly angled vertical elongate strike as opposed to a punch. Do they hold some special significance? (L to R: L-5, C-93; L-6, C-141; L-11, C-258)

The AVM

The earliest critiques on the Kensington Rune Stone pointed out that AVM must mean *Ave Virgo Maria*. This abbreviation has not been found in the Christian church literature of medieval or modern times or in other texts or runic inscriptions. A runic inscription found on a burial cross in the 1920s in Greenland did have AV MA for AVe Maria. Perhaps the V in AVM stands for Virgo after all, with AVM meaning "Hail Virgo Wisdom," as a code clothed in the expected meaning of "Hail Mary." Does the AVM altarpiece from St. Sulpice church in Paris, with its beautiful gild, provide a link to the AVM on the Kensington Rune Stone (see color section, plate 43)? Whether or not this piece conveys the chalice and sword image is still another question that cannot be answered at this time.

A 19th century French Masonic ashlar appears to contain the symbolism AVM. Does this heark back to the AVM carved in Latin on the Kensington Rune Stone? Could the A be the mason's divider and the V the mason's square, with M standing for wisdom? Again it's a fair question we cannot answer at this time.

This wood carving exhibits a 19th century French Masonic ashlar (prepared stone block). Notice the apparent symbolism of conjunction of the chalice symbol V and the sword symbol Λ. Does M stand for wisdom in this case? (Beresniak 2003: 123)

Letter	KRS Rune	Expected	Comment
A	ᚷ	ᛉ	Symbol of the chalice and the sword?
b	ᛒ	ᛒ	St. Bernard's beehives, but conventional. He is the patron Saint of bees and beekeepers. A beehive was his symbol.
d	⌐	⌐	Conventional, but mirror imaged.
e	✝	✝	A cross, four corners of the mason square
f	ᚠ	ᚠ	Conventional
g	ᚷ	ᚠ	Conventional
h	ᚼ	ᚼ	Conventional, but with the six angles of the beehive hexagon.
i	ᛁ	ᛁ	Conventional, but also represents a sword symbol?
k	ᚴ	ᚠ	Conventional Latin k, corner angle of a mason square?
l	ᚱ	ᚱ	Conventional
m	ᛦ	ᛦ	Conventional
n	ᛏ	ᚾ	Conventional
o	ᛂ	ᛂ	Two mason square symbols?
p	ᛒ	ᛒ	St. Bernard's beehives
r	ᚱ	ᚱ	Conventional
s	ᛋ	ᛋ	Conventional
t	ᛏ	ᛏ	Conventional
th	ᚦ	ᚦ	Representing St. Bernard's beehive?
u	ᚢ, ᚤ	ᚢ	Conventional
w, v	ᛦ	ᚢ	Chalice?
ä	ᛇ	✝	Crossed church ogives?
ö	⊕	ᛏ	Templar sacred geometry?

This table shows the Kensington Rune Stone runes with the explanations of possible Templar alterations from the expected rune.

The Dotted 10s

The punched 10 on the face side of the Kensington Rune Stone inscription in **ᛡman** (10 men) is followed on the side inscription with **ᛡmans** (of men). There must be a reason that the Arabic ten was used in place of the expected pentadic 10 (**ᛏ**). It could be that the dot is meant to represent one half of the Arabic 10, which is of course 5.

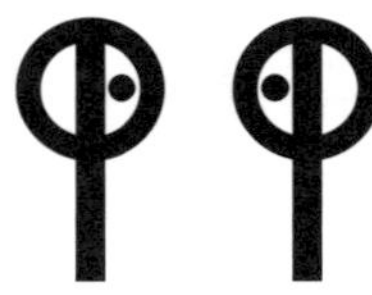

There are two tens on the Kensington Rune Stone, and each is followed by the only initial Ms on the inscription, 10 man (10 men) and 10 mans (10 of men). (L-7, C-165, L-10, C-215) (SFW: 2002)

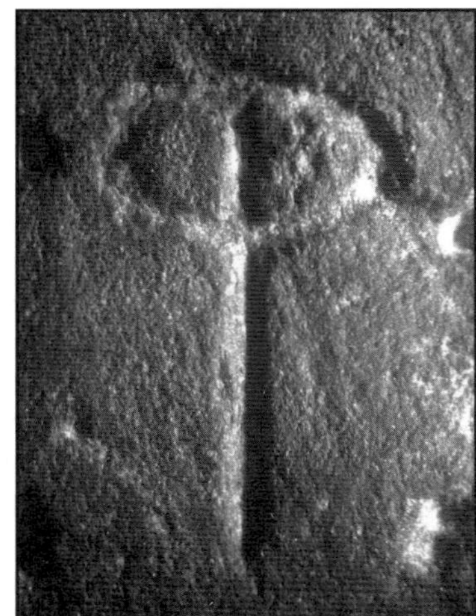

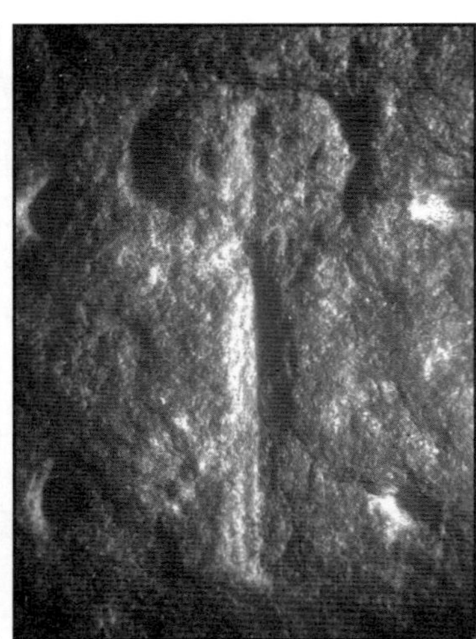

The Pentagon

There is no mistake that the Knights Templar and Cistercians firmly believed they were in possession of supernatural knowledge based on the fantastic mathematics derived from the pentagon. This was their secret, and explains their fervent belief in the rightness of their cause. The planet Venus creates the perfect pentagon with its five conjunction positions, A, B, C, D, and E, made with the Sun over an eight year period. It follows the sun around and is seen clearly in both the morning and night sky.

Note that an infinite number of micro-pentagons are created within the pentagon. In like manner an infinite number of macro-pentagons can be created to accurately measure any space (Haagensen and Lincoln, 2002).

The pentagon has the ratio of the Golden Proportion; i.e., AF is to FC as FC is to AC in the ratio Φ = 1.61803 ... Φ is the Greek letter for F, which is called phi.

If you select a line of length 1+ x and then say that the ratio is 1 to x as the ratio x to 1 + x, one gets the equation $1/x = x(1+x)$ since the ratios are equal. By clearing the fractions one then gets the identity $1 + x = x^2$.

It turns out that this algebraic equation governs the value of Φ in the same way, that is $1 + \Phi = \Phi^2$. This equation in layman's terms means that the square $\Phi^2 = 2.61803$, (obtained by adding 1 to Φ) and that $1/\Phi + 1 = \Phi = 1.61803$ leading to the obvious result that $1/\Phi = \Phi - 1 = 0.61803$.

In geometry the length of the diagonal of a 2 x 1 rectangle is the square root of 5 = $\sqrt{5}$. Guess what, add 1 to $\sqrt{5}$ and divide by 2 and you get the Golden Mean again, i.e., $1.618103\ldots = (1+\sqrt{5})/2$. The boxed face of the Kensington Rune Stone is a 2 x 1 rectangle as well. This indicates the knowledge of the Golden Mean one would expect from a Cistercian carver. A look at Varhem Abby Church shows how the nave is made up of four equal squares just as the side corridors.

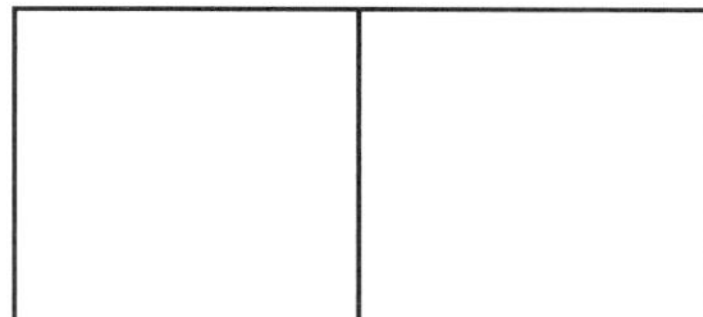

The diagonal of a 2 x 1 rectangle (made up of two equal squares) is the square root of five. The boxed outline face of the Kensington Rune Stone is two squares and was obviously dressed to obtain this 2 to 1 ratio.

We learned how to take the roots of a quadratic equation in high school algebra. Given the equation $\Phi^2 - b\,\Phi - c = 0$, then the positive root is given by the formula $[-b + \sqrt{(b^2 - 4ac)}]/2a$. Here the coefficients are a = 1, b = -1, c = -1 and substitution yields the Golden Mean as $(1+\sqrt{5})/2 = 1.631803$.

Knowing that some members of the Teutonic Knights used the Golden Mean we theorized that perhaps the dot in the 10s indicated the 10th term of the series on the Kensington Rune Stone to the 5th decimal place or the opposite. We quickly concluded that it would have to mean 10 iteration terms. By inspection the Date Series 1, 2, 3, 6 and the Text Series II 1, 1, 2, have the same start as the Fibonacci series, but both converge to 1.61803 converges in 11 iteration terms. On the other hand the inverse $1/\Phi = 0.61803$ converges in 10 iteration terms.

The Kensington Rune Stone text series I, which is: 8, 14, and 22 obtains Φ in ten iteration terms accurate to the 5th decimal place: The ratio of the 10th iteration is 2728/1686 = 1.61803, = Φ to the 5th decimal place, which is 0.00003

The codes on the Kensington Runestone are like a Russian doll. As soon as you discover one doll, the next one appears. We had no idea that all three series converge to Golden Mean numbers in 10 iterations accurate to 5 places. The Fibonacci Series itself converges in six iterations taken on the same basis as the Text Series I: 8, 14 and 22.

	KRS	KRS	KRS	Fibonnachi
	Text Series II	1362 Date Series	Text Series I	Series
				1
	En (1), en (1) , 2			1
				2
				3
		1		5
	1	2	8	8
	1	3	14	13
	2	6	22	21
Iteration Term	Iterations	Iterations	Iterations	Iterations
1	3	9	36	34
2	5	15	58	55
3	8	24	94	89
4	13	39	152	144
5	21	63	246	233
6	34	102	398	377
7	55	165	644	
8	89	267	1042	
9	144	432	1686	
10	233	699	2728	
11	377	1131		
Golden Mean				
6th term				1.61803
10th term	0.61803	0.61803	1.61803	
11th term	1.61803	1.61803		

This table is of Fibonnacci like series on the Kensington Rune Stone with iterations converges to the Golden Mean of 1.61803 and is rounded to five decimal places.

The Kensington Rune Stone 10s each have a dot, one in the left and one in the right semi-circle of the 10. Has the carver, as a code, let it be known that the tenth term after 22 would be accurate to the 5th decimal point? That is something we will let the reader decide, and perhaps uncover a better explanation. The series has the characteristic that one must always add terms to the series by summing the two preceding numbers. The reader can easily duplicate the tables of series by hand calculation.

This procedure will always lead to the Golden Mean of 1.61803…, but it would take a few more additional terms than the 10 achieved with 24 and 22 or the 6 term that can be achieved with Fibonacci's 13 and 21. The original Fibonacci series—1, 1, 2, 3, 5, 8, 13, 21—will be as accurate to the fifth place if only 6 terms are added after 21. If the pentadic numbers on the Kensington Rune Stone are placed in a series, they yield 1, 2, 2, 3, 6, 8, 14, 22, which is quite close to Fibonacci's series.

One thing is for sure: the Teutonic Knights understood Arabic numbers from banking alone, since Fibonacci introduced Arabic numbers to the bankers of Florence in 1202.

Scandals in Scholarship

While the main thrust of this book is to focus on our own evidence and research, we also feel it is important to take a look back and try to understand how the Kensington Rune Stone came to be considered a hoax in the first place. The fact that the Kensington Rune Stone was an unresolved issue for so long is in part due to the numerous mistakes made by scholars along the way. Our goal in this chapter is to present the problems we have uncovered factually and attempt to put into perspective why the inscription has been so difficult for the "experts" to figure out.

The most glaring problem with determining the veracity of the Kensington Rune Stone is that there was a rush to judgment based upon incorrect assumptions about the runic language. For example, in 1910 Anderson stated, and it was repeated by Moltke in 1949, that the runic age in Scandinavia was over by the year 1300. The runic age was not over on Gotland, which was the exception to the rule, a fact made clear by runologist Otto von Friesen (1933). In the 1960s, the runes of the Bergen Wharf in Norway were discovered and it was then realized that runes were used there well into the 1500s, just as they were on Gotland.

Another incorrect assumption was first advanced by Professor George Flom in 1910 when he wrote that Old Swedish was "a well known language." Flom created a list of words found on the Kensington Rune Stone that were not found in Old Swedish as proof of a forgery. The problem with Flom's argument is that Old Swedish has since been proven not to be a well-known language at all in 1910, a fact demonstrated by the thousands of research papers on Old Swedish published since that time. He did not consider the fact that the Old Swedish dictionary wasn't even finished until 1918 and that the planned Old Swedish Dictionary Supplements were to be issued during the period 1918 to 1975. Flom was by no means the only scholar to trip himself up when it came to the Kensington Rune Stone. In this chapter we will concentrate on the scholars who stumbled significantly in their research as well as the few who made errors in judgment and conduct.

Helge Gjessing

The logical place to begin is with the longest word in the inscription, which occurs on the second line. In Holand's 1908 book, *De Norske Settlementers Historie* he argued that the word was **opdhagelse**. A year later, Magnus Olson's brightest student, Helge Gjessing, responded to Holand's claim regarding this word. In his write-up Gjessing assumed the þ-rune stood for d, which made it the modern Swedish word opdagelse (discovery). Gjessing didn't consider that the þ-rune stood for either "th" or "t" in the initial syllable position in 1362 and didn't consult the existing references. Had he done so, he would have found optagelse = *uptakilse* (a taking-up) in the 1906 section of the Old Swedish Dictionary. A mistake by a student is one thing, but amazingly no other linguists since Gjessing have caught the point either. They all assumed Gjessing was right and never checked it.

uptakilse = *optägelse* = taking-up, ascension. *Aff mine vptkilse (assuntione)* = from my (of herself Mary) taking-up (ascension). uptäkt = uptagilse =optagelse (taking up).

uptakilse (op-. -täkilse), *f. upptagande (till himlen),* (*Marias*) *himmelsfärd.* änkte jäfwadhe ieronimus . . . aff mine (*d. v. s. Marias*) vptäkilse (*assumtione*) *Bir* 3: 160. iak orsakadhe jeronimum för aff mine optakilse än nu skal jak kungöra thik the optakilsina sannind *ib* 161. *ib* 162. — **uptakilsa dagher (op-),** *m. dag för upptagande (till himlen).* mina modhir optakilsa dagh til himerikis (*d. v. s. Marias himmelsfärdsdag*) *Bir* 3: 307.

Iv 2690. **4)** *upptaga, afrödja, sätta sig i besittning af (ouppodladt el. obebygdt land).* þän som . . .

The word upptaga, circa 1347, appears in the U section of the Old Swedish Dictionary, published in 1906. Translated into English the definition cited here is, "Take up, clear away, take procession of uninhabited and uncultivated land." The student Gjessing, as well as all the other linguists, never checked this reference. If they had, the word opþagelsefarþ on the Kensington Rune Stone, which has now been interpreted as uptakilsefärd, meaning "acquisition journey, journey to acquire new land," would never have been a problem.

The amount of writing by linguists arguing that this word was definitive proof of forgery on the Kensington Rune Stone could fill a small library. All that ink could have been saved had they done basic research. While the interpretation of the þ-rune can be complicated, its meaning in this critical word relative to the Kensington Rune Stone is settled. In 2003, Henrik Williams and author Nielsen issued a joint paper that was part of the Stockholm Historical Museum's Exhibition on the Kensington Stone. The following quote speaks for itself: "*It has also been pointed out that some of the expressions would have been impossible in the Middle Ages, e.g. opþagelsefarþ which looks very much like the modern opdagelsesfærd 'journey of exploration' in Danish and Norwegian. But the fact is that a number of the apparently modern expressions can be demonstrated to have been in existence back in the Middle Ages. And opþagelsefarþ has now been interpreted as uptakilsefärd, which could mean 'acquisition journey, journey to acquire new land'. Suddenly the critique has to start again from a new direction."*

The "gang of ten," among others, who accepted Gjessing's work, including Flom (1910), Gould (1910), Anderson (1910), Jansson (1949), Moltke (1949), Nielsen (1950), Wahlgren (1958), Blegen (1968), Wallace (1971, 82, 84, 2004), and Kjaer (1994), also accepted another point forwarded by Gjessing that was incorrect. With the exception of Nielsen in 1950, the rest of this group maintained that "**from**" was an English word and another aspect of the inscription that was sure proof of forgery. Wrong again. It turns out "from" was a Swedish dialect word after all. The word forms *from* (from) and *fraam* (from) are found in the dialects of the Swedish colonies on the Estonian islands, a fact that was already published in 1881 by Vendell in Finland, for his doctor's dissertation and in 1890 by Alex Kock, the famous Swedish linguist. The prepositional word form "fram" (from) is also cited in the Old Swedish Grammar which Gjessing did not consult.

> z. b. *fram* statt *frā* (beisp. bei Kock, Arkiv VI, 31).

The word *fram* (from) occurs as a preposition in the Old Swedish Grammar in Noreen (1904: Para 248, note 2). *Fram* (from) is pictured here in place of *frå* (from) (example in Kock, Arkiv VI [1890], page 31).

Gjessing asserted two other words were English as well, these being "ded" (**dead**) and "west" (**west**). Once again Gjessing did not consult the Old Swedish dictionary, where he would have found that *vest = wäst* (west).

> **väster (wäst),** *adv. [Isl.* vestr] *L. vester, i vester;*

The word *väster = wäst* (west) as it occurred in the Old Swedish Dictionary from 1908. Vest is also a correct rendition of *wäst* (west).

The Norwegian diplomas also have the adjective "ded" (**dead**). However, Gjessing's understanding of Old Swedish grammar missed that the adjective "ded" (**dead**) was actually the noun, ded (**death**). No one ever corrected Gjessing on these words, either.

> "Effther the henne hosbonde her Jens Herne *ded* er" (as her husband, Sir Jens Herne, is dead).[78]

Ded (dead) was Scandinavian, as seen in Queen Margethe's letter from Oslo in 1390 in the Norwegian Diploma IV 586. This document was available to Gjessing in 1909. The adjective *ded* (dead) and the noun *ded* (death) can be spelled the same way. Therefore, þeþ (death) on the Kensington Rune Stone is correct for 1362.

Our readers may ask, "How could the so-called experts make these critical linguistic mistakes?" Was it a rush to judgment, poor research, arrogance, personal bias? The answer is all of the above. The downfall of proper understanding of the inscription began within months of its discovery and continues to this day. The latest attempt to dismiss the Kensington Rune Stone as modern was published as this book was about to go to press.

Tryggve Sköld

We feel it is important to include a discussion about a paper written by Norwegian linguist Tryggve Sköld that was published by DAUM in June of 2005. This paper illustrates several of the fundamental problems that have hounded the research of numerous scholars. Sköld, who is justly credited with the important discovery of the Larsson Rune Rows in 2004, asserts that it was a Norwegian who carved the inscription, not Olof Ohman. Upon reading his paper we were struck by his confident tone while he simultaneously exhibited a clear lack of knowledge of the subject matter. Sköld has also fallen into the trap of trying to breathe life into many of his predecessor's flawed arguments.

Sköld exhibits incomplete research when he dates the Larsson Rune Row to 1700 or later, based on the introduction of the double-dotted ä and ö in book printing in Sweden. Sam Jansson (1944: Fig. 60a) showed a double-dotted ö in a Swedish manuscript from 1475. A Danish manuscript from 1387 (Uldaler, 1968: 142-45) shows the double-dotted ü that is a runic letter found on both the Kensington Rune Stone (ᚤ) and the Larsson Rune Row (ᚤ). Using Sköld's own logic, based on these two Scandinavian manuscripts, the Kensington runes are consistent with the manuscript-based double dots from the 14th century. In fact, during this time Sweden, and Gotland in particular, was awash with letters written in the German language with double-dotted diacritics.

ther thu omførde meth ſtöldhom hær

In the third line of Fru Elin's book from 1476 is the first record of double dot usage in an Old Swedish manuscript. See *stöldhom* (thievery) end of line above, which proves it was a recognized form in the century following the Kensington Rune Stone. (Jansson, 1944: Fig. 60a, 124).

Based on this argument Sköld concluded that the Kensington Rune Stone represents a modern dialect after 1700 and he set out to find where it came from. However, Sköld could have saved himself some embarrassment if he had read the joint statement about the Kensington Rune Stone by Henrik Williams and Richard Nielsen at the Statens

Historical Museum symposium in Stockholm, Sweden, in October of 2003. Sköld claimed that the words **öh** (island), **ahr** (year), **mans** (of men) were not Old Swedish. These words could be Old Swedish and were reported as such at the Museum. Sköld references Erik Wahlgren's 1958 book as proof that the Rosander book was the linguistic and runological source used by the carver. It has been well established that this book could not have been used to carve the Kensington Rune Stone. Ironically, Sköld also asserts that the words **og** (and) and **skip** (ship) are Norwegian, when both appear in Rosander as Old Swedish.

andra, så att t. ex. af sun blef son, af brut blef brott, af *skip* blef *skep* (skepp), af vin blef vun (vän), af siga blef saga (säga), af firi blef fore (före) o. s. v. Från tyskan upptogos bruket af då, jemte prefixerna an, be, bi, er, ge, för (vor) und o. s. v., samt tilläggningsstafvelserna *dom*, het, skap m. fl., äfvensom från danskan *else*, *ning* och obestämda artikeln *en*, *ett* o. s. v., genom hvilket en stor mängd nya ord blefvo bildade af förut inhemska. Efter tyskan begynte man utmärka en lång vokal genom att antingen skrifva den dubbel, t. ex. *troo*, *reen*, eller tillägga ett h, t. ex. åhr, fahra, hvilket senare äfven brukades i slutet af ord, t. ex. *jagh*, *migh*, *sigh*, *dagh*, Sverighe o. s. v. För öfrigt är uti denna tids skrifter stafningssättet mycket vacklande och obestämdt genom den inverkan så många olika språk haft på den då ej ännu stadgade svenskan, så att man i slutet af tidehvarfvet finner om hvarannat tecknadt t. ex. *rike*, *riike*, *rige*, *riche*; *jak*, *jeg*, *jac*, *jach*; *ok*, *oc*, *og*, och o. s. v. (I detta sista ord har sedan tyskans *ch* bibehållit segern öfver både gamla svenskans k, latinets c och danskans …)

This section of Rosander (1882: page 63, part of section III) showed that the three Kensington Rune Stone words, skip (ship), ok (and) and og (and), shaded in gray, were Old Swedish from the period 1300-1523. Sköld claimed these forms were only Norwegian (meaning modern), and not Old Swedish. Sköld also claimed the forger only needed to use Rosander to carve the Kensington Rune Stone. This false statement was copied from Wahlgren and not based on his own reading of Rosander. An English translation of the applicable section of Rosander can be found in "The Ohman Documents" chpater.

Sköld also reveals himself to be unfamiliar with the source material that would have yielded the correct information he missed. As his reference list indicates, he obviously did not consult the Old Swedish Dictionary, the Old Swedish Grammar, or the Old Swedish diplomas from 1340-1375. He also did not consult the runes of Gotland. Sköld claims the words **ved** (by), **skip** (ship), **vore** (our), **fiske** (fishing), **röde** (red), **läger** (camp), and **og** (and) were Norwegian, but they all also appear in these documents as Old Swedish. The words **theno** (this), **fan** (found) are also found. As evidenced by his multiple references to Wahlgren, he instead relied on the flawed arguments of his predecessors who also failed to rely on these same resources.

Another point by Sköld that has been incorrectly asserted by many opponents of the Stone is that the words **ded** (death), **from** (from), **fro** (from) are English, and that **rise** (journey) is influenced by English. All of these words can be shown to be Old Swedish.

What motivated Tryggve to write an article with such questionable scholarship is unclear. Perhaps he felt obligated to write something because of his Larsson Papers discovery, or maybe there was another motivation. During an otherwise very cordial debate in Stockholm with author Wolter in June of 2004, the professor did not appreciate the comment that his predecessors had done an "incomplete and sloppy job" in their research on the Kensington Rune Stone. Tryggve respectfully defended his colleagues, many of whom he knew personally. With this latest paper, instead of taking the opportunity to try to sharpen the arguments of his predecessors by using his exciting newly discovered Larsson Papers, he chose to use the same old "dull knife."

Rasmus B. Anderson

In Rasmus Anderson's February 11, 1910, article "The Kensington Runestone Fake" that was published in *Amerika*, he listed the following evidence:

1) Route: Impossible for 1362
2) Look of the runes: They look like gravestones just carved
3) **Opdagelse**: Modern word
4) **Havet**: Used for ocean not lakes
5) **From**: Never used in Scandinavian
6) **Vinlanth, dagh, ahr**: H not used in this way
7) Runes not used in 1362: Runic age was over

None of Anderson's points are valid today.

1) This was far from impossible since the route from Prairie Island, Minnesota, to Quebec was traveled by the explorer Radisson in thirty days with fully loaded canoes accompanied by two hundred Alquonquin Indians in the 1600s. The same conditions could have existed for the Kensington party.

2) The runes were retooled and look younger than they really are. The sides of the retooled runes are old and Anderson ignored this fact even though it was outlined in Winchell's report.

3) The medieval word is not **opdagelse**. Anderson applies þ = th to **Winlanþ** > **Vinlanth**, but not to **opþagelse** > **opthagelse** > (acquisition), a 14th century word. He chose **opdagelse** (discovery) because it was a modern word and suited his purpose.

4) **Havet** (the inland lake, ocean) was used for a body of water that heaved the ship. This concept comes originally from the old Icelandic *haf* (lift). Lake Ladoga in Russia was called a *havet* (the inland sea) by the Swedes in the 1300s.

5) **From**, as the form *fram* (from) is cited as a preposition in Schlyter's Old Swedish Law Dictionary of 1877. **From** (from) is found by Vendell in the Swedish dialects of the Estonian Islands which was reported in 1881 and 1890 by Koch. Professor Anderson had access to these publications at the University of Wisconsin.

6) The spelling of **lanþ, landth, land**, and **lanð** (land) are all found in the 1300s in Old Swedish laws and diplomas. The runic digraph **gh**, as in **dagh** (day) is found in Gotlandic inscriptions. **Ahr** (year) shows the h-insert is not uncommon in the medieval diploma's of Sweden. Here again is evidence that Anderson was ignorant of Old Swedish.

7) Anderson's statement that the runic age was over was wrong. That runes were used in Gotland in the 1300's should have been known to Anderson in 1910 since it was reported by Sjöberg (1822 and 1824).

Anderson did not bother to study the geology of the Kensington Rune Stone or the Old Swedish material that was available in Schlyter (1877) and Rydqvist (1857-83). He just repeated the arguments that Prof. George Flom and Prof. Nathan Gould expressed before him. Anderson was yet another linguist whose erroneous opinions had a negative impact on the impression many people had about the Kensington Rune Stone that lingers to this day.

There seems to be a recurring theme for some opponents of the Kensington Rune Stone to present what appears to be convincing case, and then finish things off by perpetrating a hoax of their own. One could argue that was the case in 1970 when the Walter Gran interview was released. Theodore Blegen's book presented an apparently strong academic case, and what followed shortly thereafter was a confession (pseudo-confession in this case).

This was essentially a repeat of what Rasmus Anderson tried to put over with his con-founding letter of May 10, 1910, that was also published in *Amerika*. Not long after publishing his argument about the Rune Stone, he also published a pseudo-confession that, like the Gran Tape interviews, sold their case to the public by implicating Olof Ohman.

On May 24, 1910, he wrote a flowery letter that recounted a chance meeting he had in a North Dakota drugstore with Andrew Anderson, a former neighbor and acquaintance of Olof Ohman. This letter suggested that A. Anderson led R. Anderson to believe that he, Sven Fogelblad, and Ohman were involved in carving the Rune Stone. R. Anderson wrote that A. Anderson gave him "significant winks" as some cryptic way of indicating he was part of a hoax.

R. Anderson made clear his feelings that the Stone is a hoax, and wrote his letter as though he had found the elusive "smoking gun." Professor Winchell, in his pursuit of the truth, chased down every rumor and individual that might have anything useful related to his investigation. When he learned of the R. Anderson letter, Winchell wrote to both A.

Anderson and Olof Ohman to get their sides of the story. A. Anderson denied nearly everything in R. Anderson's letter, and was either lying about things he actually said or exposed R. Anderson for writing a fictitious version of their encounter. A. Anderson concluded his letter with a proclamation that he *"believed in the stone to be genuine"* which threw a bucket of cold water on all of R. Anderson's assertions.

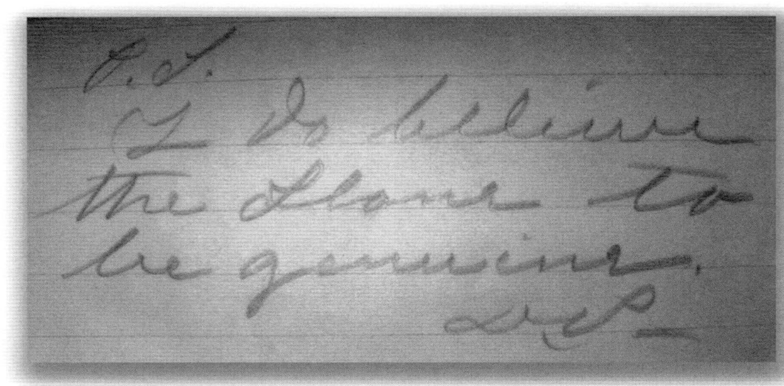

Page 6 of Andrew Anderson's letter to N. H. Winchell on June 3, 1910. (Minnesota Historical Society)
"P.S. I do believe the stone to be genuine."

Even more telling is what Olof Ohman wrote to Winchell when he learned of the R. Anderson letter and what he thought A. Anderson had said. Ohman had no warm feelings for A. Anderson, and vehemently denounced almost everything asserted in the R. Anderson letter. In fairness to A. Anderson, if he was telling the truth in his letter to Winchell, then Ohman might have softened his response and directed his anger toward R. Anderson. It doesn't change the fact that Ohman's strong denial of the claims in the May 24 letter deals a fatal blow to R. Anderson's hoax theory. Winchell summarized the problems with R. Anderson's version in notes written next to a newspaper account of Ohman's letter.

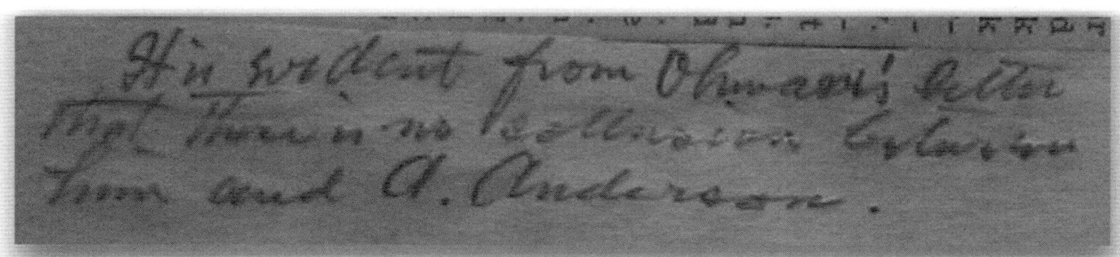

N. H. Winchell wrote these notes next to a newspaper account of Ohman's June 6, 1910 letter. (Minnesota Historical Society) *"It is evident from Ohman's letter that there is no collusion between him and A. Anderson."*

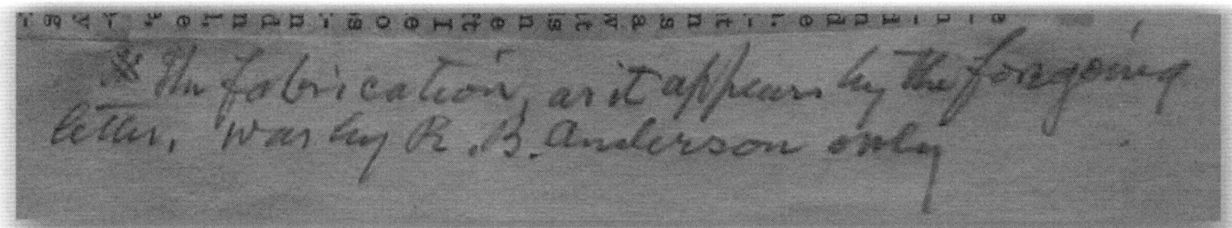

(Minnesota Historical Society) *"The fabrication, as it appears by the foregoing letter, was by R. B. Anderson only."*

This episode is one of many where a linguist, who has already concluded that the Stone was a hoax, went in search of other evidence to support his conclusion. Tragically, he blatantly ignore obvious facts, or statements, that refuted their arguments, and seemingly had no regard for anyone who might be harmed in the process.

George T. Flom

Professor Flom was one of the first linguists to declare the Stone a hoax. He also made serious errors in his pursuit of other evidence. One of the questions that we asked ourselves is: How does someone, who was obviously very intelligent, fall into such a trap? In the case of Professor Flom, his own words told us a lot about how his mind worked. His 1910 paper on the Kensington Rune Stone, laid out his linguistic arguments against it with a significant amount of editorial commentary. Newton Winchell reviewed the Flom paper on July 19 and commented on it on July 20, 1910. Professor Winchell wrote comments in the margins, often chiding Flom for inaccuracies and what he considered inappropriate commentary. Perhaps the most telling statement that Winchell clearly took exception to was in the footnotes on page 4 of Flom's paper.

> from Douglas County, Minnesota. While knowing that the runological-philological questions involved are the only ones that have scientific value, he has upon special request also undertaken an investigation of the general external evid...

Winchell underlined and obviously questioned this statement in a footnote at the bottom of page 4 of George T. Flom's 1910 paper on the language on the Rune Stone. (Minnesota Historical Society)
"While knowing that the runological-philological questions are the only ones that have scientific value..."

This sentence sums up what he believed was the only discipline of knowledge that was important with regard to evaluating the authenticity of the stone. Winchell was certainly justified at being surprised (to say the least) by Professor Flom's lack of understanding and/or respect of the scientific geological value of the investigation. One wonders where Professor Flom learned that runology and philology were "scientific" fields in the first place. Perhaps what he wrote is not what he really meant. Regardless, his words come across as someone who, at least, does not understand the scientific method, and at worst, he presents himself as arrogant with a narrow view of the complex Kensington Rune Stone problem.

Professor Flom's impact on the debate was significant for many decades. His name was continually added to the list of accomplished linguistic experts that had pronounced the stone a hoax. It mattered little that in his 1910 paper, not a single proof of forgery in Flom's linguistic analysis stands today. Perhaps what was more effective than his linguistic arguments was his charismatic and highly persuasive personality. No doubt aware of these skills and the political nature of the debate, this enabled him to better sell his linguistic points, especially to others whose minds were likewise already made up. One example of this likely impact is found in a letter that Warren Upham wrote to Professor Andrew Fossum on August 1, 1916.

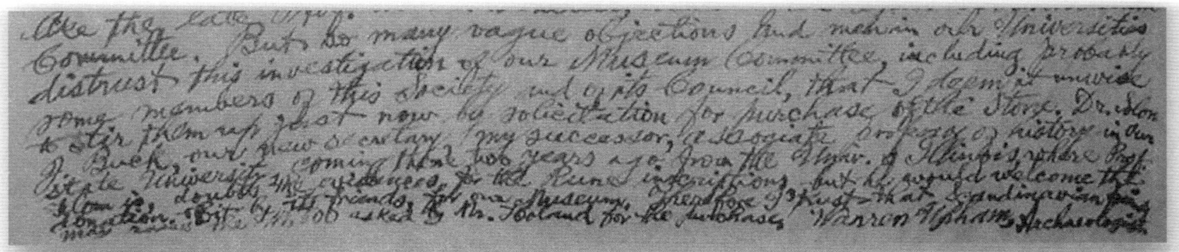

The excerpt is from a letter written by Warren Upham to Professor Andrew Fossum on August 1, 1916. (Minnesota Historical Society) *"But so many vague objections and men in our Universities distrust this investigation of our Museum Committee, including probably some members of this Society and or its Council, that I deem it unwise to stir them up just now by solicitation for purchase of the stone. Dr. Solum J. Buck, our new secretary, my successor, associate professor of history in our State University coming there two years ago from the Univ. of Illinois, where Prof. Flom is, doubts the evidence for the rune inscriptions, but he would welcome the donation by its friends, for our museum. Therefore, I trust that Scandinavian friends may raise the $1,600 asked by Mr. Holand for the purchase."*

The final word on the works of Professor's Flom and Rasmus Anderson were succinctly summarized in the notes that Newton Winchell wrote on the blank pages at the end of Flom's paper. It seems appropriate to let the wise words of the person who knew both men to objectively summarize the situation at that time.

These notes were written by Newton Winchell on a blank page in the back of George Flom's paper on the Kensington Rune Stone on July 20, 1910. (Minnesota Historical Society)

"This energetic discussion brings out important new facts, which everyone who is seeking only the truth will welcome, but everyone will be at liberty still to make such application of the facts as his own judgment dictates. The results reached by Flom are open to two elements of distrust.

1. His denial, instanter, prior to any investigation, of the genuineness of the stone. He has not shown the mental status of a frank and open-minded investigator.

2. He, and R.B. Anderson are sharp, business and personal rivals of Holand and contestants before the Scandinavian people of the Northwest in the publication of historical and statistical works on the settlement of the Northwest by Scandinavians. Such rivalry has broken out in flagrant personal attacks in the newspapers by one upon the other, and Anderson has culpably misrepresented some facts, and has manufactured others. The same having been published in his paper "Amerika" at Madison, Wis. Mr. Holand by his activity and the greater sales of his printed works has provoked them to intense jealousy. Mr. Flom has accepted some of Anderson's fabrications."

Sven B. F. Jansson

Jansson's stumble was prompted by the words of a respected archaeologist who apparently had the nerve to offer an opinion about studying the linguistic aspects of the Kensington Rune Stone.

Quoting Brøndsted (1949) in *Aften Posten* (Evening Post), Copenhagen on May 5th, *"My main opinion is that the Kensington Stone deserves a renewed modern study by competent linguists. In this context it is not sufficient to be merely a Viking Age researcher and only be familiar with the Runestone material of the Viking Age. We must ask opinions from qualified Middle Age linguists. One will then learn to what extent their judgment unanimously runs against the stone or whether linguists with insight will allow certain possibilities to open up. But surely the latter. And in that case the stone's patrons will have the comfort of knowing that by the time the next half century has passed such possibilities will have grown stronger"* (Jansson, 1949: 403).

This reasoned assessment by Brøndsted should have stood on its own merit. Apparently Jansson couldn't help himself and felt compelled to chime in on behalf of his profession. His words should also be considered on their own merit.

Quoting Jansson (1949: 403), *"For the opinion of philological science is in truth completely clear, in the same way as it always has been and it always will be: the inscription on the Kensington Stone is a forgery. Brøndsted suggests in other words that we have to ask for an opinion from "qualified Middle Age linguists." This has certainly already been done in advance, but it will do no harm to do it again. But watch out that you take note of what they say and do not silence their voices as methodically as hitherto has been the case. I do not believe for example that American, English, or German scholars of the Nordic languages will be offended if I say that in that case one should first accustom oneself to research in the Nordic languages in the lecture theatres of Scandinavia. One ought to confine oneself to the professors of the Nordic languages, though I am the last to deny that even outside the circle of professors there are one or two to be found who are in a position to evaluate the question. For my part I would be extraordinarily surprised and disappointed if one were able to find a single academic teacher in the area of Nordic philology in Iceland, Norway, Denmark, Finland, or Sweden who did not endorse the opinion on the Kensington Stone which I have expressed here. Brøndsted's idea that "by the time the next half century has passed" the position could have changed in favor of the Kensington Stone reveals a view of cultural development which must be said to be very pessimistic."* English translation by Colquhoun (2002: F40).

Jansson (1949) had mainly worked on Viking age inscriptions and failed to consult the medieval diplomas, the Old Swedish Dictionaries (1884-1918), or the work of Alex Koch (1890). This is why he was able to state that the words **from, west,** and **ded** were English and that **opþagelse** (taking up) was the modern *opdagelse* (discovery). After Jansson's prohibition, no one disagreed with him about his views on the Kensington Rune Stone the rest of his life.

Erik Moltke

Quoting Moltke (1949/50: 49-50), *"Yes, the objective observer of the developing argument could say, then we must conclude that there is a conflict between the runologist and the mineralogists, since the opinion of the latter is that the patina of the runes was several hundred years old.*

"But that conflict has been resolved. In the course of his investigation of the stone and its inscription Brøndsted (an archaeologist) discovered that the H that Holand had himself inscribed on the stone some forty years before had already acquired a certain patina, and this in spite of the fact that the stone since that time had been indoors and had not been exposed to wind and weather. Against this objective argument the subjective evaluation of the mineralogists must give way; in a discussion of the age of the runes one dare not put any weight on their opinion.

"Accordingly there should barely be any reason to offer too much time on the historical linguistic study of the inscription, about which one can say that more or less every word form in it requires an excuse for its presence on the stone if the inscription is from the fourteenth century; and excuses are in any event insufficient to justify forms such as **opdagelsesfard**, **rise**, **og**, **se**, **efter***, and* **ahr***, which on the contrary quite unceremoniously, together with* **from** *(from) and* **ded** *(dead) (English from and dead), can be explained as modern 'archaisms' and howlers.*

"As a linguistic and runological source from the fourteenth century, the Kensington Stone is rejected. On the other hand one can say that this stone represents the beginning of America's runic age." Translated from Danish by Robin Colquhoun (2002: F57-8).

It would be hard to take these silly statements about the weathering aspects by Moltke seriously, if it were not for the harmful impact they have had. One wonders how Moltke and other runologists, archeologists, and linguists would respond if a geologist were to pass along such uninformed opinions in their disciplines. Perhaps it is telling that geologists have confined their opinions to the subject which they were qualified to discuss. Obviously Moltke did not read Winchell's (1909) report to the Minnesota Historical Society on the age of the runes. (Hanson, 2002: Appendix 1).

As far as his points about the language are concerned, Moltke has merely repeated the points of Flom (1910), Gould (1910), and Anderson (1910) regarding, **opdagelsesfard**, **rise**, **og**, **se**, **efter**, **ahr**, and **ded**. All of these linguistic forms can now be accepted as Old Swedish dialect forms.

The files of the Minnesota Historical Society show that Moltke, Holvik, and Wahlgren were conspiring regarding the Kensington Rune Stone. When Holvik reported that he had found Ohman's original draft of the inscription, Moltke jumped it as if it was fact.

> clumsy language. Of course my article is unnessecary ~~after~~
> ~~yeerxxfind~~ when you have found Ohman's original draft of
> the inscription, but now let us kill this fancystone and
> do it thoroughly. And I think that the j-rune and the
> points above o and a are sufficient background for the
> remarkable "colloquial" language af the inscription.
>
> Yours sincerely
>
> E. Moltke

The end of this letter, written by Erik Moltke to J. A. Holvik, on December 13, 1949, sums up Professor Moltke's sentiments about the Stone, in no uncertain terms. This private correspondence is consistent with what he published in the learned journal, *Antiquity*, (No. 98, June 1951, page 90). (Minnesota Historical Society) *"To show how every Scandinavian scholar regards the inscription I will quote what Professor Jon Helgesson, professor in Icelandic at the University of Copenhagen, said to me when he read my first article on the Kensington Stone: 'In my opinion the inscription on the Kensington Stone is such that no philologist with any self-respect could in any decency write about it; any more than an archaeologist would trouble to publish a grave-find of the Iron Age if he found a telephone book under the urn.' In my heart of hearts I agree with Jon Helgesson. On the other hand there has been so much fuss made about this inscription that a stop must be put to it."*

These writings sum up the attitude of most linguists who have passed judgment on the inscription and declared it a hoax. For decades their "scholarship" was like the pack mentality of wild dogs, feasting on the Kensington Rune Stone carcass.

Erik Wahlgren

The low point in the history of the Kensington Rune Stone debate for those who favor the Stone's authenticity arguably was the 1958 book by Erik Wahlgren, *The Kensington Stone: A Mystery Solved.* Regardless of what side of the argument an individual might prefer, any reasonable mind would find this publication a disappointment. Professor Wahlgren's book is an all-out personal attack on Hjalmar Holand. It's certainly possible to find fault with Holand and his voluminous publications, and to be fair, the professor does make some valid, albeit mostly minor, points. However, the mean-spiritedness and derogatory nature in which the entire book is presented casts more than a little doubt on the objectivity of Professor Wahlgren.

Wahlgren's (1958: 132) statement regarding Rosander, *"Very little beyond these four pages is required to penetrate the orthographic rationale of the Kensington inscription,"* is a blatant assertion that is simply not true, based on the runic evidence to the contrary in Rosander itself. Clearly, Wahlgren was obliged to translate the parts of Rosander that were required to support his book. Instead, readers were mislead into thinking he was presenting sound linguistic research. His deception tricked not only an unsuspecting readership, but other linguists who trust his research to this very day. It is also curious that Blegen (1968) did not see fit to translate this key document that was used in support of the Kensington Rune Stone forgery theories.

Professor Robert A. Hall Jr. in his 1994 book, *The Kensington Rune Stone: Authentic and Important,* dedicated an entire chapter on the inappropriate and unprofessional manner in which Professor Wahlgren wrote his book (Chapter 15: "Wahlgren on Kensington", pp. 94-104). Hall systematically categorized Wahlgren's voluminous speculations, conjectures, condescending remarks, mis-leading statements, and sometimes vicious personal attacks into an outline that has to be read to be fully appreciated. Author Nielsen personally corresponded with Professor Hall of Cornell for over ten years and met with him and his wife Prof. Alice Colby-Hall at their home in Ithaca, New York, in the spring of 1987, and at the Linguistic Association of Canada and the United States (LACUS) in Toronto during July of that same year. He was a kind, polite, and reserved gentlemen who clearly was uncomfortable in launching his own attack.   The apologetic tone of the introduction to Chapter 15 rings sincere as he described feeling compelled to act by the egregious nature of Wahlgren's book.

We feel compelled to point out some glaring examples to illustrate the nature of Wahlgren's techniques:

Speculation – On page 106 Wahlgren expounded about why Ohman mentioned the existence of a whetstone, saying, *"The fact that Olof Ohman took the trouble to point out the whetstone during a discussion of the runic carving should certainly have prompted an investigation of the possibility of its connection with the carving and of Ohman's motive in mentioning the matter, inasmuch as self-incriminating admissions are often made by way of unconscious confession."*

Conjecture – On page 46 he summarized a cryptic discussion about when and where the stone was reportedly displayed in public in the town of Kensington shortly after its discovery by saying, *"The likeliest answer is that it was not on display at all."*

Condescending Remarks – On page 83 he categorized any arguments that were favorable to the authenticity of the stone by saying, *"…the arguments in favor of the Kensington stone are almost exclusively Holand-made rather than natural."*

Personal Attacks – On page 95, this statement speaks for itself: *"But to publish all of Holand's blunders or misstatements is not necessary here. He knows quite well what his philological disquisitions are worth."*

Whatever legitimate points Wahlgren had to offer lost their effectiveness after he compromised his credibility by the overt mean-spiritedness of his arguments. The documents cited in the historical time-line of this book offer a straightforward, unemotional, and factual rebuttal to many of Wahlgren's points. To be fair, one wonders if his argumentation would have been tempered somewhat if he had an opportunity to review N. H. Winchell's field notebook. On page 106, Wahlgren wrote that the notebook had not yet been found at that time. It was eventually located a few years later and its contents proved one of the Professor's statements to be true, *"There can be no question that it (Winchell's notebook) would contribute a great deal to enlighten us on questions of major importance to the Kensington question."*

The professor made a couple other statements that were definitely true, however, he was thinking about aspects of the inscription as opposed to the geologic features of the Stone, which have a lot to say. Page 58: *"Only science can give the answer, through the application of research methods that have won general acceptance in the branches of science concerned."* Page 25: *"In the final analysis the Kensington inscription stands or falls by its own testimony."*

Wahlgren tried hard to win the argument by listing all the linguists, runologists, historians, and archaeologists of the "first rank" who had pronounced the Stone a hoax. His list is long on opinion, but short on facts. On page 26 he noted that (in 1958) the public was more aware of publications in favor of the Stone than articles against it. His book was the first publication in a public awareness campaign to reverse the positive momentum Holand had generated. The following review of Wahlgren's book in 1965 puts forth an interesting perspective.

Quoting Stoylen (1965:8), *"Holand was no doubt at times too opinionated, but that should not permit Wahlgren to perform a hatchet act of abuse in the guise of scholarship of Holand's good name and repute...."*

"Wahlgren has far from solved the mystery surrounding it, nor has he enhanced whatever statue he may have as a scholar. His numerous accusations, insinuations, and innuendoes against the reliability and veracity of various individuals detract from his 'purported' (a favorite term of Wahlgren) solving of the mystery which still is a mystery. Scholarly skepticism is one thing, but cynical, semantic legalisms camouflaged as research done with a chip-on-the-shoulder attitude certainly are out of place in a work which 'purports' to some semblance of scientific reliability.

"Wahlgren...complains of Holand's 'incapacity to guide us in the exacting discipline of textual criticism...his pretences to responsible scholarship,' etc. A whole chapter is devoted to Holand's 'blunders and misstatements'; otherwise the book is interspersed with expressions of 'his naïveté,' 'his being a reported linguistic authority,' 'a professional promoter,' 'serenely defi-

ant to all "learned criticism",' etc. Furthermore, Holand is accused of falsification of drawings and the shadowy use of affidavits, 'a humbug and fraud.' Olof Ohman, the finder of the stone has been compromised into silence, supposedly by Holand. Flaaten, Ohman's neighbor, who was a witness that Ohman had found the stone, and others could not be relied upon. …

"'What one chiefly criticizes in Mr. Holand,' writes Wahlgren, 'is not his naïveté, nor yet his arrogance toward men of learning, but rather his complete lack of respect for the purpose and function of scientific inquiry itself.'"

Aslak Liestøl

In 1966 the Norwegian runologist Aslak Liestøl examined the Kensington Stone in Alexandria, Minnesota. He was the next runologist to examine the Kensington Rune Stone after the Swede Sven Jansson in 1949. Quoting Liestøl (1966), *"More than twelve thousand rune signs have been found among the Bergen [wharf burn layer] material. They do not include a single one that could explain any of the at least seven strange forms occurring on the Kensington alphabet."* Liestøl (1966) failed to consider that Gotland had different runes than Bergen with just as rich a medieval tradition as Bergen when it came to runes.

What Liestøl failed to mention is that the þ-rune on the Kensington Rune Stone is always used for "t" or "th" in initial position (or first syllable) of a word and eth "ð" in medial or final position (second, third, or last syllable). This means that **op(th)agelse** (taking up) is the actual word in question on the Kensington Rune Stone, not **op(d)agelse** (discovery), which is well documented to be medieval. It was this assertion by runologists that þ stood for "d" that made them sure the Kensington Rune Stone was modern.

Among the Bergen runes was one inscription from Gotland (N 670) that had a dotted R, but Liestøl missed the dotted Rs on the Kensington Rune Stone during his cursory examination in 1966.

Theodore Blegen

For anyone who has sought information about the Kensington Rune Stone controversy the 1968 publication by Ted Blegen, *The Kensington Rune Stone: New Light on an Old Riddle*, is probably the most widely known book on the subject. His denunciation of the Stone as *probably* a hoax was generally regarded as the official stance on the Stone. Part of the reason his book has received such high acclaim is because of his reputation as a thorough researcher and historian. Sadly, some of our harshest criticism is now directed at the person who holds the title as "Mr. Minnesota History." Professor Blegen wrote what appeared to be a scholarly work in 1968, but it was really a convoluted and hard-to-follow presentation of information. A careful study of his works reveals two critical errors.

The first error was to allow himself be swooned by the linguists and crown them with a certain level of infallibility. Blegen (1968: 3), *"Runologists of Sweden, Denmark, and Norway have declared the Kensington inscription to be a product of the nineteenth century— a hoax, a fraud, or as Professor George T. Flom described it in 1910, a 'modern inscription.' The testimony of the runologists, based upon studies of the symbols and words carved in the stone, cannot be set aside by lay opinion."* We have shown how they did not (and many still do not as evidenced by Sköld) do the necessary research to back up their claims. Blegen's mistake was not to realize that the runologists could be wrong. Or did he?

It turns out that Blegen did have prior knowledge of problems with Erik Wahlgrens' work, but still embraced his runological and linguistic arguments. Blegen should have heeded the words of Dr. Aslak Liestøl. Blegen wrote the following in an April 29, 1966, letter: *"Yesterday I had a conference of an hour or more with Dr. Aslak Liestøl, the runologist from Norway. Apropos of Wahlgren, I suggested that his book was marred by many errors on the purely historical side, circumstances of the find, etc. Dr. Liestøl commented that his linguistic sections were equally marred. The book, though its major conclusion was right (namely, that the inscription is a hoax), was not to be depended upon on runologically. He went on to say that the speculations about Ohman's 'humor' were merely fantasy. I thought he was also skeptical of the Wahlgren idea of some mystic explanation of AVM."*

On page 123 is what we consider to be the fatal flaw in the book. Professor Blegen wrote about what aspects of the Stone he considered important: *"What matters is the sum total of the historical, runological, and archeological evidence,"* adding, *"The total on the runological and historical side is, in my judgment, conclusive. The inscription is a fake."* The question we must ask the professor is, "what about the geologic aspects of the Stone?" Blegen has completely ignored the conflict with Newton Winchell's work. Blegen stated on page 72 that "Despite his [Winchell's] first impression, he concluded that the inscription was indeed old [Winchell estimated it to be about 500 years old]; the state geologist William O. Hotchkiss, estimated their age as *'at least 50-100 years'*. The next question is, "why?" The answer is simple. Blegen had to ignore the geology because the weathering evidence could not be reconciled with his hoax theory that charged Ohman, Fogelblad, and Anderson with the forgery.

We find it hard to forgive the professor for this gross oversight since he relied so heavily on the information compiled in Professor Newton Winchell's field notebook. However, there is no mention of Winchell's December 9, 1909, report on the geological aspects of the Stone. In reality, he couldn't talk about the report because it was in direct conflict with his conclusion. It is mystifying to us how this could happen to someone who was held in such high regard. We can't help but wonder if Professor Blegen realized this dilemma. Should he have trusted the respected Wisconsin and Minnesota state geologists who decided the inscription was old, or believe the runologists who stood firmly against it? We must all keep in mind that he was near the end of his life and may have felt pressure to complete the book. He died within months of the book being published. The possible anxiety over his mortality could have added to the difficulty of trying to solve this complicated problem. One can almost feel his indecisiveness buried between the lines in his book, but he displayed no compunction against blaming Ohman, Anderson, and Fogelblad without a shed of evidence against them, while the geologist's firm evidence was discarded.

It is ironic that at the University of Minnesota's Twin Cities campus "Winchell Hall" and "Blegen Hall" stand side by side, yet Blegen never mentioned that Winchell considered the Kensington Rune Stone to be genuine based on the weathering of the inscription. Blegen's chief scandal was to reject Winchell's geology.

As a matter of record, it should be noted that during their investigation in 1910, the Minnesota Historical Society translated all the Scandinavian documents for Winchell and others researchers. Winchell read them all and annotated his observations extensively. Ironically, what they prove is that he understood the Kensington Rune Stone inscription *better* than Gjessing, Gould, Flom, Anderson, and after him Jansson, Moltke, Wahlgren, Wallace, and Blegen.

Blegen's (1968: 65) statement, *"The modern author of the inscription not only came from the Dalecarlian region, Flom believed, but was an immigrant from somewhere between Orsa (where Ohman originally came from) and Mora in North Helsingland, Sweden"* is seriously in error. Ohman came from Forsa in North Hälsingland, but Orsa and Mora are situated in Dalecarlia, contiguous to the southwest from Hälsingland. The fact is that the dialects are in no way similar. Flom's premise regarding an immigrant from Dalecarlia is not supported by the difference in dialect to that found on the Kensington Rune Stone.

Olof's father was Olof Olsson, who lived on the farm near Kallange in Langby, but who originally came from Bjorkmo in Forsa Parrish. Karin's (Olof's wife), mother was Brita Danielsdotter and her father was Daniel Pallmen, a tailor in Överby. Överby is situated just across the main road which is the same place where Olof's wife was born.

Einar Haugen

Haugen was a vocal opponent of the Kensington Rune Stone who also passed judgment on the three interesting rune stones found together in Maine in 1969, with completely flawed arguments. He blatantly framed the argument by asserting that Ahr ᛈᛈ, on the Spirit Pond Inscription Stone, stood for A.D. 1010, with no supporting evidence. By using this guess, he was then able to say that the language was too modern for the 11th century. If the Easter calendar is used, the ᛈᛈ could represent the 10th row and 10th column which gives the year 1401, and **ahr** ᚤᚠᚱ, which is also carved on the stone and would yield the year 1402 (Nielsen, 1993). Suddenly, the inscription for this time period begins to make sense in Scandinavian. Haugen was mystified by the runic combinations þ✳ and ✳þ, but they commonly occur in Old Swedish manuscripts of the 1300s. These combinations also occur on some runic inscriptions in Gotland.

Haugen also asserted that the j-rune ᚠ was used on the Spirit Pond rune stones and copied from the invented rune ᚠ on the Kensington Rune Stone. He was also ignorant of the fact that his "so-called" j-rune was used in the 14th century Mariaklagen and Scandia Law and is not an invented rune. Many of the words that Haugen could not read as Scandinavian now clearly are. Further, Haugen did not report that weathering was found in the runes which could have ruled out the modern hoax theory that he so heavily espoused.

The authors have offered to provide the Maine Museum in Augusta a non-invasive geological examination of the Spirit Pond rune stones at no cost. Hopefully, these interesting artifacts can be thoroughly studied in the future.

Birgitta Wallace

Birgitta Wallace wrote an article that discussed the Kensington Rune Stone entitled: "Vikings in North America – New and Old," that appeared in *Viking Heritage Magazine*, 4/2003, pp. 3-9. The article addressed the work of both authors that we feel compelled to comment on. Wallace was apparently referring to author Wolter when she wrote the following: *"A geologist as well as others, commented on the freshness of the rune cuts."* This statement misrepresents at best, and is intentionally misleading at worst. The only thing that appeared fresh about the rune cuts was the retooling, or scratching out of the runes shortly after the Stone was discovered by Ohman. The geologists who have examined the inscription (Winchell, Hotchkiss, and Wolter) all said the *original* inscription was weathered and old.

These next two passages were clearly directed at author Nielsen. *"Foremost among them is Richard Nielsen, a petroleum Engineer with no linguistic training or knowledge of Old Scandinavian languages."* Author Nielsen, who is not a petroleum engineer, does not have formal linguistic training, but then, most formally trained scholars have been unable or unwilling to do the required research for the Kensington Rune Stone inscription. His knowledge of Old Scandinavian languages was competent enough to co-author a paper on the Kensington Runes Stone in 2003 with Professor Henrik Williams, the head runologist at the University of Uppsala, in Sweden, (See appendix B, page 531) and to correspond since 2000 with Professor Michael Barnes of University College London for advice on runic and linguistic matters pertaining to the Kensington Rune Stone.

"Richard Nielsen, undaunted, has scoured medieval diplomas and other documents for corroboration that the forms on the stone could be medieval exceptions from the norm. If Nielsen is right, the whole inscription is a collage of unique anomalies." Fortunately, author Nielsen did scour the medieval diplomas to find the forms that fit together very logically. What is puzzling is why an archaeologist, like Wallace, can assert to be qualified to make a statement about medieval language in the first place.

The authors of course do not take offense from the slight-of-hand mis-statements. However, we do take offense to Wallace's blatant disregard for the integrity of Olof Ohman. The following statements in her article are examples of her decades-long attack on Ohman's reputation: *"Two things make it clear that the inscription is a joke, not a recording of a 1362 event: Ohman himself, and what is probably a paper draft of the inscription."* Wallace has yet to produce one shred of evidence to implicate Ohman of anything related to the inscription other than its discovery. Her accusations directed at Ohman are reprehensible and should be retracted. "Probably a paper draft" is a blatant assertion with no evidence to support it.

"Another neighbor, John P. Gran, believing he was dying, confessed to his son that he had helped Ohman make the inscription." If Wallace had listened to the Gran Tapes carefully, she would have realized that Walter Gran *alleged* that his father made allusions to his son that he helped Ohman carve the Stone, which is hardly the confession she leads her readers to believe occurred.

These statements by Wallace are nothing more than veiled attempts to deceive people into believing the Stone is a hoax. The fact is, she has no evidence to prove her case after striving for over thirty-five years as a consistent naysayer to do so. If there is a fraud to be found anywhere it is in Wallace's scholarship. The sad part is that she is regarded as credible and that her research meets the standards of professionalism her title implies. These statements have been published by various media outlets and the Smithsonian Institution in Washington D.C., who assumed her work was properly researched. Our nation's museum and its history deserve better. Her cheap shots at the authors are an act of desperation upon the realization that she hitched her wagon to the wrong horse. There is one thing she could do to try and make matters right: Birgitta Wallace should issue a public apology to the Olof Ohman family for falsely accusing Ohman of being a liar.

In the first sentence of her section on the Kensington Rune Stone she wrote that Ohman was a "stone mason," a statement that she simply does not provide any traceable reference for. During our visits to Sweden in 2003 and 2004, the Ohman relatives confirmed that Ohman was a carpenter and scoffed at the notion of his ever having been involved in stone work. Further, this question had already been investigated by N. H. Winchell (1910), who reported in his field notebook that, *"Ohman has not known to be a stone mason. He was a carpenter."*

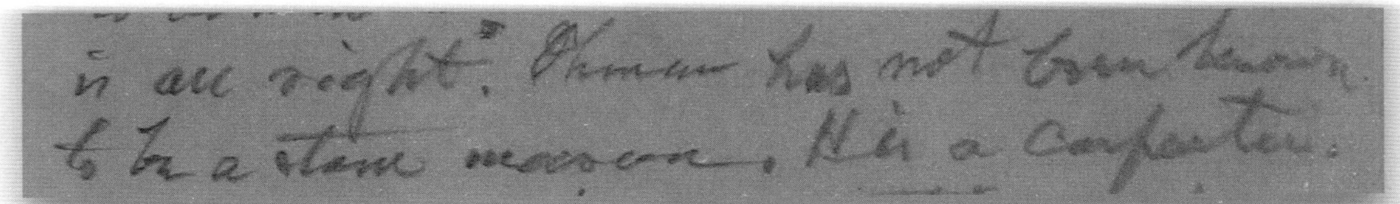

An entry made on page 42 into Winchell's notebook on March 18, 1910. (Minnesota Historical Society)
"Ohman has not been known to be a stone mason. He is a carpenter."

What is truly mystifying is that Wallace cites Blegen's book in her references, where Winchell's entire notebook has been reproduced. There is no excuse for a blatant error like this, and this is just one example of the many insinuations Wallace has put forth over the years to create an air of guilt of Olof Ohman's guilt that doesn't exist. It is shameful and dishonest.

Wallace is also completely unreliable with her quotes. Quoting Wallace (1984: 474) *"'I might say, at the offset, that the perfect preservation and the freshness of the angles and all the cutting of the characters that constitute the record on this stone appears to be an objection to its alleged age. On first examination the impression was made on my mind that it was too lately inscribed. That impression remains.' Winchell (13 December, 1909). Thus the lack of weathering is a good indication of the recent date of the Kensington inscription."*

Winchell did not say *"the lack of weathering is a good indication of a recent date of the Kensington inscription."* This is a pure invention by Wallace who ignored what Winchell actually stated. Winchell's entire quote is as follows (what Wallace quoted is in bold), ***"I might say, at the offset, that the perfect preservation and the freshness of the angles and all the cutting of the characters that constitute the record on this stone appears to be an objection to its alleged age. On first examination the impression was made on my mind that it was too lately inscribed. That impression remains,*** *but I have to admit that I have not any experience of the duration of such cuttings on such a stone. According to the date on its face the inscription was made 547 years ago. If it is compared with glacial markings on quartzite, which must have been formed at least seven thousand years ago, preserved by some drift covering, there is not much difference in the sharpness and the exposed angles."*

This is a true scandal of scholarship since Wallace has in essence falsified what was stated by Winchell. If there is a fraud to be found anywhere it is in the scholarship exhibited by Wallace.

Ole Landsverk

One of the strongest supporters of the authenticity of the Kensington Rune Stone during the 1960s and 1970s was a researcher who believed the inscription contained secret messages called cryptograms. Ole Landsverk was a brilliant physicist who learned about Old Norse cryptography from Alf Mongé, a famous code-breaker during World War II. They wrote a book together on the subject in 1967. In his 1969 book, Landsverk was adamant that the presence of cryptograms within the Kensington inscription was proof of its authenticity.

In part, his cryptography involved rune counting, based on their numerical value in the runic alphabet, to spell words and decipher messages. Although there is historical evidence of hidden messages in runic inscriptions, Landsverk's method had several problems when applied to the Kensington Rune Stone. The main problem is that he tried to have it both ways when it came to the spalled area on the second line. While acknowledging the presence of an i-rune at the start of the second line in the likely intended word þeno (this) when it served his purpose, Landsverk then ignored the same rune by assuming the empty space was previously occupied by four runes rather than three, so he could make his number counts work. Author Wolter's microscopic investigation in 2002 has positively identified the first rune in the second line as an o-rune (ᛂ). Even if one assumes the runic word ᚦᛂᚾᛂ = þeno was not intended here, the presence of the o-rune invalidates his dating method. His credibility was compromised by trying to "force fit" his cryptograms into the inscription.

The spalled area where the second line of the inscription begins appears to have originally contained the word þeno (this), which is recreated here by inserting ᚦᛂᚾ in front of ᛂ :. The o-rune (ᛂ) at the end of this word was identified by microscopic observation by author Wolter in 2002.

Landsverk's analysis also depended upon his assumption that the words **og** (and), **from** (from) and **mans** (of men) were misspellings for **ok** (and), **fro** (from) and **man** (men), which research today indicates is not the case. These issues made his subsequent cryptogram messages impossible. For these and other reasons, the cryptographic work of Landsverk and Mongé (1967) was roundly rejected by Liestøl (1968) and Kahn (1968).

In 1986 Wahlgren wrote the following criticism of Landsverk in no uncertain condescending terms, *"The methods and Landsverk's explanation of it are complex and, according to him, foolproof and exact to the day, though not to the hour. He can date the Kensington Stone to 24 April 1362. Experts in cryptography like the American Kahn and the Swede Karlgren have published reviews that pulled the method to pieces, but they have not shaken Landsverk's credibility with the true believers."*

Author Nielsen discussed these issues with Landsverk during a visit to his home in Rochester, Minnesota, in late July 1987. While he stubbornly defended his position and was clearly unhappy with Nielsen's message, he was not personally offensive, as people like Einar Haugen reported when his ideas were challenged. During this visit Landsverk showed a draft of a paper he intended to publish in response to Wahlgren. Landsverk died shortly thereafter, and attempts by the authors, with Darwin Ohman, to locate the draft in Landsverk's extensive papers during our visit to Luther College in January of 2005 were unsuccessful.

What is truly unfortunate is the neglect Landsverk's excellent work in 1961 has received, including interviews with important witnesses in the Kensington area, due to the uproar over his cryptography. Landsverk's unsupportable cryptography theory created a credibility problem for advocates of the Stone and a flashpoint for criticism and ridicule that set back serious work on the Kensington Rune Stone.

Hjalmer Holand

To many people who believe the Kensington Rune Stone is genuine, Hjalmar Holand is the hero who wrote numerous papers and eight books that championed its authenticity for over fifty years. While he deserves much credit for his relentless effort in the face of fierce opposition to his work, he was far from the saint that many believed he was. In fact, most of the criticism he received was due to his own rather flippant treatment of critical subject matter. Due to his fervent belief in the circumstances of the discovery of the Kensington Rune Stone, he was convinced that the language would be vindicated. His conviction resulted in a fierce polarization of opinions, Holand on one extreme and his opponents on the other. Together with his lack of documenting important linguistic points and a sometimes arrogant and bombastic style, he incited many of his opponents who ultimately conspired to bring him down. Their efforts to combat Holand often became the focus of their arguments rather than seeking the truth about the Rune Stone.

Holand's legacy with the Kensington Rune Stone began in 1908, less than a year after he acquired the Stone with the publication of his first book, *De Norske Settlementers Historie*. On page 18, Holand wrote about the discovery and included important facts that he did not properly document. He wrote that the annual rings of the aspen tree were counted and *"found to be at least 25 years."* It is quite reasonable that a farmer would know how to count annual rings and it very likely was done in the case of the tree that the stone was found under. However, there has never been any documentation that the annual rings were actually counted. Holand would be chastised for years about his reporting of the age of the tree. He could have avoided a lot of confusion, and not given such ammunition to his opponents, by properly documenting such important evidence. On the same page Holand wrote, *"The names of at least twelve men are available who insist the stone had been there at least as long as the tree."* Yet, he didn't list them.

When the Norwegian Helge Gjessing (1909) responded to Holand's discussion of the Kensington Rune Stone he was unmoved by the mere twenty-five year age of the tree and stated that there were many immigrants in the area around Kensington well before this time. Holand (1910b) then responded that the tree was forty years old on estimates of the tree's diameter based on affidavits he helped to procure with Dr. Hoegh in the summer of 1909. Holand never mentioned the annual tree rings after his *Harper's Journal* article of 1909. To make matters worse the age of the tree continued to grow in his subsequent publications. By his 1940 book, *Westward from Vinland*, Holand argued that because the tree was reportedly sickly it "was at least seventy years old." He then argued how impossible a forgery was, but issues like the "growing tree" only served to challenge his opponents to refute him.

He was inconsistent about the date of the discovery, that over a period of almost fifty years evolved from August to November 8, 1898. Wahlgren made a legitimate, though overstated point about the discovery date discrepancy. His other strong opponent, Johan Holvik, turned the conflicting discovery date into his convoluted re-burial theory. Wahlgren also scored a valid, though minor, point about Holand's 500-foot estimate of the discovery site from Nils Flaaten's house. The distance was actually closer to 1,250 feet. Holand likely figured the difference in distances was a minor point. It may not have been an issue at all if Ohman and the others who made their estimates, had clarified whether they meant yards or meters. However, even the most insignificant errors became an opportunity for his opponents. In the end, Holand's Achilles heel was his all-encompassing argument that included the many metallic artifacts, mooring stones, and the Paul Knutson expedition he described as the Kensington party. Throughout his eight books he tried to tie all these lines of evidence together into a neat package. This over-simplistic story was attacked on many fronts and left the Stone's credibility battered and bruised.

Holand believed in the discovery story and therefore wasn't bothered by the linguistic problems thrown up by the likes of Chester Nathan Gould, George Flom, Rasmus Anderson, Erik Moltke, and Erik Wahlgren. He felt they were judging the Stone on the information then available in Old Swedish, and believed that future information would provide vindication. He was right about this, but in his later years he did not devote time to this study. Had he continued studying the runes he may have discovered the important dotted Rs in 1930. After his 1932 book, he did not follow the developments in the Old Swedish Dictionary supplements and the publications of the diplomas of the period 1361-2 that were published in 1953. In these publications, he would have discovered useful confirmations for the Kensington Rune Stone language forms.

In Holand's defense, neither Moltke nor Wahlgren bothered to do this research, either. However, it does explain why little progress was made on the Kensington Rune Stone in the 20th century since only documents in the 19th century were relied upon by researchers. For all the mistakes that Holand made in his research the thing he is most culpable for is the way he treated Olof Ohman. The world will never know for sure what happened on the day he took possession of the Stone in 1907. The two men clearly did not see eye-to-eye about the issue of ownership, and the debate between them raged for over almost three decades until Ohman's death in 1935. In Holand's mind, he had rescued the Stone from obscurity and indifference, and proved it to be genuine, thereby earning the right to claim ownership. We invite the reader to ponder this issue after reading the chapter, "Who Owns the Kensington Rune Stone?" In our opinion this was Holand's most egregious stumble during his long and storied history with the artifact.

Johan Holvik

J. A. Holvik is a character who weaves throughout the story of the Kensington Rune Stone for fifty years. His passion to try to solve the mystery evolved into a long and tortured obsession that eventually became his undoing. Sadly, his relentless assault on the Rune Stone's acceptance undermined his own credibility and had a devastating effect on the Ohman family.

Ironically, his first involvement with the Stone was as a theology student with a background in linguistics. Holvik was asked by the Museum Committee of the Minnesota Historical Society to review the Almquist book that originally belonged to Sven Fogelblad. When Fogelblad died in 1897 at the home of Andrew Anderson, the Anderson's acquired his book collection since he had no other family in America. Betsy Anderson was a cousin of Karin Danielsson (Ohman), and she gave the book to the Ohmans after the discovery of the Stone to help them decipher the inscription. Holvik concluded that the information in the book was insufficient to carve the Kensington Rune Stone. Many years later however, he advanced several "discoveries" that in his mind proved the Stone was a hoax and that Ohman had perpetrated it. The discussions that follow reveal the motives of Professor Holvik and his profound negative impact on the controversy and the Ohman family.

Professor Holvik zeroed in on the statements made in the Holand affidavits that the Stone was found, "about 500 feet from Nils Flaaten's house." He claimed they were inconsistent with the reported location on a hill on Ohman's property. Holvik went to great lengths to show that based on these accounts, the Stone would have been found in the slough on Flaaten's property. He compounded the confusion by suggesting that because of the apparent uncertainty of what month the Stone was found that there might have been *two stones*. These ventures into rampant speculation with no basis in fact should have been ignored shortly after being presented. One reason for their longevity is that they were embraced and given credibility by Erik Wahlgren in his 1958 book. The antagonists were so driven to put down the Stone that they ignored simple facts that refuted their assertions.

The location of the discovery of the Stone is marked with a United States flag in this 1910 photograph. Nils Flaaten's farm can be seen in the distance. The individuals pictured are L to R: Nils Flaaten, an unknown man, and Olof Ohman.

Everyone associated with the discovery of the Stone was able to locate the same spot on the hill on Ohman's farm. Witness estimates of five hundred feet were obviously incorrect since the exact location was already well known. The lengths that Holvik and Wahlgren went to in order to prove their point was absurd. Their motives however, become abundantly clear when reading their voluminous correspondence. This communication also included well-known Danish linguist and Rune Stone opponent Erik Moltke. This "three-headed monster" conspired diligently to present a grossly distorted picture of the circumstances surrounding the discovery of the Stone. Their justification was the belief that the linguistics had proven the Stone false; all they needed was a hoaxer and a plausible story. Their other motivation was their intense hatred of Hjalmar Holand and his success.

Holvik let his feelings about Holand be known in this December 7, 1952 letter to Wahlgren. (Minnesota Historical Society)

I sent one copy of your article to Moltke and suggested that he bring it to the attention of the other warriors in league against this stupendous hoax perpetrated by Holand in foisting his tale upon a public so willing to believe.

In this November 23, 1953 letter to Erik Wahlgren, Professor Holvik let his true feelings flow about Holand and the Stone. The sense of a conspiracy among the individuals he cites resonates strongly in many of the letters he wrote and received. (Minnesota Historical Society)

3. Your permission to let Erik Moltke see your letter and also the delightful letters exchanged by you and Bjørndal. He has also reviewed the Strandwold monstrocity, and as you know he is vitally interested in all that goes on over here in the runestone fight. I told him that you have made a local study and that you are presenting your findings at the MLA.

No doubt our friend Holand has sent you a copy of his latest product and announcement of his next masterpiece. If not, you ought to know at once and be prepared for the worst. So I send you both an offprint and his letter to me, which in case you survive the reading thereof you will kindly go to the expense of returning to me at your convenience.

Much power to you in your very important undertaking. The MLA is a forum with wide radiation. Moltke in SS, Wahlgren at MLA, and Brøndsted in The Smithsonian Report form a constellation that will mark 1953 as the year of light through the dark clouds rolled up by fake scholarship to over-shadow the thruth in the matter of a cleverly faked runestone.

Very sincerely yours,

J. A. Holvik

P. S. - Three stones? Just an idea. But thre "drafts"? Very likely! More about that later. However, not matterial.

Professor Holvik should also be remembered for his relentless assault on the credibility of Olof Ohman. It began when he visited the Ohman farm on October 8, 1949. He had a talk with Amanda Ohman, who apparently was the only family member at the farm that day. Holvik convinced Amanda to let him borrow both a family scrapbook that contained Swedish newspaper articles, and a Swedish encyclopedia written by Carl Rosander. She asked that the items be returned, which Holvik promised to do.

It is important to put this visit into the proper context. Amanda had returned to the family farm shortly after her husband, Joel Carlson, had passed away, the previous year. The year before that (1947) her mother Karin had also passed away leaving her with much to mourn. Manda had no children of her own, and perhaps felt that the only place she could find happiness was where she had lived as a child. In addition, Amanda had lived her entire life under the shadow of suspicion that her father had perpetrated a hoax on the world. When Holvik showed up that day, he convinced her that he would be able to clear the Ohman name with the contents of the scrapbook and the Rosander book.

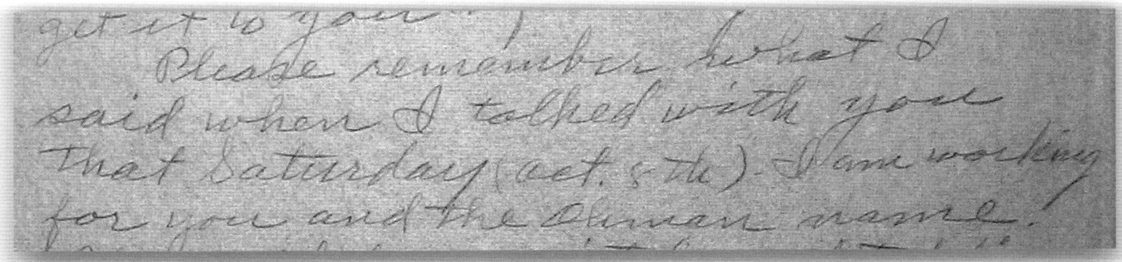

An excerpt from a letter written by J. A. Holvik to Amanda Ohman-Carlson on October 25, 1949. *"Please remember what I said when I talked with you that Saturday (Oct. 8th). I am working for you and the Ohman name."* (**Minnesota Historical Society**)

Holvik had convinced Amanda of his good intentions. However, any hopes Amanda had were quickly dashed upon receipt of the first of four letters he sent to her in a period of eleven days (October 15 to October 25, 1949). Holvik made a crass offer by sending a check and offering to buy the Rosander book for $5.00.

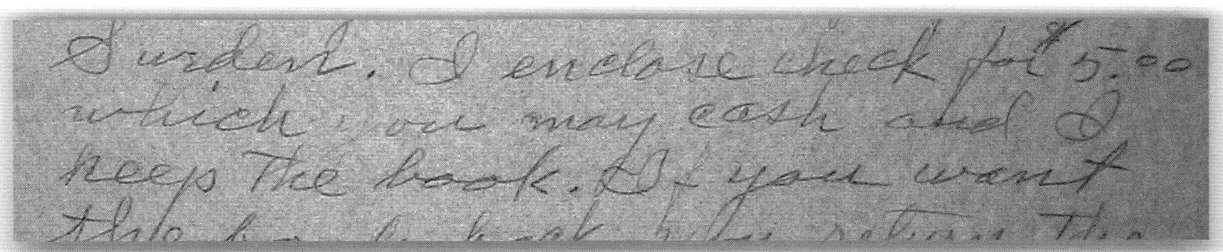

Excerpt from a letter written by J. A. Holvik to Amanda Ohman-Carlson on October 15, 1949. *"I enclose check for $5.00 which you may cash and I keep the book."* (**Minnesota Historical Society**)

He might have had more success had he returned the book first and then offered to buy it. Amanda's decision was swift and sure; she returned his check immediately.

On October 16, 1949, the day after receiving Holvik's check and offer to purchase the Rosander book, Amanda wrote back asking him to return the book. (Minnesota Historical Society)

"Kensington, Minn.
Oct. 16-49

Dear Sir

Am returning check as we don't want to sell this book we really want to keep it. So please return it at once. Did look over books here but am sure there is none Mr. Holvik would care for. Return Skolmästaren we value it as a keepsake.

Your(s) truly
Manda Ohman"

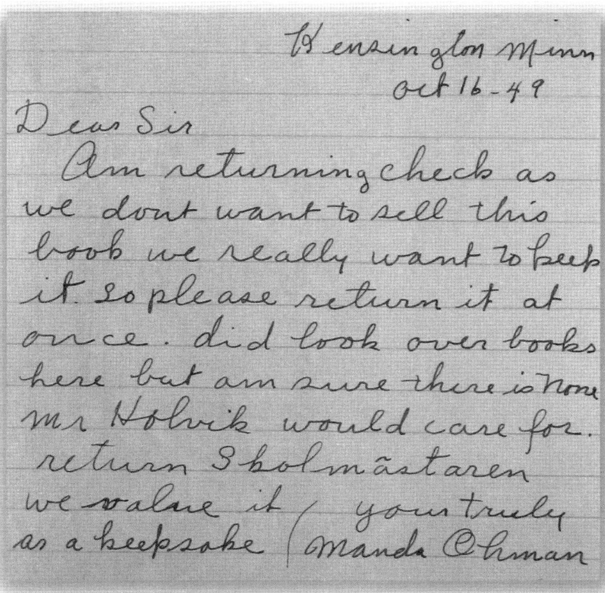

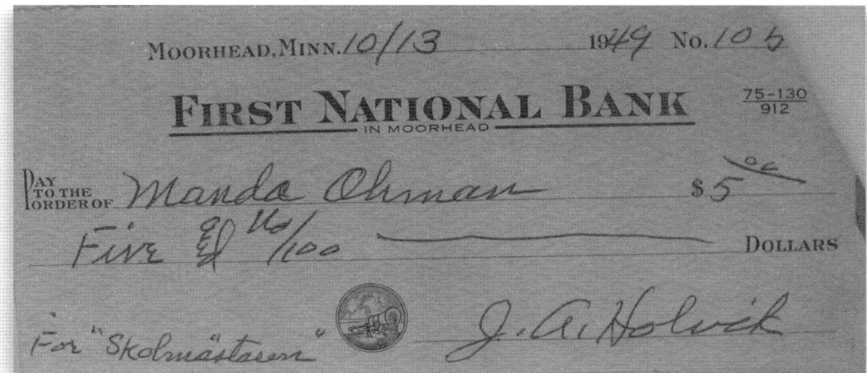

Amanda returned Holvik's $5.00 check to him in her letter of October 16, 1949. (Minnesota Historical Society)

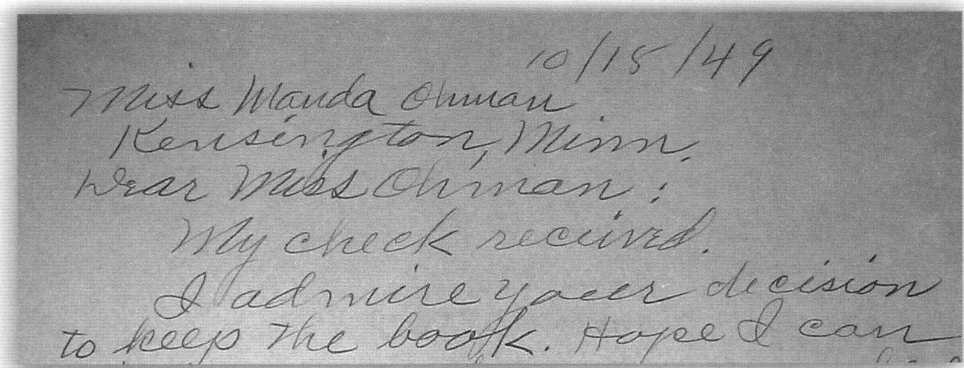

This excerpt appeared in a letter written by J. A. Holvik to Amanda Ohman-Carlson on October 18, 1949. (Minnesota Historical Society) *My check received. I admire your decision to keep the book."*

We can only speculate as to what her thoughts might have been, but she obviously became suspicious and may even have felt that her good intentions might backfire. On October 16, 1949, those fears were realized when the *Minneapolis Tribune* published an article in which Holvik claimed that he had new evidence that proved her father had carved the Stone after he discovered the blank stone in the roots of a tree. This article raised the ire of the Ohman family, and on October 25th Holvik received a letter from attorney Arley Bjella, of Williston, North Dakota, on behalf of Edward Ohman.

```
Dear Professor Holvik:

I am writing this letter to you at the request of one Ed Ohman of Zahl,
North Dakota, relative to the story which appeared in the October 16
issue of the "Minneapolis Sunday Tribune". If you will recall, in
that story you were quoted as saying that evidence shows that the rune-
stone was blank when taken from the ground, and the inscription carved
at a later date by Olof Ohman, the father of Ed Ohman, for motives which
can only be guessed at now.
```

Attorney Arley Bjella wrote a letter to J. A. Holvik on behalf of Edward Ohman, on October 25, 1949, expressing his displeasure over accusations made in a *Minneapolis Tribune* article. (Minnesota Historical Society)

Holvik's rather curt response rings hollow, especially his claim that he admired Edward's father and Sven Fogelblad. There's no indication of where Holvik got the information that Ohman and Fogelblad were "old friends"; there is no evidence to suggest that the two were anything more than casual acquaintances.

> to get somewhere. Since 1909 I have tried to get all available inform-
> ation about his dad and his old friend Sven Vogelblad, both of whom I
> admire highly in so many ways. I am sure I know more about both and

This excerpt is from the letter J. A. Holvik wrote on November 1, 1949 to the attorney representing Edward Ohman. (Minnesota Historical Society)

Several letters were exchanged over the next weeks and eventually the Ohmans decided to turn their attention to getting the borrowed items back. Both Edward (directly) and John Ohman (through an attorney) asked for the items to be returned. Eventually, Holvik did return the Rosander book, but he never returned the scrapbook (The scrapbook is now in the Minnesota Historical Society library). This tumultuous period culminated with Amanda taking her own life on April 19, 1951, by hanging herself at the farm. She was 58 years old.

There is no doubt that several issues were weighing on her mind. The recent deaths of her mother (November 19, 1947), husband (August 26, 1948), and her brother Edward (December 9, 1950) must have been devastating. The timing of these deaths, especially Edward's only four months before her own death, must have been weighing heavily on her mind. One could easily argue that she also felt terrible guilt about Holvik's accusations. Even though it is clear that she was misled as to his true intentions, one can only imagine how she felt when his accusations became public. Her attempt to help exonerate her father's reputation and restore the family name had backfired. This might have been one of the final straws of unhappiness that led to her death.

In 1949, Holvik wrote: *"The oldest sketch [of the Kensington Rune Stone] is published in the Corcordian today for the first time anywhere. This sketch of the runestone was sent in a letter by J. P. Hedberg of Kensington to Swan J. Turnblad of Minneapolis. The letter is dated January 1, 1899. Mr. Hedberg called the sketch an exact copy of the writing on the Stone brought to him by Olof Ohman. Both the letter and the sketch were filed in the archives of the MHS in August 1925. I found it there last month."* This text is repeated in Moltke (1953: 12).

Unfortunately, Holvik failed to report that the Hedberg sketch was published 26 years earlier in the newspaper of Swan J. Turnblad on February 28, 1899. He did not realize that the sketch he found was actually the Siverts copy that was sent to Olaus Breda at the University of Minnesota. The Sivert's copy was found alone at the University of Minnesota in 1925 and then sent by itself to the Minnesota Historical Society by Blegen himself where it was filed with the Hedberg Letter and other materials. It was Holvik's assertion that the copy he found belonged to the Hedberg Letter. Holvik's claim that the copies were pre-inscription drafts was his own creation with no evidence whatsoever to support it. This fabrication was accepted by Moltke and Wahlgren, and from there it took on a life of its own.

Professor Holvik can be criticized for numerous scandals in scholarship and conduct. However, his treatment of an important first-hand witness to the discovery was nothing less than criminal. Though Holvik tried to silence this witness, the testimony of Willie Sarsland is considered here for the first time.

The Willie Sarsland Letter

The Kensington Rune Stone article that appeared in the *Minneapolis Tribune* on October 16, 1949, triggered more than just the Amanda Ohman tragedy. Holvik's claim that Olof Ohman found the Stone blank and then carved the inscription prompted a new discovery witness to write a very important letter. On November 14, 1949, Willie L. Sarsland of Ludlow, South Dakota wrote a letter to the director of the Minnesota Historical Society, Dr. Harold Cater. Sarsland wrote that he was threshing wheat on the Ohman farm the *September* day that the Stone was found. He also wrote that he and his threshing crew helped Olof Ohman clean out the inscription, and offered to give more information.

NOV 15 1949

Ludlow, S.D.
Nov. 14 1949

Dr. Harold Cater
Historical Society
St. Paul, Minnesota

Dear Dr. Cater :

An article has been sent me which states that new evidence shows that the runestone was blank when taken from the ground and the inscription carved at a later date by Olof Ohman. This is untrue. The Ohman family and our family were neighbors. I was threshing for Olof at the time, September of 1898.

He was grubbing trees when he unearthed this stone and hauled it home. His intentions were to use it for a door step — but by handling it he noticed it had some kind of carvings on it. It was during the noon hour, Olof, myself and my threshing crew started to remove some of the shale & deposits and the more we worked we noticed that some one had carved on this stone.

There is a lot more I can tell you about the

165

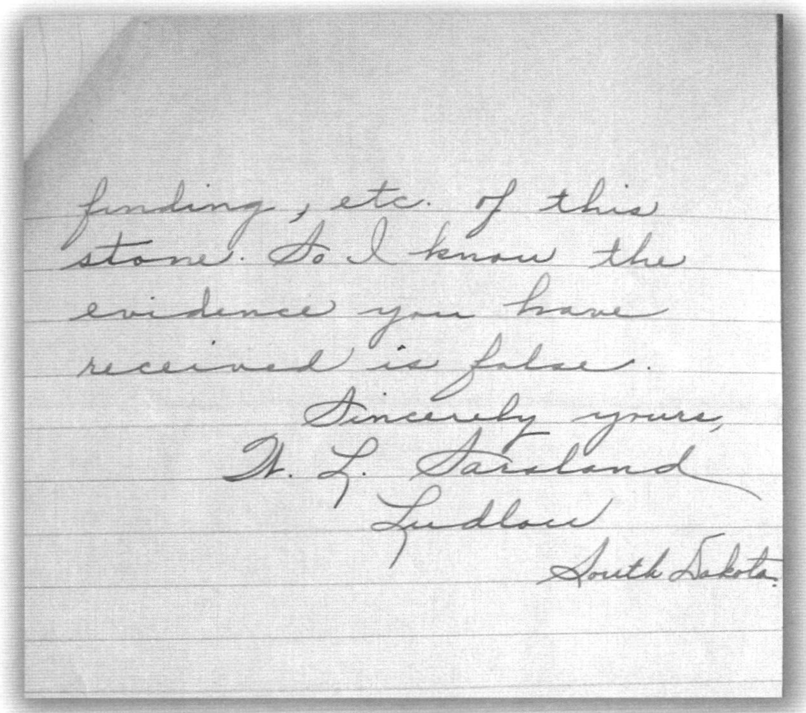

This is the three-page letter written by Willie L. Sarsland sent to then director of the Minnesota Historical Society, Dr. Harold Cater, on November 14, 1949. (Minnesota Historical Society)

Ludlow, S. D.
Nov. 14, 1949

Dr. Harold Cater
Historical Society
St. Paul, Minnesota

Dear Dr. Cater:

An article has been sent me which states that new evidence shows that the runestone was blank when taken from the ground and the inscription carved at a later date by Olof Ohman. This is untrue. The Ohman family and our family were neighbors. I was threshing for Olof at the time, September of 1898. He was grubbing trees when he unearthed this stone and hauled it home. His intentions were to use it for a door step—but by handling it he noticed it had some kind of carvings on it. It was during the noon hour, Olof, myself and my threshing crew started to remove some of the shale and deposits and the more we worked we noticed that someone had carved on this stone.

There is a lot more I can tell you about the finding, etc. of this stone. So I know the evidence you have received is false.

Sincerely Yours,

W. L. Sarsland
Ludlow, S. D.

Dr. Cater obviously found the letter very interesting, and to his credit he passed the letter on to Babcock, who was the curator of newspapers, for analysis. Babcock wrote back to Dr. Cater and stated that his opinion of the letter was, "distinctly unfavorable." Among Babcock's complaints was that Sarsland's name had not been mentioned during Winchell's investigation during two trips to Kensington in March, 1910. It was a valid question for Babcock to ask.

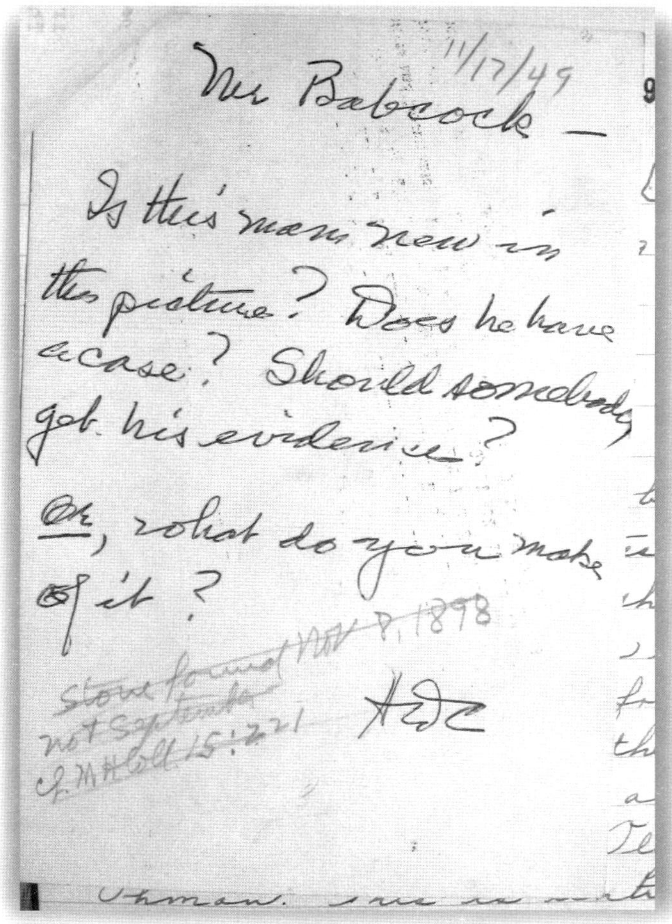

This note, written by Minnesota Historical Society director Harold Cater, was attached to the Sarsland letter and forwarded to Babcock for study on November 17, 1949. (Minnesota Historical Society)

Mr. Babcock,

Is this man new in the picture? Does he have a case? Should somebody get his evidence? <u>Or</u>, what do you make of it?

HDC (Harold Dean Cater)

Memo re Sarsland Rune Stone Letter

November 28, 1949

Dear Dr. Cater:-

I have studied the attached letter relative to the Kensington Rune Stone from Mr. W. L. Sarsland of Ludlow, South Dakota, with much care and interest. The following points occur to me:

1) This letter purporting to give details of the finding of the Stone was written fifty one years after the event in question. Why did this man not come forward with his evidence at or near the time, 1898, or at least in 1910 when the investigation was going on?

2) The name of W. L Sarsland does not appear among those listed in the Minnesota Historical Society report of 1910 as "present at the finding, or immediately thereafter." These were ; "Olof Ohman, his sons Olof Emil Ohman, 12 years of age, and Edward Ohman, 10 years of age, and Nils Olof Flaaten, owner of the adjoining farm." ("The Kensington Rune Stone," in Minn. Hist. Collections, 15: 221). I have never run across mention of the Sarsland name.

3) Mr. Sarsland in his letter states that the stone was found in "September of 1898," whereas the above report shows that it was found on November 8 of that year.

4) The letter states that "I was threshing for Olof at the time, September of 1898. . . . It was during the noon hour, Olof, myself and my threshing crew started to remove some of the shale & deposits, . . .".
A) It is highly unlikely that Ohman would have had a threshing crew at work as late as the second week in November. Olof, indeed, was grubbing out trees when the supposed find was made. Under usual farm practice, every available man, especially the farm owner, is completely occupied with the threshing and puts everything else aside for it. "Grubbing trees" would normally be farm "busy work."
B) If this man had a threshing crew in 1898, he must now be approximately 70 years old, but his memory of the details is remarkable.

5) The handwriting of the letter gives no indication of having been done by a man of seventy or so; in fact it looks like a woman's writing. Further, the letter is highly literate, correct in form and accurate in grammar, spelling and punctuation. Occasional unusual words like "shale" and "deposits" are used. I would judge that someone other than the ex-thresher wrote the letter to you, including the signature.

6) The only immediate contribution of this person to the Rune Stone discussion is the categorical statement that the inscription was on the stone when found, and that he helped to clean it.

My reaction to the Scarsland letter is distinctly unfavorable, but I would suggest that it be referred to Professor Holvik at Moorhead, since he is far more conversant with all phases of the matter than anyone else with the possible exception of Mr. Holand, the chief advocate and proponent of the Kensington Rune Stone.

Respectfully submitted,

Willoughby M. Babcock
Curator of Newspapers

The memo, with an analysis of the W. L. Sarsland letter, sent by Babcock to Dr. Harold Cater on November 28, 1949. (Minnesota Historical Society)

Dr. Cater then forwarded the Sarsland letter, along with Babcock's analysis, to Holvik, and asked him to investigate the matter. On December 2, 1949, Holvik wrote a memo back to Dr. Cater acknowledging that he had received the material and would check into it.

November 29, 1949

Professor J. A. Holvik
Department of Norse
Concordia College
Moorhead, Minnesota

Dear Professor Holvik:

Thank you for your letter of November 22. I am sorry that I was out of town and did not receive it until now so that I could not wire you about the appointment on the day you proposed.

Enclosed are copies of three different papers; one, a letter to me from a Mr. Sarsland of November 14; two, a memo from me to Mr. Babcock (Curator of our Newspaper Department) dated November 17; and three, a memo from Mr. Babcock to me dated November 28.

MHS Director Harold Cater wrote this memo to Holvik that included the Sarsland letter and the Babcock analysis on November 29, 1949. (Minnesota Historical Society)

December 2, 1949.

Dr. Harold Dean Cater
Historical Society
St. Paul, Minn.

Dear Dr. Cater:

Thank you so much for the memo and copy of the Sarsland letter. Information on that letter will be sought.

Holvik wrote back to Dr. Harold Cater on December 2, 1949, acknowledging receipt of the Sarsland letter. (Minnesota Historical Society)

A careful search of Holvik's papers filed after December 2, 1949, when Holvik acknowledged received the material and promised to look into the matter, revealed no evidence that he did so. This is confirmed by the fact that the Sarsland name does not appear in any subsequent publications about the Rune Stone. It is not unreasonable to suggest that Professor Holvik intentionally ignored the Sarsland issue, for if the Sarsland testimony turned out to credible it would have been in direct conflict with Holvik and his hoax theory about the Stone being found blank by Ohman, carved later, and replanted under the tree. The whole Sarsland/Holvik mystery gets even murkier in another letter found by the authors in Holvik's papers at the Minnesota Historical Society on September 16, 2004. A letter typed by Holvik, to Mr. Willoughby Babcock, was laced with sarcasm about the Sarsland letter that he reportedly read at 6:30 a.m. that same morning. The professor first typed February, crossed out the month, and then typed March 1, 1949, though the letter was typed in 1950.

Professor Holvik waited over three months before responding on March 1, 1949 [sic 1950] to the Sarsland letter that was forwarded to him by Dr. Harold Cater on November 29, 1949. The date of this letter to Babcock is obviously incorrect and must be March 1, 1950. The opportunity to conduct an interview with Mr. Sarsland was lost forever when Sarsland passed away on February 16, 1950. (Minnesota Historical Society)

Concordia College
Moorhead, Minnesota

J. A. HOLVIK
DEPARTMENT OF NORSE
DIRECTOR OF BAND

~~February~~ 1, 1949.
March
(Had other dates on my mind(?))

Dear Mr. Babcock:

Have just now, at 6:30 A. M., finished reading the Sarsland letter. Waht a golden nugget. And there is more to be had from the same source? Get it, be it from her, him, it, THEM (I'LL ~~##~~ settle for THEM!). I know you are busy, but this is too good, just TOO good to pass up; and I am sure I couldn't get a squack out of him (her etc.). Please, and right soon.

When I see you, and I hope ere long I can tell you a story of an apparent trap that trapped the trapper (or trappers, seemingly very much plural). Too long for now, so so long for now.

I am asking a friend of mine, Leif Hanson, student at the U to copy the stories in the early Minneapolis papers; he will have the dates. If end when he comes, kindly have the weighty tomes upward yet once and I shall be a nuisance no more – not much more – except for the micro filming, which must needs be much augmented.

A few morning cuss-words coming up on account of this %#" typewriter.

Yours,
J A Holvik.

OH OH – I nearly forgot. Your remarks were good, but GOOD.
JAH, class bound.
If you can't or would rather not write Sarsland, drop me a card.   JAH

The Sarsland letter probably would have remained in obscurity had it not been for evidence found in the Ohman family documents that came to light in the summer of 2004. Two items found pertained to Willie Sarsland and bear directly on the credibility of his letter. The first item is a newspaper clipping that was sent to Edward Ohman in a Christmas card by Willie Sarsland's widow Mathilda, in 1950. Ironically, the article was likely received at about the same time Edward passed away on December 9, 1950.

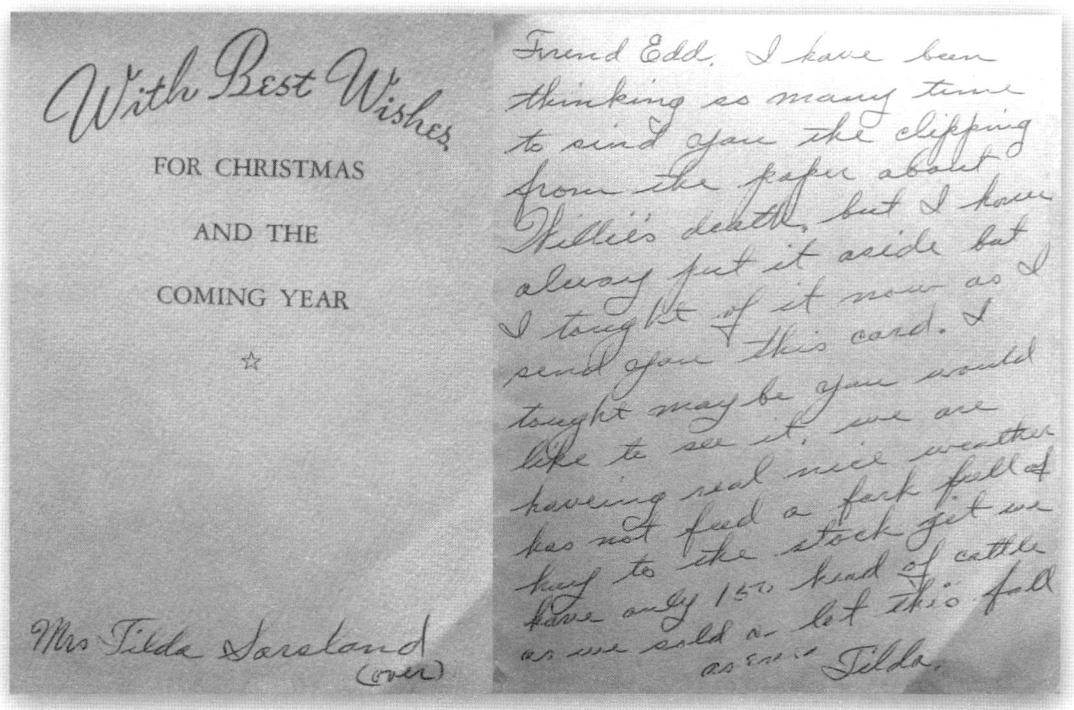

Mathilda (Tilda) Sarsland sent a Christmas card to Edward Ohman that included a newspaper obituary for her husband Willie, who had passed away earlier in the year on February 16, 1950. (Courtesy of the Ohman Family)

Friend Edd,

I have been thinking so many time(s) to send you the clipping from the paper about Willie's death, but I have alway(s) put it aside but I t(h)ought may be you would like to see it. We are having real nice weather as not feed a fork full of hay to the stock yet we have only 150 head of cattle as we sold a lot this fall.

As ever,

Tilda

In the article Sarland's words about the Rune Stone were quoted and circled in pencil by either Mathilda Sarsland or a member of the Ohman family. A subsequent search revealed that Sarsland's letter was also posted on the internet.

ranching and farming.

Before he came to South Dakota he owned and operated a threshing machine. It seems as though a threshing machine held a sort of historic significance to him as it was in the fall of 1898 while he was threshing for his neighbor Olof Ohmen, that Olof found the "Kensington Runestone". Recently the authenticity of this stone was questioned, but in Mr. Sarsland's mind there could be no doubt but what it was real as he helped remove the shale, etc. from the carvings.

He always sort of looked

A newspaper clipping from a 1950 newspaper obituary of W. L. Sarsland includes a quote by him about the discovery of the Kensington Rune Stone. (Copyright *Rapid City Journal*, all rights reserved. Used by permission.)

The second item was a picture of a woman that had been taken many years ago. The name on the back of the photo was Alma Sarsland, who was Willie Sarsland's sister as confirmed by a family tree provided to us by Sarsland relative Mark Jensen on September 11, 2004. The photo indicates that indeed the Ohman and Sarland families knew each other. In addition to the Christmas card, Solem Lutheran Church records brought forward by Mel and Mary Conrad of Kensington, Minnesota, in September of 2004 corroborate that the Ohman and Sarsland families knew each other. Alma Sarsland was in the same 1907 confirmation class with Amanda (Betsy) Ohman.

Class of 1907

Betsy Ohman, Emily Johnsrud, Ella Thompson, Lilly Traaer, Nellie Olson, Annie Moe, Augusta Rose, Lisa Gunderson, Alma Sarsland, Edwin Gran, Oscar Solum, Arthur Ohman, Albert Johnsrud, Harvey Olson

---

Amanda (Betsy) and Arthur Ohman and Alma Sarsland (Willie Sarsland's sister) were in the same confirmation class of fourteen people in 1907. (Courtesy of the *Centennial Celebration* booklet (1876-1976) of the Solem County Church in Kensington, Minnesota)

This photograph of Alma Sarsland was found among Ohman family belongings on August 23, 2004. (Photograph courtesy of the Ohman Family)

The Conrads also provided a complete obituary that indicated the Sarsland family lived in Kensington until May of 1910. In his analysis of the Sarsland letter Babcock stated that the Sarsland name is not mentioned in the Minnesota Historical Society 1910 investigation headed by Newton Winchell. The obituary states that in March 1910, Willie was filing for his homestead in Ludlow, South Dakota. Since Winchell visited Kensington in March of that year, it appears the reason why Mr. Sarsland's name is not mentioned in Winchell's report is because he was not there.

In March of 1910 he filed on a homestead in Harding county S. D. and in May of the same year brought his family where they lived on his homestead until

The February, 1950 obituary found in the Ohman documents included information of Sarsland's whereabouts in March of 1910. (Copyright *Rapid City Journal,* all rights reserved. Used by permission.)

What is especially troubling is that additional information about Sarsland would have been easy to find; a simple phone call to Sarsland could have answered many questions about the letter. Additionally, Holvik was already in communication with Amanda Ohman, and it would have been easy for him to inquire with her or another member of the Ohman family about Sarsland. Instead, it appears that the Sarsland letter was intentionally ignored by Holvik since the letter was in direct conflict with his hoax theory.

By entrusting Holvik to follow up on Sarsland's letter, the Minnesota Historical Society lost an opportunity to learn important information about the discovery of the Kensington

Rune Stone. For someone who normally would jump at an opportunity to obtain new evidence to support his case against the Stone, Holvik's objectivity is certainly called into question in light of this situation.

Babcock made another interesting observation in his analysis of the letter. He wrote, "In fact it looks like a woman's writing." It turns out that Babcock was right about this point. On October 9, 2004, one of the authors had a telephone conversation with Mrs. Irene Kralicek, of Scranton, North Dakota, who at eighty years of age is the lone surviving daughter of Willie Sarsland's thirteen children. A copy of the letter written by her father was sent to her, and she said the handwriting was that of her older sister Sally, who was twenty-seven years old and living with her parents at the time. Irene said that Sally moved back home to help her parents because Willie was in poor health. When we talked about Sally she said, "My sister had beautiful handwriting."

The signatures from the letter sent to the Minnesota Historical Society (top) on November 14, 1949, and on the tax return (below) of January 14, 1949, were *not* done by the same person. On October 9, 2004, Irene Kralicek, Willie Sarsland's only living daughter, said the November, 1949 letter was written by her older sister Sally, who was living with her parents at the time. (Courtesy of the Sarsland Family)

Irene's statement about Willie was consistent with his obituary, which said he was critically ill and bedridden from September 5, 1949, until his death on February 16, 1950.

The complete copy of the Willie Sarsland obituary relayed that he was critically ill and confined to his bed from September 5, 1949, until his death on February 16, 1950, which explains why his daughter Sally wrote the letter for her father to the Minnesota Historical Society on November 14, 1949. (Copyright *Rapid City Journal,* all rights reserved. Used by permission.)

> Since last June Mr. Sarsland had not been feeling too well and in August he was admitted to the Belle Fourche hospital for treatment, but there wasn't much that could be done for his heart ailment, only rest and care. From Sept 5 until his death he had been critically ill and confined to his bed. He endured his pains and suffering with much courage and patience.

On October 23, 2004, Irene provided us with one more piece of evidence that helped to tie up any loose ends. She wrote us a letter stating that it was indeed her sister Sally who had written the letter for her father. Along with her letter, Irene included a three-page letter written to her by Sally on October 8, 1958. The handwriting in the letter matched the Sarsland letter perfectly.

Irene Kralicek's sister Sally wrote to her On October 8, 1958. The handwriting matched the handwriting of the Sarsland letter proving that Sally wrote the November 14, 1949 letter for her ailing father. (Courtesy of the Sarsland Family)

Prior to the discovery of the obituary, the Sarsland name held no significance to investigators of the Kensington Rune Stone. These revelations suddenly made a relatively innocuous interview recorded in 1961, very interesting. Ole Landsverk interviewed Arthur Osterberg on September 20, 1961, who said the following, *"Naturally quite a number of people viewed the rune stone and also the stump and the roots of the tree that grew over the stone, while these were all on display in Ohman's yard. But I cannot name such persons. However, my brother-in-law, William Sarsland, told me that he was a member of a sixteen-man threshing crew at the Ohman farm and that they had inspected and discussed these objects."* (Landsverk, O. G., 1961, page 75). This forgotten interview became important corroboration of the Willie Sarsland story.

Kensington, Minn.

I was born in 1882 and am therefore about 79 years of age. This community has been my home except for a few years elsewhere. I lived here in 1898, the year that the Kensington runestone was found, and the years following.

Olaf Ohman hauled the stone into his yard on a stone boat. His neighbor, Nils Flaten, helped him load it. This was common knowledge in this community at the time so I heard it from several sources. I do not know the exact number of days after the discovery that this happened but it was certainly less than two weeks.

Naturally quite a number of people viewed the runestone and also the stump and the roots of the tree that grew over the stone, while these were all on display in Ohman's yard. But I cannot name such persons. However, my brother-in-law, William Sersland, told me that he was a member of a 16 man threshing crew at the Ohman farm and that they had inspected and discussed these objects.

The stone was on display about two months here in Kensington. Naturally many people inspected it here and speculated on what the symbols might be. I recall that parts of its surface were still caked with dirt. People would brush the dirt away in order to try to make out the symbols.

Signed *Arthur L. Osterberg*
Arthur Osterberg
Date *Sept 10 – 1961*

The affidavit given by Arthur Osterberg on September 10, 1961. Arthur makes reference to his brother-in-law Willie Sarsland, who told him he was a member of a sixteen-man threshing crew at the Ohman farm the day the Kensington Rune Stone was found. (Luther College Archives, Decorah, Iowa)

Based upon the evidence presented here, there is no reason to believe that Willie Sarsland was anything other than a credible witness to the discovery of the Rune Stone, therefore the contents of his letter are extremely important. The Sarsland letter contains a key statement that finally answers one the most important questions about the Kensington Rune Stone: When was the Stone discovered? It has been published for decades that the Stone was found in November (8th) based on second-hand sources, including N. H. Winchell. However, the five first-hand witnesses (Olof Ohman, Edward Ohman, Nils Flaaten, Sam Olson, and Roald Bentson on July 20, 1909) who signed affidavits said it was found in August of 1898. It was this conflict over the August and November months that Holvik took advantage of to craft his hoax theory. He claimed that Ohman found the Stone blank, wrapped in the roots of the tree, then carved the inscription, reburied it, and dug it up again in November. The confusion over the discovery has now been cleared up by the Sarsland letter and by the important testimony in Edward Ohman's 1949 interview with the Minnesota Historical Society. In that interview, Edward said, *"As a rule we came home from school and brought lunch out to Dad."* The question now became: When did school start in 1898?

On October 23, 2004, Mel and Mary Conrad provided us with the school start dates for Douglas County in 1898-99. For district 63 where the Ohman children went to school, the term began on September 5th. This means the stone was found after that date, which is consistent with the Sarsland letter that stated the Stone was found in September. Sarsland also wrote that he was threshing on the Ohman farm that day, which very likely would have been in September, and been an activity that would have helped him to recall the month.

ALEXANDRIA POST NEWS, NOV. 10, 1898.

DOUGLAS COUNTY TEACHERS—1898-9.

DIST NO.	NAME.	ADDRESS.	TERM BEGAN.	LENGTH OF TERM. (MONTHS.)
1	Prin. C. E. Payne	Osakis		
	Mrs. Hattie Stillwell	"		
	Miss Vida Bruegger	"	Sept. 5	4
	Miss Amy Bird	"		
	Miss Matilda Schultz	"		
2	Supt. J. A. Cranston	Alexandria	Sept. 5	4
3	Miss May Mitson	"	Sept. 5	5
4	Miss Susie Covel	"	Oct. 3	8
5	Miss Isabel Erickson	Holmes City	Sept. 5	3½
6	Mr. Virgil Hawley	Alexandria	Sept. 5	6
7	Miss Catherine Vivian	Osakis	Oct. 3	5
8	Miss Rena Ronning	Garfield	Sept. 15	3
9	Mr. Carl A. Wold	Brandon	Sept. 5	5
10	Miss Lydia Sture	Nelson	Jan. 1	5
11	Miss Florence Owings	Osakis	Oct. 8	4
12	Mrs. Mary Millirous	"	Sept. 5	3½
13	Miss Sadie Brophy	Alexandria	Sept. 5	4
14	Mr. John VanDyke	"	Oct. 3	4
15	Mr. R. W. Hagerman	Nelson	Sept. 12	5
16	Miss Ellen Erickson	Alexandria	Oct. 10	5
17	Miss Jessie Miller	Garfield	Oct. 3	4
18	Mr. S. E. Reed	Alexandria	Sept. 5	6
19	Miss Georgia Boyd	"	Sept. 5	3½
20	Miss Daisy Terryll	"	Sept. 5	5
21	Miss Emma Fisher	Osakis	Nov. 7	4
22		Alexandria	Nov. 7	6
23	Miss Mary Kelly	Millerville	Nov. 7	5
24	Miss Hannah Fredenberg	Alexandria	Sept. 5	4
25	Mr. Frank Smith	Brandon	Oct. 8	6
26	Mr. Carl W. Thompson	Evansville	Oct. 8	2½
27	Miss Kitty VanLoon	Holmes City	Sept. 5	8
28	Miss Jessie Sweeney	Garfield	Oct. 17	5
29	Mr. Andrew Olson	Holmes City	Sept. 12	3
30	Mr. W. A. McDonald	Alexandria	Oct. 8	4
31	Prin. H. B. Pardee	Brandon	Sept. 5	
	Miss Marie Sherman	"	Sept. 5	4
32	Miss Millie Thompson	Evansville	Sept. 5	4
33	Miss Grace Tart	Osakis	Oct. 10	5
34	Mr. J. P. Schwinghelmer	Millerville	Sept. 15	6
35	Miss Selma Kronberg	Evansville	Sept. 12	3
36	Mr. Peter Olson	Garfield	Oct. 17	5
37	Miss Harriet Roth	Brandon	Oct. 8	4
38	Miss Josephine McMahan	Melby	Sept. 5	4
39	Miss Emma Ballantine	Alexandria	Sept. 15	8
40	Miss Lilah Johnson	Nelson	Oct. 17	6
41	Mr. Jesse Curtis	Osakis	Oct. 17	4
42	Prin. Byron Emerson	Kensington	Sept. 5	
	Miss Annie Maxfield	"	Sept. 5	4
43			Oct. 17	6

DIST NO.	NAME.	ADDRESS.	TERM BEGAN.	LENGTH OF TERM.
44	Miss Clara Burkee	Urness	Sept. 5	3½
45	Miss Minnie Thoreson	Brandon	Sept. 5	3
46	Miss Belle McMahan	Parkers Pr	Sept. 5	4
47	Mr. Nels Landeen	Alexandria	Oct. 3	3
48	Mr. Adolph Olson	Brandon	Sept. 5	5
49	Miss May Norton	Evansville	Sept. 5	3
50	Miss Emma Langdon	Alexandria	Oct. 17	4
51	Miss Bertha Rolph	Scriven	Oct. 3	4
52	Miss Mary Cooney	Evansville	Sept. 5	4
53	Mr. F. H. Lyons	Leaf Valley	Oct. 17	8
54	Mr. Ralph Pennar	Brandon	Sept. 12	3
55	Miss Carrie Quam	Alexandria	Oct. 8	8
56	Mr. Jacob Pflepsen	Millerville	Oct. 17	6
57	Prin. Antoninette Johnson	Evansville		
	Miss Floy Donaldson	"		
	Miss Jennie Williams	"	Sept. 5	4
	Miss Marie Froland	"		
58	Miss Estelle Bronson	Kron	Oct. 8	8
59	Miss Mattie Pennar	Leaf Valley	Sept. 12	8
60	Miss Mary McFarlane	Alexandria	Sept. 5	3
61	Miss Gena Porter	Garfield	Sept. 5	4
62	Miss Lottie Riemer	Alexandria	Oct. 8	5
63	Miss Anna Larson	Urness	Sept. 5	8
64	Miss Mildred Stillwell	Osakis	Sept. 19	8
65	Miss Arvilla Harris	Scriven	Oct. 8	4
66	Miss Alzina Taylor	"	Oct. 8	4
67	Miss Louise Tannehill	Alexandria	Nov. 7	4
68	Miss Helen Brown	Brandon	Sept. 12	3
69	Mr. N. G. Dunning	Alexandria	Nov. 7	4
70	Miss Martha A. Urness	Urness	Sept. 5	4
71	Miss Emma Holverson	"	Sept. 12	2
72	Miss Ida Hanson	Brandon	Oct. 10	5
73			Nov. 7	5
74	Mr. N. J. Oredson	Alexandria	Oct. 8	8
75	Miss Hannah Anderson	"	Sept. 5	4
76	Mr. Elmer Sprague	Brandon	Oct. 8	8
77	Miss Hilda Erickson	Alexandria	Sept. 5	4
78	Miss Martha O. Urness	Urness	Sept. 12	
79	Joint District			
80	Miss Lilga Wicks	Kensington	Sept. 5	3
81	Miss Frida Johnson	"	Sept. 5	3
82	Miss Lena Korum	Brandon	Sept. 5	4
83	Miss Sadie Lundquist	Alexandria	Oct. 10	8
84	Joint District			
85	Mr. Louis Gumper	Belle Blyer	Oct. 8	4
86	Mr. W. W. Ruble	Osakis	Oct. 8	8
87	Miss Inez Anderson	Evansville	Sept. 5	3
88	Miss Kate Knapton	Alexandria	Sept. 5	8
89	Miss Nannie Kronberg	Evansville	Sept. 12	8

The *Alexandria Post News* of November 10, 1898, listed school information for Douglas County. The Ohman children attended school in District 63, whose term began on September 5 in 1898.

There is also a little irony with the Sarsland letter. On one hand, here was an important, gravely ill first-hand witness who took it upon himself to contact the Society, but ultimately nothing was done about it. On the other hand, the Minnesota Historical Society accepted the hear-say evidence of Walter Gran in spite of the fact that in the fifty pages of Winchell's field notebook and in his reports on his investigation of the Rune Stone, the name of the Gran family is never mentioned by the residents of Douglas County.

This portrait of the Willie and Mathilda Sarsland family was taken in July of 1949. Front row, (L to R): Mable, Sally, Mathilda, Willie, Delores, and Myrtle. Back row (L to R): Ruth, Irene, Rudy, Walt, Clifford, Lloyd, Bill, Esther, and Alice. (Photograph courtesy of Roxanne Miller, the daughter of Lloyd Sarsland)

The Gran Tapes

Perhaps the best known myth about the Kensington Rune Stone is what's often referred to as the "Deathbed Confession." This story has been used as final proof that the Stone was a hoax. It first came to life in 1967, and has evolved to the point where a Swedish encyclopedia reports that the discoverer of the Stone, Olof Ohman, confessed on his deathbed to carving the stone. This is a prime example of how disjointed the information has become about nearly every aspect of the Stone. We felt it was important to learn as much as we could about this alleged confession and try to sort it all out.

The "Gran Tapes" consist of two interviews, conducted in 1967 and 1970. The first interview was conducted by Dr. Paul Carson, Jr., an orthodontist in Edina, Minnesota, who recorded a conversation he had with his mother, Josephine Gran Carson, and his uncle, Frank Walter Gran, on August 13, 1967. During this interview Walter and Josephine alleged that their father, John Gran, said the Rune Stone was "false" and that he and Ohman carved the inscription.

```
Walter:          He said, all the time, you know he always told me, you

                 know the rune stone is false, well, like I should know....

                 how would I know, I wasn't in on the deal makin' the darn

                 thing... and he always said, you know that it is false....

                 well, what more could I say, when my father tells me that,

                 and when he could stand... or lay there in bed and then.

                 tell me that the stone was false and that, you know how we

                 made it and go and talk to Ohman  and he will tell you.

Carson:          Uh huh
```

When Walter spoke to Ohman at his father's urging, the transcript shows Ohman telling Walter "Humbug." WalterWhen Dr. Paul Carson interviewed his uncle Walter Gran on August 13, 1967, Mr. Gran reported his father had said, "…the stone was false." (Minnesota Historical Society)

Eight months later on March 8, 1968, Dr. Carson had a telephone conversation with Russell Fridley who was then director of the Minnesota Historical Society. He relayed the information about the interview to Fridley, who suggested that the Minnesota Historical Society conduct its own interview with Walter. Eventually, the proper arrangements were made and Fridley interviewed Walter Gran with Dr. Paul Carson present on January 17, 1970. The interview took place at the Viking Motel in Alexandria, Minnesota on a very cold, -12°F day. Walter's recollections were relatively vague, and he usually answered questions with rambling narratives. As an alleged witness to such an important confession he came across as flippant and unreliable. Over the course of the interview he consistently referred to well-known stories about events that many believed were proof that the Stone was a hoax. He passionately discussed these stories as if they were accepted facts that supported his claims. At times it seemed like Walter was trying to convince himself that the story he was telling was true.

```
Carson:          It seemed to me when mother was up here, you told a

                 story about Ohman and your father, at lunch time and Ohman

                 was carving a piece of wood.

Walter:          Yah, sure, yah, he was, they was having lunch, then he

                 took his jack knife out and made a few little runic     ,

                 inscriptions on a board and then he held that up and he said,

                 "Do you understand dis."

Fridley:         And you saw this?

Walter:          What?

Fridley:         And, you saw that?

Walter:          No, I didn't see that

Carson:          No, this was your Dad.

Walter:          Yah.

Carson:          And did your Dad understand it?

Walter:          Well, not then, he said he didn't and then he would

                 laught.... it would be fun, we'll fix them scripts that

                 will bewilder the people.  And they sure as hell did.
```

When Dr. Paul Carson interviewed his uncle Walter Gran on August 13, 1967, Mr. Gran said his father saw Ohman "Make a few little runic inscriptions." (Minnesota Historical Society)

The biggest problem with Walter's testimony is that many of his claims are in direct conflict with other people's testimony about important facts. For example, on page 39 of the 1970 interview transcripts, Walter said that his father claimed that Ohman carved runes on wood and allegedly said, "We'll fix them scripts that will bewilder the people." Walter was apparently unaware that in 1910, Professor Newton Winchell interviewed several people about the same rumor that was circulating in the Kensington area at the time. Winchell identified the source of the rumor as Mr. Gunnar Johnson, who claimed Ohman carved runes while working with him in the middle 1880s. It appears that Mr. Gran has inserted his father in place of Mr. Johnson in his version of the "runes being carved on wood" story.

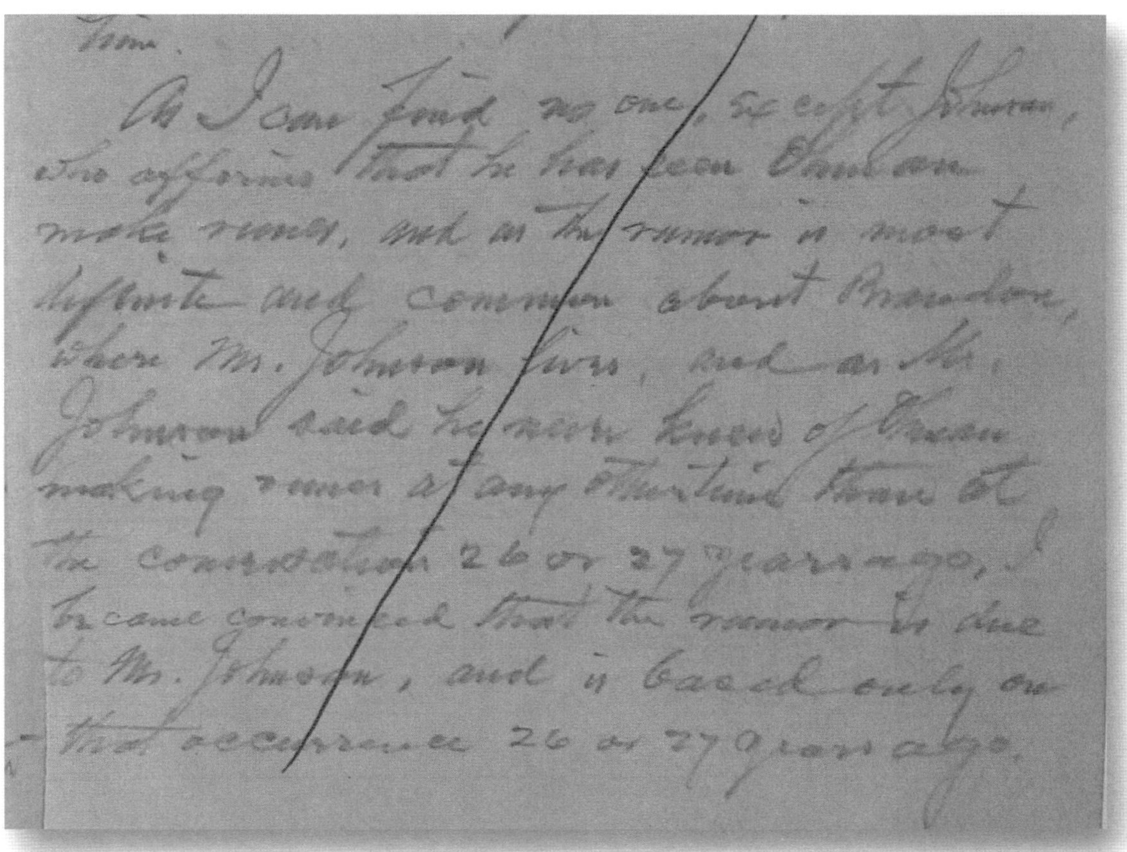

Professor Newton Winchell made this entry into his field notebook on March 19, 1910, during his third trip to Kensington. After conversing with many people, Winchell found no one except Mr. Gunnar Johnson, who could confirm that Ohman made runes. There is no mention of John Gran in any of the fifty pages of Winchell's notebook. (Minnesota Historical Society)

As I can find no one, except Johnson, who affirms that he has seen Ohman make runes, and as the rumor is most definite and common about Brandon, where Mr. Johnson lives, and as Mr. Johnson said he never knew of Ohman making runes at any other time than at the conversation 26 or 27 years ago, I became convinced that the rumor is due to Mr. Johnson, and is based only on that occurrence 26 or 27 years ago.

Letter from Olof Ohman, Kensington, Minn.,

Prof. N. H. Winchell, St. Paul.

To-day I received a letter from Northern Minnesota which in part clears up the reported rune scratches which I have been said to have made at Gunnar Johnson's when I built his house. I do not remember that I wrote any runes either there or anywhere else. And as to Gunnar saying I knew old Norse, that is a mean lie. I have never learnt the Icelandic language.

Sincerely,

Olof Ohman.

In May 1910, Professor Winchell received a reply from Olof Ohman regarding Mr. Gunnar Johnson's claim that he saw Ohman carves runes. The above letter is an English translation of Mr. Ohman's letter, which was written in Swedish. It is interesting to note that Ohman makes a statement in the second sentence where he denies ever writing runes. (Minnesota Historical Society)
I do not remember that I wrote runes either there or anywhere else.

Another problem with Walter's testimony appears on page 37 of the transcripts. Walter claimed that he saw the stone in front of the granary being used as doorstep. This is in direct conflict with Edward Ohman's testimony in his 1949 interview where he said it was never used as a doorstep.

Walter: It was intheir grainery.

Fridley: Grainery.

Walter: Yah, small grainery.

FridleyL   Do you remember seeing it there?

Walter: Yes, I wasn't very old, that time, then, us kids was
                 playing around there and then I.....noticed.... when I come
                 around there.....   (swedish)   here lies
                 the rune stone. But what the heck did we care about the run
                 stone or anything, it was only a stone, to us.

Fridley: It was used as a step.

Walter: Yah.

On page 37 of the transcript of Walter Gran's 1970 interview with Russell Fridley, Mr. Gran said the stone was used as a doorstep. (Minnesota Historical Society)

```
      Here I set down on it and started to dig in the dirt with my
hands as kids usually do and I suggested to Dad that we should take it
home and use it for a door step.

Interviewer:  Did you take it home then?

Mr. Ohman:  No, not right then.  The story goes that it was used for
a doorstep but it never was.  When I was sitting on the stone before
```

On page 1 of the transcript of Edward Ohman's 1949 interview with the Minnesota Historical Society he said that the stone was never used as a doorstep. (Minnesota Historical Society)

During the 1967 interview, Walter alleged his father told him about carving the Stone with Ohman in 1926 or 1927, which is an interesting time in the history for the Kensington Rune Stone. In June of 1927, the rally at Fahlin's Point on Oscar Lake reportedly drew over 10,000 people and was the biggest event that area had ever seen. Longtime Kensington resident Einar Bakke knew both the Ohman and Gran families, and said the Gran family resented the attention Ohman received over the Stone. The rally was held to raise money and awareness for a large monument to be built at the discovery site on the Ohman farm. People who didn't believe in the Stone surely would have frowned upon the huge out-pouring of positive attention. The timing of John Gran's alleged confession, as told by his son, seems rather curious. Because of his strong bias against the Stone, Walter apparently was compelled to make sure that the world knew of it.

On May 20, 2004, Darwin Ohman and Tom Kolberg, who personally knew Walter Gran, and are direct descendants of Olof Ohman were interviewed by Russell Fridley. They were questioned by Mr. Fridley and Scott Wolter about their memories of Walter and his testimonies made in 1967 and 1970. They described him as a friendly person who "liked to tell stories," and both recalled a particular story he told them at different times. They said Walter told them that when he hunted deer in Canada he would climb a tree and wait for a herd to come along. He reportedly then said, "I would pick out the biggest deer and jump on its back, and kill it with a knife."

Darwin and Tom were asked about a statement Walter made about the blacksmith shop at Ohman's farm, where they made the chisels, saying it was "way out in the woods." They both said the shop was in the open yard, about seventy-five feet from the house. This fact is not proof that Walter was lying, it only supports the argument that he tended to embellish his statements. Darwin said that many of the statements Walter made about his uncles John and Art were not true, and it appeared that Walter had an "axe to grind" against his uncle Art. Based on the tapes and from what he knew personally about the man, Darwin concluded that Walter was an unreliable person and that his testimony was not credible. The authors also found Walter not credible, because his recollections were often in conflict with known facts.

Walter's own testimony perjures himself when on page 154 of *Minnesota History* (Winter/1976) at the tender age of 3 he had already witnessed several important events including his direct testimony that Fogelblad carved the inscription two winters before the discovery. This point alone demonstrates how ridiculous the Gran Tapes are. The most salient fact that immerges from the Gran Tape interviews is that Fridley and the Minnesota Historical Society elected to believe the second-hand, forty-plus year-old hear-say recollec-tions of Walter Gran, as opposed to the first-hand testimony of Ohman to Winchell (1909 and 1910) and Ohman to Upham (1916). Fridley even had it both ways by accepting Walter as cred-ible when it suited his conclusion, but conve-niently ignored Walter's first-hand testimony that Ohman said John Gran's hoax story was *"hum-bug."* The interviews were released to the public under the guise of being credible evidence when there was no cross-examination of Walter, let alone any attempt to get the Ohman side of the story. In a land where a man is innocent until proven guilty, Fridley used inadmissible testimony to conclude that Ohman was a liar.

Arthur Ohman (left) and Walter Gran are pictured together in Hot Springs, Arkansas, in March, 1954. (Courtesy of the Ohman Family)

One has to wonder what would motivate an individual to discuss such a sensitive subject that they must have known would be so hurtful to such an apparently close friend. Walter said that he wanted to keep the interview quiet until Art's passing, but agreed shortly after-ward to allow it to be made public. Ironically, Art outlived the younger Walter by several years. Arthur Ohman was deeply hurt when he heard about the interviews. In May of 2004, Einar Bakke, long-time Kensington resident and good friend of both men, told us Art was devastated by Walter's claims. Einar said Art couldn't understand why Walter would say such things, even if his father had made the statements. There are a couple of things Walter says in the 1970 interview that indicate he was angry at Art. It's odd that Walter would spend time at the end of the interview, aggitatedly discussing the price Art wanted for sell-ing the Ohman farm. Throughout the interview, although he tries hard to hide it, Walter comes across as vindictive for reasons that only he knew. If his motive was to get back at the Ohmans for some unknown reason, he was far more successful than even he could have imagined. For Art Ohman, it was another deeply disappointing event related to the Rune Stone in a series that had haunted the family since the Stone was found.

There is another possibility for a motive that has nothing to do with Walter Gran. In May 2005, an Ohman relative named Arley Norlien came forward with information his parents, Christine Johnson and Arthur Norlien, had relayed to him. Christine's mother was Karin Ohman's sister, so she knew the Ohman family very well. Arley's parents also knew the Gran family, and that John P. Gran had a "falling out" with Olof Ohman, and that he "resented the attention Ohman received over the Stone." Jealously is a powerful motivator, and it could have pushed John Gran to tell his son Walter that he'd helped fake the Stone. There is even evidence that suggests what inspired Gran's envy.

John Gran was a relatively wealthy man who owned several properties in Douglas County and a fruit farm in Texas. Olof Ohman was not as well off, but he was certainly a well-known person. Gran may have resented what he perceived as Ohman's unwarranted notoriety.

Pages 84-85 of the 1912 Standard Atlas of Douglas County are the patron's reference directory. Ohman's entry is much longer than Gran's, and could have been a point of irritation for Gran.

Ohman, Olof, Proprietor of The Rhunestone Farm, S. 14, T. Solem, P. O. Kensington. 1886. It was on the farm of Olof Ohman that the historical "Rhunestone" was discovered. Mr. Ohman found the stone in 1898 under the roots of a tree. The stone bears an inscription supposed to be of Norwegian origin, dated 1362. The inscription has been examined by experts both in Norway and the United States and has been translated in part, which supports the theory that the stone was placed by the Norsemen, who visited this country prior to the landing of Columbus.

Gran, J. P., Proprietor of The Highland Farm, S. 1, T. Solem, P. O. Kensington. 1866.

Arley's story is second-hand, but it is no less credible than the second-hand hearsay of Walter Gran. Walter and his sisters may have simply been repeating what their father told them. It is possible that John is the one who made up the story as a way to get back at Ohman. Questions as to John Gran's motivation or the nature of what he told his children will never be answered definitively. Nevertheless, the geologic and runic evidence proves that someone in the Gran family was not telling the truth.

Walter Gran's Credibility

The following table contains the names and recorded statements regarding Walter Gran's credibility from people who knew him.

Witness	Age	Date	Statement	Reference
Dr. Paul Carson (Walter Gran's Nephew)	55	3-8-1968	"He wanders off on various things, but when you bring him back to the subject at hand, it's amazing how well he tells things." "If I can believe Walter,…"	Telephone conversation with Russell Fridley MHS Archives (Blegen Files)
Clarence Larson	83	11-1-1980	"He was one of the biggest liars that was ever around here."	Audiotaped interview with Ted Stoa

Witness	Age	Date	Statement	Reference
Ole Nelson	87	August, 1981	"Well, I don't think he was a man you could depend upon at all. He was up to something most of the time, into things he shouldn't be doing."	Audiotaped interview with Gordon Duenow
Martin Johnson	95	8-12-1981	"No, I don't believe that. I believe that (Gran Interview) was a joke"	Audiotaped interview with Gordon Duenow
Emil Mattson	84	8-12-1981	"No. I don't believe it. And I don't think anybody else around here that knew him (Walter Gran) believed that either."	Audiotaped interview with Gordon Duenow
Clarence Larson	84	8-14-1981	"No, he was not very dependable, that I would say."	Audiotaped interview with Gordon Duenow
Milo Spilseth	78	8-30-1981	"No, I didn't believe very much of what he said."	Audiotaped interview with Gordon Duenow
Darwin Ohman	61	5-20-2004	"...I think Walter had an axe to grind. I also believe that he liked the publicity. I mean, let's face it, he liked to tell stories, and he certainly had a good story."	Videotaped interview with Russell Fridley
Thomas Kolberg	52	5-20-2004	"...and there was some alluding that he said (Lalard Kolberg) that the Gran family was jealous of the Ohman family."	Videotaped interview with Russell Fridley
Fran Blehr	76	8-21-2004	"The simple fact was you couldn't believe one word he said." "He could almost make you believe what he was saying if you didn't know better."	Videotaped interview with Scott Wolter
Einar Bakke	92	8-21-2004	"He liked to embellish the truth a little bit."	Videotaped interview with Scott Wolter

The Ohman Letters to Sweden

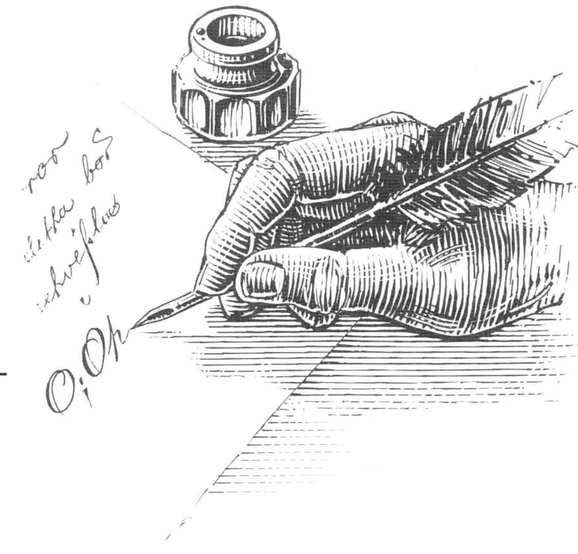

There is an important element to the Kensington Rune Stone story that has never been explored before. It has been demonstrated how much can be learned about an individual by carefully studying their written words. Everyone agrees that Olof Ohman and his family are critical characters, but relatively little is known about them. There are only a few letters written by Olof Ohman that survive at the Minnesota Historical Society; they are relatively short, and reveal little about the man who has been accused of carving the Rune Stone. In February 2004, while visiting Hälsingland, Sweden, the authors had an opportunity to meet several of the Ohman relatives. The highlight of the trip was when several of these relatives produced over forty letters written by Karin and Olof Ohman. These letters gave us the first real opportunity to understand what kind of people the Ohmans were. The letters were translated into English by Swedish historian Susanna Larsson, and in May 2004, we were finally able to read them.

The letters span a period of more than sixty years (November 9, 1879 to May 1, 1940), and originated from four different towns in Douglas County, Minnesota. Olof wrote the first ten letters during his first four-year stay in America. The first letter was written from Evansville, Minnesota, the next three were written from Holmes City, Minnesota, and the next six letters were postmarked from Brandon, Minnesota; he presumably worked as a laborer on farms in these towns. In 1883, Olof went back to Sweden, and returned to the United States in 1885. There is a corresponding gap in the letters that is consistent with the fact that he was in Sweden. Olof and Karin were married in November 1886, and had moved to Kensington by January of 1892. The letters to Sweden began again in January of 1892, after several events had unfolded. They also had brought into the world the first three of what would eventually be nine children (Olof Jr., Edward, and Arthur).

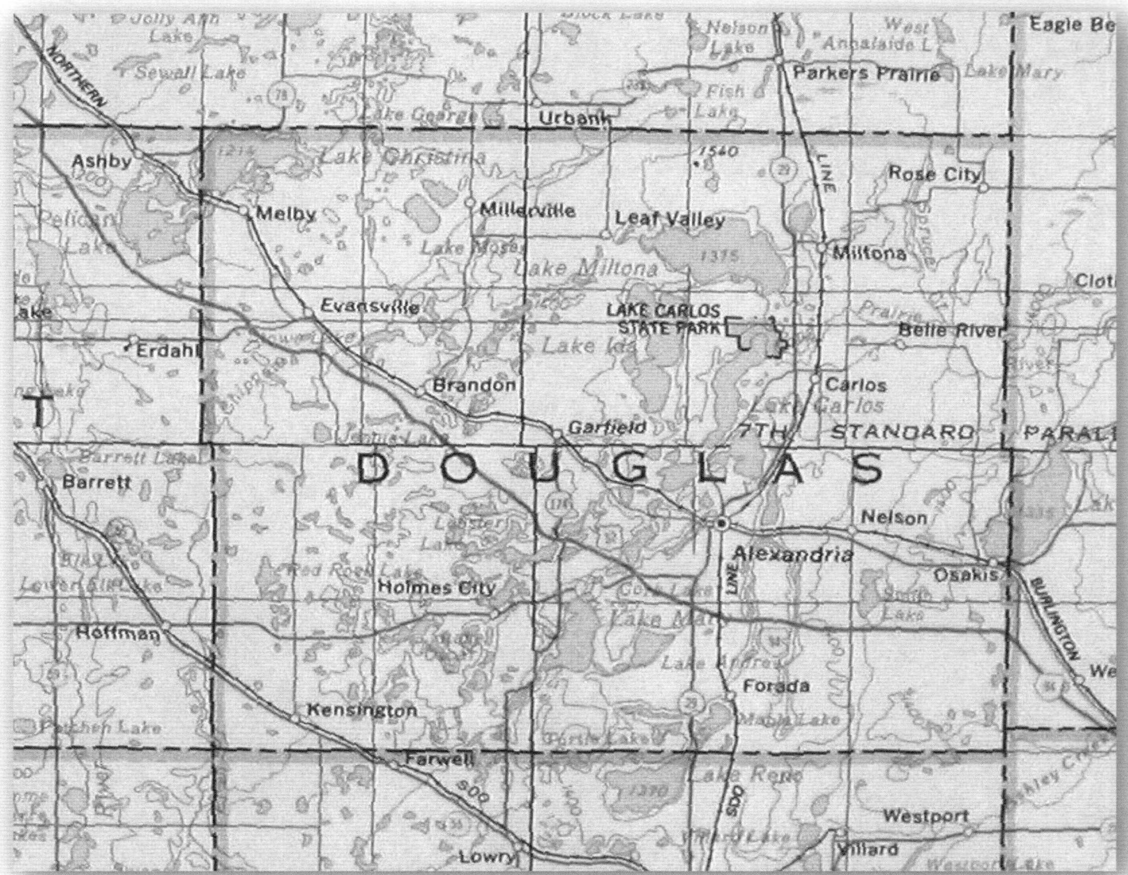

A Douglas County map shows the close proximity of the four towns, Evansville, Holmes City, Brandon, and Kensington, where the Ohman letters were written.

There are almost no letters for fifteen years between May 1895 and May 1920. This timespan includes the discovery of the Rune Stone and several important events that occurred in the years afterward. Only two letters are known from this period, written on July 22, 1906 and December 15, 1906. Surely there were many things that the Ohmans could have written to the relatives, especially concerning events surrounding the Rune Stone. On the other hand, since many of these events were frustrating and unpleasant, it could be deduced that they didn't want to burden the relatives with their troubles; reasoning that seems to be confirmed by the fact that only two letters referring to the Rune Stone have been found. They were written by a 73-year-old Olof, in April and December of 1927, discussing the rally for a Kensington Rune Stone monument at Fahlin's Point on Oscar Lake, Minnesota. Olof wrote glowingly about the event and was clearly pleased that the Stone was being regarded as a genuine artifact. He comes across as sincere and not like a person basking in the attention of a practical joke.

The letters also reveal a man who had a strong connection to his parents and two younger siblings as well as many other relatives and friends living in Sweden. In 1912, Olof made a trip to Sweden to visit his family, but his return trip was delayed until July of 1914 due to events that would lead up to the outbreak of World War I. He eventually returned to America on July 10th aboard the Lusitania, whose sinking by a German U-boat in 1917 would draw the United States into the war.

Olof Ohman stands in front of a house in Forsa Parish in Hälsingland, during his visit back to Sweden from 1912 to 1914. (Courtesy of the Ohman Relatives Association)

Olof wrote longingly about his homeland throughout the years, and often advised people thinking of coming to America not to come. He was keenly aware of national politics, and routinely talked about the plight of farmers during the Depression. He lamented the low prices for crops and livestock, and reported regularly about the many farmers who lost their land because they were unable to pay their mortgages and taxes. He often displayed empathy for those less fortunate, wondering how people survived in the cities without money or a way to feed themselves. Olof knew that as long as they had the farm, he could at least feed his family. In his later years the topic of discussion was usually the weather and reports of their relatively good health. Both he and Karin inquired often about the welfare of friends and relatives back in Sweden. The letters reveal an intelligent man who worked hard all his life.

There is no mention of the hard times that the Rune Stone's discovery brought to the family. Apparently, Olof didn't want to burden his relatives in Sweden with the troubled times that came with it. On the other hand, the Rune Stone may have been part of the reason for his negativity about America. It was likely a combination of many things. It seems he mostly longed to go back to the place where he was born and raised. The beautifully glacier-sculpted hills and valleys of Forsa Parish were always his true home.

Olof's writing style also reveals elements of his character and intelligence. His writing is very neat and legible, with a signature that shows a clear artistic flair in the Gothic style.

Olof Ohman's signature at the end of this letter written on December 18, 1880 displays an artistic flair. (Courtesy of the Ohman Relatives Association)

Chronology of Letters

The first known letter written by Olof Ohman after immigrating to the United States was when he was in the town of Evansville, Minnesota, on November 9, 1879.

(Courtesy of the Ohman Relatives Association)

1. November 9, 1879   Evansville   Olof Ohman

In the first known letter from America Olof wrote that he was living in Evansville, Minnesota at the home of another immigrant from Forsa, where he had worked in a steam mill that past summer. He also wrote that he landed in Philadelphia and listed the cities he passed through while riding the train headed for Minnesota: Pittsburgh, Pennsylvania; Columbia and Indianapolis, Indiana; Peoria, Galva, Bishops Hill, and Rock Island, Illinois; and then to St. Paul and Morris, Minnesota.

Och dertill Berät en liten del af Amerika, Jag landade i Philadelphia och gick på jernvägen till Pittsburg och vidare besodran till Columbia Indianapolis Peore Galfva Bechops Hill der gorde jag ett upprehåll i 7 dagar och sedan forssatte jag till Rockesland o.b: s att jag talade med 3 se Karllar som hörde till Olof Linds forsamling, Och vidare till Miluvake i Wiskonsen en Stad vid en Sjön i Michigan och vidare till St. Paul i Minnesota vidare till Moris sista station, Nu hvar jag lyckligt och väl framkommen till Douglas Cont, Hvaraf jag Hade den aran att Hälsa Forsboarna godag!

In the earliest known letter written by Olof Ohman, dated November 9, 1879, on page 2 he listed the cities he traveled through by train on his way to Minnesota. (Courtesy of the Ohman Relatives Association)

And then traveled the small part of America, I landed in <u>Philadelphia</u> and then went on the railroad to <u>Pittsburgh</u> and then went to <u>Columbia</u>, <u>Indianapolis</u>, <u>Peoria</u>, <u>Galva</u>, <u>Bishops Hill</u>. There I made a stop for 7 days and then continued to Rock Island. P.S. I talked to three men who belong to Olof Rindes' congregation and then on to <u>Milwaukee</u>, in Wisconsin, a city by Lake Michigan, and then on to <u>St. Paul</u> in Minnesota, on to <u>Morris</u> the last station. Now I have safe and sound arrived to Douglas County where I had the honor to say hello to the people of Forsa, Good day.

The pronoun dissa (this) and the verb "berätta" ("mention" or "report") on page 2 of the November 9, 1879 letter indicates that Ohman wrote with an A-dialect based on the use of an "a" ending. The Kensington Rune stone is carved using an e-dialect. Example: fiske using an "e" ending instead of an "a" ending for fiska. (Courtesy of the Ohman Relatives Association) *"I should also mention/report that I'm sitting and writing these lines at Lars Olsson in Lund."*

This example of Olof Ohman's writing appeared on page 2 of a letter written on November 9, 1879. (Courtesy of the Ohman Relatives Association)
"His boys Göran and Olof also each have their land. They are running the farm profession in large scale."

Letters from Holmes City

Olof Ohman wrote his first known letter from Holmes City, Minnesota, on January 5, 1880.

2.	January 5, 1880	Holmes City	Olof Ohman
3.	May 1, 1880	Holmes City	Olof Ohman
4.	May 21, 1880	Holmes City	Olof Ohman

Letters from Brandon

Olof Ohman wrote his first known letter from the town of Brandon, Minnesota, on June 3, 1880. (Courtesy of the Ohman Relatives Association)

5.	June 3, 1880	Brandon	Olof Ohman
6.	December 10, 1880	Brandon	Olof Ohman
7.	December 18, 1880	Brandon	Olof Ohman
8.	March 6, 1881	Brandon	Olof Ohman
9.	April 12, 1882	Brandon	Olof Ohman
10.	December 4, 1882	Brandon	Olof Ohman

Letters from Kensington

11.	January 29, 1892	Kensington	Olof Ohman

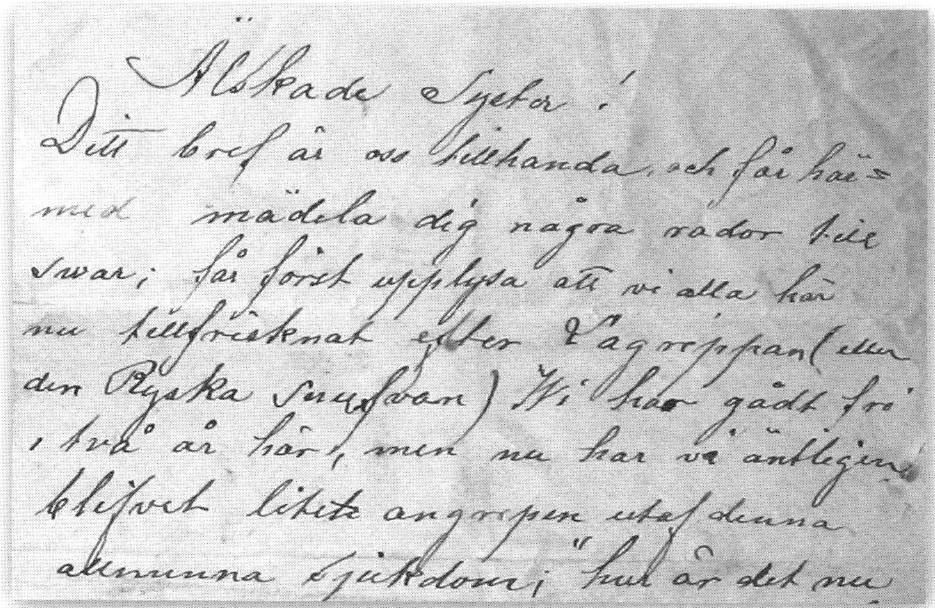

Ohman's letter from January 29, 1892 discussed how his whole family caught the flu.

Kensington, January 29, 1892

Beloved Sister,
*Your letter have arrived to us and shall here give you some answers, will first tell you that **we all have** recovered from the <u>Lagsippan</u> (or the Russian flu). **We have** been lucky not to catch it for two years, but now **we have** caught this common disease.*

12. March 24, 1892
    Kensington
    Olof Ohman

This picture of the Olof Ohman family was taken in 1893. L to R: Arthur, Olof, Edward, Olof Jr. (behind), Karin, and Amanda. (Courtesy of the Ohman Relatives Association)

13. April 1, 1894
    Kensington
    Olof Ohman

Olof Ohman wrote his third known letter from Kensington, Minnesota, on April 1, 1894. (Courtesy of the Ohman Relatives Association)

14.	May 22, 1895	Kensington	Olof Ohman
15.	July 22, 1906	Kensington	Olof Ohman
16.	December 15, 1906	Kensington	Olof Ohman
17.	May 29, 1920	Kensington	Olof Ohman
18.	March 21, 1921	Kensington	Olof Ohman
19.	January 2, 1924	Kensington	Olof Ohman
20.	February 1, 1924	Kensington	Olof Ohman
21.	March 29, 1924	Kensington	Olof Ohman

On April 28, 1927, Olof wrote about the Kensington Rune Stone for the first time in the letters to the relatives in Sweden. (Courtesy of the Ohman Relatives Association)

22.   April 28, 1927   Kensington   Olof Ohman

On page 4 of the letter Olof Ohman wrote on April 28, 1927, he wrote about the upcoming rally to be held at Oscar Lake for a monument to the Kensington Rune Stone at Oscar Lake, to be held. (Courtesy of the Ohman Relatives Association)

"I send you a clip from a newspaper that will give you the information that it is decided to build a monument on the site that the stone was found. That I have waited for, for 29 years, but it looks like it will really take place now. As long as there isn't more criticism of the same, but I am informed that runologists and archaeologists who are the learned authorities in that science in Europe have now proclaimed that it is real. A dear greeting to you."

"Signed,

"Olof Ohman"

Olof Ohman sat with his arms folded (center) listening to a speaker (blurred vertical image at left, likely Hjalmar Holand) during the rally for a monument to the Kensington Rune Stone at Fahlin's Point at Oscar Lake, Minnesota, on June 1, 1927. (Kensington Area Heritage Society)

On December 4, 1927, Olof wrote glowingly about the rally at Fahlin's Point that had taken place in June. He had reason to be happy, since the rally was the biggest event that had ever happened in the area, and it still is to this day.

23.   December 4, 1927   Kensington   Olof Ohman

On December 4, 1927, Olof Ohman wrote glowingly about the rally at Oscar Lake on June 1, 1927. (Courtesy of the Ohman Relatives Association)

"November 29 there was a big meeting in Alexandria because of the Kensington rune stone, like you saw in the news clip that I sent you. This summer, June 1ˢᵗ, there was a meeting in Oscar Lake. There were about 10,000 people there, there were also 3,000 automobiles. It was a record at the scene."

24.	February 14, 1928	Kensington	Olof Ohman
25.	May 7, 1928	Kensington	Olof Ohman
26.	January 10, 1929	Kensington	Olof Ohman
27.	April 23, 1929	Kensington	Olof Ohman
28.	September 9, 1929	Kensington	**Karin Ohman**
29.	November 30, 1931	Kensington	Olof Ohman
30.	January 2, 1932	Kensington	Olof Ohman
31.	March 12, 1932	Kensington	Olof Ohman
32.	May 15, 1932	Kensington	Olof Ohman
33.	November 11, 1932	Kensington	Olof Ohman
34.	November 14, 1932	Kensington	Olof Ohman
35.	March 6, 1933	Kensington	Olof Ohman
36.	January 2, 1934	Kensington	Olof Ohman

Olof and Karin Ohman in about 1934. (Courtesy of the Ohman Relatives Association)

37.	October 24, 1934	Kensington	**Karin Ohman**
38.	November 29, 1934	Kensington	Olof Ohman
39.	January 26, 1935	Kensington	Olof Ohman
40.	May 21, 1935	Kensington	Olof Ohman
41.	May 21, 1935	Kensington	**Karin Ohman**
42.	September 2, 1935	Kensington	**Karin Ohman**

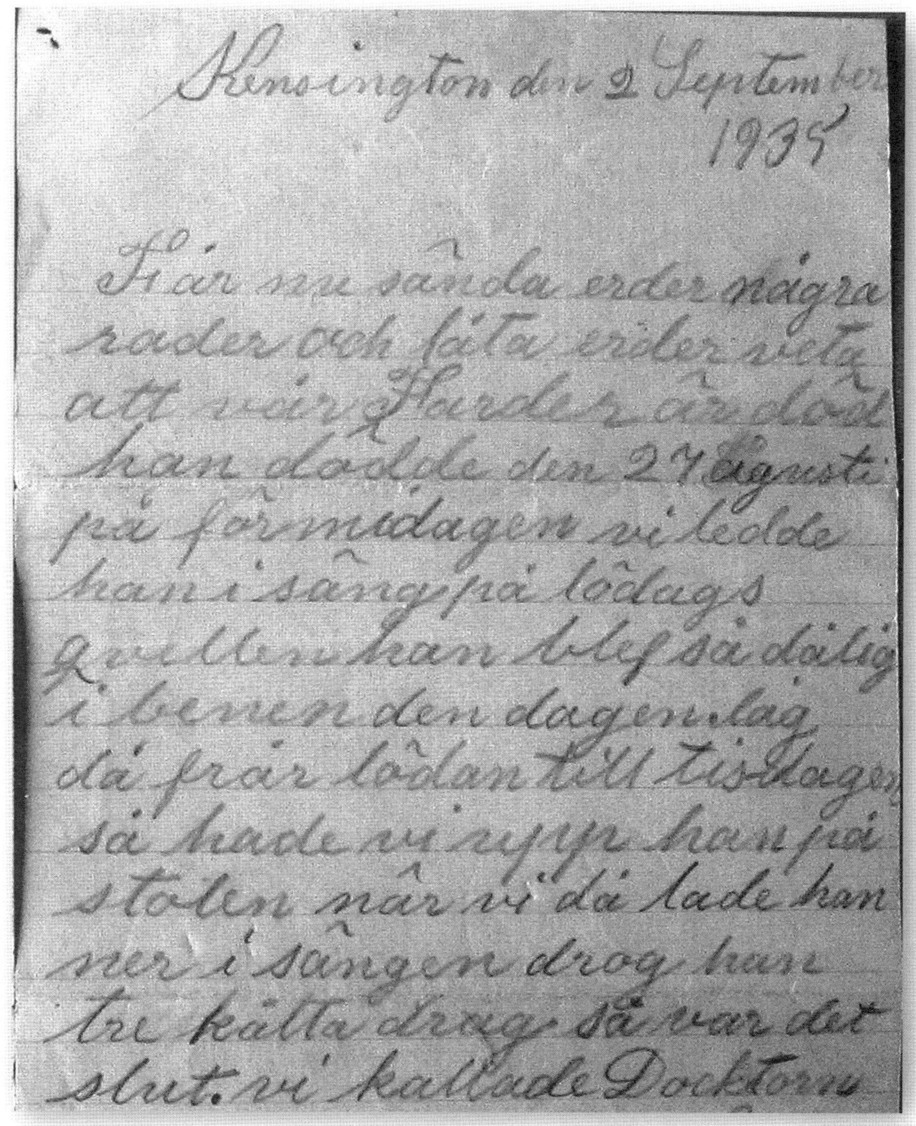

On September 2, 1935, Karin Ohman wrote a letter to the relatives in Sweden, sadly informing them of Olof's death. (Courtesy of the Ohman Relatives Association)
"I now send you a few written words to let you know that our father is dead. He died August 27th in the morning. We led him to bed on Saturday evening, he felt so bad and his legs hurt. He then laid in bed until Tuesday. That day we got him up in a chair, but when we laid him back in bed he took three short breaths and it was over."

43.	November 1, 1935	Kensington	**Karin Ohman**
44.	February 10, 1936	Kensington	**Karin Ohman**
45.	July 5, 1936	Kensington	**Karin Ohman**
46.	December 13, 1936	Kensington	**Karin Ohman**
47.	May 1, 1940	Kensington	**Karin Ohman**

As if the discovery of almost forty letters was not enough, there turned out to be more. After returning home from Sweden in February 2004, the authors kept in almost daily contact with Britta Blank about the progress of the search for more letters. Sure enough, Britta wrote back telling us about relatives who had found more letters from Olof and Karin. The whole process was very exciting and we talked about the idea of the relatives publishing a book about the letters. Britta said everyone she talked to seemed to like the idea. The enthusiasm about the letters prompted more relatives to look through their attics and basements to see what they could find. Britta herself found a couple more letters from Olof after rummaging through boxes of family belongings that spanned a time period from 1865 to 1975.

In April 2004, the relatives in Sweden formed a group called The Ohman Relatives Association. At their inaugural meeting they announced their plan to publish a book about the letters which would include photographs and translations into English and modern Swedish. This book will be a tremendous resource for historians and researchers. The letters are an important insight into the lives of a Swedish immigrant family, and into the mind of the central figure of the Kensington Rune Stone controversy.

The Ohman Documents

Research in 2004 led to the discovery of five large plastic tubs of Ohman family documents. Inside the tubs were hundreds of photographs, personal letters, newspaper articles, legal documents, and books that were saved by the Ohman family for over a hundred years. Many of the items bear Olof's signature. These important documents have never been examined by researchers, and offer a rare opportunity to learn about the life of the central figure in the Rune Stone story. Like the letters written to his relatives in Sweden, many of the letters found were written by Olof himself and several books contain his handwritten notes. After Olof and Karin died the documents ended up with Art Ohman, the last of their children to live on the farm. When Art passed away in 1984 the articles went to his sister Ida's son Lalard Kolberg. When Lalard died in March of 1997, his daughter Joanne (Kolberg) Streeter took possession of the five tubs of precious documents. No one in the family had ever carefully sorted through the documents and wouldn't have understood the significance of many of the articles even if they had.

The family located the documents in January 2004, after we asked them if they had any articles that might be useful in preparing this manuscript. It wasn't until June 30th that we were able to sit down and carefully go through the first two tubs of documents. Darwin Ohman, Joanne (Kolberg) Streeter, and author Wolter spent more than five hours sorting, reviewing, and scanning the material we felt was important. The same group was joined by Russell Fridley on July 20, and spent five more hours going through the next two boxes. On August 4th, Darwin, Tom Kolberg, Joanne, and author Wolter went through the book collection for three more hours. Several books were found that yielded important new evidence. What follows is an examination of the most relevant and important materials.

Legal Documents and Certificates

Olof and Karin held on to many of the important legal documents that most families save. These documents included mortgage deeds, stock certificates, birth and death certificates, and several funeral programs for family and friends. While most of these articles are very interesting they offer little with regard to the Rune Stone. Andrew Anderson appeared as a witness for Ohman, before a notary, to aid in the execution of a warranty deed. Mr. Anderson was previously married to Karin Ohman's cousin Betsy, and this union produced four children: Henry, Mary, Ole, and Victor (based on 1906 census data).

State of Minnesota,
County of Douglas, ss.
Village Of Kensington, On this 6th day of October.
A. D. 1910., before me, a Notary Public,
within and for said county, personally appeared Andrew Anderson (single)

to me known to be the person described in and who executed the foregoing instrument and acknowledged that he executed the same as his free act and deed.

Notary Public, Douglas County, Minn.
My commission expires, Nov. 17th, 1915.

Andrew Anderson appeared as a witness for the execution of this Warranty Deed document dated October 6, 1910. (Courtesy of the Ohman Family)

Newspaper Articles

The plastic tubs also contained several newspapers that included a six-day series of articles about the Rune Stone from April 11 to April 16, 1955. It appears that Art and John Ohman saved the articles since they were the ones living on the farm at the time. It also indicates that the Ohman boys were understandably interested in the subject of the Rune Stone. There were a few other articles in the tubs including a lengthy obituary that contains a curious, but potentially important reference to the Rune Stone.

This excerpt is from an obituary for Mr. W. L. Sarsland that appeared in a 1949 newspaper article found with the Ohman documents in July, 2004. This paragraph was circled, presumably by a member of Ohman family, and appears to support the statement by Ohman that he cleaned the inscription out shortly after the discovery. (Copyright *Rapid City Journal*, all rights reserved. Used by permission.)

Runestone". Recently the authenticity of this stone was questioned, but in Mr. Sarsland's mind there could be no doubt but what it was real as he helped remove the shale, etc. from the carvings.

What is important about this article is that if Mr. Sarsland's information is correct, it supports Ohman's statement that he cleaned out the inscription with a nail shortly after its discovery as reported by Winchell in his May 1910 report. This statement is consistent with our laboratory findings that the retooling of the inscription has given the impression that the carving is more recent than it actually is.

Photographs

The Ohman collection includes hundreds of photographs, primarily of friends, family members, and the farmstead as well as older pictures of people and places in Sweden. While the photos are primarily portraits and everyday moments, some photos provide important evidence about reported events related to the Rune Stone. In the 1970 Walter Gran interview he made a statement about the Ohman blacksmith shop being, "way out in the woods." There are several photos of the grounds around the house, taken throughout the years. The blacksmith building can be seen in some of the photos and its location relative to the house is not as remote as Mr. Gran lead people to believe. The photos provide clear evidence that Walter's memory is unreliable, but it made for a good story by a man well known for his "whopper" tales.

Two-and-a-half-year-old Joanne Kolberg played in a tub in the back yard at the Ohman farm in summer, 1951. The buildings behind her are (L-R) a storage shed, the outhouse and the blacksmith shop. The Ohman home is immediately to the left of Joanne out of the picture. (Courtesy of the Ohman Family)

Letters

By far the most interesting articles were the personal, handwritten letters and postcards. Many of the letters had some relevance to or were directly related to the Rune Stone. The letters are a treasure trove of information, and most importantly provide a clear window into the minds of Ohman family members with regard to how they felt about the authenticity of the Stone.

The first important letter in the collection was written to Olof Ohman by then secretary of the Museum Committee at the Minnesota Historical Society, Dr. Warren Upham. During Professor Newton Winchell's investigation in 1910, he borrowed the Swedish grammar book from Mr. Ohman. This letter is important because it provides proof that Mr. Ohman tried to get the book back and the Society agreed to return the book. The authors have seen the book, which currently resides in the Minnesota Historical Society library, and which has obviously not been returned to the Ohman family.

One of the letters the Ohman family had was written to Olof by Warren Upham on March 3, 1915. Professor Upham was responding to Olof's request to return the Almquist book on Swedish grammar that Winchell obtained from him. (Courtesy of the Ohman Family)

"St. Paul, Minn., March 3, 1915

"Mr. Olof Ohman, Kensington, Minn., (R.F.D.).

"Dear Sir:

"Your letter of Feb 22 is received, asking return of a Swedish grammar, which you supplied to Prof. N. H. Winchell several years ago, for aid in his investigations of the Rune Stone, your wish for its return being mainly because it belonged to another man who now wants it. On account of the unexpected death of Professor Winchell on May 2 last year, all the books which he had at his office in the Old Capitol were removed, in accordance with a bequest in his will, to be added to his former donation of a very large collection of books and pamphlets on geology, given to the Department of Geology at the State University in Minneapolis. His large lots of books in the Old Capitol therefore were so removed last summer, probably included the Swedish grammar. I have written today to Prof. William H. Emmons, head of the Department of Geology, asking him to find this book. If he can find it, he or I will mail it to you.

"Very truly yours,

"Warren Upham, Archaeologist."

There are two very curious letters in the collection that were written to Mr. Ohman by Hjalmar Holand in January, 1928. The tone of the letters is quite terse and it is obvious that Ohman and Holand are at odds over issues surrounding the Rune Stone. Both letters are written in Norwegian, Holand's native tongue. It was during this same time that Mr. Holand negotiated an agreement with ten businesspeople in Alexandria to reimburse him for his research and take possession of the Stone. It is unclear whether Ohman was aware of this agreement, but it is very clear that he felt cheated by Holand and did not trust him.

The January 17, 1928 letter, written in Norwegian, by Holand to Ohman; the tone was rather terse. (Courtesy of the Ohman Family)

"January 17, 1928

*"Mr. Olof Ohman
Kensington, Minn.*

"I thought you were interested in getting the inscription's authenticity proven, but after your last letter I don't know what to believe. Be so kind and go to Mr. Hedeen and get the statement sworn to (notarized?) and do what you can as a man so that the truth can be known. You will win with this. If you will not help in this, please send the statement back to me; I will in that case not bother you again. I enclose a dollar as payment for the postage and letter-writing I have caused you.

"Hjalmar R. Holand"

(Translation by Jim Belgum on July 14, 2004)

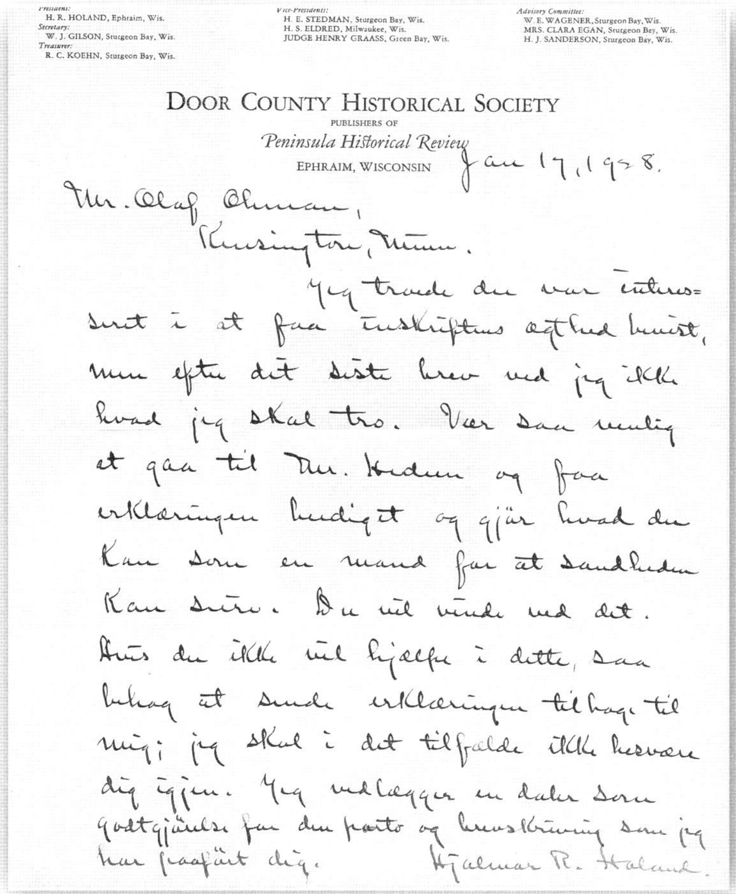

A very sad letter, filled with irony, was written to Amanda Ohman by a woman she had never met. The woman wrote about Ida Ohman's disappearance and explained that she was prompted to write after reading the series of newspaper articles on the Rune Stone in

April, 1955. She wrote that twenty-seven years earlier Ida had told her about the discovery of the Stone. The irony about the letter is that it was written to Amanda four years after her death. Her brothers Art and John received the letter and apparently decided to keep it.

A portion of the letter to Amanda Ohman from Mrs. Lillian Golden, inquiring into the whereabouts of Ida Ohman. The letter was received by Art and John Ohman, who were living at the farm four years after Amanda's death. (Courtesy of the Ohman Family)

"Minneapolis, Minn.
April 17th, 1955.

"Dear Amanda,

"I'm sure you will be surprised to get a letter from someone you have never met. I feel that I know you as you are Ida's sister and she often spoke of you. I've been reading in our daily newspapers of your father and the Rune Stone. I remember Ida told us about the great discovery your father made. While reading the other day about it I saw your name also your brother Arthur's."

The most significant letter with regard to the Rune Stone was written by Olof Ohman Jr. on April 2, 1957. This letter, written six months before he died, yields three important pieces of evidence. The first is a sketch of the tree roots around the Stone when it was found in 1898 that Olof Jr. drew on page three, a sketch strikingly similar to those drawn by his father and Sam Olson in 1910. Olof Jr's sketch has one significant difference: he drew the roots curving upward and away from the side of the Stone that bears the last three lines of the inscription. This important difference more closely coincides with the white root leaching observed on the back of the Stone. Olof Jr. was twelve years old in 1898 and likely had the clearest memory of the Ohman children who saw the Stone wrapped in the roots of the tree. While the sketch was drawn nearly sixty years after the event, its accuracy is still remarkable.

Olof Jr.'s estimate of the diameter of the tree being 9 or 10 inches is important, new, unsolicited information from a first-hand witness. The letter was written by an Ohman to his brothers Art and John, and it is reasonable to assume that none of them ever thought that this private correspondence would ever be made public for consideration in the controversy. The contents of the letter clearly indicate that the family believed in the authenticity of the Stone and in the discovery accounts of both their father and Edward.

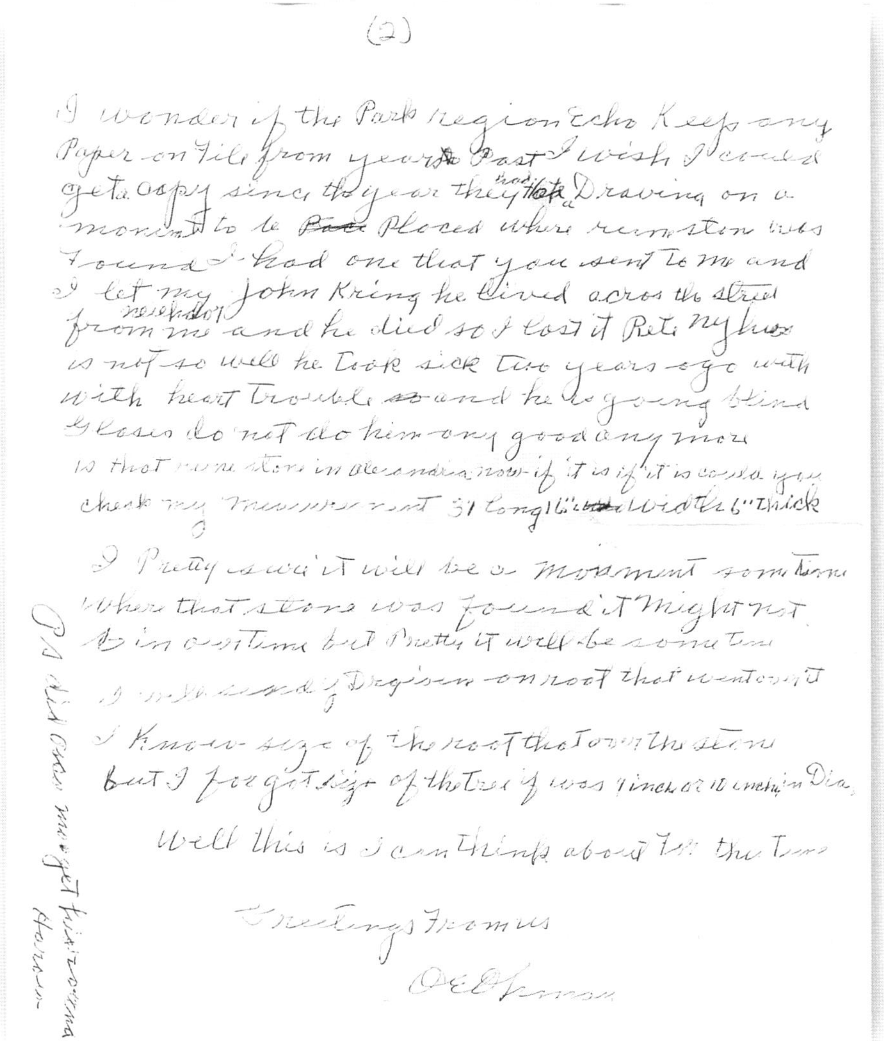

On page 2 of Olof Ohman Jr's letter to his brothers Art and John, on April 2, 1957, he wrote out the details that he could remember about the Rune Stone.

"I wonder if the Park Region Echo *keep any paper on file from years past and I wish I could get a copy since the year they had a drawing on a monument to be placed where rune stone was found I had one that you sent to me and I let my neighbor John Kring he lived across the street from me and he died so I lost it Pete Nyhues is not so well he took sick two years ago with heart trouble and he is going blind Glasses do not do him any good any more is that rune stone in Alexandria now if it is could you check my measurement 31" long 16" width 6" thick.*

"I pretty sure it will be a monument sometime where that stone was found it might not be in our time but pretty it will be some time I will send y[sic] diagram on root that went over it. I know size of the root that over the stone but I forgot size of the tree if was 9 inch or 10 inch in Dia. Well this is I can think about for this time."

"Greetings from us,

"O. E. Ohman"

Perhaps the most important letter of all those found was one written by Olof Ohman himself. This letter is the rough draft Olof wrote in Swedish to Dr. Warren Upham on March 3, 1910. Ohman's neighbor Sam Olson wrote the same letter in English that was sent to the Society with the same date. In this letter Olof asked the Society to hold the Stone until he and Mr. Holand had worked things out between them. He also stated that he told Mr. Holand that when his research was completed that he was to deposit it at the Norwegian Historical Society. Since there is not and never has been a Norwegian Historical Society, he likely meant for it to end up at the Minnesota Historical Society.

Courtesy of the Ohman Family Association.

Books

Two books are well known to have been in Ohman's library in 1910. The first is the Almquist book of Swedish grammar that originally belonged to Sven Fogelblad, and to which the Andersons fell heir when Sven died in 1897. Betsy Anderson gave the book to Ohman after the discovery of the Stone. This book currently resides in the Minnesota Historical Society library in St. Paul, Minnesota.

The second book was Carl Rosander's *The Well-Informed Schoolmaster*, which Amanda Ohman loaned to Johan Holvik in 1949. There is no evidence that Holvik ever returned the book to the Ohman family and its current wereabouts are unknown. The Rosander book was a Swedish almanac that included information about Viking age runes and language. It was also the source of lengthy discussion as the alleged source of the inscription. Even though it has been well established that the book could not have been used to carve the Kensington Rune Stone, the claim is still made by many scholars. Portions of pages 62 and 63, which include a language discussion about the Old Swedish and Middle Swedish periods, are have been translated and reproduced here for the reader to consider.

Rosander Pages 62 & 63 Translated into English by Robin S. Colquin

II Old Swedish. *From 1000 to 1300.* The link between all the countries of Northwestern Europe, which consisted of something closely akin to a common language and which made these all members of a single people, divided bit by bit, and each country adopted firstly its own government and gradually also its own language.   Old Swedish, which developed in this manner, naturally initially resembled Ancient Swedish, but was progressively converted with new words, particularly through the influence of the spreading of Christianity.   Runes, which now no longer represented secrets, became more commonly known and used as written characters, until they were gradually supplanted by the more precise and more hallowed Latin alphabet promulgated by the monks.

The new ideas that accompanied the new religion also made new words necessary, and for this spiritual language were used partly combinations of Old Swedish words such as *radband* (rosary), *skårseld* (pugartory), *vigvatten* (holy water); partly words were adopted into Old Swedish from Latin and Greek and transmuted, for example *kors* (cross) (from the Latin Crux), *font,* (font - Latin fons) *(dop) fynt* (baptism font), and in similar manner the words *altare* (alter), *bibel* (bible), *biskop* (bishop), *engel* (angel), *fest* (feast), *kloster* (cloister), *kyrka* (church), *oblat* (sacramental wafer), *prest* (priest), *predika* (preach), *psalm* (psalm), *skrifen* (writing), *signa* (sign), *tempel* (temple), *testamente* (will) and many others. The truth is that through the medium of religious teaching from foreign countries words were also imported from English, German and other languages although these are nowadays difficult to distinguish from proper Swedish words.

Notwithstanding the adoption of the Latin characters into the written language the rune þ for the <p> sound was long retained and subsequently changed, in consequence of its pronunciation, to <th>, which right down to our time has survived in both biblical and lay language. From Anglo-Saxon <o> was adopted to express <dh>. Amongst the vowels, <å> was first represented by <a> or <o> and later by <aa>; the ä-sound was written as <e> and the ö-sound with <ø>.

Besides the runestones we have various other papers which are reckoned to have originated from this period, e.g. *Vestgötalagen* (the West Gotland Law), which is believed to have been written around the year 1220, with the oldest surviving manuscript copy of it being from 1290. Moreover the Swedish literature from that time is extremely meager because when the monks, the sole teachers of the time, wrote anything, it was usually in Latin. As far as one can judge regarding Swedish on the basis of what is available, the alphabet was very indeterminate and variable, which is evidenced for example by the fact that the short word *efter* (after) is found written in no less than twenty-eight different ways such as *Abtir, Ebtir, Ibtir, Ubtir, Aftar, Ifti, Aptir, Eptir*, etc. At times the vowels or consonants were doubled endlessly, as in *Naat* (natt), *Flerre Monss*, etc.

This situation seems nevertheless to be the result of different regional dialects together with the fact that no common alphabet had yet developed for the country as a whole. If one is to judge from the Icelandic, it seems that the daily language was powerful, rich and well-regulated, and though short on vocabulary was nonetheless quite sufficient for all needs, and indeed had many words which have subsequently vanished to denote concepts for which we now lack any means of expression; the language of poetry in particular was rich, and many expressions contain an ingenuity and wisdom which show that the human understanding of our forefathers reached a much higher level than one generally imagines.

III Middle Swedish. *From 1300 to 1523.* During this period the language continued to be enriched with new words, partly from Latin and Greek through religion, which generally had the power of government in its hands, partly from German through the mercenaries in the time of the "Folkung's" regime, and partly from Danish during the Kalmar Union; as a result of student visits to Paris a good deal of expressions were even absorbed from French, particularly in relation to literature. All of this of course increased the vocabulary, but it had a detrimental influence on the national language, which constantly tottered from one set of expressions to another without specific principles and in the end produced a complete linguistic confusion.

That an increased contact with foreign peoples and their languages should have an influence on the mother tongue was natural enough. German kings with accompanying German civil servants, many German queens, and above all the Hanseatic merchants and artisans who were spread throughout Scandinavia, introduced many words and expressions from the German language, and of these we still have such words as *gesims* (cornice), *jungfru* (maid), *junker* (young nobleman), *mantel* (robe), *skymf* (insult), etc.

From Latin came the words *artikel* (article), *datum* (date), *mandat* (mandate), *plakat* (placard), *universitet* (university), etc.; from French came *kurteis* (flirtation), *penal* (bullying), *svit* (suite), *äfventyr* (story), etc., besides which Væriagarne's journeys to Constantinople were not without influence on the language. However, this situation gave a much-needed awakening to the literary scene, one contribution to which was the fact that in about 1320 the Norwegian queen Eufemia commissioned a Swedish translation of some of Germany's and France's romantic poems such as *Duke Fredrik of Normandy, Sir Ivan the Lion Knight, King Artius, Karl the Great*, etc.; it is believed that *Konungastyrelsen* (Royal Government) was written at the same time, a masterpiece in both its content and its language, and moreover the later National Laws are believed to date from this time, together with various songs, *Saint Birgitta's Revelations,* the *Life of Ausgarius*, as well as the great verse chronicle, a number of our folk ballads, etc.

The improving language during this time meant, apart from the increased vocabulary referred to above, most importantly that: harsh words were on offer in place of softer words, so that for example instead of *mer* (me), *ther* (thee), *ser* (they), *allir* (all) one began to write *mik* (me), *thik* (thee), *sik* (they), *alle* (all); nevertheless to start with the harder consonant system was retained, e.g. *gudelik, skipta* (*gudelig, skifta*) (godly, change); but as a result of Danish influence during the Kalmar Union <k>, <p> and <t> were transmuted in many words to <g>,< f> and <d>, for example *tage* (take), *skifte* (change) instead of *take, skipte*.   The old faint or sharp vowels were likewise gradually replaced by others so that for example *sun* became *son* (son), *brut* became *brott* (break), *skip* became *skep* (*skepp*) (ship), *vin* became *væn* (vän) (friend), *siga* became *sæga* (säga) (say), *firi* became *fore* (före) (before), and so on.   The use of *ch* was adopted from German along with the prefixes *an-, be-, bi-, er-, ge-, för-* (vor), *und-*, and the like, and suffix syllables *-dom, -het, -skap*, etc. as well as the Danish *else, ning,* and the indefinite articles *en, ett,* (the) and so on, whereby a large number of new words were created from old imports. In accordance with the German model one began to represent a long vowel either by writing it double as in *troo* (trust), *reen* (clean), or by adding an <h> as in *åhr* (year), *fahra* (travel), a form which later on was also used at the end of words as in *jagh* (matter), *sigh* (itself), *dagh* (day), *Sverighe* (Sweden), etc.   Moreover in the writings of these times the spelling is very variable and indeterminate because of the influence so many different languages had on the as yet unconsolidated Swedish so that at the end of the period one finds one after the other, for example *rike, riike, rige, riche* (Kingdom), *jak, jeg, jac, jach* (I), *ok, oc, og, och* (and), and so on. (In this last word the German <ch> has subsequently triumphed over the old Swedish <k>, the Latin <c>, and the Danish <g>.) Out of this chaos and confusion, which thus characterizes Middle Swedish, the language finally emerges cleaner and better established through the immortal Gustaf Vasa, from whose accession one reckons the beginning of:

IV New Swedish.   *From 1523 to the present day.*

The Ohman family also has Hjalmar Holand's 1909 book about the history of Norwegian immigration in America that he gave to Olof Ohman about that same year. Holand also wrote about the Kensington Rune Stone and on page twelve claimed the tree under which the stone was found was twenty-five years old based on a count of the annual tree rings. It was not the only time Holand mentioned tree rings in his numerous publications about the Rune Stone.

The title page of the book Olof Ohman received from Hjalmar Holand in 1909. (Courtesy of the Ohman Family)

A second book belonging to Sven Fogelblad was found in the Ohman library in August, 2004. This book of religious sermons was likely given to Karin Ohman by Betsy Anderson.

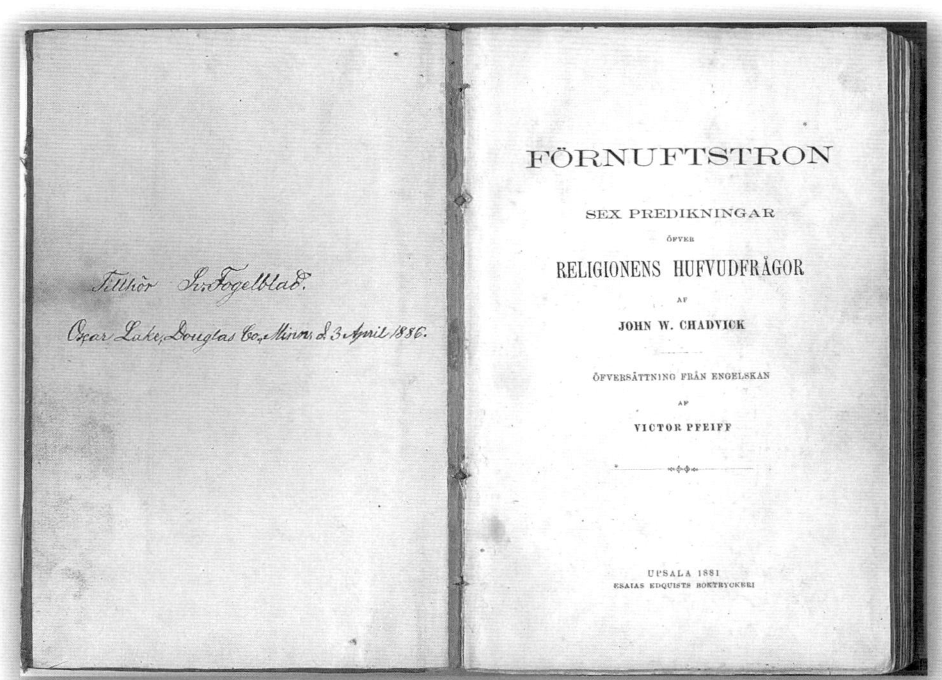

A book of religious sermons dated April 3, 1886, that originally belonged to Sven Fogelblad was found in the Ohman library on August 4, 2004. The book title in English is *Throne of Common Sense*, by John W. Chadwick. (Courtesy of the Ohman Family)

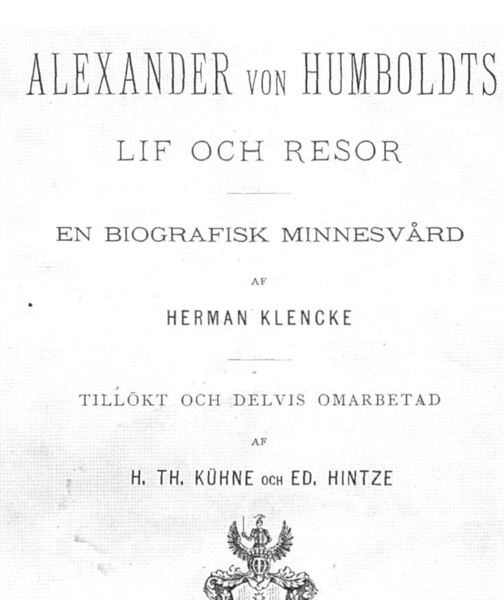

The inside cover and title page of a book in the collection contain two words found on the Kensington Rune Stone inscription that indicate Ohman did not compose the inscription. The first word, *död* (death), was written twice in his own hand. The second word, *resor* (travels), is found in the title of the book. On the Kensington Rune Stone these words are **rise** (travel), which was carved twice, and **ded** (death).

The title of Ohman's book, *Alexander von Humbolt's Life and Journeys* by Herman Klencke, contains the word travels *(resor)*. The word is spelled as **rise** on the Kensington Rune Stone. (Courtesy of the Ohman Family)

On the inside jacket of the Ohman's book, *Alexander von Humbolt's Life and Travels* by Herman Klencke, Olof and Karin wrote the birthdates and two death dates of their children. Ohman clearly understood how to spell the word death *(död)*, used twice on this page. The word is spelled differently on the Kensington Rune Stone *(ded=death)*. (Courtesy of the Ohman Family)

Ohman's library contained twenty-two books on religion, eighteen on health, seventeen on farm matters and ten on miscellaneous subjects.

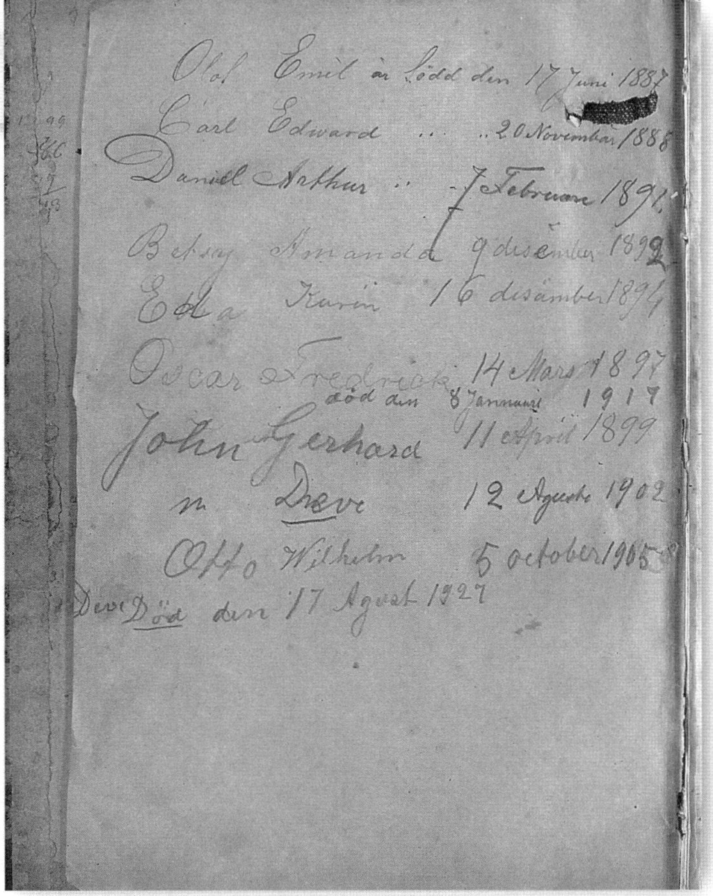

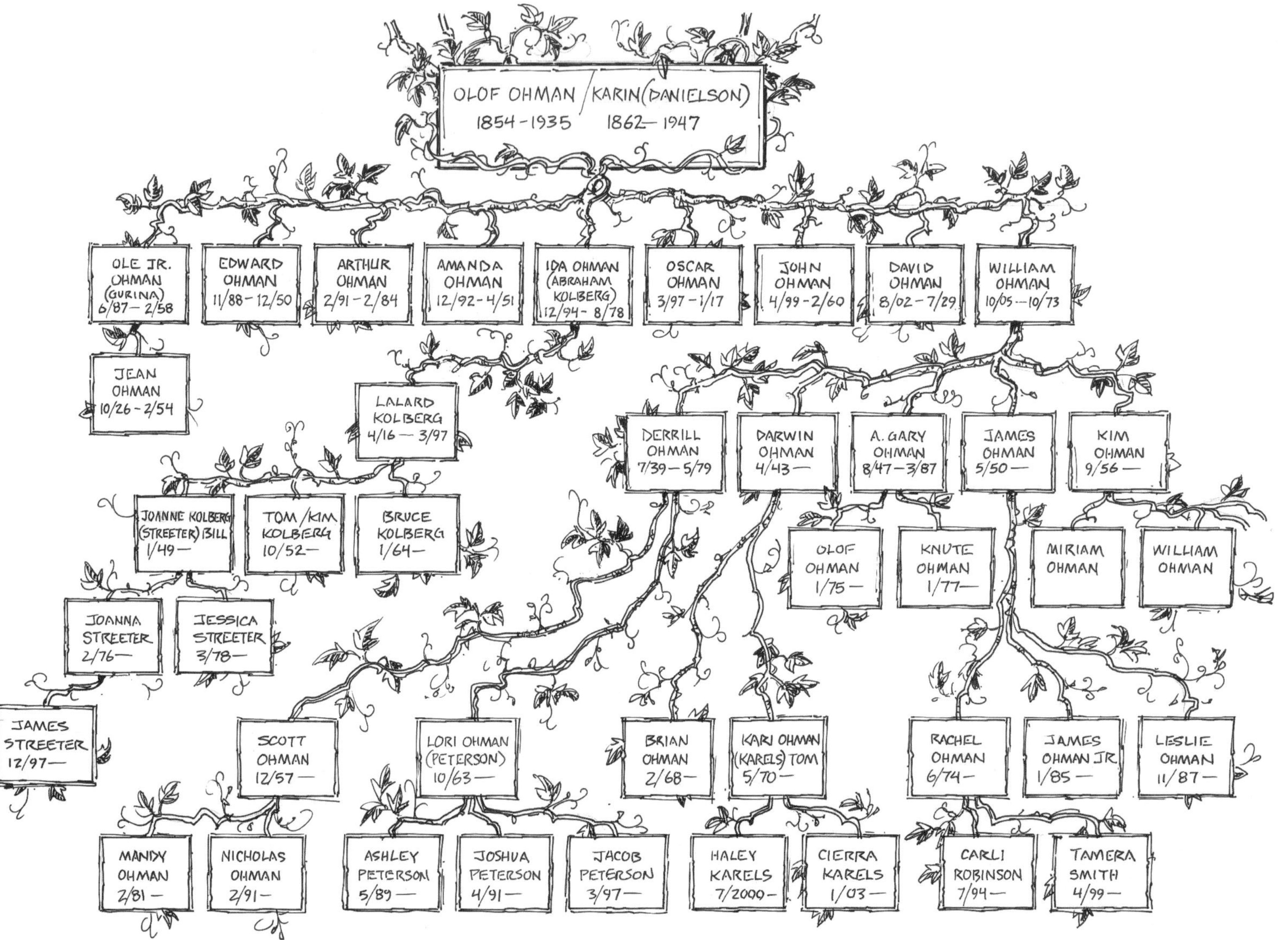

The family tree of Karin and Olof Ohman includes their nine children, seven grandchildren, fourteen great-grandchildren, eleven great-great-grandchildren and one great-great-great-grandchild. (Sketch by Dan Wiemer)

The Conclusion

The major stumbling block to acceptance of the Kensington Rune Stone's authenticity has been the lack of evidence that would allow a full evaluation of the language on the Stone; the means to interpret such evidence has only become available in the last few decades. Opinions based on this lack of evidence have been divided since the day the Stone was found. However, many discoveries have been made in the intervening years that have provided important information that makes negative opinions about the inscription obsolete. What follows are points that support the inscription's medieval origin.

Language and Runes

The analysis presented here shows compelling evidence that the Kensington Rune Stone is a medieval artifact.

1. The chief proof is the presence of the dotted Rs for the palatal R. The discovery of the Kensington Rune Stone predates the discovery of the two inscriptions in Sweden (Ukna, Sm 145 and the Lund Bone 4, Danish Rune Supplement 5) with dotted Rs by forty years. In addition, the palatal R was still in use on Gotland during the last half of the 1300s.

2. There are numerous small points of runic usage that tie the Kensington Rune Stone runes to Gotlandic practice; including the dotted L, double "r", double "l", a bind-rune in **hafþe** (had) for "fþ", use of: "þ = t" in initial position, "t" for "d", and the Latin k for the k-rune.

3. The double-dotted runes for ä (Ẍ), ö (ᛟ̈), and ü (ᚿ̈) appear to have been adopted from German manuscript practice, as also happened in Danish manuscripts in the later 1300s with ü (Uldaler 1968: 142-5).

4. The hooked X appears to be an adaptation of the X-like rune for a. To our knowledge, the only other place the hook is found in medieval records, besides the Spirit Pond Rune stone in Maine, is in the signature of the explorer Columbus (*American Heritage Dictionary* 1973: 69, autograph).

5. All the heretofore nagging traits on the Kensington Rune Stone—the word forms "g" in **og** (and), "h" in **ahr** (year), **öh** (island) and **här** (are), from (from), **hafþe** (had), and **vaR** (were) are explained by the runic practice of Gotland.

6. The continued presence of both "þ" and "t" in medial and final position even after 1400, rather than "d" in Gotlandic inscriptions confirms the origin of the Kensington Rune Stone in Gotland almost on this point alone. These words on the Kensington Rune Stone are **farþ** (journey, **hafþe** (had), **veþ** (by), **röþe** (red), **bloþ** (blood) and **þeþ** (death) (See Lye Church inscription G 99 in the color section, plate 25).

7. The continued presence of "þ" for "t" in the initial position helps validate **optagelse** (taking up) and **teno** (this). In 1362, **opþagelse** (taking up) could never be considered to be **opdagelse** (discovery) since "þ = t" in the late 1300s in Gotland (Snædal 2002: 208).

8. Moltke (1949) asserted that "þ" stood for "t" on the Kensington Rune Stone, but Moltke avoided explaining that **deno** (this) was not to be found in Scandinavia dialects. This allowed him to claim that **opdagelse** (discovery) was proof of a modern forgery, claiming that "opdage" was not used until circa 1700. Actually Moltke's fellow Dane, Stautrup (1947: Vol 5 index), cites **opdage** (discover) in New Danish from the 1500's as a loan word.

9. The use of the gh-digraph on the Kensington Rune Stone is found on two Gotlandic inscriptions (Othem Church G 283 and Lärbro Church G 294).

10. The use of initial word divider after the first letter of the first word as in **g : öter** (Götalanders) is also found in two inscriptions (Othem Church G 282 and G 283) in Gotland (Snædal 2002).

11. The use of the Easter table for dating was unique to Gotland in medieval times, so it is a clear indicator that the Kensington Rune Stone inscription traits have their chief origin in Gotland.

12. The writer of the Kensington Rune Stone is placed from East Götaland due to the occurrence of the final "t" in **havet** (inland sea, sea) and the e-dialect, his knowledge of the Swedish laws, his knowledge of the matins from Vadstena Nunnery, East Götaland with the Kensington Rune Stone hybrid prayer "AVM: Save from evil."

Another point that merits mention is the significant advancement in the greater understanding of medieval language and runes. All the words on the Kensington Rune Stone that were not known to be Old Swedish in 1898, have since been found to be so. Ironically, the discovery of the Larsson Papers in March 2004, which were initially thought by many to be the final proof of forgery are in fact just the opposite. There will undoubtedly be more discoveries made now that the Kensington Rune Stone inscription has become an object of serious study.

The linguistic discoveries made in the last several years have lead to much better understanding of the message the carver intended. The following is the best translation of the inscription to date:

The Face:

1.

8 : g : öter : ok : 22 : norrmen : po :
Åtta göter and tjugotvå norrmän på
Eight Götalanders and 22 Norwegians on

2.

...o : opþagelsefarþ : fro :
(denna?) upptagelsefärd (= uppodlings- eller plundringsresa) från
(this?) reclaiming (or plundering) journey

3.

vinlanþ : of : vest : vi :
Vinland alltför väst. Vi
far to the west from Vinland. We

4.

hafþe : läger : veþ : 2 : sk⅃ar : en :
hade läger vid två …skylar??? en
had a camp by two shocks (shelters) ??? one

5.

þags : rise : norr : fro : þeno : sten :
dagsresa norrut från denna sten.
day's jouney from this stone.

6.

vi : var : ok : fiske : en : þagh : äptir :
Vi var och (= för att) fiska en dag. Efter (att)
We were fishing one day. After

7. ᛘᛁ : ᛯᛆᛘ : ᚼᛂᛘ : ᚠᛆᚿ : 10 : ᛘᛆᚿ : ᚱᛟᚦᛂ :

vi : kom : hem : fan : 10 : man : röþe :
vi kom hem fann vi tio man röda
we came home we found 10 men red

8. ᛆᚠ : ᛒᛚᛟᚦ : ᛟᚵ : ᚦᛂᚦ : AVM

af : bloþ : og : þeþ : AVM :
av blod och död. Ave Maria.
from blood and death. Ave Maria

9. ᚠᚱᛅᛂᛚᛋᛂ : ᛆᚠ : ᛁᛚᛚᚢ :

fräelse : af : illu :
Frails ifran undo.
Save from evil.

The face side of the Kensington Rune Stone inscription that contains the first nine lines of the inscripiton. (SFW)

"Eight Götalanders and 22 Norwegians on (this?) reclaiming (or plundering) journey far to the west from Vinland. We had a camp by two ??? one day's jouney from this stone. We were fishing one day. After we came home we found 10 men red from blood and death. Ave Maria. Save from evil."

The Side:

10.   ᚺᚯᚱ : ᛈ : ᛉᚷᚾᛊ : ᛉᛏ : ᚺᚷᛈᛏᛏ : ᚷᛏ : ᛊᛏ :

   här : 10 : mans : ve : havet : at : se :
   (det) är tio man vid havet för att se
   There are 10 men by the sea to look

11.   ᚯᛒᛏᛁᚱ : ᛉᚬᚱᛏ : ᛊᚴᛁᛒ : ᚠ : ᚦᚷᛉᚺ : ᚱᛁᛊᛏ :

   äptir : vore : skip : 14 : þagh : rise :
   efter våra skepp fjorton dag(ars) resa
   after our ships fourteen days journey

12.   ᚠᚱᛉᛉ : ᚦᛏᛈ : ᚤᚷ : ᚷᚷᚱ : ᚠᚠᚠ :

   from : þeno : öh : ahr : 1362 :
   från denna ö. År 1362.
   from this island. Year 1362.

The split side of the Kensington Rune Stone inscription contains the last three lines of the inscripiton. (SFW)

"There are 10 men by the sea to look after our ships fourteen days journey from this island. Year 1362."

One could argue that the context of the message indicates there are two inscriptions; one on the face and one on the side.

The Physical Aspects of the Kensington Rune Stone and the Weathering of the Inscription

The foundation of the case for authenticity lies with the physical evidence. The first step was to **document as many facts as possible** about the physical aspects of the stone including the weathering of the inscription. The next step was to **formulate interpretations that best fit the facts**. The final opinion about the age of the inscription is based upon a consideration of all the interpreted facts (See "The Geology of the Kensington Rune Stone," page 13). The following statements represent our conclusions about the most important physical aspects of the stone we have studied:

1. Root Leaching

The two white lineations on the glacial back side of the Stone are consistent with prolonged contact with young tree roots. Because of the striking similarity of the root leaching pattern on the Stone and the sketches made by three different witnesses (Olof Ohman in July 1909, Olof Ohman Jr. in April 1957, and Sam Olson in March 1910) who saw the roots around the Stone, it can be concluded with reasonable certainty that **the root leaching was made by the same tree roots under which the Stone was found.** In fact, if an earlier tree had roots in contact with the Stone then another, different root leaching pattern would be present. Another curious aspect of the root leaching is that the white lineations have never been discussed prior to our investigations. Surely they must have been noticed, but why are they not mentioned in any previous report or correspondence? The likely reason is that the story of the discovery was never questioned early on, making discussion of the root leaching pattern unnecessary. Decades later the story of the discovery was questioned by people like Erik Walgren and Johan Holvik. They also made no mention of the root leaching, which was either not noticed or simply ignored by doubters who would have had to find an alternate explanation for the marks.

2. Scratching Out of the Runes (Retooling)

The scratching out of the runes with a nail (retooling), reportedly by Olof Ohman shortly after the discovery, has led to confusion and bias. We are confident the runes were scratched out because of our own initial impression of the inscription's appearance. The scratches give the inscription a distinct, fresh-looking, recently carved appearance. Close inspection of the characters reveals weathering along the unscratched sides or walls of the grooves.

The well-developed rust-colored iron oxide deposits within this original groove on the split side have been cut through. Roughly 90% of the inscription has been scratched out or "retooled." (SFW)

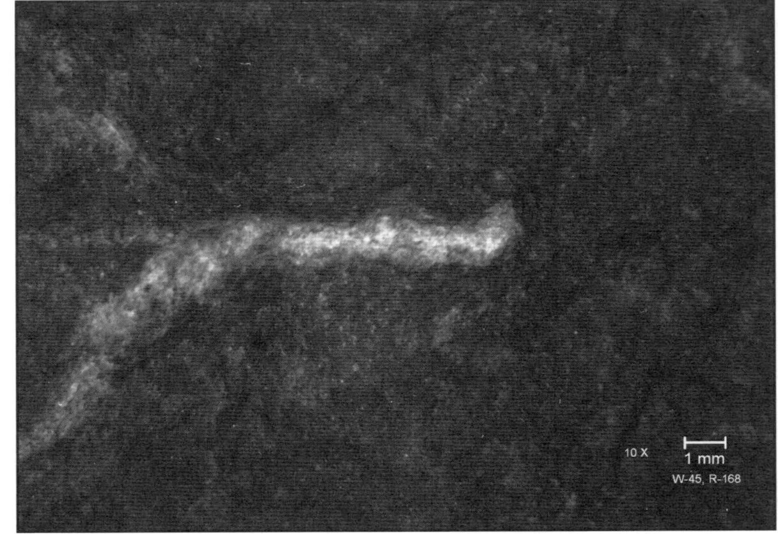

References to the runes being scratched out are documented at least 10 times by investigators over a 105-year period. The psychological effect upon investigators caused by the fresh appearance of the inscription is difficult to quantify. However, it has clearly caused bias about the age of the inscription and is an aspect of the controversy that has not been considered before. Based upon the initial impact the retooling had on us, the negative first impression of the inscription's age on investigators in the past must have been quite profound. The retooling is a critical factor that must be considered when evaluating the Stone. It falls upon doubters to give a reasonable explanation for why Ohman cleaned the inscription with a nail if he was involved in a hoax.

The retooling of the inscription is also important when considering potential weathering of the inscription *after* the discovery. Consider the myth of the Stone being used as a doorstep. If the Stone had been exposed to weathering from 1899 to 1907, when Holand took possession of it, we would expect some iron oxide deposits from freshly exposed pyrite crystals within the scratched out runes. Lack of observable iron oxide staining is consistent with Edward Ohman's testimony in 1949 that the stone "never was" used as a doorstep, and therefore was not exposed to weathering during this eight-year period.

3. Pyrite Evidence

Fortunately, Mr. Ohman did not scratch out the entire inscription. Several characters on the split side were not scratched and exhibit significant weathering. Most notable are iron oxide-coated pits within the grooves, produced by pyrite crystals that had completely weathered away. The Stone has not been in a weathering environment since its discovery, as evidenced by the lack of pyrite weathering in the bottom of the scratched out runes; the pyrite crystals had already weathered away when Ohman pulled the Stone from the ground. When we compare these pits with the still active-ly weathering pyrite crystals in the carved characters of the AVM Stone, it means **the pyrite in the Kensington Rune Stone inscription, as of June, 2005, would have taken at least twenty years to weather away**. Twenty years prior to the discovery of the Rune Stone Olof Ohman was still in Sweden (Ohman immigrated to the US in 1879). This means Olof Ohman could not have been involved with carving the Stone, making a 19th century hoax by Ohman impossible.

4. Mica Weathering

Based on comparison of the weathering rate of biotite mica in slate tombstones with the weathering of biotite in the Kensington Rune Stone, the inscription has been weathering for longer than about two hundred years. Our investigation has shown that the highly weathered biotite minerals on the two hundred-year-old slate tomb-stones had begun to fall off the surface. Since all the mica minerals on the original man-made surfaces (the entire split side, the contiguous flaked areas and the unscratched runes) have weathered away, the inscription must be at least two hundred years old, which puts the origin of the inscription back to at least the late 17th century.

5. Points to Ponder

A thorough analysis of the Kensington Rune Stone cannot be complete until a few important points are understood. There are reasons the Stone has been such a vexing mystery for over a century. Sitting in the 21st century with the benefit of hindsight makes the analysis much easier. The first point is that since the Rune Stone was found there have been amazing **advances in research science and information technology**. By leaning more on the scientific evidence as opposed to opinion, subjectivity is reduced and the question is considered more objectively, on the facts.

Another key problem has been the way many investigators have pursued their inves-tigations. Our research into these investigations showed that those who found the Rune Stone to be a hoax employed **improper method**. They started off with a con-clusion and then went looking for evidence to support it. This approach leads to incomplete and incorrect conclusions that have been repeated numerous times. The document search revealed that many investigators used this flawed approach, which is inherently biased and leads to unsupportable conclusions about the Stone.

> While the present writer has from the first time he saw the inscription never had any doubt upon this point, he

This statement on page 41 of Professor George T. Flom's April 1910 paper shows clearly that he formed an opinion about the Stone prior to any investigation. The same flawed method was employed by most researchers who concluded the inscription was a hoax. (Minnesota Historical Society)

These investigators failed to employ the **scientific method**. Scientific method dictates that facts are documented first, then a hypothesis or theory is formulated that best fits the facts. The next step is to test the theory, and re-test it. If the results are consistent and repeatable, then the theory has validity. This process was employed by Professor Newton Winchell in 1909-10, and then repeated in 2000 by Scott Wolter and other geologists. It should come as no surprise that their conclusions are consistent.

Remember that the method of investigation is divided along the lines of discipline. Those who have concluded the Stone is a hoax have been primarily linguists, runologists, historians, and archaeologists, all fields highly opinion driven and loosely referred to as "soft sciences." These are the same fields that our research found investigators employing improper method. For opinions to be as divided as they are there had to be a reason why opinions are as divided as they are; this difference in method appears to be the answer.

The document search also uncovered another reason for the flawed investigations of the past. It seems that the controversy over the Rune Stone often brought out the worst in people. Many have exhibited **bias and personal pique** that motivated them to put down others who disagreed with them, rather than objectively perform their research. Time and again problems of the human condition got in the way, and further clouded the controversy.

Olof Ohman

It is important to realize that standing at the center of the controversy is the credibility of the Stone's discoverer. Olof Ohman has been described by researchers, family, and friends, as a serious and honest man. The same individual emerges from the almost fifty known letters he wrote to family members in Sweden. Analysis of his library of over fifty books, magazines, and plat maps indicates he was an intelligent and well-read man. There is no evidence that suggest Ohman was a prankster or practical joker. It is well-documented that he repeatedly denied being involved in the creation of the inscription. In addition to the detailed notes made by Winchell from his conversations with Ohman, there are three documents where in Ohman made important statements; two were written responses to inquiries by Winchell during his investigation in 1910.

Ohman's first statement is at the start of his letter to Newton Winchell dated June 6, 1910. Ohman wrote a heated denial to the statements linguist Rasmus Anderson attributed to Andrew Anderson. Ohman began the letter by stating why he had not made any comments previously with regard to the authenticity of the inscription (See Timeline page 387).

In both the original June 6th, 1910 letter and the newspaper translation of Olof Ohman's letter to Newton Winchell, Ohman explained why he had not taken part in the discussion of the Rune Stone. (Minnesota Historical Society)

Kensington, Minn., June 6, 1910.
Prof. N. H. Winchell,
St. Paul, Minn.
My intention has been not to take part in any discussion of the Kensington rune stone, for the simple reason that I do not understand the far-fetched arguments which the learned offer in regard to the same. But when

The second example of a direct statement by Ohman appears in a translated letter he wrote to Winchell.

have made at Gunnar Johnson's when I built his house. I do not remember that I wrote any runes either there or anywhere else. And as to Gunnar

A transcribed letter from Olof Ohman to Newton Winchell written in the summer of 1910, in which Ohman denied ever carving runes. (Minnesota Historical Society)

From our perspective, this aspect of the controversy is pretty straightforward. If there was a hoax going on, then the discoverer of the Stone, Olof Ohman, must have been involved. There is no plausible explanation for how he could have unwittingly discovered somebody else's practical joke. Since Mr. Ohman denied making the inscription and never changed his position for thirty-seven years after he found the Stone, there are only two possibilities: he was either lying, or he was telling the truth. To say that he was a practical joker is simply an excuse to make him the "fall guy" for a hoax theory.

What many people seem to have missed is an obvious contradiction that has never really been properly addressed. Every person interviewed who ever met Mr. Ohman believed he was an honest man, including his neighbors, friends, family, and many of the Kensington Rune Stone investigators as well. Therefore, since Mr. Ohman said he didn't do it, it can't be a 19th century hoax.

> **32**
>
> But the question is again asked, What is the origin of the Kensington stone?—for the veracity of the finder is not doubted. There are witnesses to the fact that it

The top of page 32 of Professor George Flom's 1910 paper on the Kensington Rune Stone, where Professor Winchell underlined the statement during his review.

Those who have concluded that the Kensington Rune Stone is a fake have unwittingly committed an egregious error: they ignored the geological work of Newton Winchell. Professor Theodore Blegen's 1968 book about the Kensington Rune Stone is largely responsible for the present general opinion of the public that the Stone is a hoax. As detailed an investigation as Blegen performed, his conclusion suffers a fatal flaw that is hard to understand. Even though Mr. Blegen made extensive use of Winchell's field note-book whenever it helped to support his conclusion, he ignored Winchell's geological find-ings. Blegen was not alone in this regard. Everyone who has concluded the Stone is a fraud has also conveniently ignored or tried to marginalize the geological aspects. Perhaps it took over ninety years until the next detailed forensic geological examination took place because of diminished regard for the previous research.

The Conclusion

The Kensington Rune Stone question can also be considered as a problem of logic that begins with a simple premise: The Kensington Rune Stone is either a 19th century forgery or it is centuries old, presumably carved in the 14th century based on the date of the inscription. If the inscription is not a hoax, then each aspect of the Stone should yield evidence that is consistent with the inscription being centuries old, including the physi-cal aspects of the Stone, the language and runes, the honesty and integrity of Olof Ohman, and the history of the Stone since its discovery. The same must also be true if the Stone is a hoax. Based on the argument of logic, the answer to the question should become obvious if the facts are thoroughly researched and carefully documented. After careful consideration of the facts, the preponderance of the evidence in every aspect points in one clear direction. **The Kensington Rune Stone was not carved in the 19th century**.

For a long time it seemed that people thought the truth about the Stone could only be found in the runological and linguistic aspects of the inscription. The language and runes certainly are important, but the work performed to date by both American and Scandinavian scholars is far from complete. Far too little work in this area has been per-formed due in large part to the fact that the Stone was dismissed long ago. Since the phys-ical evidence indicates that the inscription cannot be a 19th century hoax, then the inscription must also make sense. The discovery of the Larsson papers in 2004 provided proof that there is more information to be discovered about the language and runes. We are confident that if a sincere effort is made by linguists, they will find additional evidence.

The history of the Kensington Rune Stone has played itself out like a dysfunctional courtroom drama. In this case, the most important witness with reliable factual information is the Stone itself. As Erik Wahlgren said in his 1958 book, *"The stone must either stand or fall on its own merit."* As Winchell, and authors Wolter, and Nielsen have discovered, the Stone stands quite tall and has a lot to say. For more than one hundred years however, few others have bothered to listen. What this all means depends on who you talk to. For us, it seems appropriate to repeat the words that Professor Newton Winchell wrote to Hjalmar Holand on August 10, 1911 as he tried put the status of the Kensington Rune Stone situation into perspective. His summary is a good as anyone's.

The final paragraph in the letter N. H. Winchell wrote Hjalmar Holand on August 10, 1911, summarized the controversy pretty well. (Minnesota Historical Society)

"I think the stone will withstand these loud preliminary skirmishes in Norway, and when the sober, thoughtful investigators of that country have had time to carefully poise the issue on the real evidence, the voice of Norway will be heard in defense of the stone, and finally the Norwegians, whether in America or in the old country, will approve and boast of the Kensington rune stone as their most valuable historic relic.

Very Truly,

N. H. Winchell"

The evidence makes a powerful case for authenticity of the Kensington Rune Stone inscription. However, the most compelling proof of all came to light in January 2005 with the discovery of two amazing codes within the inscription. These discoveries evolved after our years of extensive research into the history of Scandinavia and runic inscriptions from medieval times. As has been presented, it was on the island of Gotland that the unique runic characters of the Kensington Rune Stone and the Larsson rune rows, were found. This in turn led to the desire to learn more about the history of the island and the people who lived there during the 13th and 14th centuries. The presence of a Cistercian Monastery, Gutnalia, founded on Gotland in 1164 from its mother abbeys in Småland and East Götaland became the focus. The photo library of the Kensington Rune Stone inscription that was generated in 2002 identified numerous previously unidentified features. With the Cistercians in mind, we considered the possible significance of these mysterious punches and crosses. Gradually, a picture emerged that has come together into what now appears to be a perfect fit. After considering this new information we now propose our thesis as to who carved the Kensington Rune Stone, and why they came to North America.

Post-Script

The La Vérendrye Stone

The authors have presented compelling evidence that the Kensington Rune Stone inscription was created by a person affiliated with the Cistercians and the Teutonic Knights (likely a chaplain) who was acquainted with the runic practice on the Island of Gotland during medieval times. The next question to pose is how the Stone was buried in the land that eventually belonged to Olof Ohman. If we continue with the idea that the Teutonic Knights and the Hanse were closely involved during the middle 1300s then a strongly plausible scenario emerges that involves one of the most mysterious artifacts in history: the La Vérendrye Stone. While debate about the Kensington Rune Stone raged over the past century the La Vérendrye Stone lurked in the minds of investigators as somehow being connected. Winchell, Holand, Blegen, and others speculated about a possible connection if the stone was carved in runes.

In 1736, the French explorer Pierre La Vérendrye set out from Montreal, Canada, to explore the continent along with his two sons Charles and Louis Joseph. In addition to trapping and trading with the Indians, La Vérendrye had another purpose for his trip. He set out to claim land for France. To establish proof of his claim he buried up to twelve lead plates in the ground across North America. In 1738, La Vérendrye gave a lead plate to a Mandan chief at what is now Pierre, South Dakota.

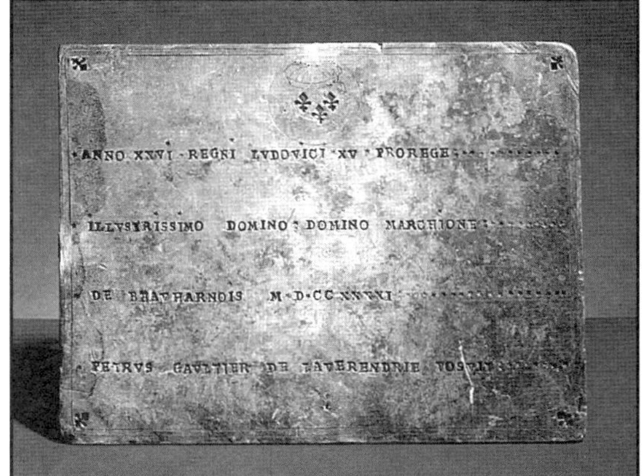

Discovered on February 16, 1913 near Pierre, South Dakota, this plaque was cast in Quebec and transported to the Missouri River by Louis-Joseph La Vérendrye. The text indicates that Pierre Gaultier de La Vérendrye intended to claim possession of the territories discovered: *"Year 26 of the reign of Louis XV. For the King, most illustrious lord. By the Marquis de Beauharnois, 1741. Placed by Pierre Gaultier de La Vérendrye."* Pierre's sons, Chevalier and Louis La Vérendrye, buried this lead plaque. Carved on the back of the plaque it reads, *"Placed by Chevalier and Louis La Vérendrye March 30, 1743."* (Photographs courtesy of the South Dakota Historical Society)

In 1743 the French Canadian explorer brothers Chevalier and Louis La Vérendrye, sons of Pierre, buried an inscribed lead tablet on a bluff overlooking present-day Pierre. Telling the local inhabitants they were commemorating harmony with the native peoples, they were in fact claiming the area for France, the land of the entire future Louisiana Purchase.

The 7" x 8" lead plaque was re-discovered by Fort Pierre high school students in 1913, and is now on display at the South Dakota Cultural Heritage Center in Pierre. It reads, *"In the twenty-sixth year of the reign of Louis XV, the most illustrious Lord, the Lord Marquis of Beauharnois being Viceroy, 1741, Peter Gaultier De La Vérendrye placed this."* The Vérendrye Plaque is considered one of the most significant historical finds in the northwestern United States. Today the site of the plate is a national historic landmark.

In 1742, the La Vérendrye sons left Fort la Reine in Manitoba, Canada, for Fort Mandan. From there, they headed west on horseback to find the Pacific Ocean. On their first visit to the Mandan village in the 1730s, horses had not yet reached the northern plains from the Spanish settlements in the Southwest. Thanks to the horses the sons went on to see the Rocky Mountains near Pincher Creek to the south of the present city of Calgary, Alberta, on January 1, 1743. They apparently planted a smaller lead plaque that was dated March 30, 1743, along the Old Man River, that would eventually be discovered in 1906. This plaque, while smaller, has the same date as the South Dakota plaque, March 30, 1743, but would not be recognized for what it was until 1961 (Parry 1988). Both plaques have the same stamped inscription text on the front face, but with unique spacing. The back side appears to have been carved with a knife by the same individual with identical texts but unique letter spacing and variations.

Canadian researchers believe that the Pincher Creek plaque is a modern promotional copy of the Fort Pierre plaque. The Pincher Creek plaque if actually found in 1906, a fact not reported until the 1960s, can hardly be a copy of the Fort Pierre plaque that was found seven years later. When this book went to press the location of the 1906 plate was unknown. The authors are currently working with Canadian historians to locate the artifact.

Chevalier and Louis La Vérendrye placed a different plaque near Pincher Creek, at the foot of the Rocky Mountains in Alberta, Canada that was discovered in 1906. This plaque has the same text on the front as the Fort Pierre plaque. However, the spacing and variations of the inscription carved onto the back indicates that it was carved by the same person at a different time. (Pincher Creek plaque images courtesy of the *Pincher Creek Echo*, February 9, 1961)

The Ft. Pierre plaque found in 1913 was likely brought back by the party after being inscribed at Old Man River, and buried or lost at a later date at Ft. Pierre. According to his journal, their father also presented a plaque at Ft. Pierre to the Mandan chief residing there in 1738. This plaque was not buried and has not yet been found. La Vérendrye's sons made another important discovery on their journey to the Rockies that would set in motion the mystery that finally appears to be solved.

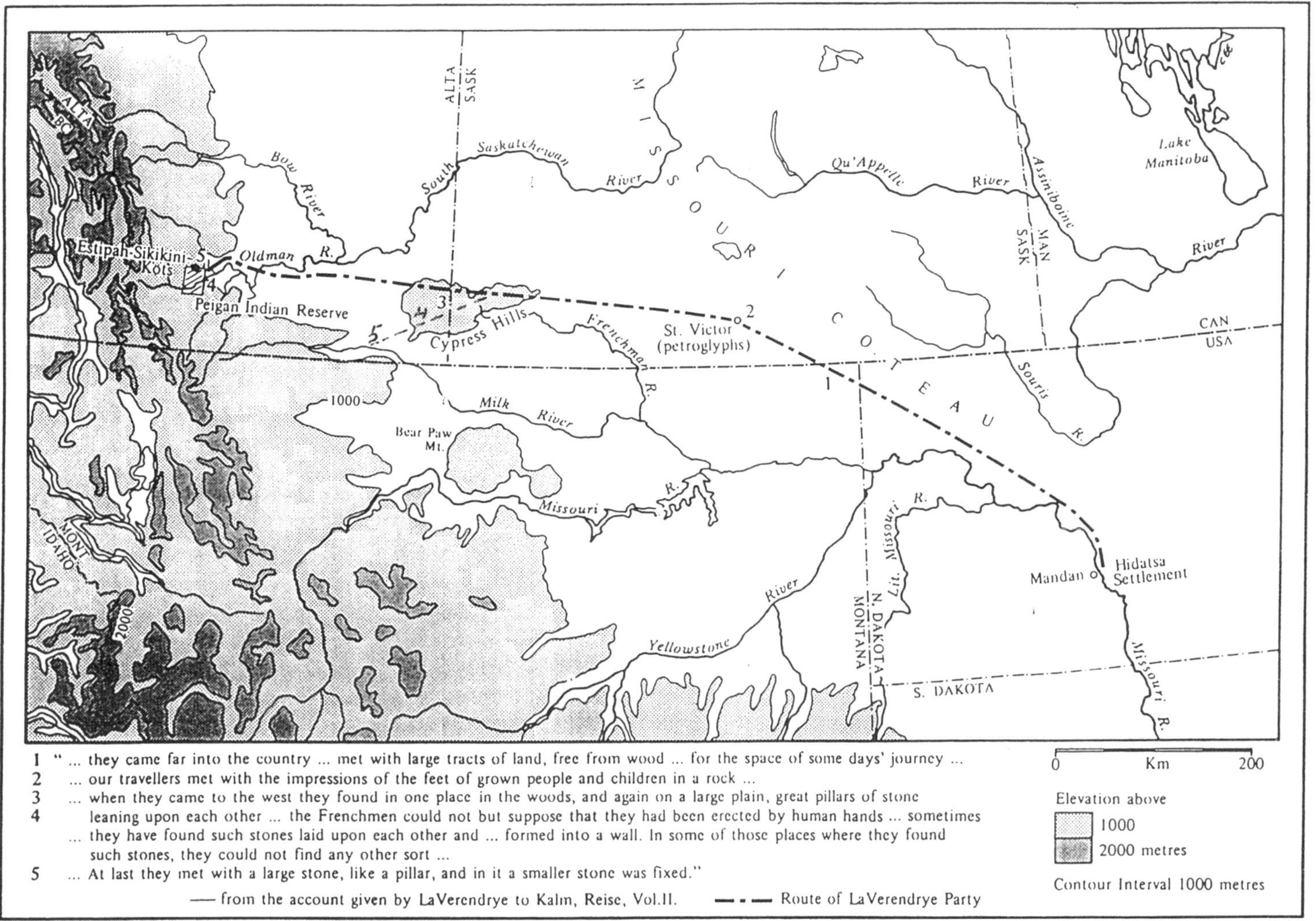

The dashed line marks the route made by brothers Chevalier and Louis Joseph La Vérendrye to the Rocky Mountains near Calgary, Alberta, in 1742. 1 denotes the plains, 2 is the site of the feet and hands in rock at St. Victor, 3 and 4 denote the Cypress Hills where a wall of columns was found with wooded hills and 5 is the site on the Milk River with the pillar thought by some to have held the La Vérendrye Stone. Map is courtesy of Buff Parry of Edmonton, Alberta, Canada. (Buff Parry, 1988)

The La Vérendrye party's route led across the plains from Fort Mandan to St. Victor, where the hands and feet inscribed in rock can be seen. As they continued west the wooded cypress hills could be seen with its fence-like wall of tall natural limestone pillars in series. Later they camped in sight of the Rocky Mountains. They apparently returned beside the Milk River, a tributary of the Missouri River. At a spot just north of the present Montana border near the top of one of the limestone columns they found a small recess that appeared to have been cut into the column. Inside this opening they found a stone that was inscribed on both sides and was approximately 1 by $\frac{1}{2}$ feet in size. They removed the inscribed stone and took it with them back to their fort in Manitoba and subsequently delivered the stone to their father.

Pierre La Vérendrye's sons reportedly found an inscribed stone inside the opening at the top of this limestone column found along the Milk River in Alberta, Canada, in 1743. The man standing next to the column is local resident Ronald Bear. This photo is courtesy of Warren Dexter who took the photo in 1982. In a telephone interview with author Wolter on June 21, 2005, Mr. Dexter said he revisited this site in 1998 and that petroglyphs had been damaged by gunfire from vandals who used the column for target shooting. Further, he said other sculptures on adjacent rock had been destroyed by river erosion that undercut the cliff allowing them to fall into the river. The column now stands within inches of the cliff and eventually will suffer a similar fate. (Photograph courtesy of Warren Dexter)

In 1743, the father, Pierre La Vérendrye, returned to Quebec with the strange inscribed stone and after examination by Jesuits the language was tentatively identified as Tartaric script. Subsequently, it was shipped to France, addressed to the secretary of state of France, Philippeaux Conte de Maurepas.

At a dinner six years later in 1749, Pierre La Vérendrye met a Swedish scientist named Pehr Kalm. Kalm had been sent to North America by the famous Swedish botanist Carl Linné to perform research and collect botany samples. During this fateful meeting, which took place at the Chateau St. Louis in Quebec City, La Vérendrye discussed the inscribed stone with Kalm. In Kalm's memoirs entitled, *Peter Kalm's Travels, Volumes 1 to 4*, he wrote what La Vérendrye had told him about the discovery of the stone. "*...stone was fixed, which was covered on both sides with an unknown characters. This stone, which was* *about a foot of French measure in length, and between four to five inches broad, they broke loose and carried to Canada with them, whence it was sent to France to the secretary of state, the Count de Mauripas. What became of it afterwards is unknown, but they think it is yet preserved in his collection. Several of the Jesuits, who have seen and handled this stone in Canada, unanimously affirm, that the letters on it are the same with those which, in the books containing the accounts of Tataria and are called Tatarian character; and that, on comparing both together, they found them perfectly alike. All that the Indians could say of these stones was that they had been in those places since time immemorial. The places where the pillars stood were near nine hundred French miles* (approximately 1600 standard miles) *westward of Montreal."* (*Archaelologia: Miscellaneous Tracts relating to Antiquity*, Society of Antiquaries of London, Volume VIII) Kalm's memoirs serve as the first reported account of the stone's discovery by La Vérendrye, who died just a few months after their meeting.

The upper script is from along the Yenisey River, in Siberia (Moltke in Brøndsted 1950). When compared to the normalized runic rendition on the lower line, the possibility exists that the inscription could be either runic or Tatarian.

A runic rendition of Tatarian script from the Yenisey River in Siberia shows how easy it would have been for the priests in Canada to have thought the script was runic even if it was Tatarian script or in fact vice versa.

One should keep an open mind about the origin of the stone because both the Cistercians and the Teutonic Knights were in close contact with the Mongols in Russia during the 1200s. In 1240, the Teutonic Knights and the Poles were defeated by the Mongols in eastern Germany at Lieglitz. After this battle and another in Hungary, the Mongols turned back to Mongolia upon the death of the Khan. Except for Russia, they never returned to Europe again. Obviously, any number of mysterious items from the East could have been acquired during the 13th century from the Mongols. It must also be remembered that a trade route extended for centuries from Siberia across Alaska then down to the east of the Rockies and subsequently across the plains all the way to Alabama. If the stone's script is Tartaric, it could be just another trade item that for some reason was venerated by the Cree Indians living along the Milk River.

The Teutonic Knights also kept Mediterranean contacts to the east until they moved their base from Venice to Marienburg in Prussia, in 1309, only two years after the fall of their brother organization, the Knights Templar, in France on Friday, October 13, 1307.

We postulate that the Kensington party consisted of men backed by mutual Cistercian and Teutonic Knight interests, carved and buried the Kensington Rune Stone as a land claim to provide future proof of discovery just as La Vérendrye's two sons did further west roughly 380 years later. The confirmation code of the pentadic date within the inscription would have prevented any successful future alteration, thereby protecting the 1362 date. The evidence that the Kensington Rune Stone was buried immediately after being carved is supported by the fact that the surface of the Stone exhibits no physical evidence of being placed upright in the ground. The relatively fast-weathering white triangular calcite on the lower left face side exhibits no evidence of differential weathering, which would be present had it been exposed for a prolonged period.

This Viking age rune stone on exhibit in the Statens Historiska Museum in Stockholm, Sweden, exhibits a clearly defined boundary below the inscription where the stone was in the ground. The Kensington Rune Stone does *not* exhibit any obvious weathering profile or boundary line that would indicate it was set upright in the ground for a prolonged period of time. (SFW)

Our land claim thesis might also provide a logical explanation for the numerous unexplained holes in large glacial boulders found in the vicinity of the Kensington Rune Stone discovery site. Hjalmar Holand believed these holes were used by Norse explorers to secure iron rings which were then used to moor their boats. The location of many of the holes are at elevations, both above and below past and present waterways making his "mooring stone" theory highly problematic. The practical and plausibility problems exposed Holand, and the Rune Stone, to intense criticism from opponents. However, the fact that many of the holes have been documented to predate the European settlement leaves open the possibility of a connection to the Norse. We believe there is a more plausible explanation for the holes.

If the intention was indeed a land claim then there must have been a method for relocating the buried stone(s) at some point in the future. Perhaps the holes were cut into glacial boulders and bedrock found throughout the Midwest to provide a "bread crumb" trail for a returning party. Many of the holes reportedly follow waterways and would be logical routes for early explorers. To relocate the area of a buried land claim stone may have been as simple as a difference in the depths of the cut holes. Once an area was identified the other marker stones could then have been located to form a grid. The next step could have been to plot intersecting lines and find the previously buried stone. During a preliminary review by the authors of the known holes found in glacial boulders in the vicinity of the Kensington Rune Stone discovery site, a surprising discovery was made. Researchers Judi Rudebush and Dale Johnson generated a map that plotted the location of several stones with triangular holes in the vicinity of the Ohman Farm. We drew three lines between the stones and they all intersected at the approximate spot where the Rune Stone was found. This is of course just a theory that needs to be developed by compiling and analyzing data from the hundreds of known holes in rocks found across the Midwest. Validation of this theory would be certain if another rune stone were found!

The triangular hole cut into this large glacial boulder is located on "Skraeling Hill" at the Ohman farm near Kensington, Minnesota. In this 1941 photo, Hjalmar Holand points to another triangular hole in a boulder around which a rock pile was made on the Nils Flaaten farm. The location of both boulders can be used along with other boulders with holes to plot lines that intersect at the approximate location of the Kensington Rune Stone discovery site. (SFW and the Wisconsin Historical Society)

This satellite photo shows the location of ten glacial boulders with triangular holes in the vicinity of the Ohman Farm. Three lines can be drawn through these marked holes that intersect at the actual location where the Kensington Rune Stone was discovered. The Flaaten 1 boulder was moved to its present location when the park was developed in the early 1980s. The original position of this boulder was located using photographs taken in the 1941.

Our theory of a land claim in the Kensington area is bolstered by the fact it is a unique location in North America since it is the apex of a three-watershed system. The watersheds between the Mississippi, Great Lakes basin, and the Red River valley all converge near Kensington and this site would have served as a strategic outpost. In the early 1800s, the area was the best hunting grounds in all the plains, and various tribes shared this territory that marked the border zone between the open plains and the dense woodland forests.

It is also possible that it could have been a Cistercian and Teutonic Knight party from Gotland who not only carved the Kensington Rune Stone, but they could also have carved another runic inscription and placed it in the limestone column at the Milk River. Why they chose to bring the Milk River stone this far into North America is unknown, but at least the journey across the plains and back would have been relatively easy going by following the Missouri river system. The fate of the La Vérendrye stone upon its arrival in France is open to speculation. The French may have hidden or possibly destroyed the stone, to ensure their Mississippi Territory could not be subject to an earlier Scandinavian claim. What is known is that the stone was placed in the column prior to 1743. Until evidence is presented that supports an alternate hypothesis, the Kensington party stands as one of the strong candidates, together with a Siberian trade scenario. As this book goes to press the authors are continuing their investigation into the whereabouts of the La Vérendrye stone, regardless of what type of script it contains.

Who Owns the Kensington Rune Stone?

The Kensington Rune Stone is an amazing artifact for many different reasons. It has touched the lives of many people across three centuries, and if it could talk, the Stone would have interesting stories to tell. One of the most interesting stories would be the account of the conversation between Olof Ohman and Hjalmar Holand that August day in 1907 when Mr. Holand took possession of the Stone. Mr. Ohman apparently thought little of the Stone when Holand first came along. They agreed that no money changed hands, and it's safe to assume that Ohman believed what the experts had told him nine years earlier—the Stone was a fraud. What harm would it do to let the obviously sharp-minded researcher take the Stone and study it? He probably thought that it wasn't doing anything constructive sitting inside the granary shed collecting dust, so why not?

It's also safe to assume that when Holand left the farm that there was enough good will between the two of them that Ohman believed Holand would eventually make things right with him. Did that happen? Apparently not. In fact, a series of documents and letters between 1908 and 1930 outline a sequence of events that left issues unresolved. One of the most interesting questions that has never been answered is: Who owns the Kensington Rune Stone? We asked ourselves who owned the Stone after reading what appears to be the first letter Hjalmar Holand wrote to Professor N. H. Winchell at the Minnesota Historical Society, dated August 3, 1908. (See timeline page 410)

The question of ownership begins with the initial discovery by Olof Ohman. There has never been any doubt that the Rune Stone was discovered on Ohman's land. He unearthed the Stone and it became his personal property. The Kensington Rune Stone was first taken to Kensington, then it traveled to Chicago, and eventually was returned to the Ohman farm in the spring of 1899. From that point, the Stone sat idle until the pivotal event regarding ownership occurred in August, 1907. There is no doubt that Holand took physical custody of the Stone from a willing Ohman on that initial meeting.

What is in doubt is the arrangement between them. It is an interesting choice of words for Holand to say that Ohman "presented me with the Stone." There is no evidence that any written agreement was made between them, and whatever oral understanding there was became muddled soon after. In 1908 when his first book was published, *De Norske Settlementers Historie*, Holand proclaimed himself the owner of the Stone and presented a copy of the book to Ohman. Holand then exercised what he thought was his right to ownership on January 11, 1910, when he offered to sell the Kensington Rune Stone to the Minnesota Historical Society for $5000.

An excerpt from the first page of the January 1, 1910 letter Holand wrote to Professor Winchell. (Minnesota Historical Society) *"In reply to your inquiry of today I will say that my price on the Runestone is $5000.00."*

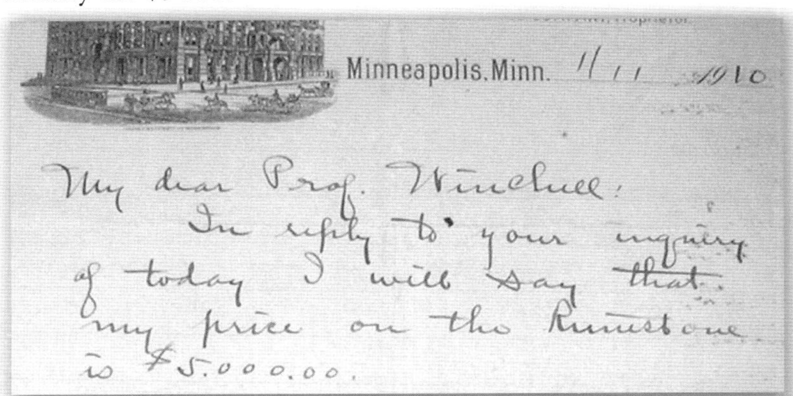

In addition to the steep price tag, Mr. Holand also offered an impassioned sales pitch about the merits of the Stone. He expounded on the virtues of the Stone, including its rightful place in history and the appropriateness of having it permanently housed at the Society. He also made it clear in his January 11, 1910 letter that, at least in his mind, he was the Stone's rightful owner.

An excerpt from the second page of the January 11, 1910 letter Holand wrote to Newton Winchell. (Minnesota Historical Society) *"I have, however, decided that I would not avail myself of my position as owner of the stone to ask a higher price."*

The Minnesota Historical Society apparently became suspicious about Holand's claim of ownership and decided to look into the artifact's provenance. With Winchell heading up the investigation, the Society authorized him to make three trips to the Kensington area. Winchell investigated several questions related to the Stone and the issues surrounding the transaction between Ohman and Holand. After several interviews with Mr. "O" and other individuals, Winchell made an entry into his field notebook on December 2, 1909 stating he'd received confirmation of Ohman's intent when he turned the Stone over to Holand.

Entry made on December 2, 1909, on page twelve of Winchell's field notebook. (Minnesota Historical Society) *"Mr. Sam Oleson confirms the statement of Ohman, that the stone was not given to Holand for his personal property."*

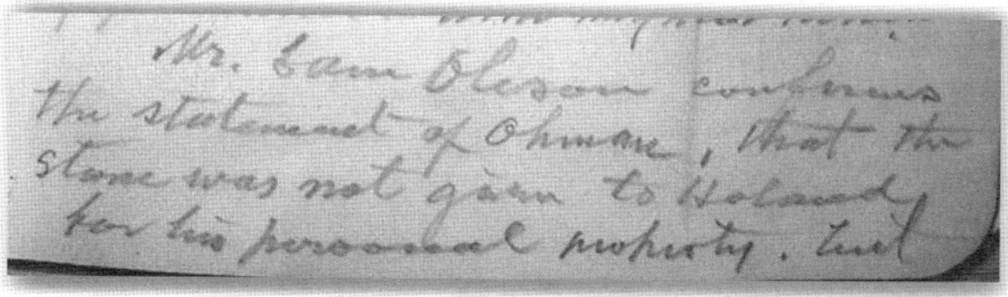

At the end of Winchell's field investigations, the Society found itself in a very sticky predicament. On one hand, Holand was offering the Stone—a significant addition to the Society's collection whether it was genuine or not—for sale. On the other hand, their own investigation revealed that Ohman had not sold or relinquished ownership of the Stone to Holand. While neither party denied that Holand took physical custody of the Stone from a willing Ohman, the understanding between them of the Stone's future most certainly was unclear. Holand justified his actions in a couple ways. First, he repeatedly wrote about how much research he did to prove the Stone's authenticity. Second, there was no reminder from Ohman, since there is no evidence or documentation that Holand ever spoke or corresponded with him for nearly fourteen years after Holand took his affidavit in July of 1909. Whether the void in communication between the two was by design or circumstance is unclear, but it does seem odd that Holand wouldn't have periodically informed Ohman of his progress and intentions. If the arrangement had been clear, then the sequence of events outlined in several important documents likely would not have occurred. In fact, it is obvious that things were not at all amicable between them. During the Society's research into the Stone's ownership they received a letter from Ohman, translated into English, and dated May 7, 1910, that spelled out his personal position on Holand and the Kensington Rune Stone in no uncertain terms.

Page two of the March 7, 1910 letter written by Sam Olson for Olof Ohman to the Minnesota Historical Society. (See timeline page 417) (Minnesota Historical Society) *"I further will ask you to please retain the Rune Stone until Mr. Holand has settled this question of disposing same with me, and the Norwegian Historical Society."*

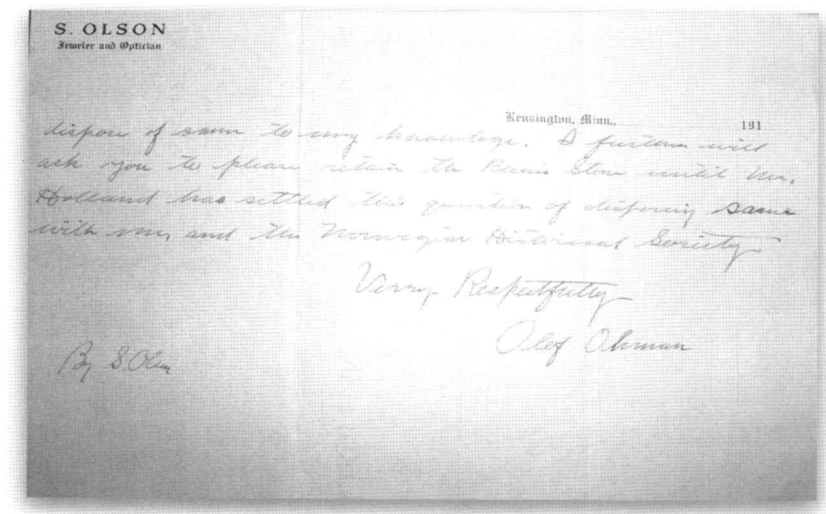

On June 21, 2004 the original draft of the letter written by Ohman in Swedish was discovered among Ohman family documents. Olof Ohman's descendants in Minnesota had saved the letter, unaware of its significance.

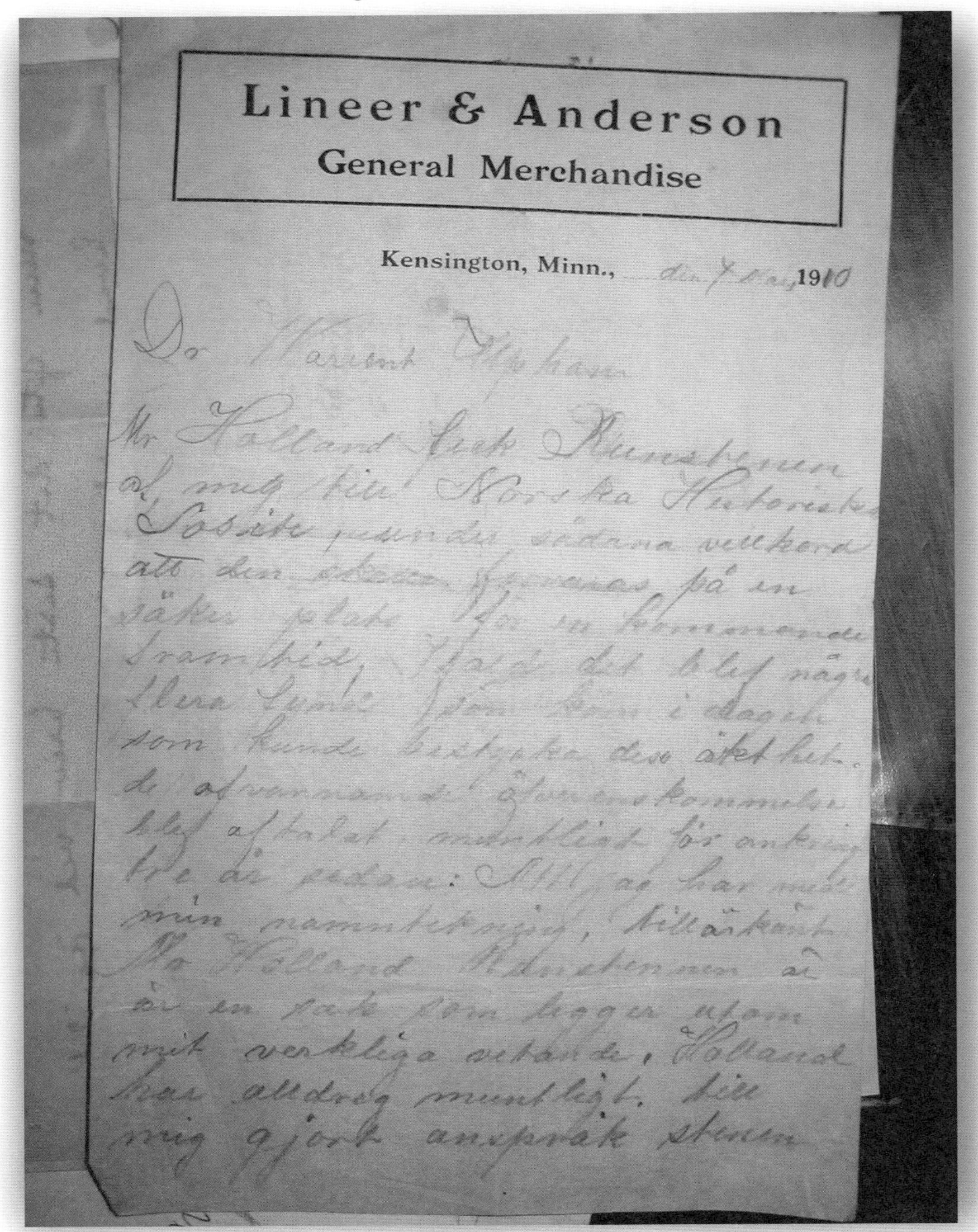

The original draft of the March 7, 1910, letter Olof Ohman wrote to Warren Upham, found among numerous personal documents retained by the descendants of Olof Ohman on June 21, 2004. (See page 417 for translation.) (Courtesy of the Ohman Family)

The Society apparently never informed Holand of this letter, though it prompted Winchell to demand Holand to clarify his claim of ownership with some type of documentation.

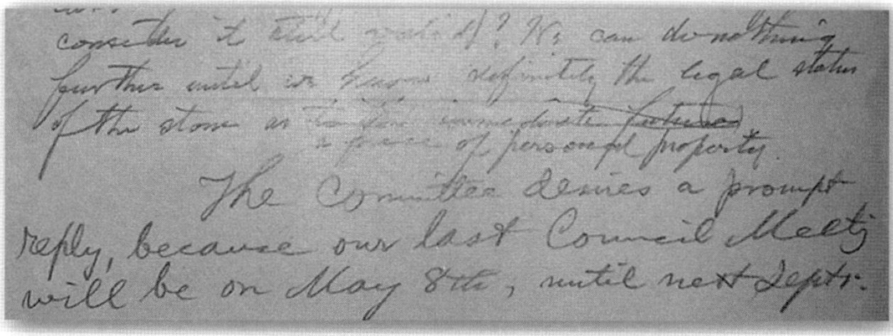

Museum Committee Letter to Holand, authored by Newton Winchell, dated April 15, 1911. (Minnesota Historical Society) *"We can do nothing further until we know definitely the legal status of the stone as a piece of personal property. The Committee desires a prompt reply, because our last Council meeting will be on May 8th, until next Sept(ember)."*

While waiting for Holand's reply, the Society did what they could to clear the way toward acquiring the Stone. Andrew A. Fossum and Torbjorn A. Sattre were sent to visit Ohman and purchase his rights to the Stone. They agreed to a down payment of $10 with an additional $90 to be paid when, and if, an agreement was reached with Holand. Fossum and Sattre completed the first phase of the Ohman agreement on April 19, 1911.

Bill of sale between Olof Ohman and the Minnesota Historical Society, dated April 19, 1911. (Minnesota Historical Society)

The Society surely struggled with this whole dilemma. Holand relentlessly pressured the Society to make a decision, and wasn't the least bit shy expressing his displeasure with the continuing delays. The issue was further clouded by doubts of the Stone's genuineness by some members of the Executive Council. Fate seemed written between the lines with regard to the Society's decision to pursue the Stone, given the ominous tone in the letter Winchell sent to Holand on April 30, 1911.

```
think would be acceptable to the Museum Committee.  You must understand

that, while personally I think the stone is valid and vindicated, I wish

to have unanimous consent to our action in the Committee and also in

the Executive Council.


                                    Very truly,

                                        N. H. Winchell,
```

Museum Committee letter to Holand dated April 30, 1911. (Minnesota Historical Society)

After what surely must have been a heated debate, the Society voted to return the Stone to Holand. The original letter sent to Holand was presumably destroyed in the fire at his home in 1934. However, the committee notes outline the reasons they declined to purchase the Stone. Notably missing is any reference to the issue of ownership.

A page of notes used for a letter from N. H. Winchell to H. R. Holand on May 9, 1911. (Minnesota Historical Society)

"At the meeting of the Council, May 8, 1911, it was ordered that, as the option has expired the stone be returned to Mr. Holand. The objections to the continuation of investigation, according to the within plan were:

"1. Doubt whether the Society had the right to invest the money of the state in that way.
2. The stone is fraudulent.
3. The price (5,000 doll[ar]s) is too high.

"The only good objection was that of Mr. Bailey viz the expense of the trip to Europe would be probably about $2000, which, with the purchase, would require $7,000 which was more than the Society could raise. NHW."

This letter prompted an angry reply from Holand, who threatened legal action if the Stone was not returned to him immediately.

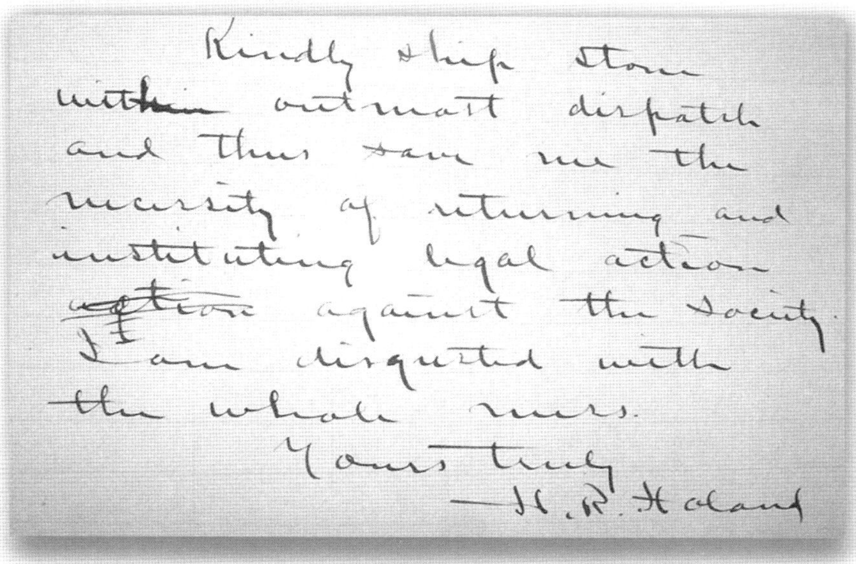

Page 2 of the May 12, 1911 letter Holand wrote to the Minnesota Historical Society. (Minnesota Historical Society) *"Kindly ship stone with outmost dispatch and thus save me the necessity of returning and instituting legal action against the Society. I am disgusted with the whole mess."*

In reading Holand's words it is clear that, at least in his mind, he believed he had clear title to the Stone. After receiving the Stone from the Society, Holand left for Europe to pursue his investigations of the inscription. Since the Society never acquired the Stone, they never paid Olof Ohman the $90 balance that was a part of their purchase agreement with him. Their tentative agreement of April 19, 1911 was invalid. Andrew Fossum's opinion seemed to sum up the situation succinctly.

The top of page 1 of the May 15, 1911 Fossum letter to Minnesota Historical Society (Minnesota Historical Society) *"If we had known that the Minn. Hist. Society would not make any use of the right to the stone, we should not have bought it."*

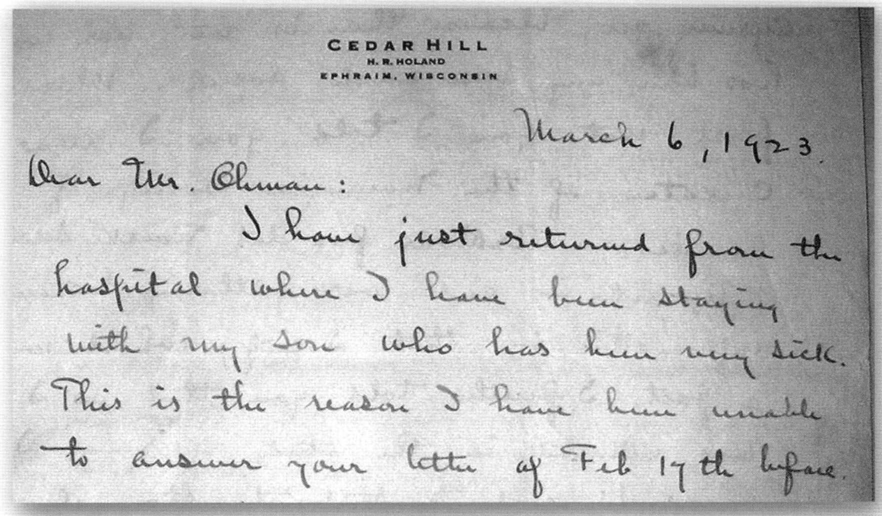

An excerpt from page two of the May 15, 1911 Fossum letter to the Minnesota Historical Society. (Minnesota Historical Society) *"It is my opinion that if the Hist. Soc. will not use the right to the stone, it should [have] returned the papers to Mr. Ohman…"*

As the days turned into years one can only imagine the frustration and anger Olof Ohman must have felt. Not only did he feel cheated by Hjalmar Holand, but he also endured the scorn and ridicule of many people in the Kensington community and around the world who suspected him of being involved in a hoax. Most people assumed that Ohman let the issue go after the fiasco with the Minnesota Historical Society. He most certainly did not!

On April 9, 2003, Mel and Mary Conrad from Kensington, Minnesota came forward with some very interesting information. They brought out an Ohman family scrapbook that had been saved in a bank vault in Kensington. Inside the scrapbook were three letters that dealt directly with the issue of the Stone's ownership. On March 6, 1923, Hjalmar Holand wrote a letter to Olof Ohman, in English, and explained his position with regard to the Stone. He told Ohman that he only wanted to be paid for research at the Minnesota Historical Society, but did not tell Ohman that he had offered to sell it to the Society for $5000. As was often his custom, Holand began his letter to Ohman with a "woe is me" story.

Excerpt of the March 6, 1923 letter from Hjalmer Holand in reply to Olof Ohman. (Courtesy of the **Ohman Family**) *"I have just returned from the hospital where I have been staying with my son who has been very sick. This is the reason I have been unable to answer your letter of Feb. 17ᵗʰ before."*

Holand was obviously responding to an inquiry from Ohman about the Stone. In his customary, witty way Holand tap-danced his way around Ohman's inquiry with empty promises.

The end of the March 6, 1923 letter from Holand to Ohman. (Courtesy of the Ohman Family)
"If circumstances should so shape themselves that I should later obtain some compensation for all I have spent on this research – if this should happen (which I don't expect) and if you are then in need, I shall be glad to give you something in consideration of your part in the matter. In the meantime you are in a better position to help me than I you."

Olof Ohman and Hjalmar Holand pictured together at Fahlin's Point on Oscar Lake, Minnesota, on June 1, 1927. The uncomfortable body language of the two men appears to make sense in light of the contentious circumstances surrounding ownership of the Rune Stone at that time. (Photo courtesy of the Runestone Museum)

By the end of 1927, the relationship between the two men had deteriorated. On June 21, 2004, two letters written by Holand to Ohman surfaced when members of the Ohman family brought forth several boxes of personal items that belonged to Olof and Karin. Unlike the 1923 letter, these letters were written in

Holand's native Norwegian. It's unclear why Holand switched languages, but it was intentional, and it could be argued that it was a deliberate attempt by Holand to send some kind of subtle message. Regardless, Ohman did not trust Holand and was in no mood to cooperate with him.

It is quite clear that Olof Ohman had lost all trust in Hjalmar Holand, based on the beginning of this January 1st, 1928 Holand letter to Ohman, written in Norwegian. (Courtesy of the Ohman Family)
"I have received your letter in which you say that you are not convinced that Dr. Hoegh's papers are lost and that you therefore refuse to write a new statement about finding the Runestone. No one will naturally hold you responsible for this, but you can well understand that a man's papers live on after his death. I can't believe therefore that you yourself think it is a valid ground to refuse to sign (or endorse) the statement." (Translation by Jim Belgum).

In 1930, Ohman had reached the end of his rope with Holand, and made one final attempt to get the Stone back. This time however, he obtained legal help since he obviously felt he would get nowhere by dealing with Holand directly. Mr. Holand responded to the attorney's inquiry by telling him that the Stone was already sold and that he would not give Ohman any compensation. He said that Ohman had slandered him, then quoted Shakespeare to make his point, mocking Ohman.

The end of the January 13, 1930 Holand letter to the Ohman family attorneys. (Courtesy of the Ohman Family) "*I used to think that if I ever received anything for it I would remember Mr. Ohman with a part of the amount. However, later I heard reports from different quarters that Mr. Ohman was slandering me. His misrepresentations even crept into the press. I therefore decided that charity in that direction was wasted. You remember the words of Shakespeare: 'Who steals my purse steals trash;... but he who steals my good name takes that which is no good to him, but makes me poor indeed.' Therefore, beyond the five dollars which I originally offered Mr. Ohman, I will not go one cent.*"

After Holand avoided the ownership issue for twenty-three years, who could blame Ohman for having negative things to say if in fact he did. In the end, Holand gambled and won that Ohman, while clearly having the energy and desire to pursue the matter, did not have the funds to sue him over the Stone. The third letter is the response from a law firm to Ohman, regarding their opinion about the legal status of his claim against Holand in reference to the Stone.

The letter written to Olof Ohman on January 23, 1930 by the law firm he hired in an attempt to pursue a claim against Hjalmar Holand. (Courtesy of the Ohman Family)

GEORGE W. FRANKBERG
WILLIAM P. BERGHUIS
ALBERT P. FRANKBERG

FRANKBERG, BERGHUIS & FRANKBERG
ATTORNEYS AT LAW
SUITE 5, IVERSON & LEE BUILDING
FERGUS FALLS, MINNESOTA

January 23, 1930

Mr. Olof Ohman
Route No. 1, Box 56
Kensington, Minnesota

Dear Mr. Ohman:

We have your letter of January 21 in which you enclose a letter dated March 6, 1923 from Mr. Holand.

We wrote Mr. Holand recently making a claim in your behalf on account of this Rune Stone and we received a letter from him dated January 18, 1930 which we enclose to you and you will see what he says.

It seems to us, Mr. Ohman, that you perhaps have a claim against Mr. Holand on account of this stone but he will not pay unless you sue him and if you wish to enforce payment from him we think you had better take it up with some attorney somewhere near Ephraim, Wisconsin where he lives because the suit would have to be brought there and we could not handle it from this distance without a great deal of expense.

It would seem to us that you have a legitimate claim against him and we hope that you will be able to collect something.

Yours very truly,

FRANKBERG, BERGHUIS & FRANKBERG

By

GWF:HB

Encls.

This sad episode in the Kensington Rune Stone story only added to the hardship that the Ohman family endured. It would seem that the ownership question was settled once and for all when Holand sold the Stone to the "Committee of Alexandria People." He had certainly convinced himself that it was his right to do so, but feeling righteous in his own mind did not make him legally right. Since there has never been any documentation of a transfer of ownership from Ohman, it appears that the Stone was never Holand's personal property to sell, regardless of how much time and effort he put into "proving its authenticity." A very good moral case, possibly legal case, could be made that the Kensington Rune Stone still belongs to the Olof Ohman family.

In January of 2005, a meeting was held at the Community Center in Kensington where area leaders met to discuss the idea of converting the Ohman Farm, which is presently a Douglas County Park, into a national monument. Darwin Ohman addressed more than thirty people in attendance about what the Ohman family would like to see if the monument were to be realized. He said the family would be very pleased to have the farm be honored in such a way.

When asked about the Rune Stone, which is currently housed in Alexandria, Minnesota, he said the family would like to see it return to the farm where it was discovered if a suitable facility were constructed, such as a state-of-the-art interpretative center. He said the family wanted to see Olof's wishes be granted by having the Stone placed where it could be properly displayed and studied. He also made it clear that the family had no intention of pursuing the Stone as their personal property. He said, "The Stone doesn't belong to anyone, it belongs to everyone."

My Experience with the Kensington Rune Stone

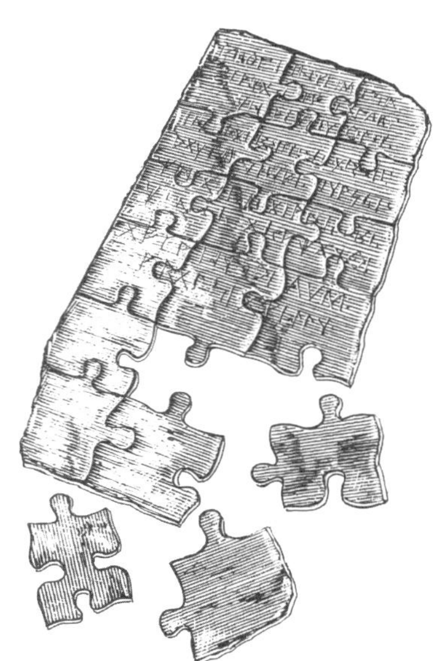

"What is the Kensington Rune Stone?" Those were the first words that came out of my mouth as Barry Hanson relayed the story to me over the phone the first time he called, on July 13, 2000. As he told me the incredible tale of this Minnesota legend, I thought to myself, "Why haven't I heard of this thing before? Did I miss school the day they talked about this?" When he asked me if we could perform an examination of the physical features on the Stone I said we sure could. I gave Barry, who had been appointed the coordinator of research by the Runestone Museum in Alexandria, the same speech I give to all my new customers. I told him that we could certainly perform a laboratory analysis of the Stone and try to determine the age of the inscription.

"However" I said, "You need to be prepared for the possibility that we may end up giving you an answer that you won't like. And regardless of which way the testing goes, you're still going to have to pay me. If you're comfortable with those conditions, then we're all set."

Barry paused for a moment and then in a serious tone replied, "That's fine."

I didn't know it at the time, but this unusual slab of stone would be unlike any other "rock" project I had ever been involved with. Barry and I agreed that we needed to discuss further details about the work plan and background information. Our first face-to-face meeting was on July 10, 2000. From the beginning it was obvious that he was an ardent supporter of the Stone's authenticity. He had a strong, deliberate presence and firm ideas about the scope of testing that he thought should be performed. It was interesting how quickly he jumped into the controversy surrounding the Stone, and relayed his disdain for individuals who did not hold similar views. He was certainly knowledgeable about all aspects of the Stone, but I was more interested in talking about what type of work our laboratory would be doing. A mouse in the corner probably would have enjoyed listening to our conversation. As part of Barry's presentation he alluded to the high-profile nature of the

Kensington Rune Stone, and how we should consider the benefits of furthering a worthy cause. In other words, we should feel moved to perform as much gratis work as we could. I could appreciate his point.

The Geologic Dream Team

After Barry left I thought long and hard about the entire story. I made a point to ask several acquaintances and friends if they had heard of the Kensington Rune Stone and to my surprise, most of them had, and the general consensus was that it was a hoax. I wondered how I could not have caught a whiff of this story at some point in my life. After considering the situation and the potential ramifications I decided to bring in a little help. I picked up the phone and called the University of Minnesota-Duluth geology department to find my college advisor and geology mentor, Dr. Charles L. Matsch. I told Charlie about the project and asked if he would be interested seeing the Stone and offering a few suggestions. He had heard of the Stone and not only did he agree to come down, but suggested I invite some other geologists to review the Stone as well. We made a list that included two more of my former professors, Dr. John Green and Dr. Richard Ojakangas; two retired University of Minnesota professors, Dr. Paul Wieblen and Dr. Robert Johnson; and Ken Harris, a glacial geology expert at the Minnesota Geological Survey. Because of the Stone's high profile, I wanted to get as much input as I could from this accomplished group that I like to call the "Dream Team" of Minnesota geologists.

On July 14, 2000, the Kensington Rune Stone arrived at American Petrographic Services for the first time. I went to the lobby and Barry introduced me to the director of the Runestone Museum, LuAnn Patton. She had short blond hair, a warm, friendly smile, and I would soon learn that we were the same age. LuAnn introduced me to a museum board member, Ken Anderson. Ken is a tall, friendly gentleman with a bushy beard who helped Barry and me load the heavy crate onto a two-wheeler so we could bring it up to the laboratory. Under LuAnn's watchful eye, Ken opened the crate and the three of us lifted the heavy Stone onto a mobile table. I focused my gaze on the tabular-shaped Stone for the first time. It reminded me of a crudely made tombstone. The inscription was very clear and I was struck by how fresh the carved characters appeared. In fact, my first impression was that the inscription did not appear to be very old. Whatever its age, it looked as though it had been skillfully carved by someone working with a hammer and chisel. Within a few minutes the lab phone rang; my three professors from Duluth had arrived.

It had been almost twenty years since I had last seen them all in the same room together, and I was thrilled that they had made the effort to come. Besides being terrific mentors, all three brought excellent credentials and experience in different geologic areas that related to the Kensington Rune Stone. Charlie Matsch is a professor of glacial geology, John

Green is an expert in optical mineralogy and Dick Ojakangas is a world-renowned expert in sedimentary petrology with extensive knowledge of Precambrian (over 600 million years old) graywackes. His experience and help proved invaluable in 2003, when he performed extensive thin section review of the Kensington Rune Stone and compared them with metagraywacke samples of drill cores from northern Minnesota in an effort to locate the probable bedrock source.

After brief introductions they pulled out their hand-lenses and immediately began to pore over the Stone. The room got very quiet as they made their examinations and after a few minutes the phone rang again; Bob Johnson and Paul Wieblen had arrived. What happened next surprised me. When Paul entered the lab he was greeted by my former professors as though he was royalty. They obviously knew Paul and had great admiration for him. He is highly respected in the geologic community, and best known for being hired by NASA in the late 1960s to head up the research on the moon rocks that the Apollo moon landings brought back. As they gathered around the Stone I was thrilled to have the input of such an accomplished group.

The Kensington Rune Stone was examined by a team of noted geologists at the American Petrographic Services Laboratory on July 14, 2000. L to R, Dr. Richard Ojakangas (kneeling), Dr. John Green, Dr. Ken Harris, Gerard Moulzolf, Scott Wolter, Dr. Charles Matsch, Barry Hanson, Dr. Robert Johnson and Dr. Paul Weiblen (kneeling). (Photograph taken by LuAnn Patton, used by permission.)

The team spent more than three hours examining the Stone and bouncing ideas off each other. At one point we flipped the Stone over to examine the back side. The most obvious feature we all noticed immediately was the pronounced glacial scratches called striations, all relatively deep and aligned nearly parallel to the long dimension of the Stone. Since there were no striations on the other sides of the Stone, and all but one side of the Stone had the same weathered appearance, there must have been special circumstances at work. I threw out the idea to the group that the Stone was probably still part of the bedrock as the glacial ice passed over, creating the striations. The Stone must have been plucked out and carried within the glacial ice, where it was protected from further abrasion. When the ice eventually melted, the Stone was left as an erratic (loose) boulder with the striations present only on the back side.

The other prominent feature on the glacial back side were two white, roughly parallel and undulating lineations across the Stone roughly perpendicular to the striations. Paul Wieblen was the first to say something. He quietly pointed to the marks and said, "These features kind of look like roots." It seemed unbelievable for a feature related to the Stone's discovery to have gone unmentioned. I ended up spending considerable time studying the marks and would eventually conclude that they were related to the tree under which the Stone was found.

I thanked each of the geologists before they left, and felt more confident about the work plan I had chosen to pursue. It wasn't until the following day that I could focus my full attention on the Stone. We had recently purchased an articulated arm for the microscope and it worked perfectly for examining this larger-than-normal sample. With LuAnn sitting nearby, and Barry poised across the Stone from me, I focused the microscope within the characters and was immediately bothered by what I saw. In several areas I could see pencil lead and ink from clumsy or careless observers of the past. It made me wonder if the consensus of negative opinion made people feel that it was unnecessary to exercise care. What disturbed me even more was that it was quite apparent that the entire inscription on the "face" side had been scratched out with a sharp instrument. This "retooling," as we like to call it, was also present on the side of the Stone even though the cuts appeared to have been applied with generally less force than the face side. Thankfully, approximately a dozen characters on the left side did not appear retooled at all.

While examining the unscratched or "original" characters I noticed that several contained reddish-brown iron oxide deposits. I pointed these out to Barry and he asked if they indicated significant age. Even though they looked like they had been there for a long period of time, I really wasn't all that impressed initially. Assuming these deposits were the by-product of decomposing pyrite crystals, I relayed to Barry how they could develop relatively quickly depending on the conditions that were present; perhaps in as little time as a year or two. The next thing I noticed made my brow furrow with disappointment. On the top line of the side was a character with heavy iron-oxide deposits that had been clearly and deeply cut through, and I assumed the grooves had been cut in the recent past. Eventually I would learn that this was not the case, and these retooled iron-oxide deposits would become an important piece of evidence.

In addition to the iron oxide, I noticed several characters had a white coatings within the grooves. I expected the material to be calcite, a common deposit found on glacial erratics, because there was a good amount of secondary calcite on the back side of the Stone, though this material was whiter in color. A small scraping examined under the polarized light microscope showed, to my surprise, that it was gypsum. Even though gypsum is occasionally found as a secondary deposit, these curious gypsum deposits within the runes would bother me until Barry mentioned the Smithsonian Institution in Washington, DC had made three casts of the Stone in the late 1940s. These deposits had to be remnants from the gypsum-based plaster used to make the casts. Now it all made sense; modern plaster is made using gypsum with powdered calcite as filler material, but older plaster was made using pure gypsum.

The Core and Chip Samples

Over the next two days we made observations and took photographs. I felt pretty comfortable with the reflected light observations we had made, and knew it was time to get into thin section work to identify the mineral make-up of the Stone. The only proper way to do thin section analysis is to cut a core sample from somewhere on the Stone. I figured this would be a sensitive issue and wondered how our new friends would react to it. To my surprise they took to the idea very well.

October 3, 2000 was coring day, and we brought the Stone down to the materials lab on the first floor. As the Stone was placed on two 4″ x 4″ boards and the coring machine brought into position, I got the video camera ready to record this special event.

I decided that I wanted to take the core where the white root-leaching branched off. In addition to the white root-leaching, I also wanted to take a closer look at a perfectly straight, fine, dark line traversing the surface of the Stone. I believed it was either a sedimentary bedding plane or a fracture, but the core would answer the question definitively. Once the coring machine was in position we rolled the cameras and gave Don Gherman the thumbs up to proceed. The spinning $1^1/2''$ diameter diamond-studded barrel began cutting cleanly into the Stone as the water pumped in to cool the barrel slowly flowed away from the hole. Everyone's eyes were riveted, especially LuAnn's. I tried to reassure her with an occasional calm wink, but she told me later it didn't help. As the core barrel slowly inched its way into the Stone, I glanced at our nervous museum director. LuAnn was smiling and chatty, but I knew this was her way of keeping herself calm. I tried to reassure her that we were taking the core from the back side, and not affecting the inscription at all. I'm sure I made her a nervous wreck.

After about ten minutes, the core barrel had penetrated the planned 2″ depth, so Don turned off the water and core machine and slowly pulled the barrel out. Everything had gone perfectly. I offered Barry the honors of breaking off the sample, handed him a screwdriver and a crescent wrench to use as a hammer, and showed him where to place the screwdriver. I told him to give it a firm whack, but he lightly tapped the top of the screwdriver; he was being a little too careful. I realized he was uncomfortable and asked him to let me do it. With one good, hard hit, the core broke off perfectly at the bottom and we pulled out a perfect core sample. Everyone breathed a sigh of relief and the relaxed, easy smile returned to LuAnn's face.

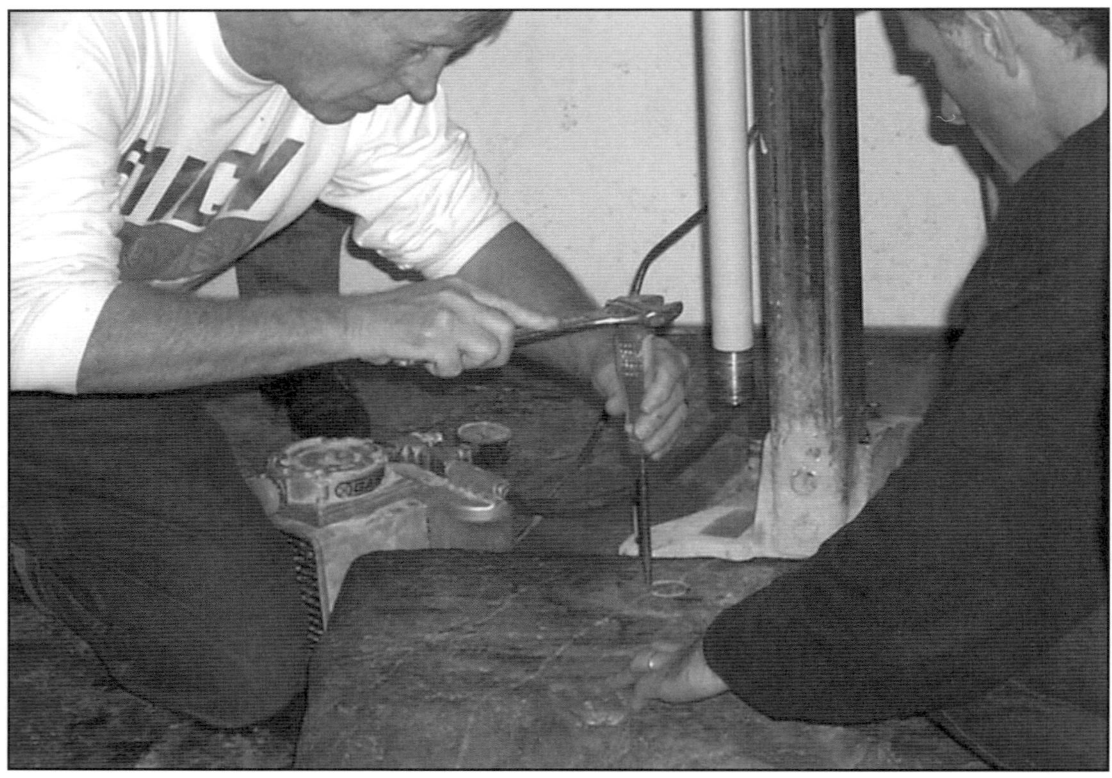

Barry Hanson lightly taps a screwdriver trying to break off the core sample drilled from the back side of the Kensington Rune Stone on October 3, 2000. (Photo by LuAnn Patton, used by permission)

In addition to identifying the mineralogy through thin section examination in our lab, I was able to gain an understanding of the freshly fractured and glacially weathered surfaces by traveling to the Materials Research Laboratory at Iowa State University and examining the core sample using their scanning electron microscope (SEM). Using this equipment I was able to learn the exact chemical composition of the minerals and how they were distributed throughout the Stone. The mica minerals that looked so fresh and pristine on the broken surface at the bottom of the core had completely weathered away on the glacial surface. We needed to know the condition of the micas of the man-made surfaces, and the only way to do that was by taking another sample in the area made at the same time as the original inscription.

We observed several curved fractures along the bottom edge of the side of the Stone that contained the last three lines of the inscription. These were impact fractures, and indicated to me that this entire side of the Stone had been intentionally broken off. This side's color and texture are completely different from the other glacial surfaces. Whomever carved the inscription had intentionally shaped the Stone before carving the inscription. LuAnn and I talked about this surface and agreed it was important enough that we should try to get another opinion about the split side. Ironically, one of the retired professors who came to the lab had a daughter who was an experienced stone carver. We called Bob Johnson, and he put us in touch with his daughter Janey Westin, who said she'd be happy to come over and examine the Stone.

On September 21, 2000, Janey showed up at the lab eager to help out. She is a strong-willed woman who not only didn't take long to agree that the curved features we observed were purposeful impacts, she also pointed out several additional impacts on other edges. Even though I was certain in my own mind that the Stone had been intentionally broken, having a stone-carving expert express the same opinion was important. At this point, it seemed pretty straightforward that we could get the information we needed about the weathering of the inscription by taking a sample from anywhere on the split side. This side had been fashioned before the inscription was carved, and presumably at the same time. I only needed a small sample to test in the SEM. By now the Stone was back in the museum and Barry had returned to his home in Wisconsin. I picked up the phone, laid out the plan to LuAnn, and we made arrangements to go to the museum in Alexandria to take another sample. This time the method for obtaining a sample wasn't quite as sophisticated.

On October 21, 2000, while on our way to collect fossils in South Dakota, my family and I stopped at the Rune Stone Museum. Brian Williams, a member of the Rune Stone Museum board of directors, let us in and helped remove the glass cover over the Stone. The Stone sat nestled in its metal cradle, angled slightly backward from vertical. We had brought all the necessary equipment: a small sledgehammer; a $^1/_2''$ steel chisel; and a five gallon bucket to catch the chip sample. I picked an area in the lower third of the split side away from the inscription, asked my son Grant to hold the bucket, and carefully put the chisel into position. With one quick stroke I struck the end of the chisel and heard a small piece fly off and hit the bottom of the bucket. "Good catch Grant," I said. The chip was the perfect size and it didn't obviously deface the Stone.

When the chip went into the SEM I was pretty excited; this was the moment of truth for us in our investigation of the micas. I thought the micas would probably be in bad shape if the weathering was old. When the first image came into view at 500x magnification, I was shocked at what I saw; or by what I didn't see. The mica minerals on the weathered side of the chip sample were gone, completely weathered away. A smile formed on my face as I realized what the image before me meant. It takes longer for these minerals to weather away than Olof Ohman, or anyone else living in his time, had been alive. My initial instincts during those first few hours of examining the Stone turned out to be right. The only scenario that made sense scientifically was that this inscription could not be a 19th century hoax.

The American Institute of Professional Geologists

As the investigation began to wind down, I asked Barry about how the museum wanted to use the information we were gathering, and he said he wanted have the test results presented at an upcoming archaeological conference in St. Paul. I was feeling comfortable with what we had learned about the Stone and how I could present the information, but I also thought about how nice it would be if I could give the findings a trial run. I came up with an idea that, if I was able to pull it off, would provide a professional critique of the results as well as a practice run. I called Bruce Johnson, the current President of the Minnesota Chapter of the American Institute of Professional Geologists (AIPG).   The AIPG is an organization of knowledgeable professionals that I had been president of in the past; I also knew that they would give Barry and me honest feedback. The Midwest Plains Archaeological Conference was scheduled for November 10, 2000, which did not give us a lot of time since I had called Bruce in late October. Bruce was able to get the scheduled speaker for the November meeting to move his talk back a month.

AIPG luncheons are held the first Tuesday of every month except June, July, and August. The September meeting is always trumped by our annual fall field trip, so our presentation was the first for the group in five months. We had a good turnout of about sixty-five geologists at the Ramada Inn in Roseville, Minnesota, and almost all of them had some knowledge of the Kensington Rune Stone. Barry gave his presentation first, speaking primarily about how the Stone was found and where others had gone wrong in their investigations, leading them to conclude the Stone was a hoax. I then laid out the geological findings in the most factual and unemotional way that I could.

Once we finished we took questions. Overall, the comments were very favorable toward the work we had done. I was a little surprised, but felt good that my geological peers did not have any major objections. With the archaeological conference only a couple of days away, I thought about using two slide projectors so the audience could see two images at the same time in hopes of contrasting the differences between the SEM images of the fresh and weathered surfaces for maximum impact.

Midwest Plains Archaeological Conference

The day before the conference I was finally able to meet the fellow I had heard so much about from Barry and LuAnn. Dr. Richard Nielsen arrived at the APS lab and introduced himself. A stocky fellow, about six feet tall with a gray goatee and a steely gaze, Dick was sixty-seven years old. Dick is a doctor of engineering by profession with a masters degree in mathematics. I would later learn that in his younger days he was an officer in the Coast Guard and had lived several years in Denmark. He was extremely knowledgeable about runes, but was self-educated and as I would find out later, not an academic "scholar" at a prestigious university. To many academics he was regarded as an amateur not worthy of the time spent discussing a long-ago dismissed subject like the Kensington Rune Stone.

Barry had been keeping Dick informed of our progress, and he had many questions about our work. Dick and I sat at the microscope and as I took him through my findings he was especially intrigued about the micas, quickly grasping my explanation of the weathering. I had many questions for him too. I was very curious about the inscription and exactly what it said, so he then explained a few details about his work. What struck me was that he'd been the first to study medieval diplomas from the same time period as the date on the Stone. He said he was finding plenty of new information that was consistent with the linguistic aspects of the Kensington Rune Stone inscription. It all sounded very intriguing to me. The next day all three of us got the chance to tell our stories.

LuAnn and Al Patton, Ken, and Barry came by the office with the Stone and then followed my wife Janet and me to the Radisson Hotel in downtown St. Paul. We checked in to the conference at 1:30 p.m., a good ninety minutes before our presentations were to start.

We found the room for our presentation and started to get set up. We all agreed that it would be a good idea to have the Stone displayed during the session because it lent an air of seriousness that set the appropriate tone. By 3:00 p.m. the room was full, with over a hundred people. There were several people in attendance who I didn't know at the time, but would eventually get to know quite well. One was a senior archaeologist from the University of Wisconsin in Milwaukee named Alice Kehoe. Dr. Kehoe spoke about 14th century history making it quite likely that a Norse party made it to what would one day be Minnesota. This information was all new to me and it was fascinating. I thought that if the weathering was consistent with the Stone being very old, then the history should also make sense and apparently it did. Next, Dick spoke about the various aspects of the runes, words, numbers, and dialect of the inscription being like the walls of a house; all the pieces had to fit together or the house (inscription) would fall. His presentation was also very compelling. Barry gave a nice introduction to the work we did in the APS laboratory and then it was my turn. I had both projectors ready and as I approached the point in the talk where I showed the SEM photos of the various surfaces, I could tell that most of the audience understood my points. When the slide of the split side surface with the missing micas came up, there was a hushed collective gasp in the crowd. They all understood the point at once. It was a moment I will never forget.

After my presentation I sat down next to Janet, who was smiling with approval. The next speaker was a gentleman that I didn't know, a physician named Dr. Jon Polansky. Jon talked about his job overseeing the research and development of new medicines, then favorably critiqued the research that all of us had performed. I didn't know whose idea this was, but it was a damn good one, because it put an unbiased stamp of approval on the work and gave the session a very nice finishing touch. When the session was over there was a festive mood to the crowd. Someone said that the well-known critic of the Kensington Rune Stone, Birgitta Wallace, had attended the session. I had heard much about her in the few months I had been involved with the Rune Stone, and Barry had made his disdain for her work known (later documented in his 2002 publication, *The Trial of Olof Ohman*). I didn't have an opinion about her one way or the other. I had, however, become very interested in the controversy, and wanted to meet as many of the key characters as I could.

The Kensington Rune Stone at the Midwest Plains Archaeological Conference in St, Paul, Minnesota, on November 10, 2000. L to R: LuAnn Patton, Jon Polansky, Scott & Janet Wolter, Alice Kehoe, Richard Nielsen, Barry Hanson, and Ken Anderson. (Photo by Tom Reiersgord.)

Birgitta had already left the room by the time we finished answering questions. LuAnn, Al, Barry, Janet, and I were not going to stay for the dinner and hear Birgitta's keynote address about the Rune Stone. Our group stayed long enough for us to have one drink at the social gathering before dinner. I wanted to meet her and decide for myself what kind of person she was. I didn't know what she looked like, so while Janet and I strolled in together, Barry helped us locate her. Within a couple minutes Barry pointed her out. Janet and I moseyed up while Birgitta finished her conversation with another person. I introduced myself, to which she replied in a slightly chastising but friendly tone, "I know who you are, I heard your presentation." I quickly interjected that I was not there to confront her about her views on the Rune Stone. I explained my interest in the controversy and that I simply wanted to meet some of the key participants. To her credit, she accepted my explanation and instantly warmed up to us. Birgitta has a charming demeanor, and I could see her being very persuasive. I introduced her to Janet and we had a very good visit.

The conference was quite a learning experience. I had my first taste of the passion and the politics involved in this controversy, my first lesson on the complex issues surrounding this Stone. I was beginning to understand the differences between the scientific process that is my world as a geologist, and the way of doing business in the fields of archaeology, history, and language. There are not just subtle differences; the disciplines are often worlds apart in the way they approach things. To me, the physical aspects of the Stone, like the thousands of concrete and rock samples I've examined, contained the evidence that tells a straightforward, factual story. As far as I was concerned, all aspects of the Stone, including the language and the runes, took a back seat to the geology. I wasn't used to people not wholeheartedly accepting our test results, and it would be a while before I could get my arms around what was really going on with the controversy.

With the conference over, all that was left to do was to complete the written report. The results of our testing breathed new life into the ongoing discussions of the Kensington Rune Stone's authenticity. The feedback from the conference was generally positive, and LuAnn Patton and the members of the Rune Stone Museum board of directors seemed pleased with our work as well. In the spring of 2001, Barry resigned as coordinator of the research and all my communication about the Rune Stone from that point on went through LuAnn and Dick. I decided at this point that I was no longer going to charge for my time for the work I did on the Stone. I had been drawn in by the controversy and wanted to continue to get to try to get to the bottom of the mystery. I felt I brought some unique skills and perspective to the problem and needed to stay involved. Besides, something was definitely wrong in this case, and I thought I might be able to help figure out what it was.

Before resigning, Barry did us all a favor by getting Paul Weiblen to take an independent look at the core and chip samples from the Stone. Although retired, Paul still had access to the geology department's electron microscope at the University of Minnesota. Paul performed some microprobe work on the samples and offered some ideas for additional work that might help us better understand the weathering rate of the minerals in the Stone. What I felt was most important was Paul's review of Newton Winchell's work with the Stone more than ninety years earlier. Paul gave Winchell high marks for his intelligent and reasoned insight in developing his opinions; I would eventually come to the same conclusion about Winchell's work in the not too distant future.

The AVM Stone

On May 24, 2001, the Kensington Rune Stone was back in our lab for some additional observations. LuAnn accompanied the Stone as usual, and she, Janey Westin, and I went about our work. I noticed that LuAnn and Janey were acting a little squirrely. I can't really explain what they were doing specifically, but there was something going on with them. Around lunchtime I suggested we go get something to eat. I went to my office to check messages before we left, and LuAnn followed me in, closing the door behind her. She leaned against the door and looked at me with a silly grin on her face and said, "Janey found another rune stone." Not comprehending what she had said at first I said, "She found a what?" I called Janey to my office and she had the same silly grin on her face.

A week and half earlier, on Mother's Day, May 13, Janey and her father Robert drove up to Rune Stone Park at the Ohman farm outside Kensington to hike around looking for mooring stone holes in glacial boulders. They paddled a canoe out to a little island in a shallow, marshy lake due north of Rune Stone Hill and spent the day hiking around the island where they found four mooring stones. It was getting late in the day and the sun was starting to set when Janey and her dad headed back to their canoe, but to get there, they had to climb over a large pile of field-cleared glacial boulders on the west end of the island. Janey said she stopped for some reason to look back where she had just walked when something caught her eye. Carved into the top of one of the boulders, in 2″ tall letters, she saw "AVM." At first she couldn't believe her eyes. Janey and her father were well versed in the Kensington Rune Stone and realized a connection right away. She said there was more to the inscription and wanted me to take a look at it. When she was finished telling her story I was ready to jump in the car that instant.

We made plans to head up to the island three days later on Saturday, May 27, 2001. Janey, Bob, and I stopped first at the farm to talk to the farmers on whose property they had found the stone. This was the same farm that was previously owned by Nils Flaaten, Ohman's neighbor who saw the Stone, the tree, and the roots the day the Kensington Rune Stone was found. We knocked on the door around lunchtime and a pretty blonde woman answered. It was a strange moment trying to figure out what to say to her even though we had talked at length about what were going to say. We figured that the land owners must have known about the history of the Kensington Rune Stone and we wondered how they would respond. We feared they would want nothing to do with anything related to the Kensington Rune Stone, let alone another rune stone. After discussing several strategies we decided the honest straightforward approach was best. It turned out to be the right one.

Arlen and Ruby Sabolik could not have been more cooperative. They saw eye to eye with us on pretty much everything we wanted to do, and they gave us permission to go out to the island, saying they would come out a little later after wrapping up a few chores. We unloaded our canoe and paddled the hundred yards or so across the water. As we approached the island I entertained myself with the possibility that this might have been where a Norse party had camped. My first impression as I walked onto the island was that this would be a perfect place for a party to camp in hostile territory. Surrounded by water and old growth trees that would make for a perfect camouflage; you could easily see out, but it would be difficult to see in. The island is roughly teardrop shaped, 150 yards long and 100 yards wide with a gently sloping elevation that rises to about ten feet above the lake. The east-west property line between the Saboliks to the north and the Park property to the south cuts the island roughly in half. Along the full length of the property line are large boulders that were cleared from the surrounding land. Arlen and Ruby later told us that the lake formed when the outlet stream that drained the area was dammed five years earlier. The dam raised the water level about five feet, creating the lake. Before the dam was put in the land now under water had been cornfields.

Janey and Bob led me to the pile of large rocks and stopped in front of the stone. The area was lush with underbrush, but the inscription on the large boulder was easily visible. A shudder went down my spine as I pulled out my hand-lens and began examining the stone. It is a light pinkish-tan-colored granite gneiss with a very pronounced $2^1/4''$ wide band of light to medium gray biotite schist that cross-cut the middle of the inscription at about a 45 degree angle. The inscription is roughly centered on the top side of the boulder and appeared to be weathered. When I starting looking closely at the characters in the lighter colored, granitic areas, I noticed what looked like very small, brown, circular, iron oxide stains, in the middle of each was a tiny, dark mineral with a slight metallic flash. Curiously, these stains were only within the carved letters; I couldn't find any staining on any other part of the boulder. Something wasn't right. If these were weathering pyrite crystals they shouldn't be there if the inscription was carved hundreds of years ago. For that matter, I wouldn't expect these stains if the carving were just over a hundred years old. I would learn that neither scenario I considered was the correct one.

The other thing that seemed odd was that the characters cut in the dark gray schistose band were white and looked relatively fresh. This was a clear tip-off, but I put the apparent inconsistency away for the time being. Looking back now, it's obvious that my gut was telling me something was not right about this inscription. I didn't pursue my hunch at that time in part because I was caught up in Janey and Bob's excitement. Whatever doubts lingered in my mind I certainly wasn't going to bring them up now. I knew eventually I would have time to more carefully study the stone later; now was not the time to start drawing any conclusions, and in the back of my mind I kept thinking about the many quick opinions that had been made regarding the Kensington Rune Stone that turned out to be erroneous. There would be plenty of time to formulate an opinion later.

The stone was intermittently covered with yellow lichen that partially obscured the inscription. After careful deliberation amongst the three of us, we decided to remove the lichen to allow us to inspect all parts of the inscription with the exception of the lower left leg of the "A." While Janey carefully scrubbed the lichen off with water and a brush, we heard Arlen and Ruby paddling to the island. When they made their way to the boulder pile we had several questions to ask them.

Arlen said he had cleared the fields and made the pile of boulders. He also said that the lichen had only grown on the rocks in the last five years, since the outlet stream was dammed. Ruby interjected that she remembered Arlen saying he thought he'd seen some scratches on a boulder several years back, and the comment jogged Arlen's memory. They recalled joking about how it might be another rune stone. Arlen was unsure if this was the same rock, but I was convinced that it was. Soon the sun went down and darkness set in. Arlen and Ruby went back to the house while the three of us prepared for round two of our investigation. Using a flashlight, we highlighted the inscription and could finally see it clearly. The inscription read,

AVM: ᚱᚨᚹᚨᚱ: ᛏᚢᚢ:

We took a lot of photographs and recorded video. Around 1:00 a.m. we paddled off the island and drove to our hotel in Alexandria, though it was hard to fall asleep that night after such a memorable day.

On Monday, May 29, 2001, I called Dick after faxing him a hand drawn copy of the inscription. He said all the runes could have been copied from the Kensington Rune Stone, except one; the second rune on the second line was a special "S," very different from the "S" (ᛋ) rune on the Kensington Rune Stone and only found on the island of Gotland in the 14th century. He faxed me a couple examples of inscriptions that had this special rune and sure enough, it was the same rune. Dick believed it was highly unlikely that a forger would know about this rune, and based on this he thought it likely that the inscription could be genuine. Now I was really confused. On one hand, the iron-oxide halos and the fresh-looking characters in the schistose band were saying, "not old"; and on the other hand, that "S" rune was saying "very old." My mind was further clouded by the excitement of Bob, Janey, and her mom, Betty. I tried to be patient, and hoped that eventually I would get the stone into the lab to examine it. I also kept in mind a saying I'd heard a long time ago that seemed appropriate in this case: Never make a decision until you have to. The one thing I did have was the luxury of time.

Fortunately, I was working with some very bright people. Bob is a retired University of Minnesota professor and was married to an intelligent woman. Betty and Bob had raised four daughters including Janey, all of them bright and thoughtful women. Bob, Janey, Arlen, Ruby, and I formed a committee to plan and make decisions about what to do with the stone. After several meetings we agreed that we had to figure out a way get the stone off the island. We feared that if word got out about the discovery of another rune stone people would come around and possibly deface it. We knew that the stone needed to be examined in our laboratory in the same way as the Kensington Rune Stone. We also felt that if the island had been a camping spot, we needed to have an archeological assessment performed.

I put in a call to the Minnesota Historical Society and spoke with then curator of artifacts Chuck Diesen, who suggested I call Christina Harrison. Christina performed a dig on Rune Stone Hill in 1976, and she was intrigued with the story of the new stone. On May 30, 2001, Christina met with Bob, Janey, and me to look at slides of the stone. She thought the inscription was interesting and agreed that an archaeological assessment was the proper next step, but she also related the difficulties she experienced during the dig. Many of the local people who were supporters of the Stone thought she was incompetent when she didn't find anything. The experience had clearly left a bad taste in her mouth, but it didn't deter her from helping us.

Over the course of the next several days the local archaeology rumor mill began to churn, and negative stories about Christina and several other people began to reach me. When I talked to Christina about what I'd heard, she acknowledged that the profession is highly political and that if you're not part of the inner circle, you don't get contracts. When I brought up Mike Michlovic's name, an archaeologist who was recommended to Janey, Christina said that he was well respected. Mike was also known as someone highly skeptical of the Kensington Rune Stone. Personally, I didn't really care what he thought about the Kensington Rune Stone, I cared if he could do a good job. I called Mike on June 19, and after we discussed the project he agreed to work with us. Mike suggested a "Phase I" archaeological assessment and explained that the Phase I included two traverses across designated areas where approximately a dozen test holes were dug. Each hole was about a foot across and roughly eighteen inches deep. The idea is to get through the soil horizon into natural, undisturbed glacial material, which is then screened for artifacts or any evidence of previous human activity. Mike offered to let me work as an assistant to help keep the costs down.

The other major task we faced was figuring out a way to get the stone off the island. LuAnn suggested we talk with her husband Al about his good friend and fellow sheriff's deputy Brad Lake. Janet and I had met Brad on an earlier trip to Alexandria and he seemed to be the kind of guy who would love to help. On June 18, 2001, I called Brad and told him the story and what we wanted to do, and he responded enthusiastically. The next time the committee met our plans for the AVM Stone seemed to be falling into place. We set the date of Monday, July 9, for the extraction. Arlen and Ruby thought a Monday would be best because there would be fewer people at the park, and our activity on the island would draw less attention.

Looking north from the top of Rune Stone hill at what my family called "Tick Island" where the AVM Stone was found in a pile of field-cleared boulders under the trees on the west end of the island. (SFW)

The weather was perfect as Janet, Grant, Amanda, and I drove out to the Sabolik's farm for a pre-extraction meeting. The meeting was videotaped with the committee members in attendance, Brad and his brother Bruce, LuAnn and her husband Al, Dennis Anderson, and a friend of Arlen and Ruby's named Pryce Score. Pryce is the president of the bank in Kensington and was there to give the Saboliks advice. We all sat around the kitchen table as Brad explained the carefully considered plan he and Dennis Anderson had devised. Dennis is an Alexandria businessman with a strong desire to help, and he provided much of the equipment we needed to do the job. The meeting ended at noon just as Mike Michlovic and Christina Harrison arrived, and we all made our way to the island, where Janey and I led Mike and Christina to the stone. They both examined it but had relatively little to offer. Mike and Christina walked the island and discussed a plan for the archeological assessment. Mike estimated that a Phase I assessment would involve two to three people and could be completed in one day, and Christina volunteered to help out.

While Janey and I were talking to Mike and Christina, the extraction team of Brad, Bill, Al, and Dennis were getting all the gear into place. The Douglas County Sheriff's office let us use their 16-foot flat-bottomed rescue boat, and Dennis brought cables, chains, and a heavy duty four-wheeler. At around 1:30 we began extraction, with the video-camera rolling to record the event. The first thing we needed to do was move the boulders surrounding the AVM Stone. It was a hot, sunny day. Fortunately there were several large trees that provided plenty of shade; unfortunately the shade provided a haven for mosquitoes. After an hour or so the boulders closest to the AVM stone were moved and we began digging the dirt out from underneath it. It turned out the stone was considerably larger than our original estimate of 1500 pounds, but in spite of this we were able to successfully roll it onto a 1971 Chevy car hood that served as a sled. Using the "come-along" with chains, greased boards, and Dennis on his ATV, we slowly moved the stone to the other side of the island. Once we had it onto a slight downward sloping grade we removed the chains and come-along for the final push to the pontoon boat. The last forty yards to the boat would be done in one final sprint. The greased 2″ x 10″ x 16′ boards were positioned under the sled, and every available free body pushed against the stone as Dennis revved his ATV. The sled started moving and we ran and pushed as it gathered speed. Once the stone got going, those of us pushing either fell down or followed as Dennis raced directly into the lake. The water and mud was flying from under the wheels of the ATV until it and the sled came to a stop in about a foot of water.

The pontoon boat was rigged with a ramp and cradle made from 4″ x 4″ wooden beams that the sled eventually sat on. The sled with the stone was pulled onto the boat using the come-along and chains. Once the stone was secured, six of us took a position around the boat, and made our way across the lake, wading slowly through the waist-deep water with the precious cargo in tow. After about a half an hour we reached the shore where Arlen was waiting behind the wheel of his John Deere tractor. A cable was attached to the sled and Arlen dragged the stone off the boat, across his cornfield and into one of his large metal sheds for temporary storage. After a lot of good planning and hard back labor, the job was successfully completed at about 6:30 p.m.

After the successful removal of the AVM Stone from the island, the extraction crew was tired and wet, but happy and proud. L to R: Bill Lake, Dennis Anderson, Janey Westin, Al and LuAnn Patton, Scott Wolter and Brad Lake (Photograph by Amanda Wolter).

The following morning, July 10, Dennis Anderson provided a private conference room for a post-extraction meeting of the AVM Stone committee. Janey, Bob, Betty, Arlen, Ruby, LuAnn, and I were present. Plans were made to contact Mike Michlovic to go ahead with the Phase I assessment the last week in July, (July 25 or 26) and to have a press release about the discovery of the stone sometime in August. I felt that now was a good time to bring up the issue of physically testing the stone. To my complete surprise Bob strongly objected. "You're not cutting into that stone." He felt the physical testing would not be convincing to people who do not believe in the Kensington Rune Stone. Also, he had not seen the report of the work we did on the Kensington Rune Stone. I was surprised to hear his reasoning, and found both arguments to be rather poor. I had a hard time understanding where he was coming from, because he had attended the presentation of our work in November the previous year.

I found myself in terrible quandary. My first inclination was to strongly challenge Bob, but doing that would put Janey in a bad position. I extended an invitation for Bob to come to our lab so I could show him our results as well give him a copy of my report. The meeting adjourned and we all went home feeling satisfied about the work we had accomplished, but I felt awkward the whole ride home. I had assumed that we would be testing the stone before the press conference, but now the plan had changed, and I felt like an outsider within a group of people I had grown quite close to. I don't know if I realized it or not at the time, but that "gut" instinct that had been slowly gnawing at me from the first day I saw the stone was back. Regardless of the setback for testing the stone, we continued on with the plans that the committee had agreed to.

July 25 was set for the archaeological dig. On July 23, I contacted an old football buddy who was now a reporter at the *Minneapolis Star-Tribune* newspaper about doing a story on the stone. He suggested Peg Meier, who has been writing about the Kensington Rune Stone for twenty-five years. It was at his suggestion that we brought her in so she could write a better story. I called Janey, since this was her discovery, and she was receptive. I called Peg, who decided it would be a good idea to come along for the Phase I dig.

Peg brought photographer Stormi Greener along to document our work. At the end of the day we all thought the Phase I assessment had gone very well. Mike, Dean, and Christina did a professional job, fully cooperated with our requests, and answered all of our questions. They dug a total of fourteen test holes (approx. 1′ x 1′ x 16-20″ deep) and found several artifacts that clearly indicated previous human habitation. The items included: three siliceous flakes (chalcedony, chert, and quartz), two pieces of charcoal, two mammal teeth fragments, and one large mammal bone fragment with a charred edge, two apparent knife cuts, and one clear cut edge. Mike said the island would be registered with the Minnesota Historical Society as a habitation site that was most likely Native American. Although they did not find any direct evidence of Norse habitation, they could not definitively rule it out. Mike would complete his report within a few weeks.

As we should have expected, Peg started to put pressure on us to run the story as soon as possible so she wouldn't lose the "scoop." At the same time, I was pressuring Janey to get the stone to our lab before the press conference, but the decision was made to hold the press conference first. The press conference was to be held on August 11, 2001, in the town of Kensington. In the week leading up to the press conference I went on a family vacation to the Upper Peninsula of Michigan. On our way back home, two days before the announcement, we stayed in Duluth. I tried not to let the idea of the untested stone bother me, but in the end, I couldn't do it. That morning in Duluth I decided I wasn't going to attend the press conference. When I called Janey to tell her I wasn't coming she was disappointed, but understood my reasoning. I didn't have anything to say since we hadn't done any testing yet. Peg wrote a great story that appeared on the front page of *Minneapolis Star-Tribune*. There was a lot of excitement, but all I could think of was getting that stone into the lab.

The next morning Janey and her dad, Bob, brought the stone to the lab. I was relieved when Bob gave me his blessing to take a core sample and do whatever I felt was necessary. First, we obtained a core sample from the back side of the stone through the same geologic zone as the inscription. Over the next several days I examined thin sections of the core to better understand the make-up of the stone. I also spent a lot of time examining the iron oxide stains around the pyrite grains within the carved characters. Both the iron oxide staining and the fresh-looking characters in the biotite-rich schistose band were driving me crazy because they did not fit with a weathering profile of roughly a hundred years, let alone hundreds of years. I didn't know what to do. There was too much excitement surrounding the AVM stone and I just wasn't comfortable with any conclusion. Eventually, I decided to put the stone away for a while and write my report later. I told myself that I would wait until things settled down and write the report after the first of the year. Once I made that decision the unsettled feeling in my gut started to go away.

On November 6, 2001, I received a call from Barb Averill with the Minnesota Historical Society. She told me two women had just written a letter to the Society, taking responsibility for carving the AVM Stone in 1985. It seemed hard to believe at first, but as she read the letter to me everything fell into place. I'd had a problem with the two scenarios I considered because they didn't fit the weathering profile that I had observed. Suddenly the fresh-appearing biotite and the actively weathering pyrite grains made sense. They had only been weathering for sixteen years! The most unbelievable part was how the women described the creation of the second letter on the second line; the "Gotland S" that was such a rare and unique rune was made by accident! The forgers described how the chisel had slipped and chipped out an extra piece of rock. It turns out my gut feeling had been right the first time I saw the oxidation halos within the inscription. The "AVM" Stone was a fake.

11/05/2001 10:02 FAX 651 297 3343   MN HISTORICAL SOCIETY   ☑001

Post-It™ brand fax transmittal memo 7671   # of pages ► 2

To Scott Wolter	From B Aversid
Co.	Co.
Dept.	Phone # 651-297-3931
Fax # 647-2744	Fax # ---

Note: We received on Oct 23 —

Minnesota Historical Society
345 W. Kellogg Blvd.
St. Paul, MN 55102-1906

September 5, 2001,

To the Minnesota Historical Society,

We, the undersigned (Kari Ellen Gade and Jana K. Schulman), were part of a group of five persons who carved the rune stone (the so-called 'AVM–stone') that was discovered on May 13th, 2001, in Kensington, Minnesota. The stone was carved on Saturday, June 8th, or Sunday, June 9th, 1985, and, at the time, we were graduate students in the Programme of Germanic Philology at the University of Minneapolis, Minnesota. During the spring quarter of 1985 we all attended a seminar on runic inscriptions, taught by Professor Anatoly Liberman, and the last couple of weeks of that course were devoted to "famous fakes," among them the Kensington runestone. Upon the completion of the course, we were inspired to make an excursion to Alexandria to visit the museum, Ohman's farm, and the site of the discovery of the Kensington stone. At the time, we also considered carving another inscription in that vicinity to see what would happen if it were discovered.

On June 8th (or 9th) we drove up to Alexandria, bringing along, among other things, a hammer, a chisel, and the Kensington runic alphabet. After having visited the museum and the farm, we drove out to the hill on which the KS had been found. Because the environment was less than ideal (too public) for our venture, we decided to walk down the hill and out to a forested elevation that looked like an island in the middle of a meadow stretching north-westward from the 'Kensington' hill. It took us approximately 15-20 minutes to reach it (the going was a little difficult, and one of us [Schulman] got caught in a barbed wire fence and had to have a tetanus shot when we returned to Minneapolis). When we arrived at the 'island,' we looked for a suitable stone and found one with a fairly even (but gnarled) surface sticking up from the ground. We proceeded to carve the inscription previously agreed on, namely, "AVM : " in the Latin alphabet (as inscribed on the KS), and "1363 : " in the Kensington alphabet (the date being one year later than the date given on the KS—we thought that might lead to interesting speculations about potential survivors from the alleged attack). The process of carving was quite cumbersome because the surface of the rock was hard and had coarse strands in it. After having carved the first two words, we decided to add the word "alu" in the Older Fuþark on a line below. This magic pagan formula is sometimes found on bracteates, and we thought it would counterbalance nicely the Christian invocation "AVM" at the beginning of the inscription (if this were indeed intended to mean "Ave Maria" by the person or persons who carved the KS). When carving the l-rune, the chisel slipped on the down stroke of the upper bar, and a piece of stone broke off in the upward direction. After the inscription had been completed, we wanted to turn the stone over so that the inscription would face downward and be more difficult to detect. We were unable to do that, however, because the stone apparently stuck firmly in the ground. Hence we covered it up with branches and leaves and left.

We had no knowledge of the discovery of the stone prior to the press release in Minneapolis in August of this year, and at no point were in any contact with the persons who discovered it. Over the years, however, we have made no secret of the location and nature of the inscription, and several people had knowledge of it. Among them were eleven students enrolled in a seminar on "Runes and Runic Inscriptions" (G625) taught by Gade at Indiana University in the spring of 1998.

Kari Ellen Gade
Professor and Chair
Department of Germanic Studies
Indiana University, Bloomington

Jana K. Schulman
Associate Professor
Department of English
Southeastern Louisiana University

A letter received by the Minnesota Historical Society on September 5, 2001 from five former University of Minnesota graduate students who claimed responsibility for carving the "AVM" Stone inscription in June of 1985. (Minnesota Historical Society)

Subject: AVM Stone "Prank"

To: Jana K. Schulman, Kari Ellen Gade, and your three nameless friends,

I should start off by introducing myself. My name is Scott Wolter and I am the forensic geologist who has looked at both the KRS and the AVM Stone in my laboratory. I was also involved in the documentation and extraction of the AVM Stone after it's recent "discovery". I should also be up-front and say that I write this letter with extremely mixed emotions. I am trying to balance my obvious anger and disappointment over this recent revelation, with my admiration and the respect for the two people who had the guts to take responsibility for perpetrating this hoax. I think you all are beginning to realize now how much time, money and energy has been wasted because of this college "prank". Personally, I have no regrets about my involvement with AVM Stone. I have met many wonderful and dedicated people who helped our team along the way. I have also been able to enjoy this past summers' experience with my wife and two children. I cannot, however, speak for the other people who expressed great sadness, embarrassment and disappointment. I'm sure at some point you will hear from them.

I shared an analogy to this situation in a conversation I had with Kari this morning that I think is appropriate. If a person dialed 911 and said they were having a heart attack, were rushed to the hospital and emergency personnel went to work on them, who is the fool if the person sat up on the gurney and said, "Ha ha, it was all a big joke!" I apologize to no one for how we conducted ourselves and am proud of the work we did. We documented everything, safely removed what may have been an important historical artifact and brought it to a laboratory for proper scientific investigation. As I have said for some time now, the AVM Stone was not doing very well under the microscope. As much as I was pulling for it personally, it wasn't holding up. I will publish the specifics at a later date.

What is by far the biggest potential tragedy of this unfortunate event is the political fallout that this is having on the Kensington Runestone. In my report of our investigation of the physical features we observed and documented, the KRS stood tall. My conclusion is that the weathering is consistent with the KRS having been in the ground much longer than any fraud theory suggests. The only evidence we have to put it anywhere in time, is the date on the stone - 1362. Not surprising, the first in-depth and honest research on the language of the KRS, absolutely puts every word, number and runeform in the 14th century. When properly researched, without bias or academic arrogance, the truth about Olof Ohman and the related history of the 14th century, supports the authenticity as well. It's all there if one wants to find it. What I fear the most is that history will repeat itself and put the KRS back in the shadows of ridicule and indifference. People were just beginning to see the light of the evidence that has always been there.

You have followed in the footsteps of your miss-informed predecessors. I can certainly forgive a bad decision of youth, but I am repulsed by the apparent lack of remorse and compassion for the people who were put-out by your prank ("she felt some excitement and amusement, she feels no regret and expects no retribution." *Minneapolis Tribune, pp. A11, November 6, 2001*.). I wonder if your words won't come back to haunt you. As for the three cowards who did not have the courage to sign your letter, they will have to live with themselves.

Scott F. Wolter
President
American Petrographic Services Inc.

The somewhat emotional response letter I sent to several people on November 7, 2001 after reading what the carvers of the AVM Stone wrote to the Minnesota Historical Society.

After hanging up the phone I laughed at myself for being so silly and not being able to figure things out sooner. The problem was that I'd only considered two possibilities for the inscription's origin when there was a third possibility. In spite of this, I was proud of myself and everybody else involved for the way we handled the whole affair; we treated the stone as though it were a genuine artifact until it could be properly examined. The best news about the AVM Stone was that we now knew the age of the inscription, and this knowledge could be used as a control sample to create a weathering profile to compare with the Kensington Rune Stone inscription. I asked Arlen and Ruby if they would leave the stone outside so the inscription could continue to weather, and promised that I would visit periodically and see how both the pyrite and biotite were weathering. My first visit back to the stone was May, 2003; Arlen and Ruby had placed the stone in the middle of their flower garden. When I took out my hand-lens and inspected the inscription, I saw the pyrites were still actively weathering and the biotite looked fresh.

I visited again on June 19, 2004, and the pyrites were still going nineteen years after the stone was carved. This is significant because nineteen years prior to 1898, Olof Ohman was still in Sweden; he hadn't yet immigrated to Minnesota. The pyrite weathering proved that Ohman could not have been involved in a hoax. It is ironic that a practical joke by disbelievers of the Stone turned out to be extremely important evidence.

Kensington Rune Stone Forum

In February 2002, I received a call from a professor in the archaeology department at the University of Minnesota, named Guy Gibbon, who said he wanted to get together to talk about the Kensington Rune Stone. We met at my office and visited for about an hour. Guy is a warm, intelligent fellow who was easy to talk with. He explained that his position on the stone was neutral, and he thought there might be an opportunity with the renewed public interest. We talked about trying to assemble experts from various disciplines to discuss potential research, and it seemed like a great idea to get people together from different fields to talk about the Stone. We were excited by the idea, and agreed to put together a list of people to help plan some kind of event.

One of the things I've enjoyed most about this experience with the Kensington Rune Stone is the opportunity to meet new people and to learn new and interesting things. The planning committee we put together certainly was an aggregation. Guy suggested a former researcher at the University of Minnesota named Tom Trow who could help organize such an event. Tom is a very bright fellow who plays his cards close to the vest, sharp witted and not afraid to be confrontational. Normally I wouldn't get along with a guy like Tom, but I liked him right away even though we are two very different people. The first couple of meetings were at the home of Tom Reiersgord, a retired attorney, and the next few meetings were hosted by Bill Jacobson. Both Tom and Bill had a long-time interest in the Stone. Another member of the committee was Rhoda Gilman, a retired teacher and political activist who had worked at the Minnesota Historical Society (MHS) for thirty-five years. She knew both Russell Fridley and Theodore Blegen, and held both in high regard. Rhoda was able to give me personal insight into Professor Blegen, who I had been researching at the Minnesota Historical Society. She understood the problem I had with the fact that Blegen used Winchell's field notes extensively in building his case against the Stone, but ignored all of Winchell's geologic work. Whether it was intentional or not, the good professor tried to have it both ways in his book. It seems that in the thirty-five years since the book was published, this problem had yet to be pointed out.

From the outset, we had people with opinions both pro and con about the Stone's authenticity, and consequently each time the committee met we spent at least half the time discussing various aspects of the Stone. In spite of the fact that we often disagreed we were able to organize a pretty good event. The conference was set for April 2, 2003. It took more than a year to get everything into place, but it was well worth the effort.

Tom Reiersgord

One of the real gentlemen I met throughout this whole Rune Stone experience was a retired attorney who lived in Edina, Minnesota, named Tom Reiersgord. I first met Tom at the Midwest Plains Archaeological Conference. He smiled widely as he introduced himself at the end of our presentations. A tall, thin man in his mid-seventies, Tom was a strong advocate for the Stone. We talked briefly among a small group and he said he had a book coming out soon which would detail his theory that the Stone spent considerable time with Native Americans after it was carved by the Norse. The most interesting thing to me was that he believed the Stone was carved at a different location, then moved, and buried where it was eventually found by Olof Ohman. I didn't pay much attention to the idea at the conference.

The next time I heard from Tom was shortly after the AVM Stone discovery was published in the newspaper. Tom called to ask how our testing was going, and he told me that if the AVM stone turned out to be genuine, then just about everything he wrote in his book would be debunked. I told him I had no idea what the age of the inscription was because we still had a lot of work to do. I remember thinking for a guy who had just published a new book, *The Kensington Rune Stone: Its Place in History*, whose basic premise could be shot down not long after its release he was taking things pretty well in stride. He even had a sense of humor about it. I told him it was premature to draw any conclusions about the stone, and it turned out to be good advice. During this conversation Tom told me he was battling cancer. He had been studying the Stone for many years, but it was finding out about his illness that prompted him to finish his book. Tom was one of the first people I thought of when I heard about the confession letter that was sent to the Minnesota Historical Society.

Not long after the AVM stone saga, I took time to read Tom's book. He had signed a copy for me and asked for feedback. In his book, Tom speculated that the Kensington party carved the inscription in the presence of Native Americans near Lake Mille Lacs, and tied in historical references that could be related to the Kensington Rune Stone. He speculated that eventually the Stone was brought westward and buried where it was found. I remember saying to myself several times as I read that it was a bit of a stretch. Tom didn't take any offense with those who disagreed with him. When I told him what I thought about certain things in the book he smiled and said, "Yes, it's a bit of a stretch, but it is possible." He admitted using some of his experience as a lawyer in his argumentation, and ultimately I had to agree with the possibilities.

One of the first times I had a chance to visit at length with Tom was on the afternoon of September 15, 2002. He called and asked if I would look at a picture of another curious find in Minnesota called the Elbow Lake stone, which many people thought it might contain a runic inscription. We sat down in the study of his older, comfortable home and he pulled out a black and white photograph of the stone. I knew right away it was not a runic inscription, because the circular object was a fossil. There was an ammonite in one corner, and the apparent texture of the rock was reminiscent of limestone. People could be confused about this stone, because the lines between the two circles looked a little bit like runes. When I explained the features to Tom he accepted my opinion. Overall, it was great fun to sit down face to face and get instant feedback to my questions about his book.

We discussed his idea that there might be proof that the Stone was carved at a location other than where it was found. He cited a giant flake of greywacke found at Nichol's Bay, on Lake Mille Lacs, first mentioned in a publication by Jacob Brower. There is a picture of the flake in Tom's book, reproduced from N. H. Winchell's 1911 publication, *The Aborigines of Minnesota*, (plate IV, of scrapers, page 462B). Tom suggested that since I was a geologist who knew the Kensington Rune Stone pretty well, I should try to locate the flake to see if it matched the Stone. I remember thinking it was a long shot, but I told him I would try to find it some time.

When Guy Gibbon and I were thinking of people to help out on the event planning committee, Tom was the first person I thought of. Tom's wife Camilla would drop him off at Bill Jacobson's home for the planning meetings, and I would give him a ride home. Those rides together gave us time to talk about people on the committee who we disagreed with regarding the Stone. One night on our drive home, Tom told me about a local organization he was a member of, called the Manuscript Society. He asked if I would be willing to give the group a presentation about the document search I was working on at the Minnesota Historical Society during their next meeting on Friday night, February 28, 2003.

The dozen or so people who came were very nice, though Janet and I joked later that it had been quite a while since we were the youngest people at a social gathering. I had recently found some really interesting things related to the Kensington Rune Stone that I was excited to share with a group for the first time. Since most of the material I presented was new to me, I was a little more animated than I might otherwise have been. At one point I scolded Theodore Blegen for how he had ignored Winchell's geologic work, when one of the guests spoke up. A woman who knew Professor Blegen personally reminded the group, and me, of his prestegious background, including his tenure as the Dean of Graduate Studies at the University of Minnesota.   Blegen was a mentor to her father, and she called him "Uncle Teddy." I sheepishly acknowledged her comments and apologized for my exuberance. I learned a valuable lesson that night and toned down the opinionated part of my presentation.

At the Kensington Rune Stone Forum at Fort Snelling, Tom gave a short and dignified summary of his ideas. Like everyone else who presented, there wasn't enough time to discuss anything at length. Tom wasn't feeling great, but he still had that ever-present smile on his face, and he enjoyed the conference and all the positive energy that was being put into researching the Kensington Rune Stone. Tom lost his battle with cancer in September, 2003. I wasn't interested in Tom's ideas at first, but my thinking evolved. I've tried to look at the various arguments about the Stone within a logical framework, and when I did this with Tom's ideas, they took on a different light. To me, it boiled down to this: the Stone was found near the crest of a hill, buried several inches deep, with the inscription side down. The processes of erosion would be in effect on the hill, as well as frost action which would tend bring a rock to the surface, so there is no plausible way to explain the Stone having been buried by nature. The Stone had to have been intentionally buried by man. It seems that whomever carved the stone intended for it to stand upright, partially buried in the ground. If the carvers didn't bury the Stone, who did? Most likely it was found by Native Americans. We will never know for sure what happened, but this point is where Tom's book becomes very interesting. This possible association with native people just as adds another dimension to ponder in the collection of Kensington Rune Stone mysteries.

Some attendees of the Kensington Rune Stone Forum at Historic Fort Snelling in St. Paul, Minnesota on April 2, 2003, had dinner at the St. Paul Grill after the event. L to R: LuAnn Patton, Camilla Reiersgord, Tom Reiersgord, and Helen Tanner. (SFW)

The Barnes Review and the Smithsonian Institution

In March 2002, I received a call from someone with a publication in Washington D.C. called *The Barnes Review*, asking if Dick and I would be willing to come to Washington and give presentations about our work on the Kensington Rune Stone. After discussing the opportunity we thought it would be a good idea to try to line up a presentation at the Smithsonian Institution during our visit. We knew full well that consultants who have offered opinions about the Kensington Rune Stone had the Smithsonian thoroughly convinced that the Stone was a hoax. Birgitta Wallace was the primary source of the Smithsonian's negative opinion of the Stone. Ms. Wallace had co-authored the highly criticized chapter 29 in the Smithsonian publication edited by Fitzhugh and Ward, *Vikings: The North Atlantic Saga.* In chapter 29 Wallace wrote three pages on why the Stone was a hoax. Researcher Michael Zalar had taken her to task on thirty-nine specific points in those three pages, and to say the least, found her work less than scholarly. We also knew that if they accepted our invitation that we would be received with mixed emotions. What made the prospect of our visit more difficult for the Arctic Studies department was that their high-profile "Vikings" exhibition was currently traveling the country with the Kensington Rune Stone displayed as an "unknown." Aware of our position, I sensed hesitation on the other end of the line when I called with the offer to give a presentation.

The museum operator put me through to Elisabeth Ward, the contact person in the Arctic Studies department. Elisabeth was very friendly, but a little guarded during our initial conversation. She said a presentation of the latest research sounded like a good idea, but that she would have to run it by her superior, Dr. William Fitzhugh. Bill had co-authored chapter 29, but when I met him a year before our DC trip he back-peddled, saying Birgitta Wallace had written about the Kensington Rune Stone and that he had simply edited the chapter. I assured Ms. Ward that we were not on any kind of military mission; we wanted to present the research as a courtesy, because we thought the Institution would be interested. Elisabeth and I talked again a few days later and set up a time in conjunction with our *Barnes Review* trip to D.C.

Shortly after we arrived at the conference we realized that the attendees were indeed an interesting collection of people. We didn't hear many of the other presentations, but the few we did hear tended to get the crowd riled up. When it was our turn, Dick and I wanted to get into the spirit a little bit so we made our points with a little more verve. I even got a few people to yell in agreement, "Hear, hear!" Overall, we were treated very well and appreciated the opportunity to speak to such a spirited group. As enjoyable as the *Barnes Review* experience was, our main goal on the trip was to meet with the people at the Smithsonian Institution. Our appointment was set for Friday, June 14 at 10:00 a.m.

A banner hanging behind the speaker's podium displays the *Barnes Review* mission statement for their Third Annual Conference held in Washington, D.C. Dick and I each gave presentations about the Rune Stone at the conference on June 15, 2002. (SFW)

Dick, his oldest son Tom, LuAnn, and I met in the hotel restaurant for breakfast and then started our trek to Washington Square. Our nation's capitol is a special place, and walking along the mall admiring the magnificent buildings gives even the most cynical a reason to be optimistic and proud. We walked in to the Natural History Museum with that same sense of pride and the feeling that we were doing the right thing. We waited in the lobby while Ms. Ward was paged; within a few minutes she appeared and graciously introduced herself. Elisabeth's warmth and professional demeanor made us feel welcome as she escorted us to the fourth floor of the museum where the staff offices, classrooms, and many artifacts not currently on display were housed. As we walked along the hallway I looked up at the high ceilings and noticed the busts of humans from ancient tribes sitting on top of what must have been at least ten-foot tall specimen cabinets. Walking through these halls reminded me of the final scene in the movie *Raiders of the Lost Ark* where the Ark of the Covenant is wheeled into a huge storage room filled with endless rows of mysterious boxed-up artifacts.

Eventually Elisabeth led us into a classroom where we set up our computer and projector. A few minutes later, Dr. Ives Goddard, a linguist; Iris Hahn, a linguistics intern; and Dr. Sorena Sorenson, a geologist, arrived and introduced themselves. Dick knew Dr. Goddard, who had been a student of Einar Haugen at Harvard, and had explained earlier that he was a harsh critic of the Kensington Rune Stone inscription. I presented on the geological aspects of the Stone first, watching Dr. Sorenson to gauge her reaction to the points I made. As a fellow geologist, hers was the opinion that mattered most to me. At one point I noticed Sorena was leaning forward in her chair with her elbows on the table, engaged with my presentation. I took this as very positive body language. A moment later I happened to glance to the other end of the table and saw Elisabeth looking at Sorena with a somewhat puzzled look on her face. She saw that Sorena was interested and seemed unsure how to react.

I spoke for close to an hour and a half, and then asked if there were any questions. Sorena's only question was whether Professor Winchell's report had ever been published in a scientific journal. I almost laughed thinking, "that's it." I assumed that if she had no other questions then she didn't have any major problems with my findings. I told her I would get back to her about Winchell's publication since I wasn't sure what the answer was. Then it was Dick's turn. He also presented an hour and a half, after which Dr. Goddard asked several questions in a caustic manner. In my opinion, he was quite arrogant and bordered on rude as he challenged various linguistic points. Dick is a gentleman who I have never seen "take the bait" and become combative in his argumentation. True to form, he remained calm and never lowered himself to the point of making derogatory or demeaning comments. He stuck to the facts and carried himself with confidence because he knew that he has done his homework.

It was hard to say whether he made any headway with Dr. Goddard, but I think everyone in the room believed the time invested was worthwhile. Later that night over dinner and a beer, Dick, Tom, LuAnn, and I talked about our day at the museum. We agreed it would be some time before we'd realize what, if any, benefit our presentations would generate. If nothing else, we felt we had successfully achieved good will that might pay off down the road.

LuAnn Patton, Elisabeth Ward, Richard Nielsen, and linguistic intern Iris Hahn, pose for a photo at the Smithsonian Institution's Museum of Natural History in Washington, D. C., on June 14, 2002. (SFW)

Lars Westman's Visit

On September 3, 2002, a Swedish journalist by the name of Lars Westman paid a visit to my office to talk about our work on the Stone. Lars was very friendly and instantly likeable, with a warm and calm demeanor and a heavy Swedish accent. Dick had previously explained to me that Lars was known as the "Walter Cronkite" of Sweden, and I wanted to help him any way I could. He asked me about our testing, and for the next three hours we looked at images on my computer while I told him the whole story. He was very interested, and even excited by our findings, and said he would write a favorable article and try to get the Stone to travel to Sweden.

Lars had never had barbeque before, so that night he enjoyed take-out barbeque dinner at our house. We got him ready for bed with a couple of margaritas, which he also enjoyed. Lars charmed everyone with stories about Sweden, saying some day we would come visit him there. It sure sounded like a good time to me!

The next morning Lars accompanied me to the office. Dick arrived from Texas at noon, and shortly after he and Lars set off for a trip to Alexandria to see the Stone. The two of them spent three days running around the area, and on their way back to Minneapolis they stopped by our house for a final visit. While we were sitting in our half-finished remodeled family room, a package was delivered. Inside were three copies of Barry Hanson's two-volume work on the Kensington Rune Stone. The three of us went through the book and enjoyed the entertaining fictional trial of all the scholars who had opposed the Stone.

In September 2002, Swedish journalist Lars Westman traveled to Minnesota to investigate the latest research for a story he was working on about the Kensington Rune Stone. Lars visited the Wolter home on September 7, 2002. L to R: Janet, Amanda, Scott, Grant, and Lars (Photo by Richard Nielsen).

Before heading to the airport, Lars thanked us for our help and hospitality, and promised to throw a "fantastic" party when we came to Sweden. As he drove away with Dick, I hoped to some day attend that party. I would find out in the not too distant future that Lars Westman was a man of his word.

Bryant Mather Review

Over the course of 2002 I had asked several geologists for a peer review of my Kensington Rune Stone report. There was one person I felt would be the toughest critic, someone I had known for about ten years, who had provided me with valuable insight on another highly controversial subject: concrete. He reviewed my manuscript for the book, *Ettringite: Cancer of Concrete,* and wrote a spirited foreword without mincing one word in it. Dr. Bryant Mather was the one of the nation's foremost experts on concrete and had recently retired, but was still serving as the director emeritus of the Structures Laboratory for the US Army Corp of Engineers in Vicksburg, Mississippi. Bryant was an honorary member and past president of both the American Concrete Institute (ACI) and the American

Society for Testing Materials (ASTM). He had authored almost eight hundred technical papers and reports, and I knew he would be able to give my report on the Kensington Rune Stone a critical, but fair technical review.

I had spoken with Bryant and he talked about his struggle with prostate cancer. He was 85 years old and resigned to the seriousness of his situation, but vowed to fight through it. His mind and wit were as sharp as ever when I asked if he would review my paper, he replied in his typical "Mather monotone" voice, "Certainly." I sent my paper to Bryant in the middle of October, 2002, and figured he'd get to it pretty quickly because whenever I'd sent something to him in the past, he usually had it back to me within two weeks. I didn't think much about the review for the first couple of weeks, but toward the end of November I started wondering if something was wrong. I checked my mail every day as the calendar turned to December. On Thursday, December 5th I was at the Minnesota Concrete Conference at the University of Minnesota, when an announcement was made at one of the sessions that Bryant had passed away the previous day. Everyone associated with the concrete industry knew Bryant and was greatly saddened that one of the true giants was gone. Not only was I sad about his passing, I also felt bad that he hadn't been well enough to review my paper. I told myself repeatedly that I should have sent it to him earlier, but soon I was resigned to the situation and had moved on.

After lunch on December 9th, I was sorting through my mail when I noticed the return address on a letter that made me jump out of my chair: US Army Corps of Engineers, Vicksburg, Mississippi. I tore open the letter and sure enough, it was Bryant's review of my paper. I was emotionally torn between the excitement of knowing that he had finished the review and dread that he had ripped me to shreds. I was also a little freaked out that his letter had arrived five days after his death. I assumed that his co-workers had cleaned off his desk, found the review, and sent it to me. As I read his review I chuckled at several of his typical picky comments, most of them about my grammar. At the end of his letter he wrote about the cancer that he knew was going to get him, and I read the words of a man who had fought a courageous battle but was resigned to his fate. He said he thought the report was "well written" and that our hypothesis was plausible. He signed off with his signature salutation, "Cheers, Bryant."

Kensington Rune Stone Digital Photo Library

Dick and I had talked about photographing each and every rune under the microscope since the Stone first came to the lab in fall, 2000. By late 2002, I was able to carve out some time to do the scope work and made arrangements with LuAnn to have the Stone come to the lab. I worked on the project all weekend, taking over six hundred digital images with low- and high-angle reflected light. What surprised me was finding several punches in many of the runes that hadn't been noticed before. An extra leg at the bottom of a "thorn" rune on the fourth line was the most surprising. It is an intentionally carved line. There are about a dozen thorn runes in the inscription, but this is the only one like this. I had no idea what this unusual rune meant, but it definitely meant something, so I called Dick. He thought it might be a combination of two runes, called a "bindrune." Dick said he would discuss it with Professor Henrik Williams, a linguist at the University in Uppsala, Sweden, to see if they could make sense of it.

All the runes were photographed and organized into folders, and a CD of all these images was given to LuAnn when the Stone was returned to the museum in Alexandria.

The digital photo library will be useful to present and future researchers. This never-before-seen two-legged "thorn" rune was discovered using low angle light. (SFW)

Minnesota Historical Society Document Search

As the 2002 holiday season wound down, I realized that there was time to turn my attention to another aspect of the controversy. I knew there was a wealth of information about the Kensington Rune Stone at the Minnesota Historical Society (MHS), only a ten minute drive from my office. The History Center building is finished inside and out with marble and granite, and it looks like a palace. The first day I walked in I didn't know where to start, so I trotted up to the library desk and asked for information about the Kensington Rune Stone. I was impressed with the knowledgeable staff who enthusiastically helped me become comfortable locating the documents I was looking for. I was anxious to find several items, but the one thing I most wanted to locate was Newton Winchell's original field notebook; to me it was the "Holy Grail" of the Kensington Rune Stone story. I'll be the first to admit that I am favorably biased toward this accomplished pioneer of Minnesota geology. Anyone who knows anything about Professor Winchell respects his accomplishments and the kind of man he was. In fact, one of the goals of my research was to learn as much as I could about the man I consider the one clear voice of reason and wisdom among the many characters in the Kensington Rune Stone story. Winchell played a pivotal role during the crucial period of time between 1908 and 1911. I couldn't wait to see what I would find.

Newton Winchell

On February 4, 2002, I visited the Minnesota Historical Society library for the first time. I started with Winchell's personal papers, and found that there were twenty boxes of material on file. While waiting for the first box to be retrieved for me, I decided to see if I could find someone who might be interested in the photo library of the inscription, thinking the Society should have a copy for their archives. I was introduced to the curator of manuscripts, Craig Wright, who agreed to sit down with me in a conference room, where I ended up giving my entire PowerPoint presentation. Craig received the presentation enthusiastically and gave me permission to use my digital camera to photograph whatever documents I wanted. The convenience of having digital images of original documents saved me a lot of research time and was invaluable in writing my reports and this book. Craig suggested that at some point I compile everything I've assembled about the Rune Stone and give a copy to the Society, which at the appropriate time I plan to do.

The first box I requested was Winchell's personal letters, and it was great to see how caring and compassionate Winchell was when writing to family members. The letter that touched me the most was actually written by his son Alexander on March 5, 1905. Alexander wrote about the arrangements he made for his father at the Mayo Clinic, where Newton was to have an operation for a problem with his prostate. Alexander implored his father to have the operation before leaving on an extended trip to the west coast, and told his father that he would pay for the operation and to not give him any grief about it. After reading the letter I thought about how proud Winchell must have been of his son.

The end of the letter that Alexander Winchell wrote to his father on March 14, 1905. (Minnesota Historical Society) *"One more thing I want to emphasize—in deciding this question the matter of cost should not be considered at all. I shall be glad to pay all the costs if you have the work done. Do not let that factor of the case affect your decision at all. Do not think, either, that I would be <u>giving</u> you any money—it would be only repaying you a small part of what you have given me."*

The second box contained ten of Winchell's geological field notebooks. I looked through six or seven of them and became discouraged, thinking that the Kensington Rune Stone notebook might be in a different place. The Information Desk confirmed my suspicion that the Kensington Rune Stone material was filed separately. They pulled a listing of the material in that file and sure enough, Winchell documents were listed. I filled out a request slip and went back to the table to wait for the material to be brought up. I started to put the notebooks I'd been looking at back in their box to return them, but decided to kill some time checking out the last couple books. I felt a strange kind of connection with Winchell and thoroughly enjoyed scanning neat, meticulous notes. I rapidly paged through the final book, trying to finish the job and move on to the next box when a familiar pencil drawing caught my eye. In the middle of the last notebook, there was pencil sketch of the tree roots growing over the Kensington Rune Stone, the same drawing that appears in Blegen's book. I felt an eerie and exciting chill as I paged through the notes more carefully. I had come so close to missing this important notebook.

The author, feeling relieved after finding N. H. Winchell's field notebook at the Minnesota Historical Society library on February 11, 2003. (Photo by MHS staff member)

I proceeded to photograph all fifty pages of the notebook that pertained to the Kensington Rune Stone. By the time I finished, my shirt was littered with small pieces of paper that had fallen out of the books, brittle with age. These old documents were literally falling apart. When I mentioned to Craig Wright that he should put this valuable notebook in a safe place, he agreed and made arrangements for the book to have special viewing procedures.

While poring over Winchell's papers, I found several eye-opening documents. As interesting as the personal letters and the notebook were, I learned more about the professor's intelligence by reviewing two publications by prominent American linguists of the time. Winchell learned enough about the language on the Stone to comment on various aspects of the linguistic arguments of George T. Flom and Olaus Breda, who each wrote lengthy papers detailing why they believed the inscription was a hoax. Winchell carefully reviewed these papers and wrote comments in the margins where he was quite blunt in his criticism of Breda, and pointed out several interesting statements by Flom.

Comments written by N. H. Winchell after his review of O. J. Breda's 1910 paper on the Kensington Rune Stone. (Minnesota Historical Society)

"'That article is not worth the paper it is printed on.' Mohn, Ed. Norwegian American.

"Prof. Breda sent in an English abstract of the above article, prior to its publication. It is a mass of ridicule and opinionated assertion without any bearing on the merits of the stone."

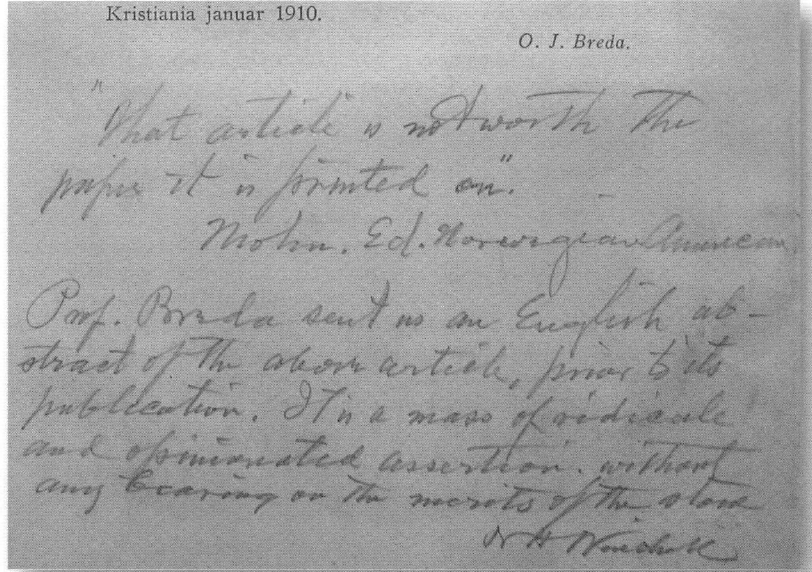

Overall, I was struck by how diligent, thorough and reasoned his logic was throughout his investigation. The glowing reviews I'd heard about him as a geology student were overwhelmingly confirmed. I was even more impressed by how he was able to develop an opinion about the weathering of the inscription with the relatively archaic microscopic equipment at the time. The powerful scanning electron microscopes we have today made my job relatively easy. On the other hand, he had the benefit of personally interviewing Ohman, his family and other witnesses to gather facts and insight; resources that can never be duplicated. It was reassuring to know that the early geologic work on the artifact was performed by someone so competent and wise. I was somewhat relieved when I read that his conclusion was the same as mine, however, after thinking about it a while I realized that I shouldn't have been surprised. He used essentially the same geologic techniques and methods, so the results *should* be repeatable with similar conclusions.

Over the course of the next several weeks I spent dozens of hours at the library and uncovered a lot of important information, amazed at the huge number of documents related to the Kensington Rune Stone. I took over three thousand digital photographs of pages I considered to be relevant documents. By far the most interesting group of documents was the hand written letters of various individuals involved in the controversy, the most prolific of whom was Hjalmar Holand. There were seventy-two letters that he wrote to Winchell and Warren Upham, some eight to nine pages long. I was frustrated at not being able to read either the initial inquiries that prompted a return letter or finally the reply of other letters. In April 2003, while checking a reference in Blegen's book, I discovered the correspondence that had eluded me to this point. Professor Blegen had spent time looking through these same books, for many of the letters are referenced in his 1968 book. Eventually, I would also become very familiar with these important, voluminous documents.

Letter Press Books

In the first box of the Letter Press Books the bindings on the six volumes were so badly deteriorated that they had almost completely fallen off. I pulled the first volume out of the box and noticed a red string that was tied around the book. I gently pulled loose the knotted red string tied around the book, and carefully opened the two-inch thick book to reveal the fragile rice-paper pages. I delicately turned each page so I wouldn't tear it, though in spite of my concerted efforts, I still occasionally tore a page. A few pages were already damaged almost to the point of being lost forever.

These pages were copies of the handwritten letters sent by the Museum Committee of the Minnesota Historical Society, nearly all of them from the years 1908 through 1916 written by then secretary Warren Upham. The letters were recorded in these books when the ink from his pen bled through the paper he was using to compose the letter, on to the rice paper underneath. Each book represents one year and contains over a thousand pages. I scanned each page for familiar names or key words that were related to the Kensington Rune Stone, until slowly but surely the holes in the correspondence filled in and a clearer picture emerged of the events surrounding the Kensington Rune Stone investigation from 1909 to 1911. The letters detailed the laborious process the Museum Committee went through when making its decision whether or not to purchase the Kensington Rune Stone from Hjalmar Holand.

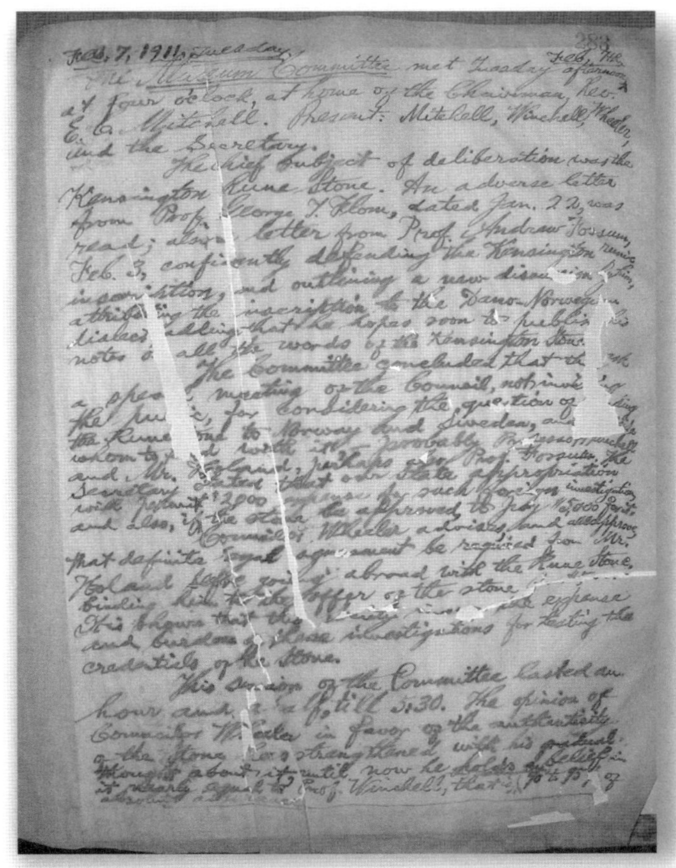

The rice-paper pages in the Letter Press Books were so fragile that some were in very poor shape. This badly damaged page from 1911 had to be fully re-assembled like a jig-saw puzzle so it could be photographed. (Minnesota Historical Society)

Warren Upham

Professor Warren Upham was tireless, often writing the same lengthy letters about a particular event to several individuals, though it must have taken a huge amount of time each day to compose them. His writing style changed when he wrote to classmates and family members, and his feelings about many topics, including the Kensington Rune Stone, were revealed when he wrote to the people he was close to. He had a great amount of respect for Professor Winchell, both professionally and personally. In 1910 and 1911 however, Upham's position on the authenticity of the Stone was 50-50. He was clearly influenced by the negative statements of linguists such as George Flom. This uncertainty led him to vote against purchasing the Stone in spite of the anxiety he must have felt, knowing he was in conflict with Winchell over this important decision.

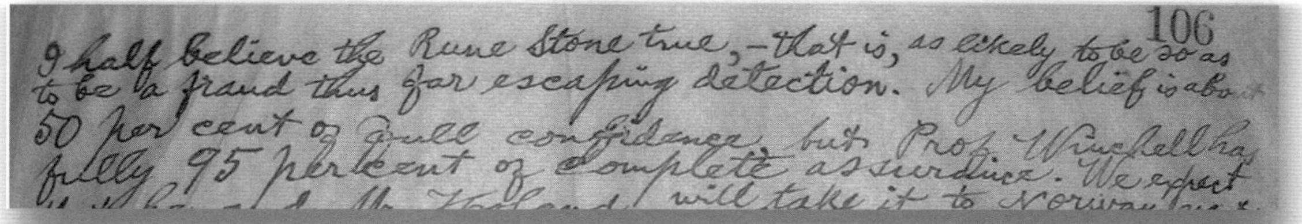

On December 30, 1910, Warren Upham wrote a note at the top of page 106 about how he half believed in the Rune Stone. (Minnesota Historical Society)
"I half believe the Rune Stone true,—that is, as likely to be so as to be a fraud thus far escaping detection. My belief is about 50 per cent of full confidence, but Prof. Winchell has fully 95 per cent or complete assurance."

Of course no one was more disappointed than Hjalmar Holand, and his anger is clearly evident in his replies upon hearing the Society's decision. After digesting all the correspondence and thinking about what might have been going on in the minds of the key players during this tumultuous time, I came away thinking that the questions about the Kensington Rune Stone had been handled well. These were some of the brightest and most well-reasoned people of their time, and although they couldn't reach a consensus, the issue was handled professionally. I have doubts that there would be people of the same intelligence and character to rise to the challenge were the process repeated today.

As I continued flipping pages though the days, weeks, months, and years of letters Upham recorded, the subject of the Kensington Rune Stone began to fade. However, I could not pull myself away because I kept stumbling onto interesting subjects or a scientific paper Upham had written in longhand. With a strong background in geomorphology and glacial geology, I was thrilled to read his papers on Glacial Lake Agassiz (March, 1913) and how Minnetonka and Minneapolis got their names (December, 1916). It was a pleasure to read about his trips around the state researching a book that would eventually be published in 1920, *Minnesota Geographic Names*. There was no real reason for me to continue reading the letters within these books for information about the Rune Stone, but I burned many hours combing the roughly 5,000 pages between 1912 and 1917. Each time I was about to quit, I'd find something interesting or tell myself, "fifty more pages and that's it." My persistence would pay off.

In May of 1916, Upham took a trip to do research for his book, and the train took him through the town of Kensington. On a whim he decided to stay and walk the 3 ¹/₂ miles to the Ohman farm to meet Olof and his family. When Professor Upham returned to the Society he wrote a flurry of letters to Holand and others about his visit with Ohman. He was so impressed with Ohman's honesty and candor that his opinion was changed about the authenticity of the Stone. This fateful visit and its impact have never before been discussed by Kensington Rune Stone researchers. Even the highly respected and thorough researcher Theodore Blegen, who spent considerable time looking at the Letter Press Books, apparently did not find these important letters.

I immediately thought back to the letter that Ohman wrote to Upham on December 9, 1909, after being invited to visit the Society and meet its members. Winchell had already met Ohman at least three times and understood his character and how it impacted the stone; Upham had not. In the letter, Ohman wrote that he could not afford to come to St. Paul and that his presence was not necessary. How might the vote have gone if the Society had insisted on a visit and paid Ohman's expenses and lodging. The Stone would likely be on display at the Minnesota Historical Society today instead of a small museum in Alexandria.

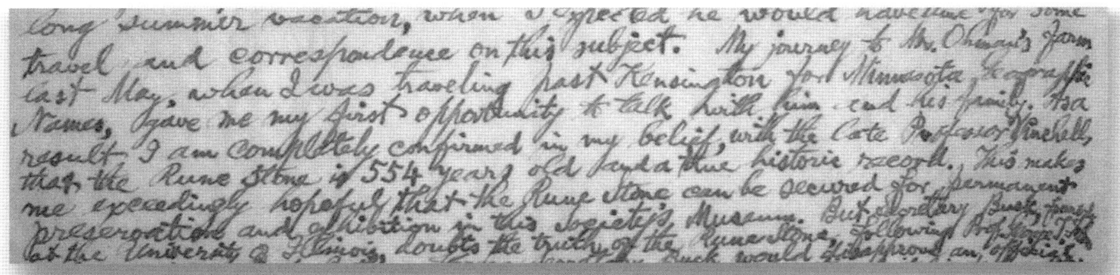

One of the many letters, this one dated November 14, 1916, that Warren Upham wrote over the course of a year and a half period after meeting Olof Ohman and his family in May, 1916. (Minnesota Historical Society) *"My journey to Mr. Ohman's farm last May, when I was traveling past Kensington for Minnesota Geographic Names, gave me my first opportunity to talk with him and his family. As a result I am completely confirmed in my belief, with the late Professor Winchell, that the Rune Stone is 554 years old and a true historic record. This makes me exceedingly hopeful that the Rune Stone can be secured for permanent preservation and exhibition in this Society's Museum."*

Hjalmar Holand

In addition to learning as many facts about the Kensington Rune Stone story as I could, one of my other goals has been to learn about the key individuals involved, and I found the personal letters revealed a great deal about how people's minds worked. In my opinion, the prolific Mr. Holand was the most enigmatic individual of all. The man who emerges from these letters is highly intelligent, strong willed, diligent, and thorough, but also forceful in his opinions to the point of arrogance with regard to the Rune Stone. He certainly wasn't shy about his feelings towards the people who disagreed with him. He had little time for anyone who disagreed with him, which made his efforts to get his message across more difficult. Holand made enemies who, in part because of his abrasive and confrontational style, went out of their way to undermine his work.

Hjalmar Holand's sometimes abrupt style comes through in this August 3, 1908 letter to N. H. Winchell. (Minnesota Historical Society) *"I told Dr. Upham that I would write a paper on the Rune Stone for 35.00 as I absolutely cannot and do not write for nothing."*

The Holand letters sometimes give a sense that his research on the Kensington Rune Stone was the only thing going on in his life. This was certainly not the case. Mr. Holand experienced an especially trying event that jumped out in a letter dated August 17, 1910.

A tragic event related by Holand in an August 17, 1910 letter to Winchell. (Minnesota Historical Society)
"Your letter came just as I left Ephraim with the bodies of two young ladies from Chicago visiting at my house who were drowned while out boating with a young man. It was a very sad affair. My own two children accompanied them but were resuscitated after more than an hour's doubtful work."

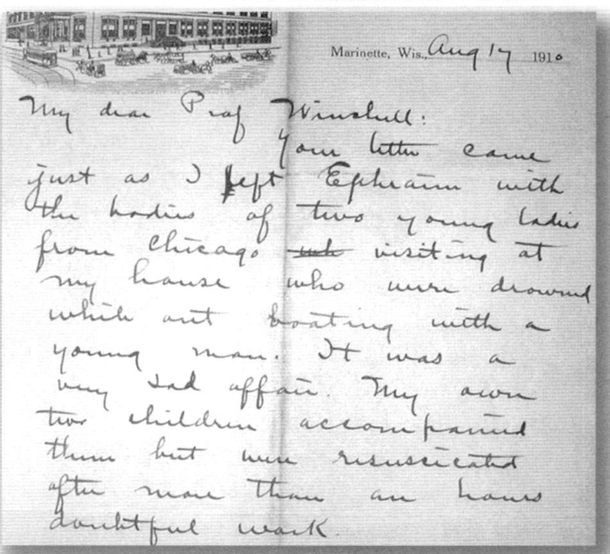

Perhaps one of Holand's most enduring qualities was his tenacity. Approaching the age of ninety he was still working hard on the Kensington Rune Stone when he wrote to Theodore Blegen. Holand also wrote a response to the scathing accusations of his work that appeared in the 1958 book by Erik Wahlgren, *The Kensington Rune Stone: A Mystery Solved.*

Holand wrote wistfully at the end of this letter to Theodore Blegen on November 7, 1960. (Minnesota Historical Society)
"I hope you are enjoying good health. I am feeling fine and have had no aches or pains, except for the death of my wife, for years."

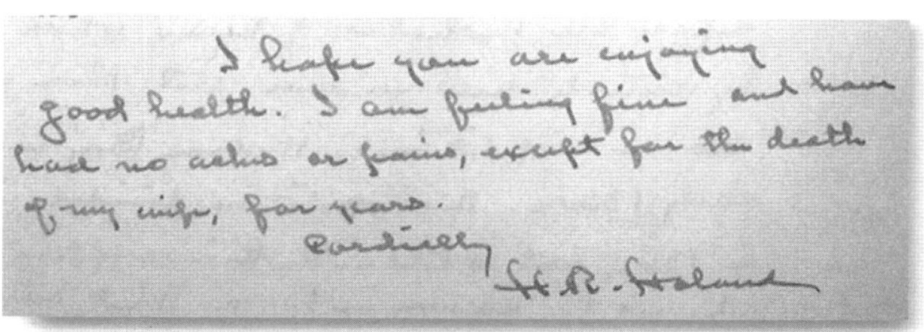

There would have been more interesting and important documents to research had it not been for the fire that burned Mr. Holand's home to the ground in 1934. All of his records, letters, and photographs were destroyed. Nevertheless, his letters at the Minnesota Historical Society present a different perspective on the controversy that I felt was important in order to have a complete understanding of the complex issues and personalities involved.

The Tombstone Study

The idea to perform a tombstone study came to me as I tried to think of a way to determine how long it took for the mica minerals in the Kensington Rune Stone inscription to weather away. The concept is really pretty simple. Small chip samples could be taken from the polished or carved surfaces of tombstones of various ages. Death dates on the tombstones provide an exact record of how long the exposed minerals have been weathering, and from these samples we could see how long it takes for the key minerals to weather away. Since the micas were completely weathered away in the original inscription of the Kensington Rune Stone they were the perfect minerals to focus the research on. Of the four mica minerals present in the Stone (biotite, cerrusite, chlorite, and muscovite), I chose biotite because it contained iron and weathered the fastest.

Now that I had a viable methodology I needed to think through the practical issues of actually performing the work. First, I wrote up a list of criteria. Important items included: finding tombstones that were in a similar weathering environment as the Kensington Rune Stone, making sure the grain size of the minerals was the same, collecting samples from both above and below grade, and obtaining permission to collect the samples. As I worked through the study in my mind, I realized that I needed to learn more about the monument business. For instance, I needed to know whether or not surface treatments are now, or ever were used to help preserve monuments.

I also thought long and hard about sampling the tombstones, and whether this research was in any way disrespectful to the deceased. I believe that most people would be excited to participate in a worthwhile experiment that might help solve an important question of history, and as fate would have it, the tombstone study got off to an unexpected, but terrific start.

In late October 2002, Dick and I met in Boston, Massachusetts, to spend a couple of days looking at other Rune Stones that have been found along the northeastern coast of the US. The tiny town of Bourne, Massachusetts is home to the Bourne Stone, reportedly brought to the Pilgrims by Native Americans to be used as a step for a church being built for the Natives in 1658. We found the stone at a small 250-year-old trading post in Aptuxet, Massachusetts, and were startled at how its size and shape are similar to the Kensington Rune Stone. The geology of the stone however, is quite different. This flat and tabular stone is yellow-pink granite gneiss, with a strongly developed foliation. The inscription is very crude and didn't look very much like runes to me; some carved figures on the stone could be Indian petroglyphs. As I scanned the inscription trying to look past the dark charcoaled lines I could see other man-made lines that were not darkened. I asked our host, Ms. Eleanor Hammond with the Bourne Historical Society, if she could lend me a flashlight and turn off the lights. It was a cold, wet, overcast day, and when the lights were turned off it got very dark inside the trading post. I took the flashlight and cast the light at a low angle to highlight the carved characters. Dick and I could easily see that there was much more than what had been charcoaled. The other thing was that, given the reported history of the stone, it was not a modern hoax.

We talked with Eleanor about possible future testing ideas, and she seemed excited about our suggestions. We thanked her for allowing us to see the stone, then we jumped into the rental car around noon and then headed north to Maine.

The Bourne Stone sat in a corner on the floor at the Aptuxet Trading Post near Bourne, Massachusetts on March 5, 2003. (SFW)

During the four hour drive we had time to talk about all kinds of things. I explained to Dick how the tombstone study would work and why I thought biotite would be the best mineral to focus on. We saw bedrock outcropings all along the way to Maine and I stopped a couple times to show Dick some beautiful mica-rich schist. Since we were scheduled to see the Spirit Pond Rune Stones the next morning I asked Dick to give me some background information about them. The three cobble-sized inscribed stones were found weathering on beach gravel along an inter-coastal waterway in 1969. Copies of the inscriptions were sent to Einar Haugen, a prominent linguist at the University in Uppsala, Sweden. He recognized characters similar to the well-known Rune Stone in Minnesota, and declared them fake. The stones are now housed at the annex building in Hallowell, Maine, where Dick had made an appointment for us to review them. We were only able to see two of the three stones because the "Inscription Stone" was on display in the Smithsonian Institution's "Vikings" exhibit that was currently at the Science Museum of Minnesota in St. Paul.

We made good time driving and decided to see if we could see the rune stones before the building closed at 4:30 p.m., but unfortunately, the doors were locked when we got there just after 4:00 p.m. While Dick tried to find a way to get in, I waited in the car thinking about my wife and kids back home, who were getting ready to go out trick or treating without me. I felt bad being away for Halloween, but it was the only time we could both get away. The sky was just beginning to darken as I scanned the area, and I suddenly realized that the local cemetery was right next to the building I was sitting in front of. A big smile spread across my face as I thought about what Dick and I could do for the next couple of hours on Halloween night.

When Dick returned he saw the rows of tombstones and was just as eager to start wandering around. As we entered the cemetery, we noticed a parked van with three teenagers in it, doing something next to the building. We had no reason to disturb them so we continued on. The cemetery was quite large so we had hundreds, if not thousands, of tombstones to look at. The tombstones nearest the annex building were the youngest, generally made of granite and gneiss, both hard and durable rocks. Older gravestones were mostly made of marble. In the growing darkness, we could easily see how the marble inscriptions were harder to read because they were weathering at a much faster rate than the granite stones. The marble tombstones dated from the 1930s back to about the 1850s. As we ventured further in, the geology of the tombstones changed once again. They became a dark gray to black color and were made of a rock type I am very familiar with. These tombstones were older than the marble tombstones and still had clearly legible inscriptions, in fact they looked as though they were carved yesterday even though many of them were over two hundred years old. These tombstones were made from a metamorphic rock, called slate.

Dick began asking me questions about slate when it suddenly dawned on me that these were the perfect stones to collect samples from for the tombstone study. I excitedly began to tell Dick that they were comprised almost entirely of biotite, one of the key minerals of interest in the Kensington Rune Stone. Biotite is the fastest weathering of the micas in the Kensington Rune Stone, and these tombstones appeared to have a similar grain size; both factors were critical to the experiment. In addition, the oldest tombstones extended into the ground, which would allow for both above and below grade sampling; almost all of the younger monuments were set onto a small concrete pad at ground level. The more we talked about it the more it seemed that we had found the perfect place to obtain samples for the tombstone study.

By now it was completely dark, and we were wondering how my kids, Amanda and Grant, were doing trick or treating back home. I just had to tell them that Dick and I were wandering around in an old cemetery on Halloween night, so I pulled out my cell phone and called home.

After we had combed the cemetery for more than two hours, it was time to find a hotel. We were making our way back to the car when we noticed several jack-o-lanterns glowing in the darkness where the teenagers had been working, so we walked closer and found that they had set up a Halloween memorial to a recently deceased friend. Nick must have been a Rock fan, because his friends had carved the likenesses of Jimi Hendrix and Bob Marley into two of the pumpkins.

While returning to the car, Dick Nielsen and I came across a jack-o-lantern memorial that some teen-agers left for their friend Nick on Halloween night, 2002, in the Hallowell Cemetery in Hallowell, Maine. (SFW)

We awoke at about 6:00 a.m., excited from the wild night in the cemetery, and anticipating seeing the Spirit Pond Rune Stones in a few short hours. Our appointment to see the stones wasn't until 9:30 a.m. so we decided to head to a place by the cemetery that Dick had spotted the previous night, called "Grinders." Grinders are a type of stuffed sandwich popular in New England. We ordered coffee and rolls and found a booth that looked out over the Kennebec River. The sun was just peeking through the leafless trees on a cool, clear late fall morning. We were over twenty miles from the ocean, but could still make out the river slowly rising as the tide moved in. Dick gazed out at the river and said softly, "They would have come here." He spoke with knowledge and experience from his years at sea as a young man in the United States Coast Guard. He sipped his coffee and spoke with disdain about how people put limitations on where the Norse explorers could and could not go. They were sailors, he said, "Damned good ones too. This area of New England would be the perfect place for them to come for wood, furs, and trade with the Indians. They were probably coming here for centuries."

When the topic switched back to the tombstone study we talked about what kind of information we needed prior to sampling. I told Dick I had to learn more about the monument business. I didn't know how long a tombstone sat around before it was sold and carved, or if the monuments were ever coated with a weatherproofing sealer, for instance. As we chatted, it dawned on me that Janet had put the kids' most recent school pictures into my wallet before I left, so I dug them out to show Dick, never noticing the local couple a few booths over. With a heavy New England accent the woman asked, "Are those pictures of your kids?" I went over to the smiling couple in their fifties and showed them the pictures. They quickly realized from our accents that we were visitors, and they asked us what we were doing in Hallowell. We told them about the Spirit Pond Rune Stones, which they had not heard of before.

I then explained in a humorous way that we'd spent the previous night in the cemetery looking at tombstones. They smiled as I explained that I was interested in talking with someone in the monument business, then Tony looked as his wife Linda and they both started to laugh. Tony reached over and put his cap on his head. Dick and I couldn't believe the words we read across the top of his hat, "Maschadri Monuments." We all laughed, realizing that *they* owned the local monument business. Tony offered to show us around since their office was right next door. Fate sure seemed to be working for us that day.

We still had more than an hour before our appointment, so we finished our coffee and walked over to their shop. The old wooden building was very small, and tools of the trade were scattered throughout the inside. Dick and I peppered Linda and Tony with questions and they graciously answered every one. A large wooden door at the back side of the building opened to a yard area, and when I peered outside I saw tombstones strewn about, all down the bank next to the river. When I looked closer I could see that they all had names and dates on them. Tony explained that people often upgrade a loved one's tombstone with a newer monument, and the old ones were tossed into this area. He knew what my next question would be before I could ask it. He went back inside and returned with a hammer and chisel, handed them to me, and said, "Go ahead and take all the samples you want."

Rows of white marble and dark gray slate tombstones stand in a section of the Hallowell Cemetery with two-hundred-plus year-old graves on November 1, 2002. (SFW)

Dick chuckled as I chiseled off small chip samples from several stones and put them into sample bags. The death dates were clearly inscribed, so labeling the sample bags was a breeze. There was just one big problem: none of these tombstones were made from slate. The samples we took would be great for the overall database, but they weren't going to work for the Kensington Rune Stone. We talked to Tony and Linda about the possibility of taking samples from stones in the cemetery, and asked who we should contact to obtain permission. Again they looked at each other and smiled. Tony said that he was one of the three members of the board of trustees for the Hallowell cemetery and would talk to the other members about helping us out. It was only 9:00 a.m. and we were already having a fantastic day.

We thanked our new friends for all their help and headed off to our appointment with the Maine Maritime Museum archaeologist, Dr. Bruce Bourque. Bruce is tall, rather quiet and reserved, but very bright and accommodating. He pulled out a shoebox-sized, cardboard box that contained the rune stone artifacts. I removed them from their bubble-wrap packing and used their microscope to examine both the "Folk" and "Map" stones under low magnification. Both stones were well rounded beach cobbles. The Map Stone looked like a fine-grained meta-basalt or greenstone, and at first I thought the inscription looked a little silly. There was a crude map with runes on one side and carved objects on the other that included what looked like the head of a Native American. As I zoomed in closer to examine the carved lines my initial skepticism began to fade as I saw what looked like obvious weathering. I could not say anything about the age associated with the weathering at that time, but I knew this inscription needed to be examined more thoroughly.

The carved face of a Native American appeared weathered on one of the Spirit Pond Rune Stones called the Map Stone. This figure is roughly 1¹/₂″ high. (SFW)

The Folk Stone appeared to be a medium-grained granite, with a thirteen character runic inscription. I immediately recognized the open "R," the "hooked X," and "crossed L" runes as being the same as those found on the Kensington Rune Stone. This inscription also had a couple things that the Kensington Rune Stone does not have. The second rune on the top line is actually two runes combined together in what is called a bind-rune. The Kensington Rune Stone also does not have a rune like the first one on the top line of the Folk stone. On close inspection of the carved areas I noticed weathering that appeared to indicate that some time has elapsed since the inscription was carved. Here again, I felt the stone needed to be studied to learn more about the relative age of the inscription.

The Folk Stone has thirteen runic characters in the inscription. The second rune on the top line is actually two runes combined together into what is called a "bind-rune." (SFW)

We thanked Dr. Bourque for allowing us to review the stones, and by 11:30 a.m. we were on our way. Driving back to Boston we talked about what a great trip we'd had. I was excited knowing we had a place to collect the samples for the tombstone study, so that as soon as I got back home I went to work getting things set up so we could go back to Hallowell. Tony Maschadri made arrangements with the other two trustees of the cemetery and I scheduled my visit back for the first week of March.

I flew into Augusta, Maine, on March 5th and found a nice old-fashioned Swedish motel to stay in on the outskirts of town. The morning was clear and cold as I arrived at Tony and Linda's office, ready to go to work. We had a quick strategy session to make sure we had the proper tools, sample bags, and that we knew where we needed to go to minimize our time in the cold. It was about 5 degrees with nearly a foot of snow on the ground. There obviously weren't going to be any below-grade samples collected that day. At 10:00 a.m. we headed out to the cemetery.

The top of the snow had crusted over enough so we could walk without breaking through. I had a general idea of where the older stones were from our two-hour visit on Halloween night. Tony knew the cemetery well and asked if I knew about the stone in the tree. As we made our way to northeast part of the cemetery, closest to the river, I asked him, "What stone in the tree?" He smiled and led me to a row of slate tombstones that ran along the top bank of a hill right next to the railroad tracks. He walked up to a huge maple tree and pointed to its base, where I was stunned to see that the tree had completely engulfed a tombstone and lifted it more than a foot out of the ground until the slate tombstone was resting at about a 30 degree angle from its former vertical position. I couldn't find a date on the stone because it was covered by the tree. The stones nearby were about two hundred years old, so we assumed this one was about the same age.

Tony Maschadri stands next to a large maple tree that completely engulfed a tomb-stone and lifted it out of the ground. Tony and I collected twenty-four chip samples from slate tombstones at the Hallowell Cemetery on March 6, 2002. (SFW)

I couldn't help but think of the Kensington Rune Stone and how appropriate this scene was: an inscribed stone in the firm grip of a tree.

One of the first things I noticed after kneeling down next the first tombstone we sampled was how crisp and sharp the inscription was; it looked freshly carved. As I gazed at the two-hundred-dred-year-old inscription I had a good feeling about using the biotite as my study mineral. The minerals appeared to be holding up like I thought they would, but the real answer about their condition wouldn't be known until we put the chip samples in the microscope. Most of the tombstones were ornately inscribed over the entire front side, which meant we could take our sample close to the edge and not deface the monument. When I set the chisel against the stone and lifted the hammer to strike I had a momentary twinge of anxiety. What if the whole stone split in half? I knew this wouldn't happen, but since I'd never done this before that fear of the unknown crept in a little bit. The hammer struck the chisel and a small black flake flew off. I examined the area the flake had come from and could barely see the mark. I smiled at Tony, who smiled back approvingly. I slipped the chip into a sample bag, and labeled the bag with the death date and name of the decedent. It seemed appropriate to give credit to the individuals who were participating in the research.

The Therasa Stratton tombstone exhibited little apparent weathering even after two hundred years. (SFW)

Tony and I spent more than three hours collecting twenty-four chip samples. By the time we got back in the car it was just after 1:00 p.m. and our fingers were so cold we could barely bend them.

Later that afternoon I made my way the History Museum in Augusta to give a presentation for Dr. Bourque and the historical society staff, among whom were two geologists, a husband and wife. I was hoping they would see the value of having the Spirit Pond rune stones undergo similar testing as we had done with the Kensington Rune Stone. Since the Spirit Pond stones are currently considered fakes I tried to make the point that there was nothing to lose and everything to gain. Overall, they said that while the information was very interesting, they thought we would prove our case only if we took a sample from one of the Kensington Rune Stone runes. I explained that such sampling was unnecessary given that the chip taken from the dressed side represented the same weathering profile as the runes. I left feeling like they needed time to mull over the idea of testing. Hopefully, there will be an opportunity to examine the Spirit Pond stones more carefully.

The next step for me was to get down to Iowa State University and put the tombstone samples into the scanning electron microscope (SEM) there. I set up a date with Jerry Armenson for the 25th of March. I rented a car at the Des Moines airport and cruised the 30 miles north to Ames. When I arrived around 10:00 a.m., Jerry had the scope ready to go and started loading four or five samples at a time. The first order of business was to determine the mineral grain size, and it turned out that most of the samples we took were much larger in size than the Kensington Rune Stone micas. In fact, only three of the twenty-four samples had the proper grain size, but they were almost a perfect match. Ironically the three tombstone samples we could use were from the stones of Lowell, Dummer, and Dummer.

Jerry Armenson provided valuable assistance in operation of the laboratory equipment used to analyze the tombstone samples. The scanning electron microscopic work was performed at the Iowa State University Materials Research Laboratory in Ames, Iowa, on March 25 and 26, 2003. (SFW)

As the work progressed over the two days we spent on the scope, and we became more familiar with the state of the biotite minerals on the surface of the samples, a couple things became clear. First, the biotite grains had clearly undergone significant degradation. The sharp and distinct edges of the once-fresh mineral grains had become rounded and frayed, and the flat basal surfaces had started to develop pitting as the individual grains were beginning to expand and separate. If allowed to continue to weather, these degraded minerals would eventually exfoliate and fall off. In spite of the severe deterioration of the biotite minerals they were largely still intact on the surface. Since the average age of the three samples was just over 194 years, it must have taken longer than that for the biotites, and the other mica minerals, to completely weather away on the original inscription of the Kensington Rune Stone.

I smiled when I realized what this meant. The weathering of the inscription pre-dated the possibility of anyone in the 19th century being involved in a hoax. I finally had a number of years to apply to the weathering of the Kensington Rune Stone. I was proud, knowing that this evidence got Olof Ohman off the hook once and for all. The first group of people that would hear these test results were attendees of the Kensington Rune Stone Forum, scheduled for the following week. The timing had worked out perfectly.

Russell Fridley and the Gran Tapes

Time and time again, people who believe the Stone is a hoax bring up the "Death Bed Confession." When I first listened to the tapes late in the year 2000, I considered it hearsay evidence and not credibile. Nevertheless, many people have been strongly influenced by it. I had listened to the tapes and read the transcripts of the interviews with two siblings of John Gran, Walter and Josephine. The 1970 interview was conducted by Russell Fridley when he was the director of the Minnesota Historical Society. John Gran allegedly told his son Walter that he and Ohman had carved the Stone. What I found interesting is that when Walter pressed his father for details, his father said, "Go ask Ohman." Walter reportedly did ask Ohman, who essentially told him that his father was lying. If John Gran had been involved in a hoax, why didn't he give any details? The Kensington Rune Stone mystery must have been something that he thought about a lot. Ohman was a neighbor and the Rune Stone is the biggest thing to ever happen in the area. The only thing that made sense to me is that John Gran made up the story about being involved in a hoax in order to prompt Ohman to confess. Nothing else explains why he would tell his children such a story, because there is no evidence that gives his "confession" any credibility.

Walter and Josephine weren't necessarily lying. In fact, I'm sure they believed their father was telling the truth. But if they believed their father was telling the truth, why did they wait so long to come forward? Consider that these interviews took place around the time that Theodore Blegen's book, *The Kensington Rune Stone: New Light on an Old Riddle*, came out. In the book, Blegen alludes to the interviews without using names, but shortly after his book was released they became public. The timing seemed awfully curious to me.

Hoping to get a little more information about the interviews, I decided to see if anybody at the Minnesota Historical Society was there at that time the interviews were conducted. I learned that Russell Fridley was retired and living in St. Paul, so I gave him a call. Russ was very open to getting together. I invited him to lunch and on February 5, 2003, he came by my office. I had envisioned Russ to be a cold, smug, ardent detractor of the Stone with a closed mind on the subject. I couldn't have been more wrong. We hit it off right away, and I found him to be very likeable, and receptive to the information I shared with him about our work. I asked him about the Gran interview and he was candid. He said that both Walter and Josephine were credible, and he saw no reason at the time to doubt them. He was impressed with the work we had done and said that no one had ever shown him any evidence like this before. My conspiracy theory about these interviews and Blegen's book now seemed pretty silly.

Russell Fridley and former long-time MHS staff member Alan Woolworth stand next to the Kensington Rune Stone at the Kensington Rune Stone Forum held at Historic Fort Snelling in St. Paul, Minnesota on April 2, 2003. (SFW)

The Kensington Rune Stone Forum at Fort Snelling

The planning committee had everything ready leading up to the Kensington Rune Stone Forum on April 2, 2003. The list of invitees read like a who's who from the various disciplines related to the Kensington Rune Stone. We decided that the meeting would be closed to the public and the media, with the exception of Peg Meier, who promised to not write an article about the event at the time. Archaeologist Larry Zimmerman and his staff at Fort Snelling set up tables with a large screen for slides and digital presentations. Guy Gibbon was the moderator, and assured us that he was going to be firm about time limits to keep the schedule on track. LuAnn had made the necessary arrangements to have the Stone there, and it was a nice touch. I was excited because I had just completed the SEM work on the tombstone samples, and this would be my first opportunity to present the findings. Both Elisabeth Ward and the new linguist intern, Iris Hahn, from the Smithsonian Institution were coming. The timing worked out well for Elisabeth, because the "Vikings" exhibition was in its final month at the Science Museum of Minnesota in St. Paul, which was the final stop on its three-year tour of the United States. Elisabeth had been hired by the Smithsonian to coordinate the exhibition and act as a liaison with the media. This was the perfect job for her because she is not shy about being in the spotlight. One of the perks of having her attend was that she volunteered to give a private tour of the exhibits to all interested attendees the night before the Forum.

I volunteered to pick up Elisabeth, her boyfriend David, and Iris at the airport the day before the Forum. I dropped them at their hotel in St. Paul and said we'd see them that evening at the Science Museum. Janet and I arrived at the museum with several others around 7:00 p.m., and we made our way up to the exhibition hall where it was quiet. We had the place nearly to ourselves. Elisabeth gave us an excellent tour, and went into much more detail than we would otherwise hear. It was obvious that she was proud of the exhibits that she had helped put together. One of the last parts of the tour included a large reproduction of the Vinland Map, which Elisabeth assured us was not medieval in origin. I knew that the artifact's origin is highly controversial and not as certain as Elisabeth's opinion of it. I also cringed that the one Spirit Pond Rune Stone I hadn't seen in Maine last November, the "Inscription Stone," was displayed as a fake. Even though it was behind clear plastic I managed to get a decent look at it. It had a much longer inscription on both sides. The flat, foot-long rock looked like a mudstone. I also noticed that the stone was beginning to delaminate along the bedding planes. I wanted to reach in and grab that stone so I could fix it, but I had to console myself with the hope that some day we'll get that stone under the microscope!

The "Inscription Stone," one of the three Spirit Pond Rune Stones, as it was displayed in the Smithsonian Institution's "Vikings" Exhibition at the Science Museum of Minnesota in St. Paul on April 1, 2003. (SFW)

Before we knew it, three hours had gone by and the museum was closing. Elisabeth got a little carried away, but she could certainly be forgiven since this marked the end of the project she had spent nearly five years of her life on. We all thanked her and headed home. On Wednesday April 2nd, we made our way to Fort Snelling for the start of the Forum. There was anticipation in the air when we arrived at Fort Snelling on Wednesday, April 2nd, to find a lot of other people were arriving. No one had any grand illusion that everyone would walk away believing the Kensington Rune Stone was genuine. We knew people who would argue against it, but if nothing else we went into the Forum with the hope that we would educate people with information about the Stone that had never been heard before. We also saw it as an opportunity to establish new relationships and open the lines of communication between different disciplines.

Guy did an excellent job as the moderator and kept things moving smoothly. The line-up included:

Guy Gibbon (Anthropologist) – Introduction

Alice Kehoe (Anthropologist) – 14th Century Europe
Kirsten Seaver (Archaeologist) – Responder

Scott Wolter (Geologist) – Tombstone Study
Richard Ojakangas (Geologist) – Meta-graywacke Origin

Dick Nielsen (Engineer) – Linguistics
Iris Hahn (Linguist) – Responder

Larry Zimmerman (Archaeologist) – 19th Century America
Rhoda Gilman/ Russ Fridley (Historians) – The Gran Tapes

Mike Michlovic (Archaeologist) – Related Artifacts
Tom Reiersgord (Historian) – Responder

At the lunch break I was given an extra fifteen minutes to explain how the digital photo library of Kensington Rune Stone runes was created and organized. I made a CD for every invited guest and took them through it to help them better understand and use it. I know Dick was frustrated because he didn't have the opportunity to respond to points raised by Iris or others, points Dick knew more about than anyone. We talked about the possibility of a bigger conference that might be generated from interest at this forum. I think people came away knowing the Kensington Rune Stone was far from a decided issue, and that there was much more to come. It was also nice to have Scott Ohman and his wife Diana in attendance; they represented the Ohman family in a dignified way.

Attendees enjoy dinner at the St. Paul Grill in St. Paul, Minnesota, after the Kensington Rune Stone Forum on April 2, 2003.   L to R: Scott and Diana Ohman, Alice Kehoe, Dick Nielsen, and Richard Olson. (SFW)

Runo Löfvendahl

Lars Westman would occasionally send an e-mail about his progress getting the Stone to visit Sweden. The article about the Kensington Rune Stone that Lars had written in *Vi* Magazine the previous November had struck a chord with many people in Sweden, and prompted interest from the Historiska Museum in Stockholm. Lars also put me in contact with a geochemist named Runo Löfvendahl, who had an extensive background in studying the weathering of Viking era rune stones in Scandinavia. Lars asked if he could give my report to Runo to review and I agreed. I received my first e-mail from Runo on January 7, 2003, and on January 14, Runo sent me a list of twelve questions regarding my report, which I quickly answered.

Runo hadn't seen the actual Stone, so he was taking much of what I said on faith, and while e-mail communication is wonderful, it's no substitute for face-to-face communication. I could tell by his questions that he is an intelligent gentleman. Being a person of many words, I wanted to tell him every detail, and be sure that all of his questions were answered, but that would have to wait for another time. I also wanted to meet Runo so I could gauge what kind of a man he was. I worried that he might be like so many people who had stumbled due to laziness or arrogance, though he didn't seem that way in his correspondence. Besides, with a geologic background I felt he had to be a pretty down-to-earth guy. I would have to wait several months to find out, and fortunately I would not be disappointed.

The Kensington Crew

On April 9, 2003, LuAnn called and said a couple from Kensington had some letters that had been kept in the bank vault in town for many years and they wanted me to see them. The letters involved correspondence between Olof Ohman and Hjalmar Holand and they had never been seen by anyone outside of Kensington before. LuAnn asked if I was interested in seeing them and I emphatically answered, "You bet I am!" She also asked if I would give a presentation about the document search when I came to see the people in Kensington; I agreed and we set the date for April 25th. I brought the family up with me the night before and we stayed at the Holiday Inn in Alexandria. The big indoor pool helped make these trips more bearable for the kids, and Janet was pleased the hotel allowed dogs so our little dachshund, Fritz, could come.

We had dinner with Diana Ohman and her son Nick, and discussed what might eventually happen with the Stone. We talked about how good it was that the Ohman family was involved with the Stone again instead of shying away from it. Scott Ohman told us how tough things had been for his grandfather, and his great-grandfather Olof, but it seemed like things were finally going to be set straight. I told them I would be sure to give Nick a little extra attention during my presentation to his class the next day.

The following morning at Voyager Elementary School, I told the kids about our testing and explained the history of the Stone. I made an effort to make sure they knew that their classmate's great-great grandfather had nothing to do with making the Rune Stone.

By 1:00 we were in Kensington, where the president of the bank, Pryce Score, who I knew well as a member of the Rune Stone Museum board of directors, was waiting. He led us to the basement of the bank, where several tables and chairs had been set up. I fired up my laptop as people trickled in. One of the surprise visitors was Ruby Sabolik, who we hadn't seen since all of the excitement with the AVM Stone almost two years before. Soon there were a dozen people gathered around. I presented the information I'd found at the Historical Society that I thought would interest them, and interested they were. At one point, Eleanor Gunderson, a senior resident of Kensington said, "You are the first scholar that has ever come here that said something positive about the Stone." I told her, "I am not a scholar, I'm a geologist, but if you want to call me an expert, that's fine." They seemed eager to talk, so I started asking questions.

These long-time residents of Kensington, Minnesota were anxious to hear, and to talk about the Rune Stone on April 25, 2003. L to R: Einar Bakke, Ralph Gunderson, Donny Olson, Eleanor Gunderson, Pryce Score, June Flaaten, Lou Score and Ruby Sabolik. (SFW)

Both Eleanor and her husband Einar were 91 years old and knew the Ohman family very well. Einar said he was close friends with Art Ohman and remembered Olof as an old man. As a kid he played at the Ohman farm almost every day for years. When I asked him about Olof he said, "He was a nice, quiet, and honest old man." He then added, "The Grans were jealous of the attention that Ohman got over the Stone; the families didn't get along." They also wanted me to know the names of the two men with rifles in the 1927 photo of Ohman and the Kensington Rune Stone taken at Fahlin's Point in 1927 (See "Kensington Rune Stone Timeline" page 442): Gilbert Hanson and John Ecklund.

After the presentation, Mary Conrad pulled out the letters that LuAnn had told me about. These letters were found in a box of miscellaneous papers that belonged to the Rune Stone Park Foundation board, which stored them at the bank. I sat at the table and began reading. One of the letters was from a law office to Ohman, responding to his inquiry. The other two letters were written by Hjalmar Holand, one to Olof Ohman in 1923, and the other to his attorneys in 1930. Holand's letters dealt directly with the issue of the Stone's ownership, which had obviously been festering for a long time. Other important details in the letters only reinforced what I had found at the Historical Society. Another thing that came through in the letters was that Holand was not the hero many people had made him out to be. Mary had several scrapbooks with newspaper articles dating back to the 1920s, so I took out my digital camera and started snapping pictures. After close to three hours Janet and the kids were ready to go home. I thanked everyone for coming and especially Mary for bringing out the scrapbooks and the letters. It would not be long before we were back to visit our friends again.

Before heading back home, we stopped at the Lutheran Church cemetery a mile out of Kensington and took a walk around. Amanda and Grant found dozens of garter snakes among the tombstones. We found the family plots of Nils Flaaten, John Gran, and Olof Ohman. I took pictures of the monuments on a warm and sunny afternoon, and as I walked among the tombstones of these men, I wished that I could sit down and talk to them. It would've been fun to ask John Gran if he really said what his children alleged, or to ask Nils and Olof about the discovery that day over a a hundred years ago. Before we left I stood over Olof's grave and told him that we would keep working on it.

Kurt Malarstedt Visit

A couple of weeks later we were on our way to Kensington again. This time we had along another visiting Swedish journalist, Kurt Malarstedt. Kurt stopped by my office for an interview on May 10, 2003, and the next day we headed west on Hwy 94 towards Alexandria. Dick had flown up from Texas to meet Kurt and several Kensington residents at the old barn on the Ohman farm. Einar Bakke was there, along with long-time area residents Gil and Marjorie Moe. Since our last visit I'd thought a lot about some of the things that Einar had said, and wanted to ask him more questions. I knew this visit would be interesting because Gil was one of the colorful characters who had worked hard on the Kensington Rune Stone for many years with researchers Arne and Leland Peterson and Marion Dahm. These guys had located and mapped hundreds of mooring stones around the region and believed they knew where the "ten dead men" mentioned in the inscription were buried. They were all staunch believers in the Stone and we were about to get a sampling of Gil's enthusiasm.

Gil had been in poor health, but Marjorie said he rallied when he heard we were coming up to talk about the Rune Stone. His hearing was quite poor, but he was as enthusiastic as a man could be in his fragile condition. He'd recently turned eighty-six and even though his body was really struggling, his friendly demeanor and willingness to help were undaunted. After the introductions I asked Einar and Gil a few questions about the Gran family. I hadn't found any evidence that anyone had ever tried to get to the bottom of what might have motivated John Gran and his children. Einar said he was born in Gibbon, Minnesota, in 1912 and had moved to Kensington in 1921. The Bakkes were neighbors with the Grans, and their families "got along pretty good." When Gil realized who we were talking about, he chimed in, saying Walter Gran "was a bum." Einar was more diplomatic, saying Walter sometimes, "stretched the truth." Einar thought that John Gran was jealous of the attention that Ohman received over the Stone and wanted to make trouble. Einar looked away, troubled, and recalled what Art Ohman said to him one day, "We didn't have time to carve any rock." Both Gil and Einar agreed, "The Ohman family was really bothered that people thought they did it."

We didn't uncover any startling revelations about why John Gran would say he carved the Stone with Ohman, although it was interesting to hear that the families were not friendly. One thing has always bothered me. If Gran was involved in a hoax, why didn't he tell everyone about it back then? It's odd that he would only tell his children in such a cryptic way. That Ohman denied Gran's claim means the confession has little credibility. Dick Nielsen pointed out that John Gran, who was from Härjedalen in Sweden, had a Swedish "a"-dialect, like Ohman, leaving both of them incapable of authoring the inscription because of the fundamental way they used their native language.

Gil also talked about how he and Marion Dahm had located several things related to the Norseman by "using the rods." I gave Gil a puzzled look and he said, "I'll show you." He reached into a bag that Marjorie was carrying and pulled out two 1/8″-diameter copper rods with a 2″ long bend at one end. He explained how, with the proper energy, the rods would cross when they located something you requested. There was an uneasy chuckle in the room, so I asked Gil to give us a demonstration. He got up and enthusiastically started to explain. Karl had been taking notes for his story back in Sweden. He looked like a guy with a sense of humor so I caught his eye and winked as Gil put me into position. "Ok, we're going to put a woman and man opposite each other and see if the rods can tell the sex." He asked Marjorie to stand opposite me and then tapped our wrists with one of the rods. Gil walked slowly between us, holding the rods out in front of him. Amazingly, the rod that he had tapped on my wrist swung and pointed toward me, and the other turned and pointed to Marjorie. I asked him to repeat it and the same thing happened again.

I asked Gil if he could teach me how to use them. He paused and said, "Well, I don't know, you might be kind of dense." The group roared with laughter, and I told him, "Come on Gil, I'm coachable." He agreed and we changed places.

I put my hands out at chest level and was about to begin walking when Gil said, "Stop, you have to take your shoes off first." I complied and started again, but when I passed between Gil and Marjorie the rods didn't move. I tried my best to let the energy work, but apparently Gil was right: I was too dense. I asked for one more try, and this time when I passed between them I tilted my fists slightly outward, and the rods slowly swung out. When they pointed directly at Gil and his wife, he excitedly yelled, "You got it!" Everybody laughed and clapped, and I couldn't help but grin. Gil gave me the rods as a gift and said he thought there was hope for me.

Mary and Mel Conrad brought along a couple more scrapbooks, and inside one of them was a picture of the Ohman's granary taken shortly before it was torn down in 1972. I showed Einar the picture and asked him if the Stone had ever been used as doorstep. He said that Art Ohman told him they kept it underneath the slanted part on the side, "Where Art used to park his car." I asked Einar if he would show us where the granary used to be, he led us outside and pointed out the spot. Einar walked around the Ohman homestead and pointed out where things used to be, talking about events that had taken place. Einar paused at the back of the old house. "There's been a lot of sadness here too." He told us how two of Olof and Karin's children, David and Amanda Ohman, had committed suicide at the house. Einar's stories made me wish the walls could talk.

The group that met at the Ohman farm in Kensington, Minnesota on May 11, 2003 to talk about the Ohman family and the Rune Stone. Standing, L to R: Kurt Malarstedt, Einar Bakke, Mary Conrad, Mel Conrad, Marjorie Moe, and Pryce Score. Sitting, L to R: Dick Nielsen, Gil Moe, and Scott Wolter. (SFW)

The Heavener Rune Stone

There are other rune stones in North America, and I wanted to check some of them out. I didn't have any grand plans that we could authenticate them, but I definitely got the bug to see them. Dick suggested we travel to Oklahoma, home of the Heavener Rune Stone, which he said was very interesting. We could get a personal tour from Gloria Farley, one of the first people to study the stone and champion its authenticity. Janet and the kids were fired up to take the road trip, so on June 18, 2003, we packed up the Explorer and started for Oklahoma. This part of the country was new to us and we were awed by the beauty of the Arkansas Ozark Mountains. I scanned the roadside geology as I drove, and convinced the family to pull over and explore a small abandoned quarry. The limestone rock layers were full of crinoid fossil parts that looked like miniature Life Saver candies, so we collected several samples to add to our rock garden back home. Little did we know, we brought along something else when we left the quarry: chiggers. Amanda and Grant were the first ones to itch, but as we rolled into Heavener the following day, all four of us were scratching away.

Dick drove up from Houston and met us at Gloria's house around 11:00 a.m. on June 19, 2003. At 88 years old and struggling with diabetes, Gloria moved a little slow, but had a razor sharp mind to go along with her firm determination. Her home was filled with books, pictures, and artifacts from her decades of work pursuing evidence of ancient cultures in America. I scanned the wall where her awards and acknowledgements from respected people hung. This woman had purpose, and after a few minutes of small talk she insisted we hop in the car to go see the rune stone. Gloria directed us through town and up a fairly high mountain where we parked the car. Gloria was in large part responsible for the creation of Rune Stone Park, and when we walked into the gift shop everybody knew who she was. She asked for the key to the structure that was built to protect the stone from the elements. Although she wouldn't be able to make the hike, she had seen the stone many times since the first time in the spring of 1928. She shooed us on as we made our way down the stone and mortar steps to the bottom of a ravine.

Gloria Farley and her two sons, Mark and Scott, posed for this 1965 photo with the Heavener Rune Stone. The eight character inscription was pecked roughly ½″ deep into a several-ton sized quartzite slab and was reportedly seen by Native Americans as early as 1830. (Courtesy of Gloria Farley)

We located the wooden structure, unlocked the door, and Dick, Grant, Amanda, and I crawled inside through the small door. It was cramped inside with the massive quartzite slab that had fallen away from the cliff and into the ravine at least a few thousand years ago. The foot-tall characters of the inscription were carved into the once-horizontal surface of the slab that now stood vertical. While the structure certainly protected the stone against being defaced, the moist environment inside the shelter was a breeding ground for lichen and fungus. The inscription was coated with a quarter-inch thick, light green layer of lichen. Gloria told me I could take a small sample of the stone along the edge that was over two feet away from the closest character. Since the inscription was carved into a flat bedding surface of the quartzite, I could get an idea of the weathering profile of the stone from a sample within that layer. After obtaining a small, roughly one inch square by ½ inch thick sample we took several photographs and headed back up the trail.

We jumped back into the car and drove over to the Kerr Museum near the town of Poteau. Inside the museum Gloria showed us other inscriptions, and wondered if I could date any of these inscriptions, which looked very different from the Heavener Stone. Carved into relatively soft sandstone, they exhibited little if any weathering. As much as I wanted to help answer questions that she had been pondering for decades, I told Gloria that I wasn't optimistic about testing them. I could see the disappointment her face as she said in her soft Oklahoma drawl, "Well, alright." I told her I was quite intrigued with the Heavener stone. I showed her the noticeable weathering rind along the broken edge of the sample I'd taken and said I'd put it under the scope as soon as I got home. If the surface with the inscription had been weathering for at least a couple thousand years, then a sample from one of the runes might tell us something about the relative age. Dick said the inscription was carved using older, Viking age runes that dated to about the year 700 A.D. If the inscription is authentic then it is over twelve hundred years old, enough time for the characters to have developed a noticeable weathering profile. If there is little or no weathering profile within the runes, then the inscription probably isn't very old. The only problem is that we would need to cut a small sample from one of the runes.

As we drove back to Minnesota I kept thinking about Gloria, and wondering if we could answer the question about the Heavener Stone for her. I also caught myself weaving over the highway from scratching the itchy chigger bite welts that had formed on my legs and torso.

Under the microscope the Heavener sample had a beautifully developed weathering profile, so I called Gloria and told her I thought a sample from the runes could potentially tell us a lot. She said she'd work on getting permission to obtain a sample, but after several inquiries by both Gloria and me we were unable to secure the permission we needed. The work could be done at any time, and by comparing samples from other man-made surfaces of known age in the area (split rock, dimension stone, graffiti, etc.) an estimate of the relative age of the inscription might be possible. I would love to test that sample for Gloria, who does not have the luxury of time.

Michael Barnes Visit

On July 17, 2003, there was a lot of excitement at the APS lab. First of all, the Bourne Stone had arrived for an examination, and I invited several people over to take a look at it. The other reason for the excitement was that both Dick Nielsen and his friend from England, one of the top runologists in the world, were also coming to visit the lab. Professor Michael Barnes of University College in London had spent considerable time helping Dick with his research into the Kensington Stone. Dick holds him in very high regard, and was excited to have him visit Minnesota. The professor had driven from Chicago with his wife and friends, and when they came by the lab mid-morning we had other visitors examining the Bourne Stone. Janey Westin had stopped over, along with archaeologist Larry

Zimmerman and one of his colleagues. Michael joined the group and they all carefully examined the inscription. Michael and Dick discussed the crudely cut lines along one edge of the stone, but couldn't figure out with any certainty what language it was. They said it could be a very old runic inscription, but the extensive weathering and wear made it impossible to say for sure.

Professor Barnes is one of the very few experts in his field who has taken the time to consider the Kensington Rune Stone inscription seriously. For years, Dick has been making linguistic points about the stone that have mostly fallen on deaf ears. Since Michael has taken time to consider Dick's points, he has seen that many of them have merit. He was intrigued enough to make the effort to see the stone and to learn more about the other evidence. After an hour or so with the Bourne Stone, I offered to share some information with him about the Kensington Rune Stone. We went into the training room, where I fired up my laptop and the projector and proceeded to fill over an hour with information that he calmly and quietly took in. I talked about both the physical testing and the document search, which was a lot to process, but I could almost hear the wheels turning in his head. The Professor gave me some helpful feedback about not getting too emotional when presenting the information, because it could take away from what he called very compelling evidence that supported the Stone.

I was impressed with the professor and could easily see why Dick thought so highly of him; not only is he extremely intelligent and knowledgeable, but he is also a very nice guy. Dick offered to escort Michael's party to see the Kensington Rune Stone and the Ohman farm. Dick smiled and winked at me as they left; I knew what he was thinking and I couldn't have agreed more. This was the kind of intelligent, thoughtful guy we wanted to consider the merits of the Kensington Rune Stone and I was sure that I would be seeing him again.

Professor Michael Barnes surveys the Bourne Stone Inscription at the American Petrographic Services laboratory on July 16, 2003. L to R: Janey Westin, Dick Nielsen, and Professor Michael Barnes. (SFW)

While the Bourne Stone was at APS we quickly determined that we would not be able to employ the same techniques for relative age dating of the inscription that had worked so well with the Kensington Rune Stone. The biggest problem was that we didn't know the weathering history of the stone before it was first documented the 17th century. The surface of the stone had also experienced significant physical abrasion, making it difficult to decipher which features were man-made and which were natural. We decided that if we couldn't help date the inscription maybe we could help determine what was actually carved into the stone. We made an old-fashioned pencil rubbing of the entire stone, which became the primary "map" of the inscription. We also reviewed the inscription using low angle light to highlight the carved lines, employing both artificial light in a darkened room, and natural sunlight after wheeling the stone outside on a cart on a sunny morning. The low angle light really made the carved lines stand out and we penciled in the lines on the map that conformed to the rubbing. Next we examined the characters under the microscope to identify tiny fractures in minerals that were likely produced by purposeful impact to see if the lines we'd mapped by light and the rubbing made sense.

At this point the inscription looked vastly different from the characters that had been charcoaled by investigators in the 1970s. Most notable was an obvious human hand, or bear paw, that had been missed. Larry Zimmerman, an expert on Native American culture, confirmed the hand was a common petroglyph carved by many Native American cultures. Even though the inscription had taken on a very different look we were still unsure about many of the other well-worn lines. To try to confirm the lines in these areas I decided to try something different. A couple of blocks from our laboratory are the offices for the Services for the Blind. One day over lunch I walked in and just laid out the idea as simply as I could to the friendly receptionist. I thought a sightless person might be able to use their highly developed sense of touch to identify the carved lines. Unlike a sighted person, I reasoned that a blind person wouldn't be influenced by what they could see on the stone and would therefore be completely objective. The receptionist said it sounded very interesting and thought she knew who might be able to help. She led me to the lunchroom and introduced me to Charlotte Czarnecki. I told Charlotte about my idea, and she immediately offered to help. I didn't know what to expect, but figured we had nothing to lose by trying.

On August 15, 2003, Charlotte arrived at the APS offices. We escorted her into the lab and explained what we wanted to do. One of the geologists, Sherry Malecha, worked with Charlotte to record on our map what Charlotte thought felt like carved lines. I set up my video camera to record the session and told Charlotte we were ready when she was. Charlotte leaned over and placed her hands lightly over the inscription. Sherry took Charlotte's hands and guided her to several of the obvious carved characters to help her get her bearings. When Charlotte said she was ready I turned on the camera and let her do her thing. After roughly an hour, Charlotte said she thought she was done. Sherry had used a pink highlighter to mark the lines that Charlotte identified. I looked at the map and was impressed with her ability to locate the obvious lines as well as the areas we were unsure of.   Charlotte had taken the exercise seriously and did a terrific job.

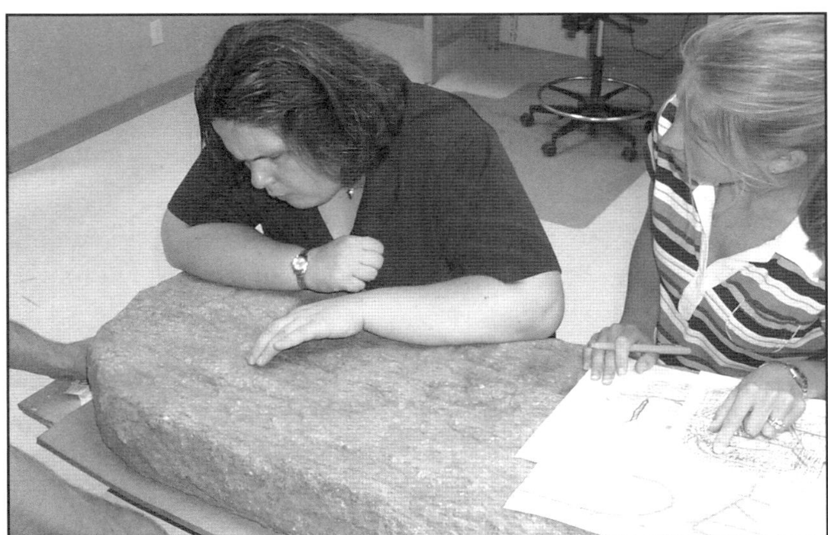

Sherry Malecha records the carved lines on a map as they are identified by Charlotte Czarnecki, who is visually impaired, on August 15, 2003. Ms. Czarnecki agreed to help identify man-made carved lines of the Bourne Stone inscription. (Photograph by Karen Nobbe-Stevens)

After Charlotte's examination we went back to the microscope and examined the areas of divergence identified using the other methods. When the final review of the questionable lines was complete we finished the map, and although we were unable to perform any relative age dating of the inscription, we were confident that we provided a more accurate map of the Bourne Stone inscription.

The final map of the Bourne Stone inscription was made using pencil rubbing, low angle light, microscopic review, and the tactile documentation of the carved lines by a visually impaired person. Decades of foot traffic wear when the stone was reportedly used as a doorstep made identification of the carved lines extremely difficult (dashed lines). (**SFW**)

Noman's Land Island

During our conversations about the history of investigations into the many other rune stones found in North America, Dick often referred to an inscribed boulder discovered on a small island off the coast of Massachusetts. This island was inhabited by fisherman for over a century until the 1930s when it was acquired by the United States military and used as a bombing target during World War II. It has been uninhabited since then and is currently a wildlife sanctuary under the jurisdiction of the federal Fish and Wildlife Service. The Noman's Land Island stone was discovered along the beach by Annie Wood in 1927. In 1928, a researcher named Edward Delabare visited the island and took several photographs of the inscription. The inscription is comprised of thirty-five runic characters arranged into four lines and dated to the year 1016. Dick had written a paper about the inscription and thought it looked very intriguing. Dick's analysis was based entirely on the relatively poor quality black and white photographs taken by Delabare. He was interested enough that he thought it should be studied further. I told Dick that we should go see if we could find it. He knew me all too well and his grin told me that he was ready to go.

Noman's Land Island rune stone sits among the rocks and sand on the beach during low tide (left). The close-up photo at right shows that the inscription was likely chalked incorrectly. (Photographs were taken by Edward Delabare in 1928.) (Copyright Reynolds DeWalt Printing, Inc. New Bedford, Massachusetts. All rights reserved. Used by permission.)

Dick said if we were going to go out there we needed to make the proper plans. He told me he had a couple of friends who live in Massachusetts who could help us, and a few days later we were in contact with Jim Mavor and Gonzalo Leon. Both Jim and Gon are smart guys and long-time residents of Woods Hole. They were both excited about gong out to the island and went right to work making arrangements with state and federal agencies to obtain permission and access to the island. Jim said the best time to go was during low tide when the weather and the ocean would likely be the calmest. The date we set was August 27, 2003.

Dick and I flew to Boston on August 26, 2004, and drove a rental car down to Jim and his wife Mary's house in Woods Hole. Dick's son Tom Nielsen flew in to join us, as did a photographer named Lincoln Morrison. Lincoln was hired by United International Film Corporation to chronicle the trip for a documentary film about the Kensington Rune Stone. Lincoln, Tom, and I stayed in a quaint summer cottage near the harbor. We awoke at 6:00 a.m., showered and then drove over to Jim's where Mary had coffee and fresh fruit waiting for breakfast. By 8:30 we had made our way to the dock and met up with Gon and other members of our party. Gon introduced us to the two guides who ran the 31-foot charter boat, and the representatives with both the Massachusetts and federal Fish and Wildlife Service. The scenic trip to the island took just over an hour and it was a beautiful warm day with a very slight high level haze. We rounded Gay Head on the southern tip of Martha's Vineyard, and approached the glacial moraine island on the northern side and anchored in ten feet of water about fifty yards from the gravel beach. Gon had rented a small flat-bottomed skiff that ferried us all to shore.

On shore we were greeted by Brian, Larry, and Bob, three engineers with an engineering company called Tetra Tech. They had been hired by the federal government to locate and remove unexploded ordinance and other objects associated with the island's past as a target training center over six decades ago. They ferried us on four-wheelers to the staging area near the center of the roughly one mile wide, two miles long island. We signed release forms and listened to a briefing about the history of the island and current safety concerns. Bob was the demolitions expert, and he warned us not to stray from the trail or touch anything metallic that could be an unexploded bomb. After twenty minutes it was time to head out to find the rune stone. I opted to walk to let the others ride on the four-wheelers and got a healthy head start when the rest of the group was delayed. I marveled at the beauty of the island as I strolled along on a perfect warm and sunny day. I'd walked about a mile before the group on the four-wheelers caught up, just as the trail was getting near to the shore. I noticed a ravine that led down an embankment to the beach, and decided to hike down the 30-foot embankment and walk along the beach while the rest of the group motored down the trail. As I reached the bottom of the sandy cliff I looked to the northwest and spotted the familiar landmark from the 1928 photos about a quarter-mile away. Whale Rock, the landmark from the old photos, was sitting in the surf getting pounded by the waves.

Before hiking down the 30-foot embankment to walk along the beach, I spotted Whale Rock in the distance (flat boulder seen in the water on the right side of this image). According to Edward Delabare's photographs, the Noman's Land Island rune stone was in the water right next to Whale rock. (SFW)

It was a satisfying moment, realizing that I had found where the rune stone was supposed to be. The sky and ocean were beautiful shades of blue as the scene was lit by warm sunlight. I felt a rush of adrenaline and my pace quickened to a trot. When I reached shore near Whale Rock I quickly discarded my shirt and back-pack, pulled off my hiking boots and put on the beach slippers that Jim had lent to me. I walked into the surf, the cool water climbing up my legs as I waded into the waves. I saw what I thought was the top of the rune stone, barely protruding above the waves just a few feet from Whale Rock. As I approached the stone the water was waist deep and the roughly two-foot waves were tossing me around pretty good. To make matters more difficult, the otherwise sandy bottom was littered with slippery glacial boulders. I finally made it to the stone and sensed that it had to be the right rock. Unfortunately, it was completely covered with seaweed and barnacles that made actually seeing the inscription impossible. I waded back to shore and grabbed a scrapper, then went back and started to remove the barnacles.

As I started to scrub the barnacles off the stone, the rest of our party began trickling onto the beach. Jim immediately shed his clothes and waded out to join me, because of the rough surf he could only get to the back side of the stone. Even though he couldn't see the inscription he was exhilarated that we had actually found the stone. Tom Nielsen also waded out and helped clean off the stone, but it was a tough job because the waves kept crashing over the stone, forcing us to pause after only a few seconds of scrapping. After an hour or so we had removed as much off the barnacles and seaweed as we could and started feeling the surface for grooves. It was difficult trying to feel for the inscription while getting tossed around by the waves. I even went back to shore to carefully look at the Delabare photos to orientate myself as to where the carved characters were supposed to be. Finally I felt what had to be the "M" in the middle of the inscription, so I took several photos of the stone and waded back to shore. When I told Dick, Gon, and Jim that I'd felt the inscription they all smiled broadly. We felt a great sense of pride over our accomplishment; we had found the stone!

Tom Nielsen stands on Noman's Land Island rune stone, which was in three feet of water at low tide. Wave action over many decades has pulled sand from beneath the stone, allowing it to steadily sink. (SFW)

When I waded back to shore the second time I noticed a rusted metal object lying between the rocks, partially covered with seaweed. I looked at the 3-foot long steel cylinder with one end flared open and called to Bob. I jokingly asked if it was a bomb, and at first he said, "No," but when he flipped it over we noticed three round areas on the side that looked like dials of some kind. Bob smiled and said, "Yep, it's a bomb alright." He dragged the partially exploded shell onto the beach, where it served as a marker for the stone and a symbol of the island's past.

By 3:30 p.m., after spending over two hours at the site, it was time to head back. As we made our way along the shore I noticed how the sandy banks were rapidly eroding from the constant pounding of the waves. I could see several large boulders that had started out on the top of the banks were slowly sliding down to the beach. The countless large boulders that were already on the beach and in the surf had experienced the same process, including both Whale Rock and the rune stone. If the rune stone had started out on the cliff and slid down like these boulders, it made sense that the inscription was still upright as it must have been in the distant past.

As Tom Nielsen and I walked back along the trail we marveled at the beauty of the island that perfect August day. We talked about the Norse people that may have been to the island and what they might have done here. As we took in the colorful cliffs of Gay Head I couldn't help feeling antsy about getting that stone off the island. Like everyone else, I'm anxious to clean the stone off and see what is left of the inscription.

The Kensington Rune Stone Travels to Sweden

Throughout the winter and spring of 2003, while things with the Kensington Rune Stone were quite active in Minnesota, there was activity in Sweden as well. By April, LuAnn Patton, director of the Rune Stone Museum, was busy making arrangements with Kristian Berg, the director of the Historiska Museum in Stockholm. The Historiska Museum wanted the Stone to come, and they wanted LuAnn, Dick, and me to come, too. When I found out we were going to travel to Sweden I got pretty excited. The Stone had been to France and Norway with Hjalmar Holand in 1911, but this would be the first time ever that the Stone would go to Sweden. Over the summer, plans were finalized, including a three month exhibition of the Stone with a conference when it arrived the first week in October. Dick and I were formally invited to give presentations about our research at the conference, which was to be held at the Historiska Museum.

The promotional poster from the Historiska Museum's exhibit of the Kensington Rune Stone in Stockholm, Sweden. The photo used was taken at Fahlin's Point, Minnesota, in 1927. L to R: Gilbert Hanson, Olof Ohman.

Dick decided to fly to Sweden early with the stone from Chicago, and on October 16, when the Stone was unpacked, he and several Swedish linguists and other researchers examined it for a day before it was put on exhibit. On October 21, 2004, it was my turn to fly to Sweden. LuAnn, her daughter Jillian, and I took off from Minneapolis and $5^{1}/_{2}$ hours later made a stop in Reykjavik, Iceland. We changed planes and took off, landing in Stockholm just before noon local time. As the plane descended, I could see the landscape looked just like Northern Minnesota. Even before we landed I liked Sweden. After picking up our bags and going through one last security check, we found Lars Westman waiting to pick us up. It was great to see him and he seemed happy to see us.

During the twenty minute ride into Stockholm I was struck by the beauty of glacially-scoured bedrock that revealed wonderful geology along road cuts. I was looking forward to was seeing real Viking age rune stones, and Lars assured us that we would see many of them very soon. He dropped us off at our hotel, and although small, its room were comfortable. I didn't care, because I didn't plan on spending much time there except to sleep. After being awake for nearly twenty-four hours sleep was exactly what I needed. I awoke at from a two-hour nap and met Dick Nielsen, LuAnn, Jill, and Lars in the lobby. We walked to a restaurant that was one of Lars' favorite haunts. Pictures and caricatures of famous Swedish writers lined the walls. Everyone in the restaurant knew Lars, and dinner was delicious. After dinner we met with filmmakers Ed Larson and Nick Giest in the lobby of the hotel. They were colleagues of Lincoln Morrison there to capture many of the events for Ed's documentary. Dick and I joined them for a nightcap and then it was off to bed where we crashed hard!

The next morning I woke up feeling rested and went down to breakfast at the hotel's buffet. Although I normally skip breakfast, the food was so good I ate it every day. It was cold and overcast as I headed off to find the Historiska Museum. I'd checked the map and it looked like about a mile walk, so I passed on taking a cab. I was excited to walk through the streets of a city in a country I had never been to. There seemed to be a disproportionate number of attractive people, due in part to the fact that everyone was thin and appeared to be in good health. There was nowhere near the number of overweight people typically seen in the United States. The city was clean, and the architecture of the centuries-old buildings was beautiful.

Dick had taken a cab and was waiting in the lobby of the museum. We checked in at the front desk and asked for the director, Kristian Berg. After a few minutes, an attractive young woman named Susanna Larsson greeted us. Susanna was a museum intern and led us upstairs to the staff offices, where she introduced us to several staff members and we were told that Runo Löfvendahl would be meeting with us around noon. When Runo arrived I finally had my chance to visit with him in person, after trading many e-mails. Runo said he had viewed the Stone for a couple hours when it first arrived, and we discussed a few points that he had questions on. I did my best to explain my reasoning, using images on my laptop. He told me he looked forward to hearing my formal presentation and eventually doing his own work on the Stone.

Our meeting was cut short for a 2:00 press conference, but even in this first brief visit I was impressed with Runo, and glad that he was in charge of the investigation team looking at the Stone and reviewing my report. The press conference was held at the Kensington Rune Stone exhibit on the second floor of the museum. The display was well done and featured artifacts from the 14th century displayed in the room along with the Stone.

This skull of a medieval warrior was found wrapped in chain mail, and was part of the Kensington Rune Stone exhibit at the Historiska Museum in Stockholm. (SFW)

When Dick, Runo, and I entered the room several reporters and a couple television cameras were already gathered. The press conference began promptly at 2:00 p.m. when Dick answered a question about how he first became interested in the Kensington Rune Stone. The next person to speak was a respected Swedish linguist named Helmer Gustafsson. Helmer was quite happy to speak, and did so for what seemed like twenty minutes. He spoke with conviction, though about what I didn't know. He was speaking Swedish so I kept leaning over to ask Dick what he was talking about. Dick, who speaks Danish, but not Swedish, couldn't make out everything he was saying, but it had something to do with a recently discovered inscription in a remote part of northern Sweden. This runic inscription was carved in wood using an alphabet very similar to that on the Kensington Rune Stone. The inscription was dated, using pentadic numbers in the Arabic style like the Kensington Rune Stone, with the year 1907.

Eventually, we learned that Helmer was proposing that the runic tradition of the Kensington Rune Stone was used in this remote part of Sweden into the early 1900s. I am no expert, but this theory seemed silly to me. First, this inscription was dated almost ten years after the discovery of the Kensington Rune Stone. Dick and I were sure there was a simpler explanation for it. If it was carved with similar runes couldn't it have been copied from the Kensington Rune Stone? It's likely that even in remote areas of Sweden news of the Kensington Rune Stone's discovery would have been known by 1907. Dick observed that the carver used the symbol (ϙ) for ten instead of zero, suggesting they didn't understand pentadic numbers.   The timing of the announcement of this strange inscription's discovery on our first day in Sweden seemed odd, but it would not be the first unusual discovery during our time in Sweden. Unfortunately, we would have to wait until we saw the inscription to know more.

Runo was the next to speak, and he also spoke in Swedish. Judging by the look on his face, he was being careful about what he said. By the time Runo finished his interview the television media had to leave. We answered questions from the local newspaper reporters until about 4:00 p.m. We stayed at the museum until the formal celebration to officially open the exhibition began at 6:00 p.m. At 6:00, Dick and I were back in the Kensington Rune Stone exhibit as a growing crowd of people milled about. I was introduced to a man in his thirties with a heavy blond beard wearing a period costume. He was a rune master named Kallie Runestar who had several questions he wanted to ask me about the Kensington Rune Stone, and we ended up firing up my laptop and visiting for over an hour. It was very interesting to talk to someone who was an expert at carving inscriptions into stone. We discussed the features of the Kensington Rune Stone inscription that he knew a lot more about than I did. He agreed with many of my observations, such as the impacts made along the edges of the split side as the carving broke off part of the previously larger stone, and the flaked areas adjacent to the carved lines.

My conversation with Kallie ended when I was introduced to the American ambassador to Sweden, Mr. Ambassador Charles A. Hombold Jr. I appreciated meeting the ambassador, but I was actually more interested in talking to Kallie. At 7:30 p.m. we were ushered into the main assembly room for several formal presentations. Kristian Berg, the ambassador, and Lars Westman kindly delivered their speeches in English as a courtesy to their American guests, and welcomed us to Sweden. As I listened to Lars speak eloquently about the "Rune Stone Mystery," I thought about how happy he must have felt now that the Stone had made it to Sweden. A year and a half before when he had visited us in Minnesota, Lars wanted to have the Stone visit Sweden where he said, "We will all have a big party." I smiled, thinking that his wish had come true.

At breakfast the following morning, I practiced my speech while Dick and Professor Barnes critiqued me. We were allotted only twenty minutes each to present our material, and knowing how long-winded I can be, neither of my cohorts thought I could do it. Talking very fast, I was able to give my abbreviated forty-seven slide version in a little over fifteen minutes. I told them I could do it if I had to. After breakfast, Dick and I took a cab to the Nordiska Museum where Dick had an appointment to look at wooden calendar staffs carved with runes and pentadic numbers. Dick explained to me that farmers used the calendar staffs in 15th, 16th and 17th centuries. We were asked to wear white gloves while examining the three- to four-foot-long artifacts. At one point a staff member asked us why we were so interested in the staffs that to date no one had even requested to look at. I thought to myself that it was for the same reason there was so much confusion about the Kensington Rune Stone; no one had done the research necessary to figure it out. Examining these symbols allowed me to find for myself the numbers that Dick said many scholars assumed were not used centuries ago.

Dick Nielsen and I examined calendar staffs that were used by farmers in Sweden during the 16th and 17th centuries at the Nordiska Museum in Stockholm on October 23, 2003. The handle on this staff shows the Pentadic numbers 1 through 19, curiously absent from this staff is the number 9. (SFW)

The conference at the museum was scheduled to start at 2:00, and as the time approached a crowd of over two hundred people gathered. The moderator was an experienced Swedish journalist named Catherina Ingelman Sundberg, with Svenska Dagbladet, who set strict ground rules for the speakers and people in the crowd with questions. The first three speakers were Lars Westman, LuAnn Patton, and Professor Barnes. Lars gave an overview of the Kensington Rune Stone mystery and LuAnn did her usual professional job of representing the Rune Stone Museum. Michael Barnes talked about the need to exercise care when dating the age of inscriptions, and cited examples of various ages occurring at a site in England. After the coffee break, Dick, Helmer Gustafsson, and I each gave our talks. Dick discussed linguistic aspects of the Kensington Rune Stone and cited documentary sources to illustrate his points. I knew he was frustrated when Catherina asked him to stop; he had many more good examples that he just didn't have time for.

The conference started getting fun when the questions came after Dick's talk. The person who stood out the most was the Norwegian runologist, Professor James Knirk. I had heard him mentioned several times in the past few years and was able to witness him for myself. He is small in stature, with a rather serious tone. Obviously quite intelligent, he clearly believed the Stone was a 19th century artifact. He asked questions after Dick's presentation, or rather, made statements about aspects of the language. Other people also had questions, but what I remember most was how Knirk dominated the discussion by continually bringing up problems he had with the language and talking over people's heads. At one point he raised his hand and said, "I have to hurry and leave, but I have four remarks to make." Catherina warned him to keep it short, which he ignored. After taking a couple minutes to make his first point, he started in with his second remark, but Catherina cut him off. She then thanked the professor and moved on to the next question.

Finally it was my turn to present, and I was eager to get started. I was a little bit worried because of the time limit, so I jumped right in. I made sure to keep calm. I looked out over the crowd and saw a few smiles form as I made my points about the Stone. The images projected onto the screen were sharp and clear, and when I was finished the enthusiastic applause seemed genuine. After the brief question and answer session was over, Catherina thanked everyone for their participation and the presentations were over. The crowd was energized and several people told me how much they appreciated the geologic information. If a poll had been taken after the presentations about the question of authenticity, I think the Stone would have done well.

After the crowd had cleared, Lars Westman took Dick, LuAnn, and me to the docks on the archipelago in Stockholm. Lars led us to a large boat where a party was being sponsored by *Vi* magazine. It was a beautiful affair and everyone was in great mood. Kristian Berg was both happy and relieved that the exhibition opening and the conference had gone well. When we sat down for dinner a white-haired man I remembered seeing in the crowd at the presentation insisted that I sit with him. He introduced himself as Per Lillestrom, an archaeologist who co-wrote a book with the famous anthropologist Thor Hyerdahl. He was a big supporter of the Stone and wanted to know more details about our work. Before taking my seat I asked Runo Löfvendahl if he would join our table. Per and his wife Elisabeth shared some wonderful stories about their travels, and throughout the evening, Lars and his boss, Göran Gynne, proposed numerous toasts with Swedish whiskey that warmed both my body and my attitude.

Göran Gynne and Lars Westman with *Vi* magazine were our hosts for a wonderful party on a boat in the archipelago of Stockholm on October 23, 2004.

It was a good opportunity to visit with Runo. He was very complimentary of my presentation and said I had done a convincing job of showing evidence that the inscription was not a 19th century hoax. We talked about what his investigation team would do with the Stone and told him he would probably have many more questions. I leaned in close to Runo and told him I wanted him to approach his investigation with the goal of trying to prove me wrong. "If you and your team come to a different conclusion about the Stone, with supporting evidence, I will accept it," adding, "however, if you cannot find evidence to refute my findings, then my conclusions stand."

After the party, Michael Barnes and I decided that the exercise of walking back to the hotel would serve us well the next morning, plus it gave us a chance to talk about the day's events and what it all meant. The professor is not only a brilliant man, he has a good sense of humor, though I can't say much for his sense of direction. On this night at least, he got us a little turned around and we went several blocks out of our way. It didn't matter though; we had more time to enjoy the beautiful city and each other's company.

I woke up on October 24, 2004 excited that I would finally get a chance to see some Viking age rune stones. Lars picked me up at the museum at noon and we headed west of Stockholm. The first rune stone we stopped to look at was just off the road next to a large, open field. Lars translated the information sign next to the stone and told me it was over a thousand years old. It amazed me to think that this inscription had been sitting in this same spot, essentially undisturbed, for all that time. Every stone we looked at had been raised at least nine hundred years ago. Most of the inscriptions were carved into granite or granite gneiss, and even though the rock was relatively stable, many of the stones showed significant wear and tear from centuries of weathering. Parts of many inscriptions were illegible or had spalled off, but we also saw that some had been repaired. Each stone was more interesting than the last and I made a point to photograph every one.

At one point we were riding through a wooded area along a winding, narrow road when Lars leaned over and said, "You will like this next one." Lars maneuvered around a couple more bends in the road and pointed to a ridge of glacially smoothed bedrock. I looked closely at a lighter colored area of the ridge and suddenly realized that an inscription was carved into it. A light snowfall from the previous evening framed the beautiful, winding rune-filled ribbons of the inscription. The person who carved into this rock must have been a highly skilled rune master. Lars pointed out the human figure at the top, which was very rare. I climbed around on the slippery outcrop, struck by how beautiful the inscription was. Of the fifteen or so rune stones we saw this one was definitely my favorite. As we drove back to Stockholm I thanked Lars for the personal tour, and he said I would see more stones the next day when we took a tour bus to see Gripsholm Castle.

The Lindö rune stone (U 236) stands next to a road in a field and was one of over a dozen Lars Westman and I saw during our tour of rune stones. (SFW)

The Viking age rune stone (Sö 179), circa 1000 AD, was found inside the Gripsholm Castle tower in 1827 and then moved outside in 1930. Translated into English the inscription reads, *"Tola raised this stone in memory of his son Harold, Ingvar's brother. They fared like men far after gold and in the East gave the eagle food. They died southward in Särkland."*

I awoke the next morning after another restless night, unable to quiet my mind. Everything I saw here was so new and interesting that I had a hard time getting to sleep almost

every night. I went to the lobby where Lars was waiting with the bus. LuAnn, Jillian, Michael Barnes, Dick, Lars, and I rode the 45 minutes out to tour Gripsholm Castle. As we walked outside the castle we stopped to examine two famous rune stones. Michael Barnes was especially interested in these rune stones, and after everyone else moved on, I stayed with the professor to listen and ask questions. He was interested in the geologic input I had to offer as well, and I told him the inscriptions were carved into granite and red sandstone. Michael then translated both stones for me with great enthusiasm. I enjoyed seeing someone passionate about their work, and in spite of a biting wind with temperatures in the teens (Fahrenheit) we both fought the cold and thoroughly enjoyed these ancient inscriptions.

Dick Nielsen talked about the inscription on a rune stone standing outside Gripsholm Castle near Stockholm, Sweden, on October 25, 2003. L to R: Michael Barnes, LuAnn Patton, and Lars Westman. (SFW)

The Swedish National Art collection is housed inside this early 16th century castle. We spent about three hours walking through the three floors, enjoying the paintings that date back to the 1300s. Important figures of Sweden's past came to life in these amazing works of art.

After lunch we drove further west and north to see more rune stones in the farm fields of the lake country. We had to keep a sharp eye out looking for rune stones that were sparsely scattered through the fields and woods. We found a church that had six rune stones, including one that had been built into the foundation. Lars took us to another site marked with a rune stone and containing several grave mounds. Nestled among the mounds were several large stones that had been raised in the shape of Viking ship.

Dick Nielsen and Lars Westman ponder a rare group of stones raised to form the shape of a Viking ship among the burial mounds in the Aasa grave field on October 25, 2003. (SFW)

We saw over thirty rune stones on this trip and thousands of amazing artifacts, some dating back almost two thousand years. It was a tremendous learning experience and best of all we made many new friends in a beautiful country. Dick and I had said that our main goal on this trip was to convince people in Sweden that the Kensington Rune Stone should be removed from the "Dustbin of History" and become an object of serious study. Judging by the strong interest from the media in Sweden both while we were there and in the days after we returned, we felt that we had accomplished our goal. A few days after returning to the States I received an e-mail message from Runo. I opened the message and read what he wrote with surprise and delight. He was impressed with my presentation in Stockholm. I hoped that eventually I could send a message to him with similar sentiments about the work that he was just beginning.

>——Original Message——-
>From: Runo Löfvendahl
>Sent: Wednesday, November 05, 2003 6:51 AM
>To: Wolter, Scott
>Subject: Kensington
>
>Dear Scott,
>
>thanks a lot for your inspired lecture on the stone and your improved
>manuscript, the photos of the runes inclusive. We have got a much
>fuller picture of the stone after studying it for a few hours, but of
>course that is only a beginning. Many thanks also for going through
>your manuscript with me, clarifying some important issues. In the near
>future I will go through your photo documentation of the runes and
>word dividers. Think your demonstration of the progress of weathering
>of pyrite and micas shows that it will be extremely difficult to
>maintain, that the stone is a 19th century fake. We will try to go
>through your manuscript very carefully, and pose you further questions.
>
>Runo

Darwin Ohman

After returning home, we received numerous e-mails about all the media attention the Kensington Rune Stone had generated in Sweden. LuAnn also received a request for the Stone to go to the Hälsinglands Museum in Hudiksvall in northern Sweden before it returned to America. The museum thought it was appropriate for the Stone to travel to the province Olof Ohman had emigrated from in 1879, even if it was only for a few weeks. The museum also invited both Dick and me to come to Hudiksvall and participate in events there. We were told that there were several descendants of the Ohman family in Forsa who wanted to meet us; Dick and I saw this as a great opportunity to learn more about Olof Ohman and the area he was from. In spite of difficulties with some members of her board of directors at the Rune Stone Museum, LuAnn was able to get approval to extend the Stone's stay in Sweden a couple more weeks.

As the second trip to Sweden approached, I was talking more with Scott Ohman, trying to persuade him to go with us. We also talked about trying to locate Olof's scrapbook, and suggested that his uncle Darwin might know where it was. When I called Darwin he was quite pleasant and seemed eager to meet. On Thursday, January 29, 2004, I knocked on the door at Darwin's home and a smiling, white-haired man welcomed me. After I introduced myself, Darwin lead me into his kitchen where I fired up my computer. I wasn't really sure where to start so I began by showing him the timeline for this book, and I explained that Dick and I wanted to tell the story of the Kensington Rune Stone as a time-line of facts. Darwin showed great interest and seemed impressed with the work we had done. When I showed him the chapter, "Who owns the Kensington Rune Stone?" Darwin looked at me and said, "That's a good question isn't it?" I explained to him that I thought the Ohman family still owned the Stone because Olof never gave up ownership, and I thought I had the documents to prove it. We talked about family members that he had known. Darwin said that Art Ohman had lived the longest of Olof's children and that he had many memories of his Uncle Art. He also talked about his father William, the youngest of Olof and Karin's nine children, and Scott's father Darrell, who was one of Darwin's four brothers.

I threw a lot of new information at Darwin that he hadn't heard before, and he admitted to being a little overwhelmed. He said he wished that he could go to Sweden with his nephew Scott and me and meet the relatives, and I assured him that there would be another opportunity sooner rather than later. His nephew Tom had brought over a box of photographs for us to look at. He led me into his heated garage, poured me beer, and put on some classic 50s music. He asked me if I would do him a favor and handed me a CD case. He said he wanted me to give the relatives in Sweden some of his music. I was surprised to learn that he belonged to a group called the Original Pretenders that was playing in the background. He said they only recently got back together after playing music many years ago.

Darwin Ohman signed a CD by his band, the Original Pretenders, during our visit on January 29, 2004. (Courtesy of the Ohman Family)

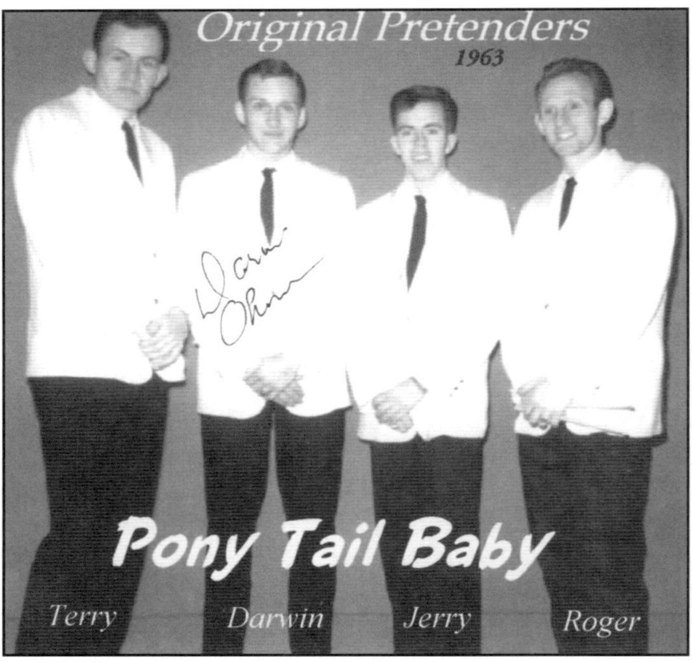

We turned our attention to the box of photos, and I felt like a kid at Christmas digging through his stocking, finding candy and presents. There were many photos that dated back to around 1900, and I knew who most of the people were. A couple of times, I had to tell Darwin who the people were in his own family photos. Two photos in particular stood out from the rest. The first was a picture of five people, three of them sitting in chairs. We could clearly see Olof on the right, but the identities of the others were mysteries. We both thought that because of the delicate furniture the picture might have been taken in Sweden, but Olof looked older than he was when he traveled back to Sweden in the early 1880s. I photographed the image to show it to the relatives in Sweden who might be able to identify them. There were several other photographs of people we couldn't identify and Darwin suggested we show them to Einar Bakke in Kensington. After visiting for almost five hours I left for home feeling like I was ready for Sweden.

Three days before departing I made one final trip to the Minnesota Historical Society to re-photograph several documents I needed for my presentation. I decided to make efficient use of the time while waiting the fifteen or so minutes for a box to be retrieved. I had been telling myself for months that I would listen to the audiotape of Edward Ohman's 1949 interview at the Science Museum of Minnesota; I had already read the transcripts.

I sat down at a table with a cassette deck, put on the headphones and inserted the tape. I wasn't sure what to expect and hadn't really thought much about it beforehand. After the introductions Edward Ohman was asked to tell his story. When Edward began speaking his voice was clear, strong, and deliberate. He spoke slowly, with a slight accent, and explained what happened the day the Stone was found. His voice resonated with credibility, and I scolded myself for not listening to the recording earlier.

A few minutes into the tape an idea popped into my head and I turned the machine off. I thought, "Wouldn't it be great if the people in Sweden could hear this?" I ejected the tape and went to the information desk, knowing the librarians could veto my idea to copy the tape and play it in a public forum. The staff was well aware of my project and had been helpful from the first day I walked in. Fortunately, they immediately picked up on the idea and signed the approval slip for me. It turned out to be an idea that would reap much benefit in Sweden.

The Stone Travels to Hälsingland

On February 2, 2004, I boarded an Iceland Air jet for my second trip to Sweden. This time Dick and I were headed to a province called Hälsingland, two and a half hours north of Stockholm by train. Our destination was the Hälsinglands Museum, located in a small coastal city on the Baltic Sea called Hudiksvall. The museum is near the parish of Forsa, in the Hälsinglands province, that Olof Ohman emigrated from in 1879. This trip was different from the one to Stockholm in October when I had come to talk only about the geologic work we did on the Stone. This time I wanted to discuss the history of the Stone since its discovery. Meeting his relatives and seeing where he came from was a golden opportunity to learn more about the man at the center of the controversy than any previous Kensington Rune Stone investigator had.

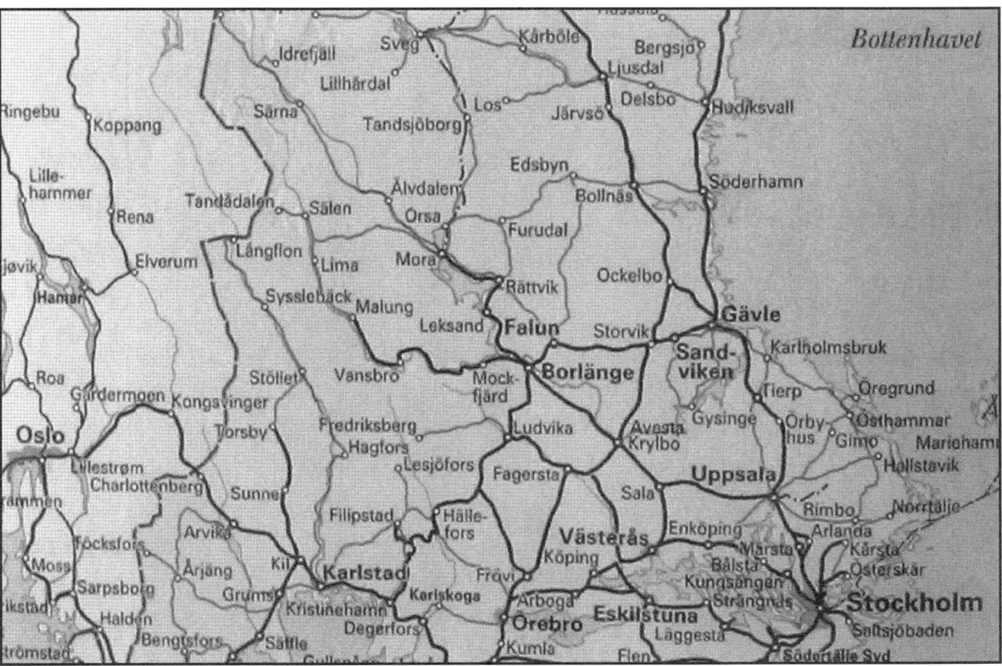

The Hälsinglands Museum is located in the city of Hudiksvall, Sweden, about a two and a half hour train ride north of Stockholm. (©Lantmäteriverket Gälve 2005)

I caught the train to Hudiksvall at the Arlanda station at Stockholm airport. The trip took about two and a half hours including stops at Uppsala, Gävle, and Söderhamn. It was a very comfortable, smooth ride through a beautiful wooded countryside blanketed in snow. I especially enjoyed the landscape littered with glacial boulders, and thick evergreen trees that reminded me of northern Minnesota. When I got off the train I was met by Susanna Larsson, who I knew from the Statens Historiska Museum in Stockholm. She had been hired to help plan and assemble the Kensington Rune Stone exhibition for the museum in Hudiksvall. We walked along the harbor about four blocks to the Hälsinglands museum, where Susanna led me to the offices and introduced me to the director of the museum, Gunilla Stenberg. The three of us sat down to visit and I quickly realized that like Susanna, Gunilla is also an intelligent and hard-working woman.

My three friends at the Hälsinglands Museum who put up with me for nine days. L to R: Susanna Larsson, Lars Nylander, and Gunilla Stenberg. (SFW)

Susanna had already made Gunilla aware of my strong interest in the Kensington Rune Stone research, and at one point Gunilla turned to me with a wry smile and asked if I would be interested in seeing letters written by Olof Ohman. "What letters?!" I said. They both smiled and she explained that the relatives of the Olof Ohman family had found letters written by Olof and Karin, and loaned them to the museum for the exhibition. My mouth fell open and stayed open as they led me to another office where they put three boxes on the table in front of me. Inside the boxes were letters and old photographs of the relatives who had immigrated to America and settled in Kensington. I felt like I'd discovered a buried treasure. I recognized the pictures of Olof and Karin, including one of Olof as a young teenager. Most of the letters were written by Olof, a few were penciled by Karin. I wanted to start reading them right away, but got no further than the city and date at the top. They were all written in Swedish. I grudgingly accepted that analysis would have to wait. I thought about photographing the pictures and letters with my digital camera, but decided to wait. Fatigue from the trip was setting in, and I knew would have plenty of time later to do a good job.

The next morning, February 4, 2004, I made a bee-line for the museum to start photographing the letters. The office where the letters were kept belonged to another person at the museum who I would get to know well. Lars Nylander was 26 years old, and with his soft-spoken, mild demeanor was a person that I instantly liked. He was in charge of researching the Ohman history and shared some newly discovered facts with me. Lars informed me that Olof had made a trip back to Sweden to visit his relatives in 1912, and that in addition to the letters, the relatives had loaned the museum two trunks that Olof used on his trip to be part of the exhibit. After digitally photographing the old photographs and letters, we walked over see where the exhibition was being prepared for the grand opening that was to be held in four days. Even while still under construction, I could see it was similar to the exhibit in Stockholm, with the biggest difference being the addition of the personal items that the local relatives had made available. The Kensington Rune Stone exhibit area was on the third floor with the personal items, and in the back room were the two trunks. Lars pointed out that the smaller trunk was used on Olof's trip to Sweden. He lifted the lid and showed me where Olof had written a note in Swedish, "Olof Ohman's American coffin on his last trip to the country 1912."

The two trunks used by Olof Ohman on his trips to Sweden (smaller trunk) and then back to Kensington. He left for Sweden in 1912, and after being delayed due to the outbreak of World War I, returned to the States in July of 1914. (Photo by Scott Wolter)

Later that day I went back to my flat to prepare for the debate which was to be held the next day. This was the first official event sponsored by the museum where Dick and I would present evidence in favor of the Stone, and linguist Helmer Gustafsson and archaeologist Mats Larsson would argue against it. Professor Henrik Williams was set as the moderator and this would be my first opportunity to meet him. Since the debate was primarily a discussion of the language and runes, I asked to present my opening statement first. I wanted to talk about the improper investigation methods used by linguists and other researchers in the past, with the message that if they wanted to call themselves scientists, then they needed to adhere to the scientific method. I also wanted to recite the words N.H. Winchell had written at the end of George Flom's 1910 paper. Winchell certainly understood the methodological problems of Flom and many other investigators, who had begun with a conclusion, then went looking for evidence to support it. Whether they realized it or not, their "scientific approach" was nothing more self-determined results. My goal was to point out the mistakes of the past and hopefully keep Helmer and Mats focused on the facts, instead of their opinions.

It was an unusually warm February morning on February 5, 2004 when I got up and caught the 8:57 a.m. train to Uppsala. When I arrived at 11:00 a.m., Dick Nielsen, who I hadn't seen since Stockhom in October, was there to greet me. It was great to see him again. The two of us caught a cab to the University and made our way to Henrik's office, where I found him every bit the gentleman that Dick had described, and I liked him immediately. We visited for half an hour or so then decided to grab some lunch. As the three of us walked to the restaurant, Henrik pointed out the on-campus cemetery and gave us a personal tour of the Domkyrkan Church. Henrik shared tidbits about the history of this incredible building that was over a thousand years old, and pointed out parts of two rune stones that had been laid into the floor.

What was once the top part of a Viking age rune stone is now part of the floor in the Domkyrkan Church in the city of Uppsala, Sweden. (SFW)

After lunch in a gorgeous renovated wine cellar from the 1200's, the three of walked to the train depot for the trip back to Hudiksvall. When we boarded the train we met up with Helmer Gustafsson, who had begun his trip in Stockholm. Helmer and Henrik sat together while Dick and I worked on his presentation on my laptop. About half an hour away from Hudiksvall, Henrik and I switched seats so I could visit with Helmer for a while. I still had my laptop going and we talked about Newton Winchell's work. He seemed genuinely interested in learning about Winchell as I showed him images and documents. Before we knew it, the train had pulled into Hudiksvall. We all walked together to their hotel and agreed to meet in an hour and go to the debate together. At 5:30 we walked across the street to the meeting room where a crowd was gathering.

As we waited for the debate to start I was introduced to Mats Larsson. At just after 6:00 p.m. Henrik called the debate to order before a standing room only crowd of more than two hundred people. After a short welcome and discussion of the ground rules, Henrik introduced me as the first presenter. I had only ten minutes to speak so I quickly went through my summary of the scientific method, and finished by asking our opponents if there was another possibility to explain the inscription that they had not fully explored. As Dick Nielsen had proposed, I asked if the Kensington Rune Stone could be a Latin manuscript carved in runes on stone. My question seemed simple enough and I hoped that it would prompt a meaningful discussion. Boy was I wrong! After relatively reserved opening statements from Helmer and Dick, it was Mats' turn to speak and the fireworks got started.

After the debate on February 5, 2004, I had a chance to pose for a picture with the moderator, Professor Henrik Williams. (Photo by Susanna Larsson)

He began by trotting out many of the old arguments that opponents have offered before, speculating that the "Hedberg Copy" was a pre-inscription draft, without any evidence to support the idea. He also chided Dick for a word he discussed in one of his previous papers and to emphasize his point he directed a personal insult at Dick, saying, "You know nothing about Old Swedish." As surprised as everyone was by the inappropriate comment, I was even more taken aback by what happened next.

Mats walked to the projector and put an overhead on the screen with what appeared to be a list. He said it was a list of the conclusions reached by a team of experts in Stockholm, headed by Runo Löfvendahl, that had examined the physical aspects of the Stone and my report. He put a card over the list so the audience could only see one apparent conclusion. I strained my eyes at the tiny script and read that the split side of the Stone had *not* been intentionally split off as I had suggested in my report. I only caught a glimpse of the other points, but I clearly saw the final verdict at the bottom of the overhead. It read that my conclusion about the inscription being greater than two hundred years old was "fantastic."

At first, I wasn't sure if what I was seeing things right. Then the shock began to wear off, and I started to get mad. First of all, what was an archaeologist doing presenting the results of a geologic investigation? Second, why was he giving a presentation that Runo Löfvendahl should be giving? Third, if these actually were the results of the geologic team's investigation, where was the evidence to support these conclusions? I had a hard time containing myself, but somehow I did. Sensing the crowd was becoming uneasy, Henrik interjected and reminded Mats that this was a civil debate, then wisely allowed Dick to be the first responder. Dick calmly acknowledged Mats' personal comment, but did not respond in kind. Instead, he elegantly addressed the point, and finished by asking both Mats and Helmer for evidence to support their claims.

When it was my turn to respond, I forcefully explained my conclusion about the split side using five digital images of the side as evidence that it had been worked. I looked at Mats and asked for his evidence, but all he could say was, "These are Runo's conclusions." The whole thing was ridiculous. I couldn't believe anyone would throw out the unsupported, alleged conclusions of someone else's work. I couldn't help but think what would've happened to me if I had done something like that in the US. My professional geologist's license would be revoked and I'd be out of a job. I couldn't understand why Mats thought he could get away with that.

Eventually, we were all given five minutes to present closing arguments. I was still pretty hot and forcefully summarized the conclusions of both my geologic report and the Minnesota Historical Society document research. I finished by saying, "If these were the conclusions of the investigation team, I will reserve my judgment until I hear these results, with the supporting evidence, from Runo. Until that happens, my conclusions stand." My words must have sounded good to some people, judging by the applause from some of the crowd.

When the debate was over, we immediately walked over and shook hands with Mats and Helmer. There was a tiny part of me that wanted to strangle Mats, but the more I thought about it, the more I realized that what had happened was really a good thing. The way Mats had conducted himself probably backfired and made Dick and me look more credible. It wasn't until the debate ended that I realized how many of the Ohman relatives were in attendance, when they came up and warmly greeted us. I recognized Elvi Sandberg and Britta Blank, who we'd first met in Stockholm. Britta especially expressed her surprise and disappointment over Mats' behavior, saying, "People in Sweden do not treat their guests that way." I told her that it wasn't that big of a deal and tried to minimize the situation. She looked away and with a disappointed tone said, "This Stone makes people do strange things." The irony and appropriateness of what she said struck me as funny. It was a phrase I'm sure I'll use often in the future.

Britta invited Dick and me to her farm, and said she would pick us up at 3:00 p.m. the next day. All the participants and planners of the debate were invited to a lovely meal and drinks sponsored by the City of Hudiksvall. It was nearly 10:00 p.m. by the time we left for the dinner. Mats couldn't stay for the meal, but he did stay long enough to pose for a friendly photo with Dick. As it turned out, the ambush tactics Mr. Larsson used at the debate would come back to haunt him.

After the lively debate in Hudiksvall on February 5, 2004, Dick Nielsen playfully makes a fist with Mats Larsson. (SFW)

On Saturday February 7, the Ohman relatives invited Dick and me along on a bus tour around the village of Forsa to learn more about the history of Olof Ohman before he came to America. Britta Blank sent her son Joakim and his girlfriend Ann-Sofie Holmberg to pick us up at the museum. When we arrived in Forsa, there was a whole crew of relatives waiting for us and a big tour bus ready to go. As Dick and I introduced ourselves trying hard to remember all the names, we noticed a familiar, but very tired looking face. Scott Ohman had just arrived and seemed overwhelmed by the warm reception he'd received from people he was related to but had never met before. As we boarded the bus I recognized many faces from the large crowd at the debate. It turned out that the Ohman relatives had been well represented that night.

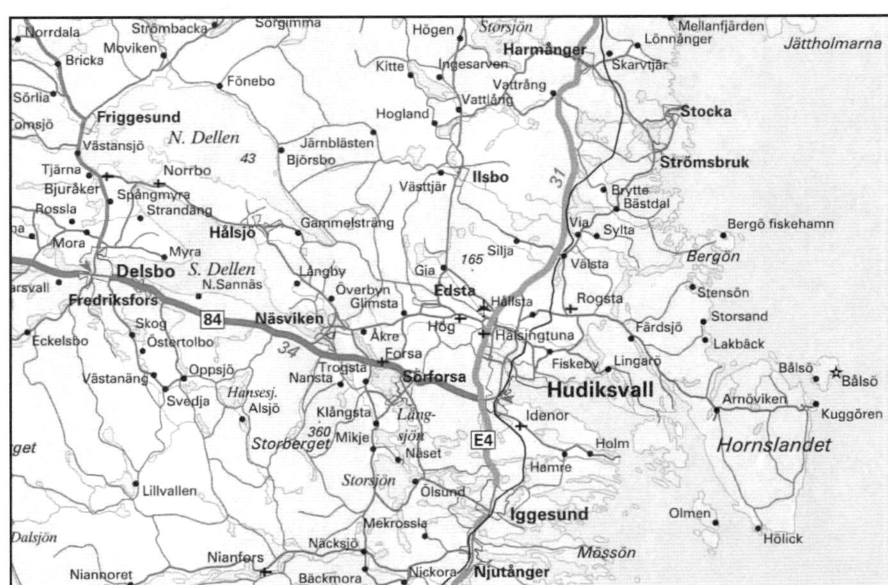

Ohman's homeland of Forsa is roughly five kilometers due west of Hudiksvall. The Dellen Lakes are part of a crater formed after a meteorite impact occurred roughly 90 million years ago. (©Lantmäteriverket Gälve 2005)

Our first stop was at a group of old farm houses arranged in a "U" shape on a beautiful plot of land where we all got out and walked around. The group gathered in the center of the houses. Standing on the landing at the front door of the center house was an older man who lived there. We crowded around the steps in front of him and listened as he began to tell the history of the farm. He could only speak in Swedish, which was fine for most of the group, but fortunately, they had arranged for Susanna to translate the speech into English for the Americans.

The current owner of the farm read from his notes in Swedish, which were translated into English by Susanna Larsson on his right, telling us about the history of the farmhouse where Olof Olsson, Olof Ohman's father, was born in 1787. (SFW)

This farm is more than two hundred years old, and had once belonged to Olof Ohman's father, Olof Olsson. We piled back into the bus and went a couple miles down the road to a vacant field where the bus stopped next to an old fieldstone food cellar. Britta told us over the loudspeaker that the cellar was all that remained of the farm where Olof Ohman was born in 1854. The house was moved many years ago and had since been torn down. Several of us got off the bus to take pictures, including Scott Ohman. Scott is a quiet man, so it was hard to tell what he was thinking as he walked the grounds where his great-grandfather was born so long ago. It was fun to be there as he saw these places for the first time.

The last stop was at another farm where Olof worked before he immigrated to the United States in 1879. While riding on the bus we visited with relatives who told us stories their parents and grandparents had told them about Olof and his family. They said he was a general farmhand and very skilled in carpentry and pointed out farms along the way where he had worked his trade as a carpenter,. Never once did I hear anyone say anything about him working with stone or being a stonemason. Around sundown, the bus pulled up to where we had started the tour. The relatives had a big meal planned and as we made our way to the building for dinner we were greeted by members of the local media who wanted to take pictures. They asked everyone to get together for a group shot and asked Scott Ohman to stand in front. I chuckled to myself knowing how uncomfortable he was being the center of attention. At the Fort Snelling forum last April, Scott had been very shy about being interviewed by the media. This time it was different. Even though he was hesitant, he was enjoying the experience.

Scott Ohman from Alexandria, Minnesota, (center) poses for a photo with over thirty of his Swedish relatives in Forsa, Hälsingland, Sweden, on February 7, 2004. (SFW)

On Sunday, February 8, 2004, the museum was scheduled to open the Kensington Rune Stone exhibition with a ceremony on the steps leading to the third floor. Dick had to return to Texas for business and reluctantly missed the event. Gunilla had asked me to say a few words and to keep it under three minutes. I had only been here for a few days and already she knew that I like to talk. The ceremony started at 1:00 p.m. and people were jammed on the spacious stairway above and below us. Gunilla welcomed everyone, and then introduced a beautiful thirteen-year-old girl from Hudiksvall. She eloquently read a statement in English about Swedish immigrants, the main theme of the exhibition. It was my turn next and I actually kept my speech close to three minutes. The mayor of Hudiksvall gave the final speech, and then cut the ribbon leading to the exhibit on the third floor. The crowd poured in and for the next two hours I answered questions about the Rune Stone. There was no doubt that the Kensington Rune Stone was of great interest to the people here, opinions about its authenticity were mixed. We were quoted or pictured in the newspaper almost daily, and after a few days, people on the streets started to recognize me. It felt strange and gave me a real sense of how interested people here were in the Stone.

The Kensington Rune Stone sat behind glass in the exhibit that opened on February 8, 2004, at the Hälsinglands Museum in Hudiksvall, Sweden. (SFW)

Even though I had already had a wonderful trip, the best was yet to come. The relatives scheduled another bus trip for Monday, February 9, that took us further west into Hälsingland. We boarded the bus at 9:00 and many of the same people who were on the first trip came along on this one as well. Ulla Nylander and Britta were our guides, and they used a microphone and loudspeaker to tell us about the various sites. Not long after the tour started a rumor circulated on the bus that a relative had found new Ohman letters, but I was pretty tired from the previous day and wasn't sure if what I heard was real or not. At midmorning the bus wound its way through the beautiful snow-covered countryside toward the Dellen Lakes, about fifteen miles west of Hudiksvall. These two large lakes were formed when a meteorite hit the earth about 90 million years ago, and the resulting crater eventually became the two large lakes that form a circular structure. The relatives wanted to make sure that I saw this geologic wonder.

At noon the bus pulled into a attractive lodge near a ski resort in the town of Järvsö, and we all went inside for a buffet lunch. I sat with Lars, Susanna, Britta, and Scott Ohman. Sitting across the table were three older folks who were siblings, two sisters and their brother. It was hard to communicate since they didn't speak English, so all we could really do was trade smiles and gestures. They were related to Olof, but I didn't know how. After lunch we hit the road again and made our way to another small museum called The House of Migrants, in Alfta. As the bus pulled into the parking lot, Britta Blank came up and told me about the newest letters that had been found the previous night. I said that I had heard something about it, but didn't know any details. She indicated the back of the bus where three men were sitting by themselves. She pointed to one of them and said, "Sven-Erik Johansson found the letters last night and brought them with him. Would you like to see them?" My eyes widened and I quickly sat up, "You bet!" She led me to the back of the bus and introduced me, and I asked Sven-Erik if I could see the envelope with the letters. As he handed me the envelope I called for Lars and Susanna. I gave Lars and Susanna a letter randomly grabbed from the collection and said, "Start reading you guys; in English please."

The letter Susanna had was written by Olof and was dated December 4, 1927. She started reading the letter, and giving Scott Ohman and me bits and pieces of information in English. Soon her eyes widened as she realized what she was reading. Olof was writing about the Rune Stone! He was telling his relatives about the rally at Oscar Lake, held on June 1st that year. He was happy that after twenty nine years the Stone was finally being recognized as genuine. Of the forty or so letters that had surfaced so far, this was the first one in which Olof Ohman discussed the Kensington Rune Stone.

Lars' letter was just as exciting, although in a different way. Written by Karin Ohman and dated September 1, 1935, she wrote to the relatives in Sweden about Olof's death. Lars began reading aloud, then shortly he stopped translating. His eyes began to well up as he silently read to himself.

During the bus tour on February 7, 2004, Lars Nylander became engrossed in a letter Karin Ohman wrote in 1936 describing Olof Ohman's death to his relatives back in Sweden. Scott Ohman listened reflectively as Lars read the letter aloud. (SFW)

After an enlightening tour at the small museum, I got back on the bus and quickly photographed the letters before it started moving. The wheels in my head were turning, trying to figure out the quickest way to get the letters translated. I was anxious to read what Olof and Karin had to say about their family and the events going on in their life at that time. These letters were like finding a treasure chest full of literary gold!

The bus pulled up to the museum in Hudiksvall at 5:30 p.m. and already it had been an exhilarating day. My document search talk was scheduled for 7:00 so I had a little bit of time to get ready for it. I set up my laptop with the projector they provided in the lobby of the museum and got ready to go. As the room began filling with people and a few minutes before starting, I decided to add a few pictures that Darwin Ohman had let me photograph before I left. The one that really had me curious was of Olof and the four other people sitting in the delicate chairs. I thought that if I had time at the end I'd show the pictures on the screen and see if anyone knew who those people were. At 7:00 p.m. the room was full with about fifty people, mostly Ohman relatives. The setting was one I'll never forget: next to me as I spoke was a genuine, six-foot-tall Viking age rune stone on my left and a replica of the Kensington Rune Stone on my right.

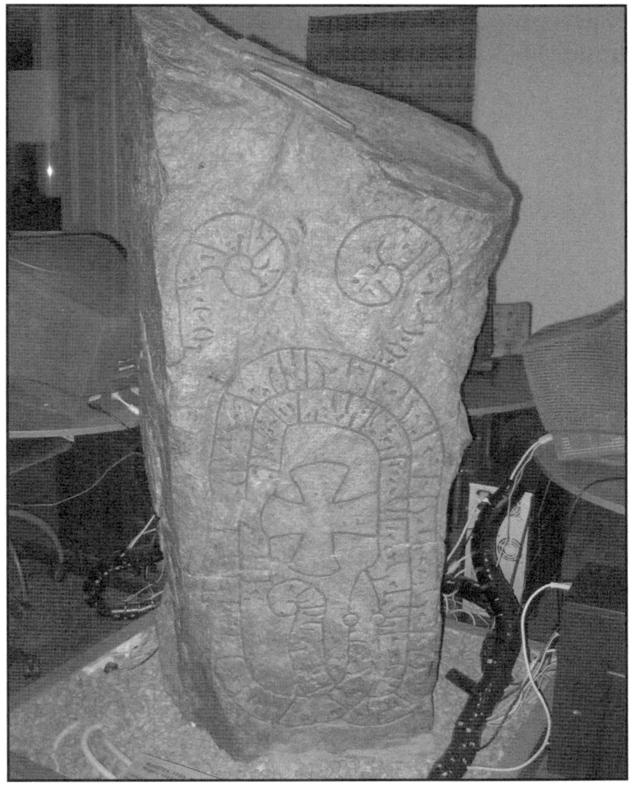

This Viking age (approximately 1000 A.D) Malsta rune stone stands among computer terminals at an internet café in the lobby of the Hälsinglands Museum in Hudiksvall, Sweden. This extremely rare inscription was carved into a granite glacial boulder using abbreviated runes and is one of the few of its kind in Scandinavia. (**SFW**)

I was very excited about giving this talk, since I felt I had done my homework well. I thought the evidence I found explained how past researchers had gone astray in their relentless pursuit to find the Stone a hoax. In Stockholm last October, I had come as a geologist interested only in discussing the work I had done on the Stone. As much as I wanted to talk about the document search then, it was not the appropriate time. Finally the time had arrived. Not only did I present evidence to explain how the Stone had come to be considered a hoax, but I also presented compelling evidence that shed light on Ohman's character. This evidence supported the fact that he was an honest man who had nothing to do with a hoax. Best of all, I would be presenting this evidence to people who genuinely cared about what I had to say.

After roughly an hour I finished what I thought was one of my most inspired talks. I looked around the room and could see that many of the relatives' eyes were filled with tears. For the first time, they had heard some heartbreaking stories about how the Stone had impacted the Ohman family in Kensington. As if they weren't emotionally moved enough, I played the first five minutes of the 1949 Edward Ohman interview tape I'd copied from the Minnesota Historical Society archives. Edward's voice was credible as he described finding the characters on the Stone that his father had pulled from the ground. When I stopped the tape I found myself standing in front of a silent group of people on the verge of being overcome with emotion. The moment was both wonderful and a little awkward, and I felt like I needed to do something to lift the mood. I remembered the pictures I had loaded into the presentation before I started, so I clapped my hands together and said in an upbeat tone, "Hey, does anybody want to look at pictures?" They agreed and I flashed the picture of Olof and the four strangers up on the screen.

Olof Ohman is pictured with his sister's family in this picture taken in Sweden in 1912. L to R: Margta Göransson, Johan Göransson, Anders Göransson, Olof Göransson and, Olof Ohman. (Courtesy of the Ohman Family)

As soon as the picture appeared there was a reaction. Sitting in the front row were the three siblings who I had traded smiles with at lunch earlier in the day. They suddenly sat up, pointed at the screen and talked excitedly in Swedish. I asked Britta what they were saying and she said that the woman was their grandmother Margta, who was Olof Ohman's sister. The man in the middle was her husband Anders and the boys standing behind them were their two sons. The younger boy on the left was Johan, the father of the three siblings. Suddenly the mood in the room lifted, because the siblings' joy at seeing a photograph of their own family that they had never seen before. While they were excitedly talking about the photo I handed Britta a pencil and paper and asked if she could get them to write the information down, and before they left I promised I'd get prints made for them as soon as I got back home.

Scott Ohman sits behind the three siblings who identified unknown people in an Ohman photograph as their father and grandparents. This picture was taken just after an emotional presentation at the Hälsinglands Museum on February 9, 2004. Front row, L to R: Gunhild Eklund, Bertil Göransson and Lilly Larsson. (SFW)

The presentation I had thought about for months had gone even better than I had hoped, and the Ohman relatives were more kind and genuine than I imagined they could be. I thought about how the synergy of all these events was in large part responsible for the number of Ohman letters that had surfaced. I had no doubt that more letters and other information would come to light now that these people were energized. It felt good, knowing I had played a role in that.

With all the great things that had already happened, the day I most looked forward to was the one when Runo and I would have time together to talk about the geology of the Stone. When I had met him in Stockholm I was so impressed and relieved that he was the man who would head the team of scientists to review my report and carefully examine the Stone. I was completely blind-sided when Mats Larsson presented what appeared to be the results from Runo's investigation team; I couldn't understand how Runo had allowed such an incident to take place. I had assumed he would share his questions and results with me personally before discussing them with anyone else, and I couldn't imagine that the man I had met in Stockholm would intentionally let this happen, so I refused to pass judgment until I talked to him. Runo called the museum on Saturday, and we made plans to meet on Tuesday, February 10, 2004.

On Tuesday morning I walked down to the train station and met Runo at 9:00 a.m. As we walked back to the museum, I filled him in on what had happened at the debate. He apologized profusely and said he had no idea that comments he had made in private would be used by Mats in that way. Runo seemed genuinely disappointed.

At the museum I introduced him to Susanna and Gunilla. I had already told Gunilla how impressed I was with Runo, and they seemed to hit off right away. I listened as they spoke in Swedish for several minutes over coffee in the lobby. Gunilla had agreed earlier to have her people remove the glass case over the stone so we could have direct access to it. After he and Gunilla had their visit, I pulled out my computer and shared a few points in the document search talk that I felt were relevant to what we would be discussing. Runo was also interested in Winchell's work, so we looked at examples of his careful research. After an hour or so of discussing past research, we went up to look at the Stone.

On February 10, 2004, Runo Löfvendahl and Scott Wolter spent seven hours examining the Kensington Rune Stone at the Hälsinglands Museum. Runo takes a close look at a scraping of gypsum from one of the runes while Scott Wolter looks on. (Photo by Susanna Larsson)

The first point I wanted to discuss concerned the split side being broken off, and it didn't take long for me to realize what Runo's objection was to this critical point. When reading my report, he thought I meant that the entire surface on the side had impacts from where the carver had chiseled it, and said he couldn't see the impacts anywhere else but along the edges. Suddenly it dawned on me that his confusion was my fault; I hadn't explained the impacts clearly enough in my report. I clarified to Runo that the impacts were only on the edges of the side where the carver had "scored" the Stone before breaking a large piece off, probably with a single blow. The carver likely did this a couple of times to create the surface on the side that tapers near the bottom end. Runo nodded his head in agreement as I explained my interpretation, and suddenly, this potentially major point of disagreement was gone. I felt a huge sense of relief. I thought about how my whole trip would have been worth it even if this was the only thing I accomplished.

We discussed the scratching out of the runes (re-tooling) which Runo was still struggling with. When we discussed my work on relative age dating of mica using tombstones, I agreed with his point that it is a new method that needs further study for full acceptance.

He, in turn, agreed when I said that because this work is new, doesn't mean that the results are not correct. Further, he also acknowledged that further study may show that my results are totally correct.

As Runo and I examined the Stone, the museum continued giving tours and we often found ourselves surrounded by giggling schoolchildren. It was nearly 6:00 p.m. when we finally felt like we had covered everything. I asked Runo if we could write down some the points we had agreed on, which left us little time before his 7:00 train left for Stockholm. We felt good about the highly productive time we spent together. As we walked together back to the train station, he told me again how sorry he was about what had happened with Mats. I told him it didn't matter, and that I wouldn't worry about any future statements unless they came directly from him. He also said that he would not have much time to work on the Stone, but that he would issue a final report. He didn't give me a timetable as to when that might be, though. I wasn't really worried, because I knew that if his team had found any serious problems with my work I would have heard it right away. I thanked Runo for making the effort to come and see me. As he boarded the train for Stockholm I let out a big sigh of relief. His team had not been able to refute my findings, and I was glad to know that he really was the quality person I met in October.

On the last day of my trip, February 11, 2004, Anders Holmstedt gave me a tour of the local rune stones in Hälsingland. Anders is a former director of the museum, and probably the most knowledgeable person there is when it comes to rune stones in this part of Sweden. Rune stones are relatively sparse in Hälsingland and we only saw five that whole day. By far the most impressive was a rune stone in the cemetery of the Hälsingtuna Church in the town of Hög. It is the largest rune stone in all of Sweden. It was bitterly cold when Anders and I walked up to it, but it was something I had to see. It seemed appropriate that the finale of the trip was seeing the biggest rune stone in all of Scandinavia.

On February 11, 2004, I saw the Hälsingtuna rune stone, the largest in all of Scandinavia. (Photo by Anders Holmstedt)

The Exhibition in Kensington

Upon my return from Sweden it took me a few days to mentally sort through everything that had happened. The excitement over the discovery of the Ohman letters was still high. I traded emails with Britta Blank almost every day, and she relayed that old letters continued to surface as relatives searched their closets and attics. On March 6, 2004, Britta wrote that she herself had found two more letters written by Olof. When I called her, she explained that she'd found them after several hours in her attic sorting through boxes of photographs, letters, and other belongings from 1860 through 1975. I teased her about being a pack-rat, and laughed when she told me matter-of-factly, "People in Sweden never throw anything away."

As energizing as the discovery of the letters was, all was not wonderful in Hälsingland. Britta explained that Mats Larsson had contacted Ohman relatives trying to get access to some of the letters. A chill went down my spine when she told me that one relative said that Mats asked if the relative would be offended if he wrote anything negative about the letters. To this I asked Britta, "After seeing how Mr. Larsson conducted himself at the debate do you trust him?" She quickly answered, "No!," so I told her, "I wouldn't let him get near the letters. He proved that he is not an objective investigator and will no doubt write something negative about Olof, no matter what is in the letters. If he published a biased, negative opinion that served his pre-formed conclusions, you might never be able to undo the damage."

I suggested that the relatives should all get together and publish a book about the letters. The letters could be photographed, transcribed into modern Swedish, and translated into English. I said, "You should sell the book and let everyone have access to them at the same time." Britta liked the idea and said she would talk to the relatives about it. I also asked her if I could get permission to have Susanna Larsson translate the letters because I wanted to write about them as well. She said she would check with the rest of the relatives and get back to me. On March 16, 2004, she wrote back saying everyone liked the idea of doing a book together, and that they trusted me to do what I thought was best with the letters. I assured her that I would not publish anything without running it by the relatives first.

As thrilled as I was about the letters, my excitement was tempered by the deteriorating situation at the Runestone Museum in Alexandria, Minnesota. On March 6, 2004, LuAnn resigned as director after almost six years of service. As hard as it was for her, it was the right time to move on, and like other things in life, when one door closes another one opens somewhere else.

The first door to open presented the opportunity for the City of Kensington to be the host of the Hälsinglands Museum exhibit. When LuAnn resigned, all of the museum's volunteer staff resigned as well. In response, the bewildered board of directors chose to close the museum so they could regroup. Ironically, it was the same time as the Hälsinglands Museum was ready to move forward with the exhibition, but now there was no director at the Runestone Museum to work with. Gunilla and Susanna asked me what they should do and I suggested that they approach the City of Kensington about hosting the exhibition. I knew Mel and Mary Conrad would be excited about the idea, and felt confident that the community would support it. Besides, LuAnn was available to help them. To top it all off, Kensington had just completed construction of a brand new community center that would serve as the perfect venue for the exhibition.

The community center in Kensington, Minnesota, was near completion on this overcast day on March 13, 2004. (SFW)

On March 13, 2004, I was asked to give a presentation in Kensington about the two trips to Sweden, and to announce plans for the exhibition. Darwin Ohman offered to drive and we left at 7:30 that morning. Darwin was well-informed about the whole situation with the Runestone Museum and was motivitated to get involved with the new plan. Darwin and I had a lively conversation that made the two hour drive seem like only a few minutes. Near Kensington I pulled out Susanna Larsson's translation of the letter Karin Ohman had written about Olof's death; the one Lars Nylander had read on the bus in Sweden. I told Darwin that I wanted the letter read to bring the exhibition, and the Ohman letters, into the hearts of the community members. I asked if he wanted to read it at the presentation. He said it was a good idea, but he wanted someone else to do it. We both agreed that LuAnn would be the right person to read it.

We had set up a 10:00 a.m. meeting in the town café to interview Einer Bakke. Darwin was excited, and he told me about the good times they had together years ago. When we arrived, Mel and Mary Conrad and Pryce Score had everything ready in the back room of the café. Duane Sprouls, the Mayor of Kensington, came by to meet us and before long

Einar strolled in.   For a guy over ninety years old he was pretty spry, and had a very sharp mind. He was excited to see Darwin and after a little catching up, we all sat down at a table. I turned on the video camera and watched as the two old friends looked at pictures and traded stories about the Ohman family, neighbors, and friends. It was a great time and I was glad that we decided to record this precious moment.

After lunch, we all went over to the old community center to get ready for my presentation. People began filing in as I fired up my trusty laptop and by 1:30 the room was full.   More than eighty people showed up for the presentation, which is a really good turnout in a town the size of Kensington. I decided to give both my presentations, about the geology of the Kensington Rune Stone and the document search, and although I spoke for over an hour and a half, everyone still seemed engaged. I shared slides from the trips to Sweden, and LuAnn got up to read the letter written by Karin a month after "Father" died. The room was silent as she read the short and concise sentences. The emotion in Karin's words jumped off the pages as she wrote about her sadness and uncertainty of a future without Olof. I looked over at Darwin, who was hearing this letter about his grandfather's death for the first time. His moist red eyes betrayed his sadness, but the words were therapeutic as well.

After LuAnn finished the letter, I made the announcement that the exhibition from Sweden was coming to Kensington. At first everyone was quiet, but as they heard more details it slowly began to sink in. Duane read a letter from Gunilla who said how the Hälsinglands Museum was looking forward to working with Kensington on bringing the exhibit to America. When Duane finished the letter the crowd applauded enthusiastically. They knew they had been handed a tremendous opportunity and were ready to seize it. As I packed up my gear, Darwin came up and told me he'd promised Einar we'd meet him at the bar for one beer. When we walked in Einar was sitting at the bar, and a big smile came to his face when he saw us. Darwin seemed right at home with his old friend, and soon more stories started flowing in the relaxed atmosphere. We had one beer, as promised, so we'd have time to stop at the Ohman farm before heading back to the Cities.

Old friends Einar Bakke and Darwin Ohman share stories and a beer in Kensington on March 13, 2004. (SFW)

Our next stop was a few miles down gravel roads familiar to Darwin, to his grandparents' homestead. When we pulled up next to the old barn, Mel and Mary were waiting in their truck with keys to the house. The farm is now a Douglas County park and the Ohman house has been designated a historic building. As we walked toward the house Darwin stopped at a sign posted out in front that read, "Turn of the Century House." Darwin looked around, puzzled, and asked, "Why isn't it called the Ohman house?" Mary explained that when the park was first set up, no one had asked the Ohman family for permission to use the name so they just called it that. Darwin smiled and said, "Well, you have permission now."

The sign outside the residence at Rune Stone Park was changed from the "Turn of the Century House" to the "Ohman Family Farm House" in April of 2004. (Photograph courtesy of Mel and Mary Conrad)

Mary unlocked the door and the four of us gathered in the small front living room. It had been over thirty years since he had last been inside the house. As Darwin peered around he told us how he used to come visit his uncles John and Art back in the late 1950s and 1960s. Mary took notes as Darwin searched his memory to give her details about the interior. The Conrads planned to repaint the house and get it ready for the upcoming exhibition. As we climbed the steps to the second floor bedrooms we could all sense Darwin's emotions rising. He paused at the top of the stairs and then walked over and pointed to a corner against the west wall. "John used to sleep right here, and Art's bed was over in that corner." Darwin walked into a tiny adjacent bedroom and with slightly welling eyes muttered, "When I came to visit, this is where I slept."

We went back downstairs and into the kitchen; we could tell where the old stove used to sit because of the cracks in the ceiling. As we made our way toward the summer kitchen in the back, Darwin paused in the short hallway leading to it. He looked up at the open 2 x 4 rafters and said, "This is where Amanda hung herself." Amanda was Darwin's aunt who committed suicide at the house in April of 1951, at the age of 58. We all stood for a moment pondering the despair of her final moments 53 years earlier.

After walking out the back door, we talked about what it must have been like for Olof and Karin to raise nine children in that well-built, but tiny house. If those walls could talk we would have been there for a long and interesting story.

It had been a highly informative and emotional day for Darwin, but he seemed excited and happy as we drove back. He talked about how great it was to see his old friend Einar and the farm again, and about how bothered he was over what had happened with the Stone, and to his family, for so many years. I told him I thought it was time the Ohman family got involved with the Stone again. Darwin explained that over the years many people had come by looking for a quote from him for an article or news story. He said he didn't really care about any of that and usually declined, but this time was different. He said, "I'm excited about all this and I'm ready to get involved now." These words came as sweet music to my ears.

The Larsson Papers

The linguistic debate about the Kensington Rune Stone inscription took an astonishing turn on March 10, 2004, when Professor Henrik Williams sent Dick, LuAnn, and me an e-mail informing us of a "sensational" new discovery. The find consisted of two sheets of paper from a collection that had been recently donated to the Institute for Dialectology, Onomastics and Folklore Research in Umeå, or DAUM.

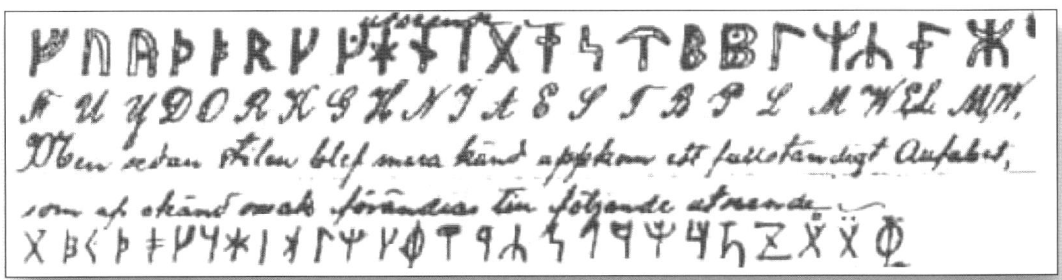

Two rune rows in the Edward Larsson papers reportedly written on April 16, 1885, when Larsson was eighteen years old. The alphabets in this document are strikingly similar to the alphabet of the Kensington Rune Stone, and curiously contain six of the runes that linguists said never existed. (Courtesy Institute for Dialectology, Onomastics and Folklore Research in Umea (DAUM))

As I read Henrik's letter and his report on the documents, I couldn't tell which way he was leaning at first. When I got to the end of his report I was stunned by the morose tone of his hastily written linguistic eulogy for the Kensington Rune Stone. He had proclaimed the rune rows in the Larsson papers to be the "missing link" he thought would never materialize, saying they proved the Stone had a 19th century origin. Henrik also asked Dick and me if we thought he had missed anything in his analysis of the papers, and after discussing it we both agreed that he had. He said that a story about the documents was going to hit the Swedish media the next day, so we didn't have a lot of time to get back to him. Dick immediately went to work on the linguistic questions, and I responded to Henrik from a different angle. I reminded him of the dilemma he was in due to the geologic work both Winchell and I had done. I wrote that since the weathering of the inscription was very old, it stood like the "Rock of Gibraltar" in the way of his 19th century theory. "One of us is wrong," I said.

Henrik stood by his report at first, saying from a linguistic standpoint the Larsson rune rows fit a 19th century explanation very nicely, but he acknowledged that Dick had made some good points as well. Dick's first observation was that the brothers Larsson had made some obvious errors, indicating he had copied the rune rows from some unknown earlier document. The age of the earlier document is unknown, and further, that document could have been copied from an even earlier document. The point was that these rune rows could well be centuries old.

Dick's second point was that the half dozen special runes were the same ones linguistic experts had said for over a century didn't exist; they asserted that the carver had invented them. If these papers were indeed authentic, then they proved that these "invented" runes existed after all, and that the runologists were wrong about this point. Dick also said, "If the experts didn't know about this rune row until now, what else don't they know about?," and offered the conclusion that these "sensational" papers actually helped prove that Olof Ohman couldn't have carved the Stone. Henrik agreed that Dick's points had merit and that it was too early to draw any conclusions about the documents until they had been thoroughly studied.

Several days after that first frantic day, Dick and I received e-mail messages from friends in Sweden, concerned about a television program that focused on the impact that the Larsson papers had with regard to the Kensington Rune Stone. From the feedback we received, it sounded like it was one-sided against the Stone, with our friend Helmer Gustafsson reportedly betting a portion of his salary that the inscription originated in the 19th century. Several experts from various disciplines also offered opinions on the program, but as disappointing as the program was, it was not unexpected. This rush to judgement was a repeat of what happened a century before. This would only be the first volley of negativity that the Larsson papers would generate.

On April 8, 2004, an article appeared in the *Minneapolis Star-Tribune* entitled, "Runestone Takes Some More Lumps." The article had an extremely negative take on the Kensington Rune Stone that was largely based on Henrik's paper, written weeks earlier. I called Peg Meier, who had written the article, and asked her how the information came to her attention in the first place. She said Mike Michlovic had forwarded the e-mail to the newspaper. It annoyed me that Mike had never bothered to check with anyone about the validity of Henrik's private correspondence, and was apparently was only too happy to forward the report in the hope it would be published. I forwarded the article to Henrik, knowing he would be upset when he read it, and with a hint of sarcasm wrote, "Congratulations Henrik, you made it into the newspapers in America." He was upset right, along with many Kensington Rune Stone supporters who sent angry e-mails to the *Star-Tribune*. Each day I checked the paper to see if there was an article or editorial to put the Larsson papers into proper perspective, but nothing was forthcoming.

In subsequent telephone conversations with Mike, he told me that he had heard about Henrik's correspondence from colleagues in Sweden. Mike was quoted in the article as saying the Larsson papers had confirmed his suspicions about the Stone being a hoax. Aside from finding it irritating that he sent the information in the first place, his opinions in such an article seemed inappropriate regardless of which way he leaned. I could never understand why any archaeological opinion was relevant with regard to the Rune Stone. Since the Stone was pulled from the ground by Ohman, archaeologists consider it to be out of context. Since past excavations at the discovery site have not found anything, there are no archeological aspects to discuss. However, these facts have not slowed archaeologists who felt moved to make pronouncements from volunteering opinions about all aspects of the controversy. The *Star-Tribune* article was only the latest example of the fascination some have with the opinions of people from a discipline that really has nothing tangible to offer. All I could do was roll my eyes and think, "Here we go again, another totally misconstrued briefing from the media about the Stone." The whole episode made me think about a line from the famous American baseball player Yogi Berra, "It's just like déjà vu all over again."

Brigitta Wallace

On April 1, 2004, I boarded a plane to Halifax, Nova Scotia, to interview arguably the most controversial figure in the history of the Rune Stone living today. I had spoken with Birgitta Wallace a few times leading up to this trip, and was both excited and a little nervous. We had talked a lot about specific pieces of evidence and as hard as I tried to not be combative, I caught myself raising my voice a few times. Over the course of our conversations it became evident to her that I knew my facts pretty well, and I could feel her confident air fade a little. We ended our last call before the trip by agreeing to disagree, but the tone of our conversations was always cordial.

Halifax was wet, rainy, and overcast as I drove the rental car to the Holiday Inn Express Hotel near downtown. The power was out at the hotel when I checked in and after finding my room with the help of a flashlight, I went to the restaurant and had a cold salad and a beer. As I watched the raindrops splash against the window I thought about the questions I wanted to ask Birgitta. I reminded myself to not be confrontational and to act professional. It turned out that my mental "pre-game" warm-up would serve me well.

When I pulled into the driveway of her home I sat in the car for a moment to admire the view of Halifax harbor. Her husband Rob answered the door and welcomed me in. A smiling Birgitta came down the winding staircase in the large open entryway and greeted me warmly. She led me to her sitting room where a cozy fire was crackling in the fireplace and hundreds of books packed the shelves that lined the walls surrounding the room. I set up my video camera and laptop computer while Birgitta made a pot of tea. At about 11:00 a.m. we sat down for the interview.

I began by explaining the purpose of my visit, that we were working on a book about the Kensington Rune Stone. I assured her that I wasn't there to argue, only to ask questions. I began by showing her the general layout of the book on my computer. When I got to her name in the biographies section, I turned on the video camera and asked questions about her background. She began by talking about her education and how she worked as a volunteer at the Carnegie Museum in Pittsburgh until she earned a permanent position in 1963. Birgitta really perked up when I asked her about her experience at L'Anse aux Meadow with co-discoverer Anne Stine Enstad. Her first trip was in the summer of 1964 and she relayed the excitement of the team finding the first artifact (weaving spool) that indicated that a woman had been there. I could relate to her thrill of discovery, as I've been fortunate to have made many exciting rare finds of my own while hunting for Lake Superior agates and Green River fossils.

I asked about her research into the Kensington Rune Stone. She said she traveled to Minnesota in the fall of 1965 and spent six weeks looking primarily into the Norse-related artifacts that had reportedly been found in the region. During her time in Minnesota she spent two weeks in St. Paul at the Minnesota Historical Society researching the Stone. I asked her what evidence had most influenced her conclusion that the Stone is a hoax. She looked at me and in a cryptic tone and said that her opinion changed when she realized that Ohman was not the ignorant farmer that many people said he was. "He was very intelligent and a deep thinker; that was obvious from the articles he saved in the scrapbook." Her words prompted me to think about the letters in Sweden. Even from the preliminary information I had gleaned from them with the help of the relatives and my friends at the Hälsinglands Museum, it was obvious that Ohman was a very intelligent man. I told her that I agreed that he was smart, but reminded her that his intelligence wasn't proof of anything.

Toward the end of the two-hour interview I felt like we had covered most of the topics I'd hoped to discuss. For my last question I asked Birgitta how she thought she would be remembered in the history of the Kensington Rune Stone. She paused for a moment and then wistfully said, "I think I will be remembered as someone who did some good work, and as somebody who made some mistakes." I was surprised to hear her say these words. Admittedly, she wasn't referring to anything specific, but I think it was her way of saying that she didn't have the Kensington Rune Stone mystery completely figured out yet.

On the flight back to Minnesota the following day I reflected on our visit, and a couple of things occurred to me. Birgitta was only twenty-one years old when she began her research on the Stone, and just beginning her professional career. The 1960s was a time when there was a virtual hurricane of negativity surrounding the Stone. Rune Stone opponents like J. A. Holvik, Erik Moltke, Erik Wahlgren, Theodore Blegen, and others were leaving their mark on the debate, and things culminated with the Gran Tapes interview in January of 1970. Each factor drove a nail in the Kensington Rune Stone coffin. It would have been very easy for anyone to be influenced by these respected researchers, especially someone young, with little experience and new to their field. In recent years Birgitta has become a lightning rod for criticism, some of it quite deserved. I sensed little energy for debate on her part, and in a way, perhaps a burden was being lifted from her shoulders. I'm sure in her mind the question of authenticity is settled. Although, as time and new facts have emerged, the firm resolve of her opinion seemed to have softened. I felt a little like a torch was being passed, only now it was being carried in a new direction.

The Ohman Interview

Another annoying part of Peg Meier's article in the *Star-Tribune* was that Michlovic mentioned the "Deathbed Confession" as additional proof against the Stone. It re-kindled my interest in listening to the "Gran Tapes" again. In June 2001, the former curator of artifacts at the Minnesota Historical Society, Chuck Diesen, had given me a copy of the original transcripts and the audio cassette tapes. When I listened to them at that time, I found Walter Gran's testimony to have so little credibility that I didn't take them seriously. It was nearly three years later and after having heard them referenced so many times by so many people, including a college professor, I decided we could no longer ignore them. The final straw came when it was pointed out to me in Sweden that one of their encyclopedias made reference to the tapes.

In the 1993 edition of the Swedish encyclopedia under the Kensington Rune Stone, there is a reference to a deathbed confession. Susanna Larsson provided the translation below in April, 2004. (Photograph by Susanna Larsson)

Kensingtonstenen, stenhäll med runinskrift, enligt uppgift hittad 1898 under en trädrot på en svenskägd farm vid byn Kensington, Minnesota, USA. Inskriften uppger att 8 "goter" och 22 norrmän landsteg i denna trakt 1362, dvs. mer än 100 år före Columbus. Trots att runologisk expertis i Skandinavien omedelbart underkände inskriftens autenticitet gav den upphov till en omfattande skriftväxling. Den slutade först 1976 då det klargjordes att "upphittaren" strax före sin död erkänt att han och några vänner tillverkat inskriften som ett skämt. *Litt.:* F. Hedblom, "Kensingtonstenens gåta äntligen löst", *Svenska landsmål och svenskt folkliv* 1977.

"The Kensington stone, stone with rune inscription, accordingly found 1898 under a tree root on Swedish-owned farm by the village Kensington, Minnesota, USA. The inscription tells that 8 "Goths" and 22 Norwegians entered the land in these parts in 1362 that will say more than 100 years before Columbus. Even though experts in Scandinavia immediately failed the inscriptions authenticity it started a wide writing exchange. It ended first in 1976 when it was known that the "founder" right before his death confessed that he and some friends carved the inscription as a joke."

I decided to call Darwin to find out what his thoughts were on the subject. Darwin was unaware of the connection between the deathbed confession and Walter Gran, so when I asked him about Walter he had no idea why I was asking. A large grin formed on his face as he told me that he knew Walter. Darwin chuckled and said, "Walter was quite a story-teller. He also liked to have a few belts." It was hard not to chuckle myself because this was very similar to what other area people who knew Walter had said when I talked to them in Kensington. I then asked Darwin to tell me what he remembered about Walter. Darwin said in the late 1950s when he was about twelve years old, he visited his uncles Art and John at the farm. He remembered Walter being there, and how after a few drinks he told a hunting story. Walter reportedly said that when he lived in Canada he used to go deer hunting a lot, and to get his deer he would, "climb a tree, and when a deer came along he'd jump on the deer and kill it with a knife."

Darwin chuckled at the memory and asked me why I wanted to know about him. I told him about the deathbed confession interview to which he expressed great surprise. Darwin was stunned that his uncles' good friend would say something like that. As we talked about what might have motivated him, the word that Einar Bakke used when I talked to him about Walter the previous spring came to mind: jealousy. Walter's father, John Gran, and Olof Ohman reportedly didn't get along. Einar thought Gran was jealous of the attention that Ohman received over the Stone. His words also made me recall something Mary Conrad had previously said, "Isn't it interesting that Walter said his father's alleged confession took place around 1927? That was the same year that the Ohmans received so much positive attention during the rally at Fahlin's Point. I'm sure they probably didn't like all of that." Einar also said Walter liked to tell stories, and we laughed in agreement when I suggested that Walter might be a "Bullshitter." These separate inquiries confirmed my own skeptical opinion about Walter, formed after listening to the tapes.

The Gran Tapes were the topic of discussion again on April 13, 2004, when Russell Fridley and I rode back from Alexandria after we'd each given a presentation about the Stone at a teacher's workshop sponsored by the Minnesota Historical Society. Russ expressed great interest in the information contained in the Minnesota Historical Society documents I had presented; most of it he had never heard before. During our conversation I told Russ what Darwin had said about Walter Gran, and asked him how long it had been since he had listened to the tapes. He said it'd been at least twenty years. The conversation was stimulating, but my stomach prompted me to suggest we stop at Dairy Queen for some ice cream. While walking back to the car shoveling spoonfuls of Oreo Blizzards into our mouths, Russ came up with a great idea. "Do you think Darwin would let me interview him?"

I knew Darwin would like the idea, and told Russ I'd run it by him. Darwin was very receptive and we all met for lunch on April 21, 2004. The two of them hit it off right away, and while they chatted I thought about the irony of this meeting. Most people who knew anything about the history of the Kensington Rune Stone considered Russell to be Minnesota's spokesman on behalf of those who believe the Stone is a hoax; such people would have scoffed at the idea of Russ sitting down to talk with an Ohman. People will be surprised to find out what a pleasant and open-minded a guy Russ is.

We kicked some ideas around and eventually agreed to do the interview with all three of us participating. Russ volunteered to write up a list of questions for Darwin to review. Darwin in turn would write down a few questions he wanted to ask Russell, and I would do the same. Darwin also suggested that his cousin Tom Kolberg should be part of the interview, since he knew Walter as well. No one had any objections so we told Darwin to invite him. We also agreed that we wanted to complete the interview before the exhibit in Kensington, which was scheduled to open in mid-June. Russ suggested that if Darwin agreed to it, a press release could be issued during the exhibition to announce the results. After Russ left, Darwin and I stayed behind a few extra minutes to talk. He said he was very impressed with Russ and excited to do the interview. We also talked about the fact that the Ohman family's chance to tell their side of the story was long overdue.

On May 20, 2004 I got to work early and had my desk cleared off by 8:30 a.m. I carried recording equipment and my video camera into the conference room at our American Companies offices and started getting things set up. My friend Rick Olson, who had lined up the use of the recording equipment, came by to make sure I didn't mess things up. Ricky had worked as a cameraman and producer with a local television station for ten years and knew exactly what to do. Shortly after 9:00 a.m. Darwin walked in with a man of a similar build and a warm smile who introduced himself as Tom Kolberg, a great-grand-son of Olof and Karin Ohman. At 9:30 sharp, Russell arrived and introduced himself to everyone. We all chatted for a few minutes, and then we were ready to get started.

After identifying ourselves for the record, Russell began the interview by asking Darwin about his family and upbringing. It was a comfortable setting, and everyone was cordial and prepared. Russell's calm, easy demeanor set a pleasant tone and he injected a little humor at the appropriate time. He had obviously done this many times before. Darwin presented himself well and came across as very credible. He and Tom had reviewed the Gran interviews the previous night, which allowed Tom to get comfortable with the sub-ject matter, so Tom's intermittent comments were to the point. When Russell finished his questions for Darwin, it was Darwin's turn to ask me questions about my interpretations of Walter's testimony. I began by pointing out several inconsistencies, including specific points where Gran's statements were in conflict with documented facts. I tried to keep my answers short and direct.

When it was my turn to ask questions, I asked Darwin and Tom to talk about their uncles Art and John, as well as what kind of person Walter Gran was. Both men said he was a nice enough guy, but, "Boy did he like to tell stories." They chose their words carefully, and it made me think about what other people who knew him said about Walter in interviews I'd read. Walter was a bullshitter.

After my questions, Russell gave a closing statement. He remained skeptical about the authenticity of the inscription and listed his reasons why. I responded to Russell's comments, and felt I was able to effectively rebut his points without being disrespectful. Then Russell asked a question I wasn't really prepared for. He asked me if I had ever seen a document in which Olof Ohman denied carving the Rune Stone. I searched my brain, but couldn't think of anything. Ohman had denied it, but I didn't know if such a statement had been recorded anywhere. It was a good question. I knew one thing for sure; as soon as we finished the interview I was going to find a record of Olof denying involvement in concocting the Stone. Russell's final question was for Darwin.

"Why do you think Walter agreed to do the interview, knowing it would hurt his close friend Arthur Ohman?" Darwin wistfully listed his reasons and concluded that, "Walter had an axe to grind against Art for some reason," adding, "In my opinion Walter has zero credibility." In spite of Russell's skepticism about the Stone, he appeared to have some doubts about Walter's testimony.

The recording lasted a little more than ninety minutes, and we all walked out feeling like things had gone well. On my way home from work I dropped the audiotapes off with Rick so he could make copies. Later that night I watched the videotape and still felt good about things, except for that one question from Russ. I knew that Ohman spoke to his innocence of any involvement with creating the Stone in a document somewhere, I just had to find it. I knew of two statements in which Ohman addressed questions about his involvement that were written in his own hand, both in letters responding to inquiries from N. H. Winchell (May, 1910 and June 6, 1910, see pages 421 and 424-5).

As important as these statements were, it seemed like there should be more. It would take a few days, but eventually I found what I was looking for. On May 25, 2004, while on my way to Sweden for the third time, I had three hours to kill on a layover in Chicago. I fired up my laptop and started looking over Minnesota Historical Society documents I hadn't read in over a year. I was revising my PowerPoint presentation for Stockholm, so I started reviewing the documents from the beginning. My haphazard maze of reading led me to Winchell's review of Professor George Flom's 1910 paper on the Rune Stone, and I decided to read again.

Professor Flom was arrogant and flippant with his opinions, but he does deserve credit for making the effort to meet with Mr. Ohman. In mid-April of 1910, Flom traveled to

Kensington and interviewed Olof and his family. While reading of this encounter I found what I was looking for on page 40 of Flom's notebook. Ironically, in the written words of one of the strongest denouncers of the inscription's authenticity came the strong denial by Ohman that he had carved the Stone.

A strong denial from Olof Ohman of any involvement with carving the inscription, found on page 40 of Professor George Flom's 1910 paper on the Rune Stone. (Minnesota Historical Society)

been said, says he has no knowledge of runes. To me he disclaimed "the ability to make such an inscription." But Ohman also denies having made the inscription. He volunteered a denial of that, evidently thinking that I knew that the suspicion is directed against him and his denial was very emphatic." But the latter does not

The Third Trip to Sweden

After all the fallout from the Larsson Papers and the developments with the Gran/Ohman tapes, I felt a strong drive to set the record straight in Sweden. So much had happened in the seven months since my last visit, in many ways it felt like seven years had gone by. To me, one last presentation about the history of the controversy seemed like a fitting end to the fourth year of my odyssey with the Stone.

The impetus for this trip began on April 29, 2004 when I received an e-mail from Kristian Berg saying he would be delighted to host my presentation at the Historiska Museum in Stockholm. Later that day we spoke on the phone, and I warned him that many people would not like everything I had to say, but I promised to finish on a positive note. He wasn't the least bit concerned and welcomed the controversial nature of the presentation. Kristian is no stranger to controversy at the museum, which had hosted other exhibits in the recent past that were hotly debated. It takes great courage to lead such a prestigious institution into what can be politically risky territory. He clearly believed that many people are resistant to learning new things and that sometimes they need a little push. In the case of the Kensington Rune Stone, some people need a good hard shove.

On May 26, 2004, I arrived in Stockholm at 7:30 a.m. after an eight-hour flight from Chicago. Unable to get any sleep, I decided to walk over to the Historiska Museum to see if I could find Kristian Berg or Ola Olsson.

Ola greeted me warmly when I found him, and escorted me to their offices where we sat down to discuss plans for the the following week's presentations. The format would be debate-style with my opponent the eighty-two-year-old man who discovered the Larsson Papers, Professor Tryggve Sköld. My tired eyes widened and my anticipation elevated another notch. Ola also informed me that Henrik Williams was going to say a few words at the event.

After a train ride to Hudiksvall the next day, Britta Blank greeted me at the Hälsinglands Museum and gave me a ride to their farm in Forsa. She had arranged for an interview with the local paper in Hudiksvall and I visited with reporter Chatarina Wilkins and her sister Monika, who had interviewed me at my home in Chanhassen a few weeks earlier. Chatarina's article appeared the next morning in the paper that promoted the upcoming debate, as well as Monday's annual event at Britta's historic farm, which would be open for public tours. After the interview, Britta gave me a tour of the farm where family members were hard at work preparing for the open house. She said there might be hundreds of people stopping by if the weather was good. What made this year's event so special was the extra attention the Rune Stone and the Ohman letters had generated for the relatives. They were also happy and proud to have Darwin come and visit, and I enjoyed watching Darwin and his new-found family members get to know each other. In light of all the events of the previous seven months with the Rune Stone, the letters, and discovering a new and exciting chapter of their heritage, the relatives decided to form a group called "The Ohman Relatives Association." The inaugural meeting was held in the barn at Britta's farm on the afternoon of Monday, May 31, 2004. I was proud to know that my involvement had helped bring these people together.

After several days of intermittent rain and sun, the weather was sunny and perfect for the Blank family historic farm open house. Darwin and I finally showed up around 11:00 that morning and found many people bustling about, taking in the re-creation of activities at the centuries-old farm. Soon after we arrived, Lars Westman appeared with his wife and another couple. It was great to see Lars, who had volunteered to translate the speech I would give that afternoon, but I was also excited because Lars would be hearing about the Kensington Rune Stone document search for the first time. As a journalist, I knew he would find the information interesting.

Britta led us all on a tour of the old house and the various buildings that were restored and running at full tilt. The re-creations included a blacksmith's shop, woodshop, charcoal pit, sawmill, and a rebuilt machine used to make air-dried bricks from swamp clay and wood chips. Everything was handmade and operated by a member of the family. Refreshments were offered inside the hay barn on the second floor, where benches were set up for my presentation. At 3:30 people filtered into the barn, and Britta's daughter Johanna started the program by singing a few Swedish songs, accompanied by a friend who played the guitar. Her clear, beautiful voice set a pleasant tone for the audience. At 4:00 it was my turn. Lars gave a summary of the Rune Stone story to the forty or so people assembled, then turned the microphone over to me so I could start with a short summary of my geologic work on the Stone.

It was awkward to speak a couple sentences, then pause while Lars translated; I couldn't generate the same flow. I switched to the document search presentation, but before starting I looked at Lars and said, "I think you're going to enjoy this." I began by explaining how Hjalmar Holand had taken possession of the Stone from Olof Ohman, and then offered it for sale to the Minnesota Historical Society for $5000. No one in Sweden had heard this before, and Lars was clearly intrigued. I continued by telling them how the Museum Committee investigated the authenticity of the Stone, spearheaded by geologist N. H. Winchell. I always enjoyed talking about Winchell, explaining how he conducted his thorough investigation into the geology and topography of the area, the rumors, and Ohman's honesty, as well as his inquiry into the language and runes of the inscription. Each time Lars translated what I'd said it seemed to take longer for him to explain it. He even interjected commentary in both English and Swedish. His mind was busy processing this new information, which made it difficult for him to translate. By the end of my talk everyone in the room was surprised by the new information but understood the important points. Lars especially seemed to enjoy hearing the human side to the controversy.

After the presentation, Britta called the first meeting of The Ohman Relatives Association to order. They discussed the goals and objectives of the Association and voted unanimously to pursue a book project about the Ohman letters to Sweden. They also voted to make Darwin the first full member, and made Dick and I honorary members. I felt a great sense of pride, and knew they were highly motivated to promote the Ohman legacy in both Sweden and America.

Lars Westman, Britta Blank, and Darwin Ohman pose for a picture outside the baking building at the Blank family farm on May 31, 2004. (SFW)

Back in Stockholm the next day Runo called and we set up a meeting for the morning before the debate. June 2, 2004, was a beautiful sunny morning for my twenty-five-minute walk through the city to the Historiska Museum. I asked for Runo at the front desk and he appeared after a few minutes. He escorted me to his office, where we sat down to discuss the latest questions and ideas of his investigative team. The first thing I asked him for was more information about the "thousand-year-old root lineation" theory that he had discussed on the television program. After a several minutes of discussion he conceded it was just an idea that a colleague had suggested, with no supporting information or a written report. I asked for his thoughts on my theory about the split side having been broken off at the time the Stone was carved. He showed me an illustration of how the Stone would have broken free from the bedrock after the glacier scratched the back, which was exactly as I had explained it, only he proposed that the split side broke free without being scratched by the glacier. I pointed out that the problem with this idea was that if it were true, all sides of the Stone would have the same weathering profile, which was not the case. Runo said this was another person's idea, and not necessarily one that he agreed with.

The last point we discussed was the fact that the Stone is composed mainly of muscovite mica, rather than the biotite I focused on in the tombstone study. He suggested that muscovite would take much longer to weather than biotite, which I agreed with. We also agreed that the weathering process involved both chemical and physical processes that took an unknown period of time. He implied that the muscovite would take thousands of years to weather away, not hundreds. I reminded him that his estimate was probably correct if *only* chemical weathering was involved. The fact is, both chemical and mechanical processes were involved, and mechanical weathering was likely the *dominant* process. Therefore, the timing for both biotite and muscovite to weather away could very well be hundreds of years. After several minutes of discussion, I felt Runo hadn't presented any compelling evidence to refute my tombstone age estimates. His argument about muscovite served to extend my "greater than two hundred years old" estimate and appeared to fit very nicely for a weathering timeline of the inscription. After about three hours, I felt there wasn't one item in our work that he or his colleagues had found any real problem with. Runo said he was ready to write his report and would forward a copy to me when it was done. I thanked him for his time and said I'd see him at the debate later that night.

Darwin and I arrived at the museum at 5:30 to get everything set up. The debate was held in the cafeteria, so it could easily hold a good-size audience. Ola introduced us to an older gentleman who was accompanied by his wife. Tryggve Sköld was a very pleasant man who with a wry smile said that he looked forward to our "discussion" of the Stone. I assured him that I was looking forward to it as well. Before the debate started, I gave Ola a set of the tapes related to the deathbed confession, and said I hoped the museum would make them available to anyone interested in listening to them. It seemed appropriate for the museum to have copies of the oral history since it had hosted so many events related to the Stone.

At 6:00 p.m. roughly fifty people had settled into their seats as Professor Sköld and I sat next to each other at the table. Ola gave a welcoming speech in Swedish, and then introduced Henrik Williams, Runo, Lila Kitzler, and Darwin to the audience. Ola handed me the microphone to give the first presentation, and once again I gave a brief summary of the geologic work before diving into the document search. I had a little extra "zing" in my voice from the excitement of finally sharing the human side of the controversy with these people, especially with Henrik. As I finished my talk, I could tell that everyone was thinking hard about the points I'd made. The first person to ask a question was Tryggve, who took exception to my comment that the linguists in the past had done an incomplete and sloppy job. He defended his profession, as I figured he would, but talked only about the work of Scandinavian linguists, and listed several familiar names who I felt had also done a poor job with the inscription. I had already presented examples of the flawed investigations, so it made no sense to argue with him and I left it alone.

Then Runo made a few comments about my geologic work, which we had discussed earlier, and concluded by saying, "I remain skeptical." This was about what I expected from Runo and I understood why. The important thing is that he was unable to find any serious problem, which was as good as an endorsement to me. I made a point to ask Lila Kitzler if she thought her 3D profiling work would be sensitive enough to differentiate between the weathered surfaces. Since we had looked into this technology and concluded it wasn't adequate, I was not at all surprised when she said she didn't think it would be. All in all, no one on Runo's team was able to find any serious problem with any part of my geological work on the Stone and although I am the first to say that there is a lot more work that can be done on the Stone, I felt a great sense of satisfaction that the work I had performed had made a strong impression.

It was interesting to hear Trygge describe how he discovered the Larsson Papers. After his presentation we each gave our closing statements. Predictably, Tryggve concluded that the language of the Stone proved it was made in the 19th century. When it was my turn, I argued that my work made Tryggve's conclusion impossible, and pointed out that my conclusion that the inscription was older than two hundred years did not put it in the 14th century. I said, "The linguists are the only ones who can put the inscription in its proper place in time," and suggested that they "wipe the slate clean and start over." I looked at Professor Sköld, "Your remarkable discovery has proved that the linguists and runologists didn't know about the Larsson Rune Row. There's bound to be more out there, go see what else you can find."

After the conclusion of the debate, Ola invited several of us to dinner at a restaurant a few blocks from the museum. Darwin, Henrik, Runo, Ola, Tryggve and his wife Nina, all started off walking to the restaurant while I lagged behind, putting my laptop away. As I hurriedly left the museum I was met by two college-age men who I recognized from the audience. They politely asked if they could speak with me and I said, "Sure if you don't mind walking." As we walked a block behind the others they told me they appreciated that I had come from America to talk about the Stone. They explained that there was big debate going on in Scandinavia about historical scholarship. They said, "The scholars lied to us." Older scholars had an established view of history and were resistant to hearing new ideas, different interpretations, and modern evidence, and the Kensington Rune Stone debate was a classic example of this problem. I was impressed that they felt strongly enough to seek me out and express their views. They told me to keep up the good work, and I told them to keep challenging their professors and to stick to their ideals; there was no danger that I would slow down any time soon.

I thanked them for attending the debate and hurried to catch up to my party. During the dinner I called Dick in Texas on my cell phone and gave him a chance to say a quick hello to everyone. Henrik proposed a toast in Dick's honor since without him, none of the important events that occurred in Sweden, including the discovery of the Larsson papers, would have happened. The conversation was very cordial and the feeling that real progress had been made permeated the mood of the dinner. After the guests excused themselves and we said our goodbyes, Darwin said he wanted to buy a round of beers, and we had a chance to talk. With a humble smile he said he was very pleased with the evening and told me that Henrik, Tryggve, and Runo had separately told him, "Your grandfather didn't carve the Stone." Each had a different reason for their opinion, which only added to an already convincing case for the Stone's legitimacy.

Swedish linguist Tryggve Sköld visited with Darwin Ohman at the post-debate dinner in Stockholm on June 2, 2004. Professor Sköld, along with Runo Löfvendahl and Henrik Williams, told Darwin that in their opinion, his grandfather Olof Ohman did not carve the Rune Stone. (SFW)

Darwin also beamed at how Henrik had stood up during dinner to "apologize for the way some linguists had treated his family, and most notably his grandfather, in the past." It was something that Henrik certainly didn't have to do, but because he is a gentleman he knew it was the right thing to do.

As we took the last sips of beer I felt a sense of relief and contentment. I knew I had done all I could do in Sweden, and was proud of what Dick, LuAnn, and I had accomplished as a team. We had made so many wonderful new friends, and succeeded in opening up a fresh discussion about the Stone. I laughed to myself, thinking about how the Kensington Stone was like religion. The answer to the big question goes beyond documented facts and evidence, and ultimately boils down to a matter of faith. People are going to believe what they want to believe and there might never be a consensus, at least not in my lifetime. It doesn't matter though, because the most important question has been resolved. I think the world is ready to accept that Olof Ohman did not carve the Kensington Rune Stone. For me, the smile on Darwin's face was worth all the time and energy I had put into this.

On my last day in Stockholm, Kristian Berg invited me to join him and Ola for lunch. I met them in the lobby of the museum and we walked a few blocks down the street to a café where we sat and talked about the success of the debate. The museum had paid for my trip, so I thanked Kristian, then told him I knew why he'd brought me back over. With a small smile, Kristian gave me a slightly puzzled look and quietly listened. I then told them about what the two young men had said the previous night. His smile widened when I said, "You're just trying to stir the pot aren't you? The Rune Stone is a perfect example of this type of controversy in historical scholarship, and by hosting a debate with a subject that's such a hot topic it forces people to think about these issues. Am I right about that?" Kristian was almost beaming at this point and said, "Sometimes the exhibits we host are not popular with everyone."

We finished lunch and walked back to the museum, where Kristian and Ola thanked me again for coming. Since being involved with the Kensington Rune Stone I've seen many intelligent people who were afraid to speak up or tackle tough questions. The Historiska Museum, and Sweden, are fortunate to have a director with such courage and leadership.

Rune Stone Days in Kensington

There wasn't much time to unwind upon my arrival back to Minneapolis on June 4, 2004. Susanna Larsson and Anna Meyer arrived to start work on the exhibition in Kensington. A few days later, Gunilla and Lars from the Hälsinglands Museum flew over to join them, and the exhibit came to life over a period of several days. As the producer of the exhibit, Susanna felt a lot of pressure to ensure that it turned out right. She worked hard to coordinate efforts with the people of Kensington and her colleagues from Sweden. Mel Conrad served as the carpenter, while the rest of the group pieced together the Swedish immigration story with antique furniture, artifacts, pictures, and the Ohman letters. The first room highlighted life in Forsa, Häsinglands, Sweden, during the late 1880s. The next room featured a typical Swedish home, and told the story of life before the great migration. A corridor with a wooden gangway symbolized the bridge to America aboard the passenger ships that carried the Swedes to their destination. The final room represented the typical immigrant home in America, seen through the eyes of the Olof Ohman family. Several of Olof's and Karin's letters were featured in the exhibit, along with re-creations of the inventions he wrote about to his relatives in Sweden. The impressive exhibit fit perfectly inside the new community center.

On June 13, 2004, five of the Ohman relatives, including Britta, arrived in Minnesota for a visit, hosted by Darwin. Everyone was keyed up for the opening ceremonies in Kensington on June 17, 2004. As I made the two-hour drive up I-94 that clear, sunny morning, my mind was a swirl of memories and emotions. It was hard to believe so much had happened in the previous eight months, and even though I knew there was much more Rune Stone work to do, an important chapter would end on this night. The opening of the exhibition marked the culmination of a lot of hard work by many people and it would probably be the last time I would see my friends from Hudiksvall for a long time.

By 7:00 p.m. the community center was packed with over a hundred and fifty people as LuAnn Patton took the podium to welcome everyone. LuAnn's voice was emotional, and who could blame her. She had been through some very difficult times at the Runestone Museum, and this would be her last opportunity to demonstrate the leadership and class she had shown during her tenure as director. She made all the right calls during the scientific research and represented the museum with dignity and grace. This night belonged to her as much as anyone. The Mayor of Kensington, Duane Sprouls, served as a gracious host to the guests from Sweden. Britta Blank and Ulla Nylander also spoke about how the Stone's travel to Sweden had brought their families together with the Ohman relatives in Minnesota. Britta explained that although she and Ulla had been neighbors and friends for twenty-five years they only found out through this experience that they were actually related.

The Wolter family and the Ohman relatives who came to America from Sweden pose for a photograph in front of the 17-foot tall granite replica of the Kensington Rune Stone outside Alexandria, Minnesota, on June 19, 2004. L to R: Amanda Wolter holding Fritz, Janet Wolter, Grant Wolter (hat), Britta Blank, Håkan Blank, Karin Lundholm, Ulla Nylander, and Sven-Erik Johansson. (SFW)

I felt my own eyes well up watching Britta and Ulla present Darwin with a book on Swedish immigration that had both Olof's and Karin's names in it, which they said was to be passed on to the oldest living Ohman descendant in America. When LuAnn took the podium again, she read letters from Russell Fridley and Lars Westman. I knew Lars was a talented writer, but this letter was the first time I had heard his writing in English. His upbeat and eloquent words touched everyone. LuAnn thanked people who had helped make the exhibition happen, and finished by calling for Mel and Mary Conrad. These two humble people had worked hard to raise money, motivate people to help, and put in a ton of their own time doing everything they could to make the exhibition a success.

With tears in all of their eyes, LuAnn Patton presents roses and heartfelt thanks to Mary and Mel Conrad for all their hard work in making the Hälsinglands Exhibition in Kensington, Minnesota, a great success. (SFW)

Finally, as Gunilla spoke in Swedish, and Susanna translated into English, they formally announced the opening of the exhibit they had worked so hard on. As people made their way into the exhibit, I visited with Janey Westin and her father Bob Johnson. We reminisced about our time with the AVM Stone and marveled at how far things had come. The entire event turned out better than any of us had thought it could.

Later that night as the headlights zoomed past me on my ride back to Minneapolis, I felt a mixture of relief and sadness. I was proud of all my friends, who had been at their best this night. I thought about all the amazing things that had happened, and the wonderful experiences I'd had throughout the past four years, how all of our work had made a difference in the understanding of the Rune Stone. I smiled, thinking how we had all made a positive contribution to the Ohman family.

The Ohman Documents

Just as I thought that things were winding down, the biggest surprise of all came just four days after the grand opening of the exhibition in Kensington. With the relatives from

Sweden heading back in a couple of days, Darwin and his wife Ginny hosted a party at their home on June 21, 2004. I walked up the driveway and was greeted by Darwin, who started introducing me to members of his family I hadn't met before, including his daughter Carrie and son Brian, and his brother Jim, who had stopped by unexpectedly. Tom Kolberg was also there with a beer in his hand and a big grin on his face. After chatting for a few moments in the driveway, Darwin led me into the garage where we had spent most of that first night we met looking at Ohman family photos. Tom's sister Joanne Streeter greeted me, as did the relatives from Sweden who were sitting at picnic tables that had been set up for the party.

I was enjoying the pleasant distraction of greeting the Swedish relatives when Darwin slipped a piece of paper into my hand. I stared at the wrinkled paper and suddenly realized I was holding an old letter. My eyes widened as I recognized the penmanship; it was a letter written by Hjalmar Holand. Darwin, and the letter, had my full attention. I looked at the date and who it was addressed to at the same moment: January 1, 1928 to Mr. Olof Ohman. I felt like I had been hit over the head. I looked at Darwin, who stood there with a big grin like he had just given me a birthday present. My mouth was hanging open, but no words came out at first. I was finally able to ask him, "Where did you get this?" He pointed to the table next to me that was covered with papers, pictures, and books and said, "Hey, there's lots more; dig in."

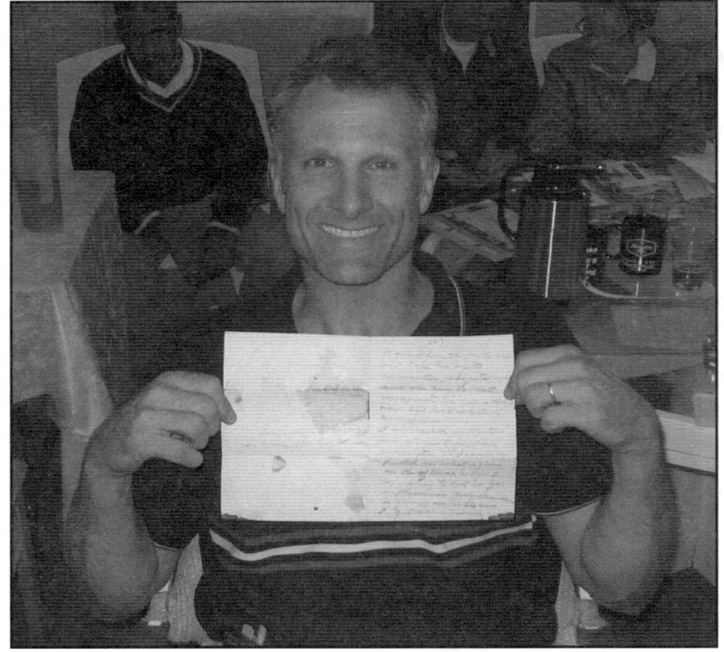

On June 21, 2004, I was obviously excited about the discovery of a letter in the Ohman documents that included a sketch of the tree roots wrapped around the Stone. Olof Ohman Jr. drew the sketch in a letter to his brothers John and Art on April 2, 1957. (Photograph taken by Tom Kolberg)

It took me a moment to collect myself, but I quickly switched from party mode to research mode. Britta and Ulla were already looking through the material, as excited as I was. Britta handed me another letter written on a half sheet of paper in a familiar, shrinking script I had seen thousands times at the Minnesota Historical Society. It was a letter written to Olof from Warren Upham. Stunned again, I quickly glanced at the date: March 3, 1915. This was a letter I never saw at the Historical Society, and I knew no one else had seen it, either. It was written in response to a letter from Olof asking the Society to return the Almquist book that Winchell had borrowed from him in 1910. The book had previously belonged to Sven Fogelblad, and Andrew Anderson and his wife Betsy had given the book to Olof after he found the Rune Stone. Dick Nielsen and I had both seen the book at the Minnesota Historical Society library, so it obviously had never been returned to Olof.

Britta pulled out another letter written in Norwegian from Holand to Olof, dated January 17, 1928. Fortunately, Britta was able to read most of it, and we heard the words laced with spite. Issues between the men were consistent with other letters from around this time. I felt like they'd found a treasure chest and we were all sorting through the loot. A plastic tub was filled with books and hundreds of family photos from around 1900 to the early 1970s. Most of the photographs were of Karin and Olof's nine children. I was especially captivated by images of the two daughters, Amanda and Ida, and joked with Tom and Darwin that I had a crush on Amanda, who was quite beautiful.

A picture probably taken around 1912. (L to R: Unknown, Christine Norlien, Ida Ohman, and Amanda Ohman.) (Courtesy of the Ohman Family)

With Original Pretenders music playing in the background, we sipped beer and pored over the materials for more than four hours. A couple of times while I was digging through the pictures, Darwin tapped me on the shoulder and jokingly asked, "Are you finding anything good yet?" At 11:00 that night, Darwin and Tom called an impromptu meeting in the garage. Darwin wanted the other family members to hear about the trips to Sweden so they could get some perspective about what was going on. For the next hour and a half Darwin, Britta, and I told our stories about the events that had occurred and what we thought it all meant. While everybody knew about the Rune Stone, they did not know about all the progress that had been made in recent years. Everyone listened intently, and the feeling in the garage was upbeat. I could sense these people were coming together and that there was strong support of the efforts being made. After all the hard times this family had endured for so long, it was the present generation that was coming together to take on the controversy as a unified force.

After thanking everyone for sharing their treasured belongings with me I left for home at about 12:30 a.m. My head was spinning with excitement and the anticipation of going through the items more carefully. What else was there and what would this new information lead to? It would only be a few days before we would find out. Eight days later, on June 30, 2004, Darwin, Joanne, and I met at Darwin's and went through everything more carefully. We scanned all the letters and dozens of photographs. As we went through the photos questions began to come up that no one had an answer for. Joanne said her father Lalard, from the age of three, had been raised on the farm by Olof and Karin. Lalard's mother, Ida Ohman, left the farm around 1915 and moved to Fargo, North Dakota, where she gave birth to Lalard in April of 1916, and married his father, Abraham Kolberg in June of that year. For some unknown reason, Ida put Lalard on a train to Kensington in 1919, and then disappeared. Joanne said Ida never came back, and that Lalard never really knew his mother or his father. It was hard for her father never to

have known his parents, and he often thought about them. The farm was an important place for him, and it was Lalard who had saved all the personal items when Art sold the farm in 1973. It was obvious that the farm was also important to Joanne by the way she talked about her father and uncles Art, John, and Darwin's father, William. Evidence of her emotional ties to the place lies in the numerous photographs of her as a child and teenager, taken at the farm from the 1950s through the 1970s.

Joanne Kolberg stands behind a steel bar placed at the Rune Stone discovery site by her uncle Arthur Ohman in this 1959 photograph. (Courtesy of the Ohman Family)

When Lalard passed away in 1997, Joanne had no idea that the many letters related to the Rune Stone were important. She did know that photographs and other items in the boxes her father kept from the farm were priceless to the family. There were many interesting things to ponder among the documents, but in the back of my mind I kept thinking about Ida and why she chose to leave her son. The three of us spent six hours scanning documents before we felt we had everything done. Joanne told us there were still two more boxes to go through, and we hadn't even started looking at the book collection.

The next time we got together at Darwin's house was on July 20, 2004. Russ Fridley had been bitten by the curiosity bug, so he joined us and we were glad to have him in on the fun. Joanne brought two more large plastic tubs filled with a jumble of papers, scrapbooks, and photographs. She said most of the stuff probably belonged to her father. Darwin, Russ, and I sat at the table as Joanne started sorting through the tubs, pulling out what she thought would be interesting. Right away she found two short letters Olof had written in Swedish; one dated 1905, and the other 1916. It was fun a few days later to read the translations that Britta did for us. The 1905 letter was Karin and Olof's will, and the 1916 letter was a poem.

Each time we found something interesting Darwin would scan the document and I'd save it in the computer. Most of the materials were personal family documents like birth, marriage, and death certificates, stock certificates, warranty deeds, and a lot of photographs. The articles spanned a broad time-frame, and chronicled what seemed to be the lives and times of a typical, rural 20th century family. Even though some of the articles prompted discussion about the character of Olof and members of his family, Russ agreed there wasn't anything that would cause even a skeptic like him to become suspicious.

At about 8:00 p.m. Russ excused himself and went home, but Joanne, Darwin, and I continued on. After a while Joanne thought she had gone through everything that looked important. When I saw that one of the tubs was nearly full I said we should really check everything before calling it quits. I dug into the tub and soon pulled out a two-page letter written to Amanda Ohman from a woman in Minneapolis named Mrs. Lillian Golden, who was a friend of Ida. I gave the letter to Darwin who read it aloud. The woman asked Amanda if she knew the whereabouts of her sister, and wrote that the last time she had heard from her was in a postcard mailed from Detroit, Michigan, twenty-seven years earlier. I felt chills go down my spine as Darwin read the letter. We all had wondered about Ida, and now realized that somebody else back then did, too. The most ironic thing about the letter was that it had been written to Amanda on April 17, 1955, almost four years to the day after she had taken her own life (April 19, 1951).

There was a somber quiet among us as we pondered the irony of the letter. We surmised that either Art or John had received the letter and held onto it as a memento of their sisters. Not long after the letter to Amanda turned up I pulled out a picture folder with a portrait of a man inside. I opened the picture but didn't recognize the person. It was an old photo, so I thought it must have been a friend of the family. Joanne noticed the photo in my hand and said she had seen that picture earlier, but didn't know who it was. I was just about to put the photo back in the tub when I noticed tiny writing in pencil at the very top of the inside cover. It said, "From Abe Kolberg, March 11, 1915." I was stunned for a second when I realized that I was looking at the man who was involved in the mystery of Ida's return of her son and her subsequent disappearance. Earlier in the evening Joanne had said she had no warm feelings for her grandfather, and that she had never seen a picture of him. I slowly looked at Joanne and said, "This is your grandfather, Abe Kolberg."

Joanne gasped slightly and looked as if she wasn't sure she wanted to see it. I handed the photograph to Darwin, who studied the picture and said, "He looks like Lalard alright." Darwin handed the photo to Joanne, who opened the cover, and through eyes welling with tears looked at her grandfather's picture for the first time.

The name of Abe Kolberg, the husband of Ida Ohman who descendants of his had never seen a picture of, at the very top of the cover of his portrait. (Courtesy of the Ohman Family)

We finally reached the bottom of the second tub shortly after 10 p.m. and I drove home more wired and awake than when I had arrived. We had found more interesting documents with important information that helped fill in some of the holes about the Ohman family history. The really great thing was that Joanne learned a little about her grandparents' mysterious past. We had gone through four of the five plastic tubs, and had only the book collection left to go through. So far we had found nothing even close to resembling a "smoking gun." We had found several pieces of evidence that supported Darwin's statements and the family's claim for decades, "There has never been a doubt about the Rune Stone." To me the most compelling thing so far was the letter Olof Jr. wrote to his brothers in 1957. If there was ever a doubt within the family Olof wouldn't have written the letter that he did, or it would have had a completely different tone. We didn't see one tangible piece of proof that Ohman had anything to do with a hoax.

On Wednesday, August 4, 2004, Darwin, Tom, Joanne, and I met in the garage one more time to look at the books. By now we knew our roles, and the process had become pretty efficient. Tom would quickly examine a book then handed it to Darwin, who would add on to Tom's comments and read the book title to Joanne, who wrote down the pertinent information on a notepad. I would quickly review the book and scan the title page, Olof's signature, and any pages with handwritten notes into the computer. I ended up slowing the process because it turned out that Olof wrote notes on a lot of pages. The notes were written in Swedish, which slowed me down even more as I hopelessly tried to read what he had written. At one point Tom paused and said, "Here's a book signed by Fogelblad." My ears instantly perked up and I asked to see the book. Sure enough, when I compared the signature in the book, it matched the signature in the Almquist grammar book I'd photographed at the Minnesota Historical Society. However, this book had nothing to with runes, it was about religion. Since all indications are that Olof was not a religious man, the book was probably given to Karin Ohman, who had a deep faith. She must have received the book from her cousin Betsy Anderson, who gave Olof the Almquist grammar book after he found the Rune Stone.

The library contained sixty-nine books, and it took us just over three hours to go through them. There was a variety of titles that seemed reasonable for an intelligent, self-sufficient farmer to have. There was even a book by Plato, *Plato's Apology, Crito and Phaedo of Socrates*, which indicates that Mr. Ohman was quite a thinker, a term I had heard used before to describe him. After studying the collection of books I had to conclude that regardless of his lack of a formal education, Mr. Ohman was a very smart man.

Runo's Report

On August 18, 2004, I opened my e-mail and saw a message from Runo. He informed me that he had attached his completed review of my geologic report, which I began to read with great interest. As I read Runo's summary of the geologic investigations, I furrowed my brow in disagreement when he wrote that Winchell had "hesitantly" reached his conclusion that the Stone was genuine. I wondered which report Runo had been reading, because Winchell was firmly convinced of his conclusion and had no hesitancy whatsoever. This was only the first of several things in Runo's report that made me question him. He agreed with points in my report that amounted to basic geologic findings, with little or no bearing on the important aspects of inscription. Runo chose to pursue "Popper's Falsification Principle" and tried to see if our results could be falsified. I was fine with this approach, but it was clear that he was going to stand behind the ideas that we had discussed in Stockholm. None of them were plausible alternate possibilities in my mind and he had offered no supporting evidence. I was also disappointed that the report questioned my ability to identify pyrite in the Kensington Rune Stone. Pyrite is a common mineral, simple to document, and I found it very puzzling that his team did not perform any scanning electron microscopy or elemental analysis. Worse yet, there was no evidence that he reviewed the SEM data that I had given him the previous October in Stockholm. The elemental maps made the presence of pyrite obvious even to a novice.

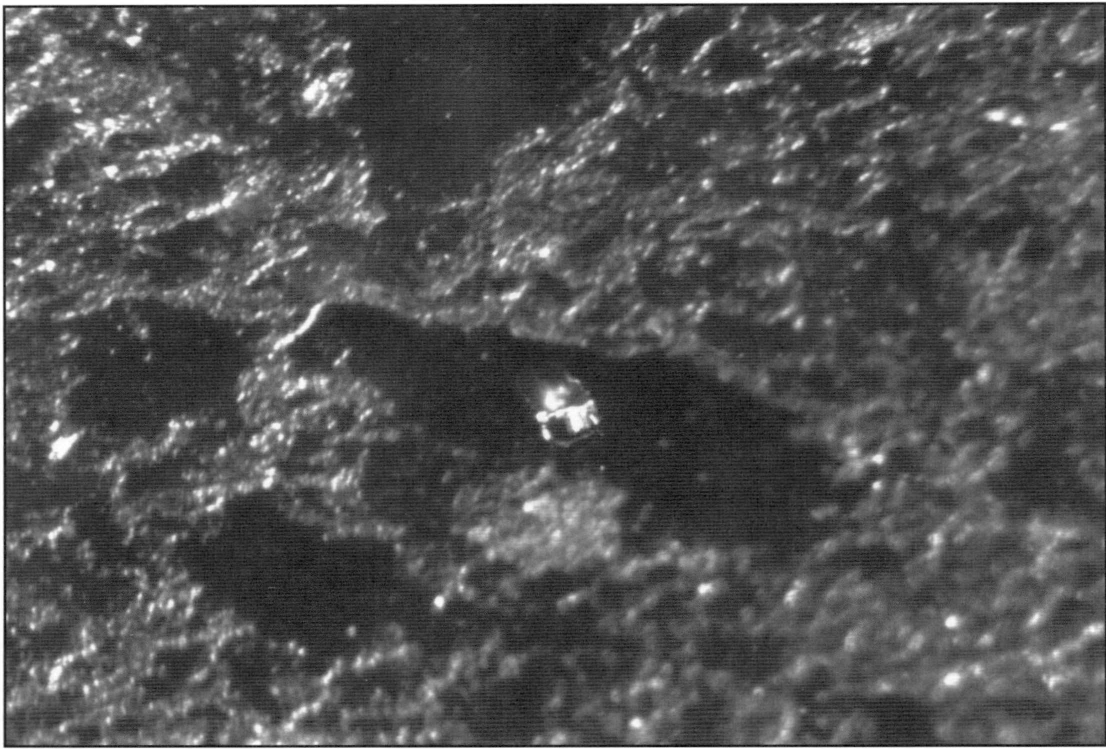

This brassy-colored pyrite crystal (0.002″ in size) exhibiting cubic habit lies within a clear quartz sand grain just below the polished surface of the core sample taken from the Kensington Rune Stone (220X).

Overall, the report was a great disappointment. One encouraging part of Runo's report was the professional rune carver's opinions about the inscription. According to this expert, the person who carved the Stone was no novice, but not a professional, who would have cut both sides of a linear rune. The carver was experienced, but not with this type of material (meta-greywacke), and had probably chalked out the text before starting to carve. The expert also said that the inscription took three to six days to carve, and since the major straight lines are 26 to 29 mm, it was unlikely that either 15 or 25 mm chisels were used.

Runo's report was long on skepticism and short on plausible alternate possibilities. I'd heard skeptical comments from Runo and others in Sweden many months before, so I wasn't surprised by the overall negative tone of his review. Runo did write that much more work could be done, which is something I certainly agree with. However, I believe the weight of the evidence and the interpretation we presented stand as the explanation that best fits with the documented facts. Our conclusions also fit nicely with the well-known axiom, "The simplest explanation is usually the right one." When I wrote my response back to Runo I stood firmly behind my conclusion: **The inscription on the Kensington Rune Stone was not carved in the 19th century, and has been weathering for longer than two hundred years.**

Ohman Presentation in Kensington

After taking some much-needed vacation time with Jan and the kids in late July, I came back from our trip to the Black Hills of South Dakota, prepared to put the "Olof carved the Kensington Rune Stone" nonsense to bed once and for all. After consulting with Dick, Mel and Mary Conrad, and Darwin, we decided to give a presentation at the community center in Kensington on August 21, 2004. Mel and Mary did their part in putting together a press release, while Dick and I worked on a new presentation. Darwin and I had another idea that we hoped would bear fruit. We decided to personally invite reporter Peg Meier to join us in Kensington on the 21st. Mel and Mary scheduled the talk for 2:00 p.m., which prompted me to propose an idea to them. I asked if there was anyone who was willing to let me interview them on camera with stories about the Ohmans or Walter Gran. I had heard several people tell interesting stories, but it seemed like this was a great opportunity to document them with the time we had before our presentation. Mel and Mary went to work, and when Darwin and I called Peg she was open to the idea.

Peg wanted to talk to Darwin beforehand and interviewed him at his house on August 10, 2004. Darwin called afterward, said they had visited for almost two hours and that it had gone well enough that Peg had decided to come to Kensington. We had discussed many times how the evidence related to the Stone presented a clear case; the problem was getting the information to the public so they could decide for themselves. Like it or not, "the truth" to the public is what they read in the newspapers or see on television. We also changed our strategy. Instead of discussing the evidence that supported the Stone's authenticity, we decided to present evidence that proved Ohman had nothing to do with a hoax. We thought it would be easier to get people interested in the Ohman story than in the details of the language and geologic aspects of the Stone. If we succeeded in getting Ohman out of the equation, eventually the question of authenticity of the Kensington Rune Stone would take care of itself.

I picked up Dick at the airport in Minneapolis at 1:00 a.m. on August 20, 2004; we hadn't seen each other since Hudiksvall in February. Later that afternoon we drove to Alexandria and checked in to the Holiday Inn. We stayed up late working on the computer in preparation for our talk, and decided to try a different approach: we would have one set of slides, and jointly present the information, which turned out to be pretty effective. It was really great to be able to work together with Dick in the same room instead of over the telephone and through e-mail. Dick brought so much knowledge and so many good ideas that rejuvenated me. I was already excited about the presentation, but Dick recharged my batteries for getting the book done.

When we arrived at the Community Center in Kensington it was about 9:30 a.m. and Peg was already there going through the Hälsinglands exhibit. Mel and Mary greeted us and led us to a room where we could conduct the videotape interviews. I set up my camera on a tripod and got ready for the first interview. Darwin showed up a few minutes later and then Dick, Darwin, Peg, and I sat down at the table with Loydd Flaaten. Loydd is the grandson of Nils Flaaten, Olof's neighbor to the east who saw the Stone in the roots the day it was unearthed in 1898. Loydd said his uncles Olaus and John Flaaten told him Ohman was an honest man and that he had nothing to do with carving the Stone. Loydd is a quiet, humble man whose family always believed in the Rune Stone.

The second person we talked to was our friend Einar Bakke. We all asked Einar questions and he shared his memories in his own unique way, clearly miffed when asked if Ohman was involved in carving the Rune Stone. He remembered Ohman and his family fondly, and found the idea that the Stone was a hoax, ridiculous.

Peg was very quiet when we talked to Mr. Flaaten, but warmed up with Einar, asked him some questions and diligently took notes. The next person we talked to was Bob Carlson, a former resident of Kensington who lives in North Dakota. Bob was seventy-five years old, and had approached Britta Blank at the opening of the exhibition in June with an interesting story he agreed to share during an interview in Kensington. Bob is a nice person who felt it was important to be there. He sounded very credible as he talked about Art and John Ohman, who he knew well, though he didn't know Edward as well. In 1947 he was eighteen years old and was working as a laborer on a farm with John Ohman and some other men. At lunchtime on one particular day, he and John caught a ride in the back of a truck and he asked John about the Rune Stone. Bob said, "John, who was a big and powerful man, put his hand on my knee and firmly squeezed it. He wasn't trying to hurt me; he was just letting me know that he was serious." He said that John looked him in the eyes and said, "Some day they will find proof that the Stone is genuine." Bob's compelling story rang true, and when I glanced over I saw a smile creep on to Peg's face as she scribbled in her notebook.

By the time we finished talking to Bob it was 12:30 p.m., so we all walked next door to the café and ordered lunch. Before we knew it there were only thirty minutes before our presentation. I set up my video camera and asked Michael Zalar, a diligent Rune Stone researcher, if he would run it for me. Gradually, the same room that hosted the emotional Hälsinglands exhibit opening two months earlier began to fill with people once again. I recognized familiar faces along with some new ones, as well. Since this presentation was about Olof Ohman we made sure to have the Ohman family seated prominently in the front row. At 2:00 sharp, Mel Conrad took the microphone and welcomed the hundred or so people in the crowd, made a few introductions, turned the microphone over to me, and away we went.

I was eager to give this presentation, and Dick and I thought we did a pretty good job. We talked for almost two hours and everyone seemed interested in our findings.

The Kensington Heritage Foundation sent out a press release prior to the presentation.

A Statement by the Olof Ohman Family about Olof Ohman

August 21, 2004

It has been almost 106 years since the Kensington Rune Stone was found on a farm near Kensington, Minnesota by a Swedish immigrant farmer named Olof Ohman. The authenticity of the 202-pound stone has been debated since that day, with no clear consensus reached by either side to this very day.

We are not here to discuss the authenticity of the stone. **We are here to present several new pieces of evidence that support the fact that Olof Ohman was not involved in carving the rune stone.** For over a century scholars from many disciplines have passed judgment about not only the rune stone, but about the honesty and integrity of Olof Ohman. Many people have been asked to give their opinion about the controversy, except for the Ohman family. They have remained silent about the stone for decades, until today. Based upon new evidence that they have had time to consider, they now feel it is time to speak out and let those interested in the rune stone hear what they have to say. The new evidence consists of the following:

1. A one-and-a-half hour videotaped interview with members of the Ohman family who knew Walter Gran, to give their side of the story with regard to the "Deathbed Confession."

2. Recently discovered documents from the Ohman family that shed new light on Olof Ohman's honesty.

3. Testimonials by two Swedish linguists, Professors Henrik Williams and Tryggve Sköld, and Swedish geologist Runo Löfvendahl, during a recent trip to Sweden that they believe that Olof Ohman did not carve the stone.

4. The recently discovered Larsson Papers in Sweden contain the remaining 6 previously unknown runes that runologists claimed Olof Ohman invented. The fact that these runes existed after all provides evidence that he did not carve the stone.

5. The discovery of 47 letters written by Olof Ohman to his relatives in Sweden, including two where he discusses the rune stone.

6. Geological evidence that proves the weathering of the inscription was much older than Olof Ohman was (44 years old) when he found the stone.

7. Recently discovered documents from the Minnesota Historical Society library collections that shed new light on his honesty and integrity.

This press release outlines the seven areas of evidence presented by Dick Nielsen and Scott Wolter at the presentation in Kensington, Minnesota, on August 21, 2004.

I closed the presentation by saying that the "Evidence was overwhelming," and that "It was now time to restore the good name of Olof Ohman, to remove the label of forger from his name." Then we asked Tom Kolberg and his sister Joanne Kolberg-Streeter to go out into the hall of the community center and pull down the construction paper to unveil the most important letters and photographs, which had been posted on the wall. It was the official, public, coming-out party for these fascinating and important documents.

As people milled about reading the letters and talking, Peg came up and said she had a couple of questions. She told me, "You've convinced me, Olof didn't do it." Her words came as a bit of a shock since I'd always perceived her as a pretty staunch disbeliever. For her to accept the evidence about Olof gave me deep sense of satisfaction and relief. Maybe other people will come around too.

Members of the Ohman family pose with their supporters in the Kensington Community Center on August 21, 2004. L to R: Tom Kolberg, Joanne Kolberg-Streeter, Scott Wolter, LuAnn Patton, Dick Nielsen, Kari Ohman Karels, Haley Karels, Darwin Ohman, and Brian Ohman. (Photograph by Mary Conrad)

On Labor Day, September 6, 2004, Peg's article appeared on page three of the Metro section of the *Minneapolis Star-Tribune*. We had waited for more than two weeks, and even though she had said it would run around that time, I was still surprised to see it. I sat in the car in front of a coffee shop and read the article. It was very positive, and for once I felt like a reporter got things right. Late in the afternoon, while at a neighborhood beach party with my family, I received a call on my cellular phone from Darwin. He had returned from being out of town and had just read the article. He was very pleased, and curious to see what would happen next. We chatted for a few minutes and after hanging up I sat down at a picnic table and watched a brisk wind blow across the lake. I thought that maybe Peg's article would begin to turn the tide of public opinion in a positive direction. If Olof is taken out of the equation it all boils down to one simple question: If Olof didn't carve the Rune Stone, who did?

The Willie Sarsland Letter

After Peg's article appeared, both Dick and I felt like this would be the perfect time to finish this book. There had been so many exciting new developments and there was a lot of new evidence to present. We had thought we were ready a few times in the past few months, but just when one thing would settle down, something else would happen that we had to follow up on. True to form, two days after the Ohman presentation in Kensington we were back in Darwin's garage looking at more documents. This time Tom and Joanne brought everything along so Dick could review it all for the first time. Joanne brought a few new things, including some photographs we hadn't seen before. One of the pictures was of a woman in a white dress with dark hair parted in the middle, who we all agreed was not a member of the Ohman family. When I turned the photo over and looked at the back I saw a name penciled at the top in very small letters: Alma Sarsland.

The Sarsland name had come up at an earlier session in a partial obituary for a man named Willie Sarsland. The obituary was undated, but based on information in the article it had to have been from around 1950.

This time I decided to look into the matter and did a Google search. Eventually, I found an anonymous posting of four letters from the Holvik file, three of which I had already seen. My jaw dropped as I read the fourth letter. In it, Sarsland indicated that he was compelled to write after reading the *Minneapolis Tribune* newspaper article of October 16, 1949, in which Holvik claimed that Ohman found the stone blank, carved the inscription, and then reburied it within the roots of the tree. Sarsland wrote that he was threshing on the Ohman farm the day the Stone was found and that he helped, "…to remove some of the shale and deposits…". After reading the letter I wondered who the heck this guy was and if his information was true. One phone call to Mel and Mary Conrad in Kensington yielded a great deal of information about the Sarsland name. That same afternoon Mel and Mary e-mailed me some details including Sarsland's complete obituary. Willie Sarsland indeed had lived in Kensington in 1898 and moved to Ludlow, South Dakota in 1910. They also sent information about Willie's sister, Alma Sarsland, who was in the same 1907 confirmation class as Amanda Ohman. The photograph of Alma in the Ohman documents made perfect sense now, and indicated that the girls were probably good friends, which also gave credibility to the Sarsland letter.

At this point I couldn't wait to search the Minnesota Historical Society library to try to find the original letter. On September 8, 2004, I began by once again searching through Holvik's file, starting from October 1949. After only a few minutes I found a memo written to Holvik from the director of the Society at that time, Dr. Harold Cater, dated November 29, 1949. Attached to the memo was a typed copy of the Sarsland letter, along with a one-page typewritten analysis by then curator of newspapers at the Minnesota Historical Society, Willoughby Babcock. I read Babcock's analysis and found his comments quite interesting. He wondered why the Sarsland name had never been mentioned before in association with the Rune Stone; specifically, he mentioned Winchell's investigation and trips to Kensington in March of 1910, which was a valid point that needed to be checked out. Another point of Babcock's struck me as somewhat odd. He wrote that the letter looked like a woman's handwriting, and concluded that his opinion of the letter was "distinctly unfavorable." After reading Babcock's analysis, I sat there puzzled for a few moments. The comment about the handwriting made me even more determined to find the original letter.

Sarsland's letter was addressed to Dr. Cater, which meant it had to be in the general correspondence file of the Minnesota Historical Society. I filled out the request slip and waited for the box to be brought out to my table, though my heightened anticipation made the ten minutes or so I had to wait seem like a hell of a lot longer. When the box was finally wheeled out on a cart, I lifted the top off and scanned the folders for the year 1949. After only a couple of moments I found the three-page stapled letter. The first thing that jumped out at me was the handwriting; it was very neat, and sure enough, it did look like a woman's handwriting! I read the original letter and then pulled out my digital camera and photographed it.

I went back to Holvik's papers and found a letter to Cater dated December 2, 1949, where Holvik acknowledged receiving the Sarsland material and promised to check into it. I kept thinking about what Holvik's reaction must have been when he first saw the letter. His jaw must have dropped in shock, for if the letter was authentic and Sarsland really was a witness to the discovery, Holvik's entire hoax theory would have gone down the drain. I started looking for any further correspondence indicating that he had followed up, as he promised. I searched from December 1949 through 1955, and found nothing. For reasons known only to him, Holvik simply ignored the letter or intentionally suppressed it. At this point there wasn't anything more to do at the Minnesota Historical Society except corral these documents in my computer and figure out what to do with them later.

Later that day I called Judi Rudebusch from Corona, South Dakota, to fill her in on what I had found. Judi is a Kensington Rune Stone researcher who told us at the Ohman presentation in Kensington that she would help us find out whatever she could about any of Sarsland's descendants in the Dakotas. When she answered the phone she had information that was just as interesting as what I had to tell her. She had contacted one of Willie's granddaughters, *and* she had contacted the only living offspring of his thirteen children! The woman's name was Irene Krelicek who was eighty years old and lived in Scranton, North Dakota. Both Irene and her niece Roxanne were excited about the news of the letter and were willing to help out. Judi gave me the phone numbers and I told her I'd call them in a couple days.

I was pretty darn excited about the Sarsland developments, but I had also found something else interesting in Holvik's file during this time: two letters written to Holvik by a man with rather shaky handwriting, named Henry Hendrickson. Hendrickson was the former postmaster in Hoffman, Minnesota, who wrote some rather cryptic things about Olof Ohman to Holvik. I was already aware of Hendrickson from Blegen's book and turned my attention to getting to the bottom of his story. On September 16, 2004, I went back to the Minnesota Historical Society to try to find additional letters from Hendrickson in Holvik's file beginning with October, 1949. Sure enough, more letters from Hendrickson were there, including the three-page letter in which he relayed his story about Ohman, as well as his own hoax theory about the Rune Stone. Hendrickson's narrative reminded me of Walter Gran and his theories; both men were long on opinions, but painfully short on evidence.

Page one of a three-page undated letter written by Henry Hendrickson in 1949 contains comments he allegedly heard Olof Ohman make in 1890. (Minnesota Historical Society)

"In Regard to the Runestone

"For J A Holvik

"In the summer of 1890 I and Ole Ohman had a long conversation about different subjects. During our talk he was carving on a piece of board with his pocket knife. Then he made a remark that he would like to figure out something that would bother the brains of the learned.
"Here are his very words in the Swedish language: Min Higsta änkass är at reppfinna nogot sonr ville bråka hjärnan jo de järde.
"Mr. Ohman was not what you may call a highly educated man he was a carpenter by trade but there was a man that was staying with him when he was visiting in the neighborhood around Kensington. His name was Sven Fogelblad he was a highly educated man he was a graduate of Uppsala college in Sweden and ordained a minister of the state church of Sweden but as he told me himself that he resigned from the church for the reason that he could not preach to people a doctrine that he did not believe himself (He was an atheist). They both liked to invent jokes Fogelblad could read and write different languages so he furnished the brains and Ohman done the work and I believe Fogelblad had books with the runic alphabet so they spelled the text out of those books.
"It is about 65 miles between lake Cormorant and Ohman's place so that is a long one day walk as the story on the stone states as would take at least two days to walk that trip as Lake Cormorant is in Becker County.

H Hendrickson"

381

In all, there were seven letters from Hendrickson in which he provided Holvik with information about people in the area around Kensington. In two of the letters (March 3, 1949 and October 13, 1949), Hendrickson told Holvik not to use his name in any publication that featured any information he provided. As far as I was concerned, if Hendrickson was not willing to allow his testimony to be part of the public record, it was worthless.

In a letter written to Holvik on October 13, 1949, Henry Hendrickson asked that his name not be used in association with the rumors he spread about Ohman or his hoax theory. (Minnesota Historical Society)

"Hoffman, Minn. 10-13-49

"J A Holvik
Moorhead, Minn.

"Dear Sir

"When you was here you said you was going to publis(h) a letter in regard the Runestone I hope you will not mention my name then or in the future. If any one should ask for it my reason for this is that I will be pestered with letters of excuses in regard to the Runestone question this I want to avoid Please grant my request

"I remain yours truly,

"H Hendrickson

"P.S. Nothing new has turned up"

As I continued working my way backwards though the file, my eye caught what was now a familiar name in a letter from Holvik, dated March 1, 1949: Babcock. When I started to read the letter another familiar name jumped out in the very first sentence; Holvik was writing to Willoughby Babcock about the Sarsland letter. How could this be? This letter was written eight months *before* the Sarsland letter, which was impossible. I took a closer look at the date and noticed that Holvik had typed February, and then crossed it out. Not only had he typed the wrong month, but he also had the year wrong, which could only have been 1950. The letter itself had a nauseatingly condescending tone and even decades later, it still reeked with deception.

In a letter from Holvik to Willoughby Babcock at the Minnesota Historical Society, the date appears to have been intentionally typed with the wrong year (it was 1950) for the purpose of hiding the actual date it was composed. (Minnesota Historical Society)

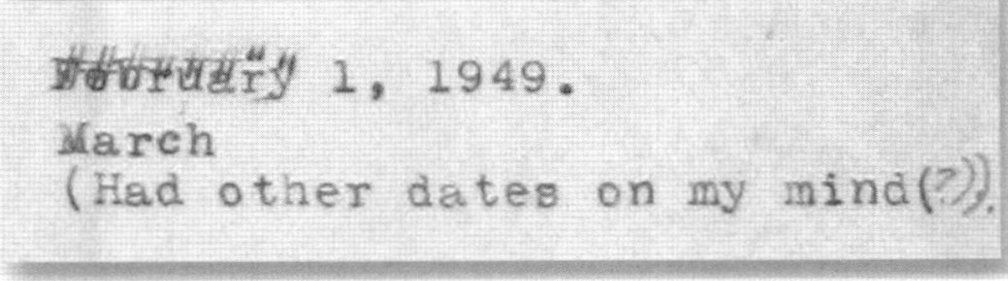

After pondering the letter a while it became clear to me that Holvik intentionally tried to bury the letter by typing the wrong date. There is no way in the world that he waited three months to read the Sarsland letter. In fact, the only reason he wrote this letter at all is because he wanted Babcock and Cater to think that he had followed up. However, he conveniently wrote this letter *after* Willie Sarsland had died on February 16, 1949. I believe Holvik knew full well that Sarsland was dead, and that neither Babcock, nor anyone else, could never interview him. I'll go even further and say that the crossed out month of February wasn't a mistake at all. He probably wrote the letter within a day or two of hearing about Sarsland's death, but thought March would look less suspicious.

On October 9, 2004, I called Irene Krelicek in Scranton, North Dakota, and asked if she had received the Sarsland letter and other documents I'd sent to her. She had received them, and said immediately that the handwriting was not her father's. "It is definitely my sister Sally who wrote that letter. Sally was living at home at the time and must have written that letter for Dad." I laughed at the irony of how Babcock's comment about "woman's handwriting" turned out to be right. A few days later I opened my mailbox and pulled out an envelope from Irene's niece, Roxanne Miller. She sent me two samples of Willie's signature, and a picture of the handsome Sarsland family that was taken in July of 1949. The signatures were definitely not the same as that on the letter, confirming what Irene had said.

Even though I felt confident that we had all the questions answered about the Sarsland letter, there was still one more thing I needed from Irene. I knew there would be people who wouldn't believe me if I tried to explain what Irene had said, so I needed proof. I called her again and asked if she would write a letter stating what she had told me. She understood the importance of my request and promised to send the letter. On October 24, 2004, I opened my mailbox and inside was Irene's letter. I was ecstatic to open it, but decided to call Darwin and open it while he was on the line along with Janet by my side so they could share in the excitement. Just as she had promised, inside was a note from her that confirmed the handwriting of the Sarsland letter was indeed Sally's. All of us were greatly pleased, but there was something else in the envelope. Irene had a little surprise for us. She included a three-page handwritten letter Sally had written to her on October 8, 1958. I read the letter aloud, frequently interrupting myself to explain how individual characters were identical to characters in the Sarsland letter. She even crossed out words she didn't like the same way in both letters. I am certainly no handwriting expert, but in my mind there was no doubt. Sally definitely wrote the letter!

On October 23, 2004, I received a note from Irene Krelicek stating that her sister Sally had written the letter for her father Willie Sarsland, on November 14, 1949.

"Oct. 18-04

"Scott-

"A short note to let you know I'm still going to send a picture of Dad & Mom in their younger yr's & one of Sally: Sorry it's taking so long!
"I'm mailing you a letter that Sally wrote to me–so you can see that my sister wrote the letter for my Dad–it wasn't Dad's signature: it was my sister Sally.
"Best get this in the mail–you will be hearing from me when I get the picture ready to go.

"Irene"

After hanging up the phone I sat back in my chair for a moment, amazed at how much information we were able to learn after all this time. I also thought about what a wasted opportunity it was that Willie Sarsland was never interviewed. Not only had Holvik spawned the most prolific hoax theory in the Stone's history, he had cleverly recruited Erik Wahlgren and others to spread it. Holvik had used his position and the credibility it afforded him to further his ideas about Ohman carving the Stone, when it was really he himself who had perpetrated a hoax. His intentional suppression of the Sarsland letter and the important information it contained amounts to nothing less than fraud.

I also thought about the impact Holvik's accusations had on so many people. His relentless assault on the character of Olof Ohman and the Ohman family was shameful. Why he was so determined to shove his ideas down everyone's throat is unclear, but he was successful to a large degree. It was he who started the legacy of the "Ohman hoax" that was taken on by Wahlgren, whose work unduly influenced future researchers like Birgitta Wallace, Theodore Blegen, and many others. I also believe that Holvik indirectly influenced a person who had become a good friend of Darwin and me: Russell Fridley. In the years after this period the negativity toward the Rune Stone grew like a cyclone through the tropics. Many people believe the final nail in the Kensington Rune Stone coffin was the Walter Gran interview of 1970. One could also say it was the crowning achievement of Holvik's grand plan to bury the Stone. For thirty-four years he was successful, even though he didn't live long enough to see it.

As fate would have it however, Holvik's suppression of the Sarsland letter turned out to be his Achilles heel. Holvik tried hard to bury him, but Willie was bound and determined to be heard. Ironically, he came back to life in an obituary that the Ohman family saved because he was someone who mattered to them. Through the help of a bunch of good people the deception was unraveled and the truth is now known. For as good as I felt about this fantastic new discovery I also felt a bit of sadness. I knew that I would have to share this important information with my friend Russ, and wondered how it would affect him. On October 25, 2004, I called Darwin to see what he thought about my writing about Holvik, the Sarsland letter and the possible impact on Russ. For several months Darwin, Russ, and I had shared any new information we discovered over lunches at a local restaurant. We all got along well even though Russ didn't agree with us on the origin of the Rune Stone. Russ told us many times that he was still skeptical and wasn't convinced yet that Ohman wasn't involved. Darwin and I tried hard not to preach or push our feelings and evidence. We only shared the information and ran our theories by him, to which he always gave honest feedback. His comments were valuable because they came from a skeptic and it forced us to think things through more carefully than we otherwise would have. Never once did I sense resentment or hard feelings of any kind. He was always a gentleman who never pulled any punches and neither did we. I know we appreciated that about him and I'm sure he did too. I couldn't help wondering how he really felt about all this Holvik/Sarsland stuff. It might have been a realization that the story he was told about the Rune Stone was all a big fat lie. If Russ felt that way he wasn't ready to tell us. I sure can't blame Russ for what he believed because everybody else in the world thought Holvik, Wahlgren, Wallace, Blegen, and many others were right too.

On October 29, 2004, my friend Wils Robinson invited another friend and me to lunch. Wils thought I would enjoy meeting his friend who was a twenty-five year-old schoolteacher named Issac Arvold. Issac was a very friendly guy who was excited to talk about the Rune Stone and to hear about the latest findings. I asked where he was from and why he chose to get a tattoo of the Kensington Rune Stone inscription. He was originally from Holmes City, Minnesota, which very near Kensington, and had grown up hearing about the controversy from his neighbors and family, who were of Swedish descent. When he decided to get body art done he wanted something deeply meaningful because it would be permanent. He had always believed the Stone was genuine and because it was an important part of the history of where he grew up and represented his heritage, it made sense to him.

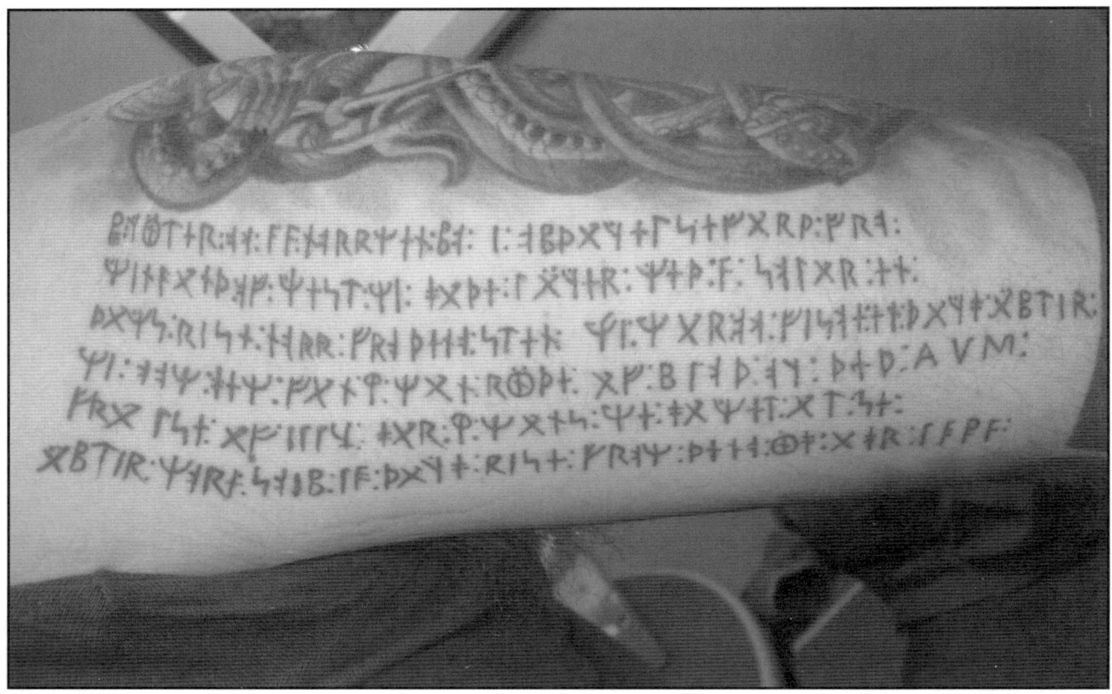

Beliefs both pro and con about the authenticity of the Kensington Rune Stone have run strong and deep for many people since the day it was discovered in 1898.   Twenty-five-year-old Issac Arvold from Holmes City, Minnesota, proudly displayed the Kensington Rune Stone inscription tattooed on the back of his upper right arm on October 29, 2004. (SFW)

I was pleased to see another example of the impact that the Stone has had on people's lives, including my own. This investigation has been one of the most challenging and rewarding experiences of my life; I have learned so much about things I never thought I would be exposed to. I have also come to know interesting and wonderful people who I never would have otherwise met. I feel like I have a whole new extended family both here in the US and in Sweden. I have learned a great deal about myself, my strong-willed personality served me well. I am also grateful to Dick for his wisdom, guidance, and friendship. There isn't another person in the world who could have done the work that Dick did, while perservering through all the adversity to finish the job. It took him twenty years, but I know he would say it was worth it. I'm so glad he chose to share that knowledge, and his trust, with me. The completion of this book is by no means the end of my journey with forensic geology; it is really only just the beginning. I look forward to many new, interesting projects that are sure to come. That's why I pick up the phone every time it rings: you never know what adventure might be waiting on the other end!

The Historical Timeline for the Kensington Rune Stone

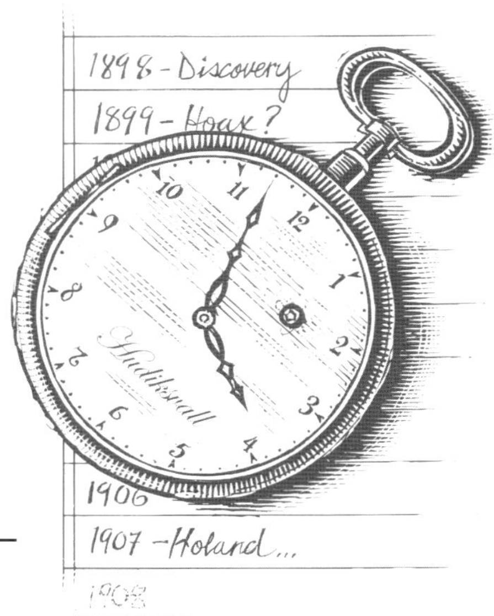

The story of the Kensington Rune Stone has been told in print a number of times, each telling usually laced with inaccurate information, as well as the writer's opinion of certain events. This type of writing has been a basic problem with the story of the Kensington Rune Stone. No one could figure out what really occurred because no one had the right information. Before any serious analysis of the controversy, there has to be an honest presentation of the documented facts. To avoid any inaccuracies or misrepresentation of important events, photographs of relevant documents, articles, or places have been included. In some cases a pertinent quote from a document highlights a particular incident. Many of the facts in the timeline represent new information for researchers, like four never-before-seen letters written by Hjalmar Holand to Olof Ohman that yield new information about these important individuals. This chronology of events is the most comprehensive to date and the story it tells speaks for itself.

The timeline spans 150 years, and is divided into eight sections that represent periods when significant actions occurred. The sequence of events is documented as objectively and thoroughly as possible. It seems appropriately to begin with the birth of the central character.

Olof Ohman Comes to America (1854 to 1898)

This period of time covers the relevant events that occurred in the lives of Olof Ohman and his family leading up to the discovery of the Kensington Rune Stone. Also listed are the dates when important documents were published prior to the discovery that could have been used by a potential forger.

1854

October 10 – Olof Ohman is born in the town of Forsa, Hälsingland, Sweden.

This stone and concrete food cellar is all that's left of the farm where Olof Ohman was born near the town of Forsa, Hälsingland, Sweden. The original house was moved to a different location and has since been torn down. (SFW)

1857/1858 – Sven Fogelblad and Claus Ljungström both attend the Bedared Parish Church in West Götaland, Sweden.

1862

January 2 – Karin Danielson, future wife of Olof Ohman, is born in Forsa, Hälsingland, Sweden.

1866 – Claus Ljungström authors a book of runes called *Runa-List.* The rune rows consisted of Viking age runes which do not fully correspond to medieval practice and certainly not to the Kensington Rune Stone.

1871 – Halvor Halvorson is given a US patent for government lot 2, of Solem Township 127 North, Range 40 West in section 14 (about 80 acres).

1877 – In Denmark, P.G. Thorsen produced a report on both the hundred-page plus *Codex Runicus* and showed one page of *Mariaklagen* runic texts. Each document is the only copy of its kind known to exist, and they contain numerous examples of the "crossed-L" or so-called "J" rune, considered to be the chief proof of forgery in the case of the Kensington Rune Stone. The *Codex Runicus* survived the Copenhagen fire of 1728 because it had been checked out of the library.

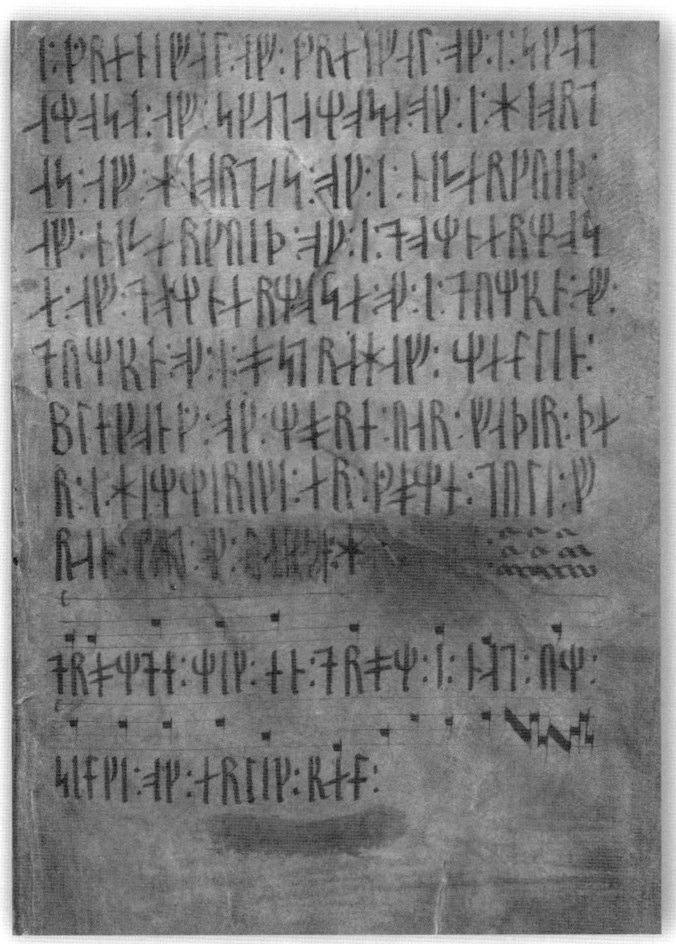

The last page of the *Codex Runicus* contains two of the so-called "J" runes (ᚠ) in the last line. (Courtesy of The Arnemagnæan Institute, University of Copenhagen, Denmark)

Page 18 of the *Mariaklagen* text contains three of the so-called "J" runes (ᚠ).

Oscar Montelius publishes the book, *Sweden's History: From the Oldest Times Until Our Days*, in Stockholm. The first volume is later published in the *Swedish American Post* between November 1897 and July 1898.

1879

June – Olof Ohman first emmigrates from Sweden to the United States at the age of twenty-five. He works as a carpenter in Douglas County, Minnesota.

1883 – Ohman goes back to Sweden.

1885 – Olof Ohman returns to the United States and spends six months in Portland, Oregon. He then moves to Minnesota and settles in the town of Brandon, where he had worked previously.

Twenty-two year old Karin Danielson immigrates from Hälsingland, Sweden, to the United States. She first stays in Bishops Hill, Illinois, and marries Ohman in Minnesota the following year.

The title page to the Oscar Montelius book of Swedish History published in Stockholm in 1877.

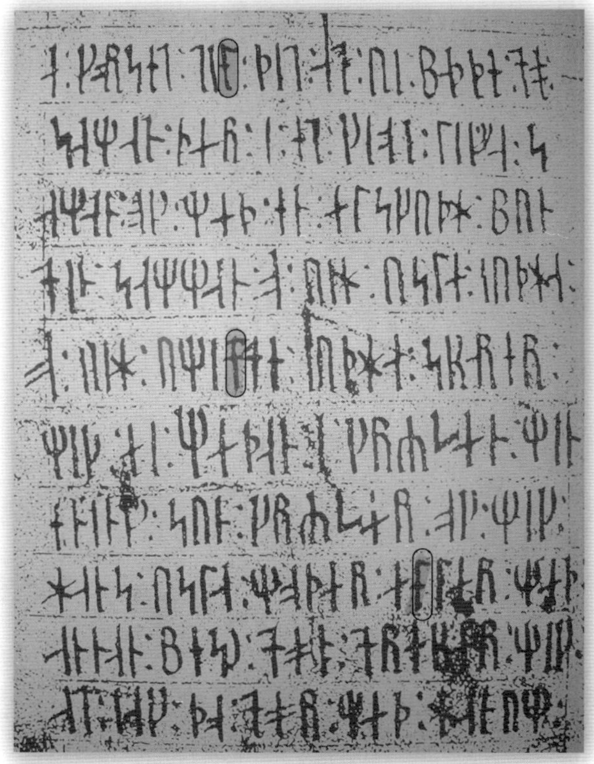

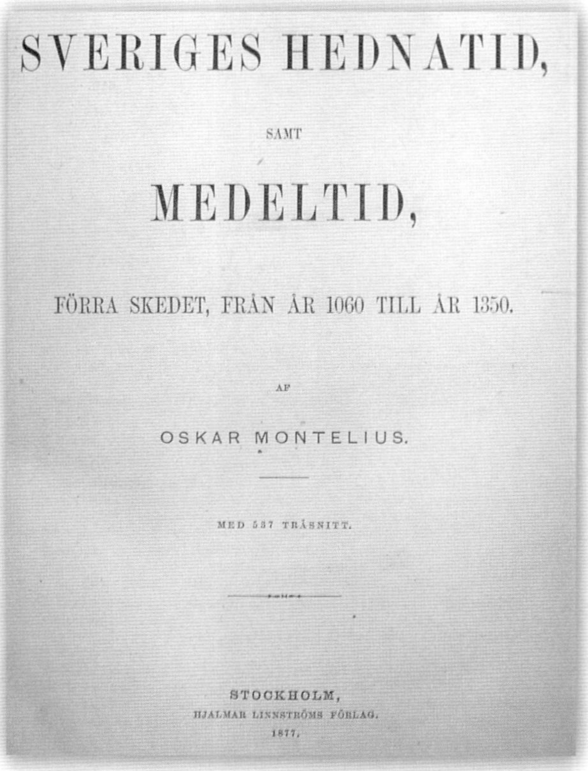

1886

November 27 – Olof Ohman and Karin Danielson are married in Alexandria, Minnesota. Pastor John E. Hedberg presides over the ceremony.

1887

June 17 – Olof Emil Ohman Jr., the first child of Karin and Olof, is born in Kensington, Minnesota.

1888 – Professor Gustav Storm publishes an essay about the Paul Knutson expedition that left Norway in 1355, and returned in 1363 or 1364. Hjalmar Holand wrote that this expedition could have been the party that carved the Kensington Rune Stone.

November 20 – Edward Carl Ohman, the second child of Karin and Olof, is born in Kensington, Minnesota.

1890 – P. Købke publishes the book, *About the Runes in Scandinavia.* The book discusses the last two lines of the *Codex Runicus,* which include the two so called "J" runes. Købke's book was referenced by George T. Flom is his discussion of the runes of the Kensington Rune Stone twenty years later. Flom (1901) missed this rune and later used it to help prove the Kensington Rune Stone was a forgery.

April 17 – Olof Ohman acquires his first parcel of property (Solum Township 127 North, Range 40 West, Section 14) via warranty deed from Halvar Stenson for $300, and was recorded on April 19, 1890.

April 19 – Ohman pays $130 to acquire a state certificate from Ole Amundson for his second parcel of property (Solem Township 127 North, Range 40 West, Section 14). This transaction was recorded on March 5, 1891. Ohman's neighbor, Nils O. Flaaten, obtains the state certificate from John Erickson for the property. These two, forty-acre sized state certificates represent the Internal Improvement Land in Section 14 shown on the 1886 plat for Solem Township. It was on Ohman's parcel that he found the Rune Stone.

Olof Ohman acquired the 40-acre northern half of the Internal Improvement Land on April 4, 1890. It was on this parcel of land that the rune stone was found.

December 3 – Ohman acquires a part of lot 2 (in Section 14), via a transfer from Halvor Stenson, for $30. This small acreage is the approximate location of the Ohman farmhouse.

1891

February 7 – Arthur Daniel Ohman, the third child of Karin and Olof, was born in Kensington, Minnesota.

March 2 – Ohman signs a copy of the book *Den Kunskapsrike Skolmästaren* ("The Well-Informed School Master") by Carl Rosander. An encyclopedia of Sweden, the book contains a section about Sweden history, and some rudimentary information about Viking age runes (page 61). Johan A. Holvik borrows this book from Karin Ohman in 1938 and reportedly returns it to the Ohman family in 1950.

Olof Ohman signed and dated (March 2, 1891) the inside jacket of the Swedish encyclopedia *Den Kunskapsrike Skolmästaren* ("The Well-Informed School Master") by Carl Rosander.

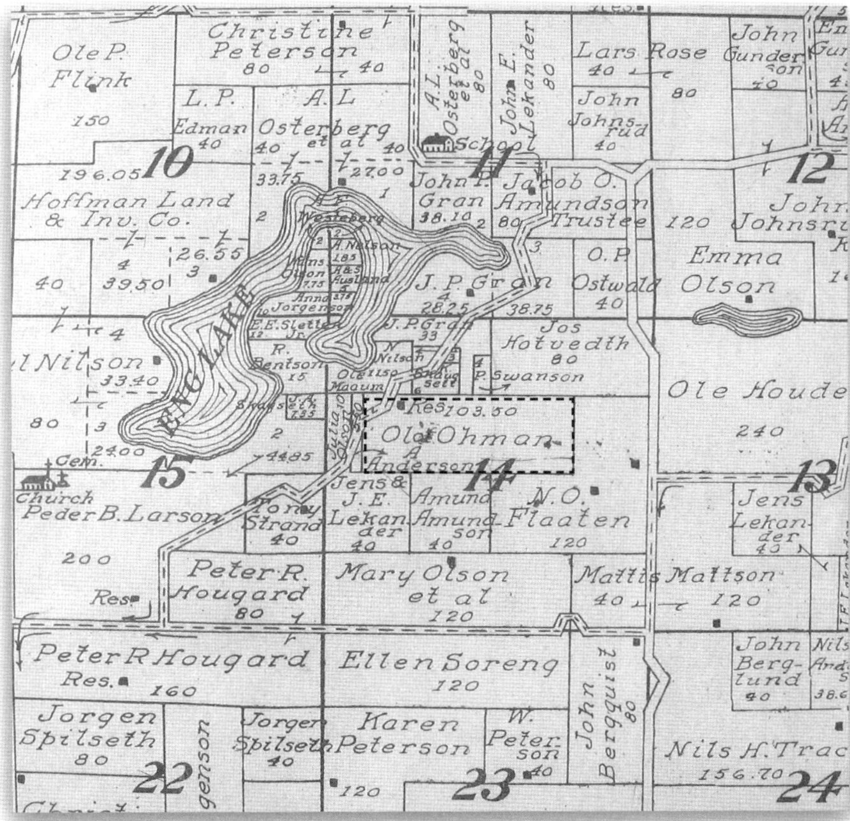

Olof Ohman owned this Solem County 1912 plat map that shows his roughly hundred-acre-sized property at the center.

1892 – Ohman and his family move from Brandon, Minnesota to Kensington and settled on the farm he had purchased.

November 29 – Ohman acquires, via warranty deed, part of lot 2 (east 12 acres of the south 40) from Halvar Stenson for $160. This transaction is recorded on December 5, 1892.

December 9 – Amanda Betsy Ohman, the fourth child of Karin and Olof, is born in Kensington, Minnesota.

1894

December 16 – Ida Karin Ohman, the fifth child of Karin and Olof, is born in Kensington, Minnesota.

1897

March 14 – Oscar Fredrick Ohman, the sixth child of Karin and Olof, is born in Kensington, Minnesota.

July 12 – Sven Fogelblad, age 67, dies at the home of Andrew Anderson, across the road from the Wennersberg Cemetery in Solem County.

1898

February 28 – Olof Ohman acquires, via warranty deed, another part of lot 2 from E. J. Moen for $50. This transaction is recorded on March 10, 1898.

The Discovery (1898 to 1900)

The period from 1898 to 1900 begins with Olof Ohman's discovery of the Rune Stone. Ohman was using a hand-powered winch to fell trees near the crest of a hill on the extreme eastern part of his land when he uncovered the Stone wrapped in the roots of a poplar tree. In the ensuing months, the Rune Stone traveled to the home of Northwestern University professor George O. Curme in Chicago for study. Numerous newspaper articles are published between January and May 1899, and the first of several translations are made from copies of the inscription supplied by Ohman and Samuel Siverts. Confusion over the origin and reason for these copies has given rise to accusations by past investigators that they were pre-inscription drafts; a misunderstanding that has haunted these copies for over one hundred years.

1898

After September 5 – Olof Ohman unearths the Kensington Rune Stone while "grubbing trees" on his newly acquired property contiguous to Nils Flaaten's farm. Mr. Flaaten is also grubbing trees nearby when the Stone is found.

This 1929 photograph shows a man pointing to the discovery site. The man in the center of the picture is Olof Ohman. (Ohman Relatives Association)

Late Fall – In an attempt to learn about the inscription on the Stone he had found, Ohman acquires a newspaper reprinting of the 1877 book, *Sveriges Historia* (Swedish History), which contains information about runes and rune stones. This was a reprinting of Montelius 1877 book, volume 1 were printed weekly from the fall of 1897 through most of 1898. Ohman signs and dated his copy of the newspaper articles in 1898. Johan A. Holvik borrowed this book from Karin Ohman in 1938 and reportedly returned it to the Ohman family in 1950. Although the Minnesota Historical Society has several pages of the book preserved on microfilm, as of 2005 the location of the actual book, like the Rosander book, is unknown. The actual newspaper articles are entirely on microfilm.

Olof Ohman signed and dated the inside jacket of a book about Swedish History that was published by the newspaper *Svenska Amerikanska Posten*. (Minnesota Historical Society)

December – Samuel Siverts' son, Ingvald, recalled that three men brought the Stone in from the Ohman farm by sleigh to the First State Bank in Kensington in December, 1898. The three men were Sam Olson, John Wedum, and Charles Lilyquist (Blegen, page 28).

December 31 – Mr. Samuel Siverts sends a copy of the inscription upon the request of Olaus J. Breda at the University, "About New Years of 1899" (Blegen, page 165). This copy has been commonly confused as being the copy made by Ohman that was sent by J. P. Hedberg to Swan Turnblad at the newspaper *Svenska Amerikanska Posten*.

The copy of the Kensington Rune Stone inscription ("Siverts Copy") that Olaus Breda received at the University of Minnesota around January 1, 1899. This document is incorrectly labeled as being sent by J. P. Hedberg on the right side of the copy. (Minnesota Historical Society)

1899

January 1 – A different copy of the inscription, the so-called "Ohman Copy," is sent to Swan J. Turnblad at the newspaper, *Svenska Amerikanska Posten*, on January 1, 1899. This copy is received with a letter written by J. P. Hedberg of Kensington, Minnesota. The Hedberg letter was found in the President's files at the University of Minnesota by Theodore Blegen in 1925, but the original copy of the inscription that accompanied the letter has been lost.

The John P. Hedberg letter was sent to the newspaper *Svenska Amerikanska Posten* on January 1, 1899. (Minnesota Historical Society)

"Swan J. Turnblad
Minneapolis

"I enclose you a copy of an inscription on a stone found about 2 miles from Kensington by a O. Ohman. He found it under a tree when grubbing – he wanted I should go out and look at it and I told him to haul it in when he came (not thinking much of it) he did so, and this is an exact copy of it. The first part is of the flat side of stone the other was on flat edge. I thought I would send it to you as you perhaps have means to find out what it is – it appears to be old Greek letters please let me hear from you and oblige.

"Yours Truly
J. P. Hedberg"

January 14 – In the newspaper *Ariel*, Professor Breda at the University of Minnesota publishes his translation of the inscription using the Siverts copy. This translation does not include the word "with" on the fourth line as found in the Hedberg-Ohman copy.

February 18 – After receiving a copy of the inscription (Ohman/Hedberg Copy), Professor Curme announces publicly on the Northwestern University campus that he had translated the inscription on the Kensington Rune Stone.

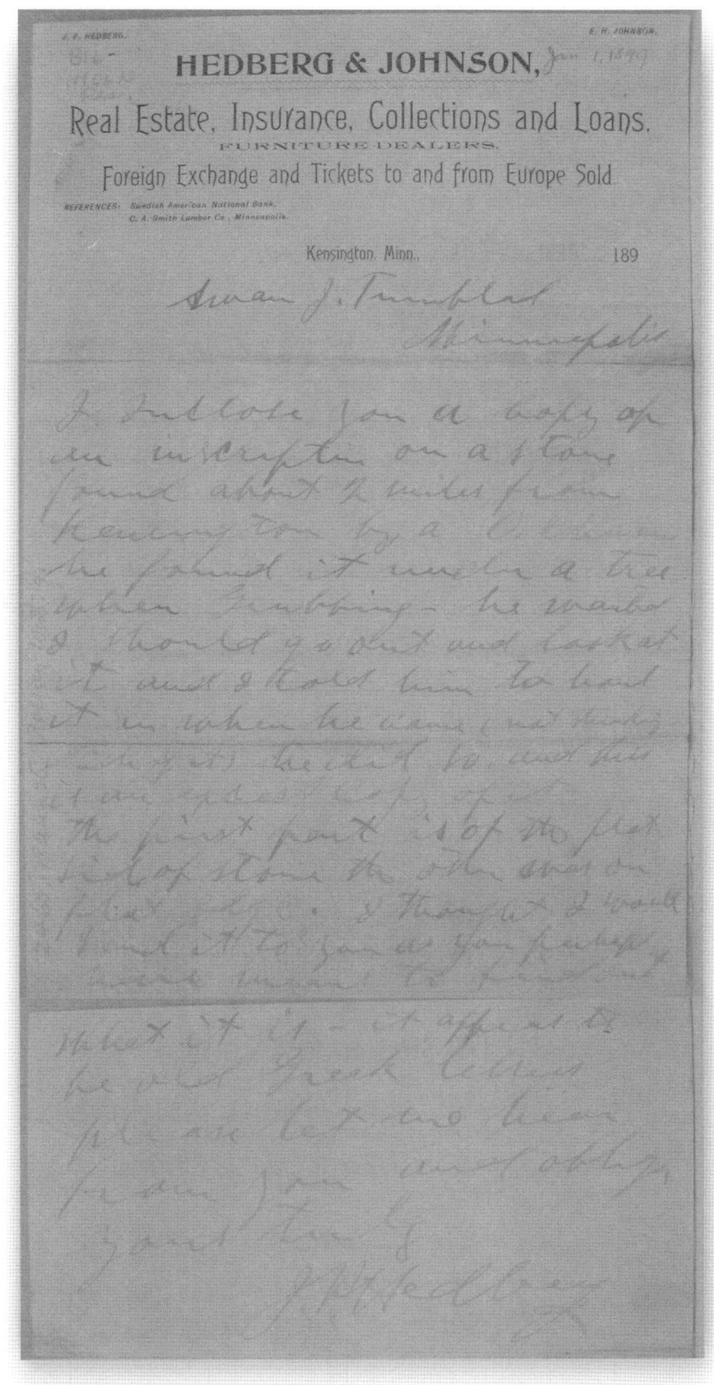

February 20 – *The Chicago Daily Tribune* reports "So much impressed with the tablet is Professor Curme that on Saturday night before the Deutsche Gesellschaft at the Phi Delta Theta house he announced publicly that he had the copies [of the] inscription in his possession and that it had been translated." Curme is quoted as saying, "I have sent to Minnesota and asked that the ground about the tree be dug up and examined. Bones can be kept intact for a longer period than 500 years if the soil is favorable and some remains ought to be found."

February 21 – The Chicago daily newspaper *The Daily Inter Ocean*, reports that "The letter [Hedberg copy] was received several weeks ago at the university [Northwestern]." Professor Curme's use of the word "with" on the fourth line in his translation confirms that this copy was indeed the "Hedberg-Ohman copy." According to the paper, "Professor Curme has asked to have a further excavation made to ascertain if possible if there is any trace of human bones there."

The Chicago Daily Tribune newspaper reports that the arrival of stone at Evanston, Illinois, is delayed and that Professor is greatly disappointed.

The *Chicago Daily Tribune* published a sketch of Professor George O. Curme in an article on February 21, 1899.

February 23 – E. E. Aaberg, a Norwegian immigrant, writes a letter to the *Skandinavien* that is published four days later on February 27. *"The hill where the stone was found was without trees when the first settlers arrived some twenty to thirty years ago. But since that time a number of aspen trees have grown up there; it was an aspen that had grown over the stone, from twenty to thirty years ago."*

The *Chicago Daily Tribune* newspaper reports that in University of Minnesota Professor Olaus Breda's opinion the inscription was modern.

The *Alexandria Post News* published the same article about the Rune Stone that appeared in the *Minneapolis Journal* on February 22, 1899.

February 24 – The *Chicago Daily Tribune* reports that Professor Breda received a letter from Sam Olson in Kensington who wrote,

"There does not seem to be any stone like it in the vicinity. There seems to be only gray granite here. No one around here knew the language of the stone and they seemed to think it Indian or something of the sort. I was much surprised when I read your letter saying it was written by the Norsemen, for I had no idea it was so old. Your suggestion that the ground around the place where it was found should be excavated will be followed, but I should prefer that a scientist be present."

A Stone Bearing Runic Inscriptions.

From the Minneapolis Journal.

A stone bearing inscriptions in runic characters, found 3 miles northeast of Kensington, in Douglas county, Minnesota, has created something of a sensation among students of early Norse discoveries in this country, and is now in the hands of Prof. O. O. Curme of the Northwestern university at Evanston, Ill., who is making a careful examination of the inscriptions.

The stone was found last November by Ole Ohman, a farmer in the southwest corner of Douglas county, while grubbing under a tree of 30 or 40 years' growth, and its position under the roots of the tree, as well as its tombstone shape and the peculiar characters, at once attracted attention.

The stone is about 30 inches long, 15 inches wide and 6 inches thick, the inscriptions being on the side and face in characters about an inch in length. It weighs about 215 lbs. The inscriptions impressed some as Greek and copies were forwarded to the department of Greek at the university of Minnesota, where it was discovered that the characters were runic, and the copies were turned over to Prof. O. J. Breda, who has charge of the department of Scandinavian languages. After a careful examination of the inscriptions, which he discovered to be only partly in runic characters, he decided that the whole thing was a hoax. Prof. Curme of Evanston, was furnished with a copy of the inscriptions and later the stone itself was shipped to him and is now in his hands.

Prof. Breda, when seen today, stated that on first blush, when the inscriptions were first submitted to him as being from a possible runic stone found in the western part of Minnesota, he was disposed to laugh. No runic stones had ever been found in Minnesota and not only that but none had ever been found in America. How a runic stone of six, seven or eight centuries ago could ever have gotten within fifty or sixty miles of the western border of Minnesota, was, therefore, a question which floored him. Nevertheless he picked out the characters, which were true runes, gave value to the characters which were evidently not runes, and of which he was in doubt, and made up the following translation of the inscriptions, dashes indicating the location of words or characters which he could not make out, not being correct runes:

—Swedes and—Norsmen on a journey of discovery from Vinland west—We camped—one day's journey north form this stone. We fished one day. After we came home we found—man red with blood dead. AVM save from—Have—men at the ocean to look after our ships—days journey from this island. Year—.

This corresponds exactly (almost with a translation made shortly after the discovery of the stone and submitted by S. A. Siverts of Kensington, and is not far different from the translation made by Professor Curme of Evanston, which is as follows:

A company of Norsemen are out on expedition of discovery from the Vineland of the West. We had a camp along with two boats one day's journey north from this stone. We go out daily and fish. One day after we came home we found a man red with blood and dead. Ave (good-bye). Rescue from fire. Has one ever had a comrade such as we have had. We are on our way to look after our ship, fourteen days' journey from this island.

Professor Breda also states that there are internal evidences in the inscription that it is not authentic. The chief of these, he says, is the fact that the inscriptions seem to be a jumble of Swedish and Norwegian in late grammatical forms and here and there an English word, but all spelled in runic characters. They are not old Norse, he says.

Professor Curme seems to regard the stone as possibly genuine. His theory is that at the time the stone was deposited at the place found it was on the shores of lake Superior, which then—500 years ago—was several hundred feet above its present level, making it entirely possible that the piece of ground at the place was an island. From the inscription he infers that the explorers left one of their number to guard the camp while they went away to fish, and that when they came back they found him dead, slain, possibly, by Pottawatomies.

After a thorough investigation, photographs will be made of the stone and sent to the authorities on such matters. Professor Breda suggests as the ablest authority on runic inscriptions, L. V. A. Wimmer of Copenhagen, and Sophus Bugge, also a Scandinavian, and thinks they would have no trouble in determining without delay whether the inscriptions were genuine.

Alexandria Post News, Thursday Feb. 23, 1899 page 1

Professor Curme is reported as saying, "Professor O. J. Breda of the University of Minnesota has missed several of the most important meanings of the runes."

The *Minneapolis Journal* newspaper publishes a letter to the editor written by H. M. Wagner of Starbuck, Minnesota that included his comment, *"But it is with Professor Breda's argument as to the validity of the inscription that I differ entirely."*

H. M. Wagner of Starbuck, Minnesota wrote a letter to the editor of *The Minneapolis Journal* that was published on February 24, 1899.

February 26 – The *Chicago Daily Tribune* reports, *"Professor Curme, who has the matter in charge and who has been confident the stone at least exists, asked the stationmaster at Evanston to put a tracer on the track and see if the car bearing the relic has been sidetracked. The professor has also written to the stationmaster at Kensington inquiring as to the tablet, and expects an answer today or tomorrow."*

February 27 – The Chicago Edition of the newspaper *Skandinaven* publishes two letters to the editor about the Kensington Rune Stone. The first was written by a grocer in Kensington named E. E. Aaberg, whose letter dated February 23, 1899, contains important details about the hill where the stone was found. The second letter was written by D. L. Kirkeberg, who wrote about his interpretation of the inscription.

This letter to the editor, dated February 23, 1899, was written by Kensington resident E. E. Aaberg, and was published in the Chicago Edition of the *Skandinaven* on February 27, 1899.

"Dear Editor:

"I saw in yesterday's Skandinaven *an article about the runestone found near here last fall. Part of that was incorrect. I want* Skandinaven *to*

No. 49.

Er vist ægte.

Interessante Oplysninger om Runestenen i Kensington.

Stenen var der

Før Settlerne kom — Nærmere Beskrivelse af Stedet, hvor den fandtes.

Tydning af Runerne.

Kensington, Minn., 23de Febr.
Hr. Red.! — Jeg ser i "Skandinaven" for igaar en Beretning om den Runesten, som blev fundet her i Nærheden ifjor Høst. En Del af Beretningen er feilagtig. Jeg vil herved bede "Skandinaven at følge med Stenens videre Skjæbne; den kan maaske være af mere Betydning for Historien ved at kaste Lys over en fjern Fortid, og da især for os Nordmænd, end man antager.

Stenen er nu paa Veien til Chicago, sendt til Northwestern Universitet i Evanston, hvor "Skandinavens" Repræsentanter kan have Adgang til at faa den at se.

Om det skulde være noget Slags Jux med denne Sten, saa er der dog Bevis nok for, at det er udført, før de første "Settlere" nedsatte sig her.

Stenen blev ikke fundet i en Myr, som berettet i "Skandinaven", men paa en rund Kul, omgivet af en Myr (slough). Antagelig har hin Kul før i Tiden været en Ø, og hvad der nu udgjør hin Myr, der omgiver Høien, har vist før i Tiden været Basinet for en mindre Sø. Den Mand, som fandt Stenen, og som eier Landet rundt der, grov ikke Grøft i Myren, men holdt paa med "Grubbing". Hin Kul, som Stenen fandtes paa, var ved de første Settleres Ankomst, for en 20—30 Aar siden, træløs; men siden hin Tid er en Del Aspeskov voget op der; det var et Aspetræ, som var voget over Stenen, antagelig en 20—30 Aar gammelt.

Manden, som fandt Stenen, har ikke boet paa Landet der svært længe. Dog, hans Ærlighed er ikke at betvivle; han har hverken funnet udhugge hine Runer eller saa Stenen under hin Træstamme. Tillige har jeg aldrig seet hin Stenart forekomme her rundt, som Stenen er huggen af. Den synes at være kommen fra et Stenbrud af Skiferisten og er antagelig bragt hib ud i Baad.

Naar Jorden bliver optøet igjen, vil antagelig Stedet, hvor den fandtes, blive nøiere undersøgt. Det er vist, at Udtydningen paa Stenen vil vise, om den har noget historisk Værd og er ægte.

Hensigten med mit Brev er at be "Skandinaven" om ikke at tabe Interessen for dette Fund, men at holde Øie med Udviklingen og holbe os underrettet om Løsningen paa dette.
E. E. Aaberg.

follow the progress of the stone; it may have been more meaning for history by throwing light on the distant past, especially for us Norwegians, than people realize.

"The stone is now on the way to Chicago, to Northwestern University in Evanston, where representatives of Skandinaven *will have a chance to see it. If anything is false with the stone it was done before the first settlers came here.*

"The stone was not found in a swamp, as we read in Skandinaven, *but on a round knoll in the middle of a swamp. The knoll appears to have once been an island, and what is left of the swamp around the knoll has long since been a small lake. The man who found the stone and owns the land around it did NOT dig a ditch in the swamp. The knoll was treeless twenty or thirty years ago when the first settlers came; but since that time, aspen trees have sprouted up there. It was an ash tree, about twenty to thirty years old that had grown (roots) around the stone.*

"The man who found the stone had not lived on the land very long. However, his honesty is not doubted. He could neither have cut the runes, nor could he have placed the stone under the tree roots. Also, I have never seen that kind of stone around here like this rune stone. It must have come from a slate quarry and very likely brought here by boat.

When the ground thaws again the place where the stone was taken will be further investigated. For sure, the interpretation of the stone will show whether or not it has historical value, and is authentic.

"The purpose of this letter is to ask Skandinaven *not to lose interest in this find, but to keep eyes open to its development and keep us informed about the outcome.*

"E. E. Aaberg"

(English translation by Edna Rude, January, 2005)

February 28 – The Kensington Rune Stone arrives at the residence of Professor George O. Curme in Chicago. The Hedberg-Ohman sketch of the inscription that was sent by John Hedberg is published in the *Svenska Amerikanska Posten*. "Mr. Ohman made a transcription of the characters or runes carved on the stone and sent this through J. P. Hedberg in Kensington to *Svenska Amerikanska Posten*."

John Hedberg and Olof Ohman sent this sketch to Swan Turnblad, the editor of *Svenska Amerikanska Posten*, where it appeared on February 28, 1899. (Article courtesy of the American Swedish Institute in Minneapolis, Minnesota)

March 1 – Curme is quoted in *The Daily Inter Ocean*, as saying,
"The most positive proof that the inscription is not of the ancient origin claimed by its discoverers is the fact that the crevices which form the letters are of a lighter color than the outer surface of the stone; this could hardly be the case if the stone had been buried for the 600 years that must have elapsed provided the inscription is authentic."

The Chicago Daily Tribune reports the arrival of the Rune Stone and Professor Curme's latest translation, and that, "He doubts the antiquity of the stone."

F. Nosander of Taylors Falls, Minnesota, sends his own translation of the inscription to the *Svenska Amerikanska Posten*. The text of this letter is reprinted in Blegen (1968: 132-3).

March 2 – *The Chicago Daily Tribune* newspaper reports, "Professor Curme made an exact copy of the inscription and sent it on to Professor Adolf Noreen of the University of Uppsala, Sweden."

March 3 – The newspaper *Skandinaven* quotes Professor Curme's comments about the inscription.

The *Alexandria Post News* newspaper reprinted the article which included the Hedberg/Ohman sketch that appeared in *Svenska Amerikanska Posten* on Febrauary 28, 1899.

John F. Stewart, an amateur geologist, takes the first known photographs of the Kensington Rune Stone at Professor Curme's home in Chicago. Professor Curme's observations reported on March 3, 1899, likely result from a collaboration with John F. Steward. (See color section, plates 19 and 20)

March 7 – J. K. Nordwall of Sebeka, Minnesota, send a translation of the inscription based upon the copy in the *Svenska Amerikanska Posten*. The text of this letter is reprinted in Blegen (1968: 133-4).

On or about March 8 – Professor Curme sends a copy of the inscription to Professor Adolf Noreen, a runic expert at Uppsala University in Sweden.

The Northwestern
March 9, 1899

12   THE NORT

THE RUNIC STONE.

Last week the Runic stone, much heralded by the Chicago papers, came into the hands of Professor Curme of the German department. The *Ærial* of the University of Minnesota introduced the stone to the college world nearly three months ago.

The Runic stone was found last November near Kensington, Minn. It is a trap stone, 32 inches long, 18 inches wide, and 6 inches thick, and bears the date of 1362. In runic characters on one side and one edge of the tablet is the following inscription:

Eight Goths (from Sweden) and twenty-two Norwegians on an expedition of discovery from the Vinland of the west. We had a camp with two boats a day's journey from this stone. We went out fishing one day. After we came home we found a man red with blood and dead. Good-by, rescue from evil. We have men at the ocean to look after our ships, fourteen days' journey from this island. Year 1362.

Professor Curme is well versed in the Runic tongue, but to make sure of the authenticity of the tablet he has sent a copy of the inscription to Adolph Noren of Upsala University, Sweden, the greatest living authority on the Runic language. Runic stones are very common in Norway and Sweden, but this is the first one ever found in America. The first thought is to consider it a hoax and to treat it accordingly, yet if proved authentic, this stone will change the whole history of America. Therefore, Professor Curme is justified, as a seeker of truth, to disregard the smiles of the uninitiated and to use every power at a scholar's command to prove the sincerity of the Runic stone.

This article appeared on page 12 of the newspaper *The Northwestern* on March 9, 1899, and relates that Professor George Curme sent a copy of the inscription to Adolph Noreen of Uppsala University, Sweden.

March 12 – An article about the Kensington Rune Stone appears in the Norwegian newspaper *Morgenbladet.* The article is based on the "Siverts" copy of the inscription, which does not contain the word "with" on the fourth line of the inscription.

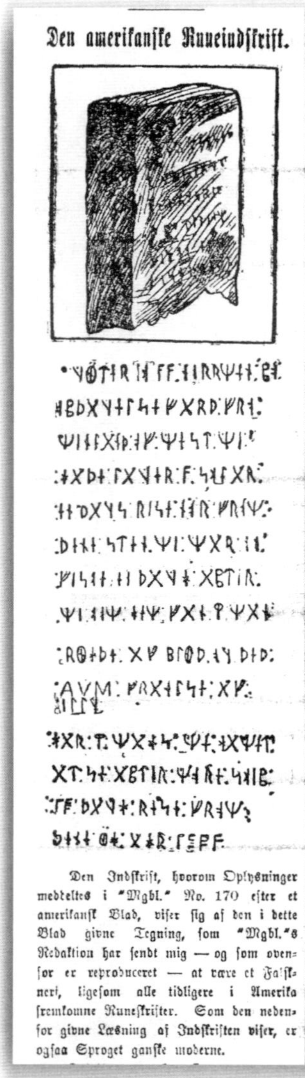

Den amerikanske Runeindskrift.

Den Indskrift, hvorom Oplysninger meddeltes i "Mgbl." No. 170 efter et amerikansk Blad, viser sig af den i dette Blad givne Tegning, som "Mgbl.'s Redaktion har sendt mig — og som ovenfor er reproduceret — at være et Falskneri, ligesom alle tidligere i Amerika fremkomne Runeskrifter. Som den nedenfor givne Læsning af Indskriften viser, er ogsaa Sproget ganske moderne.

Fabrikanten røber sig at være en svensk Amerikaner, som allerede er bleven endel amerikaniseret; enkelte engelske Ord er undslupne ham hist og her. Han har benyttet flere usædvanlige Runetegn; hvorfra han har faaet disse, kan være usikkert, men de taler ietvhertfald ikke for, men mod Indskriftens Ægthed. Maaske har han tildels selv lavet disse Tegn. Han bruger i nogle Tilfælde samme Tegn for to Lyd (saaledes for a og ä, for o og å); enkelte Gange har han af Uagtsomhed brugt et galt Tegn. Disse og andre Eiendommeligheder gjør, at jeg ikke overalt er sikker paa, hvad Manden har ment. Saavidt jeg kan se, staar der:

gøter. ok. 22. norrmen. på. opda-Gøter og 22 Nordmænd paa Opdagelsefärd. frå. vinland. of. vest. vi. gelsefærd fra vestre Vinland. Vi hade. läger. 2. sklear. en. dags. rese. havde Leir 2 Skjær en Tags Reise nor. from. dene. sten. vi. var. ok. nord fra denne Sten vi var og fiske. en. dagh. äptir. vi. kom. hem. fiskede en Dag. Efter vi kom hjem fan. 5. män. rohde. af. blod. ok. ded. fandt vi 5 Mænd røde af Blod og døde. AVM. fräelse. af illge (?)

. . . frelse fra . . .

. har. 5. mans. ve. havet. at. se. Har 5 Mand ved Havet at se äptir. vore. skip. 14. dagh. rese. from. efter vore Skib 14 Dagsreiser fra dene. øh. åhr 1462. denne Ø Aar 1462.

Usikkert er Forstaaelsen af AVM og de 3 følgende Ord samt Taltegnene, særlig det, der er læst som 5, og 2det Ziffer i Aarstallet. Engelsk er frem paa to Steder, of efter vinland og ded (engelsk dead). Foran "Gøter" i Begyndelsen har det tydelig ialfald været Meningen, at Antallet af de i "Opdagelsesfærden" deltagende Gøter skulde staa.

O. R.

The Norwegian newspaper *Morgenbladet* published the Siverts copy of the Kensington Rune Stone inscription in this article on March 12, 1899. A copy of this article was provided courtesy of Professor James E. Knirk of Oslo University.

Late March – The stone is shipped back to the Olof Ohman farm.

April 11 – John Gerhard Ohman, the seventh child of Karin and Olof, is born in Kensington, Minnesota.

April 16 – In a telegram from Oslo, Norway, Professors Gustav Storm, Sophus Bugge, and Oluf Rugh are quoted in the *Minneapolis Tribune* on April 16, 1899, as saying, "...the Kensington Rune Stone is a grand fraud perpetrated by a Swede with a chisel with a slight knowledge of runic characters and of English." (Blegen, page 166)

May 2 – Alexandria school superintendent Mr. Cleve W. Van Dyke, Executive Clerk for the late Governor Johnson, along with eleven other men, perform an excavation at the discovery site. They dig four feet down but find no artifacts or evidence associated with the Stone. Nine of Van Dyke's eleven other men included Olaus Olsen, J. P. Hedberg, Sam Olson, John E. Olson who furnished a team (of horses), Albert Larson, John E. Johnson, Emil Johnson, Gulick Landsverk, and Lars Coldberg. (Blegen, pages 170-1)

May 16 – Olaus Olson of Holmes City, Minnesota writes a letter to the newspaper *Svenska Amerikanska Posten* that is published on May 23. Among other points, Olson says, "The tree is at least twenty-five if not thirty years old." (Blegen, pages 134-136)

October 15 – John F. Steward writes a letter to Professor Ludwig F. A. Wimmer of Copenhagen, Denmark, in which he discusses his observations of the Rune Stone and the importance of establishing whether or not it is genuine. He includes his photographs that are now the earliest photographs of the Kensington Rune Stone.

A section of John F. Steward's October 15, 1899 letter to Professor Ludwig F. A. Wimmer, expressing his opinion about the Kensington Rune Stone inscription.
"The inscriptions are on the two cleavage surfaces of the stone, which have received no dressing. They are cut as with a 'diamond-pointed' tool. The grooves show no more newness than the natural surfaces of the rock; on the contrary all show age."

John Steward also relayed his opinion that the discovery of the stone was not suspicious in his letter of October 15, 1899.
"...as the circumstances connected with its finding are all favorable to age and genuineness."

1900

Around 1900 – Andrew Anderson's wife Betsy, a cousin of Karin Ohman, gives the Fogelblad copy of Almquist's 1840 book on Swedish grammar to Olof Ohman so he can learn something about the inscription on the Rune Stone.

"Mr. Öhman, when asked where and when he obtained this book, stated that he got it [Almquist book] of Mr. Anderson, who obtained it of a preacher [Sven Fogelblad]. This was on the occasion of our second visit to Mr. Öhman's house. On the occasion of our third visit he also stated that, after the Rune Stone was found, Mr. Anderson had suggested that he should take it home for the purpose of reading the rune record by means of the runic alphabet contained in it; that he did so, but found more characters on the stone than in the book, and could not translate the record, and that he had not returned the book. It transpired that later that Mrs. Anderson and Mrs. Öhman are cousins." (N. H. Winchell report of the Museum Committee, April, 1910, pages 25-26)

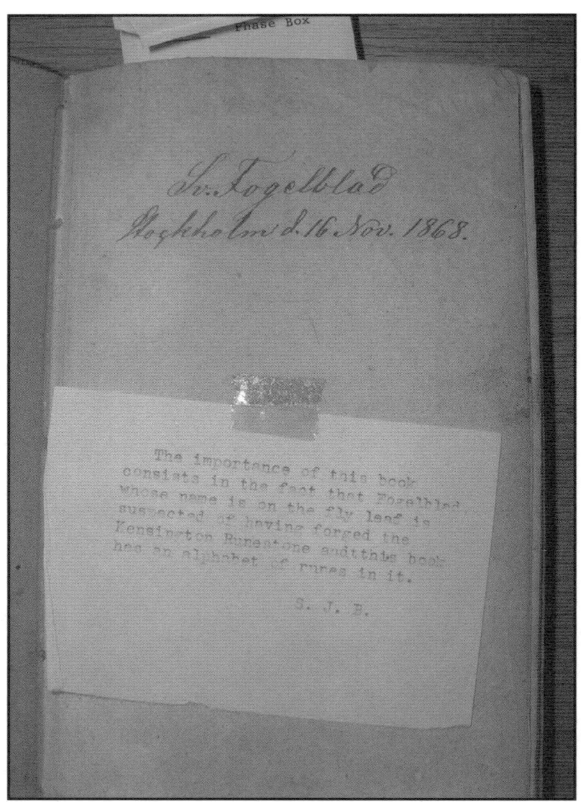

The inside jacket of the Almquist book of Swedish grammar that once belonged to Sven Fogelblad. When Fogelblad died in Andrew Anderson's home in 1897, the book became Anderson's property. The book was then given to the Ohman family after the Rune Stone was discovered. (Minnesota Historical Society)

1902

August 12 – David Ohman, the eighth child of Karin and Olof, is born in Kensington, Minnesota.

1904

August 1 – Olof Ohman signs a true copy of his original renouncement of allegiance and fidelity to the King of Norway and Sweden, as a condition to obtaining citizenship of the United States.

Citizenship document signed by Olof Ohman August 1, 1904. (Ohman Family Association)

1905

October 5 – William Otto Ohman, the ninth child of Karin and Olof, is born in Kensington, Minnesota,

1906 – Swedish philologist (expert in language and runes) Adolf Noreen publishes the first known paper about the Kensington Rune Stone which includes his translation of the inscription.

A Flurry of Activity (1907 to 1911)

This period of time was extremely important because of the investigation the Minnesota Historical Society conducted into the authenticity of the Kensington Rune Stone. The man in charge of the investigation was the accomplished geologist Newton H. Winchell, who made three trips to interview Olof Ohman, his family, and as his neighbors. The report of his comprehensive investigation was the basis for the vote of the Historical Society's Museum Committee as to whether the State of Minnesota should purchase the Rune Stone from Hjalmar Holand for $5000.

1907

August – Hjalmar Holand takes possession of the Rune Stone from Olof Ohman.

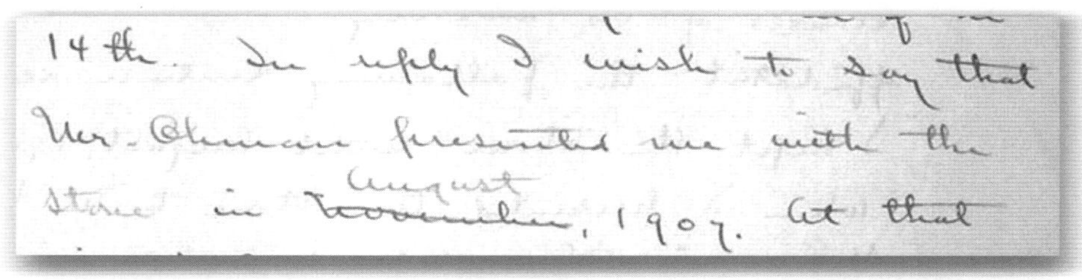

January 30, 1930 from Holand to attorneys. (Ohman Family Association)
"In reply I wish to say that Mr. Ohman presented me with the stone in August of 1907."

1908

February – Hjalmar Holand writes his first paper on the Kensington Rune Stone, *De Norske Settlementers Historie,* (Norwegian Immigrant History). Included in this paper is Holand's transcription, which omits the double-dots over the five "hooked-Xs." Holand reports the age of the tree was at least twenty-five years, based on a count of the annual tree rings.

Vinlandstogenes Betydning og Rækkevidde.   17

göter ok 22 norrmen po

opdhagelsefardh fro

vinlandh of vest vi

hadhe lager wedh 2 skjar

en dags rise nar fro

dhenne sten vi var ok fiske

en dhagh aptir vi kom hem fan

10 man rödhe af blodh ok dhedh AVM

fraelse af illy

har 10 mans ve(?) hawet at se

aftir vore skip 14 dagh

rese from dhenne öh ahr 1362.

Runestenens Indskrift.

The "Holand Copy" of the inscription appeared in *Harper's Weekly,* on October 9, 1909. (Courtesy of the Ohman Family)

August 3 – Holand writes his first known letter to Professor Newton Winchell at the Minnesota Historical Society and includes a written transcription of the Kensington Rune Stone inscription.

The beginning of the first known letter H.R. Holand wrote to Newton Winchell at the Minnesota Historical Society on August 3, 1908. (Minnesota Historical Society)

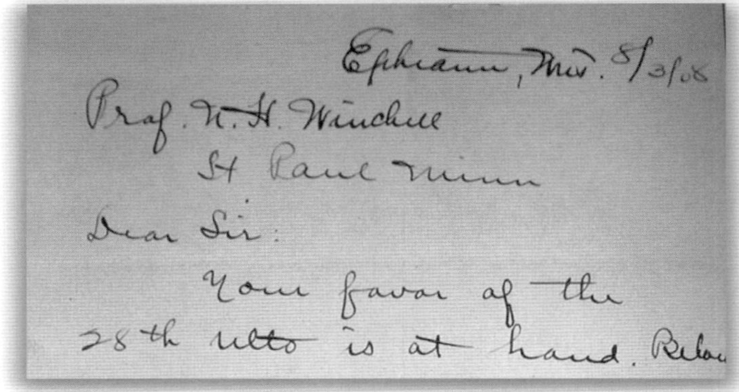

1909

May – Helge Gjessing publishes an article, "The Rune-Stone from Kensington," in *Smyra* in response to Holand's letter to Magnus Olsen in Oslo, enclosing his 1908 article on the Kensington Rune Stone. Gjessing writes that a tree twenty-five years of age did not preclude white settlers from carving the inscription. (Symra, 5: 113-126)

Holand writes his response on the subject, "The Kensington Stone's Language and Runes; Answer to Mr. Helga Gjessing," which was published in *Smyra*.

July – P.P. Iverslie published a paper entitled: "The Kensington Stone" in Kvartalskrift (5: 13-21).

July 20 – Olof Ohman, Nils Flaaten, Roald Benson, Samuel Olson, and Edward Ohman sign affidavits about the discovery of the Kensington Rune Stone. These statements are given in Douglas County, Minnesota, and signed by witnesses R. J. Rasmusson [notary public], and George H. Merhes.

October 9 – Holand publishes another paper on the Kensington Rune Stone, "An Explorer's Stone Record which Antedates Columbus," in *Harper's Weekly*, 53:15.

November 29 to December 2 – N. H. Winchell makes his first trip to Kensington.

Newton Winchell's first entry into his field notebook during his first trip to Kensington, dated November 29, 1909. (Minnesota Historical Society)

November 30 – Winchell described glacial geomorphology and writes in his field notebook that he collected rock samples of the discovery site. He also speaks with Ohman and his sons, who describe the discovery and history of the stone up until Hjalmer Holand took possession of it in 1907.

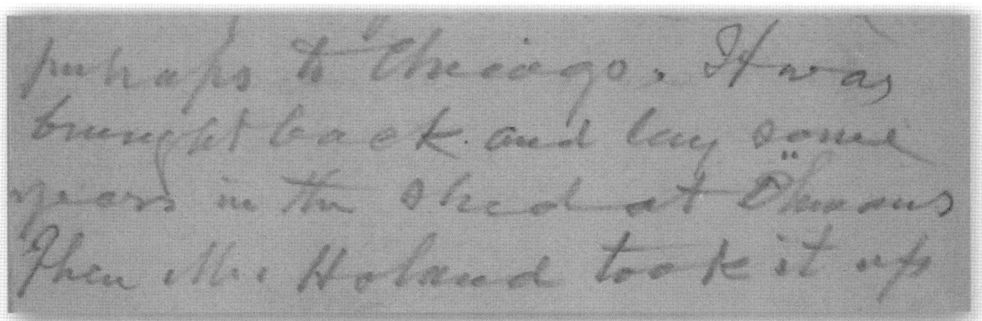

An excerpt from page 3 of Newton Winchell's field notebook entered on November 30, 1909. (**Minnesota Historical Society**) *"It was brought back and lay some years in the shed at Ohmans then Mr. Holand took it up."*

December 1 – Winchell collects more rock samples and records observations at an ice-covered Pelican Lake to investigate the possible connection of this location with the "skerries" referred to in the inscription.

December 2 – Winchell interviews Sam Olson, who discussed letters from Professor Curme in Evanston, and relates that Ohman said *"…the stone was not given to Holand as his personal property…"* He also talks with Ohman who asks Mr. Winchell to *"…not let it go from St. Paul, not even on loan to Mr. Holand to take to Chicago, but to keep it."*

December 6 – N. H. Winchell completes his report (11 pages) about the physical and geographical attributes related to the Kensington Rune Stone.

December 9 – Olof Ohman writes a four-page letter in Swedish to Warren Upham at the Minnesota Historical Society describing the discovery of the Kensington Rune Stone.

Kensington den 9 Dec 1909

Mr Warren Upham.

St Paul

Eder skrifvelse är mig tillhanda, och får upp-läsa, att mina tillgångar i ekonomiskt hänseende icke tillåter mig att infria vid eders Societys meeting. och ej heller jag kan inse att min närvaro är nödvändig. på eder fråga öfver Runstenens finnande de får jag upplysa att nämnda sten är funnen under en asprot

Af meddan teknad utseende, af roten stennen var inbäddat mellan dessa rötter med runorna vänd nedåt samt runorna på sidan vänd emot järtroten, som vi kalla på farmar språket, jag hoggde af den yttre roten som vi ser på tekningen och även järtroten på samma plats som det visas på tekningen sedan fäll trädet och stennen var blätat

Jag såg att stennen var ben, jag helt enkelt satte grubban under den och vände. den undra sedan upp så att runorna kom upp min pojk Edvar är född 1888. han var vid ikring 10 år han säg först att det var någonting ritat på stenen. Pojkarne trodde att de har funnit en Indo Allmanacka,

Jag själf såg ochså att det var någonting skrivit. men att läsa hvar för mig ett mysterie, Jag är svensk, född i Helsingland men jag har aldrig sedt någon runsten för stennen jag 44 fot ne varande sten läs vel, Aspträdet var omkring 6 tum i diameter,

Aktningsfull

Olof Ohman

This is the original four-page letter that Olof Ohman wrote to Dr. Warren Upham on November 9, 1909. (Minnesota Historical Society)

Kensington, Minn.

Dec. 9, 1909.

Mr. Warren Upham,

St. Paul,

Your communication at hand, and in reply will say that on account of financial shortcomings I will be unable to attend the meeting of your society. Furthermore I do not consider that my presence would be necessary. In regard to the find of the "Rune Stone" will state that it was found under the root of an Asp tree as indicated below. (See original letter). The stone lay imbedded between the roots of the tree with runes downward, the runes on the side being turned toward the tree. I cut the outside root at the spot indicated and then the main root whereupon the tree fell, exposing the stone. I observed that the stone was flat and I simply put my grub axe under it and turned it over so that the runes came in sight. My son Edward (born 1888) was the first to notice the inscription. The boys thought we had found an Indian Almanac. I also observed that something was written on the stone, but was unable to read it. I am a Swede, born in Helsingland, I have never seen a rune stone before. The stone lay 44 feet above the present water level. The Asp tree was about 8 inches in diameter.

Respectfully,

Olof Ohman.

An English translation of the four-page letter that Olof Ohman wrote in Swedish to Warren Upham on November 9, 1909. (Minnesota Historical Society)

December 15 - N. H. Winchell writes a one-page statement that was favorable to the authenticity of the Kensington Rune Stone.

N. H. Winchell wrote a letter to the Museum Committee on December 15, 1909, stating that the Rune Stone was genuine. (Minnesota Historical Society)

"I have personally made a topographical examination of the place where the Kensington rune stone was found, and of the region northward to Pelican lake where the skerries are located, to which the inscription refers, and I am convinced from the geological conditions, and the physical changes that the region has experienced probably within the last five hundred years that the said stone is not a modern forgery, and must be accepted as a genuine record of an exploration in Minnesota, at the date stated in the inscription."

December 27 – Hjalmar Holand sends copies of the affidavits of Edward Ohman, Roald Bentson, and Nils Flaaten that Mr. Holand and Dr. Knute Hough had obtained to the Minnesota Historical Society. These affidavits, as well as those of Olof Ohman and Sam Olson, are transcribed in Blegen (1968), pages 137-141.

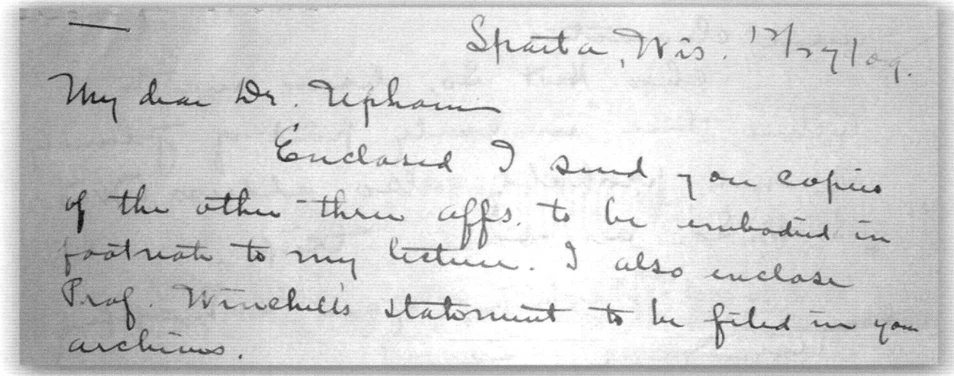

The beginning of the cover letter attached to the three affidavits Mr. Holand submitted to the MHS. (Minnesota Historical Society)

"Sparta, Wis. 12/27/09

"My dear Dr. Upham,

"Enclosed I send you copies of the other three affs. [affidavits] to be embodied in footnote to my lecture. I also enclose Prof. Winchell's statement to be filed in your archives."

1910

January – O. J. Breda writes a nine-page summary about the Kensington Rune Stone entitled, "The Kensington Stone," that was published in *Symra*, 1910, pp. 70-80. On page 2 he wrote, *"And the language! That it was not Old Norse was clear at a glance…"*

P.P. Iverslie writes a second article entitled: "More on the Kensington Stone" that was published in Kvartalskrift (6: 8-16).

January/February – Warren Upham writes an article titled, "The Kensington Rune Stone, Its Discovery, Its Inscriptions, and Opinions Concerning Them," in *Records of the Past*. He makes the following statement about the stone's weathering: *"When we compare the excellent preservation of the glacial scratches shown on the back of the stone, which were made several thousand years ago, with the mellow, time-worn appearance of the face of the inscription, the conclusion is inevitable that the inscription must have been carved many hundred years ago."*

March 2 – Warren Upham writes to Prof. Winchell that ten linguistic experts (Professor Magnus Olsen, his associate Helge Gjessing, Professors O. J. Breda, Gisle Bothne, Julius

E. Olson, Rasmus B. Anderson, George O. Curme, Starr W. Cutting, Chester N. Gould, and George T. Flom) who reviewed the inscription (or copies of the inscription) declared that it must be a modern forgery. He also suggests to Winchell that he inquire into the characters of Ohman and Holand.

Warren Upham's March 2, 1910 note to Prof. Winchell suggesting he inquire into the character of Ohman and Holand. (Minnesota Historical Society)

"Therefore, in your expected journey the later part of this week to Kensington and vicinity, as much information as possible should be gathered relating to honesty or dishonesty or both these men, to learn also whether Mr. Holand knew and visited Mr. Ohman before August, 1898, when the stone was found, and whether the former has relatives or friends whom he visited so early anywhere in that region."

March 3 – N. H. Winchell makes his second trip to Kensington and interviews T. A. Saettre and the Reverend O. A. Norman, who say Holand was never in the region until the time he took possession of the Stone from Ohman. (Winchell Field Notebook)

March 4 – W. O. Hotchkiss, the state geologist of Wisconsin writes a letter to the Minnesota Historical Society stating, *"…the old runes are at least fifty to one hundred years old unless some artificial process has been used to produce the weathered appearance."*

An excerpt from the March 4, 1910 letter written by W. O. Hotchkiss, the Wisconsin state geologist, to the Minnesota Historical Society. (Minnesota Historical Society)

Winchell interviews John E. Johnson, and Sam Olson. Mr. Olson describes the probable age of the tree (*"at least ten years old & was more likely twenty to thirty years old[.]"*) whose roots were wrapped around the Stone, and makes a sketch. (Winchell Field Notebook)

Mr. Olson says a party visited the excavation site in the spring of 1899 and saw the stump of the tree the Rune Stone was found under. Ohman tells Winchell that the tree was an *"asp"* or aspen, which was also known as a trembling poplar. (Winchell Field Notebook)

An entry made on page 26 of Winchell's notebook on March 4, 1910. (Minnesota Historical Society)

"About in the spring (May) of (1890?) Mr. Sam Oleson and a party visited the place and made some excavations where the stone was found. He saw, and all his party saw the stump of the tree that grew on the stone."*

* This entry was clearly changed at some point and is a mistake. The year should have been recorded as 1899. Either Winchell changed his mind and recorded what (the year) Mr. Olson actually said or the date was changed at a later date.

March 5 – Winchell interviews Joseph Hotvedt, who was of the opinion that Ohman may have made the inscription, and was the *"only man I have found who doubts the authenticity of the stone."* Winchell later speaks with his livery man, who makes light of Mr. Hotvedt's statements.

Entries made on page 32 in Winchell's notebook on March 5, 1910. (Minnesota Historical Society)

"My livery man made light of the statements of Mr. Hotvedt as to Mr. Ohman's making the rune record. 'You can't go much on what he says. He is always off and contrary.' It will be noted that he (Hotvedt) confirms the aspects of the roots – which is fatal to his idea that Ohman made the inscription, since by all opinions the tree was older than the residence of Öhman on the farm."

March 7 – Sam Olson writes a letter to the Minnesota Historical Society for Olof Ohman, in English, asking them to retain the Kensington Rune Stone and not return it to Hjalmar Holand.

This letter to Warren Upham at the Minnesota Historical Society, dated March 7, 1910, was written by Sam Olson for Olof Ohman. In it, Ohman tells the society not to return the Rune Stone to Hjalmar Holand. (The second page of this letter is on page 239) (Minnesota Historical Society)

"Dear Sir,

"Mr. Winchell called on me a few days ago and informed me that Mr. Holand was negotiating with the State to dispose of the Rune Stone to the State, the said stone found on my place. Mr. Holand got this Stone from me for the Norwegian Historical Society under the condition that is should be retained in a safe place for future reference in case there should appear more evidence that the stone was proven genuine. The above agreement was made about three years ago and that Mr. Holand did not receive the stone as his individual property, therefore has no right to dispose of same to my knowledge. I further ask you to retain the runic stone until Mr. Holand has settled the question of disposing the same with me, and the Norwegian Historical Society.

"Very Respectfully,

"Olof Ohman

"By S. Olson"

March 9 – Professor George O. Curme writes a letter to Winchell saying that he was not an expert in Old Norse, and that an opinion about the inscription should come from Norse scholars in Scandinavia. (Blegen pages 162-164)

This excerpt appeared on the first page of a letter written by Professor George O. Curme on March 9, 1910 to N. H. Winchell. (Minnesota Historical Society)
"My opinion ought not to have much weight."

March 12 – Former Kensington resident J. P. Hedberg writes a letter to N. H. Winchell to answer questions about the discovery of the Stone. Mr. Hedberg says he saw the stump and roots of the tree the Stone was found under, and said he copied the inscription and sent the copy to Turnblad, who then sent it to the University of Minnesota. (Blegen pages 169-70)

J. P. Hedberg's letter back to N. H. Winchell answering questions about the Rune Stone. (Minnesota Historical Society)
*"March 12*th *1910*

"Mr. N. H. Winchell
"St. Paul

"Dear Sir!

*"Your letter of the 10*th *(inst.) in regard to the Kensington rune stone as it is called. In the first place the stone was brought in to my office in Kensington by the finder Olof Ohman. I took quite much interest in the same. I copied the same and sent copy to S. J. Turnblad who sent it to the State University but Prof. Breda thought it was a fake.*

"In the spring of 1890 [sic 1899] I together with some others went out and did some digging where the stone had been found and will try and answer the following questions.

"1. Yes I saw the stump and roots.

2. The big root was was grown as a bend and I am quite sure if we have had the stone there it would have fit-ted in. It could not have grown on side of stone.
3. As said, large root ran on top of stone.
4. It is hard to say how old the tree was but it was quite large and must have been many years old, anyway a great deal older that the settlements there. I had quite a talk with one Nils Flaaten an old farmer that was along and helped Ohman to grub. I considered him absolute [sic] reliable – he was along and grubbed the tree and dug out the stone and his statements confirmed absolutely with Ohmans [sic]. While I know very little about runes I never considered the stone a fake.

"Very Truly Yours,

"J. P. Hedberg"

March 17 to 19 – Winchell makes his third trip to the Kensington area.

March 17 – Winchell travels to Elbow Lake, Evansville, and Ashby, Minnesota to investigate the rumor about Ohman carving runes. He interviews Mr. Saettre whose opinion concurrs with the livery man about Hotvedts' reliability. He also interviews O. A. Normann and O. G. Juul. (Winchell Field Notebook)

March 18 – Winchell travels to Brandon, Minnesota to interview O. F. Olson, and then to Moe, Minnesota to talk with the Reverend M. B. Juul. Later that day in Kensington, Winchell speaks with S. Olson, who called Ohman, Fogelblad, and Andrew Anderson *"queer characters."*

An entry made on March 18, 1910 in Winchell's notebook on page 41. (Minnesota Historical Society)

"These three (Ohman, Fogelblad and Anderson) are all Swedes, and if there be any fraud in it it lies with one or all of them."

March 19 – Winchell has a long talk with Ohman, who says Fogelblad had died at Andrew Anderson's house before Ohman found the Stone. Winchell also asks Ohman about the Gunnar Johnson rumor. (Winchell Field Notebook)

March 26 – Holand writes his fourth article on the Kensington Rune Stone, "A Fourteenth-Century Columbus," published in *Harper's Weekly*, 54:25. Holand reports in this paper that, *"In the opinion of many expert woodsmen, it could not have been less than forty years old growing as it did, in a dense shaded forest."* There is no explanation as to why the alleged age of the tree increased from twenty-five to forty years.

April 4 – Swedish linguist Otto Von Friesen writes a letter to the Minnesota Historical Society saying the Kensington Rune Stone inscription is a modern forgery.

The excerpt above is from a letter written by Otto Von Friesen to the Minnesota Historical Society on April 4, 1910. (**Minnesota Historical Society**) *"The inscription is fabricated in modern time by a man who was partly acquainted with runes but where this partial knowledge failed, he created himself new characters."*

April 14 to 19 – George Flom travels to Kensington with an unnamed witness to interview Olof Ohman and his family about the Stone. Professor Flom also interviews Mr. Peterson, and visits four hours with Mr. Samuel Olson.

On page 33 of his 42-page paper on the Kensington Rune Stone Professor George Flom wrote that he visited the Kensington area in April of 1910. (Minnesota Historical Society)

April 20 – Johan A. Holvik writes a letter to N. H. Winchell with his conclusions,
> *"After comparing in detail the Kensington inscription with the book [Almquist Grammar from 1840] bearing the name of Sv. Fogelblad,…. To summarize: the difference in rune system, and the so-called 'errors' in the inscription, with some parallel correct forms in the book, make it evident that there is no connection between the inscription on the Kensington Rune Stone and the book bearing the name Sv. Fogelblad."*

April 21 – The Minnesota Historical Society Museum Committee approves the 76 page report by N. H. Winchell titled, *Report of the Kensington Rune Stone*, with the following resolution:

Resolved, That this Committee renders a favorable opinion of the authenticity of the Kensington Rune Stone, provided that the references to Scandinavian literature given in this Committee's report and accompanying papers be verified by a competent specialist in the Scandinavian languages, to be selected by this Committee (Bothne), and that he approve the conclusions of this report;

Resolved, That this action of this Committee be reported to the next meeting of the Executive Council, and that Mr. Holand be so informed.

April 25 – Professor E. Louis Elmquist writes a letter to N. H. Winchell, suggesting ways to get help understanding the inscription. (MHS Archives)

May 6 – Professor George T. Flom delivers a paper about the Kensington Rune Stone at the Illinois State Historical Society Annual Meeting in Springfield, Illinois. This address is published as a 42-page paper by the Illinois State Historical Society.

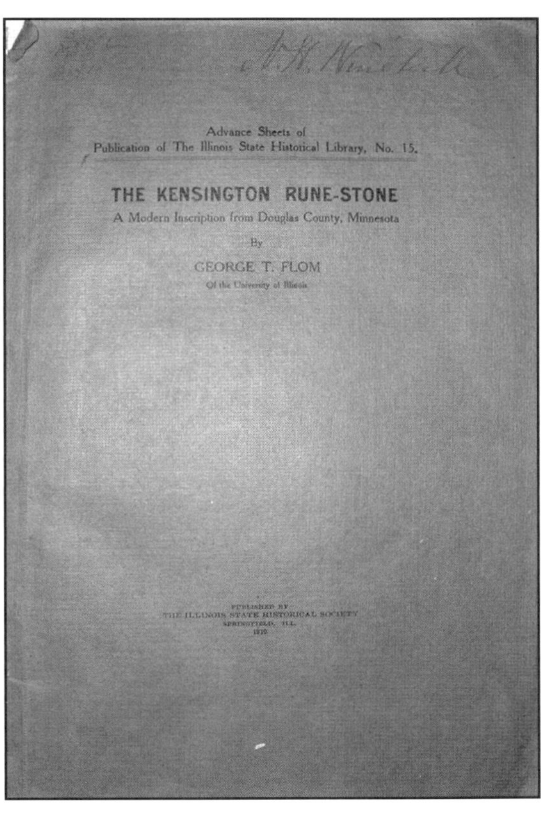

The cover page of N. H. Winchell's copy of Professor George T. Flom's 1910 paper on the Kensington Rune Stone. (Minnesota Historical Society)

May 16 – Olof Ohman writes a letter to the Minnesota Historical Society (transcribed into English), where he denied ever carving runes.

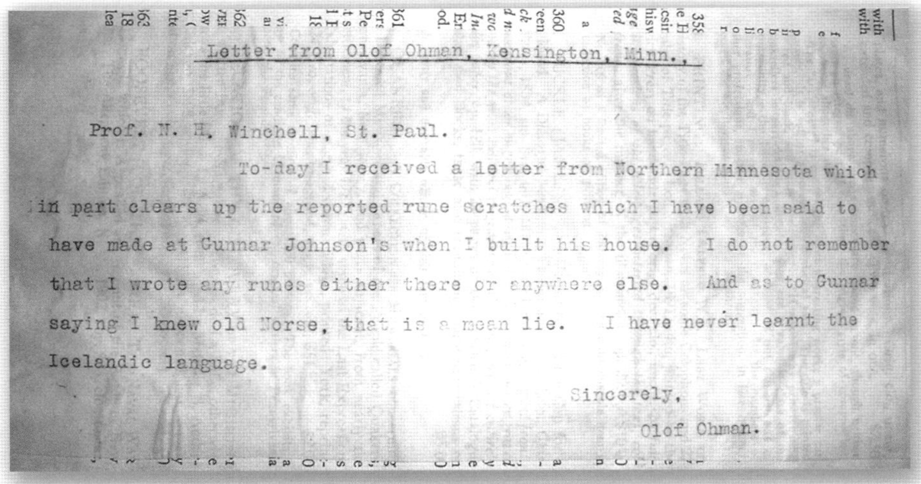

Letter from Olof Ohman, Kensington, Minn.,

Prof. N. H. Winchell, St. Paul.

To-day I received a letter from Northern Minnesota which in part clears up the reported rune scratches which I have been said to have made at Gunnar Johnson's when I built his house. I do not remember that I wrote any runes either there or anywhere else. And as to Gunnar saying I knew old Norse, that is a mean lie. I have never learnt the Icelandic language.

Sincerely,

Olof Ohman.

This undated transcription of a letter written by Olof Ohman was pasted into a notebook. The letter was probably written in May 1910, shortly after Winchell returned from his third visit to the Kensington area to investigate the circumstances surrounding the discovery of the Stone. (Minnesota Historical Society)

May 24 – Norse scholar Rasmus B. Anderson writes a letter to the editors of *Amerika* discussing an interview he conducted with Andrew Anderson, a former resident of Hoffman, Minnesota and acquaintance of Olof Ohman. R. Anderson implies that A. Anderson led him to believe that Ohman, Fogelblad, and A. Anderson were responsible for carving the Stone after some "significant winks."

THE KENSINGTON RUNE STONE ONCE MORE.

Amerika. 27 May. 1910

DRAW YOUR OWN CONCLUSIONS.

On the 17th of this month I lectured at Stanley, in the western part of North Dakota. In a drugstore in that city, a gentleman came and shook hands with me and deluged me with compliments. If he had been an Irishman I would have been sure that he had kissed the Blarney stone. The stranger was dressed in the plainest working clothes and the spots of dry mud showed that he was fresh from work. He was a very intelligent man and well educated. He could quote Swedish poetry and Greek and Latin words and phrases with absolute accuracy. He was well up in history, poetry and philosophy. I admired him not because he showered compliments on me and gave me a cigar, but because he, a man of so great intelligence and education, did not feel above common work. I asked him who he was. He told me his name was Andrew Anderson, that he was a Swede, that he in his younger days had been a student at the celebrated Upsala university, and that in 1882 he had quit the university, packed his books and emigrated to America settling in Hoffman, Minn., where he now owns a nice farm. He had for years worked on Jim Hill's railroad and was now at Stanley as foreman on a dump on the great railroad magnate's road.

Hoffman, Minn.! I asked him if that was not near Kensington and if he knew a man by name Olof Ohman, on whose land a rune-stone had been found. He said he was a neighbor of Ohman's, and that he and Ohman were brothers in law. Olof Ohman had come from Helsingeland in Sweden in 1875 and had settled near Kensington. He is a well-to-do man. He was educated as a mechanic in Sweden and is well skilled in the handling of all kinds of tools. Ohman is not a college-bred man, but has always been a great reader. His favorite books are Alex. v. Humboldt's "Cosmos" and a work in Swedish called "The Gospel of Nature" Then I asked Mr. Anderson, what he knew about Rev. Fogelblad. He answered: "Rev Fogelblad made his home at my house and died there about ten years ago". This Fogelblad, Anderson claimed, left the Lutheran church because he could not endorse its tenets, but the fact is, he was deposed on account of his dissolute habits. He was a graduate in theology of the Upsala university and came from Sweden direct to Minnesota where he lived as a literary tramp. Anderson and particulary Fogelblad were well versed in the runes. Anderson had brought with him from Sweden a book by the great scholar Fryxell on the Swedish runes. This book he loaned to Ohman, and the three, Fogelblad, Anderson, and Ohman frequently discussed the runes when they were together, Fogelblad writing long sentences in runic on paper and explaining them to Ohman. He wrote a book called "The Age of Reason". It has no important bearing on the subject, but I may add that the three, Fogelblad, Ohman and Anderson were all proud to consider themselves wholly emancipated from the dogmas of the Christian faith.

Thus we here have Olof Ohman, who settled near Kensington in 1875 and on whose farm the notorious rune-stone was found at the root of a young tree in 1898, Rev. Fogelblad, who came to Minnesota about the same time and Andrew Anderson, who settled there in 1882. All three were deeply interested in runes and either one of them was capable of producing the rune-stone in question.

From a runic, linguistic and historical standpoint the Kensington rune-stone is a fraud on the face of it.

Mr. Andrew Anderson, whom I can best describe as a diamond in the rough, did not in my long and interesing interview with him admit that either one of the three had had anything to do with the much advertised Kensington rune-stone, but he gave me some significant winks. We parted in the small hours of the morning as the best of friends.

Now, gentle reader, draw your own conclusions.

Rasmus B. Anderson.

May 24. 1910.

The end of the published letter written by Norse scholar Rasmus B. Anderson on May 24, 1910, and published in the newspaper *Amerika* on May 27, 1910. (Minnesota Historical Society)

June 3 – Andrew Andrew sends a letter in English addressed to N. H. Winchell, responding to the claims made in R. B. Anderson's letter of May 24.

Andrew Anderson's letter to N.H. Winchell responding to the alleged statements he was said to have made in R.B. Anderson's letter of May 24. Written on June 3, 1910, the letter was published in the *Norwegian American* on June 10, 1910. (Minnesota Historical Society)

Stanley, N. D., June 3, 1910.

N. H. Winchell,
   St. Paul, Minn.

Dear Sir:—

Yours of June 1st at hand and contents noted. Yes, I got a copy of Mr. R. B. Anderson's paper, "Amerika", because I subscribed on it. I can't understand how Mr. Rasmus B. Anderson could write such an interview. I never told him half of what he got into his paper. I told him that if Fogelblad had written the runes they would have been correct. I said that Fogelblad could possibly have written the inscription on paper, and Ohman could have chisled the runes on the stone, as he is a mechanic of trade. But I never said that he done it. I further said that I didn't believe in it at all, that they had created the stone, or "runes." I told him that Fogelblad was too honest for such a thing as that. Fogelblad had nothing to do with such a reproduction. Ohman wouldn't be able to produce an inscription of runes; so that settles it for all time. I have written "Amerika" in the Swedish language, and corrected his mistakes, and I do hope he is honest enough to give it space. I have also written ""Svenska Amerikanska Posten", and I wish that paper would publish my article, and that will settle this controversy, as far as me concern. Anderson made a student of me too from the University of Upsala. He got so mixed so he seems to not know what he is talking about. This is all I got to say this time. It is hard to write in a railroad camp after quitting time where it is about 75 men talking at the same time, but I feel justified to be able to give you this information.

Yours for truth,
ANDREW ANDERSON.
   Care J. Newville.

P. S.—I do believe the stone to be genuine.

June 6 – Olof Ohman writes a letter in Swedish to N. H. Winchell, responding to statements made by Andrew Anderson alleged in R. B. Anderson's letter of May 24.

(Right) Olof Ohman wrote this letter to N. H. Winchell on June 6, 1910, and it was published in *Norwegian American* on June 10, 1910. Ohman angrily responded to the alleged statements of Andrew Anderson in R. B. Anderson's letter of May 24. The handwritten notes on the right side of the article were made by N. H. Winchell. (Minnesota Historical Society)

"It is evident from Ohman's letter that there is no collusion between him and A. Anderson.

"The fabrication as it appears in the foregoing letter, was by R. B. Anderson only."

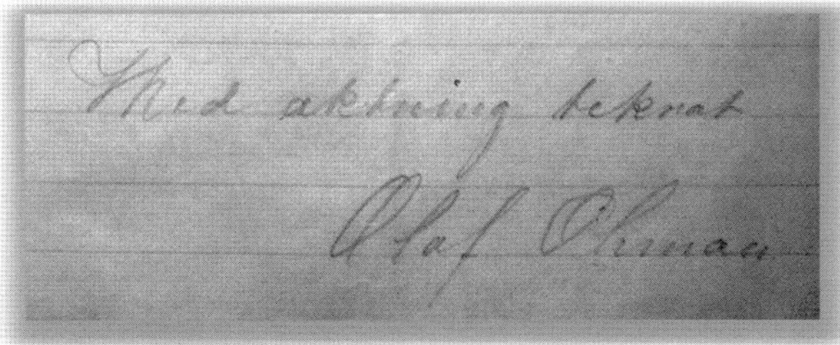

Olof Ohman's signature on page 5 of his June 6, 1910 letter to N.H. Winchell. (Minnesota Historical Society)

July 16 – Hjalmar Holand obtains a signed affidavit from Olof Ohman, written in Swedish, (transcribed in Swedish on page 44) describing the dimension of the poplar tree slice samples that he cut down on his property. Ohman was accompanied by Dr. Knut Hoegh and H. Holand.

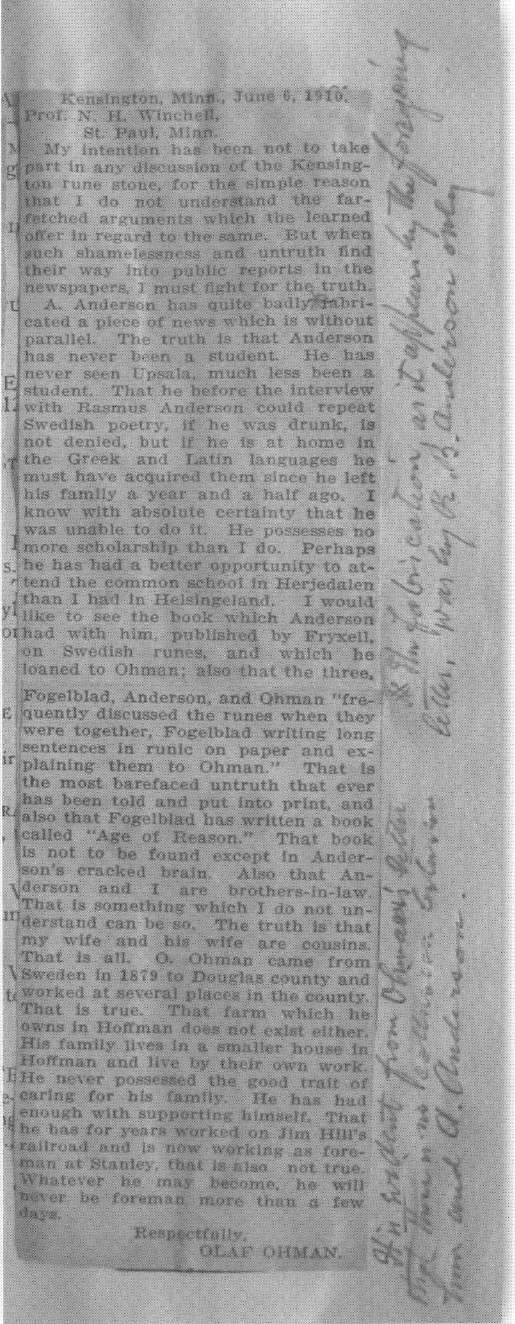

Kensington, Minn., June 6, 1910.
Prof. N. H. Winchell,
    St. Paul, Minn.

My intention has been not to take part in any discussion of the Kensington rune stone, for the simple reason that I do not understand the far-fetched arguments which the learned offer in regard to the same. But when such shamelessness and untruth find their way into public reports in the newspapers, I must fight for the truth.

A. Anderson has quite badly fabricated a piece of news which is without parallel. The truth is that Anderson has never been a student. He has never seen Upsala, much less been a student. That he before the interview with Rasmus Anderson could repeat Swedish poetry, if he was drunk, is not denied, but if he is at home in the Greek and Latin languages he must have acquired them since he left his family a year and a half ago. I know with absolute certainty that he was unable to do it. He possesses no more scholarship than I do. Perhaps he has had a better opportunity to attend the common school in Herjedalen than I had in Helsingeland. I would like to see the book which Anderson had with him, published by Fryxell, on Swedish runes, and which he loaned to Ohman; also that the three,

Fogelblad, Anderson, and Ohman "frequently discussed the runes when they were together, Fogelblad writing long sentences in runic on paper and explaining them to Ohman." That is the most barefaced untruth that ever has been told and put into print, and also that Fogelblad has written a book called "Age of Reason." That book is not to be found except in Anderson's cracked brain. Also that Anderson and I are brothers-in-law. That is something which I do not understand can be so. The truth is that my wife and his wife are cousins. That is all. O. Ohman came from Sweden in 1879 to Douglas county and worked at several places in the county. That is true. That farm which he owns in Hoffman does not exist either. His family lives in a smaller house in Hoffman and live by their own work. He never possessed the good trait of caring for his family. He has had enough with supporting himself. That he has for years worked on Jim Hill's railroad and is now working as foreman at Stanley, that is also not true. Whatever he may become, he will never be foreman more than a few days.

Respectfully,
OLAF OHMAN.

Kensington den 16 Jule 1910
Skifverna a. b. c. d. är alla huggnad på min egendom i narhoten af vad Runsten var funnen. under samma skogs-förhallande, skifven a är afsamma storelse som tradet hvar vuxen afver sten. nun bäde a och . C. är fran mycket frodigare strad, an det som stod afver stenen, c och d. är ifrån trad som i sin vaxkt som mer liknade Runstens tradet. men är cirka 3/8 kummar mindre i tversnet an detta. Olaf Ohman.

A type-written, Swedish transcription of the July 16, 1910 letter written by Olof Ohman. (Minnesota Historical Society)

July 19 and 20 – N. H. Winchell reviews and comments on Professor George T. Flom's paper on the Kensington Rune Stone.

(Right) N. H. Winchell's notes on when he received, reviewed, and commented on George T. Flom's paper on the Kensington Rune Stone. (Minnesota Historical Society)

September/October - Holand writes an article entitled: "Are there English words on the Kensington Runestone?" in Records of the Past (Washington D.C., 9:240-45)

December 30 – Warren Upham writes a miscellaneous entry stating that he half believes the Rune Stone true.

The Kensington Rune-Stone

AN ADDRESS
by
GEORGE T. FLOM

Delivered before The Illinois State Historical Society at its Annual Meeting, May 5-6, 1910 at Springfield, Illinois

Received about July 12. 1910.
Examined July 19. Commented on July 20. 1910.

Entry into Minnesota Historical Society archives letterpress book, Volume 16, page 106, by the Museum Committee secretary Warren Upham. (Minnesota Historical Society)

"I half believe the Rune Stone true, — that is, as likely to be so as to be a fraud thus far escaping detection. My belief is about 50 percent of full confidence, but Prof. Winchell has fully 95 percent of complete assurance."

1911

February 7 – Four members of the Minnesota Historical Society Museum Committee, E. C. Mitchell, N. H. Winchell, Councilor Wheeler, and Warren Upham, meet to discuss the Rune Stone. A letter from Professor George Flom opposing the Stone's authenticiy is read, as is a letter written by Professor Andrew Fossum defending it. The committee agrees that a special meeting is to be held to discuss sending Winchell and Holand to Norway to study the linguistic aspects of the Stone. They also agree that the state appropriate $2000 for the foreign study in addition to $5000 to purchase the Stone if the resolution is approved.

February 24 – Andrew Fossum writes an article entitled, "Study in Language in the Kensington Runestone leads to Satisfactory Results" in the Norwegian American, pages 1, 3, 6.

April 19 – Olof Ohman signs a bill of sale with the Minnesota Historical Society for $10 to purchase his rights to the Kensington Rune Stone. The agreement is that the $90 balance will be paid when Ohman acquired the ownership rights from Hjalmar Holand (See document on page 239).

May 5 – The Minnesota Historical Society's board of directors votes against purchasing the Kensington Rune Stone from Hjalmar Holand with state funds, and recommends that the purchase be made with private funds.

May 10 – Warren Upham writes to Ohman that the Minnesota Historical Society would not be paying the $90 balance owed to him for his rights to the Stone.

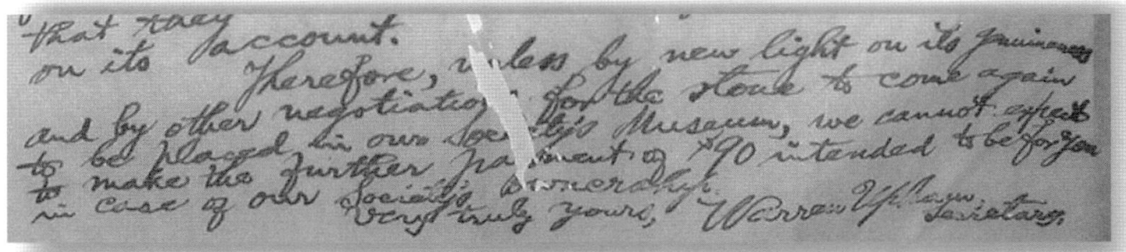

Warren Upham's letter to Olof Ohman that the Society would not make the $90 payment for his rights to the Stone. This entry was made in the Minnesota Historical Society archives letterpress book, volume 16, page 562, on May 10, 1911. (**Minnesota Historical Society**)

> *"Therefore, unless by new light on its genuineness and by other negotiating for the stone to come again to be placed in our Society's Museum, we cannot expect to make the further payment of $90 intended to be for you in case of our Society's ownership.*
>
> *"Very Truly Yours,*
>
> *"Warren Upham*
> *Secretary"*

May 11 – The Minnesota Historical Society sends the Kensington Rune Stone back to Hjalmar Holand.

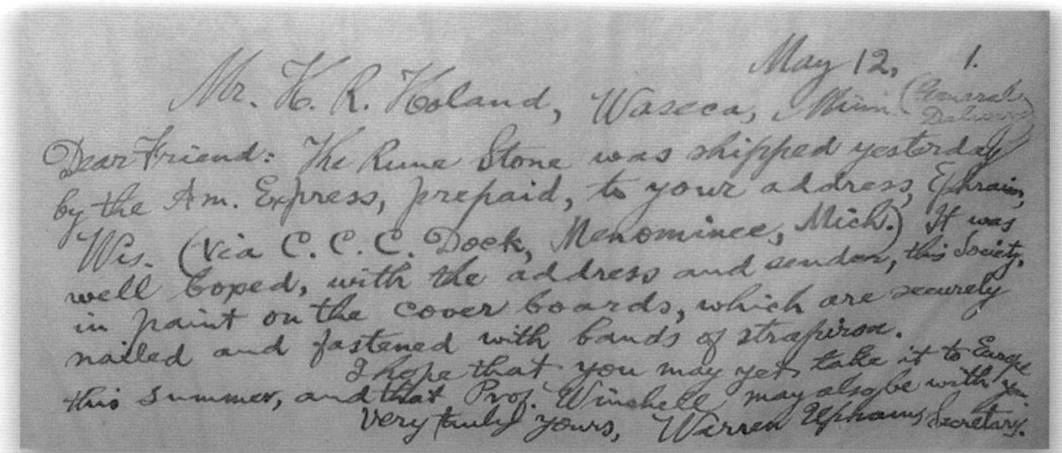

Entry by Museum Committee secretary Warren Upham to Hjalmar Holand on May 12, 1911 into Minnesota Historical Society archives letterpress book, Volume 16, page 584. (Minnesota Historical Society) *"Dear Friend: The Rune Stone was shipped yesterday by the Am. Express, prepaid, to your address, Ephraim, Wis. (Via C. C. C. Dock, Menominee, Mich.) It was well boxed, with the address and sender, this Society, in paint on the cover boards, which are securely nailed and fastened with bands of strapiron.*

"I hope that you may yet take it to Europe this summer, and that Prof. Winchell may also be with you.

"Very Truly Yours,

"Warren Upham
Secretary"

Holand Goes to Europe (1911)

This relatively short period is important because of the unfortunate seeds that Hjalmar Holand planted during his nearly two-month long trip to Europe after the Minnesota Historical Society declined to purchase the Stone from him. He was determined to find the La Vérendrye Stone in France, and to convince the scholars in Scandinavia that the inscription was genuine, but he failed on both counts.

1911

May 30 – Hjalmar Holand sails from New York to Europe with the Kensington Rune Stone on the ship "Cecilie."

The beginning of Hjalmar Holand's three-page letter to Warren Upham, written the day before leaving on his trip to Europe on May 29, 1911. (Minnesota Historical Society)

"*May 29, 1911*

"*My dear Dr. Upham:*

"*I sail tomorrow on the Cecilie, North German Lloyd, and will arrive in Ronen [France] June 5th.*"

June 5 – Hjalmar Holand arrives in Ronen, France.

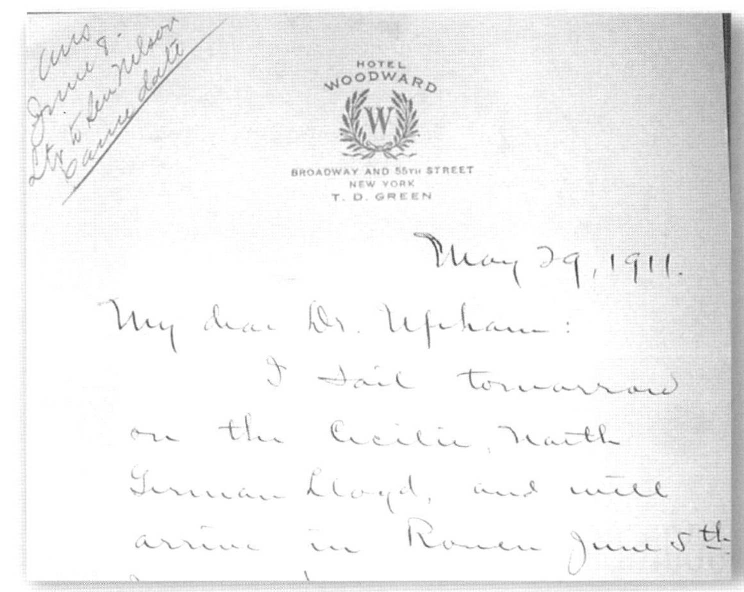

of this supercilious indifference. When I was in Washington lately I therefore appealed to Senator Knute Nelson to persuade our Secretary of State, Mr. Knox, to make an official request on the part of the United States upon the French government to find this stone. Yesterday I received from the senator a copy of his letter to Mr. Knox in which he lays the matter fully before the secretary and it is therefore likely that a thorough official search will soon be made.

In addition I have enlisted the services of the ablest private individual in this field in Paris. This is Prof. Waldo Gifford Leland who now for four years with four assistants has searched the French archives for material on our colonial history under the Carnegie institute auspices. He is intimately acquainted with these archives and ought to find whatever documentary reference there is to this stone if any is in existence.

Finally I have personally, in company with M. Dogsie, a French scholar, searched the Paris museums if perchance the stone should be deposited there. We searched through the Musee de Cluny, Musee Guimet, the Ethnological, the Mineralogical, and Bibliotique Nationale. In the last I was interested in finding a number of inscribed stones from Carthage, 2,000 years old. I was struck by the remarkable similarity of the weathering with that of the Kensington stone. ering the two one cannot

June 10 – Hjalmar Holand and Professor Oscar Montelius, Swedish Royal Archivist, engage in a lively dispute over the Kensington Rune Stone at the closing session of Congress in Paris, France.

June 19 – While in Paris, Holand authors an article chronicling his efforts to locate the La Vérendrye Stone. He writes about personally searching several Paris museums with French scholar, M. Dogsie.

Part of a letter that Hjalmar Holand wrote on June 19, 1911, while in Paris that appeared in the *Norwegian American* on July 14, 1911. (Minnesota Historical Society)

July 1 – Professor Alexander Bugge of the Department of History at the University of Christiania, Norway, writes a letter to the newspaper *Aftenposten* characterizing the Kensington Rune Stone as a fraud.

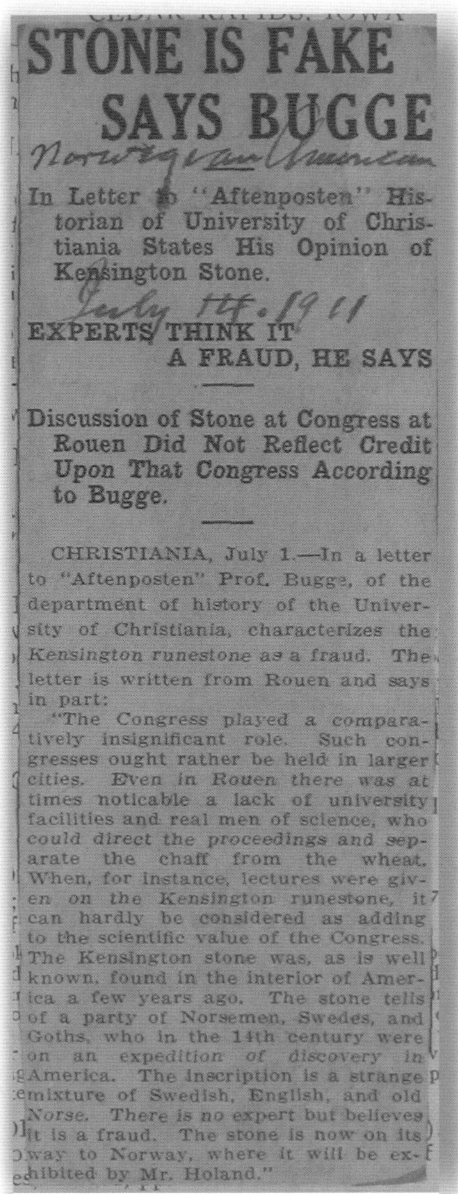

STONE IS FAKE
SAYS BUGGE

In Letter to "Aftenposten" Historian of University of Christiania States His Opinion of Kensington Stone.

EXPERTS THINK IT
A FRAUD, HE SAYS

Discussion of Stone at Congress at Rouen Did Not Reflect Credit Upon That Congress According to Bugge.

CHRISTIANIA, July 1.—In a letter to "Aftenposten" Prof. Bugge, of the department of history of the University of Christiania, characterizes the Kensington runestone as a fraud. The letter is written from Rouen and says in part:

"The Congress played a comparatively insignificant role. Such congresses ought rather be held in larger cities. Even in Rouen there was at times noticable a lack of university facilities and real men of science, who could direct the proceedings and separate the chaff from the wheat. When, for instance, lectures were given on the Kensington runestone, it can hardly be considered as adding to the scientific value of the Congress. The Kensington stone was, as is well known, found in the interior of America a few years ago. The stone tells of a party of Norsemen, Swedes, and Goths, who in the 14th century were on an expedition of discovery in America. The inscription is a strange mixture of Swedish, English, and old Norse. There is no expert but believes it is a fraud. The stone is now on its way to Norway, where it will be exhibited by Mr. Holand."

This article appeared in the *Norwegian American* on August 4, 1911. At the end of this article Professor Haegstad referred to himself as a scientist. (Minnesota Historical Society)

This article appeared in the *Norwegian American* on July 14, 1911. (Minnesota Historical Society)

July 11 – Holand gives a lecture on the Stone at the University in Christiania, Norway. He is challenged by Professor Haegstad, who proclaims, "It is false!"

"IT IS FALSE!"
SAYS HAEGSTAD

"I, Under No Circumstances, Will Be Connected With This Stone or Its Story," Says Norwegian Professor, of Runnestone.

STATEMENT FOLLOWS
ADDRESS BY HOLAND

Well Known Philologist Gives Reasons for His Beliefs That Stone Is a "Fake."

By ORLANDO INGVOLDSTAD.

Special to the Norwegian-American.

CHRISTIANIA, July 11.—The Kensington stone, once a live issue among a few Norwegian-Americans, has been given a second death-blow by the learned Prof. Hægstad. The scientists of the university unanimously pronounced the stone a "fake" shortly after it was found in 1898. This was done in writing by Prof. Bugge. But not satisfied with the decision of European scientists, the owner of the stone, Mr. H. Rued Holand came to Norway with the intention of proving to the learned Norsemen that they were mistaken in their condemnation of his protege.

July 12 – Hjalmar Holand writes a letter in response to Professor Haegstad's arguments against the Stone. Holand's letter appears in *Norwegian-American* newspaper.

HOLAND REPLIES TO HAEGSTAD

Nor. Am. Aug. 4. 1911

Exponent of Kensington Stone Answers Arguments Advanced By Professor of University of Christiania.

***

DISCUSSION CENTERS ON LINGUISTIC FORMS

***

American Author Presents Series of Replies to Points Mentioned As Condemning the Stone.

***

By H. R. HOLAND.

Special to the Norwegian-American.

CHRISTIANIA, July 12.—At my lecture before the University of Christiania yesterday Prof. Hægstad advanced a number of arguments in support of his belief that the Kensington inscription is a modern forgery. His conclusion in this matter has of course been long known in America, but we have not hitherto been made acquainted with his reasons for condemning the inscription. I have therefore thought it would interest the readers of the Norwegian-American to learn his objections. The following points are what I after conversation with others can remember of his arguments:

The first part of Hjalmar Holand's July 19, 1911 seven-page letter to Warren Upham, chronicling his trip to Europe. (Minnesota Historical Society)

"My dear Friend,

"Here I am on board for America after a most profitable and pleasant though somewhat strenuous trip."

Holand's reply in the *Norwegian American* of August 4, 1911. (Minnesota Historical Society)

July 19 – Hjalmar Holand boards the ship "Caronia" for the trip back to America.

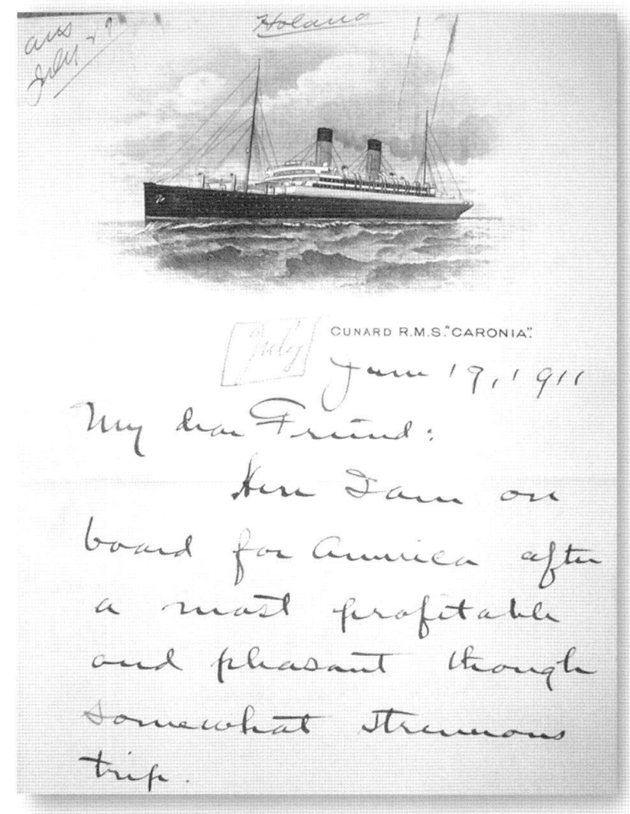

July 20 – Hjalmar Holand writes a six-page letter to N. H. Winchell summarizing his trip to Europe, expressing frustration that only one man had read a copy of the Society's report about the Rune Stone.

An excerpt from the 5th page of the letter
Hjalmar Holand wrote to N. H. Winchell on
July 20, 1911. (Minnesota Historical Society)
*"Prof Roht - The only man who had read the
report— thought the inscription must be genuine if
the stone was* <u>in</u> *situ in 1890."*

July 21 – An article written by P. P.
Iverslie in the *Norwegian American* criticizes Professor Bugge for being "behind
date" in the linguistic matters of the
Kensington Rune Stone inscription.

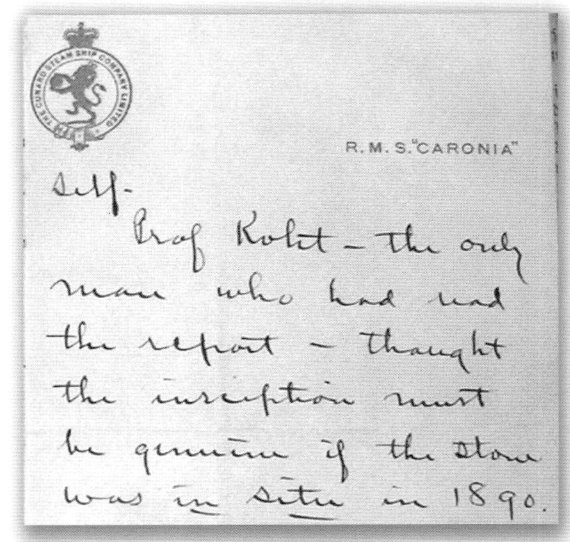

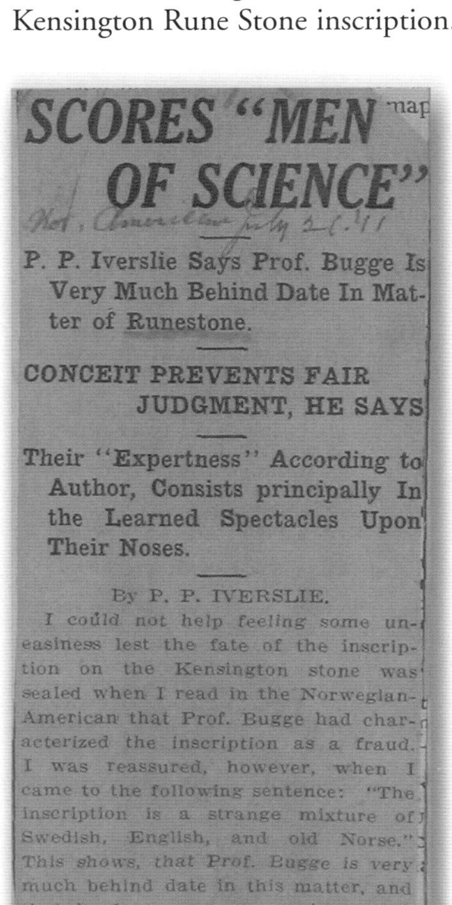

P.P. Iverslie's letter as it appeared in the *Norwegian
American* on July 21, 1911. (Minnesota Historical Society)

August 4 – Newspaperman Peer Stromme writes a
letter to the newspaper *Norwegian American* saying
that Professor Haegstad made statements without
offering any proof.

Peter Stromme's article appeared in the *Norwegian American* on August 4, 1911. (Minnesota Historical Society)

August 10 – N. H. Winchell writes a letter to Holand after his return from France, Sweden, and Norway.

"MHS
Old Capitol
Aug 10, 1911

"My dear Holand,

"I have only just now read the account in the Norwegian American, *of your lecture at the University of Christiana, and your reply to the criticisms of Hægstad on the inscription. I am struck with the similarity of the case in Norway with the early stage of the discussion in America. In both countries they cite certain evident variations from the high literary style of the date of 1362. In America these have been examined into and no longer offer stumbling blocks, in the acceptance of the record, but in Norway they have advanced no further than these linguistic stumbling blocks. Hægstad's whole argument is about on a par with Flom's and has no more force. It remains for some philologist in Norway (whom Hægstad seems to call a "scientist"), who has not in precipitate judgment already condemned the stone, to dispassionately and thoroughly investigate it. The repetition of the old objections which have been sufficiently removed in America, may at first blush before an audience which is not well informed on this special question, appear sufficient to disprove the inscription, and in Norway, as in America, may carry the day temporarily against the stone. But it is quite likely that, after a little time given to more detailed study by some experts, the truth will appear to be on the side of the runestone. I do not consider the result of the Norway meeting, even as reported by some of the old enemies of the stone in our American papers, as fatal, or even as seriously damaging to the stone, for the same stage of the investigation has been passed through in America.*

"Further, there are certain topographical and physical elements in the case, and in my judgment these weigh so strongly and fundamentally in favor of the stone that it appears to be that the little linguistic irregularities must be made to stand aside or be explained in con-

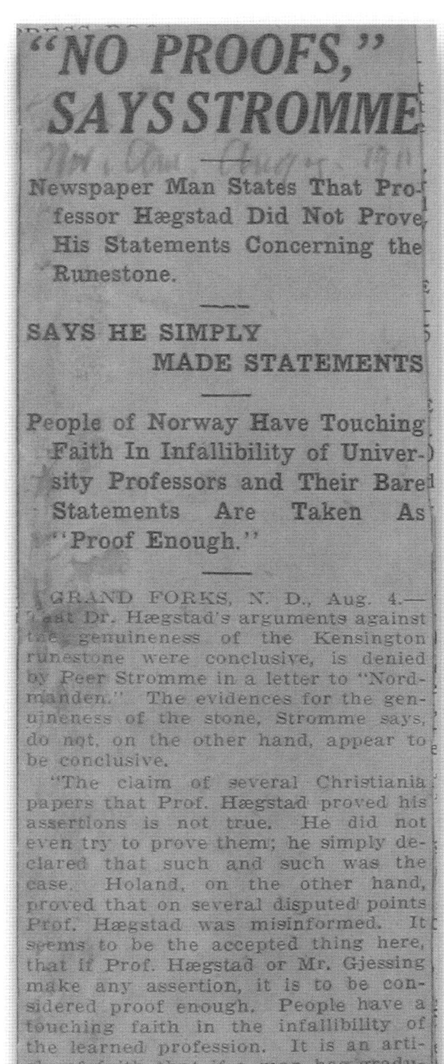

"NO PROOFS," SAYS STROMME

Newspaper Man States That Professor Hægstad Did Not Prove His Statements Concerning the Runestone.

——

SAYS HE SIMPLY MADE STATEMENTS

——

People of Norway Have Touching Faith In Infallibility of University Professors and Their Bare Statements Are Taken As "Proof Enough."

——

GRAND FORKS, N. D., Aug. 4.—That Dr. Hægstad's arguments against the genuineness of the Kensington runestone were conclusive, is denied by Peer Stromme in a letter to "Nordmanden." The evidences for the genuineness of the stone, Stromme says, do not, on the other hand, appear to be conclusive.

"The claim of several Christiania papers that Prof. Hægstad proved his assertions is not true. He did not even try to prove them; he simply declared that such and such was the case. Holand, on the other hand, proved that on several disputed points Prof. Hægstad was misinformed. It seems to be the accepted thing here, that if Prof. Hægstad or Mr. Gjessing make any assertion, it is to be considered proof enough. People have a touching faith in the infallibility of the learned profession. It is an article of faith that if a man has graduated from the University of Norway, he must of necessity know more than all the scientists of America."

formity with these elements. A certain ancient king is said to have given the orders that the tide of the ocean should not advance so as to disturb him. I have no doubt that his hearers acclaimed him great and applauded his wisdom; but it is also said that the king was obliged to remove from his place or be overwhelmed by the superior force that carried the great tide. So with the runestone, as it appears to me, and as it appeared to be when I first gave attention to it, and I stated in my first paper concerning it – there are geological (physical) aspects of the question (which absolutely require that the stone's story be correct). These are fundamental and cannot be set aside by verbal technicalities such as are, to this date, brought up to disprove it. They stand impregnable while a light combat rages about them among the scouts. When the line of battle reaches these fundamental truths they will assert their power. No one has, as yet, attacked those important bulwarks of the rune stone. They are discussed in the report of the Museum committee of the Minnesota Historical Society.

"Still, even as the discussion now stands the…technical linguistic difficulties are apparently removed by your dignified reply to Prof. Hægstad published in the same number of the Norwegian American. *The only lingering uncertainty lies in the word* opdagelse. – i. e. *whether it could have existed in 1362 under the primitive form* opdage, *else being a terminational and unobjectionable suffix.*

"The elementary state of the discussion in Norway is amusing and at the same time vexing, because it goes out to the "Verdict of Norway." On the contrary it is only the loud blast of the first onset of the opponents of the stone who, having already announced their views (viz. Bugge and Hægstad), make a show of bravery in standing by their posts. The same took place in America, where similar loud blasts were found to consist almost wholly of noise, and gave the stone more help than harm after the smoke blew away.

"Again it is quite amusing to read of Hægstad's statement that the stone is <u>composed of a soft material</u>. On the contrary, it is harder than granite, standing next to pure quartzyte in hardness. It is also…sophomoric in Prof. Hægstad's address, in the first instance to scout "flowery discourses and flights into the speculation" and in the next instance to say that all he seeks is "The path of Truth." Thus impugning the contrary to the adherents of the stone. But the adherents of the stone are as fond of Truth and as adverse to flowery discourses as he can be, and they might, perhaps, with more justice accuse him of the very same faults, for he has not always fairly presented the truth, and has himself resorted to flowery language with all its stealthy sting.

I think that the stone will withstand these loud preliminary skirmishes in Norway, and when the sober, thoughtful investigators of that country have had time to carefully poise the issue on the real evidence, the voice of Norway will be heard in defense of the stone, and finally the Norwegians, whether in America or in the old country, will approve and boast of the Kensington rune stone as their most valuable historic relic.

"Very truly

"N. H. Winchell"

September/October – Holand writes an article entitled "The Kensington Runestone Abroad" in Records of the Past (Washington, D.C., 10: 260-71). In this article Holand brags about how smart he is compared to the Scandinavian runologists and linguists he had met.

September 8 – P. P. Iverslie writes a seven-page, typed, single-spaced letter to Professor Julius Olson in Madison, Wisconsin, where he strongly attacked Professor Olson for statements against the Kensington Rune Stone in a recent interview.

"Victory!" There is absolutely nothing new against the authenticity of the inscription brought to light. Nothing better has yet appeared on that side then the article of the student Gjessing.

Respectfully,

P. P. Iverslie.

Excerpt from a typed copy of a letter written by P. P. Iverslie to Professor Julius Olson that appeared in the *Norwegian American* on September 8, 1911. (Minnesota Historical Society)

October – P.P. Iverslie wrote an article entitled, "Runestenen: Nagtet Optagelse in Minneapolis Tichande" in Kvartalskrift, 7: 6-11.

The March to Authenticity (1912 to 1949)

The years from 1912 to 1949 were marked by a slow but steady march toward scholarly acceptance, led by the Stone's champion, Hjalmar Holand. He gave impassioned lectures, wrote articles, and published three books. Ultimately, he was successful in achieving a level of acceptance when the Kensington Rune Stone was displayed for a year at the Smithsonian Institution as a genuine artifact. Along with the rest of the world, Olof Ohman and his family did the best they could through World War I, the Depression, and World War II.

1912 – Olof Ohman travels to Forsa, Hälsingland, Sweden, to visit his relatives. Inside the lid of the trunk he writes in Swedish, "Olof Ohman's America coffin, on his last trip to the home country 1912."

Inside the lid of the trunk that Olof used to carry his belongings on a visit to Sweden is the year (1912) he took the trip. (SFW)

1913

July – J. J. Skørdalsvold publishes a seven-page article called "Kensingtonstenen," in the Norwegian journal, *Kvartalskrift*. This article was favorable toward authenticity with regard to the language on the stone.

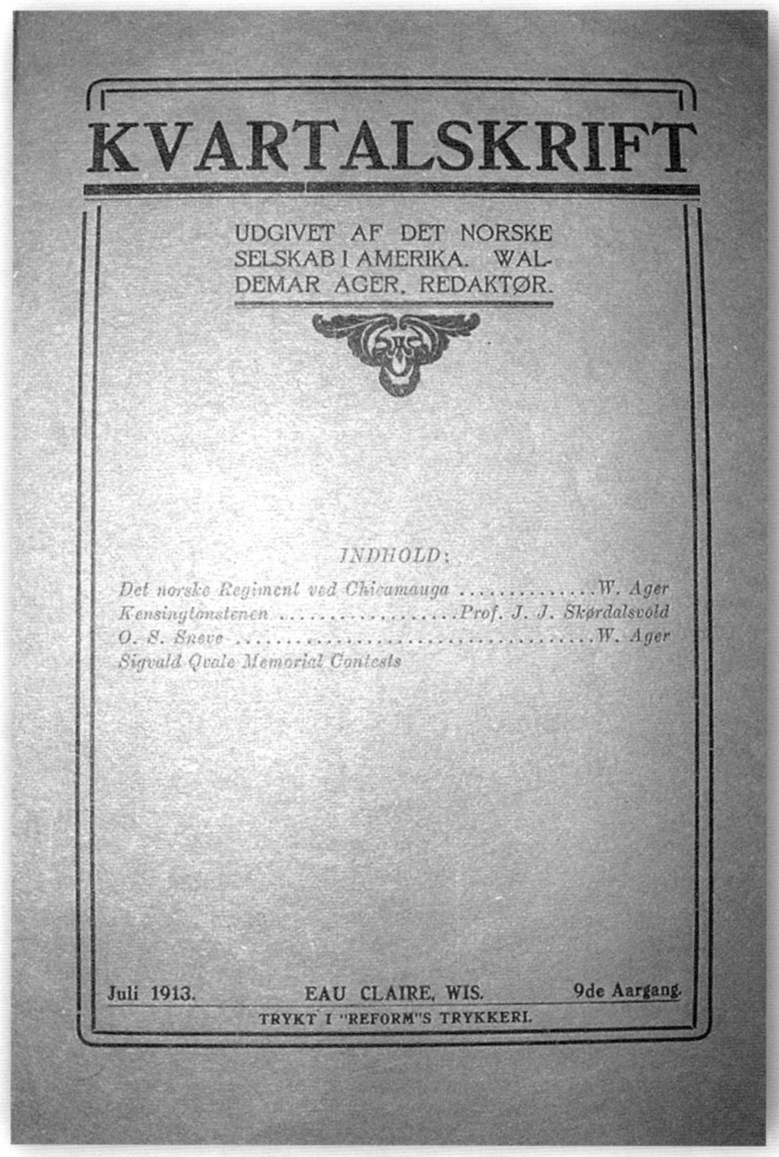

The cover page to the July, 1913 issue of the Scandinavian journal called *Kvartalskrift*. Included is a seven-page paper about the Kensington Rune Stone written in Norwegian by Professor J. J. Skørdalsvold. This document was one of many that Winchell had translated. Winchell arranged for all Scandinavian language documents pertaining to the Kensington Rune Stone to be translated into English. Later arguments by Wahlgren that Winchell could not read these documents were baseless. (Minnesota Historical Society)

November 24 – N. H. Winchell writes a letter to Professor J. J. Skørdalsvold, thanking him for sending an English translation of Skørdalsvold's July, 1913 *Kvartalskrift* article about the Rune Stone.

St. Paul, Minn.
Nov. 24, 1913.

Prof. J. J. Skordalsvold,

919-21 Ave. So.

Minneapolis, Minn.

My dear Sir:-

Your article, translated into English, has just been received, and I enclose herewith my check for $7.00 which is the sum you specified, for the translation.

Your article is a distinct contribution to the discussion, and will carry weight with American as well as Furpean scholars, and I wish to thank you, in the name of the committee of the Historical Society, for your careful consideration of some of the objections which have been brought against the stone. It requires only candid and critical consideration of the case to enable any one with unprejudiced mind to discover quickly that no objection of permanent validity has as yet been produced against the stone. Flom's objections especially, when not actual contributions to the genuineness of the stone, the opposite of his intention, seem to me to have little or no bearing on those points which are important and crucial in such an investigation, and on Breda and Flom most of the European objection has been built up--a mountain raised from a mole-hill.

As time elapses passion will subside, and the true issues will be perceived by fresh discussions such as yours, and the final result will be based on reason rather than on rage.

The Committee of the Historical Society are following the instructions if the executive council, and are cautiously continuing the research, with the intention of rendering a final report in due time.

With renewed expression of thanks

Very truly,

N. H. Winchell

The letter from Professor N. H. Winchell to Professor J. J. Skørdalsvold, sent on November 24, 1913. (Minnesota Historical Society)

1914

January – P.P. Iverslie writes an article entitled, "The Kensington Stone and Vinland's relation" in Kvartalskrift, 10: 3-10.

May 2 – Professor N. H. Winchell dies in a hospital in Minneapolis, Minnesota at the age of 75.

July 10 – Olof Ohman arrives back in the United States after crossing the Atlantic on the passenger ship "Lusitania."

The passenger record for Olof Ohman, who traveled back to the United States from Sweden aboard the ship Lusitania in July 1914. (All rights reserved. www.ellisisland.org) (Used by permission.)

Name.	Ohman, Olof
Ethnicity:	U.S. citizen
Place of Residence.	Kensington, Minn.
Date of Arrival:	July 10, 1914
Age on Arrival:	60y
Gender:	M
Marital Status.	M
Ship of Travel:	Lusitania
Port of Departure.	Liverpool, England, UK

A U.S. citizen

1916

May 15 – Warren Upham visits Olof Ohman and his family in Kensington for the first time.

This entry was made into Warren Upham's field notebook (Page 61) after visiting the Ohman farm in Kensington, Minnesota, on May 15, 1916.
"Very muddy roads, and raining on way out, I walked 3 ¹/₂ ms. each way; was at Mr. O's house an hour, 1:10 to 2:10. Saw Mr. and Mrs. O., Olof E., older son, and Arthur, a son about 25 years old, younger that the one who noticed the runes."

May 24 – Warren Upham makes an entry in the letterpress book about his visit to the Ohman farm on May 15.

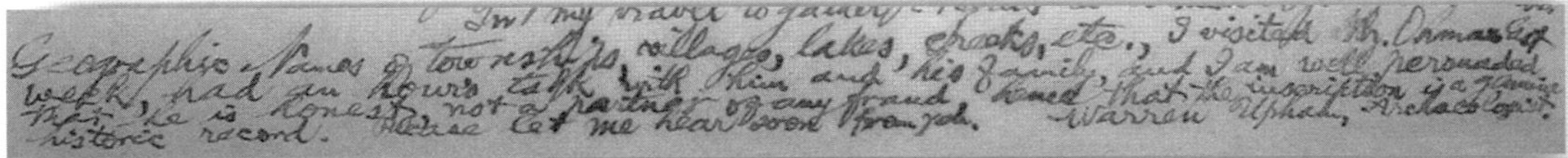

Entry into MHS archives letterpress book, Volume 19, page 875, by the Museum Committee Secretary Warren Upham, to Professor Andrew Fossum, on May 24, 1916. (Minnesota Historical Society)
"I visited Mr. Ohman last week, had an hour's talk with him and his family, and I am well persuaded that he is honest, not a partner of any fraud, hence that the inscription is a genuine historic record."

June 14 – Warren Upham writes to Hjalmar Holand, Professor Andrew Fossum, Dr. Knute Hoegh, the Honorable Laurits S. Swenson, and Olof Ohman about his trip to Kensington, saying he is convinced of Ohman's honesty, that he believes Ohman was not a participant in any fraud, and that the Stone is genuine.

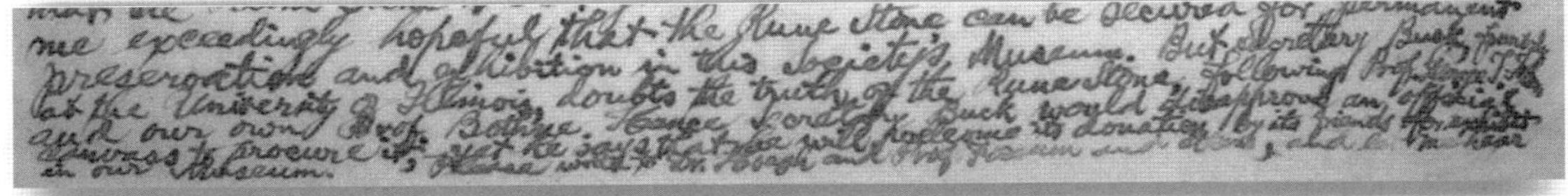

Entry into MHS archives letterpress book, Volume 19, page 923, by the Museum Committee Secretary Warren Upham, to Hjalmar Holand on June 14, 1916. (Minnesota Historical Society)
"Recently I had my first opportunity to visit Kensington and to talk with Mr. Ohman and his family. As a result, I feel confident that he is honest, not a partner or participant in any fraud, hence I am strongly confirmed in my belief that Prof. Winchell and our Museum Committee are right in accepting the Rune Stone as a true record."

October 14 – Warren Upham writes to Hjalmar Holand that he thinks the Stone is authentic, and that he urges the Minnesota Historical Society to renew negotiations aimed at acquiring it.

Entry into MHS archives letterpress book, Volume 19, page 911, by the Museum Committee Secretary Warren Upham, to Hjalmar Holand on October 14, 1916. (Minnesota Historical Society)
"But Secretary Buck, formerly at the University of Illinois, doubts the truth of the Rune Stone, following Prof. George T. Flom and our own Professor Bothne. Hence Secretary Buck would disapprove an official canvass to procure it, yet he says he will welcome its donations by its friends for exhibit in our museum. Please write to Dr. Hoegh and Prof. Fossum and ask, and let me hear."

1919

January – P.P. Iverslie writes an article entitled, "The Stone in Douglas County" in Kvartalskrift, 15: 16-25.

January 7 – Oscar Ohman dies of acute meningitis in Solem Township at the age of 19.

Oscar Ohman's death certificate was issued to the Ohman family on November 19, 1980. The death date on the certificate is different than the date on Oscar's tombstone. (Courtesy of the Ohman Family)

No. 3013—Certified Copy of Death Register in Douglas County, State of Minnesota. Miller-Davis Co., Minneapolis

No.	Date of Death			NAME OF DECEASED	Sex	Color	Married, Single or Widowed	AGE		
	Month	Day	Year					Years	Months	Days
	Jan.	8	1917	Oskar Fredrick Ohman	M	W	S	19	8	24

PLACE OF BIRTH (Township or City)	Date of Arrival in Minnesota			Disease or Cause of Death	PLACE OF DEATH (Township or City)
	Month	Day	Year		
Minn.	–	–	–	LaGuppe Acute meningitis	Solem Twp.

OCCUPATION	NAMES AND BIRTHPLACES OF PARENTS		When Registered		
	Names	Birthplace	Month	Day	Year
Farmer	Olof Ohman	Sweden			
	Karin Donaldson	Sweden	1	12	17

State of Minnesota,
County of Douglas

In District Court of Said County

I, Hazel I. Holt , *Clerk of the District Court in and for said County and State aforesaid, do hereby certify that the foregoing is a full and complete transcript of the entries appearing of record in the Register of Deaths now remaining in my said office relative to the death of the said* Oskar Fredrick Ohman *and of the whole thereof.*

WITNESS my hand and the seal of said Court hereto affixed at Alexandria *, Minn., this* 19th *day of* November *A. D. 19* 80

HAZEL I. HOLT , *Clerk*

By *Cynthia F. May* , *Deputy*

The tombstone of Oscar Ohman, with the incorrect death date (Oscar died in 1917), is located in the Solem Township Cemetery near Kensington, Minnesota. (SFW)

1923

March 6 – Hjalmar Holand writes to Olof Ohman and said he would pay him 10% of the proceeds if he ever sells the Stone.

The date on page 1, and Holand's signature on page 6 of his letter to Olof Ohman. (Courtesy of the Ohman Family)

1925 – The Hedberg letter written on January 1, 1899 was found alone in the office of the president of the University of Minnesota. The letter was then sent to the Minnesota Historical Society. A note reported the transfer of the letter in *Minnesota History* in 1925, *"A letter reporting the findings of the Kensington Rune Stone written by J.P. Hedberg on January 1, 1899, has been turned over to the society by Mr. Rodney West, registrar of the University of Minnesota."*

1927

April 14 – An article appears in the *Park Region Echo* announcing plans to build a 204´ tall monument on the spot where the Kensington Rune Stone was found.

(Courtesy of the *Echo Press*, Alexandria, Minnesota. All rights reserved. Used by permission.)

April 25 – Olof Ohman writes a letter to relatives in Sweden notifying them of the monument plans.

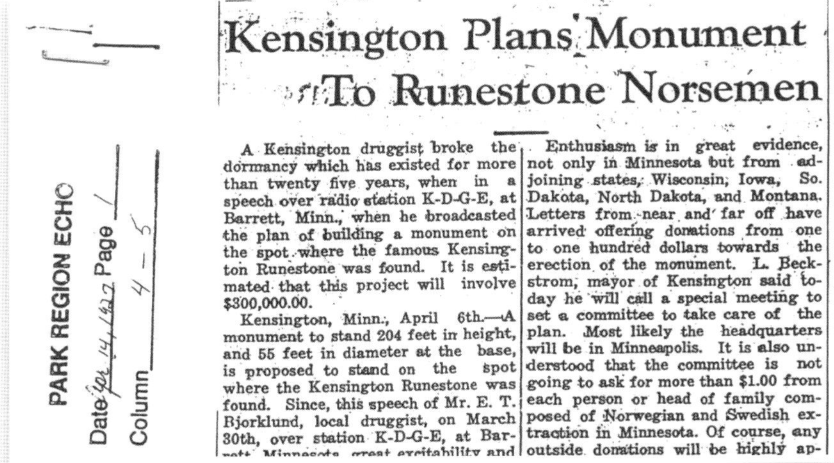

Kensington Plans Monument To Runestone Norsemen

A Kensington druggist broke the dormancy which has existed for more than twenty five years, when in a speech over radio station K-D-G-E, at Barrett, Minn., when he broadcasted the plan of building a monument on the spot where the famous Kensington Runestone was found. It is estimated that this project will involve $300,000.00.

Kensington, Minn., April 6th.—A monument to stand 204 feet in height, and 55 feet in diameter at the base, is proposed to stand on the spot where the Kensington Runestone was found. Since, this speech of Mr. E. T. Bjorklund, local druggist, on March 30th, over station K-D-G-E, at Barrett, Minnesota, great excitability and

Enthusiasm is in great evidence, not only in Minnesota but from adjoining states, Wisconsin, Iowa, So. Dakota, North Dakota, and Montana. Letters from near and far off have arrived offering donations from one to one hundred dollars towards the erection of the monument. L. Beckstrom, mayor of Kensington said today he will call a special meeting to set a committee to take care of the plan. Most likely the headquarters will be in Minneapolis. It is also understood that the committee is not going to ask for more than $1.00 from each person or head of family composed of Norwegian and Swedish extraction in Minnesota. Of course, any outside donations will be highly ap-

June 1 – A rally was held at the Fahlin farm on Oscar Lake to start the monument campaign.

Olof Ohman posed with the Rune Stone during a rally at Oscar Lake on June 1, 1927. L to R: Gilbert Hanson, Olof Ohman, and John Ecklund. (Photograph courtesy of the Ohman Family)

Several prominent individuals attended the June 1 rally for the Kensington Rune Stone at Oscar Lake. L to R: (Back row) Reverend Carl G. Zaar, Reverend Johns Hog, Reverend John Daniels, Lewis Williams, and unknown. (Front row) Iver Lee, Olof Ohman, Hjalmar Holand, and Edwin Bjorkland. (Photograph courtesy of the Runestone Museum)

This beginning portion of a longer article about the rally at Oscar Lake appeared in the *Park Region Echo* on June 2, 1927. (©*Echo Press*, Alexandria, Minnesota. All rights reserved. Used by permission.)

July 28 – An article in the Alexandria *Park Region Echo* announces the articles of incorporation had been filed, forming the Kensington Rune Stone Foundation, which planned to build the proposed 204′ monument.

November 29 – About 1,000 people attend a festival at the Armory in Alexandria, Minnesota to raise money and awareness for the Kensington Rune Stone Memorial at the discovery site on the Ohman farm. Speakers include Mayor H. W. Ludke; Honorable A.

Several Thousand People at Oscar Lake See Rune-stone Displayed

The weatherman smiled on the efforts of the Kensington boosters Wednesday to hold a huge rally for the purpose of starting the campaign to build a $300,000 monument on the site of the finding of that document in stone which tells of a Viking exploration to the vicinity of Kensington, and the first really fine day for weeks brought an immense crowd to the Fahlin farm on Oscar Lake to see the famous runestone and hear noted speakers tell its history and what it means. Only a guess can be made as to the size of the crowd, but the long double lines of autos parked across fields in every direction, and around the farm buildings and on the lakeshore would indicate that the expectations of the boosters that a crowd of 5,000 people would be on hand seemed to have been more than realized.

G. Sorlie, the governor of North Dakota; Dr. J. A. O. Stub, pastor of the Central Lutheran Church of Minneapolis; Victor Lawson, editor of the *Willmar Tribune*, Reverend M. Casper Johnshoy; Constant Larson; Gunnar Bjornson; and Hjalmar Holand. Olof Ohman is also present at the festival.

December 4 – Olof Ohman writes a letter to relatives in Sweden telling them about the events at Oscar Lake in June.

This article published on July 28, 1927, about the proposed monument at the Kensington Rune Stone discovery site included an artist's drawing of the monument. (©*Echo Press*, Alexandria, Minnesota. All rights reserved. Used by permission.)

Citizen and Alexandria Post News

TA, THURSDAY, JULY 28, 1927

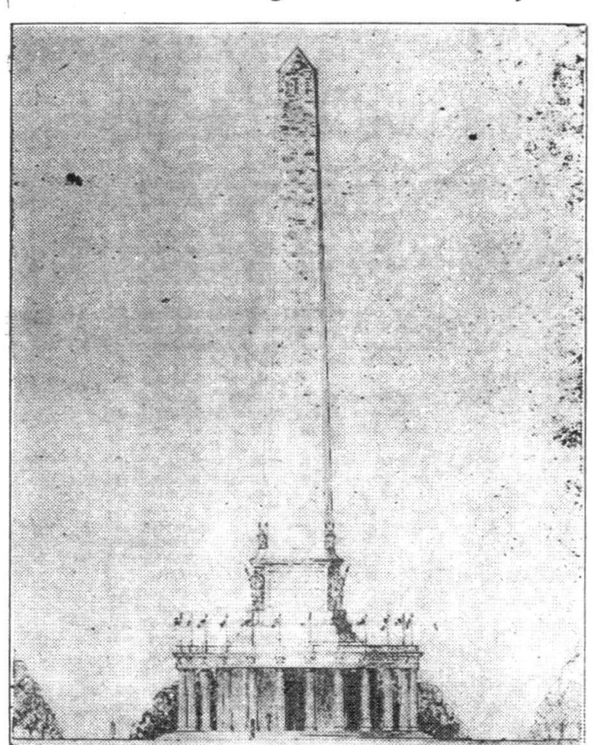

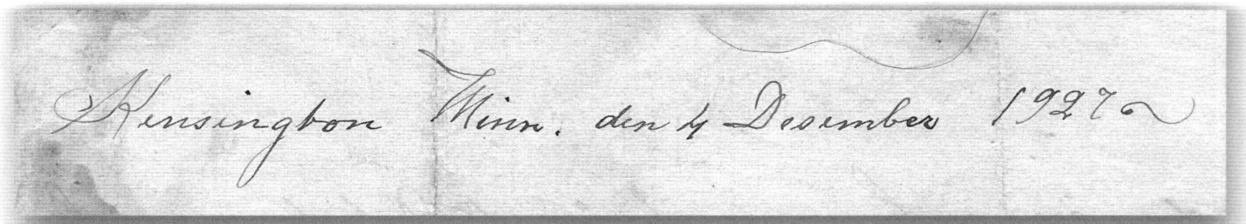

The city and date at the top of the first page of the letter Olof Ohman wrote to his relatives in Sweden on December 4, 1927. He wrote how pleased he was that after twenty-nine years a monument was to be erected on the site where the Stone was found. (Courtesy of the Ohman Relatives Assocation)

1928

Jaunary 1 – Hjalmar Holand writes a letter to Olof Ohman discussing financial terms regarding the Kensington Rune Stone.

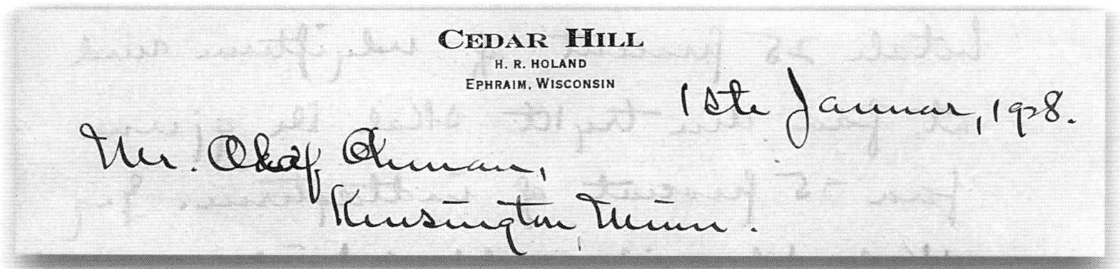

The beginning of the letter Hjalmar Holand wrote to Olof Ohman on January 1, 1928. (Courtesy of the Ohman Family)

January 17 – Hjalmar Holand writes another letter to Olof Ohman discussing financial terms regarding the Kensington Rune Stone.

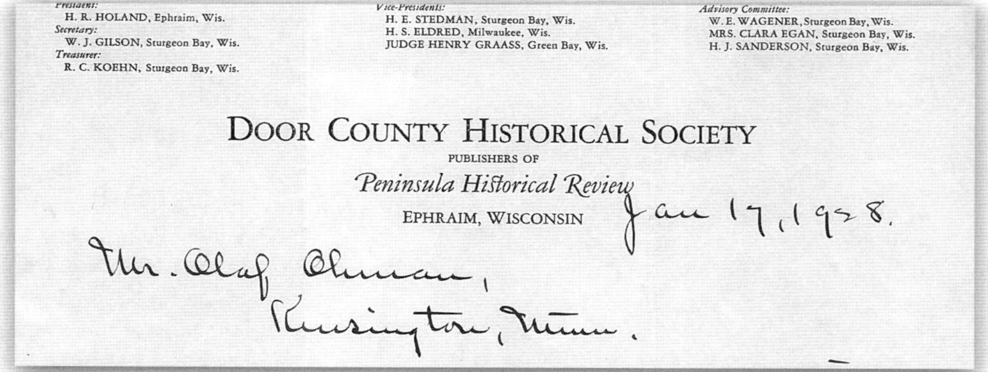

The beginning of the letter Hjalmar Holand wrote to Olof Ohman on January 17, 1928. (Courtesy of the Ohman Family)

1929

July 17 — David Ohman, son of Olof and Karin Ohman, committs suicide at the home where he was raised by shooting himself in the head with a small caliber rifle. He was reportedly despondent over his confinement to a wheelchair due to paralysis below the waist caused by a tumor on his spine.

The tombstone of David Ohman, in the Solem Township Cemetery near Kensington. (SFW)

(Left) Obituary for David Ohman from page 3 of the *Park Region Echo* newspaper on July 25, 1929. (©*Echo Press*, Alexandria, Minnesota. All rights reserved. Used by permission.)

DAVID EDWIN OHMAN

David Edwin Ohman died on Wednesday of last week, following a lingering illness of tumor of the spine from which he has suffered for the past three years. The past few months his condition was such that he was unable to use his legs and was only able to be about with the aid of a wheel-chair. Two years ago he consulted specialists in Minneapolis and also submitted to an examination at the Mayo clinic at Rochester, but his condition grew gradually worse until the end. The funeral was held from the home at 2 o'clock on Saturday afternoon with Rev. J. A. Vaage of Farwell officiating. The male quartet from Kensington sang, "Abide With Me," and Rev. Vaage sang a vocal solo. He leaves the following relatives to mourn his untimely death: his father, Ole Ohman, and his mother, his brothers, Arthur and John, living at home, and Edward and William, of Appam, N. Dak., and Olof of Viking, Alta., Canada, and two sisters, Mrs. Joel Carlson of Minneapolis and Mrs. Ida Kolberg of Detroit, Mich. All of the brothers were present and also Mrs. Carlson, but Mrs. Kolberg was absent. David was born on August 12, 1902, and was 26 years, 11 months, and 5 days old at the time of death. He had lived on the farm at home practically all his life. Interment was made in the Solem cenetery.

Ohman Boy Ends Life With Shot from Rifl

Friends of the Ohman family, prominent Solem township folks, we shocked to learn last week that Dav F. Ohman, son of Mr. and Mrs. O Ohman, had committed suicide about six o'clock Wednesday evenin

The unfortunate young man h been paralyzed from the waist dow caused by a tumor on the spine, i the past six months, and it is thoug that his mind became deranged b cause of the incurable disease fr which he suffered. While the rest the family were away from the hou he wheeled himself in the wheel ch he had to use, out into an entry wh a small calibre rifle hung on the w placed the butt of the rifle on the fl and the muzzle against his head, a reached down and pulled the trigg

An obituary notice will be found another page of this issue.

An article from page 1 of the *Park Region Echo* newspaper on July 25, 1929. (©*Echo Press*, Alexandria, Minnesota. All rights reserved. Used by permission.)

1932 – Hjalmar Holand publishes his first book about the Rune Stone, titled, *The Kensington Stone.*

Both Hjalmar Holand and Olof Ohman personally signed, most likely at different times, this copy of Holand's 1932 book, "The Kensington Stone."

1934 – Hjalmar Holand's home in Ephraim, Wisconsin burns to the ground, resulting in the loss of all of his documents and personal items. Photographs, letters, affidavits, and all other documents related to his research on the Rune Stone were destroyed.

Warren Upham dies at the age of 84.

The tombstone of Warren Upham, who is buried at Hillside Cemetery in Minneapolis, Minnesota. (SFW)

1935

August 27 – Olof Ohman dies at his home. He is 80 years old.

Obituary for Olof Ohman from page 3 of the September 5, 1935 *Park Region Echo.* (©*Echo Press,* Alexandria, Minnesota. All rights reserved. Used by permission.)

OLAF OHMAN

Olof Ohman of Kensington passed away Tuesday, August 27th at his home from a short illness.

He was born Octiber 10, 1854 in Hakingland, Sweden, and came to America in 1879. He was united in marriage in 1886 to Karin Danielson of Sweden and settled near Kensington where he has made his home since.

His wife and seven children survive, besides two grandchildren and one brother in Sweden.

Funeral services were held Friday, August 30 at Solum church, Rev. B. G. Holmes officiating.

Funeral services were conducted for Olof Ohman Friday at 1:30 from the home and at 2:00 from the Solem church. Rev. B. G. Holmes officiated. The pall bearers were Martin Molde, Haaken Peterson, John Bergquist, Pete Backlund, A. Hagstrom, Adolph Wicklund. Olof Ohman has been a resident of Solem township the past 43 years and died Tuesday, August 27.

Mr. Ohman was born October 10, 1854 at Nora, Halsingland, Sweden. He left his native land in 1879, coming to the United States and locating in Iowa. He was united in marriage in 1886 to Karren Dannelson and in 1892 they came to Douglas county, settling on a farm in Solem township.

Surviving their father are five sons, Olof of Whiting, Alberta, Canada, Edward of Appman, N. D., Arthur and John at home and William at Pinewood, Minn.; two daughters, Mrs. Joe Carlson of Minneapolis and Mrs. Ida Kolberg of Michigan. Four children preceded him in death.

Ole Ohman, well known and highly respected citizen of Solem township, passed away at his farm home three miles north of Kensington on Tuesday morning, August 27, at the ago of 80 years and ten months. Funeral services were held at the Solem church Friday afternoon, attended by a large number of relatives and friends. He was laid to rest beside his son in the church cemetery.

1940 – Hjalmar Holand publishes his second book about the Rune Stone, *Westward from Vinland.*

1944 – Erik Noreen writes a paper about the Kensington Rune Stone titled, *Amerikanska Runor* (American Runes).

1946 – Hjalmar Holand publishes his third book about the Rune Stone, *America 1355-1364: A New Chapter in Pre-Columbian History.*

1947

November 19 – Karin Ohman dies at her home. She is 86.

The obituary for Karin Ohman from page 7 of the *Park Region Echo* newspaper of November 27, 1947. (©*Echo Press,* Alexandria, Minnesota. All rights reserved. Used by permission.)

Mrs. Karin Ohman Is Buried Sunday At Kensington Rites

Funeral services were held on Sunday afternoon, Nov. 23, at Kensington for Mrs. Karin Ohman, with Rev. A. J Sheldahl of Evansville, officiating.

Services were held at the home at 1:30 p.m., followed by regular services at the Solem Lutheran church. Music was furnished by Mrs. Louis Johnson, organist, assisted by Aron Nelson as soloist.

Interment was in the Solem cemetery. The pallbearers were, Pete Backlund, Arthur Norlien, Gust Swanson, Adolph Wicklund, Martin Molde and Walter Broden

Mrs. Ohman passed away Wednesday, Nov. 18th, at 2:30 p. m. at her home in Solem township.

She was born in Forsa, Helsingland, Sweden, Jan. 2nd, 1862, and was nearly 86 years old at the time of her death.

Mrs. Ohman came to Bishop, Ill., in 1885 and a year later to Minnesota where she married Olof Ohman and settled on the farm in Solem township which was her home until she passed away.

She is survived by five sons and two daughters, Olof, Edward, William, Arthur and John and Mrs. Joel Carlson and Mrs. A. Kolberg. Her husband and two sons preceded her in death, also three sisters and one brother

The tombstone of Karin Ohman, located in the Solem Township Cemetery near Kensington, Minnesota. (SFW)

1948

February 17 – The Kensington Rune Stone is displayed at the Smithsonian Institution until February 25, 1949.

June 29 – Edward Ohman is interviewed for an article that appears in the *Fargo Forum* newspaper. Edward was in the Veterans hospital for a recurring illness. He planned to visit the farm in Kensington upon his release, to see his brothers Art and John, and his sister Manda.

Edward Ohman was interviewed for an article that appeared in the *Fargo Forum* newspaper on June 29, 1948. (Courtesy of *Fargo* (ND) *Forum*, all rights reserved. Used by permission.)

The article went on to say: "'The last time I was there, I pounded an iron pipe into the ground on the spot, but I am afraid that will eventually rot away,' he said, 'I hope now that we can place a stone marker on the spot and when I arrive home I shall talk it over with my brothers and sister. The story that we used it for a doorstep at our granary is an untruth,' he said, 'My father flopped it up with a mattock and I dusted it off and noticed the characters. We took it home, cleaned it up and set it in a shed in front of the granary. H. R. Holand of Ephraim, Wisconsin, took it to make a study of the characters. He wrote two books about it. We eventually lost title to it. For a long time it was displayed in a case in Alexandria, Minnesota.'

"During his boyhood days, (Edward) Ohman developed an intense dislike for the Stone and ran away and hid when asked to talk about it. The reason was that so many persons questioned and cross-questioned him about it many of them scholars and historians some of whom believed he and his father might possibly have carved the characters in the stone to win fame and notoriety. Ohman's eyes still blaze as he recalls the efforts of these doubting Thomases to undermine the truth of the find. 'To think that my father and I could do such a thing is utterly ridiculous,' he said. 'We never knew anything about runic characters.'

There were two other brothers in addition to Edward, Art, and John: Olof of Viking, Alberta, Canada; and William, of Pinewood, Minnesota."

September – The Kensington Rune Stone is featured in the September issue of *National Geographic Magazine*, in an article that included a photograph of Niel M. Judd, Curator of Archaeology at the Smithsonian Institution.

A photograph from the September, 1948 issue of *National Geographic Magazine*. (Copyright B. Anthony Stewart/National Geographic Image Collection.)

November 18 – Johannes Brøndsted delivered a report to the American Scandinavian Foundation where he summarized his opinion, *"After long and close study I am personally inclined to believe that this famous runic monument is genuine. But I am an archaeologist, and to my mind, the deciding point in this question lies with the philologists.... In my opinion no archaeological argument speaks against the stone."*

1949

March 12 – Dr. M. W. Stirling, Director of the Bureau of American Ethnology at the Smithsonian Institution, was quoted in the newspaper *Washington Times-Herald* as saying, "[The Kensington Rune Stone] is probably the most important archaeological object yet found in North America."

The Dustbin of History (1949 to 1982)

The Kensington Rune Stone's 1949 display as a genuine artifact at the Smithsonian Institution triggered a strong backlash against the inscription from linguists and runologists in America and Scandinavia. Papers and books written by Erik Wahlgren in 1958, and by Theodore Blegen in 1968, effectively buried the Stone as a hoax in the minds of the public. There was a storm of negativity for more than thirty years, with virtually no one able to bring balance to the discussion. This period took its toll on the Ohman family as well.

1949

October 8 – J. A. Holvik visits the Ohman farm and spoke with Amanda Ohman. She loans him a family scrapbook along with the Rosander book (*Den Kunskapsrike Skolmästaren*), on the condition that he return it.

October 16 – A story appears in the *Minneapolis Tribune* quoting J. A. Holvik as saying the Stone was blank when taken from the ground, and carved at a later date by the discoverer, Olof Ohman.

New Evidence Proves Runestone Fake, Expert Says; Investigation Demanded

A claim that new evidence casts doubt on the authenticity of the Kensington runestone was made Saturday.

J. A. Holvik, professor of Norwegian at Concordia college, Moorhead, Minn., wrote Dr. Harold Cater of the Minnesota Historical society that he believes a re-investigation of the stone is "imperative."

2 RUNES QUESTIONED

The new evidence, he wrote Cater, shows that the runestone was blank when taken from the ground, and the inscription carved at a later date by Olof Ohman, "a man of unusual learning and interests, for motives which can only be guessed at now."

Holvik said that the society's files hold a document that is supposedly the first copy of the stone's inscription, but actually an early draft of the inscription Ohman intended to place on the stone. Holvik said two alphabet characters used in the inscription are "freak" characters, or "modern" runes.

The Moorhead man also said three affidavits sworn to in 1909 concerning the stone, but not appearing in the society's report, also are open to question.

The affidavits give August as the date the stone was found, although the society's "Museum Committee Report" gives the month as November, Holvik said.

Holvik also submitted to the society a scrapbook and a history, both in Ohman's possession in 1898, which he received from Ohman's widow. The history contains two runic alphabets which contain all of the real rune characters appearing in the stone's inscription.

'PRACTICE' CITED

The home-bound volume, Holvik said, shows indications of its cover having been used to practice the writing of one particular character.

Other variations from the usual usage of characters are cited by Holvik as reasons for the society to appoint a commission of experts to examine the new evidence which he submitted.

Eight days after J. A. Holvik visited the Ohman farm and borrowed a scrapbook and the Rosander book from Amanda Ohman, this article appeared in the *Minneapolis Tribune*. (Copyright 2005 *Star Tribune*. Republished with permission of *Star Tribune*, Minneapolis-St. Paul. No further republication or redistribution is permitted without the written consent of the *Star Tribune*.)

Amanda Ohman sends a letter to Professor Holvik, and returns his five dollar check, writing that she doesn't want to sell the Rosander book and that he should return it at once.

November 14 – After reading the October 16 *Minneapolis Tribune* article, Willie L. Sarsland of Ludlow, South Dakota, writes a letter to Dr. Harold Cater, then director at the Minnesota Historical Society. Mr. Sarsland writes that he was threshing at the Ohman farm the day the Stone was found and helped Olof, "…remove some of the shale and deposits…" from the inscription. He also says, "There is a lot more I can tell you about the finding, etc. of this stone. So I know the evidence you have received is false." (See complete Sarsland letter page 165-166)

November 17 – Minnesota Historical Society Director Dr. Harold Cater asks the Curator of Newspapers at the Society, Willoughby Babcock, to analyze the Willie Sarsland letter.

November 28 – Willoughby Babcock sends a memo to Dr. Harold Cater with his analysis of the Sarsland letter and writes, *"My reaction to the Sarsland letter is distinctly unfavorable."*

November 29 – Dr. Harold Cater sends a memo to Johan Holvik that included the Sarsland letter and the Willoughby Babcock analysis.

December 2 – Johan Holvik writes back to Dr. Harold Cater that he has received the Sarsland letter and the Babcock analysis.

December 28 – Edward Ohman, 61 years old at the time, is interviewed by Ralph S. Thornton, Modridge S. Robb, and Bergmann Richards at the Science Museum in St. Paul, Minnesota, about the discovery of the Kensington Rune Stone.

Edward Ohman was interviewed about the Kensington Rune Stone on December 28, 1949. This photograph and article appeared in the *Minneapolis Morning Tribune* newspaper on December 29, 1949. (Copyright 2005 *Star Tribune*. Republished with permission of *Star Tribune*, Minneapolis-St. Paul. No further republication or redistribution is permitted without the written consent of the *Star Tribune*.)

1950

January 16 – Edward Ohman writes a letter to Holvik, asking him to return the scrapbook and the Rosander book he had borrowed from Amanda Ohman on October 8, 1949.

Edward Ohman's letter to J. A. Holvik on January 16, 1950. (Minnesota Historical Society)

"Kensington Minn.
1-16-50

"Mr. J. A. Holvik
Dear Sir

"Am writing you a few lines regarding the scrapbook and also the other book. Would like awful well to get them back as soon as possible. Wishing you a happy new year.

"Yours truly,

"Edward Ohman
Kensington, Minn."

February 24 – In response to comments made by Professor A. W. Brøgger, Harold S. Langland writes an article that was published in the *Norwegian Post* newspaper. Concerning the weathering of the runes, Langland said:

> *"…with great care I studied the appearance of the surface of the stone and interior surfaces of the runic letters. Having had an engineer's scientific training, including chemistry and physics, and considerable experience on the prairies and lakes of Minnesota, I am not without some knowledge of the weathering of stone surfaces. I observed the perfectly clear evidence of newly scratched marks on the stone; some of these scratches were on the surface and some were down in the runic grooves. They were very obvious, as the stone's outer surface is many shades darker than the interior. These scratches were recently made, that is, within a much shorter time than the runes themselves. The inner surfaces of the runes were as dark and weathered as the stone's exterior surface; it goes beyond the bounds of sound reasoning that those characters could have been*

recently cut and then have weathered down to the color of the stone's exterior surface in a few years.

February 27 – Edward Ohman writes a second letter to J. A. Holvik, again asking him to return the scrapbook and the Rosander book he had borrowed from Amanda Ohman on October 8, 1949.

The second letter that Edward Ohman wrote to J. A. Holvik on asking for the return of the scrap-book and Almquist book he had previously borrowed. (Minnesota Historical Society)

"Kensington, Minn.
2-27-5[0]

"Prof. J. A. Holvik

"Dear Sir,

"I wrote you 1-16-50 regarding the scrapbook and also that Sweedis (sic) book, but have not heard from you, it seems to me you had them so long a time now that you would get all the knowledge you want out of them books. So I wish you would send them as soon as possible.

"Yours truly,

"Edward Ohman
Kensington, Minn."

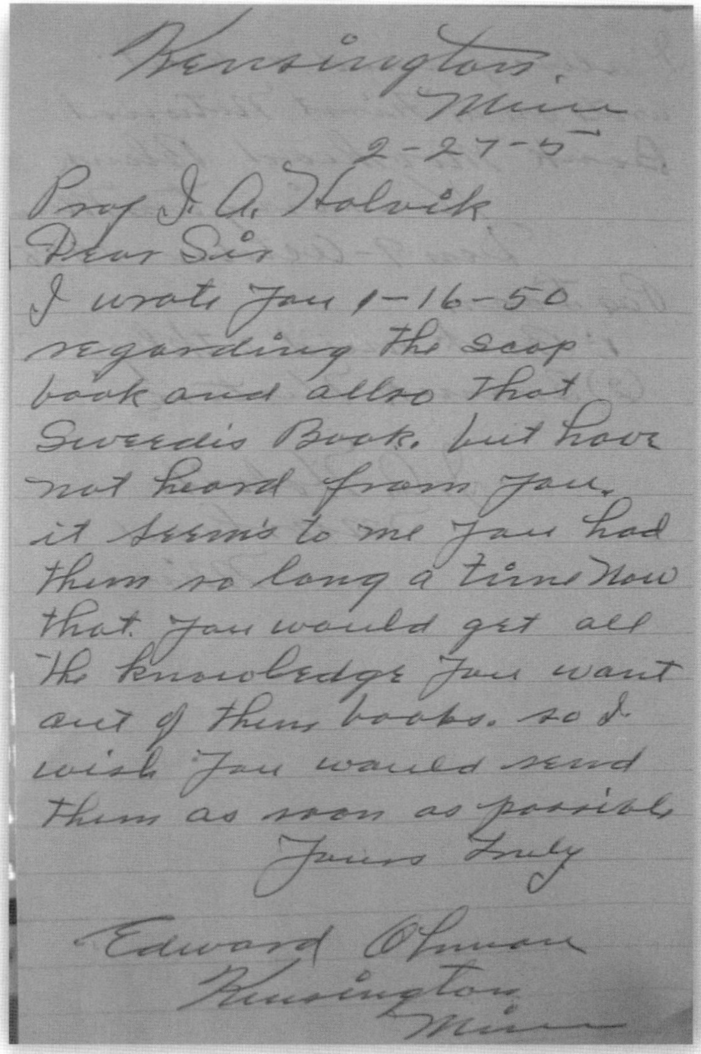

March 1 – Holvik writes a letter to Willoughby Babcock, sarcastically asking him to follow up on the Sarsland letter.

July – Sivert N. Hagen publishes an article titled, "The Kensington Runic Inscription," in *Speculum: A Journal of Medieval Studies.*

December 9 – Edward Ohman dies in Appam, North Dakota, at the age of 62.

Edward Ohman's obituary as it appeared in the *Williston Herald* on December 11, 1950.

APPAM VETERAN DIES SATURDAY

Edward Carl Ohman, 62, of Appam died in a local hospital Saturday, Dec. 9. He had been a resident of that vicinity since 1917.

Funeral services were held this afternoon in Our Redeemer's Lutheran church in Williston, with burial in Riverview cemetery. Rev Clarence Framstad officiated.

Lt. Jerry Wilder was in charge of the firing squad, with Sgt. Byron Flexhaug, Sgt. Russell Johnson, Cpl. Leland Marchant, and Cpl. Raymond Atol. The armed color guard was Pfc. Peter Korwir and Pfc. Thomas Stokke.

Flag and color bearers were U S. flag, William Fenton; VFW, C O. Harding; American Legion, Ear Gwin; DAV, Robert K. Reep.

W. W. Jeffrey and R. W. Moran were the flag folders, and Lt. Robert Jeffrey, the bugler.

Born Nov. 20, 1888, in Kensington county, Minn., Mr. Ohman grew up and attended school there, until moving to Crosby in 1911, where he was employed as a carpenter. In 1917 he moved to Appam. He enlisted at Crosby Sept. 18, 1917, and served in World War I, as a sergeant 1/c, with Hdq. Co. 338 Field Artillery, overseas from Jan. 21, 1918 to May 30, 1919. He was discharged from Camp Dodge, June 12, 1919.

Mr. Ohman was employed as a carpenter until 1928 when he owned and operated a garage until 1948.

He was a member of the VFW post at Appam and the American Legion post at Williston.

Four brothers, Ole of Viking, Alberta, Canada; Arthur and John of Kensington, Minn.; and William of Pine Wood, Minn.; one sister, Mrs. Amanda Carlson of Minneapolis, and five nephews and one niece, survive him.

Arrangements with the Sletten Funeral Home.

1951

April 19 – Amanda Ohman-Carlson hangs herself at the Ohman family farm. She is 58 years old.

Mrs. Joel Carlson Buried Monday

Funeral services for Mrs. Joel Carlson, who passed away at her home in Solum township Thursday, April 19, were held from the Walter Anderson Funeral Home in Minneapolis at 2 p.m., Monday. Interment was made in Lakewood cemetery.

Amanda Ohman was born in Solem township on December 9, 1892, and was 58 years of age at the time of her death. She grew to womanhood on the home farm and on August 9, 1924, she was married to Joel Carlson, who preceded her in death on August 26, 1948. Following their marriage they lived in Minneapolis most of the time, until recently.

She is survived by four brothers, Arthur and John Ohman of Kensington, Wm. Ohman of Pine Wood, Minn., and Olof Ohman of Viking, Alberta, Canada. Besides her husband, she was preceded in death by her parents, three brothers and one sister.

This obituary for Amanda Ohman-Carlson appeared in the *Park Region Echo* on April 26, 1951. (*©Echo Press,* Alexandria, Minnesota. All rights reserved. Used by permission.)

June – Erik Moltke, an archaeologist with the National Museum in Copenhagen, writes an article entitled, "The Kensington Stone," that appeared in *Antiquity*, number 98. It summarizes an earlier article he co-authored with Harry Anderson in *Danske Studier*, 1949-1950, which was highly critical of the Kensington Rune Stone inscription. At one point in the article, Moltke recalls a statement made by Jon Helgason, a professor of

Icelandic at Copenhagen University, who told him that Moltke intended to write about the Stone. *"No self-respecting scholar can in decency deal with this monstrosity; there is certainty [sic] no archaeologist that would bother with a grave from the stone-age if the burial urn rested on a telephone book."* Moltke further stated, *"In my heart of hearts I agree with Jon Helgason. On the other hand, there has been so much fuss over this stone, this inscription that a stop must be put to it."*

June – Erik Moltke and Harry Anderson co-author a paper entitled, "What the Learned think about the Kensington Runestone–and Hjalmar Holand." This paper is a scathing attack on Holand where Anderson asserted that the word "rise", with an "i", "is not, was not and could not be Scandinavian."

August 30 – Professor William Thalbitzer, a prominent philologist researcher and ethnographer in Copenhagen, publishes a paper entitled, *Two Runic Stones, From Greenland and Minnesota.* This paper, which is favorable to the authenticity of the Kensington Rune Stone, is published by the Smithsonian Institution in their miscellaneous collection, volume 116, number 3.

SMITHSONIAN MISCELLANEOUS COLLECTIONS
VOLUME 116, NUMBER 3

TWO RUNIC STONES, FROM GREENLAND AND MINNESOTA

BY
WILLIAM THALBITZER

(PUBLICATION 4021)

CITY OF WASHINGTON
PUBLISHED BY THE SMITHSONIAN INSTITUTION
AUGUST 30, 1951

The cover of Danish professor William Thalbitzer's paper, published by the Smithsonian Institution on August 30, 1951. (Courtesy of Smithsonian Institution)

October 8 – Hjalmar Holand gave testimony to the district court in Alexandria, Minnesota, regarding the details of how he obtained the Stone from Olof Ohman, and its eventual disposal. The court hearing was prompted by the Chamber of Commerce in order for Holand's story to be officially documented for any future purposes, including possible litigation. Holand emphasized that no one owned the Stone and the $2500 payment he had received was to pay for additional research.

Hjalmar Holand testified about the ownership of the Kensington Rune Stone in Alexandria on October 8, 1951. (©*Echo Press*, Alexandria, Minnesota. All rights reserved. Used by permission.)

1952

January 3 – In what appears to be the initial contact between the two men, Erik Wahlgren writes to Holvik inquiring about the Rosander book, the Siverts copy, and the Ohman scrapbook. Professor Erik Wahlgren publishes his first paper on the Kensington Rune Stone entitled, *The Runes of Kensington*. None of his arguments against the Stone are valid today.

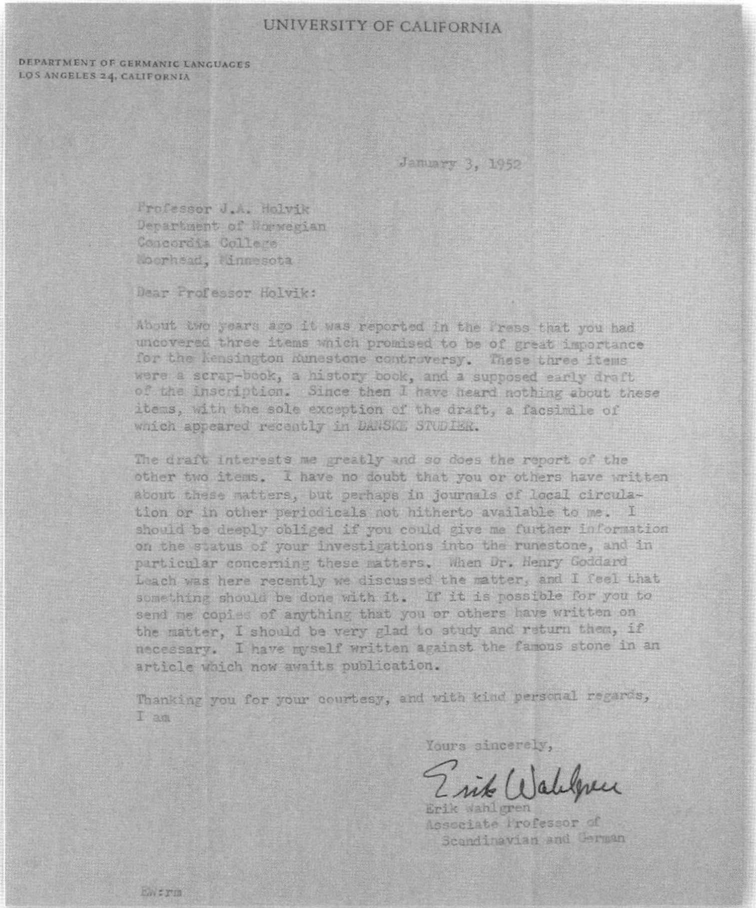

Erik Wahlgren's letter to J. A. Holvik appears to be the first contact between the two. (Minnesota Historical Society)

1953

February – Erik Moltke writes another article highly critical of the Kensington Rune Stone. Entitled, "The Ghost of the Kensington Stone," it appears in *Scandinavian Studies*, volume 25, number 1.

1955

June 4 – Einar Haugen writes an article entitled, "Haugen Doubts Kensington Runestone is Real McCoy" that appears in Capitol Times, p15.

1956 – Hjalmar Holand publishes his fourth book, *Explorations in America before Columbus*.

1957

January – An article appears in the Minnesota Archaelogist entitled, "Stones that Speak: More Evidence on the Authenticity of the Kensington Rune Stone," 21:12-18.

Hjalmar Holand publishes his 256-page autobiography, *My First Eighty Years.*

April 2 – Olof Ohman Jr. writes a letter from Viking, Alberta, Canada, to his brothers Art and John Ohman in Kensington, Minnesota, and thanks them for sending an article written about the Kensington Rune Stone. Olof Jr. wonders when a monument to the Stone will be built on the farm, and recalls the diameter of the tree it was found under being 9 to 10 inches. He also includes a sketch of the roots over the Stone that is strikingly similar to the sketches made by his father and Sam Olson in 1910.

1958

February 19 – Gurina Ohman writes a letter to John Ohman telling him about the death of his oldest brother, Olof Ohman Jr.

Gurina Ohman's letter to her brother-in-law, John Ohman, about the death of Olof Jr. (Courtesy of the Ohman Family)

"Dear John,

"Just a few lines to let you know a little about your brothers death he sure went quick was coming from up town and dropped on the way so he did not suffer the Dr. said he was gone instantly."

Spring – Erik Wahlgren publishes the book, *The Kensington Stone, A Mystery Solved.* It is a strong denouncement of the Rune Stone's authenticity.

June 3 – Erik Wahlgren writes a letter to Theodore Blegen about Ohman's sons, and the likely fallout he expects from his book.

> There is one thing I hope, and that is that Olof Öhman's surviving sons will find the burden of fear lifted from their hearts. I have tried to do them a good turn, although it was no more than they deserved. I felt heartily sorry for them during our conversation some years ago. They have suffered tragic exploitation for too many years.
>
> Einar Haugen warned me that I would make many enemies through publication of the book, for passions run high on this subject. If scholarship accepts my effort, I shall have no regrets, however. It was a wonderful challenge.
>
> Thanking you again for your thoughtfulness,
>
> Yours sincerely,
>
> *Erik Wahlgren*
>
> Erik Wahlgren

An excerpt from Erik Wahlgren's letter to Theodore Blegen. (Minnesota Historical Society)

1959

May 11 – Erik Wahlgen writes a letter to Theodore Blegen and discusses the hard times that the Ohman family have experienced, most of it due to the Stone.

> Indeed, after meeting two of his sons in 1953, I felt thoroughly sorry for them all. One of them had become a dipso; their sister Amanda had a year or two previously committed suicide; their older brothers have told people that they used to run and hide when anybody came to look at the stone. It has been a tragic obsession. To put it bluntly, they have been victimized, exploited, in a sense virtually blackmailed for the advantage of others. It is really not a pretty story. I don't know whether the following is true, but it is quite

An excerpt from Erik Wahlgren's May 11, 1959 letter to Theodore Belgen. (Minnesota Historical Society)

May 18 – Erik Wahlgren writes another letter to Theodore Blegen. Wahlgren reports receiving a letter from a man in Florida who saw a newspaper article in which someone confessed to being involved in the Rune Stone hoax.

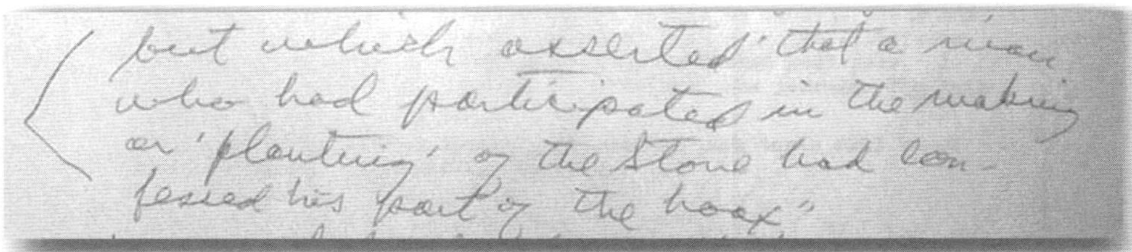

An excerpt from the letter Erik Wahlgren wrote to Theodore Belgen on May 18, 1959. (Minnesota Historical Society)

"…but which asserted that a man who had participated in the making or 'planting' of the Stone had confessed his part of the hoax."

1960

February 10 – John Ohman dies in Pinewood, Minnesota after a long battle with cancer. He is 60 years old.

The Lord is my shepherd; I shall not want.

He maketh me to lie down in green pastures: he leadeth me beside the still waters.

He restoreth my soul: he leadeth me in the paths of righteousness for his name's sake.

Yea, though I walk through the valley of the shadow of death, I will fear no evil: for thou art with me; thy rod and thy staff they comfort me.

Thou preparest a table before me in the presence of mine enemies: thou anointest my head with oil; my cup runneth over.

Surely goodness and mercy shall follow me all the days of my life: and I will dwell in the house of the Lord for ever.

In Memory Of

John G. Ohman

Born
April 11, 1899

Passed Away
February 10, 1960

Services At
Solem Lutheran Church
Kensington, Minn.

Officiating
Rev. H. N. Schey

Interment
Solem Church Cemetery

Casketbearers
Carl Carlson   Palmer Spilseth
Martin Johnson   Louis Moe
Oscar Swanson   Theodore Edman

Arrangements
Olson Funeral Home
Bemidji, Minn.

The funeral service program for John Ohman from his funeral at the Solem Church in Kensington, Minnesota. (Courtesy of the Ohman Family)

The tombstone of John Ohman, located in the Lutheran Church Cemetery near Kensington, Minnesota. (SFW)

1961

September 10 – Arthur Ohman draws a sketch of the aspen tree roots around the Kensington Rune Stone for researcher Ole Landsverk, which Landsverk publishes in October of 1961.

Arthur Ohman's sketch of the roots around the Kensington Rune Stone, drawn for researcher Ole Landsverk on September 10, 1961. (Luther College Archives, Decorah, Iowa)

October 15 – Ole G. Landsverk publishes a 77-page paper titled, *The Kensington Runestone: A Reappraisal of the Circumstances under which the Stone was Discovered.* Chapter five, "They Still Remember," features the signed statements of several residents of the Kensington, Minnesota area, including Arthur Ohman, brothers Olaus and John Flaaten, Henry Moen, and Arthur Osterberg.

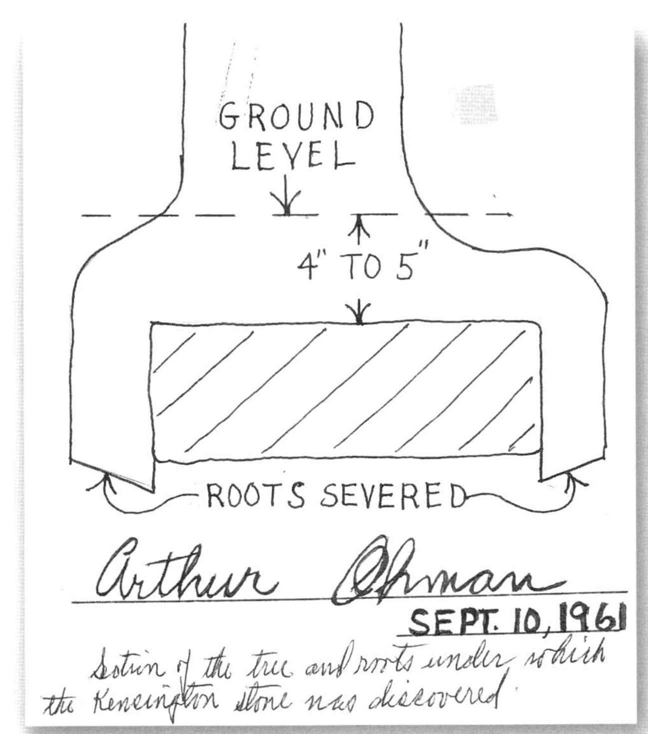

1962 – Hjalmar Holand publishes his fifth book, *A Pre-Columbian Crusade to America.*

1963

August 7 — Hjalmar Holand dies in Sturgeon Bay, Wisconsin at the age of 90.

Runestone Translator
Hjalmar Holand, 90, Dies

Hjalmar Rued Holand, Ephraim, Wis., the leading advocate of the authenticity of the Kensington Runestone, died Thursday at Sturgeon Bay, Wis. He was 90.

Mr. Holand had devoted more than 50 years to research, lecturing and writing on the runestone, discovered Nov. 8, 1898, by Olof Ohman on his farm near Kensington, Minn.

Already a recognized historian of the American Midwest and Norwegian immigration, Mr. Holand studied and translated the old Norse runic inscriptions on the stone.

Mr. Holand

He translated the inscriptions as being an account of a Viking voyage to what is now Minnesota, by "eight Goths and 22 Norwegians" in the year 1362.

He was awarded the king's medal for distinguished cultural service by King Olav V of Norway in 1957. The Supreme Lodge, Sons of Norway, honored him for his more than half century of research on the runestone in a ceremony commemorating the 600th anniversary of the date inscribed on the stone.

Born in Norway, Mr. Holand immigrated to the United States in 1884.

Survivors include two daughters, Mrs. Thomas Swanhild Johnson, Waukegan, Ill., and Mrs. Philip Vallee Ditchen, Green Bay, Wis.; two sons, Harold, Miwaukee, Wis., and Ivar, Ephraim, Wis., and five grandchildren and nine great-grandchildren.

This obituary for Hjalmar Holand appeared in the *Minneapolis Star* on August 8, 1963. (Copyright 2005 *Star Tribune*. Republished with permission of *Star Tribune*, Minneapolis-St. Paul. No further republication or redistribution is permitted without the written consent of *Star Tribune*.)

October 6 – Arthur Ohman writes a letter to Ole Landsverk and tells him that Holvik asked him to sign a letter about the origin of drilled holes on the Ohman farm.

This letter was found in Ole Landsverk's personal papers in the Luther College archives of the Preus Library in Decorah, Iowa, on December 28, 2004. (Luther College Archives, Decorah, Iowa)

"Kensington, Minn.

"Professor Holvik visited me on my farm near Kensington. At that time Holvik tried to induce me to sign a statement that certain drilled holes in rocks were mooring holes. These holes were in fact ordinary drilled holes in rocks that we were blasting. I informed Holvik of this fact, but he continued to insist that I sign the statement which I knew to be entirely false. When I persisted that these were ordinary drill holes for blasting, Holvik became very angry and left. I did not sign the statement for it was wholly false.

"Signed,

"Arthur Ohman   Witnessed by: Ludeen L Bengtsen
                                          Edwin Belgum
                                          James Belgum

"Date-Oct. 6, 1963"

1965

February 2 – Erik Wahlgren writes a letter to Theodore Blegen and refers to N. Winchell's field notebook, which Mr. Blegen had not yet located. Blegen's handwritten notes in the margin refer to how, "K[ensington]-writers go emotional."

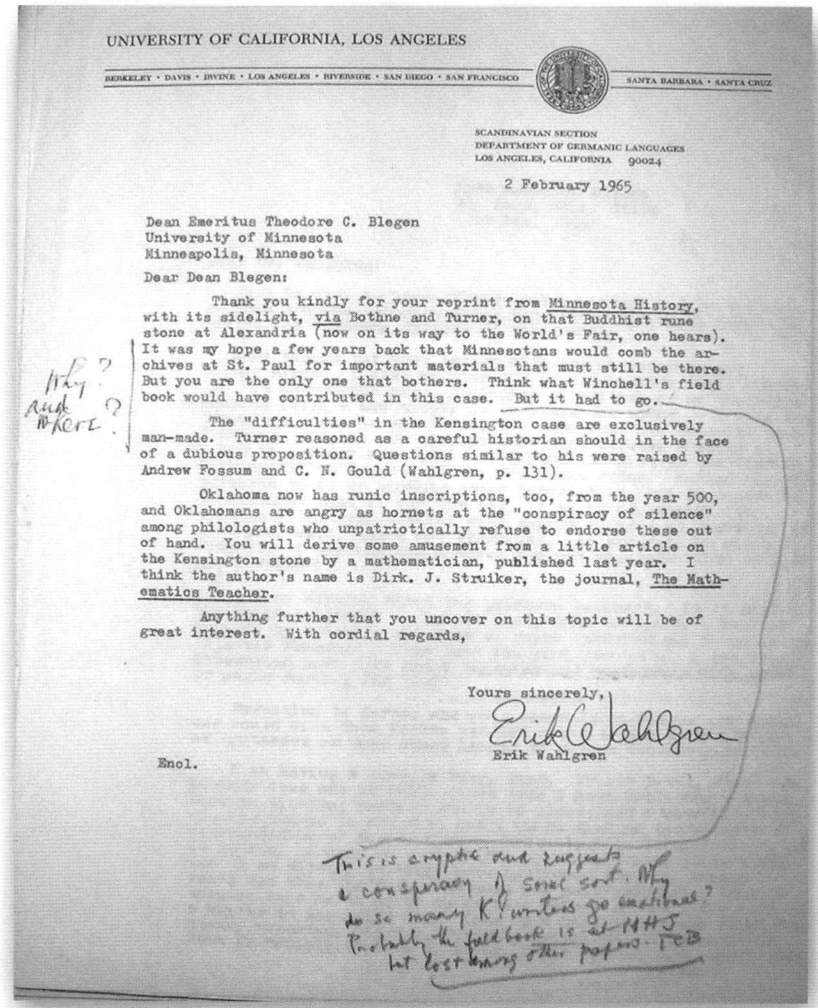

Erik Wahlgren's February 2, 1965 letter to Theodore Blegen. (Minnesota Historical Society)

February 17 – Erik Wahlgren writes a letter to Theodore Blegen discussing his disdain for Landsverk and pontificating about the "K" problem.

either cannot or will not understand rules of scholarly evidence. Landsverk I know personally. He is a mathematician and physicist from, I am ashamed to say, my own alma mater, Chicago. He nearly has apoplexy whenever he sees me.

(Minnesota Historical Society)

Well, enough. Some of the things uncovered did not seem suitable for printing, and some things I promised not to print, when I was still working on the problem. One thing gradually became plain to me, although a psychiatrist might disagree: a name prominently and often associated with the K. problem could not possibly himself believe in it. For he had access to the true facts. The disagreeable part of the controversy is that it is one in which one must choose between accepting a fraud and attacking a man.. Most of us blench before this choice.

Yours sincerely,

Excerpts from a two-page letter Erik Wahlgren wrote to Theodore Belgen on February 17, 1965. (Minnesota Historical Society)

Summer – The Kensington Rune Stone and the "Big Ole" statue appear at the World's Fair in New York.

September 1 – The quarterly publication, *The Minnesota Archaeologist*, Volume 27, Number 3, contains a lengthy review of Erik Wahlgren's book, *The Kensington Stone: A Mystery Solved*, written by Lawrence D. Steefel; Steefel's review is positive.

1966

June/July – Aslak Liestol writes an article published in *Minnesota History*, 40:59; that dealt with the runes of the Kensington Rune Stone.

> *"They were of the kind 'in continuous use by nearly all social groups' of that period, but among all 12,000 [of the runes found in Bergen] not a single one of the 'strange forms occurring in the Kensington alphabet' occurs. Mr. Liestol stated that if a runic inscription had actually been carved in the 14th century, it surely 'would have been written with the runes which the people of those days were accustomed to using.'"*

This statement is not consistent with the runes in the *Codex Runicus*, the *Mariaklagen*, or runic inscriptions elsewhere in Scandinavia, particularly in Gotland.

1967

August 13 – Dr. Paul Carson interviews his uncle, Frank Walter Gran, and his aunt, Mrs. Josephine Gran-Carson, about what they claimed to know regarding their father's involvement with carving the Rune Stone.

1968

January 26 – In a letter to Theodore Blegen, Erik Wahlgren writes negatively about Ole Landsverk's cryptographic work. He also writes about hearing a mysterious tape recording, played by Holvik in August of 1953, that dealt with the disputed ownership of the stone.

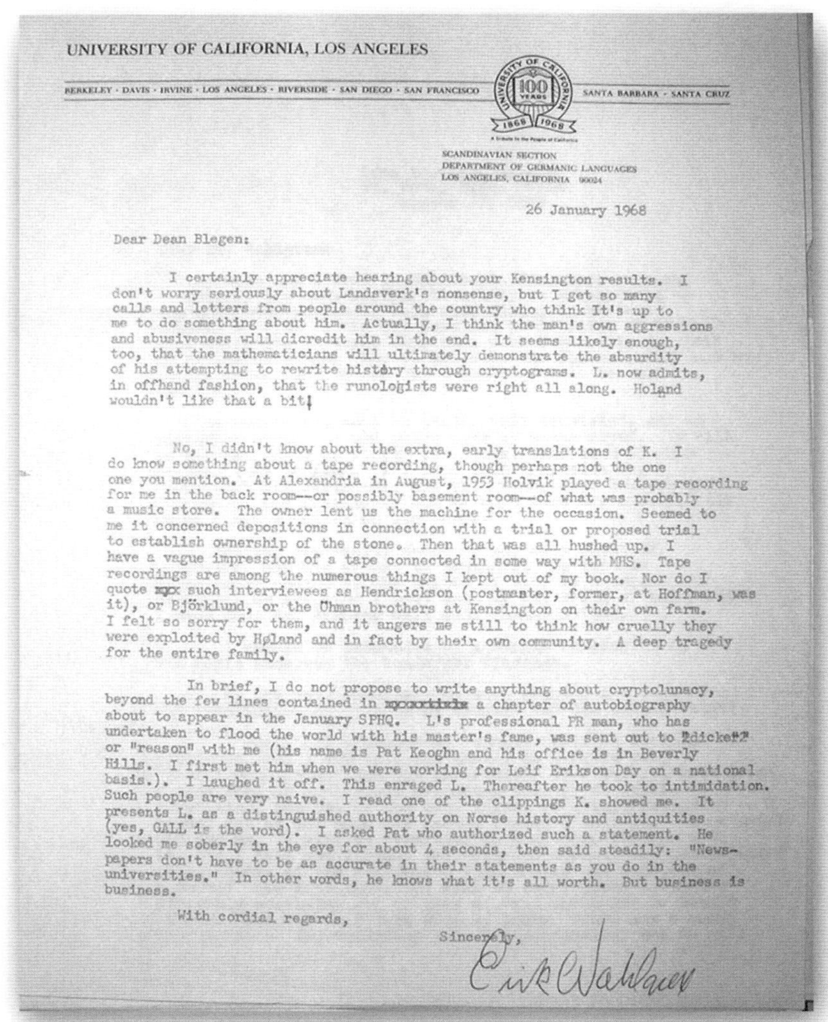

UNIVERSITY OF CALIFORNIA, LOS ANGELES

BERKELEY · DAVIS · IRVINE · LOS ANGELES · RIVERSIDE · SAN DIEGO · SAN FRANCISCO   SANTA BARBARA · SANTA CRUZ

SCANDINAVIAN SECTION
DEPARTMENT OF GERMANIC LANGUAGES
LOS ANGELES, CALIFORNIA 90024

26 January 1968

Dear Dean Blegen:

I certainly appreciate hearing about your Kensington results. I don't worry seriously about Landsverk's nonsense, but I get so many calls and letters from people around the country who think It's up to me to do something about him. Actually, I think the man's own aggressions and abusiveness will dicredit him in the end. It seems likely enough, too, that the mathematicians will ultimately demonstrate the absurdity of his attempting to rewrite history through cryptograms. L. now admits, in offhand fashion, that the runologists were right all along. Holand wouldn't like that a bit!

No, I didn't know about the extra, early translations of K. I do know something about a tape recording, though perhaps not the one one you mention. At Alexandria in August, 1953 Holvik played a tape recording for me in the back room—or possibly basement room—of what was probably a music store. The owner lent us the machine for the occasion. Seemed to me it concerned depositions in connection with a trial or proposed trial to establish ownership of the stone. Then that was all hushed up. I have a vague impression of a tape connected in some way with MHS. Tape recordings are among the numerous things I kept out of my book. Nor do I quote such interviewees as Hendrickson (postmaster, former, at Hoffman, was it), or Björklund, or the Öhman brothers at Kensington on their own farm. I felt so sorry for them, and it angers me still to think how cruelly they were exploited by Høland and in fact by their own community. A deep tragedy for the entire family.

In brief, I do not propose to write anything about cryptolunacy, beyond the few lines contained in a chapter of autobiography about to appear in the January SPHQ. L's professional PR man, who has undertaken to flood the world with his master's fame, was sent out to "dicker" or "reason" with me (his name is Pat Keoghn and his office is in Beverly Hills. I first met him when we were working for Leif Erikson Day on a national basis.). I laughed it off. This enraged L. Thereafter he took to intimidation. Such people are very naive. I read one of the clippings K. showed me. It presents L. as a distinguished authority on Norse history and antiquities (yes, GALL is the word). I asked Pat who authorized such a statement. He looked me soberly in the eye for about 4 seconds, then said steadily: "Newspapers don't have to be as accurate in their statements as you do in the universities." In other words, he knows what it's all worth. But business is business.

With cordial regards,

Sincerely,

Erik Wahlgren

Erik Wahlgren's letter to Theodore Belgen, written January 26, 1968. (Minnesota Historical Society)

January 30 – Professor Belgen wrote a letter to Wahlgren saying he would not be able to use the Walter Gran interview testimony in his forthcoming book about the Rune Stone.

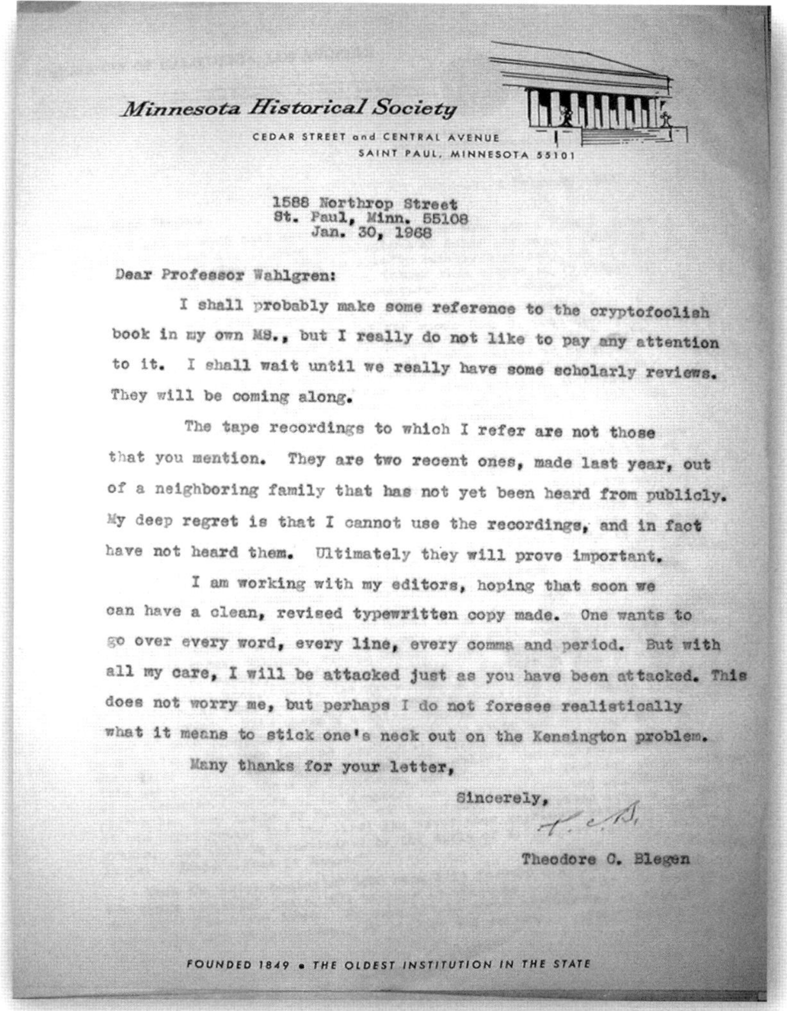

Theodore Blegen's January 30, 1968 response to Erik Wahlgren's letter. (Minnesota Historical Society)

February 4 – Wahlgren writes a letter to Blegen, expressing frustration over the voluminous mail he receives about the Kensington Rune Stone and the antagonism he feels over Landsverk's cryptographic work.

The beginning of a letter Erik Wahlgren wrote to Theodore Belgen on February 4, 1968. (Minnesota Historical Society)

March 8 – Minnesota Historical Society Director Russell Fridley has a telephone conversation with Dr. Paul Carson about Carson's uncle, Walter Gran. The two men talk about Gran's reluctance to discuss what he knew about who carved the Kensington Rune Stone.

```
Telephone conversation between R. W. Fridley and Dr. Carson, telephone
number 926-3339 -- Friday, March 8, 1968, 11 a.m.  (This is NOT verbatim)

Re:  Kensington Rune Stone
```

(Minnesota Historical Society)

June 3 – Birgitta Wallace writes a letter to Theodore Blegen, offering to read his manuscript, and apologizing for not having her own book on the Kensington Rune Stone ready for his review. As of June, 2005, Ms. Wallace's book on the Kensington Rune Stone remains unpublished.

Summer – Theodore C. Blegen concludes in his book, *The Kensington Rune Stone: New Light on an Old Riddle*, that the Kensington Rune Stone was a hoax, probably perpetrated by Kensington residents Olof Ohman, Sven Fogelblad, and Andrew Anderson.

1969

July 18 – Theodore Blegen dies in Ramsey County, Minnesota, at the age of 78.

1970

January 17 – Russell Fridley, then Director of the Minnesota Historical Society, interviews Frank Walter Gran about his father's alleged involvement with carving the Kensington Rune Stone. This interview is the genesis of what would come to be called the so-called "Deathbed Confession."

1972

Fall – The granary shed on the Ohman farm, which reportedly housed the Kensington Rune Stone from 1899 to 1907, is torn down.

Clifford Roiland points at the foot of the granary door where the Rune Stone was rumored to have been placed after it was discovered. The shed was torn down in 1972 shortly after this photograph was taken. (Photograph courtesy of the Kensington Area Heritage Society)

1973

October 30 – William Ohman dies in Pinewood, Minnesota, at the age of 68.

The Twenty-Third Psalm

THE LORD IS MY SHEPHERD; I SHALL NOT WANT.
HE MAKETH ME TO LIE DOWN IN GREEN PASTURES:
HE LEADETH ME BESIDE THE STILL WATERS.
HE RESTORETH MY SOUL: HE LEADETH ME IN THE
PATHS OF RIGHTEOUSNESS FOR HIS NAME'S SAKE..
YEA, THOUGH I WALK THROUGH THE VALLEY OF
THE SHADOW OF DEATH, I WILL FEAR NO EVIL:
FOR THOU ART WITH ME; THY ROD AND THY STAFF
THEY COMFORT ME. THOU PREPAREST A TABLE
BEFORE ME IN THE PRESENCE OF MINE ENEMIES:
THOU ANOINTEST MY HEAD WITH OIL; MY CUP
RUNNETH OVER.. SURELY GOODNESS AND
MERCY SHALL FOLLOW ME ALL THE DAYS
OF MY LIFE: AND I WILL DWELL IN THE
HOUSE OF THE LORD FOR EVER . . . . .

WILLIAM O. OHMAN

BORN
OCTOBER 5, 1905
KENSINGTON, MINNESOTA

ENTERED INTO REST
OCTOBER 30, 1973
SHEVLIN, MINNESOTA

SERVICES
OLSON–SCHWARTZ FUNERAL HOME
BEMIDJI, MINNESOTA
FRIDAY
NOVEMBER 2, 1973   1:30 PM

OFFICIATING
REV. STEPHEN KNUDSEN

INTERMENT
PINEWOOD–DODGE CEMETERY
PINEWOOD, MINNESOTA

Funeral service program for William Ohman. (Courtesy of the Ohman Family)

November 11 – Art Ohman holds an auction of many of the family belongings at the farm in Kensington.

Auction Sale!

Having sold the farm to the Runestone Park Foundation I will sell my personal property at public auction. Located 2 miles North, then ¾ mile east & ¾ mile North of Kensington. Road will be marked.

Saturday, November 10th

Sale starts at 10:30 A.M.   Solem Ladies Aid will Serve Lunch

This sale is on the farm where the Kensington Runestone was found and which has just been purchased by the Runestone Park Foundation for development as a park & camping grounds. If you have never visited the site, this is your chance to do so and at the same time have an opportunity to bid on some good antique items.

MACHINERY

1939 Ford Ferguson Tractor with new tires
Ford cultivator   Ford tandem disc
Ford 2 bottom plow   Dump rake
Triple grain box mounted on two wheel trailer
Letz Burr mill   1914 Bob sled
4 wheel trailer & wagon box
John Deere gas engine 1½ horse
1 Model T motor
2 Old gas engines   Fanning mill
2 Wheel buggy cart
Gamble super-rite 4 speed transmission, 32 inch lawn mower, used once.
Lawn-Boy self propelled 21" lawn mower

MISCELLANEOUS

Table saw   Air compressor-2
Large block & tackle   Lots of scrap iron
Platform scale   Grindstone
Bench grinder & motor
Duck boat   Leg vise
2 home made small sleds
24' home-made extension ladder
265 gallon fuel tank   Hand corn planter-2
New battery charger   2 hydralic jacks
Antenna & rotor   Lg. anvil
Lge. broad axe   Pipe cutter
Wall press drill   32 volt light plant engine
Complete tap & dye set   Electric ½" drill
3½ h.p. Torro lawn mower
Bench vise   Skill saw

FURNITURE

Old Maytag washing machine
Refrigerator
Steel Kitchen cabinet
Jungers 2 burner parlor heater, like new
GE vacuum cleaner

ANTIQUES

Oak Library table   Sewing machine
Spinning wheel, not complete
Old storage cabinet
Leather studio Couch   Small table
Old Storage cabinet
100 year old original wood box
15 gal. crock   Wardrobe
Wood & coal kitchen stove
Old oak square kitchen table
Round oak table   Wood bed
Oak dresser-2   Foot stool
Wood bed   7 kitchen chairs
Small cabinet   Wall telephone
7 old dining rooms chairs, good condition
Rocking chair   Taylors Iron
Book case with glass front
Dishes   2 wooden chests
Glass wall coffee grinder
3 Iron beds
1 set of good britching harness & collars
Hand corn sheller
2 wagon spring seats
Blacksmith tongs
40 piece tap & dye set, new
30 gallon cast iron kettle
Combination plane with 16 different blades
4 rolls lawn fence & steel gate & oak posts
Several trunks   Machinery seats
Forge   Ladder
Many, many hand tools, old & good

Savage 300 Deer Rifle
model EG99

Usual terms of sale.
Not responsible for accidents.

ARTHUR OHMAN OWNER

Mel Hagen 2101
Del Johnson 2108
Auctioneers

First State Bank
of Kensington
Clerk

The flyer distributed in the Kensington area announcing the auction sale of items from the Ohman farm in November, 1973. (Courtesy of the Ohman Family)

1976

Summer – Archaeologist Christina Harrison conducts a dig on Rune Stone Hill. Nothing of substance relating to the Kensington Rune Stone is found.

On the editor's page of the Winter/1976 issue of *Minnesota History*, Russell Fridley wrote an article entitled, "Debate Continues Over the Kensington Rune Stone," pages 149-151. Fridley wrote another article in the same publication entitled, "The Case of the Gran Tapes: Further Evidence on the Rune Stone Riddle," pages 152-154.

Archaeologist Christina Harrison at the dig on Rune Stone Hill, as three field assistants look on, in the summer of 1976. (Photograph courtesy of the Kensington Area Heritage Society)

1977 – On the editor's page of the spring/1977 issue of *Minnesota History,* Erik Wahlgren wrote an article entitled, "More on the Kensington Rune Stone," page 195. On page 196 Elden Johnson of the Univeristy of Minnesota wrote about the excavation performed at the discovery site by Christina Harrison.

1979 – Jeffery R. Redmond publishes the book, "*Viking Hoaxes in North America.* Redmond is a graduate student in Scandinavian at the University of California in Los Angeles, studying under the direction of Professor Erik Wahlgren.

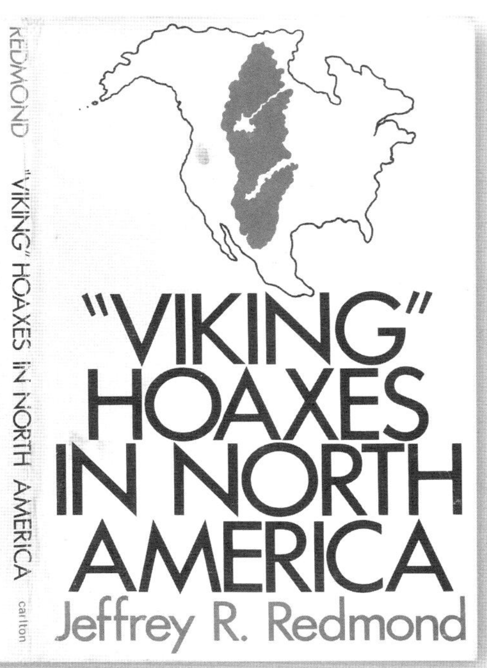

In 1979, Jeffrey R. Redmond published this 64-page book which included a denouncement of the Kensington Rune Stone. (Courtesy Jeffrey R. Redmond)

1981

August 11 to 30 – Alexandria, Minnesota resident Gordon E. Duenow conducts interviews with several elderly residents of the Kensington area who knew both the Olof Ohman and John P. Gran families. All individuals interviewed said that they did not believe Walter Gran's claim that his father and Olof Ohman carved the Stone. They all say Olof Ohman was an honest man.

August 11 – Gordon E. Duenow interviews Emil (90 years old) and Martin Johnson (95 years old), and Ole C. Nelson (87 years old).

August 12 – Gordon E. Duenow interviews Emil Mattson (84 years old), and Martin Johnson.

August 14 – Gordon E. Duenow interviews Clarence Larson (84 years old).

August 30 – Gordon E. Duenow interviews Selma (77 years old) and Milo Spilseth (78 years old).

Back from the Dead (1982 to 2000)

After 1981, things took a turn for the better for the Kensington Rune Stone, primarily because of two researchers who offered important new evidence that supported the authenticity of the Stone. These discoveries opened new dialogue and stimulated interest into what many had considered a dead issue.

1982

Robert A. Hall Jr. publishes his first book about the Rune Stone, *The Kensington Rune-Stone Is Genuine*.

Robert Hall Jr. published a book in 1982 that was favorable to the authenticity of the Kensington Rune Stone.

1984

February 18 — Arthur Ohman, the last surviving offspring of Olof and Karin Ohman, dies at the age of 93.

The obituary for Arthur Ohman that appeared in the *Park Region Echo* on February 24, 1984. (©*Echo Press,* Alexandria, Minnesota. All rights reserved. Used by permission.)

The tombstone of Arthur Ohman located in the Lutheran Church Cemetery near Kensington, Minnesota. (SFW)

Arthur Ohman

Arthur Ohman was born in Kensington, Minnesota, on February 7, 1891, the son of Olaf and Karin (Danielson) Ohman. Arthur was baptized and confirmed in the Lutheran faith and attended schools and grew to manhood in the Kensington area. He worked in lumber mills in northern Minnesota and also farmed and threshed for many people. Arthur also worked as a well driller for several years. He was the last surviving son of Olaf Ohman, the man credited with the discovery of the Kensington Runestone. Arthur died on Saturday, February 18, 1984, at the Bethany Home at the age of 93 years.

He is survived by nephews: Lalard Kolberg of Forest Lake; Darwin Ohman of Anoka; Gary Ohman of Shevlin, MN; James Ohman of Coleraine and Kim Ohman of Alaska.

Funeral services were Wednesday, February 22, 1984, at 1:00 p.m. at the Solem Lutheran Church, Kensington, Minnesota with Rev. James Radatz officiating. Interment was in Solem Lutheran Cemetery, Kensington, Minnesota.

Pallbearers were Einar Bakke, Martin Johnson, Sydney Johnson, Ernest Johnson, Oscar Swanson and Milo Spilseth.

Arrangements were with the Anderson Funeral Home.

1986

Inspired by Robert Hall's book, author Nielsen begins studying the Kensington Rune Stone. A series of papers results in 1986, 1987, 1988, 1989, 1992, 1993, 1998, and in 2005 that are published in the Epigraphic Society occasional publications. (See reference list.)

1987

August 12 – The *Echo Press* in Alexandria, Minnesota, reports the discovery of the Arabic 10, the "J-rune," and the "e-dialect" on the Kensington Rune Stone by Dr. Richard Nielsen.

1993

June 9 — Minnie Osterholt conducts an interview with a lifetime resident of the Kensington area, Ione Torgerson Bakke (72 Years old), for the Douglas County Historical Society (Accession # 93-07-OH), about the Olof Ohman family, Henry Moen, and the Runestone Museum. Mrs. Bakke's grandmother Carrie was a very close friend to Karin Ohman, and was a midwife who delivered most of the Ohman children. When asked if Olof Ohman had put the Kensington Rune Stone where it was found, Ione said, *"Absolutely did not put it there."*

Summer – Rhoda Gilman, a retired staff member of the Minnesota Historical Society, and James Smith writes an article titled, "Vikings in Minnesota: A Controversial Legacy," in the Minnesota Historical Society publication *Roots*.

Robert Hall Jr. published a book in 1994 that was favorable to the authenticity of the Kensington Rune Stone. Chapter 15 was dedicated solely to a categorical denouncement of the poor scholarship in Erik Wahlgren's 1958 book, which was highly critical of the Kensington Rune Stone.

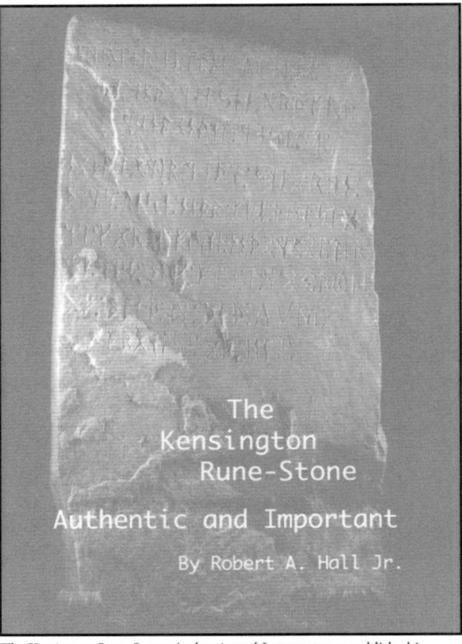

The Kensington Rune-Stone: Authentic and Important was published in 1994 by Jupiter Press as Volume 19 of the Edward Sapir Monograph Series in Language, Culture, and Cognition. This image is reprinted by permission. The volume is available for purchase for $20 plus shipping from Jupiter Press, P. O. Box 101, Lake Bluff, Illinois 60044.

1994

Robert A. Hall Jr. publishes his second book about the Kensington Rune Stone titled, *The Kensington Rune-Stone: Authentic and Important*. Richard Nielsen and Rolf Nilsestuen assisted Hall on some aspects of his book, as acknowledged by Hall.

Rolf M. Nilsestuen publishes a book about the Kensington Rune Stone called *The Kensington Runestone Vindicated*.

Rolf Nilsestuen published a book in 1994 that was favorable to the authenticity of the Kensington Rune Stone. (Courtesy of University Press of America; Lanham, Maryland)

Iver Kjar publishes a paper on the Kensington Rune Stone. It follows the old, outdated arguments of Moltke (1950, 1951, 1953).

The
KENSINGTON
RUNESTONE
VINDICATED

ROLF M. NILSESTUEN

Rolf M. Nilsestuen
5404 Woodacre Drive
Suitland, MD 20746-2297
1-301-568-8309

UNIVERSITY
PRESS OF
AMERICA

Lanham • New York • London

A New Century of Investigations (2000 to Present)

The movement begun by the linguistic discoveries of Robert Hall and Richard Nielsen continued to build momentum when new geologic studies indicated the weathering of the Kensington Rune Stone inscription was very old. In 2003 the Kensington Rune Stone traveled to Sweden for the first time, and a new era of serious research began. The next year saw renewed interest and involvement from the Ohman family in America and in Sweden, which led to new discoveries that finally exonerated Olof Ohman.

2000 – The Smithsonian Institution of Natural History in Washington D.C. publishes the book, *Vikings: The North Atlantic Saga*, in conjunction with a 3-year traveling exhibition about the Viking age Scandinavian explorers. Chapter 29, *Stumbles and Pitfalls in the Search for Viking America*, is written by Birgitta Lindroth Wallace and William Fitzhugh, and includes three pages on why the Kensington Rune Stone is a hoax.

Summer – In the *NEARA Journal* (New England Antiquities Research Association) an article appears entitled: "Factual Errors in Chapter 29, 'Vikings: The North Atlantic Saga' regarding the Kensington Stone," by Michael Zalar. In the article Zalar documents thirty-seven factual errors in Chapter 29, including what appears to be a deliberate attempt to misconstrue N. H. Winchell's assessment of the weathering of the inscription.

July 14 – The Kensington Rune Stone is brought to the American Petrographic Services Inc. laboratory for the first time. Several prominent Minnesota geologists examine the Stone for several hours and exchange ideas about how to proceed with a forensic evaluation of the inscription. The individuals who attended include Dr. John Green, Ken Harris, Dr. Charles L. Matsch, Gerard Moulzolf P.G., Dr. Richard Ojakangas, Dr. Paul Weiblen, and Scott F. Wolter P.G.

November 10 – Dr. Richard Nielsen, archaeologist Alice Kehoe, chemist Barry J. Hanson, Dr. Jon Polansky, and geologist Scott F. Wolter present lectures that are favorable to the authenticity of the Kensington Rune Stone at the Midwest Plains Archaeological Conference in St. Paul, Minnesota. The presentations include the first modern geological analysis of the weathering that confirmes Newton Winchell's conclusion that the inscription is very old.

2001

January 4 – American Petrographic Services Inc., in a report written by Scott F. Wolter, documents the geological and physical features of the Kensington Rune Stone. The report concludes that the inscription is authentic. Wolter writes the following on page 8, conclusion number 5, *"It is clear that the four man-made fracture surface types on the Kensington Rune Stone exhibit weathering (primarily mica degradation) consistent with being buried in the ground for at least decades and probably centuries. This being the case, the logical conclusion is that the Kensington Rune Stone is an authentic artifact, presumably made at the time it is dated (1362 A.D.)."*

April – Dr. Richard Nielsen publishes a 75-page paper on the language of the Kensington Rune Stone in the publication, *Scandinavian Studies*. This paper is currently available on the internet.

May 13 – On a small island in a shallow lake that partially surrounds the hill where the Kensington Rune Stone was found, Janey Westin and her father, Robert Johnson, discover the AVM Stone.

October – The Kensington Rune Stone travels to Vienna, Austria to be displayed as part of an exhibition about mysterious artifacts in history for six weeks.

November 6 – The Minnesota Historical Society receives a letter from two women claiming responsibility, along with three unnamed accomplices, for carving the AVM Stone in the spring of 1985. The women write that they were inspired to produce the "fake" rune stone after hearing about the Kensington Rune Stone during a lecture about famous fakes by Anatoly Lieberman at the University of Minnesota. The AVM Stone becomes an important control sample for comparing weathering aspects with the Kensington Rune Stone.

2002

February 24 – A symposium about the Kensington Rune Stone is held in Thousand Oaks, California. The speakers include Dr. Richard Nielsen, Barry J. Hanson, and Professor Henrik Williams from the University of Uppsala, Sweden. Professor Williams proclaimes that based upon Dr. Nielsen's work, the Kensington Rune Stone deserves further study.

June 14 – Dr. Richard Nielsen and Scott F. Wolter give a three-hour presentation on the Kensington Rune Stone at the Smithsonian Institution in Washington, D.C. anthropologist Elisabeth Ward, Senior Linguist Ives Goddard, Linguist Intern Iris Hahn, and geologist Dr. Sorena Sorenson represent the Smithsonian.

September – Barry J. Hanson publishes his two-volume book, *Kensington Runestone – A Defense of Olof Ohman the Accused Forger*.

September 3 – Lars Westman, a journalist from Stockholm, Sweden, visits St. Paul, Alexandria, and Kensington, Minnesota for an article about the Kensington Rune Stone that would be published in *Vi* Magazine.

August – Author Nielsen collects below grade samples from tombstones at the Hallowell cemetery in Maine.

November 1 – Scott Wolter and Richard Nielsen jointly present papers on the Kensington Rune Stone at the NEARA (New England Antiquities Research Association) Conference in Boston, Massachusetts.

December 31 – Scott F. Wolter publishes a report that includes a digital collection of 689 images of the entire Kensington Rune Stone inscription entitled, *Photo-Library of the Characters of the Kensington Rune Stone Inscription.* The photographs were taken using both high and low angle reflected light at magnifications ranging from 3.75 to 64 times. Several new important features of the inscription were documented during the course of this work.

Scott Wolter is pictured reviewing images of the Kensington Rune Stone under the microscope. (Photograph by LuAnn Patton)

2003

March 3 – Scott F. Wolter and Tony Maschaidri collect twenty-four chip samples for testing from slate tombstones in the Hallowell Cemetery in Hallowell, Maine.

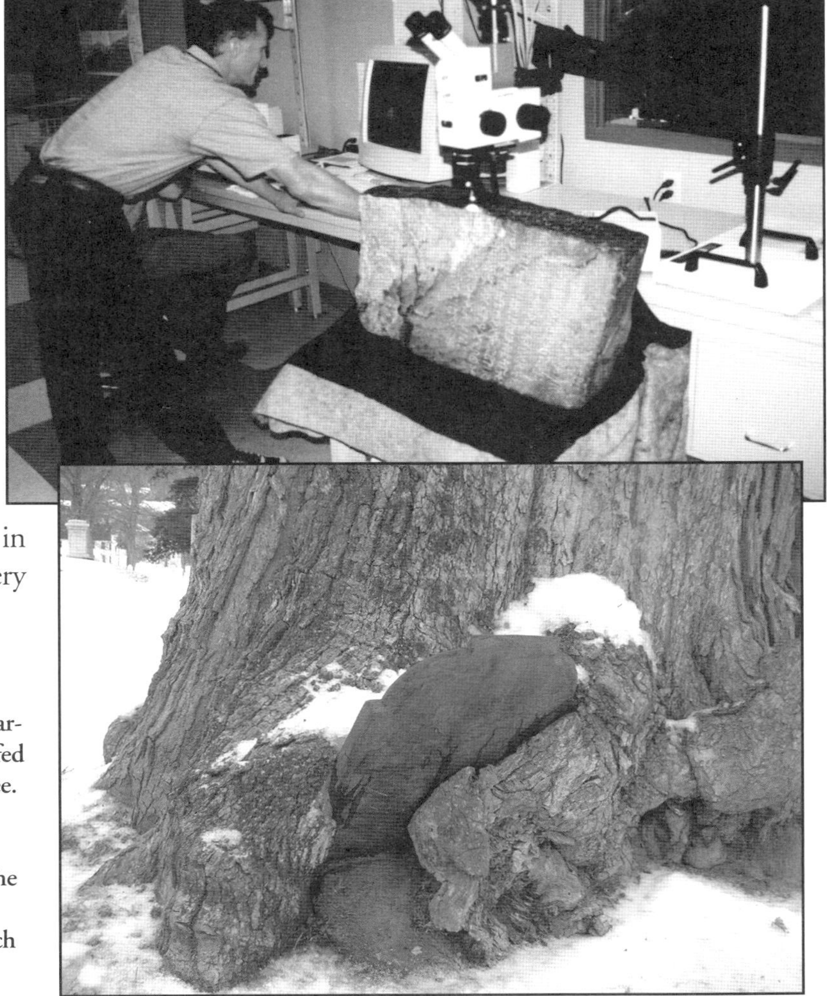

A roughly two hundred-year-old slate tombstone, engulfed and uprooted by a large tree. Twenty-four chip samples were collected for testing from slate tombstones in the Hallowell Cemetery in Hallowell, Maine, on March 6, 2003. (SFW)

April 2 – A one-day forum on the Kensington Rune Stone is held at Fort Snelling in St. Paul, Minnesota. Thirty-five invited guests from several disciplines (geology, linguistics, archaeology, history and the media) attend to discuss various aspects of the controversy.

October 14 – Scott Wolter completes a 56-page report, *The Geology of the Kensington Rune Stone*, which includes the results of the tombstone study.

October 16 – The Kensington Rune Stone arrives at the Historiska Museum in Stockholm, Sweden, for a special three-month exhibition. This was the Kensington Rune Stone's first trip to Sweden.

The Kensington Rune Stone as displayed in an exhibition at the Historiska Museum in Stockholm, Sweden, on October 22, 2003. (SFW)

October 24 – A one-day conference at the Historiska Museum covers various aspects of the Kensington Rune Stone with formal presentations by Professor Michael Barnes, Helmer Gustafson, Dr. Richard Nielsen, and Scott Wolter.

November 5 – Swedish geo-chemist Runo Löfvendahl, who attended the presentations at the Historiska Museum on October 24, writes an e-mail to Scott Wolter in reference to his presentation about the Kensington Rune Stone: *"(I) think your demonstration of the progress of weathering of pyrite and micas shows that it will be extremely difficult to maintain, that the stone is a 19th century fake."*

2004

January 29 – The Kensington Rune Stone is shipped from the Historiska Museum in Stockholm to the Hälsinglands Museum in Hudiksvall, Sweden.

February 5 – A debate about the Kensington Rune Stone is held in Hudiksvall, Sweden. Richard Nielsen and Scott Wolter argue in favor of the Stone's authenticity, and Helmer Gustafsson and Mats Larsson argue against it. The moderator of the debate, which was attended by over two hundred people, was Professor Henrik Williams.

March 5 – The Kensington Rune Stone returns to the Runestone Museum in Alexandria, Minnesota, after spending over four months in Sweden.

April 21 – Darwin Ohman and former director of the Minnesota Historical Society, Russell Fridley, meet for the first time.

May 20 – The "Ohman Interview" is conducted at the American Companies headquarters in St. Paul, Minnesota. The participants include the former Director of the Minnesota Historical Society, Russell Fridley; Darwin Ohman, a grandson of Olof Ohman; Tom Kolberg, a great-grandson of Olof Ohman; and Scott Wolter. This interview gives representatives of the Ohman family their first opportunity to go on record with their position regarding the authenticity of the Kensington Rune Stone, and the credibility of Walter Gran. Walter Gran was interviewed by Russell Fridley in 1970, and among other claims, alleged that his father told him that "he and Olof Ohman carved the Kensington Rune Stone."

June 2 – At a debate held at the Historiska Museum in Stockholm, Sweden, three attending Swedish scholars tell Darwin Ohman that they do not believe that his grandfather, Olof Ohman, carved the Kensington Rune Stone. Runo Löfvendahl, a geologist, and linguists Tryggve Sköld and Professor Henrik Williams each give a different reason for their opinion.

Participants of a debate about the Kensington Rune Stone held at the Historiska Museum posed for a picture at a post-debate dinner on June 2, 2004. The individuals pictured are (left to right) Tryggve Sköld, Darwin Ohman (partially obscured), Ola Olsson, Runo Löfvendahl, Henrik Williams, and Scott Wolter. (SFW)

June 17 – The opening ceremonies for an exhibit about Hälsingland entitled, *Hälsingland Roots in Minnesota: An Immigrant Story*, is held at the community center in Kensington, Minnesota. The exhibit focuses on the story of Swedish immigration to America as seen through the eyes of Olof Ohman. Several people from Sweden attend, including four members of the team that assembled the exhibit, Gunilla Stenberg (the director of the Hälsinglands Museum) Anna Meyer, Lars Nylander, and Susanna Larsson. Five Ohman relatives from Forsa, Sweden, also attend including Britta Blank, Ulla Nylander, Karin Lindholm, Sven-Erik Johansson, and Håkan Blank. Approximately 120 people attend the ceremony that was hosted by LuAnn Patton (the former director of the Runestone Museum in Alexandria), and Duane Sprouls, (the Mayor of Kensington).

Britta Blank from Forsadalen, Sweden, presents a gift to the Mayor of Kensington, Duane Sprouls, at the opening ceremonies of the Hälsingland Exhibition in Kensington, Minnesota, on June 17, 2004. (SFW)

June 21 – Several boxes containing hundreds of personal belongings including books, letters and photos belonging to the Ohman family are discovered by Joanne Kolberg, a great- granddaughter of Karin and Olof Ohman.

August 21 – Richard Nielsen and Scott Wolter give a two-hour presentation at the community center in Kensington. They present numerous pieces of evidence that prove Olof Ohman was not involved in any Kensington Rune Stone hoax.

September 7 – An article appears in the *Minneapolis Star Tribune* about the "Ohman Documents" and the presentation in Kensington, Minnesota, on August 21ˢᵗ.

Darwin Ohman paused to look at a photograph of his father William, which was one of many documents belonging to the Ohman family that were brought forward for researchers to examine in the summer of 2004. (Photograph courtesy of 2005 Star Tribune/Minneapolis-St. Paul)

2005

February 28 to March 3 – Scott Wolter travels to the island of Gotland in the Baltic Sea to photograph runic inscriptions on medieval grave slabs with words and characters similar to those found on the Kensington Rune Stone. Wolter photographs sixty-one churches in greater Gotland and seven churches (six in ruins) within the walled city of Visby.

Wall murals and limestone columns adorn the beautiful interior of Sanda Church which is similar to the ninety-two churches found in greater Gotland. (SFW)

May 5 to 9 – Scott Wolter makes a second trip to the island of Gotland to photograph additional medieval grave slabs and churches.

This picture of Klinte Church on the west coast of the island of Gotland shows its beautiful eight-sided spire. (SFW)

June – A paper written by retired professor Tryggne Sköld is published by DAUM (Institute of Dialectology, Onomastics and Folklore Research in Umea). In it Professor Sköld claims that the Larsson papers help prove the Kensington Rune Stone was carved by a Norwegian. In his analysis, Sköld uses many of the same incorrect assumptions that had been made by linguists for the past century.

June – A paper written in 2004 about the pentadic number in Arabic placement on the Hammerby Calendar Stick is reported to the authors via the internet. This is discussed on page 92.

Kensington Rune Stone Biographies

Anderson, Andrew (1863-1937): Farmer – Anderson was born in July 1863 and emigrated from Sweden in 1882. The 1900 census lists that Andrew (age 36) was married to Betsy (38) with six children, Peter (14), Andrew (12), John (9), Mary (7) and her twin Olof (7), and Carl (3). Ohman obtained Anderson's property in lot 2, (NW $^1/_4$, Section 14) on October 6, 1910.

In 1897, Sven Fogelblad died at the home of Andrew and Betsy Anderson, whereupon they inherited his book collection. Betsy gave Fogelblad's copy of the Almquist book of Swedish grammar to her cousin Karin Ohman in 1898 so her husband Olof could try to decipher the Kensington Rune Stone inscription *after* he found it. Theodore Blegen accused Andrew Anderson of being one the three likely forgers of the Stone. It is clear that Anderson knew Ohman since he borrowed money from Ohman many times from 1892 to 1894. The monies were paid back, albeit past their due date. However, there has never been any evidence presented that links Anderson to anything regarding to the Rune Stone.

Anderson, Rasmus B. (About 1845-1910): Linguist – Anderson was the United States ambassador to Denmark, and Professor of Scandinavian languages at the University of Wisconsin from 1868 to 1884, the first such post in America. In 1866 during his undergraduate days at Luther College in Decorah, Iowa, Anderson was known as a "dangerous person" (*Luther College: 1861-1961*, p. 76) who led a rebellion during a pastoral conference. Considered the ringleader of the group of rebels, he wrote up a list of grievances or "bill of rights," which the students signed. When Anderson refused to retract his statements or apologize, he was expelled and ordered off the campus. Years later Anderson made amends with the college and was awarded his degree. In 1883, Anderson wrote a book titled, *America Not Discovered by Columbus.*

A letter written by Anderson on May 14, 1910 was published in the newspaper *Amerika*, where he recalled a meeting between himself and Kensington resident, Andrew Anderson. In the article, A. Anderson implied that he was involved with carving the Kensington

Rune Stone with Olof Ohman. Later that year Newton Winchell wrote to both Ohman and A. Anderson about the R. B. Anderson letter. A. Anderson denied the claims in R. B. Anderson's letter, and stated that he believed the Stone was genuine.

Rasmus B. Anderson, as he appeared in about 1900, was a Professor of Scandinavian at the University of Wisconsin. Hjalmar Holand was one of his students and rented a room in Anderson's house until they had a falling out over a now forgotten dispute. (Luther College Archives, Decorah, Iowa)

Babcock, Willoughby (1893-1967): Historian – After receiving degrees from the University of Minnesota and Harvard University, the Minneapolis native began his career at the Minnesota Historical Society as an editorial assistant on August 26, 1918. During his forty year career as museum curator (1919-1946) and then curator of newspapers (1946-1958) he developed an extensive statewide microfilming program in the society's newspaper library.

At the request of director Dr. Harold Cater, Babcock performed an analysis of the Willie Sarsland letter on November 29, 1949. He wrote in his conclusion that his opinion regarding the validity of the Sarsland letter was "distinctly unfavorable."

Willoughby Babcock was the curator of newspapers at the Minnesota Historical Society and is pictured here in 1930. (Photograph courtesy of the Minnesota Historical Society)

Bakke, Einer (1912-Present): Construction Worker – Einer was born in Gibbon, Minnesota and moved to Kensington in 1921.

Einer knew Olof and Karin Ohman, their children and grandchildren. He recalls with clarity many events related to the Kensington Rune Stone that happened over the years. Einer remembers the rally at Fahlin's Point in 1927, and now lives on the opposite side of Oscar Lake. His late wife Ione can be seen as a little girl on the right side of the stage in the photograph on page 196.

Barnes, Michael (1940-Present): Runologist – Barnes is an expert in Scandinavian languages and a runologist at the University College of London in England.

Professor Barnes has provided valuable critical input to both of the authors over the past few years. Barnes traveled to Stockholm where he gave a presentation at the Historiska Museum on October 23, 2003 on the difficulty of dating inscriptions. He also traveled to Minnesota to personally inspect the Bourne Stone and visit the area where the Kensington Rune Stone was found. (See color section, plate 46.)

Bentson, Roald (Unknown-After 1910): Farmer – Bentson was a neighbor and friend of Olof Ohman who gave a joint affidavit in 1909, along with Sam Olson, about his observations of the Stone and the tree roots (Blegen, page 140).

Berg, Kristian (1959-present): Historian – Kristian studied art history and history of ideas at the Universities of Stockholm and Gothenburg, and worked at the National Board of Housing and Planning at The National Heritage Board. From1994-1999 he was head of the Heritage Department at the Swedish Ministry of Culture. From 1999-2005 he was the Director General at the Historiska Museum in Stockholm, Sweden.

Kristian hosted the Kensington Rune Stone exhibit and one-day conference at the Historical Museum in Stockholm during its first trip to Sweden in October of 2003. This exhibition brought extensive media coverage and public interest in the Rune Stone and eventually led to the discovery of the Larsson papers and new research into the artifact.

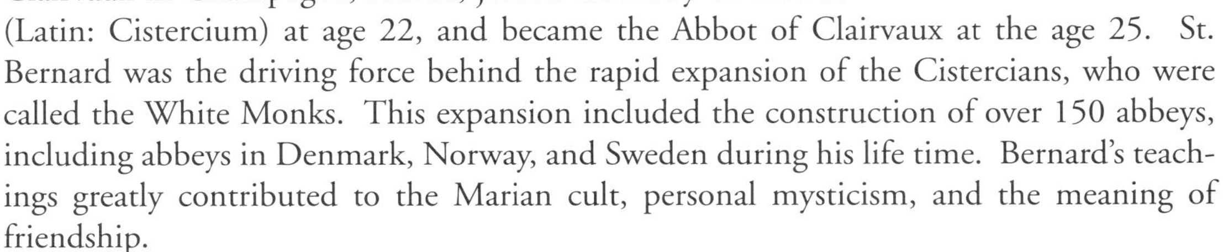

Kristian Berg was the Director General at the Historical Museums in Stockholm, Sweden from 1999 to 2005. (Photograph courtesy of Kristian Berg)

Bernard of Clairvaux (1090-1153): Priest – St. Bernard of Clairvaux in Champagne, France, joined the Abby of Cisteau (Latin: Cistercium) at age 22, and became the Abbot of Clairvaux at the age 25. St. Bernard was the driving force behind the rapid expansion of the Cistercians, who were called the White Monks. This expansion included the construction of over 150 abbeys, including abbeys in Denmark, Norway, and Sweden during his life time. Bernard's teachings greatly contributed to the Marian cult, personal mysticism, and the meaning of friendship.

He was a sponsor of the Knights Templar, wrote their charter and obtained papal recognition for them. He also organized the second crusade to the Holy Land in 1146. The Templars also participated in the crusade to rid Estonia and the entire south Baltic coast of pagans in the period 1174-1219, using Bornholm and Gotland as strategic staging areas.

Blank, Britta (1944-Present): Building Engineer/Farmer — Britta was born and raised in Forsadalen, Sweden, and has four children. She and several other relatives have been studying the history of that area and the old farms for several years.

Olof Ohman's uncle, Erik Olsson, is the great-great grandfather of Britta's husband Fleming. In October 2003, she and other descendants of Olof Ohman began to hear about the Kensington Rune Stone everywhere in the Swedish media. She sent an e-mail to the Historiska Museum in Stockholm, and told them her family was related to the discoverer of the Stone. The museum put them in contact with journalist Lars Westman, from the Swedish Magazine *Vi*, who wrote an article that helped make the meeting with the Ohman family in Minnesota possible. In February 2004 when the Kensington Rune Stone came to the Hälsinglands Museum in Hudiksvall, Britta and her relatives arranged a dinner and a sightseeing tour with about fifty Swedish relatives who met Scott Ohman, Olof Ohman's great-grandson. Scott was the first member of Olof Ohman's family ever to visit Sweden and see where Olof Ohman was born in Långby, Forsadalen. In late 2003 and early 2004, several previously unknown letters written by Olof and Karin Ohman to relatives in Sweden over a period of several decades began to show up. The relatives in Sweden formed a group called the Olof Ohman Relatives and Friends Association which knows of forty-six letters in Sweden. Hopefully, more documents hidden in drawers and boxes in Sweden and Minnesota will turn up.

Blegen, Theodore (1891-1969): Historian — Professor of history at Hamline University (1920-1927) and the University of Minnesota (1927-1939) and dean of its graduate school (1940-1960). He succeeded Solon J. Buck as the superintendent at the Minnesota Historical Society in 1931 until 1939. Upon his retirement in 1960, he returned to the Society as a research fellow until his death.

His 1968 book, *The Kensington Rune Stone: New Light on an Old Riddle* is partly responsible for the Stone being widely considered a hoax today. He concluded that three people were most likely responsible for perpetrating a fraud: Andrew Anderson, Sven Fogelblad, and Olof Ohman, but he did not consider the geological finds of Professor Winchell.

Theodore C. Blegen as he appeared in 1952 when he was Dean of the Graduate School at the University of Minnesota. (Photograph courtesy of the Minnesota Historical Society)

Breda, Olaus J. (1853-1916): Linguist – Born in Norway, he became a professor of Scandinavian languages at the University of Minnesota in 1883, and returned to Norway in 1898.

Professor Breda received a copy of the inscription directly from his fellow Norwegian Samuel Siverts of Kensington which he in turn sent to Olof Rygh in Oslo. Based on this copy the professor expressed the opinion that the inscription was a modern joke by someone who knew runes. The professor also received the Ohman/Hedberg copy sent to the University of Minnesota by Turnblad of SAP.

Olaus Breda circa 1898. (Photograph courtesy of the Minnesota Historical Society)

Brøndsted, Johannes (1890-1965): Archaeologist – He was the head of the Danish National Museum of Denmark in Copenhagen, and was considered to be the foremost Scandinavian archaeologist when he visited the Kensington Rune Stone in 1949.

Quoting Brøndsted in the *Aften Posten* (Evening Post), Copenhagen on May 5th, 1949, *"My main opinion is that the Kensington Stone deserves a renewed modern study by competent linguists. In this context it is not sufficient to be merely a Viking Age researcher and only be familiar with the Runestone material of the Viking Age. We must ask opinions from qualified Middle Age linguists. One will then learn to what extent their judgment unanimously runs against the stone or whether linguists with insight will allow certain possibilities to open up, but surely the latter. And in that case the stone's patrons will have the comfort of knowing that by the time the next half century has passed such possibilities will have grown stronger."* (See Brønsted (1950, 1953)

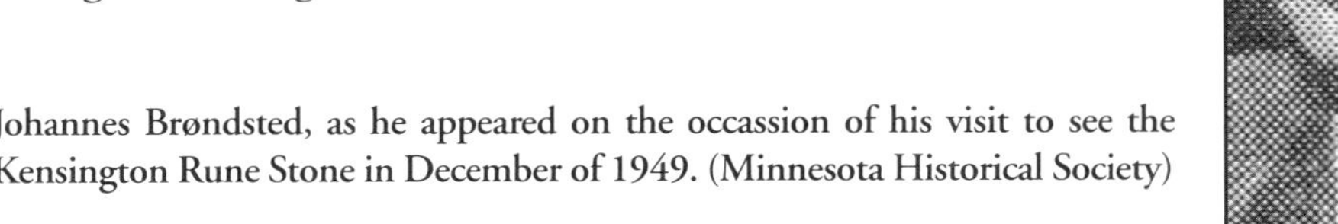

Johannes Brøndsted, as he appeared on the occassion of his visit to see the Kensington Rune Stone in December of 1949. (Minnesota Historical Society)

Bugge, Sophus (1833-1907): Linguist – Professor of Comparative Linguistics and Old Norse at the University of Christiania in Norway, Professor Bugge, along with his Danish colleague Ludwig Wimmer (1839-1920), was the co-founder of modern runology.

Bugge was the lead runologist of Norway when Curme sent him photos of the Kensington Rune Stone and a copy of the inscription in March of 1899. Professors Storm, Bugge, and Rygh were the committee that reviewed the documents, and sent a cablegram to Breda rejecting the inscription.

Cater, Harold (1908-Unknown): Historian – Cater was director of the Minnesota Historical Society from 1948 to 1955.

He received the Willie Sarsland letter on November 15, 1949, and solicited the opinion of Willoughby Babcock. Upon receiving Babcock's analysis of the letter he forwarded the documents to Johan Holvik for follow up.

Dr. Harold Cater, pictured in 1949, was director of the Minnesota Historical Society. (Photograph courtesy of the Minnesota Historical Society)

Curme, George O. (1860-1948): Linguist – Professor of Germanic languages at Northwestern University, Curme was the first linguist to examine the Kensington Rune Stone when it was shipped to his home library at the end of February 1899. He was initially skeptical of the inscription, but later observed weathering of the inscription.

de Molay, Jacques B. (1243-1314): Grand Master of the Knights Templar – Joined the Knights Templar about 1265, and was elected Grand Master in 1298. In 1307, Pope Clement V and King Philip le Bel of France gave the order in Europe to have the Templars arrested, disarmed, and imprisoned. de Molay was arrested in Paris, held for seven years, and burned at the stake in front of Notre Dame Cathedral in 1314.

While in prison de Molay created four Metropolitan Lodges of the Templars: Stockholm, Sweden in the north; Naples, Italy in the east; Paris, France in the south; and Edinburg, Scotland in the west. The Templars were forced to go underground to escape persecution, and their secret societies were born.

Flaaten, Nils (1845-1919): Farmer – A Norwegian immigrant from Tinn, Telemarken, who owned property immediately to the east of Ohman's, which he acquired in 1884. He was also grubbing trees on his own land not far from Ohman the day the Stone was discovered. Ohman called him over, and he was the first person other that Olof, Olof Jr., and Edward to see the Stone and the tree roots entangled around it. He said he had visited the site earlier in the day and never saw anything suspicious (Blegen, page 139).

A portrait of Nils and Torbjor "Tilda" Flaaten, made around 1900. (Photo courtesy of June and Lloyd Flaaten)

Flom, George T. (1871-1960): Scandinavian Linguist – Professor of Scandinavian languages at the University of Illinois, Flom was a strong opponent of the Kensington Rune Stone inscription, and delivered a paper to the Illinois State Historical Society Annual Meeting on May 6, 1910. Flom discussed the linguistic problems he had with the inscription and recounted his visit to the Ohman farm a few weeks before. In his address he outlined twenty-one points against the inscription's authenticity, not one of which is valid in 2005.

Professor George T. Flom, in about 1905. (Photograph courtesy of Minnesota Historical Society)

Fogelblad, Sven (1829-1897): Pastor – Born to Anders Anderson, a farmer in the parish of Faglum in Västergötland, Sweden, Fogelblad attended the famous Skara secondary school, was accepted at Uppsala University in 1854 as a theology student, and was ordained in 1857. He became the assistant pastor at the Bredared Parish Church in Västorgötland and served there until he resigned in1865. He immigrated to America some time from 1868 to 1870 and lived near Kensington. Fogelblad died at the home of Andrew Anderson on July 12, 1897, though his tombstone lists a different death date.

Fogelblad has been accused of being the author of the Kensington Rune Stone inscription (Blegen, 1968). Anderson's wife Betsy, and Ohman's wife Karin, were cousins, and Mrs. Anderson gave the Ohman family Fogelblad's scrapbook and the Almquist book of grammar when Fogelblad died. The data in the Ohman book collection shows that these documents were in no way sufficient to carve and compose the Kensington Rune Stone.

It has been theorized that Sven Fogelblad must have known Ljungström, since they were both at the Bredared Parish Church in 1858 and 1859. Fogelblad supposedly acquired enough knowledge of runes to author the Kensington Rune Stone inscription from Ljungström and his book of runes, but they were not sufficient to carve the Kensington Rune Stone.

The tombstone of Sven Fogelblad in the Wennersborg Cemetery in Solem County has the wrong birth and death dates. The Solem County Death Register (Book B, p. 54, line 21) lists Fogelblad's birth in 1829 and his death date as July 12, 1897. (SFW)

Fossum, Andrew A. (1860-1943): Linguist – He was Professor of Greek and French languages at St. Olof College from 1892 to 1910 before moving to teach at Park Region Luther College and Concordia College.

Fossum was a member of the Museum Committee of the Minnesota Historical Society that investigated the authenticity of the Kensington Rune Stone in 1910 and 1911. See Fossum (1911, 1918)

Fridley, Russell (1928-Present): Historian – Director of the Minnesota Historical Society for thirty-two years from 1954 to 1986.

Russ conducted an interview for the Minnesota Historical Society with descendants of John Gran, in an attempt to document the reported story of his "deathbed confession." The first interview was conducted with Walter Gran and his sister Anna Josephine in Alexandria, Minnesota, in 1970. The second interview was conducted with John Gran's other daughter, Sophie in Los Angeles, California, in 1972.

Gjessing, Helge (1886-1924): Philologist – He was the Assistant Director of Antiquities at the University of Oslo in Norway, and as a student of Magnus Olsen in 1909 he was assigned to study the Kensington Rune Stone. He issued a report in *Symra* (1909) which rejected the authenticity of the Kensington Rune Stone. None of Gjessing's runic or linguistic points are valid today.

Gould, Chester N. (1872-1957): Linguist – He received his undergraduate degree at the University of Minnesota under Professor Olaus Breda, and later became Associate Professor of German and Scandinavian languages at the University of Chicago.

Gould (1910) wrote a scathing letter about Hjalmar Holand to Warren Upham at the Minnesota Historical Society rejecting both the Kensington Rune Stone and Holand. None of Gould's runic or linguistic points are valid today.

Gran, Frank Walter (1894-1973): Farmer – Born and raised in the Kensington area, Walter knew the Ohman family well and was a close friend of Arthur Ohman for many years.

Walter was 76 years old when he was interviewed in 1970 by the director of the Minnesota Historical Society, Russell Fridley. Walter alleged that in 1926 or 1927, his father, John Gran, who reportedly thought he was dying, said that he and Olof Ohman had carved the Rune Stone. This interview was the genesis of the so-called "Deathbed Confession" and would become one of the most pervasive and distorted stories attached to the Rune Stone controversy (See "The Gran Tapes" chapter).

Frank Walter Gran in a photo from around 1917 when he was in the Army during World War I. (Photograph courtesy of the Ohman family)

Gran, John P. (1857-1933): Farmer—When he was seven years old, John emigrated from the province of Härjedalen, Sweden with his parents, his two brothers, and a sister. He married an 18-year old Norwegian girl named Anna Engeldahl, and together they had nine children including Josephine, the oldest, born in 1886, and Walter, the fifth child, who was born in 1894. Gran owned two farms, one roughly a mile north of the Ohman farm and another about three miles away and was one of the wealthiest men in Douglas County in his time. Joseph Hotvedt owned the eighty acre property sandwiched between Ohman and Gran.

Josephine and Walter alleged that John delivered a "deathbed confession" saying he was involved with Ohman in carving the Kensington Rune Stone. On August 13, 1967, Walter and Josephine recorded statements recalling conversations between Walter and his father in late 1926 or 1927. John Gran was ill and convinced that he was dying.

John P. Gran's tombstone in the Solem Church cemetery near Kensington, Minnesota. (SFW)

Gustafsson, Helmer (Circa 1940-Present): Runologist – Retired as a runologist with the Swedish Bureau of Research and Antiquities in April, 2005. Helmer and archaeologist Mats Larsson participated in the spirited debate with the authors in Hudiksvall, Hälsinglands, Sweden, on February 5, 2004. Helmer argued that the Kensington Rune Stone had a 19th century origin and was carved by a Swedish immigrant using runes that originated from the Swedish province of Dalarna. In the March 2004 issue of *Viking Heritage* magazine, Helmer claimed that the recently discovered Larsson rune row also had its origin in the Dalarna runes and probably represented a *secret* runic alphabet.

Helmer Gustafsson as he appeared on a Swedish television program about the Kensington Rune Stone in March of 2004. (Photograph by Scott Wolter, image courtesy of Vetenskapsmagasinet, SVT, Sweden)

Hægstad, Marius (1850-1927): Linguist – He was Professor of Norwegian Landsmal (popular speech) at the University of Christiania in Norway.

Professor Hægstad sparred with Hjalmar Holand in Christiania, Norway in 1911, about the language of the Stone. He made a pronouncement at that lecture, "The Stone is false!" None of his points against the Kensington Rune Stone are valid today.

Hall, Robert Anderson, Jr. (1911-1997): Linguist – Professor Hall was born in Raleigh, North Carolina, and graduated from Princeton University in 1931. He received his MA from the University of Chicago in 1935, and his Dottore in Lettere from the University of Rome in 1934. He was appointed an associate professor of linguistics at Cornell in 1946, and promoted to professor in 1950, where he served until his retirement in 1976, upon which he received the title Professor Emeritus of Linguistics and Italian. He published more than fifty books, and over five hundred and fifty journal articles and reviews.

Professor Hall wrote two books about the Kensington Rune Stone in which he emphatically proclaimed the inscription to be genuine. Hall also collaborated with author Richard Nielsen in his work on the language of the Stone beginning in 1984 and continuing until his death in 1997.

Robert Hall Jr. (Courtesy Alice Hall)

Hanson, Barry (circa 1945-present): Chemist/ Businessman – Barry and author Dick Nielsen convinced the Runestone Museum that a new investigation of the weathering in the Kensington Rune Stone runes was in order. Hanson's 2002 research is a result of his strong interest in the Kensington Rune Stone, and he worked closely with author Richard Nielsen on the book. For the first time many of the important Scandinavian publications related to the Kensington Rune Stone were translated into English in Hanson's book.

Haugen, Einar (1906-1994): Linguist – Haugen was a graduate student under George Flom at the University of Illinois. He became the department head of Scandinavian languages at the University of Wisconsin, and then held the same position at Harvard University.

He was also famous for pointing out a runic code that identified Olof Ohman as the carver. *"Some defenders of the stone have wondered why the inscription begins with eight Goths instead of twenty-two Norwegians, and it has been said that a Goth wrote the inscription. Here Professor Haugen agrees with the defenders except that his Goth is somewhat later vintage than 1362 — in fact a native of Västorgötland in the 19th century. He also suggested that the two words 'öh' and 'man' 'crucial weaknesses' in the inscription — are a reference to Ohman, the two parts separated to avoid too obvious a ploy."* (Haugen, March 7, 1968, Kensington File, Blegen Papers)

Haugen sponsored Wahlgren's 1958 book and supported George Flom's views. Wahlgren wrote in the foreword of his book, *"In equal measure this book has profited by the scholarly attention of Einar Haugen of the University of Wisconsin. Haugen has read the manuscript at three stages of its development and offered a wealth of criticism on philological and other points."* In February of 1987, author Richard Nielsen was invited to the home of Professor Haugen and his wife in a suburb of Boston for a few hours' visit about the Kensington Rune Stone. In spite of expressing amazement at his poor pronunciation of Scandinavian words, Professor Haugen listened patiently to Dick's explanation of the "J-rune" discovery in the *Codex Runicus*. The fact that the "J-rune" was previously unknown was the basis of Haugen's rejection of the Spirit Pond rune stones. Haugen encouraged Dick by saying, *"If I were a younger man,"* (he was in his late eighties at the time), *"I would seriously undertake an effort to get to the bottom of these stones, but under the circumstances I encourage you to press forward with your studies with all your vigor."*

Einar Haugen, as pictured in a Minneapolis newspaper article circa 1954. (Minnesota Historical Society)

Hedberg, John P. (1853-1933): Businessman – Hedberg was a businessman in Kensington who dealt in land, insurance, furniture, loans, and foreign currency.

Hedberg sent the Ohman copy of the inscription to Swan Turnblad at the *Svenska Amerikanska Posten* in Minneapolis on January 1, 1899. Turnblad, in turn, sent copies to the University of Wisconsin, Northwestern University, the University of Minnesota, and similar midwestern institutions. The Kensington Rune Stone was exhibited in his Kensington loan office for a period in late 1898.

A photograph of John P. Hedberg, taken around 1900. (Photograph courtesy of the Kensington Area Heritage Society)

Holand, Hjalmer (1874-1963): Historian – Hjalmar Holand will forever be known as a champion for the authenticity of the Kensington Rune Stone. He wrote numerous papers and 6 books about the Stone over a 55-year period that began in 1907 when he first took possession of the Stone from Olof Ohman.

Hjalmar Holand (third from left) posed with a group of unknown people for a photograph believed to have been taken in 1931.

Holvik, Johan A. (1878-1960): Linguist – He was a professor of Norse and Music at Concordia College in Moorhead, Minnesota.

Holvik first became involved with the Kensington Rune Stone when he was asked to examine the Almquist Swedish grammar book that Ohman gave to Winchell during his visit to Kensington in March, 1910. Holvik wrote a report stating, in effect, that the book was not the source used to carve the Kensington Rune Stone. In 1911, Holvik had a fateful lunch meeting in Oslo, Norway, with Hjalmar Holand. The two argued about the Kensington Rune Stone, and many believe this triggered Holvik's opposition, which evolved into an obsession to prove the Stone a hoax. Holvik was successful in having his arguments furthered by other opponents of the Rune Stone's authenticity, such as Erik Wahlgren, Erik Moltke, and others. Holvik died from a stroke on November 25, 1960. He is buried in Prairie Home Cemetery across from Concordia's campus.

This picture of Johan A. Holvik appeared in an article in the *Minneapolis Star* on August 11, 1951. (Photograph courtesy of 2005 Star Tribune/Minneapolis-St. Paul)

Hotvedt, Joseph (1861-1918): Farmer – Mr. Hotvedt owned the farm on the north side of Ohman's farm, which Ohman later purchased.

Mr. Hotvedt said he "saw the roots and verifies the description of their flatness, 'such as would be caused by lying against a stone'." This testimony is significant because he told Winchell in 1910 that he "doubts the authenticity of the Stone," which gave great credibility to his statement about the roots because he had no ulterior motive in promoting the roots as some indication of the Stone's authenticity.

Joseph Hotvedt is buried in the Solem township cemetery in Douglas County, Minnesota. (SFW)

Iverslie, Peter P. (circa 1850-circa 1920): Linguist – Iverslie was very active regarding the Kensington Rune Stone and published his articles in *Kvatal* (Quarterly) out of Eau Claire, Wisconsin.

Jansson, Sven B. F. (1905-1987): Runologist – A professor of Runology at the State Historical Museum, and director of the project to edit and interpret all of Sweden's rune stones, Professor Jansson wrote articles that were negative about the Kensington Rune Stone. In one, he said,

> *"For my part I would be extraordinarily surprised and disappointed if one were able to find a single academic teacher in the area of Nordic philology in Iceland, Norway, Denmark, Finland, or Sweden who did not endorse the opinion on the Kensington Stone that I have expressed here."* (Jansson, 1949: 403, F40)

As a result of this statement the Kensington Rune Stone was removed as an object of research for the next half century.

Swedish Runologist Sven B. Jansson painting a rune stone. An international symposium on runes and runic inscriptions was held in honor of his eightieth birthday September 8-11, 1985. (Photograph courtesy of the Swedish Books of Runic Inscriptions)

Kalm, Pehr (1715-1779): Botanist – Kalm was one of fifteen botany students of Carl Linné, sent around the world to collect samples that were returned to France for identification and classification. Kalm traveled to North America to find plants that could tolerate the Swedish climate and arrived in Philadelphia in the autumn of 1748. Kalm returned to Stockholm with such a fantastic collection in 1751 that over ninety of the seven hundred plants described by Linné were collected by Kalm. Kalm published an account of his travels in three volumes in 1770-71, with a fourth volume published in 1966 and re-published in1970.

Within Kalm's written accounts, *Peter Kalm's Travels*, he wrote about a conversation he had at a dinner party with Pierre La Vérendrye in 1749. The discussion was about an inscribed stone La Vérendrye's sons had discovered at the top of a stone pillar along a river near the Rocky Mountains. Kalm wrote that the stone was sent to France later that same year. Kalm's is the only known account of the inscribed stone now called the La Vérendrye stone. For over a hundred years historians have speculated that there could be a connection between the Kensington Rune Stone and this mysterious stone.

A portrait of Swedish botanist Pehr Kalm from the year 1761.

Kehoe, Alice (1934-Present): Anthropologist – Now retired, Kehoe was a professor of anthropology at Marquette University in Milwaukee, Wisconsin, from 1968 to 1999. She has been president of the Central States Anthropological Society, and of the Milwaukee Society of the Archaeological Institute of America. From 1979-82 she was on the Board of Directors of the American Anthropological Association.

Alice has been a consultant on the archaeological and anthropological perspective of the Kensington Rune Stone and has researched history relevant to the 1362 date, noting the circumstances following the Black Death, and Hanse takeover of Bergen. Kehoe prepared a case study of the Kensington Rune Stone issue for the Waveland Press series of anthropological texts for undergraduate courses teaching critical thinking. The book was published in January, 2005.

Knirk, James E. (1947-Present): Linguist/Runologist – Knirk is from Michigan and received his PhD from Yale University.

In 1984 he assisted Erik Molke in proofing Moltke (1985). In that year Dr. Knirk took over the runology section of the University of Oslo, a position he currently holds as full professor. He has commented on Nielsen (1998) and Nielsen (2002), see Knirk (1998 and 2002). Author Nielsen visited Knirk in the time frame from 1986 to 1989 and he was most helpful to his early investigation. Knirk also urged Nielsen to find a solution to the Kensington Rune Stone in one time and in one place. It seems he was right.

Kolberg-Streeter, Joanne (1949-Present): Nurse – Joanne was born in Minneapolis, Minnesota, and moved with her family to Forest Lake, Minnesota in 1955. Joanne married Bill Streeter in 1971 and they have two daughters, Joanna and Jessica.

When she was growing up, Joanne spent several weekends every summer at the Ohman farm visiting her uncles Art and John Ohman. When her father Lalard died in 1997, she took possession of the Ohman documents in his collection.

Joanne Kolberg-Streeter stands next to a picture of her great aunt Amanda Ohman-Carlson, and her grandmother Ida Ohman Kolberg at the community center in Kensington, Minnesota, on August 21, 2004. (SFW)

Kolberg, Lalard (1916-1997): Heavy Equipment Mechanic – Lalard was born in Fargo, North Dakota and is the only son of Abraham Kolberg and Ida Ohman. From the time he was three years old he was raised at the Ohman farm by his grandparents, Karin and Olof Ohman. Lalard and his wife Doris raised three children, Joanne, Thomas, and Bruce, in the house that formerly belonged to his Aunt Amanda and Uncle Joel Carlson in Forest Lake, Minnesota.

Lalard took possession of the Ohman family documents after Art Ohman's death in 1984.

Lalard Kolberg looking quite dapper in a 1932 photograph. (Courtesy of the Ohman family)

Kolberg, Thomas (1952-Present): Chemist — Tom lives in Forest Lake, Minnesota, and holds a BA in Microbiology.

Thomas Kolberg holds a book from the Ohman Library that was signed by Sven Fogelblad in 1886. Tom helped sort through the Ohman book collection with Darwin Ohman, Joanne Streeter, and authors Wolter and Nielsen in Darwin's garage on August 4, 2004. (SFW)

Landsverk, Ole (1901-1987): Physicist — After receiving his undergraduate degree from Luther College in Decorah, Iowa in 1924, his MA from the University of Minnesota in 1930, and PhD from Chicago University in 1939, Landsverk worked at the University of Chicago as a research physicist for the government from 1943 to 1946. During this time he developed a series of instruments for warning people that atomic radiation was present, and was a member of the atomic test team at Bikini atoll in 1946. In 1947 he founded the Landsverk Electrometer Company in Chicago until he turned over control to a successor in 1968.

Landsverk wrote four books on Norsemen in America after 1000 AD and on dated runic cryptography. His 1961 book, *The Kensington Inscription: A Reappraisal*, emphasized the facts and circumstances surrounding the discovery of the Kensington Rune Stone and disputed many of the unfounded assertions found in Wahlgren's 1958 work.

Author Nielsen visited Landsverk at his home in July 1987 to discuss his recent findings concerning the Kensington Rune Stone. Nielsen informed Landsverk that he had discovered the so-called modern "J-rune" in the *Codex Runicus* of ca. 1319, discussed in his paper before LACUS that month, and of the Arabic 10 on the Kensington Rune Stone from Nielsen's 1986 paper in ESOP. Dick had just come from the Runestone Museum in Alexandria, Minnesota, and reported to Landsverk that the spalled area appeared to have a word such as *þessi* or *þeno*. Dick pointed out that these three points would change the basis of Landsverk's cryptographic analysis due to the requirement for accurate number counts of the runes. While unhappy to hear that these results invalidated his suggested findings, he did not shoot the messenger.

They also discussed what appear to be runic letters on bones found in Mandan villages that Landsverk had reported in his last book. These photos were discovered in the

Landsverk Collection at Luther College. Author Wolter, Darwin Ohman, and author Nielsen visited this collection in Decorah, Iowa on December 28, 2004.

A photo found in the Landsverk papers on file at the Luther College Library on December 28, 2004 shows inscribed bones found at Mandan Indian Village sites.

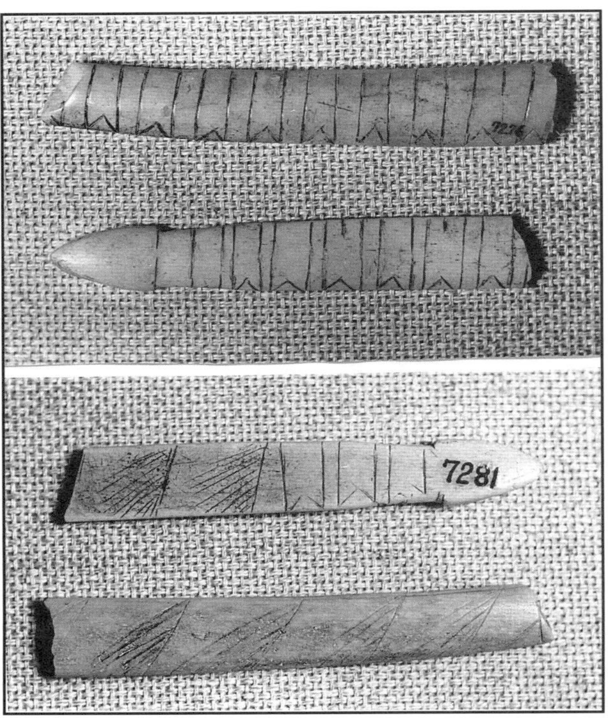

Ole G. Landsverk was an ardent supporter of the authenticity of the Kensington Rune Stone though the 1960s until his death in 1986. (Luther College Archives, Decorah, Iowa)

Larsson, Edward (1867-1950): Tailor/Musician – Larsson was from the farm Pernils (Peter Nicolas' homestead) in the village Holsåker, Dala-Floda parish, Gagnef County, in the Province of Dalecarlia (Dalarna). Following the *gesällsystem* (journeyman system) for craftsmen of the time, he would have traveled to receive his specialized training from various tailor masters. Most of his documents are hand-written music scores, but there are also books, letters, farm documents, and pictures. The collection was inherited by his son, and later by his grandchildren, who donated all his papers to DAUM.

Larsson's papers included two sheets (dated 1883 and 1885) that contained complete, previously unknown rune rows, the second of which is strikingly similar to the Kensington Rune Stone alphabet. In the fall of 2003, retired professor Tryggve Sköld recalled the documents while listening to a radio program about the Kensington Stone's exhibition in Stockholm. He wrote a paper that contained a number of important observations on the differences and similarities between the two scripts. To some linguists in Sweden, this rune row represented the "missing link" that proved a Kensington Rune Stone-type runic alphabet existed in 19th century Sweden.

A photo of Edward Larsson taken in the 1940s. (Photograph courtesy of the Edward Larsson Family)

Larsson, Susanna (1978-Present): Historian – Born and raised in Falköping, Sweden, Ms. Larsson was a co-producer of "The Riddle of the Kensington Rune Stone: A Hälsinge Story?", an exhibit at the Hälsinglands Museum in Hudiksvall, Sweden, in February 2004, and the "Hälsinglands Roots in Minnesota: An Immigrant's Story" exhibit in Kensington, Minnesota, in June 2004.

Ms. Larsson provided the English translation of most of the Ohman letters found in Sweden.

La Vérendrye, Pierre Gaultier de Varenne, Sieur de (1685-1749): Explorer – Upon the orders of the governor-general of Canada, La Vérendrye and his two sons, Chevalier and Louis, set out from Quebec in 1738 to explore the Canadian wilderness and returned in 1743. La Vérendrye buried a dozen 7″ x 8″ lead plates along his voyage, claiming land for France. In 1913, one of the plates was discovered near Fort Pierre, ND. It reads, *"In the twenty-sixth year of the reign of Louis XV, the most illustrious Lord, the Lord Marquis of Beauharnois being Viceroy, 1741, Peter Gaultier De La Vérendrye placed this."*

On April 29, 1742, Chevalier and Louis left Fort la Reine, and aided in their travels by several tribes of Natives they laid eyes on the Rocky Mountains for the first time on January 1, 1743.

The sons discovered large pillars of limestone along the Milk River on their return to Quebec, and found fixed inside an opening at the top of one of the pillars an inscribed stone which they removed and took with them. The stone was given to their father, who upon his return to Montreal that same year sent it to the French secretary of state, the Count of Maurepas, in Paris.

Linné, Carl (1707-1778): Botanist – Visited Gotland in 1741: Carl Linæus in his *Iter Gotlandicum* in Linean Society London.

Linné, who is called the "Father of Botany," sent his student Per Kalm to North America, where he met Pierre LaVérendrye in 1749.

Portrait of the renowned Swedish scientist Linné, wearing a Rosicrucian's Cross, that hangs in the National Art Collection on display at Gripsholm Castle outside of Stockholm.

Ljungström, Claes J. (1819-1882): Pastor – A native of Västorgotland and graduate of Uppsala, he was the co-pastor at Bredared Parish Church in Västorgotland from 1855 to 1859 with Sven Fogelblad. He authored the book, *The Art of Runic Writing* in 1866, with a second edition published in 1875, which was used as a textbook in Swedish schools. His book is on Viking age rune stones and its rune row were not sufficient to carve the Kensington Rune Stone.

Löfvendahl, Runo (1944-Present): Geochemist – Born in Bäcke, Sweden and raised in Bränna in western Sweden. Runo has a PhD from the University of Stockholm in isotope geology, and currently works as a geologist at the National Heritage Board of Sweden.

Runo headed an investigation team that examined the Kensington Rune Stone in 2003 and 2004, and studied the geologic aspects of the stone and carving techniques used to make the inscription.

Runo Löfvendahl at his desk in Stockholm, Sweden, on June 2, 2004. (SFW)

Moltke, Erik (1901-1984): Philologist/Runologist – He was the head runologist with the National Museum of Denmark in Copenhagen.

This photograph of Erik Moltke appears in his 1958 books. (Photo courtesy National Museum of Denmark in Copenhagen.)

Montelius, Oscar (1843-1921): Archaeologist – Montelius was the founder of the Historiska Museet (Historical Museum) in Stockholm, Sweden.

Montelius (1877) authored a book on the history of Sweden which was republished in *Svenska Amerikanska Posten* SAP (1897-1898) and republished in SAP in 1900.

This portrait of Oscar Montelius hangs at the Statens Historiska Museet in Stockholm, Sweden. (Courtesy Antiquarian-Topographical Archives (ATA), National Heritage Board, Stockholm)

Nielsen, Karl Martin (circa 1900-1987): Linguist/Runologist—Nielsen worked with Brønsted in 1950 and 1953 on the runic and linguistic aspects of the Kensington Rune Stone. He was the first runologist to acknowledge that the word "from" was, in fact, Swedish. All previous runologists had maintained that "from" was an English word only. He also wrote a discussion of the pentadic numbers on the Kensington Rune Stone in 1987.

Nielsen, Richard (1933-Present): Engineer – Born in Santa Monica, California, on November 26, the middle child of three (two sisters) children of Richard and Dagmar. He graduated from the United States Coast Guard Academy in 1955 and from the University of Michigan with a Master of Science degree in Naval Architecture and Marine Engineering in 1961. Nielsen also holds a Masters of Arts in Applied Mathematics that he earned in 1964 from the University of Michigan. In 1965, Dr. Nielsen earned a

Doctor of Technology Degree at the University of Denmark in Copenhagen. Dick has five children, Deborah Ann, Thomas Mark, Anne Marie, Kari Louise, and Richard Tage.

In 1985, after returning to the United States from Europe, he took up the study of the Kensington Rune Stone to keep his reading ability in Scandinavian languages. His study led to the discovery of the Arabic use of ten in the inscription, which led to the discovery of the "crossed-L" rune's existence in 14th century manuscripts. These discoveries fueled an extensive and continuing investigation that has lasted twenty years. He speaks Danish, reads the runic and linguistic books of Sweden, Denmark, and Norway, and is somewhat at home with the diplomas of the mid-1300s in Sweden that concern the Kensington Rune Stone.

By simply checking the data available he found *risor* (journeys) in the Old Dictionary Supplements of 1956, and the preposition *from* (from) as a dialect word in an 1881 publication in Sweden (from Henrik Williams). With the exception of Karl Martin Nielsen on *from*, all runologists and linguists since Noreen in 1906 have claimed that neither *from* nor *risor* were Swedish. Quoting Nielsen (2004) "The Kensington Rune Stone is too important to be left to the linguists, who fail to check the dictionary."

Scott Wolter and Richard Nielsen pose for a photo on April 1, 2003. (Photograph by Janet Wolter)

Noreen, Adolf (1854-1925): Linguist – He was Professor of Scandinavian Languages at Uppsala, and member of the Swedish Academy.

Noreen wrote the first published paper about the Kensington Rune Stone in 1906, in which he claimed the inscription was modern.

Ohman, Amanda (1892-1951): Business Owner – The first daughter and fourth child of Karin and Olof. Amanda, who never had children, was married to Joel Carlson, who died in 1948. Upon his death, she moved back to the family farm in Kensington. She took her own life on April 19, 1951.

Ohman, Arthur (1891-1984): Farmer – The third son of Karin and Olof, he lived on the farm until 1970. Art outlived his siblings and died on February 18, 1984, at the age of 93. He was a good friend of Walter Gran until the Gran Tape interviews of 1967, 1970, and 1972.

Arthur Ohman in a photo from about 1910. (Photograph courtesy of the Ohman family)

Sisters Amanda and Ida Ohman, around 1910. (Photograph courtesy of the Ohman family)

Ohman, Darwin (1943-Present): Engineer/Musician – Darwin is the second of the five sons of William Ohman, and a grandson of Karin and Olof.

Darwin participated in an interview with Russell Fridley in May of 2004, and provided a different perspective to Walter Gran's testimony in the Gran Tapes interviews and the alleged "Deathbed Confession." Darwin also traveled to Stockholm, Sweden, in May of 2004, where he received an apology from Professor Henrik Williams for the way his family had been treated by some linguists since the Stone was found.

Darwin Ohman holds up a book of the Ohman genealogy he received as a gift from his relatives in Sweden at the grand opening of the Hälsinglands Exhibit in Kensington, Minnesota, on June 17, 2004. (SFW)

Ohman, David (1902-1929): Farmer – David was the sixth son and eighth child of Karin and Olof. He lived at the family farm until he committed suicide on July 17, 1929, at the age of 26.

David Ohman at his confirmation in about 1915. (Photograph courtesy of the Ohman family)

Ohman, Edward (1888-1950): Farmer – The second child of Karin and Olof, Edward was working with his father when Olof unearthed the Rune Stone. From most accounts, Edward was the first one to notice the inscription, and later in his life gave an important interview about the Kensington Rune Stone to the Minnesota Historical Society on December 29, 1949, a year before his death on December 9, 1950.

Edward Ohman, about the time the Kensington Rune Stone was found in 1898. (Photograph courtesy of the Ohman family)

Ohman, Ida (1894-1979): The second daughter and fifth child of Karin and Olof, Ida moved to Fargo, North Dakota, and in 1916 she had a son named Lalard by her soon-to-be husband, Abraham Kolberg. In 1920, Ida relocated to Detroit, Michigan. Ida married again, and as Ida Erikson she lived in Detroit until her death in 1979.

Ohman, John (1899-1960): John Ohman was the fifth son and seventh child of Karin and Olof. John never married, and lived on the farm until his death from cancer on February 10, 1960.

John Ohman (right) posed for a picture with his good friend Louis Johnsrud in about 1925. (Photograph courtesy of the Ohman family)

Ohman, Karin Danielson (1862-1947): Farmer – Born in Forsa, Hälsingland, Sweden, she immigrated to America in 1885. Karin was one of five siblings (three sisters and a brother), and first settled in Bishop Hill, Illinois, before moving to Minnesota a year later, in 1886. Karin lived on the farm until her death in 1947.

Karin Ohman sits with her grandson Derrill in a 1941 photo. (Photograph courtesy of the Ohman family)

Ohman, Olof (1854-1935): Farmer – Born on October 10, in Forsa, Hälsingland, Sweden, he first immigrated to America in 1879, but returned to Sweden in 1883. Olof came back to America in 1885 and settled in Brandon. In 1886 he married Karin Danielsson, also from Forsa, and moved to the Kensington homestead in the fall of 1891. Ohman visited his relatives in Sweden in 1912, and returned to Kensington in July, 1914.

Ohman discovered the Kensington Rune Stone wrapped in the roots of an aspen (often referred to as a poplar) tree he was grubbing on his farm near Kensington, Minnesota, in November of 1898. Various hoax theories accused him of being involved in the Stone. For thirty-seven years after the discovery, until his death on August 27, 1935, he denied any involvement in a any hoax or forgery.

A young Olof Ohman in about 1872. (Photograph courtesy of the Ohman Relatives Association)

Ohman, Olof Jr. (1887-1958): Farmer – The first child of Karin and Olof Ohman. Olof Jr. and his wife Gurina had a daughter, Jean Ardell Ohman, who died from complications of diabetes in 1951 at the age of 25. Olof Jr. lived most of his adult life in Viking, Alberta, Canada, but kept in close contact with his Minnesota family until his death in February of 1958. On April 12, 1957 Olof Jr. wrote a letter to his brothers on the farm that contained important information and his recollections about the Stone.

Olof Ohman Jr. in about 1905. (Photograph courtesy of the Ohman family)

Ohman, Oscar (1897-1917): Farmer – The fourth son and the sixth child of Karin and Olof, Oscar died of acute meningitis at his home on January 8, 1917.

Oscar Ohman as he appeared in about 1916. (Photograph courtesy of the Ohman family)

Ohman, Scott (1957-Present): Business Owner – Scott is a great-grandson of Olof and Karin. Scott's father Derrill is the first of five sons of William Ohman, who was the youngest of Olof and Karin's nine children.

Scott and his wife Diana have made a strong effort to represent the Ohman family in the Rune Stone controversy. Scott traveled to Forsadalen, Sweden, in February of 2004, to meet the Ohman relatives in Sweden and to be a spokesman for the Ohman side of the family in America.

Ohman, William (1905-1973): Farmer – William was the seventh son and ninth child in Olof and Karin's family. In 1930 he moved to Bemidji, Minnesota, where he and his wife Myrtle raised five boys: Derrill, Darwin, Gary, Jim, & Kim. William passed away on October 30, 1973.

William Ohman pictured in about 1925. (Photograph courtesy of the Ohman family)

Ojakangas, Dick (1932-Present): Geologist – Ojakangas received his undergraduate degree from the University of Minnesota-Duluth (UMD) in 1955, his MA from the University of Missouri-Columbia in 1960, attended Helsinki University in Finland on a Fulbright Scholarship in 1960-61, and earned his PhD at Stanford in 1964 (all degrees in geology). Ojakangas was a member of the UMD faculty from 1964-2000 and has been professor emeritus since 2000. His main interests are sedimentology and sedimentation (including economic deposits in sedimentary rocks), iron formations, and ancient glaciations with an emphasis on Precambrian age rocks (greater than 600 millions years old).

Ojakangas performed petrographic analysis of the Kensington Rune Stone to determine the likely source of the rock type (metagraywacke) on which the runes were carved.

Dick Ojakangas stands next to the Kensington Rune Stone during the forum at Fort Snelling in St. Paul, Minnesota, on April 2, 2003. (SFW)

Olsen, Magnus (1878-circa 1965): Linguist – He was professor of Old Norse and Icelandic language and literature at the University of Oslo in Norway from 1908 to

1948. Olson assigned Halge Gjessing to investigate the Kensington Rune Stone. See Gjessing (1909).

Olson, Samual (Unknown-Unknown): Optometrist – Olson completed studies at the Illinois College of Optometry in 1895 and opened an office in Kensington as an optician and jeweler.

Mr. Olson wrote a letter to Professor G. O. Curme in January 1899, inquiring about the Kensington Rune Stone inscription on behalf of Olof Ohman. He also wrote a letter in English to the Minnesota Historical Society on March 7, 1910, on behalf of Olof Ohman, asking them to retain the Rune Stone until Ohman and Holand had worked out an agreement over what should be done with it. Mr. Olson also provided an important sketch of the tree roots around the Stone to Professor Winchell on March 4, 1910. In addition, Mr. Olson gave an affidavit as to his observation of the Stone and the trees (Blegen, page 140).

Patton, LuAnn (1958-Present): Administrator—Director of the Kensington Rune Stone Museum in Alexandria, Minnesota from 1999 to 2004.

Ms. Patton was the driving force behind the museum's efforts to get the Stone tested by American Petrographic Services in July 2000. In spite of an often hostile local environment, LuAnn was instrumental in enabling the Stone to make its historic, first trip to Stockholm, Sweden in October of 2003. The Historiska Museum in Stockholm held a three-month exhibition about the Stone which included a one-day conference that included several lectures. Among the presenters were professors Michael Barnes and Helmer Gustafsson, and the present authors Dr. Richard Nielsen, and Scott Wolter, P.G.

Reiersgord, Thomas (1932-2003): Attorney/Historian – Mr. Reiersgord published the book, *The Kensington Rune Stone – Its Place in History* in 2001. Tom's book explores the possible history of the Kensington Rune Stone with Native Americans, including the idea that the Stone was carved in one location and moved by Natives to where it was found. His book proposed the idea that the Cistercians at Gutnalia in Gotland might be involved with the Kensington Rune Stone.

Tom Reiersgord inspects the Kensington Rune Stone at the American Petrographic Services Inc. laboratory on April 21, 2002.
(Photograph courtesy of the Reiersgord family)

Roerich, Nicholas (1874-1947): Artist – Roerich was born in St. Petersburg, Russia, the son of Konstantin and Maria. Roerich studied at the Academy of Art and at St. Petersburg University and held several positions as a teacher and spokesman for the arts in Russia. In 1921, Roerich founded the Master Institute of United Arts in New York, which flourished for years until it financially collapsed during the Great Depression. Two years after his death the institution was reborn on West 107th Street in New York, where it remains today.

Roerich and his wife Helena received the Rothenburg Casket at a hotel in Paris in 1923. Helena later wrote a poem, published in 1930, that described the presence of four Ms on the casket.

This photo of George, Nicholas, and Svetoslav Roerich was taken in 1942. (Photograph courtesy of the Roerich Museum, New York)

Sarsland-Kralicek, Irene (1924-present): Rancher – Irene was born on the family ranch in Ludlow, Harding County, South Dakota, on February 24, 1924. She married George Kralicek on October 24, 1948, and they lived together until his death in 2002.

In 2004, Irene was the sole surviving offspring of Willie and Matilda Sarsland's thirteen children. She provided written testimony and an example letter from her sister Sally, which proved that Sally had written the letter for her father, which was then sent to the Minnesota Historical Society on November 14, 1949.

Sarsland-Eschrich, Sally (1921-1972): Rancher – Sally was living with her parents in Ludlow, South Dakota, in November of 1949, to help her parents because of her father's poor health. Willie probably dictated the letter about being a witness to the Kensington Rune Stone discovery to Sally, who sent it to the Minnesota Historical Society on her father's behalf.

Sarsland, Willie Levi (1875-1950): Farmer – Willie was born on September 14, 1875, in Omaha, Nebraska. His parents, Ole and Mary Sarsland, moved to a farm near Kensington in Douglas County in 1881. On July 13, 1900, he married Anna Mathilda Hedstrom, and they eventually had thirteen children. Willie moved his family to Harding County, South Dakota, in May of 1910.

Willie Sarsland was part of sixteen-man threshing crew that was working on the Ohman farm the day the Kensington Rune Stone was found. Willie wrote a letter to the Minnesota Historical Society on November 14, 1949, outlining important facts about the discovery.

Willie Levi Sarsland as he appeared in 1898 at the age of 23. (Photo courtesy of Irene Sarsland-Kralicek)

Siverts, Samuel A. (1854-1941): Banker – Mr. Siverts was the cashier at the Kensington bank at the time the Stone was found.

Mr. Siverts sent a copy he made of the inscription to Professor Olaus Breda at the University of Minnesota. Siverts also packed and shipped the Stone to Professor George Curme at Northwestern University upon his request in February of 1899.

Söderwall, Knute F. (1842-1924): Linguist – He was Professor of Scandinavian Languages at Lund University in Sweden. For eighteen years he was the editor-in-chief of the Swedish Academy's dictionary of the Swedish language.

He met Holand in 1911 and indicated that words such as "from" and "opþagelse" would not be a problem in Old Swedish. Events have proved him right.

(Courtesy of the Morris (MN) *Sun Tribune*)

S. A. Siverts, Sr., Passes

S. A. Siverts, Sr., a resident of Morris for a quarter of a century, passed away at the home of his daughter, Mrs. O. B. Carlson, in Grand Rapids, on Monday morning, Feb. 3. He was 86 years of age last November 22.

Interment was at Northfield on Wednesday afternoon, in the family lot where Mrs. Siverts was buried in 1924.

Mr. Siverts came to Morris in 1899 as the cashier of the Citizens' Bank, and continued in that capacity until about 15 years ago. He served on the city council, on the school board, and was active in church and community affairs.

Besides the daughter at whose home he died, he is survived by three sons, S. A. Jr., and Ing. T., of Minneapolis, and John of St. Paul.

Knute Söderwall as he appeared in 1912 at the age of 70.

Steward, John F. (Unknown-After 1900): Amateur Geologist – Mr. Steward took the first known photographs of the Stone at Professor George O. Curme's home in March 1899.

Steward wrote a letter to runologist Professor Ludwig Wimmer in Copenhagen, Denmark, on October 15, 1899 that described the weathering of the inscription and how the facts of the discovery supported its genuineness. He also wrote that he was sending a photograph of the Stone to Wimmer and several other scholars.

Storm, Gustav (1845-1903): Historian – He was a professor of History at Christiania University in Norway from 1877 until his death in 1903.

Professor Storm published a work on the Vinland Voyages in 1888 and was strong supporter of the position that the Sagas were of historical value. He was a member of a committee along with Bugge and Rygh who in 1899 sent a cable to Breda stating the Kensington Rune Stone was a fake.

Thalbizer, William (1873-1958): Ethnologist and philologist – Thalbizer was a professor of Arctic Ethnology at the University of Copenhagen in Denmark.

Thalbitzer wrote a paper in 1950 about the Kensington Rune Stone and the Kingigtorssuaq stone concluded that they both were likely genuine artifacts. Thalbitzer was criticized by scholars who disagreed with him about the Kensington Rune Stone. Quoting Thalbitzer (1950, page 4-5),

> *"For a long time I, too, had considered the Kensington Stone a fraud, and the late Prof. Finnur Jónsson and other Scandinavian runologists confirmed my view. However, from time to time certain fresh facts bearing on the matter have come to light, in archaeology, runology, and philology, especially Prof. Axel Kock's later studies on medieval Swedish dialects. As new light is gradually being thrown on this amazing find from the West, I cannot but waver in my doubt and am forced to see the question from a new viewpoint. Not only Holand's books but my own investigations as well have set me thinking along new lines. I now maintain that this matter in its entirety is worthy of re-study; it seems to me that, after all, the inscription may be authentic."*

The Kingigtorssuaq stone (about 10 cm long) was found in a stone cairn on a small island off northwest Greenland in 1824. (Photograph courtesy of Smithsonian Institute in Washington, D.C.)

Turnblad, Swan J. (1860-1933): Editor/Publisher – Mr. Turnblad, a Minneapolis resident, was the editor of the *Svenska Amerikanska Posten* in 1899.

John Hedberg and Olof Ohman sent a sketch of the inscription to Mr. Turnblad, who published it on February 28, 1899. Mr. Turnblad sent a copy of the inscription to the University of Minnesota, University of Wisconsin, Northwestern University, and other midwestern institutions.

This portrait of Swan Turnblad hangs on the wall at the Swedish American Institute in Minneapolis, Minnesota. (Photo courtesy of the American Swedish Institute)

Upham, Warren (1850-1934): Geologist, archaeologist, librarian – One of ten children born on a farm near Amhurst, New Hampshire, Upham graduated from Dartmouth College in 1871, served as an assistant on the geological survey of New Hampshire from 1874 to 1878, and then held the same position in Minnesota under Newton H. Winchell from 1879 to 1885. Became the superintendent and librarian at the Minnesota Historical Society on January 1, 1896 and held the post until 1914 when he became the Society's archaeologist, a position he held until his death. Upham published 321 papers and books, but his best-known publication is the book, *Minnesota Geographic Names*.

While researching for his book in May of 1916, Upham stopped in the town of Kensington and decided to walk 3 $^1/_2$ miles to the Ohman farm to visit with Olof and his

family. It was after this visit that he became completely convinced that the Kensington Rune Stone
was genuine, and lobbied unsuccessfully for the
Society to pursue a second attempt to purchase the
Stone from Hjalmer Holand.

Geologist/archaeologist/librarian Warren Upham pictured in
1915. (Photograph courtesy of the Minnesota Historical
Society)

Von Friesen, Otto (1870-1942): Runologist/
Linguist – He was a professor of Swedish at Uppsala
and a member of the Swedish Academy.

Von Friesen wrote to Warren Upham on April 4, 1910, during the Minnesota Historical
Society investigation, that the Kensington Rune Stone was a modern artifact carved by a
person who had a partial knowledge of runes, with some invented characters.

Swedish runologist Otto von Friesen wrote his notes in 1923 while standing between two gate pillars
located on the southern tip of Gotland Island in Vamlingbo Parish. To the left is the Sigraifs G 8 runic
inscription discussed in this book. (Photograph courtesy of The Swedish Books of Runic Inscriptions)

Wahlgren, Erik (1909-1984): Linguist – Wahlgren was Professor of Scandinavian and
Germanic Languages at the University of California, Los Angeles, from 1938 until he
retired in 1977.

Arguably the chief opponent of the Kensington Rune Stone and the work of Hjalmar Holand, his 1958 book, *The Kensington Stone: A Mystery Solved* condemned the Stone as a hoax, and is largely responsible for the prevailing negative public opinion. Quoting Erik Wahlgren (1952: 62-3),

> "***From*** *is not out of place in the language of Minnesota. It is unlikely that this particular question can be solved, and it is in fact unimportant to our thesis except to emphasize once more the multitude of inconsistencies barring the inscription's claim to medieval origin. It is unnecessary to account for these bastard forms, for nowhere are they more appropriate than among the homemade runic symbols from a Minnesota farm.*"

The word "**from**" in fact, is a Swedish dialect word from the colonies in the Estonian Islands.

Jeffrey Redmond (left) sits at a table with his mentor, Professor Erik Wahlgren, in this late 1960s photo. (Courtesy Jeffrey Redmond)

Wallace, Birgitta (1944-present): Archaeologist – Graduated with a degree in Nordic and Classic Archaeology from Uppsala University in Sweden, she then moved to the United States and took a volunteer position at the Carnegie Museum in Pittsburgh, Pennsylvania, eventually earning a permanent position in 1963. In 1964, Birgitta went along the eastern seaboard looking at various reported Viking age sites. She spent the summer of 1964 working at L'Anse aux Meadows in Nova Scotia, Canada, with Anne Stine Ingstad, the Norwegian director of the excavation. Birgitta spent six weeks in Minnesota in the fall of 1964, researching primarily reported Viking age artifacts and the Kensington Rune Stone.

Ms. Wallace is a well-known critic of the authenticity of several rune stones and other reported Nordic artifacts found in the United States.   In 2000, she authored a three-page article critical of the Kensington Rune Stone which contained numerous factual errors. (See Wallace 1971, 1982, 1984/5, and 2000.)

Birgitta Wallace takes a break from a dig at L'Anse aux Meadows in Nova Scotia, Canada, in 2002, in a photograph by her husband Rob. (Photograph courtesy of Birgitta Wallace)

Westin, Janey (1957-Present): Stone Carver – Westin received her degree in Japanese in 1980 from the University of Minnesota. She is a professional stone carver and sculptor who specializes in letter carving and works out of a studio in Minneapolis called Paper & Stone.

Westin and her father, Bob Johnson, discovered the AVM Stone within a quarter mile of the discovery site of the Kensington Rune Stone. While the AVM Stone turned out to be a hoax carved in 1985, it became an important control sample for comparative study with the Kensington Rune Stone. These studies, which are ongoing, indicate the Kensington Rune Stone inscription pre-dates Olof Ohman's immigration to America. Westin also offered valuable input into the methods and techniques used to carve the Kensington Rune Stone and the Bourne Stone.

Westman, Lars (1934-Present): Journalist – Lars lives in Stockholm and is a senior writer for *Vi* magazine.

Lars has written several articles on the Kensington Rune Stone that challenged the traditional ideas about the Stone by having a tone toward the authenticity of the Stone. Due in large part to Lars' efforts, the Stone traveled to Sweden for the first time in October 2003.

Affectionately holding his cat, Lars Westman poses in front of a "Stop Lars" sign given as a birthday present by his son, on October 24, 2003. (SFW)

Williams, Henrik (1958-Present): Philologist/Runologist – Professor Williams was born in Kalmar, Sweden, and graduated from Utica High School in Ohio in 1977. After completing graduate studies at University of Illinois at Urbana-Champaign in 1983-84, (graduate student and teaching assistant of Swedish), and Augustana College, Illinois, in the spring of 1988 (research), Henrik became a professor of Scandinavian languages at Uppsala University in 1990.

Henrik gave a lecture on the linguistic aspects of the Kensington Rune Stone at Thousand Oaks, California, in February of 2002, and has continued research on the inscription ever since. One of the key points of Henrik's presentation was his pronouncement that Olof

Ohman could not have carved the inscription due to differences in dialect.

> *"It has also been pointed out that some of the expressions would have been impossible in the Middle Ages, e.g.* **opþagelsefarþ** *which looks very much like the modern opdagelsesfærd 'journey of exploration' in Danish and Norwegian. But the fact is that a number of the apparently modern expressions can be demonstrated to have been in existence back in the Middle Ages. And* **opþagelsefarþ** *has now been interpreted as uptakilsefärd, which could mean 'acquisition journey, journey to acquire new land.' Suddenly the critique has to start again from a new direction."* (Williams, et al., 2003)

Winchell, Newton H. (1839-1914): Geologist – Graduated with a masters degree in 1867 from the University of Michigan, where his brother Alexander was a professor of geology, he served as the state geologist of Minnesota from 1872 to 1900. In the summer of 1874 he accompanied General Custer's expedition to the Black Hills and prepared the first report and geologic map of the interior of that unique region. Beginning in the spring of 1906, Winchell served as the head of the Department of Archaeology at the Minnesota Historical Society.

During the years 1909-10 he investigated the physical aspects of the Stone, and the topographical aspects where the Stone was found, as well as the character of the individuals involved with the discovery of the Kensington Rune Stone. He then authored a 76-page report which concluded that he was entirely confident that the Stone is a genuine artifact.

Geologist/archaeologist Newton H. Winchell about 1901. (Photograph courtesy of the Minnesota Historical Society)

Wolter, Scott F. (1958-Present): Geologist – Born in Homestead, Florida, Scott is the oldest of Fred A. and Barbara M.'s three children. Graduated from the University of Minnesota–Duluth in 1982 and worked as a field geologist in northern Minnesota with a mineral company in 1983. Twin City Testing Corporation in St. Paul, Minnesota, hired Wolter as a field construction inspector in 1985, and in 1986 he was asked to help develop and run the petrography department, which he did until 1989. In January of 1990 he started American Petrographic Services Inc., a materials forensics laboratory which specializes in concrete, aggregate, and rock. In September 2001, APS was hired to evaluate the structural concrete damaged by fire in the terrorist attack at the Pentagon on 9/11. Wolter has published two books about

Lake Superior Agates (1986 and 2001), and *Ettringite: Cancer of Concrete* (1997), as well as several papers about concrete, agates, and fossils from the Green River area of Wyoming.

Wolter was hired in July of 2000 by the Runestone Museum in Alexandria to perform an independent laboratory analysis of the physical features of the Kensington Rune Stone. Wolter's report concluded that the inscription was authentic. Additional analysis performed by Wolter from 2001 to 2004 included the generation of a digital photo library of the Kensington Rune Stone inscription, a tombstone study to determine the relative age of the Kensington Rune Stone inscription, and an extensive search of documents related to the Kensington Rune Stone at the Minnesota Historical Society and other institutions. Both he and Nielsen continue to research the Kensington Rune Stone and other reported Old Norse runic inscriptions carved in stone found in North America.

Zalar, Michael (1958-Present): Amateur Historian – Born in Duluth, Minnesota, and attended the University of Minnesota–Duluth.

Michael first encountered the Kensington Rune Stone in the spring of 1998, and has since published two articles on the Kensington Rune Stone (NEARA Journal, and Journal of the West), and an introductory booklet of facts regarding the Stone. Michael currently maintains a popular website on the Kensington Rune Stone.

Michael Zalar in 2001.

Bibliography and References

Almquist, Carl J. L. Svensk spåklära: Tredje upplagan, öfversedd och tillökad med samlinger öfver tio svenska landskapsdialekter. [Swedish language reader with collection of ten Swedish Dialects]. Stockholm: Högbergska boktryckeriet, 1840. På M. Wirsells förlag. Sven Fogelblad's copy is in the MHS library.

American Heritage Dictionary, Morris, William, Editor. 1973. The American Heritage Dictionary of the English Language. The American Heritage Dictionary Publishing Co and Houghton Mifflin Company, Boston, New York, Atlanta, Illinois, Dallas, Palo Alto.

Anderson, Magnus. 1895. Vikingefærden: Vikings Reise. Oslo: Eget.

Anderson, Rasmus Björn. Editor: 1906. Pre-Columbian Historical Treasures: 1000-1492. London: The Norroena Society.
———1930. America Not Discovered by Columbus (Eighth Edition. First Edition was 1883). Madison, WI: Leif Erickson Memorial Association.

Ariel. 1899. "Runic Monument or Mare's Nest?" Ariel, 22: 208, University of Minnesota.

Barnes, Michael P. 1990. "On Types of Argumentation in Runic Studies." In Proceedings of the Third International Symposium on Runes and Runic Inscriptions, 11-29. Grindaheim, Norway: August 8-12.

Béresniak, Daniel. 2000. Symbols of Freemasonry. New York: Assouline.

Blegen, Theodore C. 1968. The Kensington Rune Stone: New Light on an Old Riddle. St. Paul: Minnesota Historical Society.

Breda, Olaus J. 1910. "Rundt Kensington–stenen." [Around the Kensington Stone]. Symra (Decorah, Iowa). Translation in MHS Archives.

Baigent, Michael, Richard Leigh, and Henry Lincoln. 1982. The Holy Blood and the Holy Grail. London: Jonathan Cape.
———1986. Messianic Legacy. London: Jonathan Cape.

Baigent, Michael, and Richard Leigh. 1989. The Temple and the Lodge. London: Bedford Square: Arcade Publishing, US paper back.

Brøndum-Nielsen, Johannes. 1927. Dialekter og dialektforskning [Dialects and dialect research]. Copenhagen: I. H. Schultz Forlag.

Brøndum-Nielsen, Johannes and Aage Rohmann 1929. Mariaklagen (Lament of the Virgin). Facsimile and Word List for Klemming's, (1878) publication. I. H. Schultz Forlag, Copenhagen.

Brøndsted, Johannes. 1953. "Norsemen in North America Before Columbus, with linguistic Summary of Karl Martin Nielsen." In The Annual Report of the Board of Regents of the Smithsonian Institution. Washington, D. C.: Smithsonian Institution. 367–405 English translation of Karl Martin Nielsen's section by Colquhoun (2002: F-69 - F-87).
———1950. Problemet Om Nordboer I Nord Amerika Før Columbus [The Problem of Norsemen in North America Before Columbus]. Copenhagen: Årbøger for Nordisk Old Kyndighed og Historie.

Cantor, Norman F., ed. 1999. The Encyclopedia of the Middle Ages. Viking.

Collin, H. S., and C. J. Schlyter. 1827. West Göta law. Vol. 2 of Samling af Sveriges gamla lagar, VGL [Collection of Sweden's Old Laws]. Lund: Berlingska Press.

Collins, A. Jefferies. 1969. The Bridgettine Breviary of Syon Abbey. Henry Bradshaw Society, Vol. XCVI. Stanbrook Abby Press, Worcester, England.

Colquhoun, Robin. 2002. "Translations from Scandinavian Papers on the Kensington Rune Stone." Appx. F in Kensington Runestone: A Defense of Olof Ohman the Accused Forger, Barry J. Hanson vol. II: F1–F102. Kearney, NE: Morris Publishing.

Dersin, Denise. 1996. What Life Was Like On the Banks of the Nile 3050-30 B.C. Time-Life Books, Alexander, Virginia.

Durant, Will. 1950. The Story of Civilization 4 -- The Age of Faith. MJF Books, New York.

Farley, Gloria. 1994. In Plain Sight: Old World Records in Ancient America. Columbus, GA: ISAC Press.

Fitzhugh, William W., and Elisabeth I. Ward. 2000. Vikings: The North Atlantic Saga. Washington, DC: Smithsonian Institution Press.

Flom, George T. 1910. The Kensington Rune-Stone. An Address…Delivered before the Illinois State Historical Society at its Annual Meeting, May 5-6, 1910 at Springfield, Illinois. With an appendix in 1911. Cover title: The Kensington Rune-Stone: A Modern Inscription from Douglas County, Minnesota.

Fossum, Andrew. 1911. Study of language on the Kensington runestone leads to satisfactory results. Norwegian-American, February 24, 1911: 1, 3, 6.

Fridley, Russell. 1976. The Case of the Gran Tapes: Further Evidence in the Rune Stone Riddle. Minnesota History, Winter: 1976.152-154.

————1976b. "Debate Continues Over the Kensington Runestone." Minnesota History, Winter: 1976. Winter: 1976. 149-151.

Friesen, Otto von (1933) "De Svenska Runinskrifterna" [The Swedish Runic Inscriptions], pp. 145-248. in Runerne [The runes]. Nordisk Kultur VI. Stockholm: Albert Bonniers Förlag, von Friesen, Editor.

Gardell, Sölve. 1937. Gravmonument från Sveriges Medeltid [Grave monuments from Sweden's Middle Ages]. Part I Text,; Part II Photographs, l. Repr. Göteborg , Stockholm: Kung Vitterhets Historie och Antikvitets Akademien, 1945-46.

Gardner, Laurence. 1996. Bloodline of the Holy Grail. New York: Barnes and Noble Books.

————2001. Genesis of the Grail Kings. New York: Barnes and Noble Books. 2004.

Gilman, Rhoda 1993 "Vikings in Minnesota: A Controversial Legacy" from Roots 21:2 Spring: 1993. St. Paul: Minnesota Historical Society.

Gjessing, Helge. "Runestenen Fra Kensington," in Symra (Decorah, Iowa), 5: pp. 113-126 (1909). Translation in MHS Archives.

Gould, Chester Nathan (1910), Article in letter to Warren Upham, March 19, 1910. University of Chicago. Copy in MHS Archives.

Grøtvedt, Per Nyquist, 1939. "Den språklige sammenhæng mellem sørøstnorske og båhuslenske mål" [The Language Correspondence between Southeastern Norwegian and Bohus County Speech]. Mål og Minne: 156–169.

Gustavson, Helmer. 2005. "The Not so Enigmatic Runes of Kensington", Viking Heritage, March: 2004.

Gustavson, Helmer, and Sven-Göran Hallonquist. 1985. Runor i Dalarna [Runes in Dalecarlia]. Stockholm: Runverket.

Hagen, Siverts Nielsen. 1950. "The Kensington Runic Inscription," in Speculum: A Journal of Mediæval Studies, 25:321-356 (July, 1950).

Hall, Robert A., Jr. 1982. The Kensington Rune-Stone Is Genuine. Columbia, SC: Hornbeam Press.

————1994. The Kensington Rune-Stone: Authentic and Important. Lake Bluff, IL: Jupiter Press.

————1995. "Attestations as Evidence in Language History" in Nielsen (1998). pp. 238-241.

————1998. Narrative Cohesion in the Kensington Runic Text. Chap. 38 in The Emergence of the Modern Language Sciences: Studies on the transition from historical-comparative to structural linguistics in honor of E.F.K., Volume 2: Methodological perspectives and applications, ed. Sheila

Embleton, John E. Joseph, and Hans-Josef Niederehe, 255–264. Amsterdam: John Benjamins Publishing Company.

Hanson, Barry J. "The Kensington Runestone -- Physical Features, Past and Present." Journal of the West, Winter: 2001, 40:1, 68-80.

———2002. Kensington Runestone: A Defense of Olof Ohman the Accused Forger. 2 vols. Kearney, NE: Morris Publishing.

Hansen, Aage. 1962–1971. Den lydlige udvikling i dansk fra ca. 1300 til nutiden [Development of Danish Phonology from Circa 1300 until the Present]. 2 vols. Copenhagen: G. E. C. Gads Forlag.

Heer, Friedrich. 1961. The Medieval World. Winnepeg: Mentor.

Heimfrid, H. 1939. Article on Dotted Rs at Unka Church. Fornvännen, Stockholm.

Hoegh, Knut O. 1910. "Kensington og Elbow Lake stenene" [The Kensington and Elbow Lake Stones]. Symra 5 (October 2, 1909): 176–189. Translated for the Det Norske Selskab by Mrs. Davis T. Nelson. Translation in MHS Archives.

Holand, Hjalmar R. 1908. De Norske settlementers historie [The Norwegian Settlements' History]. Ephraim, WI: (privately printed). Translation by the authors.

———1909. Kensington-stenens sprog og runer: Svar til hr. Helge Gjessing. Symra, 5: 209-213. Translation in MHS Archives.

———1909 "An Explorer's Stone Record which Antedates Columbus" Harper's Weekly. 53: 15, (October 9, 1909).

———1910 "A Fourteenth Century Columbus." Harper's Weekly. 54:25, (March 26, 1910).

———1910b "First Authoritative Investigation of 'Oldest Native Document in America." Journal of American History, New Haven. 4: pages 165-184, 2nd Quarter. 1910.

———1910 "Are There English Words on the Kensington Runestone?" in Records of the Past (Washington, D.C.), 9:240-245 (Sept.–Oct 1910).

———1911. "The Kensington Stone Abroad." In Records of the Past, (Washington, D.C.), 10: 260-271, (September-October, 1911).

———1932. The Kensington Stone: A study in pre-Columbian American history. Ephraim, WI: (privately printed).

———1940. Westward From Vinland. New York: Duell, Sloan, & Pearce.

———1946. America 1355-1364: A New Chapter in Pre-Columbian History. Binghamton, NY: Vail-Ballou Press, Inc.

———1951 "Hvad mener de lærde om Kensingtonstenen" [What do the learned think about the Kensington Stone?] in Danske Studier, 46: 49-58. English translation in Colquhoun (2002: F-88 – F-97).

———1956. Explorations in America Before Columbus. New York: Twayne Publishers.

———1957. My First Eighty Years. New York: Twayne Publishers.

———1962. A Pre-Columbian Crusade to America. New York: Twayne Publishers.

Holvik, Johan, A. 1948 "J. A. Holvik Presents Basis for Belief That Rune Stone Is Modern," in Concordian, December 10, 1948, p. 4. In Minnesota Historical Society "Scrapbook," 1: 38.

———1949 "Holvik Finds New Evidence Debunking Runestone," in Concordian (Moorhead, Minnesota), November 18, 1949.

———1952 "Veteran of the Runestone Repeats his Doubts," in Minneapolis Sunday Tribune, March 2, 1952, Editorial Section, p. 3. In Minnesota Historical Society "Scrapbook," 1: 68.

Haagensen, Erling, and Henry Lincoln. 2002. The Templars' Secret Island. London: Weidenfeld Nicolson Illustrated.

Håkursen, Barbro. 2004. Runstaven på Linnés Hammarby [The runic shaft at Hammarby, home of Linné], Sweden: VT.

Hægstad, Marius. 1911. The runestone from Kensington is discussed—Prof. Hægstad denies its genuineness. Verdens gang [The Course of the World]. July 12. Quoted in Orlando Ingvoldstad, "It is false! says Hægstad," Norwegian-American (Northfield, Minn., August 4, 1911), 4.

Iverslie, Peter P. 1909. "Kensingtonstenen" [The Kensington Stone], Kvartalskrift, 5: 13–21.
———1910. "Mere om Kensingtonstenen" [More about the Kensington Stone], Kvartalskrift, 6: 8–116.
———1911. Runestenen: Naegtet optagelse in Minneapolis Tidende [The Rune Stone: Denied Publication in the Minneapolis Tidende]. Kvartalskrift, 7 (October): 6-11.
———1914. "Kensingtonstenen og Vinland's beliggenhed" [The Kensington Stone and Vinland's Location], Kvartalskrift, 7: 6–11.
———1919. "Stenen i Douglas County: Af en aldeles ulærd" [The stone in Douglas County: from a complete amateur], Kvartalskrift, 15: 6–25.

Jacobsen, Lis and Erik Moltke. 1942. Danmarks runeindskrifter. Copenhagen: E. Munksgaard, 1941-1942. 3 Volumes.

Jansson, Sam. 1943. "Svensk paleografi" [Swedish paleography]. In Brøndum-Nielsen, Johannes. Palæografi A: Danmark og Sverige [Paleography A: Denmark and Sweden]. Copenhagen: J. H. Schultz A/S Universtets Bogtrykkeri.

Jansson, Sven B. F. 1949. "Runstenen från Kensington i Minnesota" [The runestone from Kensington in Minnesota]. N. Tidsskrift För Vetenskap, Konst Och Industri, 25 (7-8): 377–405. English translation by Colquhoun (2002: F-20 – F-47).
———1987. Runes in Sweden. Translated by Peter Foote. Värnamo, Sweden: Royal Academy of Letters, History and Antiquities, Central Board of National Antiquities.

Janzén, Assar G. "Review of Hjalmar R. Holand, Explorations in America Before Columbus," in Swedish Pioneer Historical Quarterly, 8:25-31 (January, 1957).

Johnsen, Ingrid Sanness. 1990. Norges innskrifter med de yngre runer [Norway's inscriptions with the younger runes]. Ed. James E. Knirk. Vol. 6.2. Oslo: Norsk Historisk Kjeldeskrift Institutt.

Jónsson, Finnur. 1924. Interpretation of the runic inscriptions from Herjolfsnes. Meddelelser om Grønland. 67: 272–90.

Kahn, David. 1968. Letter Regarding Mongé and Landverk's 1967 Book." American-Scandinavian Review 56: 82, Spring 1968.

Kehoe, Alice. The Kensington Runestone. Chicago: Anthropology Texts/Waveland Press, 2005.

Kjær, Iver. 1994. Runes and Immigrants in America. The Nordic Roundtable Papers. The Center for Nordic Studies. University of Minnesota.

Kjær, Iver, and Erik Pedersen. 1979. Danmarks gamle ordsprog 1.1, Peder Låles ordsprog [Denmark's old proverbs 1.1, Peter Låles proverbs]. Copenhagen: Det danske Sprog- og Litteratureselskab.

Klemming, G. E. 1878. "Småstycken på Fornsvenska" [Codex Holm. A 120. Small fragments in Old Swedish (shown later to be Middle Danish-circa 1325)]. SSFS-Svenska Fornskrift- Sällskapet. 1878:161-76.

Klenche, Herman 1879. Alexander von Humboldt's Lif och Resor [Alexander von Humboldt's life and Journeys] from the 7th German addition. Stockholm.

Knirk, James E. 1995. Critique of Nielsen's "Linguistic Aspects Concerning the Kensington Rune Stone," cited in Nielsen (1998). Pp. 242-247. Reply to Knirk's comments in Nielsen (1998: 248-265).
——— 2001. "Essay on the Kensington Runestone," Scandinavian Studies 73: 1. Spring.
——— 2001b. "Umlauted Runes on the Kensington Runestone." Scandinavian Studies 73: 2. Summer.

Kock, Alex. 1890. "Några Bidrag till fornnordisk Grammatik" [Some contributions to old norse grammar]. Arkiv för nordisk filologi 6:31-34.
——— 1906. Svensk Ljudhistoria [Swedish Phonetic History]. Part 1, section 1. Lund: Gleerup, Lund, Harrassowitz, Leipzip.

Kroman, E. 1944. In Brøndum-Nielsen, Johannes. 1944. Palæografi A: Danmark og Sverige [Paleography A: Denmark and Sweden]. Copenhagen: J. H. Schultz A/S Universtets Bogtrykkeri.

Købke, P. 1890. Om Runerne I Norden [On Runes in Scandinavia]. Copenhagen: Otto B. Wrobleweki's Press.

Landsverk, O. G. 1961 The Kensington Runestone: A Reappraisal of the Circumstances under which the Stone was Discovered. Glendale, California.: Church Press, 1961. Cover title: The Discovery of the Kensington Runestone: A Reappraisal.
———1969. Ancient Norse Messages on American Stones. Norseman Press, Glendale.

Larson, Constant. 1916 History of Douglas and Grant Counties, Minnesota: Their People, Industries and Institutions. Indianapolis: B. F. Bowen & Co., 1916. "The Kensington Rune Stone: An Ancient Tragedy," vo1. 1, pp. 72-122.

Larsson, Patrik. 2002. Yr - runan [The YR rune]. Uppsala: Institutionen för Nordiska Språk, Uppsala University.

Liestøl, Aslak. "Cryptograms in Runic Carvings: A Critical Analysis," in Minnesota History, 41:34-42, (1968).

Liestøl, Aslak. "The Runes of Bergen: Voices from the Middle Ages," in Minnesota History, 40:49-59 (Summer, 1966). An appendix, "The Bergen Runes and the Kensington Inscription," is on p. 59.

Lithberg, Nils. 1953. Computus, Nordiska Museets Handlingar 29, Stockholm.

Lithberg, Nils, and Elias Wessén. 1939. Den Gotländska runkalenderen 1328 [The Gotlandic Runic Calendar of 1328]. Kungl. Vitterhets Historie och Antikvitets Akademiens Handlingar. Item 45.2. Stockholm.

Ljungström, Claes J. 1866, 1875. Rúna-list eller Konsten att läsa runor, folkskolorna och menige man meddelad. [Runic alphabets and the art of reading runes for folk schools and the common man], second edition. Lund Lund: Tryckt uti Berlingska Boktryckeriet, 1866, 2nd ed., 1875.

Lorenzen, M. 1882. Mandevilles rejse [Mandeville's journey]. Copenhagen: S. L. Møllers.

Luddy, Ailbe J. 1932. The Order of Citeaux M. H. Gill and Son Ltd., Dublin, Ireland.

Luther College (1961) Centennial Yearbook 1861-1961, Decorah: Luther College.

Mackey, Albert G. (1908) Lexicon of Freemasonry, Barnes and Noble Reprint.

Markey, T. L., ed. 1978. On Dating Phonological Change. Ann Arbor, MI: Karoma Publishers, Inc.

Massey, Keith A. J. and Kevin Massey-Gillespie. 2000. Mysteries of History!! Solved!! 5). The Kensington Rune Stone is Genuine. Massey Electronic Publishing.
———2005. "Medieval Elements in the Kensington Stone." In press with Epigraphic Society Occasional Publications, Vol. 24: 175-180, San Francisco.

Matsch, Charles L. 1976. North America and the Great Ice Age. New York: McGraw-Hill.

Minnesota Historical Society. 1910-1968. "The Kensington Rune Stone: A Scrapbook of Clippings." Minnesota Historical Society, St. Paul: 1910-1968, 2 vols.
———1910. "The Kensington Rune Stone: Preliminary Report," Minnesota Historical Society, St. Paul: Volkszeitung Co., 1910.
———1915. "The Kensington Rune Stone: Preliminary Report," in Minnesota Historical Collections, St. Paul: Minnesota Historical Society, 1915, vol.15: 221-286.

Moltke, Erik, and Harry Andersen. 1949. Kensington-stenen: Amerikas runesten [The Kensington-stone: America's runestone]. Danske Studier 45:37–63. (1950). English translation in Colquhoun (2002: F-48 - F-68).

————1950. "Hvad mener de lærde om Kensingtonstenen og Hjalmar Holand" [What do the scholars think of the Kensington stone and Hjalmar Holand]. Danske Studier 46:59–63. English translation in Colquhoun (2002: F-98 – F-102).

————1951. "The Kensington Stone." Antiquity 98 (June): 87–93.

————1953. "The Ghost of the Kensington Runestone." Scandinavian Studies 25, no. 1 (February).

————1985. Runes and their origin: Denmark and elsewhere. Copenhagen: The National Museum of Denmark.

Mongé and Landsverk. 1969. Ancient Norse Messages on American Stones. Norseman Press, Glendale.

Montelius, Oscar. 1877. Sveriges historia från äldsta tid till våra dagar: Sveriges Hednatid, Medeltid, Förra skedet, fran År 1060 Till År 1350 [Sweden's history from the earliest time to our own days: Heathen time, medieval time, first period from 1060 to 1350]. Stockholm: Hjalmer Linnstroms Forlag.

————1897-8. Sveriges hednatid samt medeltid, förra skedet, från år 1060 till år 1350 [Sweden's heathen period and the early stage of the middle ages from the year 1060 to the year 1350]. Vol. 1. Stockholm: Hjalmer Linnstroms Forlag. (Reprinted in the Svenska Amerikanska Posten, Nov. 1897–Feb. 15, 1898).

Nielsen, Karl Martin. 1950. "Kensingtonstenens runeinskrift" [The Kensington runic inscription]. AARBØGER for Nordiska Oldkyndighed og Historie. Copenhagen: Det kgl. nordiske Oldskriftselskab. English translation in Colquhoun (2002: F-69 – F-87).

————1987. "The Numerals in the Kensington Inscription," Runor and runinskrifter: The Second International Symposium on Runes and Runic Inscriptions. Konferencer 15: 175-83. Stockholm: Vitterhets Historie och Antikvitets Akademien.

Nielsen, Richard. 1986. "The Arabic Numbering System on the Kensington Rune Stone." Epigraphic Society Occasional Publications 15:47-61. San Diego.

————1987. "The Runes on the Kensington Rune Stone." Epigraphic Society Occasional Publications 16:51-83. San Diego.

————1987b. "New linguistic and runic evidence, which supports Hall's thesis that the Kensington runestone is genuine." LACUS Conference, Toronto.

————1988. "Appendix I. Linguistic Evidence that Supports the Kensington Runestone is Genuine," Epigraphic Society Occasional Publications, 17:124-78. San Diego.

————1989. "Appendix II Linguistic Evidence that Supports the Kensington Runestone is Genuine," Epigraphic Society Occasional Publications, 18:110-32. San Diego.

————1993. "The Translation of the Spirit Pond Runestones of Maine." Epigraphic Society Occasional Publications, 22: 158-217. San Diego.

————1998. "Linguistic Aspects Concerning the Kensington Rune Stone," Epigraphic Society Occasional Publications 23:189-265, San Francisco with critiques by Dr. Robert Hall, Jr. (1995), 238-41, & response, 242-3, and with critiques by Dr. James Knirk (1995),244-47, & response, 248-265.

————2000. "Proposals Concerning Early Scandinavian Incursions Into the Western States," Journal of the West, Vol. 39, Winter Issue, pp. 72-85, January 2000, Manhattan, Kansas.

————2001 "Response to Dr. James Knirk's Essay on the Kensington Runestone," Scandinavian Studies, Vol. 73.1. Spring: 2001. In Supplemental Materials (www.byu.edu/sasslink/).

————2002. "The Kensington Runestone and Evidence in Erikskrönikan, Mid-14th Century Diplomas and the Kingigtorssuaq Inscription." Appx. D in Hanson (2002). Vol. 2: D1 - D45.

————2005 "Response to Dr. Knirk's Review on the Kensington Runestone in Scandinavian Studies in Summer: 2001." In press with Epigraphic Society Occasional Publications, Vol. 24:76-98, San Francisco.

————2005b. "Progress on the Kensington Runestone: KRS Report 1998-2003." The Epigraphic Society—Occasional Papers: 24: 68-76.

Nielsestuen, Rolf M. 1994, The Kensington Runestone Vindicated, Lanham, New York London.

Noreen, Adolf. 1906. "Runinskrifter från nyare tid" [Runic inscriptions from more recent times]. Föreningen heimdals populär-ventensapliga tidningsartiklar 7:48–57.

Noreen, Erik. 1932. Fornsvensk läsebok [Old Swedish reader] Lund, Sweden: Gleerups.

————1944. "Amerikanska runor." Svensk stilparodi och andra litterära och språkliga uppsatser. Stockholm: Bokforlaget Natur och Kultur, 1944. pp. 75-82.

Northwestern. 1899. "The Runic Stone" Northwestern, Northwestern University: March 9, 1899.

Ohman, Edward. 1949. Interview by Ralph S. Thornton, Modridge S. Robb, and Bergmann Richards. Audio tape recording and transcript. December 29. Minnesota Historical Society, St. Paul.

Ohman, Olof 1909. Affidavit of July 1909. Minnesota Historical Society. Reproduced in Blegen (1968:137-136).

————1910. Letter to Warren Upham of March 14, 1910. Minnesota Historical Society. Reproduced in Blegen (1968: 158-162).

Parry, Buff. 1988. "Records Twice Found." The Pincher Creek Echo, Vol. 89, No. 01, Thursday, 9th August, 1988, Pincher Creek, Alberta.

————2005. "In Search of the Vénendrye Stone." Private report to Drs. John Polansky and Richard Nielsen covering their sponsored research of Buff Parry on this subject during the period 2001-2005.

Pike, Albert. (1871) Morals and Dogma: Ancient and Accepted Rite of Freemasonry. Charleston. Edition of 1917 printed by L.B. Jenkins, Richmond, Virginia, September: 1917.

Pipping, Rolf. 1921. Erikskrönikan [Erik's Chronicle]. Uppsala: Svenska Fornskrift-Sällskapet.

Redman, Jeffrey R. 1979 "Viking" Hoaxes in North America. New York Heathstone.

Reiersgord, Thomas E. 2001. The Kensington Rune Stone: Its Place in History. St. Paul, MN: Pogo Press.

Ronge, Hans H. 1957. Konung Alexander [King Alexander]. Institutionen for Nordiska Språk. Uppsala, Sweden.

Rosander, Carl. 1882. Den kunskapsrike Skolmästaren: Ny, genomsedd upplaga [The able, versatile schoolmaster: New, revised edition]. Stockholm: Albert Bonniers Förlag.

Rydqvist, Johan Erik. 1883. Svenska språkets lagar [The laws of the Swedish language]. 6 vols. Stockholm: Berlingska Press.

Rygh, Oluf. "Den amerikanska runeindskrift," [The American Runic inscription] in Morgenbladet (Christiania), March 12, 1899.

Saint-Hilaire, Josephine [Helena Roerich]. 1930. On Eastern Crossroads: Legends and Prophecies of Asia. New York: Frederick A. Stokes Company.

Säve, Pehr Arvid. 1864. Reseberättelser [Travel report] Manuscript in ATA, Stockholm.

Seife, Charles. 2000. Zero: The Biography of a Dangerous Idea. New York: Penguin.

Seip, Didrik Arup. 1954. Palæografi B: Norge og Island [Paleography B: Norway and Iceland]. Copenhagen: J. H. Schultz A/S Universtets Bogtrykkeri.

————1955. Norsk Språkhistorie til omkring 1370 [Norwegian Language History until ca. 1370]. Oslo: H. Aschhehoug.

————1934. Studier I Norsk Språkhistorie [Studies in Norwegian Language History]. Oslo: H. Aschhehoug.

Siverts, Ingvald T. 1964. Two letters to Theodore C. Blegen dated June 25, 1964 and June 29, 1964. Minnesota Historical Society.

Sjöborg, Nils Henrik. 1822 and 1824. Samlingar för Nordens fornälskare [Collections for Scandinavian antiquary lovers]. 2 Vols. Stockholm: Rediviva 1955. Reprint of Vol. 1 1822 and Vol. 2 1824.

Skautrup, Peter. (1944). Det Danske Sprogs Historie [History of the Danish Language]. Vol. 1. Frag Guldhornene til Jyske Lov [From the Gold Horn to the Jutland Law] (1947) Vol. 2. Fra unionbrevet til danske Lov [From The Union Letter to the Danish Law] (1970) Vol. 5. Registre [Indices], Gyldendalske Boghandel, Copenhagen.

Skørdalsvold, J.J. 1913. "Kensington-stenenen" [The Kensington Stone.] Kvatalskrift, Fall: 1913.

Sköld, Tryggve. 2003. Edward Larssons Alfabet ock Kensingtonstenens (Edward Larsson's Alphabet and that of the Kensington Rune Stone), DAUM-KATTA-Dialekt-Ortnamns-och Folkminnesarkivet i Umeå, Winter Issue 2003, pp 7-11.

————2005. Kensintonstenens Språk, DAUM, Dialekt-Ortnamns-och Folkminnesarkivet i Umeå, Summer Issue, June 2005.

Snædal, Thorgunn. 2002. Medan världen vakar [While the world wakes]. Uppsala universitet Institutionen för nordiska språk.

Steefel, Lawrence D. (September, 1965). "The Kensington Runestone." The Minnesota Archaeologist, 27:3.

Stoylen, Sigvald. 1965. "The Kensington Rune Stone," in American Book Collector, 16:6-9 (November, 1965).

Söderwall, K. F. 1884–1918. Ordbok öfver svenska medeltids-språket [Dictionary of Swedish medieval language]. 2 vols. Lund, Sweden: Berling Press.

Thalbitzer, William. 1951. "Two Runic Stones from Greenland and Minnesota." Smithsonian Miscellaneous Collections 116:3.

Thompson, Claiborne W. 1975. Studies in Upplandic runography. Austin: University of Texas Press.

Thorsen, P. G. 1877. Om Runernes Brug til Skrift udenfor det monumentale [On the use of runes for non-monumental purposes]. Copenhagen: Gyldendal Press.

Uldaler, Nelly, and Gerd Wellejus. 1968. Gammel Dansk læsebog [Old Danish reader], Copenhagen: Gyldendal.

Upham, Warren. 1910. "The Kensington Rune Stone, its Description, its Inscriptions and Opinions Concerning Them" Records of the Past, IX (January-February), 1910, 3-7.

————1913. Report on Lake Agassiz. Found in the letterpress books at the Minnesota Historical Society. March, 1913.

————1920. Minnesota Geographic Names: Their origin and historic significance. St. Paul: Minnesota Historical Society.

Van Dyke, Clive. W. 1910. Letter to Newton W. Winchell, April 19, 1910. Minnesota Historical Society. Reproduced in Blegen (1968:170-71)

Vendell, Herman. 1881. Dialect of Nökker, etc. (in Estonia). PhD diss. University of Helsingfors, Finland.

Wahlgren, Erik. 1952. "The Runes of Kensington."Studies in Honor of Albert Morey Sturtevant. Lawrence: University of Kansas Press.

————1958. The Kensington stone: A Mystery Solved. Madison: The University of Wisconsin Press.

————1986. The Vikings and America. London: Thames and Hudson.

Wallace, Birgitta. 1971. "Some Points of Controversy." 155-170. Chapter Five in The Guest for America by Geoffrey Ashe, Editor, Praeger Publishers, New York.

————1982. "Viking Hoaxes," Vikings in the West, Archaeological Institute of America, N. Y, pp. 53-76.

————1984. The Kensington stone: A Review Essay of "The Kensington Runestone is Genuine" by Robert A. Hall, Jr. The Old Northwest. 10 (4): 463–78. (1985).

Wallace, Brigitta and William W. Fitzhugh. 2000. "Stumbles and Pitfalls in the Search for Viking America". Chapter 29 in 374-384, Vikings: The North Atlantic Saga. Smithsonian Institution Press, Washington D. C. 374-384.

Weiblen, Paul W. 2001. "Report on the Mineralogical Characterization of the Kensington Rune Stone," Department of Geology and Geophysics, University of Minnesota, In, Barry J. Hanson Kensington Runestone: A Defense of Olof Ohman the Accused Forger. Kearney, NE: Morris Publishing, 2002. Vol. 2, Appendix H.

Wessén, Elias. 1937. In Svenska dagbladet [Swedish daily] April 3, 1937. Quoted in Sven B. F. Jansson in Runstenen från Kensington i Minnesota [The runestone from Kensington in Minnesota]. N. Tidsskrift för vetenskap, konst och Industri, 1949. 25 (7-8): 377–405.

————1965. Svensk språkhistoria [Swedish language history]. Vol. 1 of Phonology and Inflections. Lund, Sweden: Almqvist and Wiksell.

Wiktorsson, Per-Axel and Eva Odelman. 1996. Dalslands diplomatarium [Diplomas of Dalsland]. Åmål, Sweden: Dalslands Fornminnes- och Hembygsförbund.

Williams, Henrik and Richard Nielsen. 2003. Texten och pentadiska siffrorna på Kensington stenen [The language and pentadic numbers on the Kensington stone]. Paper presented at the Historiska Museet exhibit of the Kensington rune stone, Stockholm, October 22.

Winchell, Newton H. Professional and personal notebooks. Minnesota Historical Society, St. Paul. Reproduced in Blegen (1968: 141-158).

————1910. Report to the museum board. April 21. Minnesota Historical Society, St. Paul.

————1911. Aborigines of Minnesota. St. Paul: Minnesota Historical Society.

————1915. "The Kensington Rune Stone, Preliminary Report to the Minnesota Historical Society." Museum Committee of the Minnesota Historical Society, 1915, Minnesota Historical Society Collections V. 15, 211-286. Reproduced in Hanson (2002: Appendix 2).

Winkler, Erhard M. 1997. Stone in Architecture: Properties, Durability. Berlin: Springer-Varlag.

Wolter, Scott F. 2005. "The Geology of the Kensington Rune Stone: Relative Dating of the Inscription using the Mineral Pyrite." The Epigraphic Society - Occasional Papers 24: 99-103. 2005.

————2002. Photo-library of the Kensington Rune Stone Inscription. St. Paul, MN: American Petrographic Services Inc.

————2001. Kensington Rune Stone Investigation: Preliminary Report (#10-01120). St. Paul, MN: American Petrographic Services Inc.

————2001. The Lake Superior Agate: One Man's Journey. Eden Prairie, MN: Outernet Publishing, LLC.

————1997. Ettringite: Cancer of Concrete. Edina, MN: Burgess Publishing.

————1996. The Lake Superior Agate: Third Edition. Eden Prairie, MN: Outernet Publishing.

Wood, Annie M. 1936. Noman's Land: Isle of Romance. New Bedford, MA: Reynolds DeWalt Printing Inc.

Worm, Ole (Olaus Wormius). 1623, 1646. Fasti Daniei. Copenhagen (Hafniæ).

Zalar, Michael. 2000. Factual Errors in Chapter 29, 'Vikings: The North Atlantic Saga' NEARA Journal, Summer: 2000.

Abbreviations

Diplomas:

DL + [number] = series in Wiktorsson (1996)

SD + [number] = series in SDR.

SDR = Liljegren, J. E. (1829-) Diplomatarium suecanum (Swedish diplomas). Stockholm (I-XI). Hildebrand, Emil (1878) Svenskt Diplomatarium1348-1349 (Swedish diplomas V for 1348-1349). Riksarkivet.

SDns + [number] = series in SDnsR

SDnsR = Silfverstrope, Carl (1875-1903)-Swedish diplomas from and including 1401 - new series).

Runic Inscriptions:

DR + number = Number in Danish Runic Inscriptions. See Lis Jacobsen and Erik Moltke (1952)

N + number = Number in Norwegian Runic Inscriptions. See Magnus Olsen (1941-60), Aslak Liestøl (1980) and S. Johnsen (1990).

SRI 1-15 (1900-1981) Sveriges runinskrifter (Sweden's Runic Inscriptions), Kungl. Vitterhets historie och antikvitets akademien, Vol. I-XV, 1900 ff, Stockholm.

I	Öl + number = Number in *Ölands runinskrifter granskade och tolkade* (Södermanland's Runic Inscriptions Studied and Interpreted) by Sven Söderberg and Erik Brate. 1900-1906.
II	Sô + number = Number in *Östergöterlands runinskrifter granskade och tolkade* (East Göterland's Runic Inscriptions Studied and Interpreted) by Erik Brate. 1911-1918
III	Sô + number = Number in *Södermanlands runinskrifter granskade och tolkade* (Södermanland's Runic Inscriptions Studied and Interpreted) by Erik Brate and Elias Wessen. 1924-1958.
IV	Sm + number = Number in *Smålands runinskrifter granskade och tolkade* (Småland's Runic Inscriptions Studied and Interpreted) by Ragnar Kinander. 1935- 1961.
V	Vg + number = Number in *Västergötalands runinskrifter granskade och tolkade* (West Götaland's Runic Inscriptions Studied and Interpreted) by Hugo Junger and Elisabeth Svärdstrôm. 1940-1971.
VI-IX	U + number = Number series in *Upplands runinskrifter granskade och tolkade* (Uppland's Runic Inscriptions Studied and Interpreted) by Elias Wessén and Sven Jansson), 1940 – 1958.
XI-XII	G + number = Number in *Gotlands runinskrifter granskade och tolkade* (Gotland's Runic Inscriptions Studied and Interpreted) by Sven Jansson and Elias Wessén, 1962 and by E. Svärdström. 1978.
XIV	Gs + number = Number in Gäst*sticktlands runinskrifter granskade och tolkade* (Gäststickland's Runic Inscriptions Studied and Interpreted) by Sven Jansson. 1981.

Appendix A

Swedish Journalist Lars Westman wrote this article that was published in the October 9, 2003 issue of the Swedish publication of *Vi* magazine.

Introduction

But now the Kensington Stone comes to Sweden, at last. It's really one solitary man's effort: Richard Nielsen, amateur investigator and oil and gas engineer from Texas. He is convinced about the genuineness of the stone. And his investigations are taken seriously.

And think if he is right. It is a real dizziness in the thought: a Scandinavian crew on expedition deep into Minnesota, long before Columbus, long before Swedish Americans.

Did some of them come home? The record is silent. Did they disappear in the ocean or into the American ground, just as the stone?

It is about this that the Kensington enigma deals.

Occupied by Runes

Back and forth over the Atlantic, a daily intensive correspondence with e-mail. (SFW)

Henrik Williams is a Runologist and Professor of Scandinavian Language in Uppsala. Richard Nielsen is an offshore oil and gas engineer and amateur historian in Houston, Texas.

The cooperation between them has fused new life into the research around the Kensington Stone.

Danish-American Richard Nielsen has spent twenty years on the runes of the Stone. He has paid for the geological research on the Kensington Stone in the USA.

Without Richard Nielsen the research would have been stone dead, said Henrik Williams.

If the Stone is false or genuine it is still important, he says. It is now the truth he is striving for. But in any case he sees the Stone as clearly authentic; it is interesting if it is from the 1362, which date stands on the Stone, or if made in the 1800s.

Since its discovery close to one hundred years ago it has lived a fantastic life in the debate and is charged up from all the opposition and from all the passion it has let loose.

Henrik Williams and Richard Nielsen speak during the day and the night about the runes and the language on the Stone. The multitude of the deviations from what is known from research is enormous, he says.

He took some examples: the verbs on the Stone stand consistently in singular. They stand **vi hade, vi var, vi kom,** and **fan** instead of *hafdom, varom, komom* and *fannom*.

And mainly has the language on the Stone been seen as completely modern, he says. It seems more like it's from the 1800s than the Middle Ages the experts have said for 100 years now.

It has been the main reason that one has looked on the Kensington Stone as a forgery, done by some clever rune carver and language-gifted Swedish-American. Henrik Williams holds thereby with.

But it is not so simple.

The researchers have known too little, the Stone has never been investigated seriously. Many oddities that are found on the Stone are found in fact in medieval documents and sources. Richard Nielsen has sluiced medieval documents in search of parallels to the language on the Stone.

Henrik Williams himself retains fundamental doubts on the Stone, but has been more and more open to all possibilities.

"I am unbelievably fascinated by the Stone. And Richard Nielsen's work touches all the large problems in medieval runology."

Special Word Gets New Interpretation. The word **opdagelsefard** on the Stone perhaps does not mean *upptæcksfærd* as one thought. And the expression *upptæcksfærd* is hardly found in the middle ages.

But perhaps *uptakilsefærd* stands there, therefore *resa för att ta upp, odla upp, nytt land* (journey to take up idle and new land).

For Henrik Williams the Stone becomes more and more an adventure. Each day ther is a new e-mail from Richard Nielsen, with new possibilities of interpretation. It is a game with nuances of language and writings that hardly can be described, he says. The Stone was carved in some type of Scandinavian mixture of language, no matter whether from the 1300s or the 1800s. If it is genuine, therefore 14th century, it could have been a Scandinavian monk. If carved by a farmer in 19th century Minnesota it must have been a farmer with special knowledge in runology and medieval theology.

He must have had knowledge to use pentadic numbers; the special numbers, which are found in the 1300s are found on the Stone. But they are used in a modern style, from the decimal system; such as in the year 1362.

Runic numbers with decimal system in the 1300s is a tough nut to crack for those who believe in the genuineness of the Stone.

But Richard Nielsen has cracked runic nuts on the Kensington Stone before.

Whether medieval or 19th century, perhaps the geologists at the Bureau of Antiquities may now decide the matter, says Henrik Williams.

Appendix B

The Stockholm Historical Museum's Exhibition on the Kensington Stone

22nd October 2003

By Prof. Henrik Williams and Dr. Richard Nielsen

Introduction

Was the Kensington Runestone carved in 1362 or during the latter part of the 1800s?   Since the discovery of the Stone in 1898 the debate of this question has raged wildly.   Many amateur researchers and many Americans insisted that the inscription was from the Middle Ages.   Runologists and Scandinavian language researchers have asserted just as firmly that it is modern.   But why has the question not been resolved? How can it take more than a hundred years to demonstrate whether a document is from the 1300s or from a half a millennium later?   We will try to explain here where the complications lie.

The text on the Kensington Stone can be read on the display board.   It is quite clear the both Norwegians and Swedes from the Gutish region are named.   The inscription can have been carved in a mixed language regardless of whether it is old or new.   The Swede of today can struggle through the text with a certain amount of difficulty.   But in order to determine whether it is 100 years old or 600 years old one has actually to be a specialist.   In the 1300s we spoke Ancient Swedish in Sweden.   In the our neighboring countries they spoke Ancient Norwegian and Ancient Danish (and Ancient Gothic in Gotland).   The languages lay much closer to each other than today and could be easily understood by all the Nordic people.   It was particularly during the1300s that many changes occurred in the Scandinavian languages.   They are much easier to understand than the older ancient languages and the Viking age runic inscriptions.

Many of the runes on the Kensington Stone differ from those of contemporary inscriptions (see exhibition). Nor is the language similar to that of other texts from Scandinavia of the 1300s.   It is for this reason that the scientists hesitate to admit that that it is so old.   But they think that the language fits into the 1800s. It has also been pointed out that some of the expressions would have been impossible in the Middle Ages, e.g. **opþagelsefarþ** which looks very much like the modern *opdagelsesfærd* "journey of exploration" in Danish and Norwegian.   But the fact is that a number of the apparently modern expressions can be demonstrated to have been in existence back in the middle Ages.   And **opþagelsefarþ** has now been interpreted as *uptak-ilsefärd*, which could mean "acquisition journey, journey to acquire new land".   Suddenly the critique has to start again from a new direction.

Almost every word, even every rune, on the Kensington Stone lends itself to discussion.   But the dividing line in the debate is clear.   Many phenomena in the inscription are unexpected.   A basis for some of them is found in Middle Age texts, even if amongst rare citations.   For other phenomena no old parallels are found, or at least no convincing example has yet come to light.   But even texts whose authenticity are guaranteed show deviations.

The question is whether the number of deviations on the Kensington Stone is far too many.   Can a text from the 1300s contain so many unique and unexpected characteristics?

We will give here a couple of specific examples of the sort of problem involved.   The originators of the description are Richard Nielsen, engineer and energetic amateur researcher in Texas, and Henrik Williams, runological researcher and linguistic expert at Uppsala University.   Together they have tried to give a balanced picture of the Kensington Stone's mysteries.

The Problem with "har"
First amongst the words on the side of the Kensington Stone stand three runes, which are read as ᚼᛆᚱ **har** and which have been translated as initiating the sentence "(We) have 10 men by the sea."   This word has long represented the strongest argument against a 1300s origin for the inscription.   In the language of the Middle Ages one distinguished between the singular and plural forms of the verb.   English-speaking people, amongst others, still do this today: they say *she has* but *they have*.   In Ancient Swedish one expected *(vi) havom*, which right down until the 1940s could be written *(vi) hava* in formal contexts.

There are four other verbs in the inscription which are under the same question mark, namely **vi ha?e, vi var, vi kom** and **(vi) fan** instead of *hafdom, varom, komom* and *funnom*.   The case seemed clear: the verb forms on the Stone point clearly away from the 1300s and just as clearly towards the 1800s.

However, as Hjalmar Holand has already shown, there are actually examples of verbs written in the singular form as early as the 1300s, in spite of the fact that they obviously ought to be in the plural.   A plausible explanation of this is that the singular form demonstrably first became common in the spoken language.   A careless writer could commit a blunder and unintentionally include a form from the spoken language.   Many such examples are found, and therefore the origin of the Kensington Stone in the 1300s should not be regarded as impossible as far as this point is concerned.

In spite of this important discovery there remain two other problems with the singular form.   The first is that even though such forms pop up already in the Middle Ages, not a single one of the tens of thousands of documents where the singular form is used does so *consistently*.   It is always a case of exceptions.   The other is that the singular form of *havom* was never *har* but *haver*.   No real example of *har* is found before the year 1500 in spite of the fact that this is one of the most common words in the language.   For a moment it looks as though the problem is solved.

But then a new interpretation stands the whole question on its head.   It turns out that researchers have been slipshod on this point.   The word is not ᚼᛆᚱ **har** but ᚼᚬᚱ **här**!   So it must be a different word.   We need a verb and Richard Nielsen suggests that the word is *är* which in this case is preceded by a superfluous *h*.   The meaning then becomes "(Det) är 10 man vid havet" [(There) are 10 men by the sea].   The addition of a spurious *h* at the beginning of a word is something that occurs sporadically in the Middle Ages, also in runic inscriptions.   The deviation is unexpected but cannot be ruled out.   Moreover it represents an elegant explanation of the words **öh** "ö" and **ahr** "år".

In other words it is found that with the new reading and interpretation the word ᚼᚬᚱ cannot be used as unambiguous evidence against the Kensington Stone's 1300s origin.   But one must necessarily believe in the use of an unnecessary *h* and in the fact that this text is the only one from the Middle Ages that consistently employs single forms of verbs instead of the expected plural forms.

The Problem with the Pentadic Numerals
The fact that the Kensington Stone is precisely dated to 1362 gave rise to a sensation!   There are indeed a few runic inscriptions with self-dating, but they express their dating more circuitously.   On the church bell from Saleby in Västergötland for example it says: "When I was made, it was one thousand two hundred and twenty winters and eight from God's birth".   Documents from the Middle Ages on the other hand were dated with Roman numerals: e.g. MCCCLXII (1362).

But the unique thing with the Kensington Stone is not just that it uses numerals but partly that it uses a special kind of "runic numerals" and partly that it employs them in accordance with the modern position system.   In the Middle Ages one took as many of the different number sorts as were necessary: M (1000) + CCC (3x100) + L (50) + X (10) + II (2x1).   But today we state the number of thousands (1) + hundreds (3) + tens (6) + units (2).   The same method is used on the Kensington Stone: ΓԲԲΓ.
It is not surprising the researchers rejected the possibility that a runic inscription with this dating form could be genuine.   And in any case who has ever heard of runic numerals?   But again it turns out that the truth is more complicated than we perhaps would like.   Runic numerals have demonstrably been used in the 1300s!   They are also known from a 1600s work by Ole Worm who amongst other things deals with runic calendars.

The runic calendars were used amongst other things to keep track of the arrival of Easter, and they have nothing to do with real runic inscriptions.   The numbers that are used on the runic calendars are "pentadic," i.e. built up in groups of five, whereas our numbers are built on the ten.   In the pentadic system small cross-strokes are used for the numbers 1 (Γ) to 4 (Ի) and 6 (Ρ) to 9 (Ҏ), while the numeral 5 is represented by a half circle (Ρ) and the number ten by its own symbol (on the Kensington Stone this is Ŷ).   The system was the same but the symbol could vary somewhat in appearance.

Scandinavians in the America of the 1800s have cannot be expected to have been aware of Ole Worm's publication of the runic calendars.   They cannot therefore have copied the runic symbols from them. This should constitute a strong argument for a Middle Age dating of the Kensington Stone.   But now it turns out that pentadic runic numerals also been published in a more accessible source.   In the 1820s Nils Henrik Sjöborg published *Samlinger for Nordens fornälskare* Collections for Scandinavian Antiquarian Enthusiasts, which had a wide circulation.   It includes a tabulation of runic numerals!   It has been taken from a pocket calendar from 1601. Even people in the 1800s therefore could have been familiar with the pentadic system from this book, even if the Kensington Stone 10 is not found in Sjöborg.

The most difficult thing is to explain why runic numerals are used in such a modern way.   One would have expected a Roman equivalent of 1362, and instead of ΓΓ (22) one would have expected †††Γ.   Use of a decimal system pre-supposes knowledge of Arabic numerals.   There are few examples of the use of Arabic numerals in Scandinavia in the 1300s and even less frequent is the use of the position system, i.e. numbers like 22 and 1362.   In order to regard the Kensington Stone as a product of the Middle Ages one must accept that on this point it is unique in two respects.   It has to be accepted firstly that it is the only genuine runic inscription that uses pentadic numbers, and secondly that it is the earliest Nordic document that expresses dates in accordance with the modern numeral position system. Richard Nielsen has suggested that knowledge of the use of pentadic numbers in calendars was imported from sources outside Scandinavia (see the exhibition), but Henrik Williams does not agree that the datings are comparable.

Conclusion

The latest research shows that at any rate the language of the Kensington Stone is generally consistent with both the 1300s and the 1800s. One cannot absolutely exclude either the one or the other century. Many expressions that appear deviant in a 1800s context can derive from local dialect usage, Swedish-Norwegian language combinations, and even outright errors, conscious or unconscious, on the part of the rune carver. But a 1300s origin presupposes the same and further involves a need for other special explanations of deviations from the norm. Each person must reach his own conclusion as to where the boundary of probability lies.

The only thing that is certain is that the Kensington Stone needs to be studied further before we can reach a definite result. Whether everyone will be convinced even then remains to be seen.

Appendix C—The Language of the Kensington Rune Stone

1st Line.

8 : göter : ok : 22 : norrmen : paa :
Åtta göter and tjugotvå norrmän på
Eight Götalanders and 22 Norwegians on

2nd Line.

...o : opþagelsefarþ : fraa :
(denna?) upptagelsefärd (= uppodlings- eller plundringsresa) från
(this?) reclaiming land (or plundering) journey

	KRS Form.	Negative Assertions	What the Record Says
1		Pentadic numbers were not used in runic inscriptions.	True, but pentadic numbers first appear in the late 14th century calendars in Scandinavia
2 3	**Göter ok** (Goths and)	The end vowel in *–er* is weakened from *–ar*. (K. M. Nielsen 1950: 73, F89).	**Göter** is found in DL 75b from 1388 (Wiktorsson 1996). **Göter** cited in Rydqvist's (1883) Old Swedish Dictionary. Punches in ᛦ (g) & ᚱ (r).
4		Numbers were carved in words, but or once on G 99 (1449) in **V tihi** (five tens).	The normal 22 was rendered as ᛏ. ᚠ ᚠ eliminated carving the words *tu tighi ok tu* (two tens and two).
5	**norrmen** (Northmen)	Should be *normæn*. This word is Swedish for Norwegian.	Old Swedish had *normen* (Norwegian), but the meaning of *normæn*. Might simply be north men.
6	**paa** (upon)	"The use of *pa* (on) with nouns denoting activity, as here, is modern," (Flom 1910: 111).	**Paa** is cited in Skåne (1349) (Markey 1978: 58). Activity occurs in Dl 75, DL 75a (1388) in *pa woræ wegne* (on our behalf) (Wiktorsson 1996) & *A konungs reso* (on King's journey), SDns142 (1402).
7	[þen] o		This o-rune is likely the o-ending in *þeno* (this), which both suits the text and the space.
8	**opþagelse** **opthagelse** **optagelse** (taking up)	"*Opdagelse* is a late word." (Gould 1910). The Danish/ Norwegian *opdagelse* (discovery)" (Wahlgren 1958: 114).	It is now known that **optagelse** could simply imply "taking up land, taking booty" in Old Swedish (Williams et al 2003: 9). In manuscripts of the 1300s *th* stood for *t*, without logic, leading to forms like *Sthokholm* in SD 6491 (1361).
9	**farþ**	English '**fare.**' "*–farþ* and *skjar* should reasonably be regarded as English, as *a* can stand for *ä*" (Moltke & Andersen 1949: 55, F63).	**Farþ** appears in Söderwall (1884-1918) with an *a* in *farth*. The plural *farþir* (trips) with "a" root vowel is recorded (Hagen (1950: 323). Extra hook in ᚷ (a).
10	**fro, fraa** (from)	"The pronunciation was regularly with *a*" Flom (1910: 112).	*fra > fraa* (from) is cited in Collin et al (1827: 98, § 51) in VG II (1345-50). *Fraa* is cited in SD 6935 (1364), SD 6631 (1362) and earlier (1344).

3rd Line.   ᛘᛁᚿᚠᚵᚿᚦ : ᚯᚠ : ᛦᛐᛋᛐ : ᛘᛁ :

vinlanþ : of : vest : vi :
Vinland vesterut. Vi
to the west from Vinland. We

4th line.   ᚼᚵᚿ : ᛚᚬᚵᛋᚱ : ᛘᛐᚦ : ᛚ : ᛋᚴᚿᚠᚵᚱ : ᛐᛐ :

haþe : läger : veþ : 2 : skLar : en :
hade läger vid två …??? en
had camp by two ??? one

	KRS Form.	Negative Assertions	What the Record Says
11	Vinlanþ	Should be *Vinlandi* in dative Wahlgren (1958).	Wessén (1965: 102) shows that the dative can occur in both forms, *Vinlandi* and the accusative form *Vinland*, hence the KRS form is correct. Extra hook in ᛚ (l).
12 13	of vest, west (to the west)	"English use of prepositions may possibly lie behind the phase *of west*, which is un-known in Nordic usage, and the intended meaning is unclear." Kæjr (1994:15).	In Söderwall, *of* is Old Swedish for "extreme, too," hence **of west** (far to the west) **West** appears in Söderwall II p. 1067 as *wæst* (west) and *væster* (in a later copy from circa 1450). But, "The English 'west' " (Wessén 1937 in Jansson 1949: 394).
14	vi, wi (we)	**Vi** (we) is not found with singular verbs in the 14th c.	"we" with singular verb is in diploma DL75b (1388) in *wi hafthæ* (we had) (Wiktorsson 1996) .
15	had, haþe	"*haþe* without *f* … Oldest example is from 1385." (K. M. Nielsen 1950: 76, F72).	The form without *f*, *Jac haddœ* (I had), appears in diploma SD 7042 of 1364.
16	läger (camp).Punches: ᚬ (ä) & ᚱ (r)	"*läger* is not known in the meaning "camp" until the Reformation period." (Gould 1910).	*Lägre* (camp) is Old Swedish, but *läger* (resting place [in effect camp]) could be the form in Old Swedish of 1362. See SD 4069 (May 1, 1346).
17	veþ	"The development of *i* to *e* in open syllable before *dh* which brought about the change of *vidher* to *vedher* begins about 1400" (Flom 1910: 111).	See *wedher* in SD 6835, August 3rd, 1363. Quoting Thalbitzer (1951: 30), "the original *i* became *e* before þ the consonant from about 1300."(Kock I §30 and §47).
18 19	ᛚ skLar (2 ???).	Asserted by Moltke (1949: 48). as *skjar* (skerries) with a modern ᚠ –rune for *j*.	The special rune ᚠ was known in Scandinavia by 1319, seemingly for "yl" after a vowel. Hence, **skLar** is not "skerries," and its meaning remains unknown and enigmatic.

Apparent code marks and punches found on runes in the first four lines of the inscription above yield:

:ᛘ:ᚱ ᚷ ᛚ ᚬ ᚱ: = **gral är** (grail is). "Graal" *gral* (grail) is medieval from French.

5ᵗʰ Line.   ᚦᚷᚴᛋ : ᚱᛁᛋᛏ : ᚾᛖᚱᚱ : ᚠᚱᛆ : ᚦᛏᚾᛆ : ᛋᛏᛆᛏ :

þags : rise : norr : fraa : þeno : sten :
dagsresa norrut från denna sten.
day's jouney from this stone.

6th Line.   ᚢᛁ : ᚢᚷᚱ : ᚼᚼ : ᚠᛁᛋᛏ : ᛏᛏ : ᚦᚷᛋᚼ : ᛆᛒᛏᛁᚱ :

vi: var : ok : fiske : en : þagh äptir:
Vi var och (= för att) fiska en dag. Efter (att)
We were fishing one day. After

	KRS Form.	**Negative Assertions**	**What the Record Says**
20 21	**Enþags, dhags, dags** (day's).	Should be **ens dags** (one day's) (Fossum 1911).	SD 4986 from 1353 has *dh* for *d* in *dhag* (day). The possessive adjective ending in *ens* can be omitted in Old Swedish. Wessén 1965: 145).
22	**rise** (journey)	**"Rise" is English** (Moltke/Andersen 1949: 55). *"... dags resa* was not in use before 1599 (Wahlgren 1952: 62).	The oldest example is *en dags reyssæ* (one day's trip*)* printed in a 1506 book, believed to be from copies of the 14ᵗʰ century original (# a286, b287 in Kjær and Petersen 1979: 59).
23	**norR** (to the north) with ᚱ	Should be **nor** (K. M. Nielsen 1950: 76, F71-2).	**Norr** can be rendered *norr* in Old Swedish, Wessén (1965: 68) & Erik Noreen (1932: 226). On Gotland the palatal R was used in the 1300s (Snædal 2002), and sometimes incorrectly as here.
24	**fro, fraa** (from)	The KRS has **"fro ...** instead of *fra"* (from) (Jansson (1949: 393, F31).	SD X250 from 1373 has *fra thæn førsta daghin* (from that the first day) in accusative masculine singular *Fraa* (which is **fro**) is cited in SD 6935 (1364), SD 6631 (1362).
25	**þeno** (this).	See discussion above	
26	**sten** (stone)	As a masculine dative noun, **sten** should be *steni* (Moltke 1951: 90).	Wessén (1965: 97) showed the dative as both *sten* and *steni*. Hence, the KRS **þeno sten** is correct in either dative or accusative.
27	**vi, wi** (we)	**Vi** (we) is not cited with singular in the 14ᵗʰ c.	"we" with singular verb is in diploma DL75b (1388) in *wi hafthæ* (we had) (Wiktorsson 1996)
28	**vaR, waR** (were) with ᚱ	Should be *wi varum* (we were).	The anticipation of *o* could result in **varo : ok** for **var : ok,** as suggested to us by Prof. Barnes. On Gotland the palatal R was used in the 1300s.
29 30	**ok fiske** (fishing).	*ok* for *at* is too young (Moltke and Andersen 1949: 58, F67).	The KRS *ok* for *at* is found already by 1340 (K. M. Nielsen 1950: 81, F-78). Seip (1954: 214) refers to *ok* and *at* as used during the middle ages.
31 32	**En dagh, þagh, dhagh** (one day)		"þagh" *dagh* (day) is cited in Rydqvist IV (1863: 300).
33	**Äptir** (after).	Word was seen in a book.	Cited in Rydqvist III, a Dictionary of the 1850s.

7th Line.   ᛈᛁ : ᚴᚯᛘ : ᚽᛏᛘ : ᚠᛉᚿ : ᛩ : ᛘᛉᚿ : ᚱᚯᚦᚿ :

vi : kom : hem : fan : 10 : man : röþe :

vi kom hem fann vi tio man röda

we came home we found 10 men red

8th Line.   ᛈᚠ : ᛒᚱᚽᚦ : ᚽᚤ : ᚦᛏᚦ : AVM

af : bloþ: og : þeþ : AVM :

av blod och död. Ave Maria.

from blood and death. Ave Maria

	KRS Form.	Negative Assertions	What the Record Says
34 35 36	vi kom hem ,	Should be *wi komom hem* (we came home).	See above discussion on singular verbs in plural function.
37	(jek) fan ([I] found).	Should be *vi funnom*	fan might be have the with the carver as the inferred subject: "After we came home, (I) found 10 men … ."
38	ᛩ (10)		See 51 below.
39	man (men)	*Man* is singular (Jansson 1949: 393, F41).	The O. Swedish plural form man seems due to German influence (Ronge: 1957: 143).
40	röþe (red)		The form röþe is the only adjective modifying man.
41	af (from)	Af (from) governs the dative.	SD X 142 of 1372 has *af thetta bref* (from this letter) in accusative. Hence af (from) can be both a dative and accusative preposition.
42	bloþ, (blood)	Should be *bloþi* (blood) with dative ending (Wahlgren 1958: 109).	Wessén (1965: 102) shows that the dative can occur in duel forms, *blod* and *blodi*, hence *blod* is both dative and accusative.
43	og, ogh (and)	Og was given in Ohman's Rosander (Moltke 1951: 93).	*Ogh* (and) is found in a 14th century diploma from 1388 (Wiktorsson 1993: #75b). See og (and) from 1324 on G 182.
44	þeþ (death)	The English "dead," since the form should be *döde* (dead) (K. M. Nielsen 1950: 79).	The dative noun occurs in duel forms, such as with *deth* and *dethi* (death) (Wessén 1965: 102), hence, the word is "death" and not the plural adjective dede (dead) with the plural e- ending missing.
45	AVM (ave = hail Mary)	AVM (Ave Maria) (Noreen 1906). AVM would not be used in the 14th century (Hægstad 1911).	AV, and abbreviation for *Ave* (hail), is cited on a medieval grave cross in Greenland (Finnur Jónsson 1924: 281-2). Punch in foot of M
	Apparent code marks found in the 7th and 8th lines of the inscription above yield: and M		

9ᵗʰ Line.   � : XP : ᛁᚱᚱ :

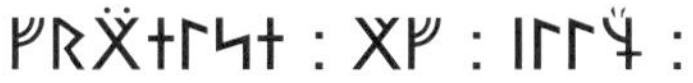

fräelse : af : illü :
Frails ifran undo.
Save from evil.

10ᵗʰ Line.   *ᚻᛅᚱ : ᛏ : ᛘᛅᚾᛋ : ᚢᛏ : ᚻᛅᚢᛏ : ᛅᛏ : ᛋᛏ :*

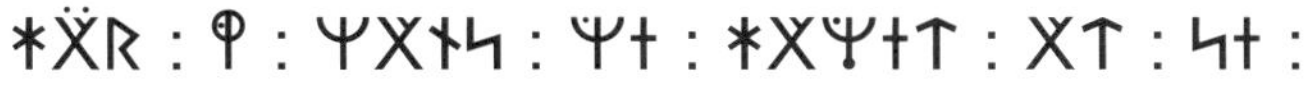

här : 10 : mans : ve : havet : at : se :
(det) är tio man vid havet för att se
There are 10 men by the sea to look

	KRS Form.	Negative Assertions	What the Record Says
47 47a	**Fräelse** (Save) [**Os** (us)]	Rosander (1882) has *frälsä os af illu*, a model for **fraelse af illu** (save from evil). (Wahlgren 1958: 137).	**Fräelse** (save) has an e-ending, rather than *ä*, as well as an inserted *e* before *l*. The KRS is missing the *os* (us) before **af** (from).
48 49	**Af illu** (evil)	"The ending *–ly* in *illy* must also be characterized as English ."(Moltke and Andersen 1949: 55, F63). The English ill *ondo* (Noreen 1906).	The Larsson rune-row used for the **u**-rune. On this basis the KRS rune ᚢ stands for *u* and yields the dative ending in **illu**.
50	**Här** (are, is)	All commenting runologists and linguists have asserted this should be *hafdom*.	This verb **här** is actually singular with a parasitic *h*, which then yields **är** (is, are). (Williams et al 2003: 10).
51	ᛏ (ten)	"Of course the symbol Ⴊ for 10 can be explained as a cipher with superimposed I, that is, a digraph for 10. (Wahlgren 1958: 119).	Zero was not used in pentadic series, since they were calendar based. ᛏ(10) Arabic placement. This symbol is the Arabic 10 known in Scandinavia from at least 1250. .
52	**mans** (of men)		**här 10 mans** (10 of man) yields "10 men are" (Williams et al 2003: 10).
53	**we**(þ), **ve**(þ) (by)	"The form *ve* is unknown in Old Swedish 'and 'is now common in daily speech" (Nielsen 1950: 77, F73).	**Ve** can certainly be a medieval contraction for **veþ.** Here **ve** can govern the accusative. þ is sometimes dropped before a consonant
54	**havet** (the inland sea, ocean)	"Should be the dative *havinu* not the accusative form. (Wahlgren 1958: 109)	**Havet** is accusative on the KRS. It could refer to the Great lakes, or Lake Winnipeg in Canada. Punch in foot of ᚢ (v/w).
55 56	**At se** (to see)		Seip (1954: 214) refers to both *ok* and *at* as being written during the entire middle ages.

Apparent code marks found on v-rune in the 10th line of the inscription above yield:

11ᵗʰ Line   ᛒᛏᛁᚱ : ᚢᛂᚱᛏ : ᛌᚴᛁᛒ : ᛁᚠ : ᚦᛉᚵᚼ : ᚱᛁᛂᛏ :

äptir : vore : skip : 14 : þagh : rise :

efter våra skepp fjorton dag(ars) resa

after our ships fourteen days journey

12th Line.   ᚠᚱᛅᚢ : ᚦᛏᚼᛂ : ᛟᚼ : ᚵᛁᚱ : ᛁᚠᛈᛁ :

from : þeno : öh : ahr : 1362 :

från denna ö. År 1362.

from this island. Year 1362.

	KRS Form.	Negative Assertions	What the Record Says
57	**äptir** (to look after)	**äptir** (after) cannot govern the accusative.	**äptir** (after) can govern the accusative. See above (Karl Martin Nielsen 1950).
58	**vore, vaare wore, waare** (our)	The accusative plural was always *vaar* (our) in Old Swedish (Noreen 1944: 80).	**Vore** (our) is found in diploma DL 75a March 22, 1388 as *worä jnseilä* (our seals) in accusative plural (Wiktorsson 1996).
59	**skip** (ships)	**Skip** should be *skipum* in dative plural (Flom 1910: 111).	**Skip** was both plural and singular in accusative (Wessén 1965: 102). **Vore skip** (our ships)
60	ᛁᚠ (14)	If from 1362, the KRS is the first Scandinavian record of these numbers.	The pentadic ᛖ (14) or the Arabic ᛉ (14), hence by analogy ᛁ ᚠ . On the other hand, perhaps it is an abbreviation for *ti ok 4* (14) as *ni ok ti* (19) in the Skåne Law or *ti ok ti* (20)) from a rhyme in the 1400s. (Rydqvist II (1857: 558).
61	**þagh, dagh, dhagh** (days')	The plural genitive e-ending.	The genitive -s is dropped in *dagsrand = dagrand.* (day's break) in Söderwall. *Tre daghæ ferd* (3 day's trip) in Danish from 1459 (Lorenzen 1882: 61, 81).
62	**rise** (trip)	**Rise** should be the plural *risor.*	This is a journey of 14 days, hence **rise** is singular.
63	**from, fraam** (from)	English "from." (Wessén (1937)	**From** is a Swedish dialect form (Nielsen 1950)
64	**theno, þeno** (this)	Neuter *theno* incorrectly modifies feminine **öh**. (Moltke 1951: 90).	Feminine and masculine genders were coalescing by 1362. See **þeno** in language section above.
65	**öh** (island)	The h is used as a vowel lengthener found in Swedish only after 1600 (Moltke 1951: 90).	The parasitic h-insert, as in **öh**, is found in Old Swedish. (Williams and Nielsen 2003: 10).
66	**ahr** (year 1362)	"h is used for a sign of vowel length in **ahr**, which is a late importation from High German" (Gould 1910).	The parasitic h-insert, as in **ahr**, can be found in Old Swedish words (Williams and Nielsen 2003: 10).
67	1362 ᛁ ᚠ ᚦ ᛁ	If dated correctly, the KRS is the first use of a pentadic date.	SD 6859 from 1363 has *Anno Domini Mccclxiij* Mccclxiij (Year of our Lord 1363).

Orthography

Letter	Rune	Comments
a	ᚷ	ᚷ A double hooked a-rune is found in **farþ** (journey)
b	ᛒ	
e	ᛂ	
f	ᚠ	
g	ᚵ	Mirror image of the normal g-rune ᚵ
h	ᚼ	Parasitic h **här** (is, are), **ahr** (year), **öh** (island).
i	ᛁ	
k	ᚴ	
l	ᛚ	ᛚ A crossed L-rune is found in the uninterpreted **sk** ᛚ **ar** (???).
m	ᛘ	
n	ᚾ	
Either o or aa	ᚮ	**po**, **paa** (upon), **fro**, **fraa, fraam**, **from** (from), **kom (**came), **vore**, **vore** (our).
p	ᛔ	
r	ᚱ	
R for palatal R sound	ᚱ	In **va**ᚱ (were). Also ᚱ in **norR** (north) on the Kensington Runestone to denote the palatal R.
s	ᛋ	
t	ᛏ	
þ	ᚦ	Medial and final position þ,ð, dh, d, th. **farth**, **fard**, **fardh**, **farþ**, **farð** (journey), **Vinlanth**, **Vinland**, **Vinland**h, **Vinlanþ**, **Vinlanð** (Vinland), **hathe, hade**, **haþe**, **haðe** (had), **veth**, **ved**, **vedh**, **veþ**, **veð** (by), **deth**, **ded, deþ**, **deð** (death)' For d in initial position **þagh** (day), **þeþ** (death), as in West Götaland Law of 1300. Initial position t, th, **opthagelse**, **optagelse** (up taking), **thenno**, **þenno**, **tenno** (this).
Either W or V	ᛘ	**winland**, **vinland**, **war**, **var** (were), **wed**, **ved** (by), **wi**, **vi** (we), **wore**, **vore** (our), **west**, **vest** (west), **hawet**, **havet** (the inland sea). ᛘ A dotted foot is found in havet (the inland sea).
Either u or y	ᚤ	**illy**, **illu** (evil).
Either ä or æ	ᚷ̈	ᚷ̈ Dotted feet are found in **läger** (camp).
Either ö or ø	⊕̈	

Almquist Word Analysis

Almquist (1340) gives examples of texts near, 1200, 1300, 1400, 1500, and during the 1500s and for each century thereafter. The only word forms used on the Kensington Rune Stone (KRS) from the Old Swedish texts are: **ok** (and) and **wi** (we). The following seventeen forms were not used and this sum represents over a fourth of the total words on the inscription:

widh and *wider* for the KRS **we?** (by) (1300 and 1400); also **we** (by). (Words #1 and 2).
land for the KRS **lan?** (land) (1300). (Word #3).
Giötha (Götaland) for the KRS **Göter** (Götalanders), with <th> used for <t> (1300). (Word #4).
Vir (we), Wij ware for the KRS **wi war** (we were) (1200 and 1500). **Wi** was used 3 times. (Words #5, 6, 7, and 8).
Effter for the KRS **æptir** (after) (1500). Used twice. (Words #9 and 10).
The form *död* (death) for the KRS **?e?** (death) (ca. 1500). (Word #11).
The form *är* for the KRS **hær** (is) (1300, 1400, and ca. 1500). (Word #12).
The form *dag* for the KRS **?agh** (day) Used and **?ags** (day's) twice. (1200) (Words #13, 14, and 15).
The form *a* for the KRS **po** (upon) (1200). (Word #16).
The form *an* for the KRS **en** (one) (1200). Used twice. (Words #17 and 18).
The form *kommo* (came) for the KRS **kom**. (Word # 19)
The form *voro* (were) for the KRS **var**. (Word # 20).
<th> was used in demonstrative pronouns in *thetta* (this) (ca. 1500), as in the KRS **theno** (this). (Words #21 and 22).
The form *aff* for the KRS **af** (from). (Word # 23)
Verbal declensions (Pages 93-98) show the um-endings in Old Swedish verbs, unlike **war** (were), **kom** (came), **fan** (found) and **ha?e** (had) on the KRS. (Words #24, 25, 26 and 27).
The form *stein* and *stin* (stone) for the KRS **sten**. (Word # 28).
The form *ok* (and) for the KRS **og** (and). (Word # 29).
The form *upp-* for the KRS **op-** (up) (1200). (Word # 30).
The form *-ilse* for the KRS **-else**. (1500). (Word # 31).
The form *mana* (of men) for the KRS **mans** (of men) (1200) (Word # 32).
The form *min* (men) for the KRS **-men** (men) (1200). (Word # 33).
The forms *skep* and *skib* (ship) for the KRS **skip**. (Word # 34).

Hence, 34 out of 56 word forms on the KRS could have been obtained from Almquist (61% of the KRS words). Most of the difficult KRS words would have been well served by this information. Almquist (1840: 249) stated that the plural form of the verb had been given up for 50 years (that is 1790). Based on the above information it is very difficult to maintain, as Blegen (1968) did, that Fogelblad could have had a hand in production of the Kensington Rune Stone inscription. He died before the Montelius' work became available in the newspapers.

Appendix D

The following pictures are of the medieval inscriptions in their entirety from which we obtained images of runes or words that appear in this book. Most of the inscriptions were carved on grave slabs that are found mortared into the stone floors of the churches on the island of Gotland. These images are reproduced courtesy of the Swedish Books of Runic Inscriptions unless otherwise noted.

G 2 Sundre Church

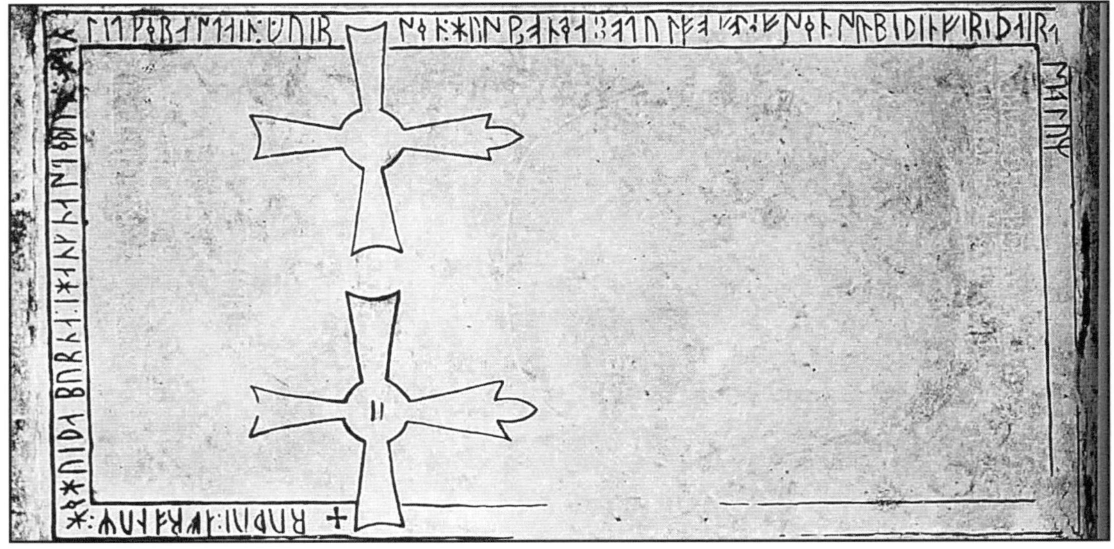

G 33 Näs Church

G 34 Näs Church (SFW)

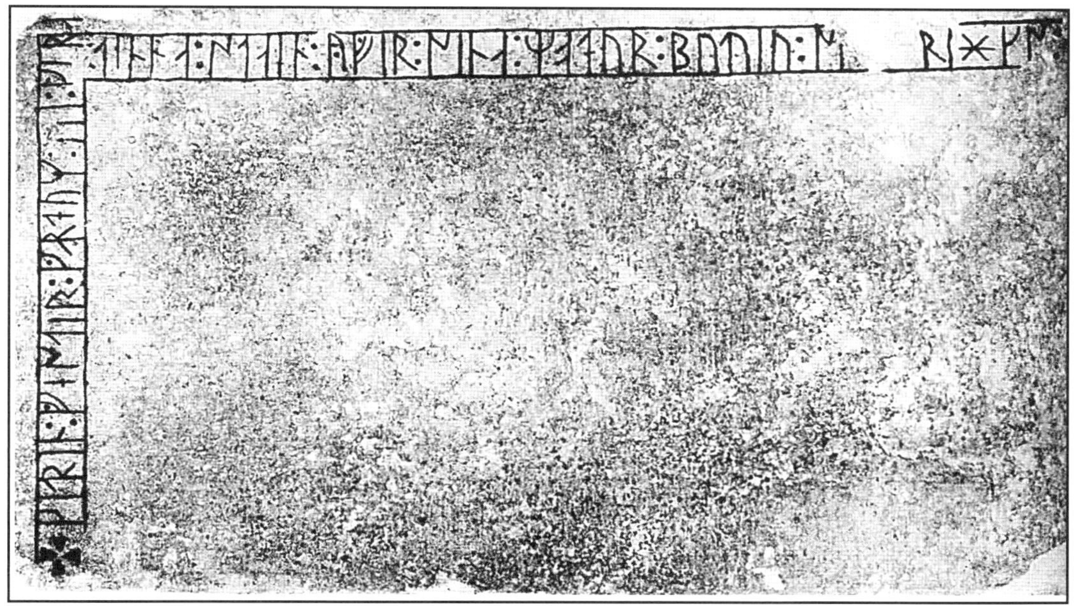

G 42 Havdhem Church

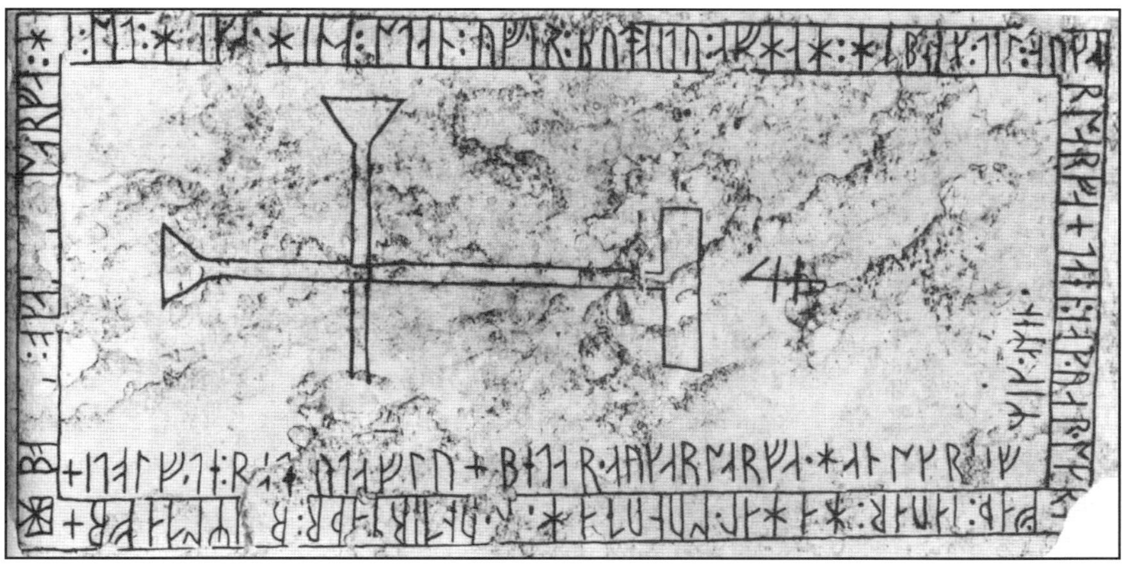

G 55 Hemse Church

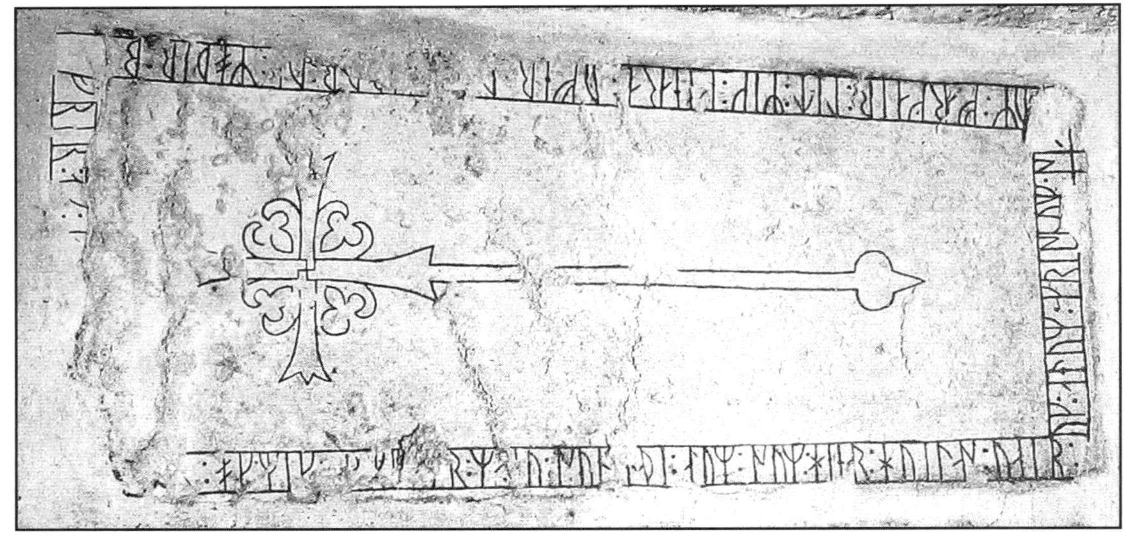

G 63 Silte Church

G 65 Sproge Church

G 70 Urgunda Church

G 100 Lye Church

G 103 Lye Church

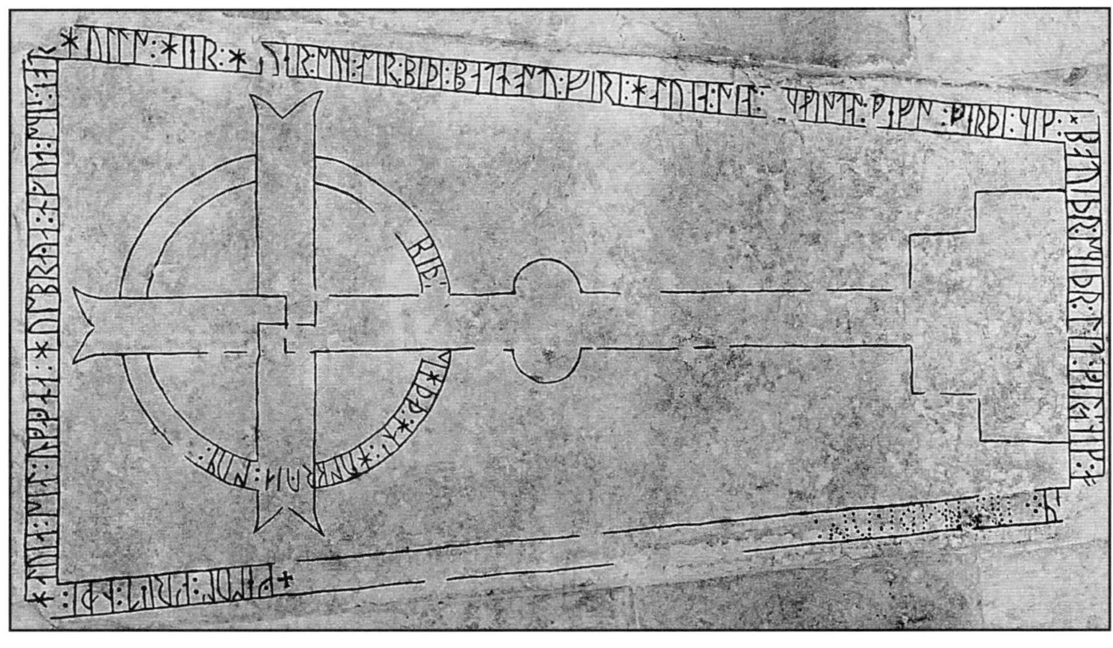

G 115 Gammelgarn Church

G 118 Anga Church

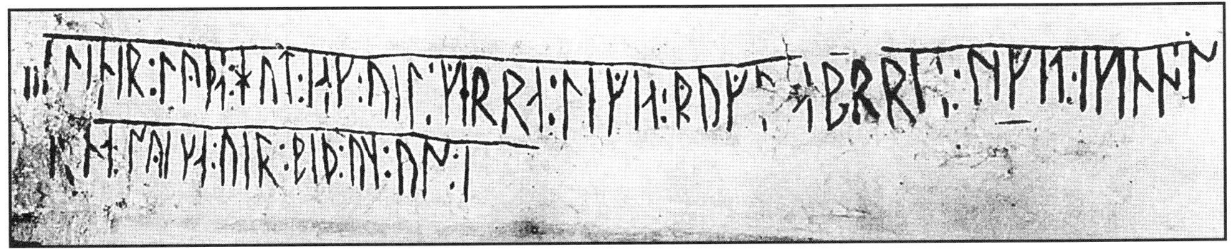

G 128 Guldrupe Church

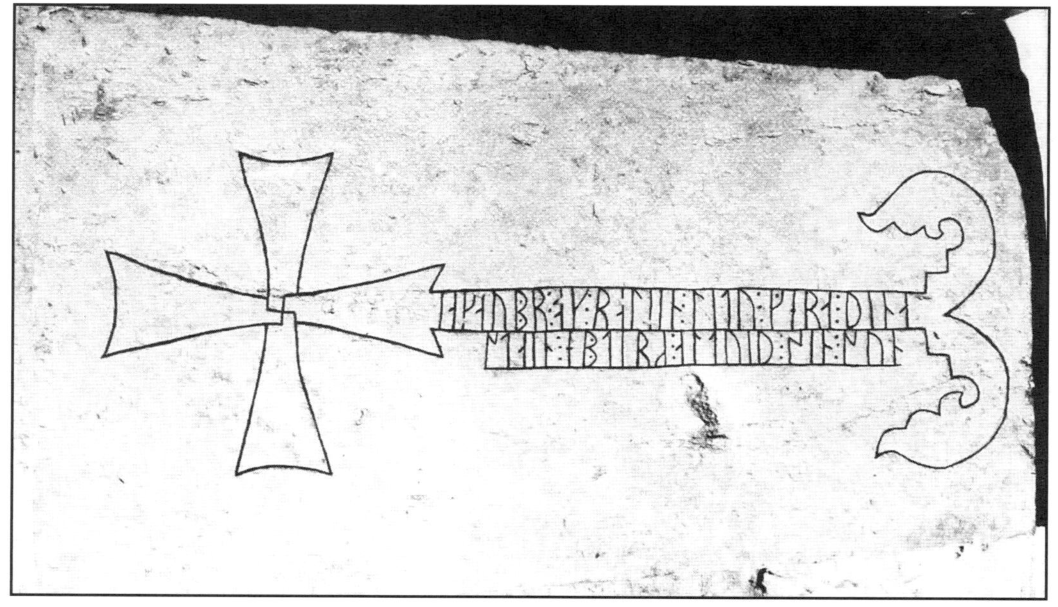

G 151 Norrlanda Church

G 163 Mulde (SFW)

G 166 Klinte Church

G 170 Hejde Church

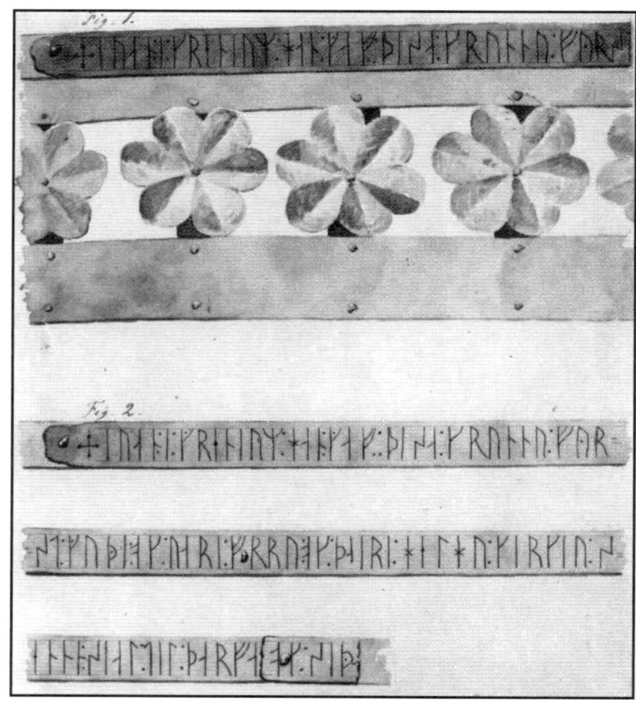

G 178 Väte Church

G 181 Sanda Church (SFW)

G 182 Sanda Church

G 192 Västergarn Church

G 215 Roma Church (SFW)

G 370 Hablingbo Church

Index of Photographs & Illustrations

Picture credits in parenthesis pertain to the image only. The captions are the comments by the authors. (SFW) – indicates photograph taken by author Wolter.